INSTITUTIONALIZING COMMON POOL RESOURCES

The Editor

Dinesh K. Marothia holds Ph.D. from the University of Alberta, Edmonton with specialization in natural resource economics. Prof. Marothia was recipient of Canadian Commonwealth Scholarship for Ph.D. degree. Having served as Assistant and Associate Professor at J.N. Agricultural University, he joined Indira Gandhi Agricultural University, Raipur in 1987 where he is now Professor and Head of the Department of Agricultural and Natural Resource Economics established through his initiative. This was the first Department under State Agricultural university system in India where teaching and research on natural resource economics was initiated.

He has held positions of member and Chairman with the Commission for Agricultural Costs and Prices, Ministry of Agriculture, Government of India. Prof. Marothia had a short stint as (founder) Director of India Natural Resource Economics and management Foundation, Anand.

INSTITUTIONALIZING COMMON POOL RESOURCES

Edited by

DINESH K. MAROTHIA

CONCEPT PUBLISHING COMPANY, NEW DELHI-110059

ISBN 81-7022-981-2

First Published 2002

Published and Printed by
Ashok Kumar Mittal
Concept Publishing Company
A/15-16, Commercial Block, Mohan Garden,
NEW DELHI-110059
Phones : 5351794, 5351460
Fax : 091-11-5357103
Email : publishing@conceptpub.com

PREFACE AND ACKNOWLEDGEMENTS

For more than two decades, I have been concerned with the roles of institutional arrangements for the renewable natural resources in general and common pool resources (CPRs) in particular. I first began to study the problem of collective action faced by individual/community using CPRs at the University of Alberta, Edmonton, during the mid 1970s where I took a series of natural resources economics courses from W.E. Phillips, T.W. Manning, J. Delehanty, T. Veeman focused on the development of alternative institutions for managing renewable natural resources. As I completed my Ph.D. dissertation I was quite excited to learn that institutional arrangements suggested therein for controlling soil erosion on agricultural lands in the Peace River Region of Alberta had received considerable attention of the policy makers. In the late 1970s and the beginning of the 1980s during my extensive visits to a number of North American universities I could further enhance my understanding about the institutional dimensions of renewable natural resources and common pool resources degradation/management through my intensive interaction with Professors R. Barrows, R.C. Bishop, D.W. Bromley, E.N. Castle, S.V. Ciriacy-Wantrup, M. Clawson, J.H. Dales, D.A. Harkin, R.H. Haveman, M.M. Kelso, A.V. Kneese, J.V. Krutilla, J.W. Mellor, V.W. Ruttan, G.E. Schuh, W.D. Seitz, T. Smith, W.B. Sundquist and E.R. Swanson. I owe a special debt of gratitude to all of them for shaping my thoughts about institutional economics of natural resources. I had also an opportunity to discuss various aspects of institutional structures with Professors Partha Dasgupta and Karl Goran Mäler at the Beijer Research Seminar organized by the International Institute of Ecological Economics at Kota Kinabalu, Malaysia, during May, 1995. I am grateful to both of them. Over the years I have benefited greatly from the series of discussions with Professors M.L. Dantwala, V.M. Dandekar, and A. Vaidyanathan on the importance of designing institutional arrangements in managing natural resources.

It is clear to me now that the problems of CPRs are the problems of linking institutions to collective outcomes; CPRs policy is institutional designing policy. Given the importance of understanding how effective are institutional arrangements to arrest CPRs degradation process, and given the involvement of researchers in diverse fields concerning these problems, it seemed to me that it was important to compile a book for learning more about the process of institutionalizing the commons.

My awareness about CPRs research conducted during the past three decades in various disciplines in India and knowing individual researchers involved in theoretical and field research helped me to identify contributors for this book and relevant topics on which they could write. All the contributors of this volume are distinguished scholars in their fields and my academic association with most of them made it especially pleasurable to edit this volume. The contributors include Anil Agarwal, B. Balasubramanian, Vishwa Ballabh, M.G. Chandrakanth, Kanchan Chopra, P.V. Dehadrai, R.S. Deshpande, Madhav Gadgil, Brij Gopal, Sudarshan Iyengar, Nandita Jain, Narpat S. Jodha, P.K. Joshi, Amalendu Jyotishi, Jagdish C. Kalla, Pradeep Kumar Katiha, R.N. Kaul, Ashish Kothari, Renzino Lepcha, I.C. Mahapatra, Kailash C. Malhotra, V.K. Misra, M.V. Nadkarni, Sunita Narain, Y.S. Negi, K. Palanisami, Vaidhya Rangesh Paramesh, Prem Shankar Pathak, S.C. Rai, R.K. Rajput, C. Ramasamy, M.S. Rathore, Ravishankar, A., N.C. Saxena, R. Seenivasan, C. Sekar, R. Selvam, Tushaar Shah, C.R. Shanmugam, Eklabya Sharma, Vandana Shiva, Nimisha Shukla, Katar Singh, Vir Singh, Maniranjan Sinha, M.S. Suneetha, P. Thomas and M.P. Vasimalai. I will be ever grateful to all of them for their contributions and patience as this volume has, due to my sickness, taken in little longer preparation than stipulated. I am grateful to my friends and well wishers for their collective prayers for my rapid recovery. I am sure their prayers were heard and answered and as a result I am back on the work track. They are all fine friends and colleagues.

During the preparation of this volume I have also greatly benefited from the interactions with Y.K. Alagh, Anwar Alam, G.S. Bhalla, M.S. Bhatia, A. Damodaran, B.D. Dhawan, V.B. Eswaran, G.S. Guha, Anil Gupta, T. Haque, S.M. Jharwal, D. Jha, Gopal Kadekodi, Shashi Kolavalli, J.P. Mishra, Mruthyunjaya, Jayant Patil, D. Ramakrishnaiah, V.M. Rao, R.M. Saleth, Abhijit Sen, Selvarajan, I.J. Singh, Kirti Singh, Samar Singh, Debashish Sircar, U.K. Srivastava, Suresh Pal, M.S. Swaminathan and A.K. Vasisht. Some of these colleagues also took the burden of reviewing the articles of the contributors of this volume. I am grateful to all of them.

I am extremely grateful to Ashok K. Mittal of the Concept Publishing Company for keeping me going and bringing this book to the market. In the process of editing this book I found a very good friend in him. His cooperation was simply beyond comparison. Finally in the preparation of this volume, my private secretary Jagrup Chandla with the Commission for Agricultural Costs and Prices, Government of India, New Delhi, and Valsala Nair of the Department of Agricultural and Natural Resource Economics (DANRE), IG Agricultural University, Raipur, C.G., extended their abundant secretarial assistance. I thank them for in equal abundance.

The volume presents a remarkable interdisciplinary assembly in which agricultural scientists, fisheries scientists, forestry experts, alternative medicine systems experts, environmental and resource economists, geographers, ecologists, anthropologists, sociologists, political scientists, physicists, biologists, botanists, environmental engineers, environmental advocates and philosophers, journalists and environmental policy analysts addressed their tasks focusing on institutions as a crosscutting theme in their writings on sustainable use of CPRs.

In preparing this volume, we aimed at the highest possible scholarly standard by inviting original articles and by carrying out a thorough peer review of the chapters. Almost each author undertook to review one or two other chapters. I also arranged for other reviewers. As a result, each chapter has been reviewed by an average of two reviewers. Most of the authors have positively responded to the reviewers' comments and incorporated them. I am extremely grateful to all the contributors for their scholarly contributions as well as participating in the peer review process.

This book addresses the fundamental casual connections linking institutions to collective outcomes in the areas concerning the common-based rural development programmes; water resources, landuse and irrigation systems; degraded lands, fisheries, biodiversity, community knowledge and alternative governance. As such it may serve as the basis for orchestrating a coordinated research programme in the different agro-climatic conditions in the country and as a framework to build-up institutional reforms to complement the structural adjustment programmes which are aimed at a sustainable management of CPRs. A large number of researchers, policy-makers, managers, dedicated individuals, community mobilizers and NGOs are working continuously to design appropriate institutional arrangements and property rights regimes for an efficient, equitable and sustainable management of CPRs. We hope that this book will stimulate increasing number of scholars to delve into theoretical and practical dimensions of institutional choice in CPRs management. We dedicate this book to the thinkers, designers and practitioners of cultural and social capital in managing the CPRs.

Date : 1-1-2001
Place : Raipur, Chhattisgarh

DINESH K. MAROTHIA

CONTENTS

V : BIODIVERSITY AND INSTITUTIONAL STRUCTURES

VI : COMMON POOL KNOWLEDGE

VII : PROPERTY RIGHTS, INSTITUTIONAL CHANGE AND POLICY PROBLEM

1 Introduction and Overview

Dinesh K. Marothia

The role of institutional arrangements is extremely important in natural resource management in general and common pool resources (CPRs) in particular under any resource governance structure (State control, private property, communal or communities control, open access, and distributed or shared governance)*. Institutions are defined as "collective action in control, liberation and expansion of individual action" (Commons 1931, p.649). Institutions include laws, constitutions (i.e. "laws about making laws"), traditions, moral and ethical structures and customary and accepted ways of doing things (Commons 1924, p.124). Institutional arrangements are applied to resolve conflicts of interest of many individuals with diverse interests and preferences. To maintain a coordinated flow of action and transactions in the conduct of any going concern, society adopts working rules which define person-to-person relations with respect to property (Commons 1931, Gonce 1971). Institutional arrangements or working rules effectively indicate the cause, effect or purpose essential for a collective action. Working rules also indicate what an individual can, must, or may or may not do, enforced by collective sanctions (Commons 1931, p.650). Collective action, as well as individual action, is influenced by scarcity. In the face of scarcity, self-interest breeds conflict and disorder (Commons 1934). Ownership becomes the foundation of institutional framework because ownership interacts with scarcity to create conflicts of interest which are "predominant in transactions". But transactions are mutually interdependent as well as conflicting. Because of this mutual interdependence the alienation and acquisition of rights of future ownership of resources among individuals would be negotiated between the parties concerned according to the working rules of society, thus creating a "certain security of expectation" or "order" (Commons 1934, 1950). Thus rights are relative, evolutionary and subject to change or limits as per needs or values of power relationships and society (Commons 1934, for an elaborative

* This section is heavily drawn from the author's earlier works (Marothia 1981,1989a, 1992a,b, 1993, 1995,1996,1997a, 1997b,1997c,1998, Marothia and Phillips 1985).

discussion and views of different school of thoughts on scarcity, resources, transaction, inequality, values and collective choice see the works of Arrow 1975, Rawls 1971, Ostrom 1976, Sen 1979, 1984, 1987, 1992, Dasgupta 1982, 1993, Bromley 1989a,b,1991, Schmid 1978).

The recognition that rights are subject to limits and changes is fundamental to a clear understanding of any natural resource policy analysis (for property rights paradigm see the works of Ely 1914, Scott 1955, Bator 1958, Coase 1960, Ciriacy-Wantrup 1963, Demsetz 1966,1967, Dales 1968, Mishan 1971, Furubotn and Pejovich 1972, Randall 1972, 1975, 1978a, 1978b, Alchian and Demsetz 1973, Samules 1974, Becker 1977, Bromley 1978, 1989a,b, 1991, Castle 1978, Schmid 1976, 1978, Marothia and Phillips 1985, Marothia 1989a, 1993, 1997a,b,c, Jodha 1996). Rights are the instruments by which any society controls and orders human interdependence and resolves the question of who gets what (Parson 1941). The interdependence can be described in terms of institutionalized cost, external effects and power (Commons 1934). Thus property is not simply a derivation of a physical fact. It also reflects a social choice of the kind of efforts that are counted in creating an image in an individual's mind about the knowledge of a person's rights. A community usually defines property rights either by a common problem or by the mutual advantage of joint action (Schmid 1972, 1976, 1978). In the absence of rules that govern through social organization, human relations settle down to a sheer play of power against power, a war of all "against all", in which individual life is "solitary, poor, nasty, brutish and short" (Long 1953). Alternative rights are of interest because of their effect on the economic performance and outcomes (Schmid 1978). Rights define potential opportunities and the opportunities of one person are shaped by the opportunities of others (Samuels 1972). Thus the opportunity sets of an individual are composed of alternative lines of action that are open because of the relative structure of rights as well as the relative capacity of the person to make use of those rights. The value of a right is also limited by the available knowledge and technology. The opportunity sets of individuals interact and condition the outcome of human transactions. The components of the institutional structure are then one of the points of leverage in changing outcomes (Schmid 1978).

Thus institutions express a society's value system and give it effect in the form of working rules. In other words, institutions or working rules order relationship among individuals within society and structure incentives in human exchange, whether social, economic or political (North 1990, for additional literature on institutions see works of Buchanan and Tullock 1962, Ciriacy- Wantrup 1963, Schultz 1968, Olson 1971, Wilber and Harrison 1978, Myrdal 1978, Dasgupta 1982, 1993, Marothia and Phillips 1985, Matthews 1986, Uphoff 1986, Söderbaum 1986, 1990, Bromley 1989a,b, 1991, Marothia 1989a,

1 Introduction and Overview

Dinesh K. Marothia

The role of institutional arrangements is extremely important in natural resource management in general and common pool resources (CPRs) in particular under any resource governance structure (State control, private property, communal or communities control, open access, and distributed or shared governance)*. Institutions are defined as "collective action in control, liberation and expansion of individual action" (Commons 1931, p.649). Institutions include laws, constitutions (i.e. "laws about making laws"), traditions, moral and ethical structures and customary and accepted ways of doing things (Commons 1924, p.124). Institutional arrangements are applied to resolve conflicts of interest of many individuals with diverse interests and preferences. To maintain a coordinated flow of action and transactions in the conduct of any going concern, society adopts working rules which define person-to-person relations with respect to property (Commons 1931, Gonce 1971). Institutional arrangements or working rules effectively indicate the cause, effect or purpose essential for a collective action. Working rules also indicate what an individual can, must, or may or may not do, enforced by collective sanctions (Commons 1931, p.650). Collective action, as well as individual action, is influenced by scarcity. In the face of scarcity, self-interest breeds conflict and disorder (Commons 1934). Ownership becomes the foundation of institutional framework because ownership interacts with scarcity to create conflicts of interest which are "predominant in transactions". But transactions are mutually interdependent as well as conflicting. Because of this mutual interdependence the alienation and acquisition of rights of future ownership of resources among individuals would be negotiated between the parties concerned according to the working rules of society, thus creating a "certain security of expectation" or "order" (Commons 1934, 1950). Thus rights are relative, evolutionary and subject to change or limits as per needs or values of power relationships and society (Commons 1934, for an elaborative

* This section is heavily drawn from the author's earlier works (Marothia 1981,1989a, 1992a,b, 1993, 1995,1996,1997a, 1997b,1997c,1998, Marothia and Phillips 1985).

have recently used the Oakerson (1986, 1992) model and its derivative forms for analyzing CPRs in various parts of the world and in the Indian context (see case studies reported using the Oakerson model in Arnold and Stewart 1991, Bromley 1992, Ostrom 1992, Tang 1992, Marothia 1993, 1996,1998, Singh 1994, Floke and Berkes 1995, Singh and Ballabh 1996). This volume addresses the problem of CPRs management from the institutional perspective rooted in concepts of property rights regimes, institutional arrangements, transaction or action costs and authority system.

This volume is divided in seven parts, preceded by this Introduction and Overview. This Chapter presents, first, an analytical overview of the papers contributed to this volume and then spells out policy relevant conclusions drawing upon the issues emerging from each Chapter under seven sections of this book and other relevant literature .

1. Commons, Development and Institutions

The four chapters that make up Part I deal with definitions, various concepts of CPRs and management regimes, contributions of CRRs in the livelihood system, causes of their erosion and the process of decline, role of institutions or social capital in rebuilding CPRs institutions and mechanism of integrating CPRs-based programmes with rural development.

1.a. Erosion of Social Capital and Decline of Commons

CPRs of land, water, forest, fisheries, wildlife and agriculture constitute an important component of community assets in India and significantly contribute towards the people's livelihood despite the decline in their area and physical productivity. All resources, including CPRs, are capable of being nationalized, privatized or managed collectively and all are equally capable of being unspecified and unmanaged. This is because a particular resource may be controlled under any single regime or more than one regime (Cox 1985 ,Gibbs and Bromley 1989, Marothia 1993, see also Marothia Chapter 31 of this volume). The nature of property rights is determined by several attributes such as physical and technical characteristics of a resource, attributes of resource users and communities and external and internal institutional arrangements designed and enforced by the community or resource management authority to protect resources (Bromley and Cernea 1989, Bromley 1991, 1992, Folke and Berkes 1995, Townsend and Polley 1995, Jodha Chapter 2, Marothia Chapter 31 of this volume). Enough evidence is available in India to show that resources managed under common property regimes have degraded into open access due to weak property rights regimes, institutional arrangements and breakdown of the authority system. Examples are also available when renewable resources in general and CPRs in particular degraded under open access system were brought back under state or private or community management regime through appropriate institutional changes. Surprisingly, many researchers who have addressed the issue of CPRs management/ degradation have grossly confused the open access situation (of Hardin's (1968) "tragedy of commons") with common property regime. As a result of the persistent confusion in the literature, many researchers and policy makers suggested privatization or State takeover of the CPRs for their management. This misunderstanding has recently been increasingly challenged by many natural resource scientists and they have documented that the breakdown in common property systems may be due to the deficiencies in specifications of property and institutional arrangements rather than in its viability as a property rights regime (Ciriacy-Wantrup and Bishop 1975, Runge 1981, Dasgupta 1982, 1993, Bromley and Chapagain 1984, Jodha 1986, 1996, Oakerson 1986, 1992, Wade 1988a, Berkes 1989, Gibbs and Bromley 1989, Bromley 1989, 1991, 1992, Bromley and Cernea 1989, Feeny et al. 1990, Damodaran 1991, Arnold and Stewart 1991, Marothia, 1992b,c,1993, 1997a,b,c, Dasgupta and Mäler 1994, Singh 1994, 1997, Singh and Ballabh 1996). Thus it is important for a researcher to analyze the situations under which a particular resource governance system is likely to yield positive or negative results in terms of an efficient, equitable and sustainable use of the resource.

In a substantive work involving 82 villages spread over 21 districts of the dry regions of India, Jodha (Chapter 2) has documented the factors which led to the decline of CPRs in terms of area, physical degradation and management system, and related them to the disintegration of social and institutional arrangements evolved and enforced by the rural community to protect and manage CPRs. Jodha (Chapter 2) identified the role of different driving forces behind the demographic changes and emphasizes that population pressure could be necessary but not the sufficient condition to accelerate shrinkage of CPRs area (see also earlier work of Jodha 1986, 1992, 1995, 1996). Negi (Chapter 3) has similarly indicated in his Himachal Pradesh study that while population has been the biggest contributor towards the pressure on CPRs land, the process of encroachment has also reduced the size and status of CPRs lands. Fragmented land holdings, land holdings in the vicinity of a forest, tiny farm sizes and acquisition of grazing lands by developmental agencies and increased pressure by outsider grazers on the grazing lands were the important factors in the process of encroachment and shrinking common pool land resources (Negi, Chapter 3). Based on a series of studies Nadkarni (Chapter 4) documented that the encroachments of CPRs were more in developed villages whereas the extent of area under CPRs was higher in the backward villages. Exogenous development with outside commercial interests, process of commoditization of collective resources, public policies and market forces resulted in the decline of CPRs (Nadkarni, Chapter 4, see also Nadkarni and Pasha 1991).

Jodha (Chapter 2) emphasizes the importance of multiple social and institutional arrangements as these arrangements are manifestations of "social capital" and erosion or collapse of these arrangements leading to a decline of CPRs (see also Jodha 1995). In other words once "social capital" depletes, CPRs become open access resource and its process of depletion begins (Jodha, Chapter 2). Local customs/social groups have played an important role in designing informal institutional arrangements for collective tasks for managing CPRs in different parts of the country (Negi, Chapter 3). For example, cultural or religious rules, both formal and informal, have worked very effectively for management of Kuhls in Himachal Pradesh (Negi, Chapter 3). Over time, however, these informal binders are seen to lose their effectiveness, and as a result voluntary participation in resource management is declining (Negi, Chapter 3). Also due to the introduction of elected village councils (Panchayats) and derecognition of the traditional social arrangement or customary system, which embodied social capital, the community lost collective stake and control over CPRs, culture of group action got replaced by individualistic tendencies, disintegration of village community started and social capital got depleted (Jodha, Chapter 2). Most of the development programmes undertaken by the State to upgrade and conserve CPRs focussed on financial and technical support without recognition of the local perception and traditional knowledge system (Jodha, Chapter 2, see also Gupta 1986, 1995, Marothia 1993). Understanding of traditional institutional arrangements may serve as an important step towards rehabilitation of CPRs as well as rebuilding of social capital (Jodha, Chapter 2 see also Jodha 1995, 1996).

1.b. CPRs-based Development and Institutional Mechanism

An institutional mechanism for coordination and integration of the CPR management plan with the plans of various departments engaged in agriculture and rural development at national, state and field planning officer levels needs to be evolved incorporating concepts of equity and sustainability (Singh, Chapter 5, see also Gupta 1995, Agarwal 1997). An institutional structure like joint forest management needs to be institutionalized which can ensure achievement of the goals of collective management, namely, equity and sustainable use (Nadkarni, Chapter 4, see also Saxena, Chapter 17). Shared resource management yielded collective outcomes in terms of positive interactions among the resource users and sustainable use of CPRs (see Chapters 14-18 and 31). In order to incorporate environmental and ecological considerations in development planning, Singh (Chapter 5) suggested formulating of a comprehensive strategy for CPRs-based development planning and management. NGOs and other volunteer agencies and community mobilizers have played a catalytic role in capacity building of rural communities (Jodha, Chapter 2). Initially, such a strategy may be adopted in selected protected areas in India, as is being already done now, and lessons learnt from these projects may be incorporated in formulating programmes for sustainable development (Chapter 5, see also Chapters 26, 27 and 28 for management of CPRs in the protected areas).

2. Water Resources, Land Use and Irrigation Systems and Institutions

In Chapter 6 (Agarwal and Narain) of this section the role of community institutions in harvesting and managing rainwater for environmental regeneration and poverty alleviation has been discussed and strategies suggested for replication of community-based management models in the similar poverty-prone areas. With an NGO initiative a village has been transformed through institutional innovations–this case is presented in Chapter 7 (Ballabh and Thomas). Problems of water management in the command areas can be solved through the farmers' participation. Institutions like Pani Panchayat can mitigate the water scarcity and build up monetary and social capital in society. This is documented in Chapters 8 (Mahapatra and Rajput) and 13 (Deshpande and Jyotishi) respectively. A range of institutional arrangements are suggested to rehabilitate the Tamil Nadu tanks in Chapters 9 (Shah et al.) and 10 (Palanisami and Balasubramanian). Technological, policy and institutional options to overcome the problem of groundwater managements are suggested in Chapters 11 to 13.

2.1. Rainwater Harvesting, Community Institutions and Ecological Poverty Alleviation

Rainwater harvesting can meet the people's basic water needs as also improve food and livelihood security. Community- and NGO-based experience of Sukhomajiri, Ralegan Siddhi and Tarun Bharat Sangh have shown that the transformation process from a state of ecological poverty to a state of sustainable economic growth demands community participation with multi-faceted dimensions and strategies (Agarwal and Narain, Chapter 6). The work of the Rajiv Gandhi Watershed Development Mission in Madhya Pradesh also shows that government agencies can learn from community-based management experiences and replicate on a large scale. In all the three cases of

Sukhomajiri, Relegan Siddhi and Tarun Bharat Sangh village-level institutions played a crucial role in developing institutional arrangements and applying them for a sustainable management of the created water resource and equitable access to the resource generated by the total village population. Multi-layered institutional development structures were created in the villages for decision-making and implementing the applied programme with participatory democracy rather than representative democracy (Agarwal and Narain, Chapter 6). In Shankerpura village of Gujarat State, interventions by Sadguru Water and Development Foundation (SWDF) in designing institutions to evolve rules and norms for sharing resources and reducing conflicts, organizing people, capacity building, and bearing the transaction costs associated with uncertainty of technology, negotiation with governments, and organization helped in restoring the livelihood system of the people (Ballabh and Thomas, Chapter 7). To manage CPRs and to understand poverty environment interface it is imperative to design an integrated village ecosystem planning with a high order of democracy in decision-making for ecological regeneration, create appropriate community-based property rights, provide to village institutions directly financial grants to increase productivity of the commons and to induce village institutions to raise substantial funds by organizing their CPRs (Agarwal and Narain, Chapter 6 and Ballabh and Thomas, Chapter 7).

2.b. Irrigation Institutions

Many success stories of irrigators cooperative societies/water users associations (WUAs) working in the command area of river basins have been documented in the past three decades. Shared resource management has been the key to the success of irrigation cooperatives/WUAs. Mahapatra and Rajput (Chapter 8) have documented the successful stories of irrigation cooperatives functioning in the command area of the river Tapi in Maharashtra, Mohini Water Distribution Cooperative Society in the Ukai–Kakrapar project command area in Gujarat, Sri Datta Water Cooperative Water Management Society in the Mula irrigation project in Maharashtra, Lower Bhavani Project—Thindal distributary in Tamil Nadu, water users association in Kerala and Paliganj distributory in Bihar. In most of these cases the State Department of Irrigation facilitated the formation of cooperatives and is still maintaining the main water courses. However, the internal institutional arrangements related to an equitable and efficient water distribution, recovery of the irrigation fees and maintenance and repairs of the canal system are designed and enforced by the members of the societies (see also Chambers 1988, Chambers, Saxena and Shah 1989, Sengupta 1991, Marothia et al. 1987, Wade 1988b). In some cases water users associations have also promoted group farming to enhance the productivity of tiny farm holdings, for example, in Kerala (Mahapatra and Rajput, Chapter 8).

2.c. Tank Irrigation: A Case for Institutional Rebuilding

For several centuries, tanks have been central to socio-ecology and irrigated agriculture in the States of Andhra Pradesh, Karnataka, Tamil Nadu and Chhattisgarh. Tanks are, however, disappearing fast; and those that remain have long since fallen into disrepair. Decades of siltation, poor organization and management, decline of compulsory labour contribution (Kudimaramat) in maintenance work, inadequate operation and maintenance budget from the government, meager revenue from tank-based activities (social forestry, fisheries, duck- and goat-rearing, grazing leases, poor collection of irrigation fees), growth of wells in tank command areas and well owners' reduced interest in tank management, and encroachments have contributed to their decline (Shah *et al.* Chapter 9, Palanisami and Balasubramaniam, Chapter 10). Most of the tanks in Tamil Nadu (Shah *et al.* Chapter 9 and Palanisami and Balasubramaniam, Chapter 10 see also Palanisami and Flinn 1988, Mosse 1997) and elsewhere (see Rao and Chandrakanth, 1984, Von Oppen 1985, Marothia 1992b) have degraded into open access due to weak institutional arrangements, property rights structures and breakdown of local authority system (see also Marothia 1993, Vaidyanathan 1997).

Government and international donors have devised programmes to rehabilitate large tanks, but by far more small tanks and tank chains are left out of these programmes. In this respect, a small programme of tank revival has been conceived and implemented by the PRADAN/DHAN Foundation, a Madurai-based development organization. Key strategic elements of PRADAN's tank programme include creation of a Water User Organization (WUO) at the tank level with strong common property interests in tank conservation by concentrating management rights, responsibilities and rewards in a clearly defined body of registered ayacutdaars, creation of new sources of on-going resource generation for sustained investment in maintenance and repair of the tank complex—essentially, through giving the WUOs rights over plantations in the waterspread area and tank bund;.and creation of upper tier organizations as co-ordinating structures which lobby with government agencies for resources and favourable policies (Shah et al. Chapter 9).

In order to produce an impact of significance Shah et al. (Chapter 9) say that PRADAN's tank programme will need to break new ground in three areas: first, to identify ways of promoting sustainable tank management in today's context; second, it needs to take a hard look at the farmer organizations it is promoting and constantly search for ways to enhance their relevance and centrality to their members; and third, work out a strategy to discourage the increasing use of well irrigation which has emerged as the prime cause of the decline in tanks in much of South India (see also Palanisami and Balasubramaniam, Chapter 10). Similar strategies may be designed to rehabilitate tanks in other parts of the country.

2.d. Groundwater Crisis and Role of Technical and Institutional Arrangements

Declining and rising water table are two distinct problems, which are threatening the sustainability of Indian agriculture have and attracted the attention of researchers and policy makers in recent years (Joshi, Chapter 11 see also Joshi, 1997). Defective irrigation pricing policy is the main cause of both rise and fall in the groundwater table. Pricing of both canal water and power is not decided on the basis of economic and ecological parameters but on political considerations, which has a very high social cost (Joshi, Chapter 11 see also Vaidyanathan 1996, Marothia 1997b). The implications of groundwater mismanagement are increase in the irrigation cost, decline in productivity, and widening income disparities. Technological and policy options are available but need effective implementation. Among the technological options, sub-surface drainage and water-saving irrigation methods (like drip and sprinkler systems) are feasible and cost-effective means to control rise in the water table. To prevent fall in the water table, besides water-saving irrigation systems, crop diversification through low water requirement crops can be introduced. Designing an appropriate irrigation pricing policy, withdrawal of all subsidies from canal water charges, and power tariff and transfer them to water-saving irrigation systems, educate farmers and organize a social movement by creating mass awareness about the beneficial effects of collective action in using groundwater, introduce effective legislative structures to control mismanagement of groundwater, strengthen the role of cooperatives or the group-oriented system, adoption of river basin approach are the effective ways to control externalities related with groundwater (Joshi, Chapter 11, Rathore, Chapter 12; see also Shah 1993, Dhawan 1995, Vaidyanathan 1996, Veeman 1978, Saleth 1994, Marothia 1997b). Institutions like Pani Panchayats should be replicated on a large scale particularly in groundwater scarcity zones for an efficient and equitable distribution of water, promoting a less-water-intensive cropping pattern and effective enforcement of the rules and regulations by Panchayats (Deshpande and Jyotishi, Chapter 13).

3. Degraded Lands and Framing of Institutional Choices

Common Property Land Resources (CPLRs) provide livelihood support to the rural poor apart from performing several useful ecological functions. Quick and significant reduction in the extent of CPLRs, largely due to the breaking down of institutional arrangements, has brought down the ratio of uncultivated land to cultivated lands. A number of experiments have been conducted in forests and CPLRs in various agro-climatic conditions involving the stake holders to design new institutional arrangements and management regimes. The problems and prospects of restoring the environmental health of the degraded lands in general and CPLRs in particular and provide income-earning opportunities to the poor through technological and institutional options have been examined by several authors and their main findings are presented in Chapters 14-18.

3.1. Sustainable Regeneration of CPLRs: Technical and Institutional Options

Iyengar and Shukla (Chapter 14) have reviewed a large variety of experiments being undertaken for the regeneration of the degraded CPLRs in the country and suggested that, to improve the situation the entire planning mechanism of the forest department may have to be altered by putting the resources under the community's control and reducing the role of the forest department to providing technical and scientific innovations in the formulation of institutions (Iyengar and Shukla, Chapter 14). Through innovative experiments undertaken by NGOs the productivity of CPLRs improved in several parts of the country (see also Parikh and Reddy 1997, Iyengar 1989, 1997 for Collective Management of CPLRS). However, the authors have observed that with the improvement in the productivity of CPLRs, the members of CPLRs development group will themselves involve in privatizing CPLRs for value addition activities. In order to have a sustainable management of CPLRs the societies will have to revive ethical codes inbuilt in the traditional institutions for designing new institutional arrangements (see also Damodaran 1990 for an elaborative treatment of policy parameters relating to common lands governance.)

Misra (Chapter 15) documented and analyzed the experience gained in accessing revenue wastelands for tree plantation for implementing the Tree Growers' Cooperative Societies (TGCS) project in different parts of India. TGCS have been organized to reintroduce a decentralized system of management of village common lands. In Misra's opinion people have potential to resolve land-related disputes at the local level and appreciate the value of regenerating and utilizing the common lands in a sustainable manner. However, politically motivated privatization of common lands and village-level politics adversely affect this process. Formulation and effective implementation of a judicious landuse policy, periodic survey for land capability classification, simple procedures for land lease to grassroot institutions and interdepartmental coordination are important for an expeditious wastelands afforestation work on which a national debate and action is needed (Misra, Chapter 15). Kalla and Kaul (Chapter 16) in their study on the socio-economic impact of joint management of common lands in the Aravalli project have observed that interventions devised by the Haryana State Forest Department in terms of regulated access to the created fodder, fuel biomass have significantly altered the income accruals towards a more egalitarian distribution and in turn better standard of living (see also Chopra, Kadekodi and Murty 1990, Mishra and Sarin 1987 for participatory approach to CPLRs in the same area). While the project has, by and large, successfully compensated for the benefits forgone owing to the regularization of access to common lands, creation of participatory management institutions, new institutional arrangements with respect to an equitable distribution of permanent assets, increase in the women specific activities to further improve their socio-economic status through active participation in planning and decision-making has reduced child labour and increased school enrolments, promoted healthy growth of biodiversity and ensured sustainability of the project after withdrawal of external support.

Saxena (Chapter 17) has assessed the fuelwood problem based on land production capabilities and access to biomass in the different regions of the country. To minimize the fuelwood deficit, Saxena argues that the major potentials exist on private, revenue and forest wastelands. However, this biological potential has not been achieved due to bio-physical-socio-economic and technological constraints and market policy and institutional failures across the regions and types of lands (see also Marothia 1988b, 1989b, Marothia and Nandi 1994). To mitigate the fuelwood scarcity and to achieve visible success in the implementation of joint forest management, Saxena has suggested several reforms like enhancing the capacity of the forest department to build up and respond to local institutions, restructuring rights and privileges over forest, policies and laws pertaining to NTFPs, working plans, silvicultural arrangements, etc. (Saxena, Chapter 17 see also Chambers, Saxena and Shah 1989 , Agarwal 1992 , Marothia 1998.)

Agro-forestry models have an adequate potential to meet the rural energy needs in terms of forage and firewood. Besides, the agroforestry models can be adopted for bioremedy of the polluted and problem sites to reclaim the area for productive use (Pathak, Chapter 18). Traditional methods for restoring degraded lands and modern technology to meet the increasing employment needs and environmental concerns under an effective institutional arrangement for resource conservation, production and marketing need to be synthesized. Organization of village institutions, their proper orientation based on the microplan and systems of award and punishment will go a long way in ensuring success of the programme. Linkages between different government departments and village-level institutions are essential to ensure the success of agroforestry programmes' implementation (Pathak, Chapter 18 see also Nadkarni, Pasha and Prabhakar 1989, Kramer and Ballabh 1992, Saxena and Ballabh 1995).

4. Institutional Arrangements in Fisheries Resources

The role of alternative property rights structures in the management of inland fisheries, development strategies for promoting open-water capture fisheries and market and non-market interventions for internalization of externalities due to shrimp farming in the coastal zones are discussed in this section.

4.1 Property Rights Crisis and Developmental Strategies

Inland waters are managed differently for fishery activities under different property and management regimes and have a direct bearing on the socio-economic conditions of fishermen (Sinha and Katiha, Chapter 19). Property rights over the river water rest with the State, however, the water flows through more than one State and is, therefore, managed by different departments. This causes multiple conflicts in the exploitation and management of riverine fisheries in terms of resource investment in the fish stock, fishing rights and implementing appropriate management regimes. Privatization of fishing rights in rivers has created social and economic inequalities in many States. A national reverine Fisheries Development Authority needs to be constituted for the development of fisheries in the major rivers of the country flowing through two or more States. The Fish Farmers Development Agency (FFDA) needs structural changes in its approach with respect to preferential allotment of ponds water, necessary credit and technical support to production oriented fish cooperatives and fishers groups (see also Srivastava et.al. 1993, Marothia 1997a). Similarly institutional arrangements need to be so designed as to regulate the efforts and limit the fish harvest to the maximum sustainable level in the estuarine fisheries. Currently, the estuarine fisheries are under an open access regime. The fisheries operations in floodplain wetlands are either under cooperative or private management regimes and require new institutional arrangements to re-examine lease policy and revitalization of cooperatives (Sinha and Katiha, Chapter 19). Dehadrai (Chapter 20) suggests that fishing laws and other allied rules for the development of inland fisheries need re-examination by an experts group comprising environmentalists, fisheries scientists and jurists. A proper mix of appropriate institution arrangements and a technological package have to be linked with production incentives under the right kind of property regimes for the inland, coastal and deep-sea fisheries sectors (Dehadrai, Chapter 20 see also Srivastava et. al. 1991).

4.b. Coastal CPRs, Shrimp Farming and Externalities

Shrimp farming has spatial and temporal externalities on the marine ecosystem and other resource-based economic sectors operating within the coastal environment (Ramasamy and others Chapter 21). Based on a study conducted on the Coromandal coast of south India, Ramasamy and others (Chapter 21) have observed that proliferation of shrimp farming has led to displacement of economically weak and marginalized people whose livelihood depends on marine fisheries. Pumping of brackish water and indiscriminate use of sub-terranean fresh water for hatcheries by shrimp farms causes salinity and the intruded salt water makes fresh water unfit for irrigation and human and animal consumption. Coastal mangrove forests are also depleting fast due to shrimp farming. To internalize the shrimp farming, market and non-market interventions are suggested by Ramasamy et al. in Chapter 21 (see also Marothia 1988a). Ramasamy et al. further suggest (Chapter 21) that the designing of a comprehensive coastal CPRs policy and institutional structures are urgently needed for the efficient use of biological coastal resources, use of environmental friendly technologies of production, conservation and sustainability, trade-off between domestic and export markets, improvement of the local people's nutritional status and livelihood security of the coastal inhabitants.

5. Biodiversity and Institutional Structures

Chapter 22 (Malhotra) in Part 5 covers sacred groves as CPRs which provide a common socio-regions space to the community for establishing harmony for the entire ecosystem and, unlike the other category of CPRs, SGs do not necessarily provide economic benefits. Medicinal plants are analyzed within the paradigm of institutional economics in Chapter 23 (Chandrakanth et al.) followed by the role of biodiversity in managing CPRs in the Himalayan region in Chapter 24 (Singh). The role of ecotourism through a participatory approach to conserve biodiversity in Sikkim is discussed in Chapter 25 (Sharma et al.). In the next two Chapters, Kothari (Chapter 26) and Chopra (Chapter 27) demonstrate the importance of revival of community-based institutions for shared resource management in protected areas. Management issues of aquatic resources including wetlands are discussed in Chapter 28 (Gopal) with an emphasis on an integrated river-basin wide watershed approach.

5.1. Sacred Groves (SGs) as Socio-religious CPRs

The institution of Sacred Groves (SGs) dates back to the pre-agrarian hunting stage. SGs are widely distributed in various parts of India, with their number and size differing, and are found among the tribals and non-tribals. SGs provide a variety of cultural, social, economic, ecological, health, psychological, religious and political functions to individuals, clans and communities and represent climax vegetations and rich biodiversity. They encompass a variety of systems ranging from truly private to community owned and managed groves (Malhotra, Chapter 22). Unlike many CPRs, SGs do not necessarily provide tangible economic benefits to the community but instead provide a common socio-religious space which the community uses to establish cohesiveness, identity, solidarity and well-being of inhabitants as also of crops and animals (Malhotra, Chapter 22). However, many groves are threatened because of the weakening of traditional beliefs, cultural and biological integrity. We need to understand the process, identify the factors that trigger a shift in the traditional value and belief systems. To understand the changes that are taking place in the institution of SGs, Malhotra (Chapter 22) suggests development of approaches and models that should help us in analyzing the nature of threats, both internal and external, that are likely to create the institutions of SGs rather than economic models.

5.b. Medicinal Plants as CPRs

Medicinal plants have been escaping the attention of both researchers and policy-makers while addressing the land-based CPRs (Chandrakanth and others, Chapter 23). The loss of medicinal flora entails huge transaction costs and intra- and inter-generational inequalities. In the context of the new economic policy and the regime of WTO, conservation and sustainable use of medicinal flora will be directed and enforced by the interplay of property and patent regimes (see also Marothia 1997d). An analysis of the magnitude and dimension of trade and trade-related benefits and costs is difficult, unless quick and appropriate efforts are made to unearth them. Policy prescriptions concerning the conservation and sustainable use of medicinal plants should be location and context specific. Chandrakanth *et al.* (Chapter 23) have advocated an approach which must consider the synergistic relations among the economic, institutional and technological factors which determine the conservation and propagation strategies of medicinal plants in forest CPRs, non-forest CPRs and in cultivated lands. The policy domain and the valuation of the contribution of medicinal plants should be pluralistic in nature leading to a blend of institutional economics and natural resource economic approaches for understanding and unravelling the intricate issues in the economics of medicinal plants and health security (Chandrakanth *et al.* Chapter 23).

5.c. CPRs Cropland Linkages

Another study conducted in the mountain areas of the Indian Himalayan region by Singh (Chapter 24) emphasizes that the production capacity and sustainability of CPRs depend mainly on the degree of biodiversity, especially the varieties of plants and their genotypes. The commons' biodiversity has an enormous bearing on the agro-biodiversity due to CPR-cropland linkages. Singh (Chapter 24) suggests that the efficient management of CPRs, with biodiversity consideration at its focus, and coupled with cropping activities, can take care of food and nutrition security to a great extent, supply many basic necessities of life, elevate the economic standard of people, provide favourable ecosystem services and infuse sustainability in the whole production system.

5.d. Ecotourism, Protected Areas and Shared Management

To promote ecotourism and simultaneously conserve biodiversity, Sharma and his colleagues (Chapter 25) stress the need for participatory approach which may link enterprise operations, conservation action and integration of traditional cultural values. The Sikkim Biodiversity and Ecotourism Project has shown that collaboration between the public and private sectors, as well as local communities, and a participatory design can produce results that contribute to conserving biodiversity assets that are of global significance (see Marothia, Chapter 31 for distributed governance concepts and application in managing CPRs).

The creation of protected areas (PAs) as conservation policies and strategies has undoubtedly saved many habitats and species from destruction, but alienated local communities from their resource base and caused severe hardships (Kothari, Chapter 26). The responsibility for the conservation of PAs rests only with the government and the line department. PAs are affected by the continued existence of conventional rights of the local people; such as grazing by livestock, harvesting of timber, collection of non-timber forest products (NTFPs), etc. Tourists also use PAs for recreation and educationists and scientists for research. Each of these uses creates a set of stakeholders with limited rights to PAs. Kothari (Chapter 26) suggests that only a partnership between conservationists and communities/social activists, and the empowerment of ecosystem-dependent communities can withstand destruction of wildlife and habitats. Changes are, therefore, needed in the conservation policy, law and administration, to allow for a much more participatory system, one which is respectful to both the needs of wildlife and the rights of humans. Such changes will have to integrate relevant community knowledge and practices, customary laws and local institutional structures, vertical and horizontal integration within government agencies, land/water use planning in a regional context within which special areas for wildlife protection are supplemented by incentives for conservation across the spectrum of human resource uses, mutual learning sessions amongst various stakeholders, open access to information, and so on. However, such a conservation strategy requires rebuilding of community knowledge, practices, law and empowerment, trust between authority and local people and political will to overcome the socio-economic and cultural constraints (Kothari, Chapter 26). But there are several examples of people and resource communities having overcome these hurdles and created opportunities for shared resource management (Chapter 26; see also Marothia 1998). Using Keoladeo National Park (KNP) as a case in point, Chopra (Chapter 27) argues that biodiversity conservation can be both more effective and less resource consuming if stakeholders are involved in a joint or shared management based on areas of complementarity in benefit cost accruals and value perceptions as perceived by stakeholders. Using the travel cost approach method to estimate the nature of tourist demand for the services of park and multicriteria approach for ordinal ranking of different kinds of values as perceived by stakeholders, benefit and cost flows from KNP to local communities and urban economy, Chopra (Chapter 27) suggests a range of institutional arrangements (both external and internal) for joint management of PAs in general and wetlands in particular (see also Marothia 1998). Singh (Chapter 5) also argues for using the PAs approach for CPRs development.

Brij Gopal (Chapter 28) emphasizes that the concept of property regimes, which suits best to specific terrestrial resources, cannot be applied to the aquatic resources without taking the entire watershed into consideration. The policy makers must consider the whole river-basin as one watershed for which an integrated planning has to be made keeping in view the multitude of resources and stakeholders as well as the cascading effect of activities in the upper riparian areas (upstream watershed) on the downstream areas. The institutional arrangements, at the level of a Village Panchayat or the State, must take cognizance of all the individual resources and various stakeholders in the entire sub-watershed instead of fragmenting it into small units for maximizing the use for one resource at a time, as well as the impact of their activities on the downstream areas (Gopal, Chapter 28).

6. Common Pool Knowledge

Shiva (Chapter 29) and Gadgil (Chapter 30) emphasize the importance of community intellectual property rights and reconciling systems of common pool knowledge resource of indigenous communities with modern approaches to the management of natural resources. Both the Chapters look at the varying conceptions of the role of common pool knowledge and indigenous people in view of the international environmental policy.

6.a. Biodiversity and Community Intellectual Property Rights

With the expansion of patents and intellectual property rights (IPRs) into the domain of biodiversity, via the trade related IPRs (TRIPRs) programme and World Trade Organization (WTO), a potential threat has been posed to the biological and intellectual heritage of our diverse communities by appropriating and privatizing their knowledge (Shiva, Chapter 29). Shiva argues for evolving a pluralistic IPR regime with a strong legal framework which makes it possible to recognize and respect indigenous knowledge, and protect the indigenous knowledge systems and practices and livelihoods based on it and the prevention of biopiracy. Shiva further argues (Chapter 29) for usufructurary rights to protect biodiversity as CPRs as it is ethically consistent with the mutual interdependence philosophy of *Vasudhaiva Kutumkam.* Entitlements, equity, sustainability and justice are built into usufruct rights since ownership is based on the concept of return on labour to provide for ourselves, our children, our families, our communities in tribal societies. Whereas IPRs on plant genetic resources or products derived from them convert the survival resource held in common by the poor into the monopoly of the rich and powerful. Often this appropriation is done under projects for "bioprospecting". Bioprospecting, in effect, leads to the enclosure of the biological and intellectual commons. In the IPRs context, to recognize the rights of community it is necessary to evolve categories of community intellectual rights (CIRs) related to biodiversity to balance and set limits and boundary conditions for IPRs, and on the monopolies of Trans National Companies (TNCs) which they are designed to create (see also Berkes, Folke and Gadgil 1994, Marothia 1997d, Gupta 1999, Gadgil and Utkarsh 1999, Mishra 1999). Community control over common resources is the only real mechanism for ensuring sovereign control over natural resources. The legal precedence of biodiversity as commons has already been established by the Provisions of the Panchayats (Extension to the Scheduled Areas) Act. This implies that any IPR regime that relates to biodiversity has to have a mechanism of institutionalizing CIRs for respecting indigenous people, protecting biodiversity and preventing biopiracy.

6.b. Synthesis of Indigenous and Modern Scientific Knowledge

Gadgil emphasizes (Chapter 30) the importance of reconciling the system of the vast pools of locality specific slow track knowledge (indigenous knowledge) of complex natural systems with those generated through fast-tract science (scientific knowledge). He advocates preparation of documents such as the People's Biodiversity Registers that take advantage of the crucial methodological advances of fast-track science to confer dignity on and enhance the utility of slow-track knowledge and could serve as very useful tools in such an endeavour. Full benefits of such an integration would, of course, flow only when supported by systems of open, public participation in the management of natural resources and a just sharing of benefits flowing from relevant commercial applications (see also Berkes 1993, Berkes, Folke and Gadgil 1994, Marothia 1997d, Gupta 1999, Gadgil and Utkarsh 1999).

7. Property Rights, Institutional Change and Policy Problem

Marothia (Chapter 31) considers the question of an appropriate level of authority through a potential application of distributed governance concepts in managing CPRs. In this chapter particular attention is paid to how rights and responsibilities would be distributed among the State and local communities under alternative property rights regimes.

7.a. Distributed Governance and Competing Models of Management

Renewable CPRs have been managed and controlled under different resource management regimes in India. Dissatisfaction with the traditional failure of "pure" community natural resource management and "pure" government control had led to great interest in distributed governance. State or government control with active local communities involvement has recently been identified as a feasible option in managing CPRs (Marothia 1998). These alternative perspectives suggest that distributed governance or shared management might prove more effective than any form of "pure" government of "pure" local community management (Townsend and Polley 1995). Marothia (Chapter 31) discusses the outcomes of the CPRs-based development programmes implemented under different property regimes for the upliftment of the rural poor in the Chhattisgarh regions of Madhya Pradesh and argues in favour of distributed governance for managing CPRs through alternative approaches of management. Marothia (Chapter 31) further advocates a major shift in the role of policy-makers and administrators to share power for promoting greater involvement of the local people in decision making and administration. He emphasizes undertaking of theoretical and empirical research studies under different agro-climatic conditions for testing the efficacy and replicability of alternative models of distributed governance in managing CPRs.

8. Conclusions and Policy Implications

The different chapters of this volume cover a wide range of CPRs case studies But despite their diversity, the chapters are woven together by a common thread— institutions to produce a collective outcome in the realm of managing CPRs. The evidence provided in this volume may be spelt out in three broad themes, namely, importance of the roles of institutions, effectiveness of institutional innovations and prospects of redesign or creating new institutions in contrast to the existing ones in managing CPRs. A number of issues have also emerged in connection with each broad theme that help to derive following policy relevant conclusions:

Cultural Capital and CPRs Management: The role of multiple social and institutional arrangements, property rights structures and determinants of resilience and sustainability of these arrangements in managing CPRs have effectively been analyzed in this volume. It has been concluded by several authors that the process of CPRs depletion begins with the collapse or erosion of formal and informal social capital (local customs/bindings, disintegration of customary systems, ethical codes, cultural and religious rules). CPRs-based development programmes have largely failed due to lack of understanding and non-incorporation of social capital in the formulation of the programmes. The importance to rebuild social capital for the rehabilitation of CPRs under the common property resource management system (CPRMS) has been brought out very clearly in this volume. Existence of appropriate institutions facilitates the effective functioning of CPRMS. In addition to the existence of appropriate institutions, willingness of the community to reform the existing institutional arrangements in the changing socio-cultural-religious-economic- political environment of the village systems and collective enforcement of new rules by the customary authority of resource management are also important factors in sustaining CPRMS. For example traditional institutions of Kuhls irrigation in Himachal Pradesh and SGs across the country are still functioning well under CPRMS even in the changing village environment with continuous social learning process.

Replicability of Community-based Institutional Innovations: Community mobilizers and NGOs play a catalytic role in designing multi-layered technical and institutional innovations intended to solve or alleviate ecological poverty through community participation in rainwater harvesting, tank management, irrigation water distribution in command areas, groundwater management, rehabilitation of CPLRs, biodiversity, common pool knowledge, fisheries and forestry resources. However care has to be taken to put appropriate property right regime(s) in their proper perspective when considering transferability from one area or resource type to another. For example, rainwater harvesting institutional innovations developed by the NGOs or *Kuhls* irrigation system may not be transferable or replicable in their exact form, but some of their basic attributes for designing institutions may be. Community-based experiences have been adopted by many government organizations and institutional mechanisms developed by communities and NGOs have been successfully replicated. Change in the mindset of politicians, bureaucrats, resource management agencies, village-level institutions is the common feature of a successful replication of community-based institutional innovations. CPRMS is a more acceptable form for replicability of community-based designed institutional innovations.

Alternative Property Rights Regimes: The role of property rights regimes, their structures, functions, enforceability and linkages with social and ecological systems in managing CPRs have been discussed in several chapters. It has been documented adequately that without well-designed institutional arrangements, and effective authority systems, property right regimes under different management systems have failed in the past and are continuing to fail and CPRs cannot be sustained over time. It has also been documented very well that no single type of property right regime can solve the problem of CPRs degradation or rehabilitation. In addressing CPRs degradation problems, attention has been carefully focussed on specific human and ecological contexts, besides the establishment of enforceable property rights regimes. Relative merits of a range of institutional attributes like formal arrangements vs. informal social norms/practices, hard law vs. soft law arrangements, alternative decision- making mechanism, alternative technical and financial arrangements in conjunction with alternative property rights regimes at different stages of CPRs development have been discussed. Several authors have advocated joint/shared/distributed management or decentralized system for managing CPRs. Joint/shared/distributed governance examines how rights and responsibilities are distributed among and within the State, resource industry/ private owners and local communities. A balance mix of external and internal institutional arrangements at different levels of decision-making is important for a decentralized management system. As several chapters in this volume point out, shared/joint/distributed governance is a viable option. Depending on the resource type, a combination of different property rights regimes may also be viable.

Common Pool Knowledge and IPRs: Threat to the common biological and intellectual knowledge via trade-related intellectual property rights (TRIPRs) programme in the area of biodiversity has been extensively discussed and pluralistic IPR regimes and recognization of community intellectual property rights have been suggested to prevent biopiracy and to set limits and boundary conditions for IPR and the monopolies of TNCS. The importance of reconciling systems of traditional knowledge with modern knowledge in managing CPRs has been emphasized in terms of the interaction between international environmental policy on the use of traditional knowledge and the implementation of local-level resource management systems that use the traditional knowledge.

Future Research Foci: Despite a large body of knowledge presented in this volume on the crucial role and relevance of institutions, there are still important research issues which need further indepth investigation for a sustainable management of CPRs. These include identification of common features of successful institutional innovations and factors that threaten the development or survival of institutional innovations across agro-climatic situations; spatial and temporal externalities generated by institutional innovations at the same level of social organization and across levels of social organizations under different models of CPRs management; comparative advantages of creating new institutions against reforming existing institutions; means to incorporate flexibility, self-correcting procedures and social learning processes into existing/new CPRs management institutions; comparative benefits of formal vs. informal social norms, hard laws vs. soft laws, alternative decision-making external and internal institutional arrangements under alternative governance or property rights structures; possibilities of integrating property rights regimes with institutional arrangements, economic arrangements and a biophysical system at local, regional and national levels for CPRs development; role of property rights regimes in connection with TRIPS, IPRS, and community intellectual property rights structures; and incorporating common pool traditional knowledge in managing CPRs. Further understanding of these and other related issues through interdisciplinary collaborative research work, like the present volume, in different agro-climatic conditions and across social organizations, will help us to contribute to the pressing scientific and policy problems which surround the human interactions with CPRs through institutional frameworks at local, regional, national and even global levels.

REFERENCES

Agarwal, A. (ed.) 1992. *The Price of Forests*, New Delhi: Centre for Science and Environment.

Agarwal, A. (ed.) 1997. *The Challenge of the Balance*, New Delhi: Centre for Science and Environment.

Alchian, A., and H.Demsetz. 1973. "The Property Rights Paradigm", *Journal of Economic History,* 13: 16-27.
Arnold, J.E.M., and W.C. Stewart. 1991. *Common Property Resource Management in India,* Tropical Forestry Paper No.24, Department of Plant Sciences. Oxford Forestry Institute, Oxford: University of Oxford.
Arrow, K. J. 1975. *Social Choice and Individual Values,* New Haven: Yale University Press.
Bator, F. 1958. "The Anatomy of Market Failure", *Quarterly Journal of Economics,* 72: 351-79.
Becker, L. C. 1977. *Property Rights: Philosophic Foundations,* Boston: Routledge and Kegan Paul.
Berkes, F. (ed.) 1989. *Common Property Resources Ecology and Community–Based Sustainable Development,* London: Belhaven.
Berkes, F. 1993. "Traditional Ecological Knowledge in Perspective". In: Inglis, J.T. (ed.) *Traditional Ecological Knowledge, Concept and Cases,* Ottawa: Canadian Museum of Nature/ International Development Research Centre.
Berkes, F., and C. Folke. 1992. "A Systems Perspective on the Interrelations Between Natural, Human-Made and Cultural Capital", *Ecological Economics* 5:1-8.
Berkes, F., and C. Folke. 1994. Investing in Cultural Capital for Sustainable Use of Natural Capital. In Jansson, A.M., M. Hammer, C. Folke and R. Costanza (eds.) *Investing in Natural Capital: The Ecological Economics Approach to Sustainability,* Washington, D.C.: Inland Press.
Berkes, F., C. Folke, and M. Gadgil. 1994. "Traditional Ecological Knowledge, Biodiversity, Resilience and Sustainability". In: Perrings, C., K.G. Mäler, C. Folke, C.S. Holling and B.O. Jausson (eds.). *Biodiversity Conservation: Policy Issues and Options,* Dordrecht: Kluwer Academic Publishers.
Blomquist, W. 1992. *Dividing the Waters: Governing Groundwater in Southern California,* California: ICS Press
Bromley, D.W. 1978. "Property Rules, Liability Rules and Environmental Economics", *Journal of Economic Issues,* 12:43-60.
Bromley, D.W. 1985. "Resources and Economic Development: An Institutionalist Perspective", *Journal of Economics Issues,* 19: 779-96.
Bromley, D.W. 1989a. "Property Relations and Economic Development: The other Land Reform", *World Development,* 17:867-77.
Bromley, D.W. 1989b. *Economic Interests and Institutions: The Conceptual Foundations of Public Policy,* New York: Basil Blackwell.
Bromley, D.W. 1991. *Environment and Economy: Property Rights and Public Policy,* Oxford: Basil Blackwell.
Bromley, D. W. (ed.) 1992. *Making the Commons Work,* San Francisco: ICS Press.
Bromley, D.W., and M.M. Cernea. 1989. *The Management of Common Property Natural Resources: Some Conceptual and Operational Fallacies,* Discussion Paper 57, Washington, D.C.: The World Bank.
Bromley, D.W., and D. P. Chapagain. 1984. "The Village Against the Center: Resources Depletion in South Asia", *American Journal of Agricultural Economics,* 66: 868-73.
Buchanan, J.M., and G. Tullock. 1962. *The Calculus of Consent : Logical Foundations of Constitutional Democracy,* Ann Arbor: University of Michigan Press.
Castle, E.N.1978. "Property Rights and the Political Economy of Resource Scarcity", *American Journal of Agricultural Economics,* 60:1-9.
Chambers, R. 1988. *Managing Canal Irrigation : Practical Analysis from South Asia,* New Delhi: Oxford & IBH Publishing Company, Pvt. Ltd.
Chambers, R., N.C. Saxena, and T. Shah. 1989. *To The Hands of the Poor: Water and Trees,* New Delhi: Oxford & IBH Publishing Co. Pvt. Ltd.
Chopra, K., G.K. Kadekodi, and M.N. Murty. 1990. *Participatory Development: People and Common Property Resources,* New Delhi: Sage Publications.

Ciriacy-Wantrup, S.V. 1963. *Resource Conservation: Economics and Policies*, Berkeley: University of California Press (revised edition).

Ciriacy-Wantrup, and R.C.Bishop. 1975. "Common Property as a Concept in Natural Resource Policy", *Natural Resources Journal*, 15: 713-27.

Coase, R.H. 1960. "The Problem of Social Cost", *Journal of Law and Economics*, 3(October):1-14.

Coleman, J. 1988. "Social Capital in the Creation of Human Capital", *American Journal of Sociology*, 94 (Supplement): S95-S120.

Commons, J.R. 1924. *Legal Foundations of Capitalism*, New York: Macmillan Company.

Commons, J.R. 1931. "Institutional Economics", *American Economic Review*, 21:649-57.

Commons, J.R. 1934. *Institutional Economics*, New York: Macmillan Company.

Commons, J.R.1950. *The Economics of Collective Action*, New York: Macmillan Company.

Cox, S.J.B.1985. "No Tragedy on the Commons", *Environmental Ethics*, 7: 49-61.

Dales, J.H. 1968. *Pollution, Property and Prices: An Essay in Policy Making and Economics*, Toronto: University of Toronto Press.

Damodaran, A. 1990. *Property Rights and the Economics of Common Lands: Exploring the Nexus in Economy: Planning and Policies*, New Delhi: Concept Publishing Company.

Damodaran, A. 1991. "Tragedy of Commons and Comedy of Common Property Resources", *Economic and Political Weekly*, September.

Dasgupta, P. 1982. *The Control of Resources*, Delhi: Oxford University Press.

Dasgupta, P. 1993. *An Inquiry into Well-being and Destitution*, Oxford: Clarendon Press.

Dasgupta,P., and K.G.Mäler. 1994. *Poverty, Institutions, and the Environmental Resource Base*, Environmental Paper No.9, Washington, D.C.: World Bank.

Demsetz, H. 1966. "Some Aspects of Property Rights", *Journal of Law and Economics*, 9: 61-70.

Demsetz, H. 1967. "Toward a Theory of Property Rights", *American Economic Review*, 57: 347-59.

Dhawan, B.D. 1995. *Groundwater Depletion, Land Degradation and Irrigated Agriculture in India*, New Delhi: Commonwealth Publishers.

Drobak, J. K., and J.C. Nye. 1997. "Introduction". In: Drobak, J.K. and J.C. Nye (eds.) *The Frontiers of the New Institutional Economics*, California: Academic Press.

Ely, R. T. 1914. *Property and Contract*, New York: Macmillan Company.

Feeny, D., F. Berkes, B. J. McCay, and J. M. Acheson. 1990. "The Tragedy of the Commons: Twenty-Two Years Later", *Human Ecology*, 18:1-19.

Folke, C., and F. Berkes. 1995. "Mechanism that Link Property Rights to Ecological System". In: Hanna, S. and M.Munasinghe (eds.) *Property Rights and the Eovironment - Social and Ecological Issues*, Washington, D.C.: The Beijer International Institute of Ecological Economics and World Bank.

Furubotn, E., and S. Pejovich. 1972."Property Rights and Economic Theory: A Survey of Recent Literature", *Journal of Economic Literature*, 10 (December): 137-62.

Gandhi, V.P. 1998. "Rapporteur's Report on Institutional Framework for Agricultural Development", *Indian Journal of Agricultural Economics*, 53:552-564.

Gadgil, M., and G. Utkarsh. 1999."Intellectual Property Rights and Agricultural Technology: Linking the Micro and the Macro Scale", *Indian Journal of Agricultural Economics*, 54(3): 327-341.

Gibbs, C.J.N., and D.W. Bromley. 1989. "Institutional Arrangements for Management of Rural Resources: Common Property Regimes". In: Berkes, F. (ed.) *Common Property Resource: Ecology and Community-Based Sustainable Development*, London: Belhaven Press.

Gonce, R.A. 1971. John R. "Commons' Legal Economic Theory", *Journal of Economic Issues*, 5:80-95.

Gupta, A.K. 1986. Sociology of Stress: Why do Common Property Resource Management Projects Fail? *Proceedings of The Conference On Common Property Resource Management*, Washington, D.C.: BOSTID & National Research Council.

Gupta, A.K. 1995. "Sustainable Institutions for Natural Resource Management: How Do We Participate in People's Plans". In: Samad, S.A., T. Watanabe and Seung-Jin Kim (eds.) *People's Initiatives For Sustainable Development: Lessons of Experience*, Kualalumpur: Asian and Pacific Development Centre.

Gupta, A.K. 1999. "Making Indian Agriculture More Knowledge Intensive and Competitive: The Case of Intellectual Property Rights", *Indian Journal of Agricultural Economics*, 54(3): 342-369.

Hardin, G. 1968. "The Tragedy of Commons", *Science*, 162:1243-1248

Hardin, G., and J. Baden. (eds.) 1977. *Managing the Commons*, New York: W.H. Freeman and Company.

Hardin, R. 1982. *Collective Action*, Baltimore: The Johns Hopkins University Press.

Iyengar, S. 1989. "Common Property Land Resources in Gujarat: Some Findings about their Size, Status, and Use", *Economic and Political Weekly*, 24: A.67-77.

Iyengar, S. 1997. "Common Property Land Resources in Gujarat: Some Issues in Size, Status and Use". In: Parikh, J. and S. Reddy (eds.) *Sustainable Regeneration of Degraded Lands*, New Delhi: Tata McGraw Hill Publishing Company Limited.

Jodha, N.S. 1986. "Common Property Resources and Rural Poor in Dry Regions of India", *Economic and Political Weekly*, 21 (27): 1169-1181.

Jodha, N.S. 1992. "Rural Common Property Resources: A Missing Dimension of Development Strategies", *Discussion Paper No.169*, Washington, D.C.: The World Bank.

Jodha, N.S. 1995. "Common Property Resources and the Environmental Context. Role of Biophysical Versus Social Stresses", *Economic and Political Weekly*, 30(51).

Jodha, N.S. 1996. "Property Rights and Development". In: Hanna, S.S., C.Folke and K.G. Mäler (eds.) *Rights to Nature: Ecological Economic, Cultural and Political Principles of Institutions for the Environment*, Washington, D.C.: Island Press.

Joshi, P.K. 1997. "Farmers' Investments and Government Intervention in Salt-Affected and Waterlogged Soils". In: Kerr, J.M., D.K. Marothia, K. Singh, C. Ramasamy and W.R. Bently (eds.) *Natural Resource Economics: Theory and Application in India*, New Delhi: Oxford & IBH Publishing Co.Pvt.Ltd.

Kiser, L. L., and E. Ostrom. 1982. "The Three Worlds of Action: A Metatheoretical Synthesis of Institutional Approaches". In: Ostrom, E. (ed.) *Strategies of Political Inquiry*, Beverly Hills, Calif: Sage

Kramer, R.A., and V. Ballabh. 1992. "Management of Common Pool Forest Resources". In: Peters, G.H. and B.F. Stanton (eds.) *Sustainable Agricultural Development: The Role of International Cooperation*, England: Dartmouth. Mass: Peter Smith.

Long, E.J. 1953. "Freedom and Security as Policy Objectives", *Journal of Farm Economics*, 35:317-322

Marothia, D.K. 1981. *An Economic and Institutional Analysis of Soil Erosion on Agricultural Lands*, Ph.D. Dissertation, The University of Alberta, Edmonton, Canada.

Marothia, D.K. 1988a. *Externalities: A Review of Alternative Approaches*, Department of Agricultural & Natural Resource Economics (DANRE), Indira Gandhi Agricultural University, Raipur (India), DANRE Research Bulletin No.2.

Marothia, D.K. 1988b. "Afforestation of Bhata Soils: Socio-economics and Management Aspects", *Indian Journal of Agricultural Economics*, 43(3): 305-309.

Marothia, D.K. 1989a. "Resource Ownership and Human Interaction: A Theoretical Exposition", *Annals of Arid Zone*, 28: 165-80.

Marothia, D.K. 1989b. "Socio-Economic Rationales of Wasteland Afforestation", *Journal of Tropical Forestry*, 5: 343-350.

Marothia, D.K. 1992a. "Village Ponds and Aquaculture Development: Issues of Inequality in Common Property Regimes", *Proceedings of the Annual Conference of the International Association for the Study of Common Property*, Washington, D.C.: National Research Council.

Marothia, D.K. 1992b. "Village Irrigation Tanks : Institutional Design for Sustainable Resource Use", *Agricultural Situation in India,* 47 (6): 479-487.

Marothia, D.K. 1992c. "Rapportear's Report on Tribal and Hill Economy", *Indian Journal of Agricultural Economics,* 47(3): 567-578.

Marothia, D.K. 1993. "Property Regimes and Institutional Arrangements: Concepts and their Relevance in Managing the Village Commons", *Indian Journal of Agricultural Economics,* 48(3): 557-65.

Marothia, D.K. 1995. "Village Ponds and Aquaculture Development: Is Conflict Inevitable?" *Invited Paper presented to the National Workshop on Poultry, Fisheries and Food Processing organized for the Honorable Members of Parliament* held at National Academy of Agricultural Research Management, Hyderabad (India), July: 4-7

Marothia, D.K. 1996. "Cooperative Management of Non Timber Forest Products: Issues of Property Rights and Institutional Structures". In: Rajagopalan (ed.) *Rediscovering Cooperation: Strategies for the Models of Tomorrow,* Vol. 2, Anand: Institute of Rural Management.

Marothia, D.K. 1997a. "Institutional Arrangements in Common Fish Ponds". In: Kerr, J.M., D.K. Marothia, K. Singh, C. Ramasamy and W.R. Bentley (eds.) *Natural Resource Economics: Theory and Application in India,* New Delhi: Oxford & IBH Publishing Company.

Marothia, D.K. 1997b. "Agricultural Technology and Environmental Quality: An Institutional Perspective—Key note paper", *Indian Journal of Agricultural Economics* 52(3): 473-487.

Marothia, D.K. 1997c. "Property Rights, Externalities and Environmental Pollution". In: Agarwal, A. (ed.) *The Challenge of the Balance,* New Delhi: Centre for Science and Environment.

Marothia, D.K. 1997d. "Property Regimes in Medicinal and Aromatic Plant Resources: Some Policy Issues", *Keynote paper presented at the National Conference on Health Care and Development of Herbal Medicines,* held at I.G. Agricultural University, Raipur (India) August 29-30.

Marothia, D.K. 1998. "Shared Management in Non-timber Forest Resources", *Invited paper presented at the International Workshop on Shared Resources Management in South Asia - The Next Step,* held at Institute of Rural Management, Anand, (India) February 17-19.

Marothia, D.K., A.P. Mukherjee, and S.K. Sharma. 1987. "Canal Irrigation System: Socio-Economic and Management Issues", *Indian Journal of Agricultural Economics,* 44 (33): 300.

Marothia, D.K., and Nandi, D. 1994. "Degraded Lands, Agroforestry and Energy Needs: Issues and Development Strategies". In: Punjab Singh, P.S.Pathak and M.M. Roy (eds.) *Agroforstry Systems for Sustainable Land Use,* New Delhi: Oxford & IBH Publishing Company.

Marothia, D. K., and W. E. Phillips. 1985. "Analysis of Natural Resource Problems Using a Synthesis of Neoclassical and Institutional Economics", *Asian Journal of Economics and Social Studies* 4(4): 263- 281.

Matthews, R.C.O. 1986. "The Economics of Institutions and the Sources of Growth",*Economics Journal,* 96: 903-18.

McCay, B.J., and J. M. Acheson. (eds.) 1987. *The Question of the Commons: The Culture and Ecology of Communal Resources,* Tucson: The University of Arizona Press.

Mishan, E.J. 1971. "The Postwar Literature on Externalities : An Interpretative Essay", *Journal of Economic Literature,* 9: 1-28.

Mishra, J.P. 1999. "Rapportear's Report on Intellectual Property Rights and Agricultural Technology", *Indian Journal of Agricultural Economics,* 54(3): 447-458.

Mishra, P.R., and M. Sarin. 1987. *Sukhomajri-Nada: A New Model of Eco-Development,* Bombay: Business India, Nov.16-29.

Mosse, D. 1997. "The Symbolic Making of a Common Property Resource: History, Ecology and Locality in a Tank-irrigated Landscape in South India", *Development and Change,* 28(3).

Myrdal, G. 1978. "Institutional Economics", *Journal of Economics Issues,* 12:771-783.

Nadkarni, M.V., and S.A. Pasha. 1991. "Developing Uncultivated Lands – Some Issues from Karnataka Experience", *Indian Journal of Agricultural Economics*, 46 (4) : 543-554

Nadkarni, M.V., S.A. Pasha, and L.S. Prabhakar.1989. *The Political Economy of Forest Use of Management*, New Delhi: Sage Publications.

Norgaard, R. B. 1985. "Environmental Economics: An Evolutionary Critique and a Plea for Pluralism", *Journal of Environmental Economics and Management*, 12:382-393.

North, D.C. 1990. *Institutions, Institutional Change and Económic Performance*, Cambridge: Cambridge University Press.

Oakerson, R.J. 1986. "A Model for the Analysis of Common Property Problems". *Proceedings of the Conference on Common Property Resource Management*. Washington, D.C.: National Academy of Sciences.

Oakerson, R.J. 1992. "Analyzing the Commons: A Framework". In: Bromley, D.W. (ed.) *Making the Commons Work*, San Francisco: ICS Press.

Olson, M. 1971. *The Logic of Collective Action : Public Goods and the Theory of Groups*, Cambridge, Mass.: Harvard University Press.

Ostrom, E. 1986. "Issues of Definitions and Theory: Some Conclusions and Hypotheses". *Proceedings of the Conference on Common Property Resource Management*, Washington, D.C.: National Academy of Sciences.

Ostrom, E. 1990. *Governing the Commons: The Evolution of Institutions for Collective Action*, Cambridge: Cambridge University Press.

Ostrom, E. 1992. *Crafting Institutions for Self Governing Irrigation Systems*, San Francisco: ICS Press.

Ostrom, V. and R. John. 1976. "Commons Foundations for Policy Analysis", *Journal of Economic Issues*, 10:839-857.

Ostrom, V., D. Feeny, and H. Picht. (eds.) 1988. *Rethinking Institutional Analysis and Development: Issues, Alternatives and Choices*, San Francisco: Institute for Contemporary Studies Press.

Palanisami, K., and J.C.Flinn. 1988. "Evaluating the Performance of Tank Irrigation Systems", *Agriculture Systems*, 28:161-177.

Parikh, J., and S. Reddy. (eds.) 1997. *Sustainable Regeneration of Degraded lands*, New Delhi: Tata McGraw Hill Publishing Company Limited.

Parson, K.H. 1941. "Social Conflicts and Agricultural Programmes", *Journal of Farm Economics*, 23: 743-764.

Randall, A. 1972. *On the Theory of Market Solutions to Externality Problems*, Oregon Agricultural Experiment Station, Special Report No.351.

Randall, A. 1975. "Property Rights and Social Microeconomics", *Natural Resources Journal* 15: 729-48.

Randall, A. 1978a. "Property Institutions and Economic Behaviour", *Journal of Economic Issues* 12: 1-21.

Randall, A. 1978b. "Contemporary Issues in Natural Resource Economics: Discussion", *American Journal of Agricultural Economics*, 60 (May): 290-292.

Rao, V.M., and M.G. Chandrakanth. 1984. "Resource at the Margin, Tank Irrigation Programme in Karnataka", *Economic and Political Weekly* (Review of Agriculture number): A 54-A54.

Rawls, J. 1971. *A Theory of Justice*, Cambridge, Mass.: The Belknap Press of Harvard University Press.

Runge, C. F. 1981. "Common Property Externalities: Isolation, Assurance and Resource Depletion in a Traditional Grazing Context". *American Journal of Agricultural Economics*, 63: 595-607.

Saleth, R.M. 1994. "Towards a New Water Institution: Economics, Law and Policy", *Economic and Political Weekly*, 29 (39): A-147-A-155.

Sampath, R.K., and R. A.Young. (eds.) 1990. *Social, Economic and Institutional Issues in Third World Irrigation Management*, San Francisco : Westview Press.

Samuels, W. 1972. "Welfare Economics, Power and Property". In: Wunderlich, G. and W.L. Gibson (ed.) *Perspectives on Property*, University Park: Penn, State University Press.

Samuels, W. 1974. "The Coase Theorem and the Study of Law and Economics", *Natural Resources Journal*, 14:1-34.

Saxena, N.C., and V. Ballabh. (eds.) 1995. *Farm Forestry in South Asia*, New Delhi: Sage Publications.

Schmid, A.A. 1972. "Analytical Institutional Economics: Challenging Problems in the Economics of Resources for a New Environment", *American Journal of Agricultural Economics*, 54:893-901.

Schmid, A.A. 1976. "The Economics of Property Rights: A Review Article", *Journal of Economics Issues*, 10: 159-68.

Schmid, A.A. 1978. *Property, Power and Public Choice: An Inquiry into Law and Economics*, New York: Praeger.

Schultz, T.W. 1968. "Institutions and Rising Economic Value of Man", *American Journal of Agricultural Economics*, 50: 1113-1122.

Scott, A. 1955. "The Fishery: The Objectives of Sole Ownership", *Journal of Political Economy*, 63: 116-24.

Sen, A. 1979. *Collective Choice and Social Welfare*, Amsterdam: North Holland.

Sen, A. 1984. *Resources, Values and Development*, Delhi: Oxford University Press.

Sen, A. 1987. *On Ethics and Economics*, New York: Basil Blackwell.

Sen, A. 1992. *Inequality Reexamined*, New York: Russell Sage Foundation.

Sengupta, N. 1991. *Managing Common Property: Irrigation in India and the Philippines*, New Delhi: Sage Publications.

Shah, T. 1993. *Groundwater Markets and Irrigation Development: Political Economy and Practical Policy*, Bombay: Oxford University Press.

Singh, K. 1994. *Managing Common Pool Resources: Principles and Case Studies*, Delhi: Oxford University Press.

Singh, K. 1997. "Property Rights and Tenures in Natural Resources". In: Kerr, J.M., D.K.Marothia, K.Singh, C.Ramasamy and W.R.Bentley (eds.) *Natural Resource Economics: Theory and Application in India*, New Delhi: Oxford and IBH Publishing Company, Pvt. Limited.

Singh, K., and V.Ballabh. (eds.) 1996. *Cooperative Management in Natural Resources*, New Delhi: Sage Publications.

Söderbaum, P. 1986. "Economics, Ethics and Environmental Problems". *The Journal of Interdisciplinary Economics*, 1:139-153.

Söderbaum, P. 1990. "Neoclassical and Institutional Approaches to Agriculture, Environment and Development". In: Csaki, C., T. Dams, D. Metzger and J. van Zyl (eds.) *Agricultural Restructuring in Southern Africa*, Windhoek, Namibia: International Association of Agricultural Economics.

Srivastava, U.K., B.H. Dholakia, S.S. Rao, and S. Vathsala. 1993. *Freshwater Aquaculture in India*. New Delhi: Oxford & IBH Publishing Co.

Srivastava, U.K., B.H. Dholakia, S. Vathsala, and K. Chidambaram. 1991. *Fishery Sector of India*. New Delhi: Oxford & IBH Publishing Co.

Tang, S.Y. 1992. *Institutions and Collective Action: Self-Governance in Irrigation*, San Francisso: ICS Press.

Townsend, R.E., and S.G.Polley. 1995. "Distributed Governance in Fisheries". In: Hanna, S. and M. Munasinghe (eds.) *Property Rights and the Environment – Social and Ecological Issues*. Washington, D.C.: The Beijer International Institute of Ecological Economics and the World Bank.

Uphoff, N. 1986. *Local Institutional Development: An Analytical Sourcebook With Cases*, West Hartford Connecticut : Kumarian Press.

Vaidyanathan, A. 1996a. "Depletion of Groundwater: Some Issues", *Indian Journal of Agricultural Economics*, 51:184-192.

Vaidyanathan, A.1996b. "Agricultural Development: Imperative of Institutional Reforms". *Economic and Political Weekly*, Special No. (Sept.): 2452-2458.

Vaidyanathan, A. 1997. "Tanks and Tanks Irrigation". In: Agrawal, A. (ed.) *The Challenges of the Balance*, New Delhi: Center for Science and Environment.

Veeman, T. 1978. "Water Policy and Water Institutions in Northern India :The Case of Groundwater Rights", *Natural Resource Journal*, 18 (3) :569-587.

Von Oppen, M. 1985. "Tank Irrigation in South India- Adapting A Traditional Technology to Modern Socio-economic Conditions", *Irrigation Symposium on Traditional Irrigation Schemes and Potential for their Improvement*, Berlin: Federal Republic of Germany, 109-118.

Wade, R. 1988a. *Village Republics: Economic Conditions for Collective Action in South India*, Cambridge (USA): Cambridge University Press.

Wade, R. 1988b. "The Management of Irrigation Systems: How to Evoke Truest and Avoid Prisoners Dilemma", *World Development*, 16:489-500.

Weimer, D.L. 1995. "Institutional Design: Overview". In: Weimer, D.L. (ed.) *Institutional Design*, Boston: Kluwer Academic Publishers.

Wilber, C.K., and R.S. Harrison. 1978. "The Methodological Basis of Institutional Economics: Pattern Model, Story Telling and Holism". *Journal of Economic Issues*, 12:61-89.

Williamson, O.E. 1994. "The Institutions of Governance of Economic Development and Reform". In: *Proceedings of the Annual Conference on Development Economics*, Washington, D.C.: World Bank.

SECTION 1

THE COMMONS, RURAL DEVELOPMENT AND INSTITUTIONS

2 Decline of Rural Commons : Role of Population Growth and Public Policies

N.S. Jodha

1. Previewing the Issues

This chapter deals with some relatively unrecognised consequences of demographic changes and equally unrecognised processes behind these changes. Our thematic focus is on rural common property resources or common pool resources (CPRs) and their changing situation following the demographic changes in the dry tropical regions of India. CPRs despite the decline in their area and physical productivity, constitute an important component of community assets in India as in other developing countries, and significantly contribute towards the people's sustenance. Hence, a need for looking at their changing status, the factors causing their decline and possible remedial measures.

In the mainstream debate on the subject the decline of CPRs is strongly attributed to population growth and the consequent land hunger leading to the inevitability of decline of CPRs (McNicoll and Cain 1990). However, without denying the association between land hunger and shrinkage of CPRs, our contention is that the above formulation explains the changing situation of CPRs only partially. A closer look at the changing CPR situation and changing features of population reveals several dimensions of the former of which, decline of area (due to increased population pressure), is only one. The other dimensions of changes in CPRs due to demographic changes are seldom recognised by the mainstream work on the consequences of population growth. The same is true about the recognition of involved qualitative aspects of population influencing the status of CPRs. This chapter, with the help of field-level studies reflects on these dimensions of the CPR and demographic changes and their causes and consequences. Accordingly, in the following discussion, we focus on CPRs as an embodiment of multiple social and institutional arrangements evolved and enforced by the rural communities for protecting and harnessing their natural resources. The erosion or collapse of these arrangements leading to the decline of CPRs, is presented as "unrecognised" or "less recognised" consequences of demographic changes. They are unrecognised because of their qualitative nature and non-visibility at the aggregative level. These arrangements are very basic in terms of inducing and sustaining community level collective concerns and group action for protection and management of CPRs. These arrangements manifest what is described as 'social capital' at micro level.

Next we deal with the factors behind the decline or erosion of social capital and related aspects, as important dimensions of demographic changes. Though increased population has negatively affected CPRs, the discussion shows that growth in the number of people affecting area and use of CPRs explains the situation only partially. Most of the factors and processes that adversely influence "social capital" and related aspects, and thereby cause the decline of the CPRs area, productivity and management, fall outside the demography of numbers. The qualitative changes in population, i.e. changes in attitudes, perceptions and functioning as social groups through reciprocity, sharing, networking, etc. are caused mainly by non-demographic factors or driving forces. These driving forces have their origin in state policies, market forces and the changing survival and growth contexts of rural communities. Admittedly, at times these changes (specially policies) might emerge as inappropriate responses to population pressure and associated poverty. For instance, state policies in India, following their failure to transfer surplus land from larger farmers to the landless, curtailed the CPR area to give land to the poor. However, in most circumstances these policies emerge independent of population growth and accelerate the qualitative processes of demographic change, influencing status of CPRs.

2. What are CPRs? Manifestations of Collective Concerns

Common property resources or common pool resources (CPRs) can be broadly defined as those resources in which a group of people have a co-equal use rights, specially rights that exclude use of those resources by other people. Individual membership in the group of co-owners is typically conferred by membership in some other group, generally a group whose central purpose is not the use or administration of the resource (*per se*) such as village, a tribe, etc. (Ostrom *et al.* 1988, Bromley and Cernea 1989, Gupta 1987).

However, looking at CPRs from the "rights" perspective may disguise the more important "obligations or responsibility" aspects of CPRs and the basic driving forces that help in shaping and enforcing the obligations. The above co-equal usage rights, responsibilities, and measures to enforce then, as mentioned earlier, are institutional arrangements evolved by a rural community to protect, manage and regulate the use of specific natural resources, which help the community in facing the constraints and risks and also in harnessing the opportunities generated by their natural resources. These tasks, for a variety of reasons, cannot be managed with the individualised adaptation strategies of the community members (Jodha 1995). The effectiveness of CPRs as a collective strategy is directly linked to the community's concern, commitment, norms and group action to enforce them. Accordingly, any land resource with shared access right to the members of a group acquires the status of CPR only with their collective involvement in its management. The collective involvement in turn is a manifestation of the community's attribute already described as "social capital". Accordingly, once "social capital" depletes (or collective management of resources declines) CPR becomes an open access resource and its process of depletion begins as the evidence presented in the paper clearly shows. However, to have a better idea of the need and basis of collective strategies (manifested through provision of CPRs), it will be useful to briefly comment on the range of services and functions performed by CPRs, which satisfy the collective concerns and needs of the community. To facilitate an understanding of the above functions, it is essential to identify CPRs. In the dry regions of India, CPRs include community pastures, community forests, wastelands, sacred groves, common dumping and threshing grounds, watershed drainages and village ponds, rivers, rivulets as well as their banks and beds. At times they are described to represent "uncultivated-half" of India.

A quick look at the products and services offered by well-managed CPRs would indicate that they are not only the sources of physical supplies and income/employment for the people especially the poor, but they are a means to satisfy several social concerns and collective needs (Jodha 1995).

(i) CPRs as a source of what is described as "bio-diversity in bush" manifest the community's concerns as well as operational norms of the people-managed biodiversity conservation systems (as against the state-managed biodiversity conservation systems in parks and protected wild), to serve current and future needs of the community and maintain positive ecosystem-social system links (Jodha 1996b).

(ii) CPRs, generally comprising fragile and marginal landscapes unsuited for cropping are occupied by natural vegetation. Besides helping in protecting and harnessing of nature's diversity by the community, by remaining outside the community's use-intensification zone (through ploughing), they help reduce the chances of erosion of fragile lands.

(iii) By influencing micro-climate, hydrological and nutrient flows in watershed contexts, CPRs act as support land for croplands and influence crop yields.

(iv) By offering multiple products and services, CPRs help in integrating the internal inequity-based diversity of community stakes in its natural resource base i.e. groups with different economic occupations can meet their diverse needs from the same natural sources, i.e. CPRs.

(v) As a part of the community's diversification strategy, CPRs (due to non-covariate flow of products and input use when compared to crop lands) help in reducing the production risks for the community and in reducing social inequities.

(vi) Finally, by providing a concrete, operational context in the form of required group action for their management, CPRs play an invisible but significant role in the maintenance and constant renewal of social capital implying attitudes, approaches, and mechanisms supporting collective concerns and action, despite internal heterogeneities of a community.

The aforementioned contributions of CPRs are not easy to quantify except in terms of indicating some proxies (e.g. higher diversity, density of vegetation in well-managed CPR units; or better performance of crop and livestock farming in villages with a better upkeep of CPRs; or very high share of CPR-generated income in the drought period sustenance income of the household). The later discussion on the bio-physical degradation of CPRs will reflect on some of these aspects. Since most of the above benefits are indivisible (and also less visible) the community with a collective concern (and not individuals) can promote and protect the sources of such gains. However, besides the collective, indivisible and invisible gains, CPRs make several quantifiable contributions towards the community's sustenance.

3. Contributions of CPRs

According to the detailed study of CPRs conducted over a period of four years, covering more than 80 villages from 21 districts scattered in seven major states in the dry tropical region of India, the important contributions of CPRs are as follows (Jodha 1986, 1992):

(i) The poor households (including agricultural labourers) and small farmers (owning less than 2 hectares of dry land equivalent) secured 66 to 84 per cent of their total fuel requirements from CPRs in different states. CPRs accounted for 79 to 84 per cent of total animals grazing days in the case of the poor in different areas. The total employment through CPR-product collection, etc., accounted for 137 to 196 workdays per poor household in different areas. This is more than per household employment days generated by public work programmes in rural areas in many states. CPRs-generated income worked out to Rs. 534 to 774 per household and accounted for 19 to 23 per cent of the total average household income from different sources. The Gini-Coefficient of income as a measure of inequity declined from 44-50 per cent to 33-41 per cent when CPR-generated income is included in household income for the village. The magnitudes of the above variables were slightly lower for medium size farm households and much lower for the large farmers in the study areas.

(ii) Yet another set of data (covering all categories of households) from the same study reflected on the contribution of CPRs to private farming. For farming operations during pre-sowing to pre-harvesting period, CPRs directly contributed 31 to 42 per cent of the cash and kind inputs used. Indirect contribution through sustaining draft animals, without private cost; sparing land from fodder cultivation for animals; sparing crop by-products for sale (rather than feeding own animals as CPRs provided the substitute source of fodder), etc., were much greater. Such resource saving, which would potentially disappear in the absence of CPRs accounted for 68-76 per cent to 84-96 per cent of total incomes or resources currently at the command of the farmers in different cases.

(iii) Finally, as a measure of collective risk minimisation strategy, CPRs contributed 42 to 57 per cent of drought year sustenance incomes of the households in different areas. The corresponding figures for non-drought years were 14 to 22 per cent respectively.

3.a. Decline of CPRs

Despite some unavoidable underestimation, the above data clearly show the rural people's dependence on CPRs and the latter's valuable contribution to their sustenance. However, despite this, CPRs are generally neglected and are declining rapidly in different areas. The decline is visible in (i) shrinkage of their areas, (ii) bio physical degradation, and (iii) loss of management systems. Table 1.1 summarises the decline of area in different states/districts covered by the study.

3.b. CPR Area Shrinkage

Accordingly, the area of CPRs had declined by 31 to 50 per cent in the studied villages of different states during the early 1980s as compared to the early 1950s, when different states introduced land reforms, which influenced the status and treatment of CPRs. As further investigations into the decline of CPR area showed, the bulk of the area decline was due to the governments' undeclared policies of privatisation of CPRs including by (i) legalisation of encroachments despite protest of villagers against it in some cases and (ii) often pre-election period distribution of land in the name of giving land to the landless. In practice 50 to 80 per cent of such privatised CPR land in different states went to the people who already had relatively more land. Consequently, the latter's average size of land holding after getting CPR land increased to 5 to 9.5 hectares per household in different states. The corresponding land holding size for the poor (ex-landless) households ranged between 1 and 1.3 hectares respectively (Jodha 1986, 1992).

TABLE 2.1: **Extent and Decline of Area of CPR Land in Dry Regions of India**

State (and no. of districts)	No. of study villages	CPR land 1982-84 (ha)	CPRs as % of total village area		% decline in CPR area since
			1982-84	1950-52	1950-52
Andhra Pradesh (3)	10	827	11	18	42
Gujarat (3)	15	589	11	19	44
Karnataka (4)	12	1,165	12	20	40
Madhya Pradesh (3)	14	1,435	24	41	41
Maharashtra (3)	13	918	15	22	31
Rajasthan (3)	11	1,849	16	36	55
Tamil Nadu (2)	7	412	10	21	50

Adapted from : Jodha 1986, where more disaggregated details are reported.

3.c. Bio-physical Degradation of CPRs

In the absence of systematic benchmark information on bio-physical conditions of CPRs in the past, the information on this aspect was collected through reconstruction of oral history and use of some unsystematically kept records. Nevertheless, it revealed some important aspects of bio-physical degradation and hence decline in productivity of CPRs. Table 2.2 summarises the details. Accordingly, not only availability of products from CPR has declined drastically but the overall extent of "biodiversity in bush" has also declined (Jodha 1996b). For collecting the same or lesser amount of CPR products, villagers (women) had to spend more time and cover longer distances now as compared to the past.

Other indicators of environmental resource degradation or decline of biodiversity revealed by Table 2.2 are: disappearance of a number of trees, and

TABLE 2.2: **Some Indicators of Physical Degradation of CPRs**[a]

Indicators of Changed Status and Context for Comparison	States (with number of villages)					
	Andhra Pradesh (3)	Gujarat (4)	Karnataka (2)	Madhya Pradesh (4)	Maha-rashtra (3)	Rajasthan (4)
CPR-products collected by villagers: [b]						
— In the past (no.)	32	35	40	46	30	27
— At present (no.)	9	11	19	22	10	13
Per hectare number of trees and shrubs in:						
— Protected CPRs[c]	476	684	662	882	454	517
— Unprotected CPRs	195	103	202	215	77	96
Number of watering points (ponds) in grazing CPRs:						
— In the past	17	29	20	16	9	48
— At present	4	13	4	3	4	11
Number of CPR plots where rich vegetation, indicated by their nomenclature, is no more available	—	12	3	6	4	15
CPR area used for cattle grazing in the past, currently grazed mainly by sheep/goat (ha)[d]	48	112	95	—	52	175

(a) Table adapted from Jodha (1992); based on observation and physical verification of status at the time of field research, compared to the situation in the past (i.e., 1950 or before) as reflected in collected oral and recorded descriptions in different villages. The choice of CPRs where plot-based data are reported was guided by the available information about them

(b) Includes different types of fruits, flowers, leaves, roots, timber, fuel, fodder, etc., in the villages. The past indicates the period preceding the 1950s. "Present" indicates the early 1980s.

(c) Protected CPRs were the areas (called "oran") where for religious reasons live trees and shrubs are not cut. The situation of CPR plots (numbering between 2 and 4 in different areas) was compared with other bordering plots of CPRs which were not protected by any religious or other sanctions.

(d) Relates to area covered by specific plots, traditionally used for grazing high productivity animals (lactating cows, working bullocks or horses of feudal landlords). Because of the commons' depletion, such animals no more grazed there.

shrubs which existed prior to 1950; non-usability of traditionally high productivity plots for high priority uses (e.g. grazing of lactating cows, etc.). A comparison of protected and unprotected plots gives a clear idea of the above changes. Table 2.2 is quite self-explanatory.

4. Weakened Management System

Physical degradation of CPRs (and also shrinkage of their area) is paralleled by a gradual decline in the social arrangements designed for management of CPRs—through regulated use, group action for upkeep and cash and kind investment for development of CPRs. This is indicated by discontinuation or absence of a number of past obligations of CPR users in the present context. Table 2.3 provides an account of such changes.

TABLE 2.3: **Some Indicators of Changes in the Management of CPRs**[a]

	Number of Villages Pursuing the Following Measures					
State (with Number of Villages)	Formal/Informal Regulations on CPR Use[b]		Formal/Informal Taxes/levies on CPR Use[d]		Users' Formal/ Informal Obligation Towards Upkeep of CPR[e]	
	In the Past[c]	At Present	In the Past	At Present	In the Past	At Present
Andhra Pradesh (10)	10	—[f]	7	—	8	—
Gujarat (15)	15	2	8	—	11	2
Karnataka (12)	12	2	9	—	12	3
Madhya Pradesh (14)	14	2	10	—	14	3
Maharashtra (13)	11	1	6	—	10	1
Rajasthan (11)	11	1	11	—	11	2
Tamil Nadu (7)	7	—	4	—	7	1

a. Table adapted from Jodha (1992).
b. Measures such as regulated/rotational grazing, seasonal restrictions on use of CPRs, provision of CPR watchmen etc.
c. "Past" stands for the period prior to the 1950s, present stands for the early 1980s.
d. Measures such as grazing taxes, levies, and penalties for violation of regulations on the use of CPRs.
e. Measures such as contribution towards desilting of watering points, fencing, trenching, protection of CPRs, etc.
f. (—) indicates nil.

Weakening of the CPR management means weakening of village-based, socially sanctioned, customary authority of village elders to manage CPR affairs, non-functioning of consensual rules ensuring contributions for CPR development, penalising the resource abusers, etc. The consequent lack of resources for maintenance of CPRs and absence of provisions against their overextraction have initiated the process of depletion of CPRs. This represents a situation where decline of "social capital" as a community asset has led to the depletion of the physical asset (CPR) of the community. Both are equally invisible to the mainstream decision makers, planners and policy makers.

5. The Process of CPR Decline

Though already alluded to in different contexts, the factors and processes of decline of CPRs are now discussed in more detail. Here we put together the factors which led to the decline of CPR in terms of area, physical degradation and management system; relate them to the disintegration of social arrangement evolved and enforced by rural community to protect and manage CPRs; look at these changes as indicators of (qualitative) demographic changes and, finally, sum up the role of different driving forces behind these demographic changes. Table 2.4 provides field-based, quantified evidence on the impact of some of the factors involved in the process of decline of CPRs.

5.a. Increased Population Pressure

The lead line of the mainstream debate on the decline of CPRs, as stated in the beginning, is to link the decline of the CPR area with the increased population, causing land hunger leading to privatisation of CPRs. While broadly agreeing to the logical formulation of argument and supportive evidence from different areas, it will not be wrong to maintain that population pressure could be a necessary but not sufficient condition to accelerate shrinkage of CPR areas. The population pressure works to reduce the CPR area provided public policies complement it in curtailing the area of CPRs.

5.b. Regressive Land Distribution Policies

At least the data from our study areas show that : (i) in several cases in spite of higher growth of population, the decline in the area of CPR was not that high. On the contrary in many villages the decline of the CPR area was disproportionately higher than increase in population. Table 2.4 (Section G) shows lesser decline in villages with a higher population growth and *vice-versa.*

TABLE 2.4: **Decline of CPR Area in the Villages Differentiated by Qualitative Changes in their Population (1950-52 to 1982-84)**

	Changes in Demographic Characteristics	Villages Covered (No.)	Decline in Area of CPRs (%)
A.	Occupational Change: Proportion of households newly shifted to agriculture		
	Higher[(a)]	27	37
	Lower	21	12
B.	Degree of Commercialisation:		
	Higher[(b)]	31	44
	Lower	28	18
C.	Factionalism, Group Dynamics:		
	Higher[(c)]	30	28
	Lower	26	14
D.	Socioeconomic Differentiation:		
	Higher[(d)]	28	42
	Lower	32	15
E.	Dependence on State Patronage:		
	Higher[(e)]	25	60
	Lower	27	16
F.	Population Growth		
	Higher[(f)]	21	19
	Lower	29	45
G.	Group Action (Social Capital)		
	Higher[(g)]	20	17
	Lower	48	46

(a) Table adapted from Jodha (1992). Households that shifted away from traditional caste occupation and became cultivators. Their proportion to total households in the village ranged from 15 to 20 per cent and 2 to 5 per cent, respectively, in the villages with "higher" and "lower" occupational shifts.

(b) Accessibility to market and related facilities are used as proxy for commercialisation. Better accessibility is broadly defined to include the situation of villages having a market centre within 2 km, availability of more than five shops in the village, regular operation of town-based trader or his agent in the village, year round bus service, etc. On the basis of presence or absence of these attributes villages are grouped as those having a "higher" or "lower" degree of commercialisation.

(c) "Higher" factionalism means presence of two or more factions in a village with vast differences in their strength and political patronage from above. Villages with "lower" factionalism lacked these features. They had factions of equal strength to be able to control each other.

(d) Differentiation reflected by values of Gini-coefficient of owned land holdings which ranged from 0.63 to 0.75 and 0.34 to 0.40 in the villages with "higher" and "lower" socioeconomic differentiation respectively.

(e) Villages, which had officially sponsored land (*Patta*) distribution more than twice during the last ten years, and had 100 per cent dependence on state grant for CPR improvement, are included in the "higher" group. The villages with "lower" patronage did not have these attributes.

(f) Total increase in village population during 1951-1981. "Higher" means 55 to 68 per cent; while "lower" means 28 to 35 per cent increase.

(g) Group action reflecting "social capital" means activities including emergency sharing, collective protests to government, negligible extent of litigation, collective charities, maintenance of village assets without government help, etc. "Higher" means presence of more than 15 collective practices; "Lower" means five or less practices.

Furthermore, in all the 82 studied villages put together, if the proportion of CPR area privatised by a deliberate effort of the government through *patta* (land title) distribution, generally around periods of elections, etc., is excluded, the remaining extent of the CPR area decline will not be more than 7 to 11 per cent of the total CPR area privatised against the present figures of 31 to 55 per cent.
Similarly, if the privatised CPR land given to those already owning land (in place of helping only the landless) is excluded, the decline of CPRs for a genuine help to the landless would range from 12 to 25 per cent of the current figure of CPR land distributed. Thirdly, the villages, which, despite political and administrative changes, were able to keep their traditional arrangements intact, and had little relief, subsidy or visits of influential political personalities, showed a much smaller (16 per cent) decline of CPRs compared to much higher (60 per cent) corresponding figure in the case of politically patronised villages (Table 2.4, Section E). The preceding observation also indicates that not only the regressive land distribution policy but the disruption of CPR management (including area protection) systems also contribute to the decline of the CPR area, by way of allowing the implementation of anti-CPR land policies. As Table 2.4 (Section G) shows, the villages with their social arrangements (social capital) intact had only 17 per cent decline in the CPR area as compared to 46 per cent in other villages. However, disruption of social capital is again an (unintended) product of reforms policies as elaborated below.

5.c. Introduction of Land Reforms

During the early 1950s, the Indian states (i.e. areas covered by our studies) introduced the land reforms programme. Besides abolishing intermediaries (i.e. feudal landlords) between the state and the peasants and giving land titles to the tillers/tenants, the land reforms also postulated provisions of imposing ceiling (limit) on land (holding) size for farmers. They intended to distribute the surplus land, to be made available through land ceiling, to the landless. Having failed in this (Ladejinsky 1972), the governments opted for the easier option, i.e. to curtail CPR area and distribute it to the landless, though, as indicated earlier, most of it went to those who already possessed land. Thus, the land distribution policies proved quite regressive in effect. However, the most significant aspect of the land reforms programme was reduced local control of local resources, which in the past had helped in evolving and enforcing several CPR management practices. Table 2.5 provides a more detailed summary of different reform policies and their negative side effects on CPRs and their customary management systems.

5.d. Introduction of Village Panchayats

Almost a parallel reform measure was the introduction of elected village councils (Panchayats), which were made the formal custodians of CPRs as well as other village affairs. In the process, the traditional social arrangement, or customary systems, which embodied "social capital" were disregarded or de-recognised. CPR management—area protection, regulated use and development—became a formal responsibility of village Panchayats. However, the latter being politically oriented bodies with external incentive systems (patronage, etc.) distracting them from the local affairs could hardly prove a substitute for the customary arrangements. Being majority vote seeking bodies they could neither regulate CPR use (by punishing the misusers) nor prevent encroachment on CPR lands. On the contrary, for the above reason (i.e. political favour for themselves as well as higher ups) they actively encouraged privatisation of the CPR area (Table 2.4, Section E). As a final consequence, CPRs in most areas were converted into open-access resources, to be overextracted and encroached upon (see Table 2.5).

The community lost collective stake and control over CPRs; culture of group action got replaced by individualistic tendencies; grabbing CPR land as a piece of private property (rather than enhancing and harnessing products of CPRs), became the guiding force. The "social capital" as mentioned earlier got depleted. The new politically driven and patronage-based incentive systems led to disintegration of the community's collective stake in CPRs and encouraged factionalism at the village level (Gupta 1987). The villages which could guard against factionalism were able to maintain their CPRs, but others could not. Table 2.4 (Section C and D) shows that the villages with high factionalism and higher differentiation also had a greater decline of CPRs compared to the others. Table 2.5 summarises the impact of the above institutional changes on the specific aspects of CPR such as the access and protection of area, usage regulation, collective sharing and group action, autonomy and flexibility, concern for local needs and perceptions; control of "free rider" problem; CPR productivity and regeneration, etc.

TABLE 2.5: **The Impact of replacing Customary Management with Formal Management of CPRs**

Variables	Situation Under	
	Customary Management (with community involvement)	**Formal Management (with involvement of state through Village Panchayats)**
Control of access and protection of CPR area	Effective prevention of encroachment and curtailment in area	Deliberate encouragement to privatisation, rapid area decline
Usage regulation	Collective rights/ obligations; regulations enforced through different devices/social sanctions/ physical measures	Common-pool resources as open access resource, little enforcement of regulatory provisions
Development, productivity promotion	Group action, obligatory/ voluntary contributions for resource mainte-nance/investment	Periodic activities depending on government grants, little people's participation
Miscellaneous items:		
— Group action/ collective sharing	— functional and high extent of participatory group activities	— periodical, formal, state-patronised activity, involving local wage labour
— Autonomy/ flexibility	— high degree of flexi-bility, location and ethnic group specificity	— generalised, uniform patterns imposed from above, insensitive to local conditions
— Local needs and perceptions	— people's needs/means key guiding factors	— perception of outsiders (e.g., government agencies) a key element
— Opportunities for grabbing common resources	— very little encroachment	— privatisation of common lands encouraged
— "Free rider" problem	— non-existent	— new type of non-contributing benefi-ciaries on the increase

TABLE 2.5 *(Contd.)*

Variables	Customary Management (with community involvement)	Formal Management (with involvement of state through village Panchayats)
— Practice of "exclusion"	— only outside villagers had no access	— on factional consideration even local villagers can be prevented
— CPR productivity regeneration, and biodiversity	— sufficient regrowth, biodiversity as permitted by the nature	— reduced regeneration and biodiversity due to depletion and use of narrowly focussed technologies
— Resource mobilisation/ self-help	— participatory activities a key factor in sustainability of common-pool resources	— increased external dependence, cost-free use/misuse of common resources

Source: Table adapted from Jodha (1996a).

5.e. Market Forces

The above changes in community arrangements attributed to the replacement of the customary arrangement by formal administrative, legal and political arrangements were accentuated by the penetration of market forces in these areas. The role of market is not new for the study areas. But in the past market-driven devices did not extend to CPRs. However, with the replacement of local community arrangements by formal top-down interventions; individualisation of people's approach to CPRs; emergence of circumstances favouring conversion of CPR land into private property, "the land-scarcity-land price" links became operative in the CPR context. Increased commercialisation of agriculture following market integration of hitherto relatively isolated dry areas with the mainstream economy further added to the strengthening of individualistic attitudes, which put a very low premium on collective action and CPRs. Table 2.4 (Section B and also A) indicates the impact of these changes on CPRs.

5.f. Side Effects of Other Developments

The other developments (e.g. top down interventions) associated with the economic transformation of hitherto subsistence-oriented backward areas,

TABLE 2.6: **Some Public Interventions affecting Customary Rules and Practices and their Consequences for CPRs**

Interventions involving common-pool resources	Customary rules and practices affected by interventions	Consequences of intervention and formal rules
Land reforms in the 1950s		
— Undeclared policy of privatisation of common resources	— Erosion of social sanctions and community authority to protect common resources, regulate their use and develop them	— Decline of common-pool resource area, overcrowding, over-exploitation and physical degradation
— Distribution of common lands for private cultivation	— Legal status to common-pool resources without an effective enforcement mechanism due to loss of customary communal arrangement, loss of community stake in resources	— Village Panchayats failed to ensure people's participation for common-resource management
— Government acquisition of common land for public purposes — Legalisation of illegal encroachments		— Common-pool resources became open access resources
Introduction of Panchayat system and other measures for common-pool resources		
— Provision of Village Panchayats (elected councils) as custodians of common-pool resources	— Replacement of traditional decision makers (e.g. village elders' group) by Panchayats	— Few village-level initiatives for common-pool resources
— Government grants and subsidies to manage and develop community lands	— Cessation of participatory management, local resource mobilisation and group action for common resources	— Default on the part of Panchayats; diversion of CPR grants to other uses
— External, formal, administrative, and legal measures extended to village affairs	— Authority and knowledge of local community ignored	— Common-pool resources became open-access resources with expected degradation and depletion
	— Failure to implement legal provisions for common resources	— Common-pool resources became legal entities instead of a collective asset, with no effective mechanisms to put legal provisions into practice

TABLE 2.6 (*Contd.*)

Interventions involving common-pool resources	Customary rules and practices affected by interventions	Consequences of intervention and formal rules
Formal production and resource upgrading programmes		
— Research and technology application on pilot scale	— Disregard of local knowledge and institutional factors, user needs and perceptions	— Area decline due to the acquisition of common lands for pilot projects
— Pasture, social forestry and watershed development projects	— Marginalisation of participatory approach, local resource mobilisation and collective action	— Reduced access to common-pool resource users
— Projects conceived from outside, sustained by government subsidy, characterised by "technique dominance"	— Alienation of community from its resources, loss of community stake in resources	— Common-pool resource development as part of development projects decided by state agencies, no local stakes.

Source: Table adapted from Jodha (1996a).

and the tendencies they promoted were also not favourable to traditional social arrangements. The disregard of traditional knowledge systems, traditional forms of group action, collective sharing and sensitivity to the problems of local natural resource base, etc., complemented the role of market forces. Concerned with the need for enhancing productivity of community natural resources, under the development plans, the states undertook several initiatives to upgrade and conserve CPRs. But all the efforts treated CPR units as pieces of land without CPR perspective (i.e. involving community participation and ownership). They focussed on fiscal support (subsidy) and technologies (e.g. for afforestation, soil conservation, pasture re-seeding, etc.), without recognition of local perceptions and traditional knowledge systems. Hence, they had little impact beyond the "pilot project areas". Table 2.6 summarises some details on the public interventions and their impact on CPRs and their management.

Besides, a few other public policies and programmes directed to enhance agricultural development in dry areas adversely affected the CPR. For instance, to meet the "land reclamation" targets, development officials also encouraged conversion of fragile CPR area into crop land by removing natural vegetation. The "grow more food campaigns" also followed the same approach in many areas. The government loans and subsidies promoted tracterisation, which facilitated extension of cultivation to fragile CPR lands at a very low cost (Jodha 1992, 1996a).

6. Belittling the Reforms? Searching for a Way Out

The point in enumerating the negative impact or rather side effects of formal reforms, market integration, the top-down development intervention, etc., is not to minimise their positive gains. Instead, our objective is to highlight their insensitivity to the CPR issues and the significant changes they brought about in the attitudes and approaches of rural communities, which represent a less recognised but major qualitative aspect of changes in rural areas. Also our purpose is to identify major underlying driving forces, which are more numerous as well as more effective than the simple increase in the number of people to accelerate degradation of community-level environmental resources. The recognition and understanding of the above phenomena may serve as an important step towards rehabilitation of CPRs as well as rebuilding of "social capital".

Though it falls outside the scope of the present chapter, still we can venture to indicate possible approaches to address the above consequences and processes of demographic changes. To facilitate this it will be useful to have a look at how the rural population individually or as a group has responded (adjusted) to the above changes. Accordingly, the net consequence of degradation of CPRs and depletion of social capital (which at this stage seem to reinforce each other) is reflected through the situation summarised in Table 1.7. The Table presents the dominant features of community approach and behaviour in the context of the depleted state of CPRs. Since the rural community is more differentiated and has individualised its approaches to CPRs, the adjustments of rich and poor people to the CPR changes show considerable differences, though the key circumstances underlying their responses are broadly common. For instance, the decline of social arrangements to manage CPRs induces the rich (and poor too) to grab CPR land; it also encourages the poor to overextract the resources without obligation or incurring private cost in the process.

Similarly, the public policies, while legalising encroachments on CPR lands with minimal penalties, and creating patronage or subsidy-based incentives, induce both rich and poor (though in different degrees) to privatise CPRs with no fear and cost.

The loss of "social capital" at the community level is the single most important factor promoting individualised behaviour vis-a-vis community resources in the case of both rich and poor. Finally, since community has no

TABLE 2.7: **People's Adaptations to Changing Situation of CPRs**

Measures adopted by Different Groups in the face of Decline in Area, Productivity and Management Systems of CPRs		
Rural Rich	Rural Poor	Rural Community (General)
Withdrawal from CPRs as users of products: (opportunity cost of labour higher than CPR product value)	**Using of CPRs** as an important source of sustenance Complementarity of CPR-cropland-based activities	**Acceptance of CPRs as open access resources:** no collective efforts to enforce users' obligations, regulations
Increased reliance on alternative options — Own biomass supplies (stall feeding, etc.) — Non-renewable/external resources (e.g. replacing thorn fencing with stone fencing, wooden cart tires with rubber tires, local wooden tools with iron tools)	**Acceptance of interior options** — Opportunity cost of labour lower than value of products of degraded CPRs — No other private cost of resource use	**Selective approach to specific CPR units:** despite general neglect of CPRs, concern for some productive units — Limited exceptions where collective arrangements still survive
Private squeeze on CPRs as assets — Grabbing CPR lands — Preventing others using seasonal CPRs (private crop lands during off-season)	**Measures reflecting desperation** — Premature harvesting of CPR products — Removal of roots/base of products — Over-crowding and over-exploitation of CPRs — Use of hitherto unusable inferior products	**Focus on "other" uses of CPRs** — Focused item in seeking government subsidy/relief, in running factional quarrels, in populist programmes, etc. — Community responds only to external directions, does not plan own activities
Approach to CPR management — Indifference to decline of CPRs — Act as influential local party to non-functioning legal system administrative super-structure for community resources	— No capacity to organise users — Extraction without obligation	**Party to non-operating legal and administrative measures :** — acceptance of external impositions without protest, etc. — Loss of "social capital" ability to act jointly

Source: Table adapted from Jodha (1992).

control over local resources they are at the receiving end and simply respond to the top-down interventions, designed for community lands (be it social forestry or rehabilitation of degraded pastures), without owning them.

Under the circumstances as briefly indicated in Table 2.7, rehabilitation and sustainable use of CPR and rebuilding of social capital are quite difficult tasks, especially when the policy environment and the present process of economic transformation are not congenial for them.

However, if CPRs, due to their ecological and economic functions, need rehabilitation; and social capital rebuilding is considered essential not only to help CPRs but also to facilitate success of other grassroot level development interventions, the situation depicted by this chapter requires change.

In this context building of a collective stake in community resources is a first step. The practical approach to do this would involve promotion of user groups of CPRs as attempted by several NGOs in different areas (Poffenberger *et al.* 1996). However, to accommodate diverse interests of economically differentiated rural communities, the CPR re-development will have to have a strong focus on diversification of products and services and an equitable distribution of gains using appropriate methods including some form of share-holding system, as tried in watershed development and pasture development projects in India (Mishra and Sarin 1987).

Besides, the above initiatives require a strong policy support in terms of a legal framework to encourage user groups; transfer of control of local resources to local communities and provision for investment in CPRs, which are presently so depleted that no community would be able to rehabilitate them on their own (Jodha 1992).

However, despite the need for user group-based collective action as well as policy and funding support from the state, the divided local communities may not have the capacity to respond to new opportunities and take up new responsibilities. Hence, the need for catalytic role of NGOs and other volunteer agencies to mobilise rural communities and help in their capacity building to undertake new responsibilities (Poffenberger *et al.* 1996). The information presented in this chapter hopefully may help the community mobilisers to understand the process by which rural communities were disempowered and their collective stakes in natural resources disintegrated. This in turn can help evolve the strategies to change the situation. A few NGOs in India have already incorporated such insights in their work plans.

REFERENCES

Bromley, D.W. and M.M. Cernea, 1989. "The Management of Common Property Natural Resources: Some Conceptual and Operational Fallacies", *World Bank Discussion Paper*, No. 57, Washington, D.C.: The World Bank.

Gupta, A.K. 1987. "Why Poor People do not Cooperate? A Study of Traditional Forms of Cooperation with Implications for Modern Organisations", In: G.C. Wanger, *Politics and Practices of Social Research*, London: George Allen and Unwin.

Jodha, N.S. 1986. "Common Property Resources and Rural Poor in Dry Regions of India", *Economic and Political Weekly*, 21 (27).

Jodha, N.S. 1992. "Rural Common Property Resources: A Missing Dimension of Development Strategies", *World Bank: Discussion Paper No. 169*, Washington, D.C.: The World Bank.

Jodha, N.S. 1995. "Common Property Resources and the Environmental Context: Role of Biophysical versus Social Stresses", *Economic and Political Weekly*, 30(51).

Jodha, N.S. 1996a. "Property Rights and Development" In: Hanna, S.S., C. Floke, K.G. Mäler, *Right to Nature: Ecological, Economic, Cultural and Political Principles of Institutions for the Environment*, Washington, D.C.: Island Press.

Jodha, N.S. 1996b. *Social Dimension of Biodiversity Management in Agricultural Landscapes*, ENVSP, Environment Department, Washington, D.C.: The World Bank (Limited Circulation).

Ladejinsky, W. 1972. "Land Ceiling and Land Reforms", *Economic and Political Weekly* 7(5-7).

McNicoll, G. and M. Cain (eds.) 1990. *Rural Development and Population: Institutions and Policy*, New York: Oxford University Press.

Mishra, P.R. and M. Sarin 1987. "Sukhomajri-Nada: A New Model of Eco-Development", Bombay: *Business India*, November, 16-29.

Ostrom, E., D. Feeny and H. Picht (eds.) 1988. *Rethinking Institutional Analysis and Development: Issues, Alternatives and Choices*, San Francisco: International Centre for Economic Growth, Institute for Contemporary Studies.

Poffenberger, M. and M.B. McGean (eds.) 1996. *Village Voices, Forest Choices: Pioneering India's Forest Management in 21st Century*, New Delhi: Oxford University Press.

3 Common Property Resource Management in Himachal Himalayas

Y.S. Negi

History of economic development is replete with instances of intimate relations and definite dependence of human beings on their natural environments. Major civilizations are noted to have developed near the abundant sources of water, rich forests and fertile lands. Thus, with such an intimate relationship, and with the manifold increase in biotic pressures on these systems, it seems normal to expect various natural resources systems of proven economic importance to be under one or the other kind of a stress. Sustainability of these systems, however, has always been the concern of humankind; as is suggested by various studies of different civilizations that portray the high status granted to numerous natural resources. Some of these resources were held in high esteem, and at times granted the godly status. In India, there is ample literary evidence of attributing divinity to mountains, oceans and other water sources, forests and other plants and even animals. Nevertheless, over the years, an increased emphasis on short term goals, both market and non-market, coupled with the manifold increase in the biotic pressure, has put many natural resource systems under great stress. The adverse consequences of this state of affairs have been alarming; and the evidence abounds of the deteriorating state of forests, depleting underground water, shrinking marine resources, polluted rivers and the general degradation of the environment. Common Property (natural) Resources (CPRs) of the Indian Himalayan region, in this respect, seem to be in a management crisis.

Ownership or title to a resource, i.e. the rights to use the same, are important factors that govern the use pattern of a resource. Depending upon the nature of rights, property may be classified as the private property, public property, common and open access property. Common property resources are important forms of natural resource endowments, defined as the class of resources for which exclusion is difficult and joint use involves subtractability, i.e. an identifiable group of people hold the rights in common and the use and management of these resources is governed by the traditional or mutually agreed upon rules (Berkes *et al.* 1995, Chen 1988, Moench 1985, Singh 1993). These common property resources are important not only for the rural poor who meet many of their subsistence needs from them (Chopra *et al.* 1990, Jodha 1986, 1992, Moench 1985, Negi 1993, Negi *et al.* 1997, Sharma and Bhati 1995), but also for the society as a whole because of many positive economic and ecological externalities that these resources generate. Further, these resources also act as the "safety nets" in terms of the basic needs of rural people in bad times. Some of these resources are being overexploited and the danger of their crossing the threshold limits is becoming more and more eminent. Population and income-driven diverse extractive pressures on these CPRs pose economic and ecological threats to the region. Natural forests, community forests, common grazing lands, some mining areas, rivers, community ponds and other sources of community drinking and irrigation water are the major common property resources that are under tremendous pressures in the Himachal Himalayas. Although the *de jure* control of some of these resources may rest with the government or an agency, yet *de facto*, many of these resources, in most cases, are used as common properties. Sustainability of these resources is now crucial; not only for the economic well-being of the people in this hilly region but also from the point of view of the larger economic and ecological implications for the country as a whole.

The use pattern and sustainability aspects of various common property resources in a region are influenced by their structure and reliability (Baker 1995). A common property resource structure can be viewed in terms of its physical and social complexity from the management point of view. Reliability, the second influencer of CPRs use, relates to the carrying capacity of the resource in relation to the varying human and livestock pressures. Another dimension of reliability is the stability of the users' rights in the long run. The present chapter assesses the status of a few representative CPRs and their management patterns in Himachal Pradesh — the most prominent hill State of the western Himalayan region. In order to establish the context, a brief background discussion on the State is also taken as under.

1. The Western Himalayan Region and Himachal Pradesh

The western Himalayan region has a total geographical area of 329,034 sq.km. The majority of the population is engaged in agriculture, inclusive of horticulture and animal husbandry. The region is dominated by the area under forests, which ranges from sub-tropical forests to those of alpine types.

Pastures and meadows are also common. The western Himalayan region is divided into three zones. In the first zone is the State of Jammu and Kashmir. This northernmost State of the country lies between 23° 17' to 37° N latitude and 74° 18' to 80° E longitude. Forests cover about 9.4 per cent of the total geographical area of 222,240 sq.km, with a per capita forest availability of 0.34 ha Livestock rearing is an important activity in the region and grazing intensity is high, estimated at about six times the carrying capacity (Khosla *et al.* 1991).

The eight hill districts of Uttar Pradesh form the second zone of the western Himalayan region. The zone exhibits a lot of physical and climatic variations and has both tropical and temperate areas. The region as a whole abounds in natural resources but lacks infrastructural facilities, especially transport. More than 65 per cent of the area is under forests which are owned by the State. The regional economy is mostly based on agriculture and forests, although agriculture constitutes only about 13 per cent of the landuse. However, more than 80 per cent of the people depend on agriculture and forests for their livelihood. Because of limitations of cultivable land area, agro-pastoral farming is practised over a large area (Shah 1996, Swarup 1991).

2. Himachal Pradesh

The third zone of the region comprises the State of Himachal Pradesh; the region of major interest in the present discussion. Himachal Pradesh is situated in the heart of the western Himalayan region. The State lies between 32° 22' to 33° 12' N latitude and 75° 47' to 79° 04' E longitude. Popularly referred to as the *Dev Bhoomi* (land of gods), Himachal is also known as the Himachal Himalayas. The word Himachal combines the Sanskrit *Hima*, meaning snow and *Achala*, referring to the mountain and literally translates to "unshakable snowy mountain". The name, Himachal, thus reminds one of the Himalayas, "the abode of snow" (Ahluwalia 1988, Joshi 1986, Singh 1985). The State has a total geographical area of 55,673 sq.km.

2.a. Topography and Agroclimatic Regions

Himachal Pradesh has a high geographic and topographic variation, ranging from the Shiwalik hills in the south to the Himalayan ranges in the north. The physical characteristics often change within very small distances and have a bearing on the climatic conditions that range from sub-tropical to temperate, and sub-alpine to alpine. These climatic and ecological possibilities have implications for landuse in different parts of the State (Negi 1993). On the basis of agro-ecological variations, the State is divided into four major agroclimatic zones, viz. (i) low hill zone, (ii) mid hill zone, (iii) high hill zone, and (iv) alpine zone.

The low hill zone comprises the areas adjoining the States of Punjab and Haryana and have some agro-ecological similarities with these plains. The elevation of the zone ranges up to 1,000 m above mean-sea-level. The zone occupies about 35 per cent of the geographical area of the State and has 33 per cent of the cultivated area of the State. Population density is highest in this zone. Climatic conditions of the zone make it relatively more suitable for agriculture; therefore, irrigation becomes of importance to the farmers. Pasture and forests cover about 40 per cent of the geographical area of this zone.

The mid-hill zone ranges up to 2,000 m above mean-sea-level, and has about 22 per cent of the geographical area of the State. The zone accounts for about 53 per cent of the total cropped area and 45 per cent of the irrigated area of the State. A major portion of the uncultivated area is in pastures. Pastures and forests cover about 29 and 40 per cent of the geographical area of the zone. The forests are limited to the north and north-eastern slopes. Forests, common pasture lands, small gravity irrigation channels (locally known as *kuhls*) are the important CPRs of the region.

The altitude of the high hill zone ranges from 2,000 to 3,000 m above mean-sea-level. About 25 per cent of the geographical area of the State falls in this zone. A high proportion of this area is under natural pastures and forests. The cultivated area is low, about 18 per cent of the total cultivated area of the State. The topography of the high hills and the alpine zone put constraints on harnessing of the natural streams for irrigation. The small gravity irrigation channels (*kuhls*) and small rainwater storage tanks are the major source of irrigation. In fact, after forests and community lands, the *kuhls* are the major CPRs of this region as well. *Kuhl* management, as we would discuss, is quite a complex though highly formalized and developed CPRs management system in this region.

The alpine zone or the high hills temperate dry zone comprises the high mountain regions and accounts for more than 8 per cent of the geographical area of the State. Rainfall is scanty and occurs in summers with an average of 20 cm per annum. The winters are severe and receive precipitation in the form of snow. The region is inhabited mostly by tribal communities of the State. Since opportunities for cultivation of crops are limited, people are also engaged in sheep and goat rearing and related cottage works.

2.b. Economy

Historically, Himachal has been a *closed book* (Mitto 1978). The princely States were small and did not attract much attention from other rulers in the plains. However, there are instances of prominent princely States in the region having been the target of the Mughals and Gurkhas. Most of these States were engaged in wars among themselves. Trade in these times was limited and the standard of living of the general public did not concern most rulers who, it seems, neither had the intention nor the resources to undertake developmental programmes (Negi 1993). Further, the lack of transport highly restricted trade and maintained dispersed, self-sufficient settlements. Thus, a typical subsistence form of economy, particularly agricultural landuse, developed in the State.

The population settlement patterns and the topography of various parts of the State make agriculture, including fruit-growing and animal-rearing, the main economic activity of the State. Since the cultivated area in different parts of the State is limited, animal-rearing is also a significant component of household activities. Animals are mainly open-grazed and only improved breeds of milch animals are stall-fed. As a supplement to pasture grasses (hay) and a small amount of cultivated fodder crops, tree fodder is also used for stall-feeding the animals. Similarly, for climatic and difficult topographic reasons, and for reasons of lack of electric power, the household energy use is typically wood-based. This is especially so in the high hills. As a result of these characteristics, the State is highly dependent on various natural resources which are mostly in the common property regimes. This close dependence on CPRs amply projects their importance to the local economy. In fact, continued pressures on these resources, with a little emphasis on their replenishment, has led to the present situation where sustainability of many of these economic and ecologically important resources is in jeopardy.

Thus, mountain ecosystems in this region, previously seen as rugged and resilient, for example, the proverbial invincible Himalayas, now constitute one of the most vulnerable ecosystems. Villages and households situated within these rapidly changing and vulnerable environments are involved in and routinely planning for risk and uncertainty management in respect of natural resources (Chen 1988, Ham 1995). Many of the activities carried out as day-to-day routines are, in fact, aimed at minimizing such risks. As in any management process, so too in CPRs management, an assessment of the magnitude and health of the resource base is thus important. Such information provides a platform to the resource managers for setting management targets and enabling them to plan for the attainment of the same. Himachal Pradesh has had a rich heritage of maintaining common property resource systems, as well as institutions related to the use of these resources (Agarwal and Singh 1996, Berkes *et al.* 1995, Singh 1961, Thakur 1996, Thakur *et al.* 1998). The present management crisis, therefore, can at best be termed paradoxical. It is in this regard that historical and current management strategies or efforts need to be analyzed so as to draw up future plans of action.

2.c. Landuse

Among the major forms of landuse, forests occupy more than 30 per cent of the total geographical area of the State. Pastures and grazing lands form about another 35 per cent. Together, these two components, along with the barren area and land put to settlements and other non-agricultural uses account for about 75 per cent of the total geographical area of the State (Table 3.1). Only about 29 per cent of the area is available for cultivation. These figures speak of a heavy dependence of the State on these land resources that are mostly considered as the common property resources. A part of these lands are also termed as the wastelands, mainly from the point of view of their suitability for agriculture. No firm estimates of the extent of so termed 'wastelands' of the State are available. However, one estimate puts the figure at 35 per cent of the geographical area (Nagpal 1991). In fact, various types of landuses in the region are linked to each other and there is a heavy dependence on common property resources. Out of the 10 types of landuses identified in a study in Kullu district of Himachal Pradesh, seven were having elements of CPR component (Davidson-Hunt 1995). Because of the interplay of *de jure* and *de facto* property rights in these resources, the commons in the study area were noted to be quite complicated. However, this is not the only isolated case of the type, because of the many mountain specificities such interlinkages are common in this hilly region.

These indicative references on landuse in the State provide some insight into the direction in which the landuse pattern has been shifting over time. It is evident that the forest area has changed most prominently over the past some years. Contrary to the general belief of a decline in the forest area, it shows an increase over time. This, however, is partly because of the reclassification of the area, as a result of which the area under the legal control of the Forest Department has increased. Different afforestation and reforestation programmes of the State Government have also contributed favourably in this regard. The area under the category "other uncultivated lands" like land under miscellaneous tree crops and current fallow shows a decline (Table 3.1).

2.d. Forests and CPR Lands

Forests are the major natural resource of the State and until recently were the major revenue earning resource for the State. Apart from the direct incomes from the sale of timber, forests also contribute to the State exchequer by way of extraction of fuelwood and fodder, grasses, resin and gums, and various valuable medicinal and aromatic plants; not to mention the invaluable services rendered for maintenance of general ecological environment. As pointed out earlier, the people in this hilly region have had an intimate socio-economic and

TABLE 3.1: **Distribution of the Geographical Area under Major Landuses in Himachal Pradesh**

(% of total geographical area)

Particulars	Temporal reference points (years)					
	1950-51	1960-61	1970-71	1980-81	1990-91	1992-93
Forests	23.69	30.80	21.76	26.96	30.85	30.57
Barren and uncultivated	6.49	4.25	4.05	4.72	5.46	4.30
Land put to non-agril. uses	7.41	6.75	5.87	5.40	5.74	5.93
Culturable waste	9.11	7.03	5.72	7.94	3.72	3.55
Permanent pastures and other grasslands	21.30	27.40	40.51	33.93	33.72	35.43
Land under misc. tree crops and groves	1.47	1.25	1.39	1.31	1.43	1.26
Current fallow	3.10	2.30	2.00	1.38	1.32	1.43
Other fallow lands	0.43	0.12	0.07	0.42	0.45	0.67
Net cropped area	27.00	20.10	18.63	19.12	17.31	16.86
Total geographical area (by village papers, '000 ha)	1941.07	2635.12	2932.50	2985.20	3367.60	3395.40

Data Source: Statistical Outline of Himachal Pradesh (various issues).

ecological relationship with their forests. Thus, the people were aware of maintaining the economic and ecological sanctity of forests while drawing various direct benefits from their forests. Hence, the hill people looked upon the forests with reverence. In fact, it was the realization and acceptance of this intimate relationship that proved of crucial importance in formalizing various user rights in the forests, when the forests were brought under formal management regimes by the government (Anderson 1886, Davidson-Hunt 1995, ODA 1994).

Legally, forests occupy about 38 per cent of the total geographical area of the State, but the effective forest area is estimated at 17 per cent only. Of the total forest area, about 98 per cent is controlled by the Forest Department and only a little above one per cent is under private ownership. Of the forest under the State control, more than 92 per cent are *protected forests* and about 5 per cent the *reserved forests*. The remaining are the unclassed forests. Since a major part of the State forests is under public ownership, the burden of meeting various forest-based demands, naturally, falls on these forests. Given the population pressure, it is, however, difficult for these forests to sustain growing demands from within and from outside the State. It has been estimated that the per capita availability of forests in the State is just about 0.9 ha by the legal classification of the forests and only about 0.2 ha according to the revenue records of forest area. Other estimates for forest area put the per capita forests at 0.31 ha of the actual forest cover in the State (GOI 1989). Forests in the vicinity of villages are mostly used as common property resources, because of traditional user rights in these forests in some cases and further because of the general lack of proper management and checks in other cases.

During the time of princely States, forests in the Himachal were not managed under a planned management regime. However, because of the low population pressure and also because of the few opportunities for trade in timber, the forest utilization strategies did not seriously consider the forest degradation scenario. In fact, there are no definite records of specific efforts made in the field of forest management during the period of *Rajas/Ranas* in the State. These rulers of small principalities used the forests as their personal properties, mainly as game reserves. Later on under the British rule forest management was formalized. As, for example, in Kangra district, the forests were placed under the control of the Deputy Commissioner, who managed the forests as per the guidelines of Barnes' Regular Forests Settlements. The Forest Department started the formulation and documentation of the regular forest management plans for different forests by preparing forest Working Plans. Subsequently, people's participation was also sought in forest management to ensure protection of forests from fires and also from the acts of illicit felling of trees. In this regard, some local people's organizations were also encouraged. Village cooperative forest societies (VCFS) or village development committees (VDC) of Kangra district, like the *kuhl* irrigation system as we would discuss, are well known in this regard.

When the then government felt the need to follow the restriction prescription for forest management, there was a feeling of disagreement on the issue among the general public in the area. In order to win the favour of the local people, the administration allotted some forest areas to the local people that were to be managed by these cooperative societies (Agarwal and Singh 1996). This was necessary because in spite of restricting many traditional rights in the forests, forest degradation had continued. To halt this process special village forests were visualized. Special *panchayats* were to be set up to manage the forests as per the simple Working Plans. Thus the VCFS were started. These societies were formed as statutory bodies under the Kangra Forest Society Rules, 1941 (Agarwal and Singh 1996). Major provisions made for the VCFS were that lands would be transferred to these societies and that the management would be conditional to the acceptance of the Working Plan. Further, to maintain the legality, it was also provided that the powers of forest officers and locally appointed *Rakhas* (forest guards) will have legal basis. These societies functioned well within the purview of their management objectives until their say, and share in the forest produce was manipulated. VCFS had the responsibility (i) to protect, improve and regenerate the forest, (ii) to manage these forests to ensure local requirements of timber, fuelwood and fodder and (iii) to strive for preventing soil erosion and degradation of the forest. However, with the deterioration of the financial position of these VCFS and with no share in the sale of timber and resin, the societies are keeping a low managerial profile. On the similar pattern the VDCs also manage a small area under forests and the produce is shared according to the norms fixed by the committee. The VDC auctions off the area annually for harvesting of grass. Some of the area is given to the people from the socially underprivileged sections within the village while some of the area is retained by the VDC for meeting various needs of its members (Bhatia 1997).

2.d.1 Common Property Lands

There are some common lands in and around the forests, the use of which is not governed by any formal rules and hence the situation is equally alarming in the use of these CPRs components of forests and non-forest areas. Some field-level estimates show this situation more clearly by using a micro-level information gathered through surveys conducted for the purpose (Table 3.2). It is evident from these figures that irrespective of the agroclimatic regions, the pressures on CPR lands have been increasing significantly over time. The pressure is relatively high in the midhill region, where the population per ha of CPR lands has increased by more than 300 per cent in 1991 as compared to 1961. Similarly the increase in the other two regions is very high; more than 200 per cent against the same benchmark of 1961.

TABLE 3.2: **Population Pressure on CPR Lands in Different Zones of Himachal Pradesh**

Year	Population/ha of CPR lands		
	Low hills	Mid hills	High hills
1961	0.69	2.73	1.00
1971	0.95	3.28	1.64
1981	1.32	5.20	1.96
1991	1.83	9.13	2.31

Source: Singh, 1995.

While population has been the biggest contributor towards the pressure on CPR lands, the increasing commercial farming and human psychology of 'making hay while the sun shines' also seems to have contributed to the encroachment pressure on CPRs. In an informal, quick and purposive survey of 27 acquaintance farmers in the mid and high hills of Himachal Pradesh, carried specially for the purpose of present discussion, it was noted that all those respondents who got an opportunity, or were tempted by the actions of others (23 respondents), had encroached upon some common property lands, mainly forest land. The primary purpose of this quick survey was not to obtain details on the extent of encroachment or the type of people involved in such practices, but to simply comprehend the trend. Thus, the figures (Table 3.3) being used in this discussion are just the indicators and the survey may need to be repeated with a sizable sample for gauging the full extent of encroachment; and that, however, was not possible to do in the present case. Nonetheless, the survey does point out or rather supports the common feeling that there is a pressure on the common property resources.

It is observed that a higher proportion of marginal and small farmers were involved in the process of encroachment up to 5 per cent of their land holding size, while a higher proportion of medium and large farmers were engaged in the higher level of encroachment. However, on an average, the proportion of medium and large farmers was higher than the marginal and small farmers. Looking at these responses from a different angle, from the angle of encroachment levels, it is noted that only about 18 per cent of the marginal and small farmers, as against 33 per cent of the medium and large farmers, were engaged in encroaching land in the range of 5-10 per cent of their land holdings. Overall picture in this regard, however, points out that the level of encroachment was more in the range up to 5 per cent of the land holding size.

TABLE 3.3: **Extent of CPR Lands Encroachments in the Sample Villages of Mid and High Hills of Himachal Pradesh**

Farm Size	Encroachment level (as % of owned land holdings) and involvement of different category farmers (as % of total farmers)					
	< 5%		5-10%		overall	
			category-wise view			
Marginal and small	52.9		33.3		47.8	
Medium and large	47.1		66.7		52.2	
Overall (%)	100.0		100.0		100.0	
			encroachment-levelwise view			
Marginal and small	81.8		18.2		100.0	(11)
Medium and large	66.7		33.3		100.0	(12)
Overall (% and No.)	73.9	(17)	26.1	(6)	100.0	(23)

Note: Figures in parentheses show the number of respondents.

Another point that came out of this analysis is that those farmers who had their land holdings in the vicinity of forests and other common property lands were involved more in acquiring such lands. The spirit behind the story of *tragedy of commons* seems to have been playing a part, so far as these land acquisitions are concerned. In this regard, it may also be noted that the farmers having more fragmented lands had higher opportunities to do the same. Two factors seem to be playing crucial roles in this case. One, that because of the fragmented holdings, farm or holding size at a given site is small, sometimes even that of large farmers. This allows people to complete their farm jobs in a relatively short period of time, compared to the sites where their land holdings are consolidated and thus relatively large. This site specific time saving plays an important psychological part and prompts farmers to utilize this time by cleaning and thus extending their farm boundaries, often in a routine manner. Secondly, farm holdings in the hills are small and most of these are qualitatively marginal. This fact, thus, acts as a driving force for farmers to extend their holdings when opportunities to do so arise, particularly in isolated far-flung areas where legal or social control over these resources is weak. Often it is noted that the process starts with those persons who have enough human or capital resources to do so. Once the process of encroachment is initiated, it brings into its fold other people having lands in the vicinity; lest they lose their chances to others. Over time, these land acquisitions are almost considered a matter of right, particularly when some socially or politically influential persons have also joined the race.

2.d.2 CPR Lands — Encroachment Process

The process of such land encroachments itself is also very interesting. It needs, however, to be pointed out at this stage that at times "encroachments" may even be unintentional. Except in rare cases, the encroachment process is incremental, and is completed over a period of time, often running into years. The process may start with the cleaning of farm or field boundaries (cutting and clearing incoming bushes, clearing eroded soil and stones, etc.). Or in other cases, it may just start with the need for strengthening of boundary fences (mostly wooden poles, and stone walls). Where there are biological fences, like where bushes are used, the growth of the same over time covers quite an area of an already small farm, and clearing of incoming branches year after year leads to a gradual extension of the field boundaries, because the outward growth does not concern the farmer. Similarly, where stone walls or wooden poles are used for fences, the decay of poles or erosion of walls require their occasional mending. In this process, again, the field boundaries are often extended. In case of wooden poles, in particular, there is often a need to relocate the same at some other point, when the soil beneath the poles gets eroded or the base of the pole becomes lose. The needful is most often done by extending the pole(s) into the common lands rather than in the tilled owned area.

Apart from these, rather inadvertent manners, of land acquisition, there are other methods that are intentionally used to encroach upon the common lands. Common among these methods is to slowly extend the portion of boundary wall at a needed point, or to relocate the pole into the common land. The newly constructed wall post or a pole fixed is then sprinkled over with humus or other such material or soil from the nearby area, so that it does not easily attract the attention of a passerby. Another way to extend farm boundaries to adjacent common lands is through gradually (and thinly) planting some fruit or common farm forestry trees in the commons. Planting methods used again are not generally the ones that are commonly in practice or the ones that are prescribed, but the modified ones which do not attract attention. While the trees are growing, the land is not tilled or dug at all. So these trees grow as the wild ones. However, when the trees attain a sizable height or age, the extended farm land is merged with the original farm without attracting the attention of the authorities. In a few cases, however, it may also be the case that this method is used in connivance with the officials who are supposed to be the guardians of these resources.

2.d.3 Pasture Lands

Pastures or common grazing lands (commonly known as *charan* or *charands*, and *ghasnies*, etc.) are another important common property lands, particularly in the higher reaches of the region. The pastures near the villages are called *juh*, *munchar* and *gochars* or *gorchars*. Those pastures at a greater distance are termed as *trakar*. High mountain pastures are known as the *dhars*, *gahars* and *nigahars* (Raina 1996, Verma 1998). Utilization of these land resources in most cases is on the basis of socio-cultural norms of a particular area. At most times, there are accepted norms that have been traditionally set by the society or the local public agencies. Local institutions like *panchayats* are also engaged in the setting up, modification and/or enforcing these norms. People have the users' or *bartandari* rights in these pastures. Bartandar is a person entitled to some rights over land or trees in the protected forests for which he/she does not hold property rights. Pasture lands are the primary source of forage for the livestock in the region because of the almost negligible area put under fodder crops. These different types of grazing lands are used by different types of users who are (i) local people, (ii) migratory animal graziers and (iii) nomadic graziers. However, whenever the grazing is discussed, it is mostly the nomadic and migratory graziers that become the reference points. Local people or farmers graze their animals in the near vicinity of their dwellings on a day-to-day basis. The other two categories of animal keepers move out of the village or dwelling places for longer duration, often months, to graze their animals. Sheep and goats are the major animals that are routinely taken to highland pastures for grazing. The nomadic graziers, *gujjars*, being the most prominent members of this group, mostly keep buffaloes and roam along their set routes for grazing their herds.

Grazing areas or pasture lands in the vicinity of the village have traditionally been so managed that grazing is restricted to the periods when it does not affect growth of grasses. Animal rearing in the hills is dependent on natural grasslands, which are the major contributor (Table 3.4) towards the total fodder requirements of a household for its livestock (Negi *et al.* 1997; Sharma and Bhati 1995, Vashist *et al.* 1998). In the recent past, these lands used to be open and boundaries only demarcated notionally among different users. Over time, however, some permanent boundary markers are being put to use. At times, it is possible to notice stone walls and wooden or even iron poles demarcating the boundary among *ghasni* users at a particular location. This is quite a deviation from the practice where the lands were informally so demarcated that each user family knew the boundaries of the village pasture lands under its control. The growing emphasis on the fixed or prominent boundary markers seems to be the reflection of the growing tendency to privatize these common lands, through the process of first gaining operational control and later claiming title to these lands. This also implies the growing population pressure on the farm lands and hence the tendency to hedge against the acute land pressures in the times to come.

TABLE 3.4: **Prominent Sources of Meeting Various Forest-based Timber, Fuelwood and Fodder Requirements in Himachal Pradesh**

(% of total use in an average household)

Particulars	Sources and proportion		
	Market	CPRs	Owned lands
Timber	92.48	7.52	negligible
Fodder (grasses)	10.90	61.66	27.44
Tree fodder	—	57.81	42.19
Agril. by-products	24.38	—	75.62
Fuelwood	17.90	50.21	31.89

Source: Negi *et al.* 1997.

Apart from the watch-and-ward, there are no special management steps taken to manage these pasture lands during the period of growth of grasses. This is because of the fact that these grasslands are vast natural lands and farmers or the users do not have the resources to modify the grass production on these lands on a scientific basis. Moreover, because of the reason that the users do not have the title to these lands they are not really interested to make any investment for the upkeep or modification of grass production process on these lands. However, in some cases, the practice of using fire after the harvesting of grasses, to clean the pasture lands of bushes, etc., is followed. The belief is that this practice helps in better grass production in the following season because of clearing of bushes and other unwanted vegetation. These grassland management practices are aimed at removal of bushes, checking weed growth in the area, and stimulation of fresh growth. Considering the grazing pressures on these lands and also the health of these pasture lands, suggestions have often been made to rejuvenate these pasture lands through seeding and fertilization. However, as noted above, the resource scarcity, both capital and labour, does not permit the users to take these measures. In fact, it is because of these reasons that in many areas the pastures are acutely infested with the lantana bushes. This is a very quick growing weed and is proving a menace in these pastures.

The harvesting of grasses (hay) is done with care to maintain the quality of the grass and to avoid the spoilage of grass due to rains. For this purpose it is important to adhere to the timings of harvesting stage. Harvested grasses are kept for drying so that the same can be effectively stored for the winters without the risk of spoilage. Different practices that are used for storage of grasses are the making of bales after drying the grass and then storing it under some roof. Secondly, the grasses are dried and stored in open, in conical heaps (*tolis*); with the help of a wooden pole in the middle. This method is most common in many parts of the State. This is because of the fact that being bulky in nature, hay storage would require quite a space if the same is to be stored under a roof. Thirdly, because of the risk of accidental fires, people prefer to store grasses in the open, even though it is cumbersome to handle the same in times of need, especially during winters.

However, in the low hills it is being felt that because of the grazing pressure, the scrub forests are under pressure. Trees are deteriorating and yielding to bushes and other such growth. The pressure is from the locally grazed animals and also from the migratory graziers. In the mid and high hills because of heavy grazing and low regeneration of grasses and other vegetation, the soil erosion and land slides are becoming common. Grazing damage is mostly in the form of browsing of the young plants and also trampling of seedlings. However, in the alpine pastures, the damage is not felt as yet by the shepherds. This must be because of the reason that grazing in these areas is done in a set rotational pattern, when the herds enter the area in a very specific season. This leaves the pastures undisturbed for most part of the year, unlike in other areas. However, there is a feeling among the shepherds that pressure is increasing because of the entry of other shepherds, who had no traditional rights in these pastures. They argue that allotment of grazing permits to them should be stopped or discouraged.

The alpine pastures are utilized mainly through the practice of open grazing and the practice of harvesting grass for storage, like in other areas, is not there. Grazing in these areas is a practice that is traditionally woven into the fabric of subsistence local economy. In fact, the grazing rights are specified in different records as, for example, forest Working Plans, Settlement Records and the Indian Forest Act. The exercise of rights in protected forests is regulated by rules framed under the Indian Forest Act (Kaushal and Gaur 1998, Raina 1996). However, in order to effectively manage forests and the pastures, government can also restrict these rights. The migratory graziers are heavily dependent on these pasture lands and their livelihood is crucially linked to the health of these pastures. Gaddies, and Gujjars are the traditional users of these pastures. They are the professional graziers having a large herd of sheep and goats, and buffaloes respectively. These traditional migratory and nomadic graziers take their herds to different areas through specified paths or grazing routes and season, each year, for open grazing in a specified areas or runs. Shepherds remain in the grazing lands for about 3-4 months. Of this the period of June-July is usually in the high alpine pastures. It is this period that exerts grazing pressures on these pasture lands.

In order to regulate grazing, the shepherds, or the animal herders are required to pay a nominal grazing fee. The grazing fee for sheep and goats in 1963 stood at Rs. 12.50 per hundred of sheep and Rs. 25 per hundred goats. Since then, the rates have gone up by about 60 per cent and these were Rs. 20/100 for sheep and Rs. 40/100 for goats in 1992, while the grazing fee for horse grazing was Rs. 2/horse in the same year (Kaushal and Gaur 1998). Since the prevailing cropping pattern does not allow for cultivation of fodder, mainly because of small size and marginal nature of land holdings, over the years, the pressure on these lands has increased because of continuous grazing and the same is also affecting the economy of the State (Rathore 1991). Grazing pressure also seems to have increased because of the result of additional permits allotted for an area and also because of the fact that many areas are closed for grazing for management reasons. As a result the grazing intensity has increased at a particular grazing site. The grazing capacity of an area varies as per the quality of grasses, the frequency of visits by the grazing herds and the size of their animal herds. Grazing incidence in the districts with the high migratory grazing practices varies from 0.08 in Chamba to 2.3 in Kinnaur and Lahaul-Spiti (Kaushal and Gaur 1998).

Although, the grazing practices are normally as per the set routine in an area, sometimes the conflict over grazing in a particular region is also noticed. In the low and mid hills and also in the high hill pasture lands near the villages, conflicts arise due to the encroachment of these lands by the people, closure by the Forest Department, or acquisition of lands by any other agency for general developmental works. Further, conflicts also arise when the people bring cattle or sheep and goats from other villages for grazing in these pastures. This happens when the local people sometimes bring the animals of their relatives or acquaintances in other areas for grazing in the village pastures. This not only increases the grazing pressure at a site but also creates an ill-will among the traditional common resource users at a site.

3. Common Property Water Resources

3.a. Drinking Water Sources

The peculiar mountain characteristics, often termed as "mountain specificities" (Jodha 1992), have a number of operational implications for natural resource use and overall development of mountain regions. Inaccessibility, marginality and heterogeneity are some among these specificities or conditions that constrain development and use of natural resources. Water is a crucial natural resource for the people of the region, like it is for the people elsewhere. However, the availability and harnessing of the water is much more cumbersome in the mountain areas. Further, because of the topography, it is not always possible to harness groundwater for daily use. As a result, people have to judiciously use and manage the natural sources of water, particularly for drinking purposes. In spite of the fact that mountains are the origin of many rivers and rivulets, hill people face acute shortage of drinking and irrigation water on account of various peculiar mountain specificities.

Natural drinking water sources in the hills are mostly in the CPR regimes. Therefore, the use and management pattern for these sources is also governed by the local societal norms for use of CPRs. However, these resources do not face the problems commonly associated with other CPRs, like lands, mines, etc. In the case of drinking water sources, voluntary actions are more prominent than in other cases. The common natural sources of drinking water in the Himachal are the natural aquifers, springs, lakes and small rivulets. Water from natural springs or geysers is allowed to collect at that place and the site is maintained or protected, so as to avoid contamination of water. For this purpose these water sources (locally called *baories*, *baolies*, or *baies*, etc.) are protected. These sources are so managed that their maintenance and water use from these sources can be ascertained and regulated, respectively. Different kinds of structures are raised to collect/store water in *baories*. For this purpose, mostly the locally available material like stones, slates and wood is used. Sometimes, at a place, one may also notice the use of bushes for protecting a water source. Socio-cultural forces/factors are seen to play an important role in water use and management of these sources. There may be set rules (depending upon the local customs) governing the water use. Thus, one may find different outlets for the people of different caste/social groups at some places or even separate *baories* for the same purpose, wherever it is feasible. In the event of lack of opportunities for these arrangements, alternative local customs develop, where people of different social groups make informal arrangements, in terms of timings or merely paying respects when persons from a higher social group are there. However, the provision of tap water in the villages is helping to dilute the stringency of these customs. The provision of tap water, in a way, is helping to bridge the gap between different social groups.

Maintenance of drinking water sources is generally a collective task, and for this purpose group meetings of water-users are held and required decisions taken. Also, in most cases, the maintenance works like desilting, repairs of walls and steps, roofs (wherever the *baories* have roofs), and paths leading to these drinking water sources are carried out by linking the tasks with some cultural/religious ceremonies. In such cases, it is easy to ascertain participation of water users. This is because of the fact that water is an essential day-to-day use item and also because people attach high significance to cultural and religious norms. Apart from these culturally formal efforts to maintain these sources, it is also seen that voluntary actions of many individuals or individual families are of importance in this regard. It is not uncommon to find an individual or a family renovate drinking water source at the time of marriage, birth (particularly after long wait and praying) in the family, and at times in memory of the their near and dear ones. With the involvement of the government through its Rural Development or Irrigation and Public Health departments, people also seek the help from these quarters for the maintenance purposes. Drinking water sources for animals (called *kufars* or *dibbers*) are similarly maintained, but these are generally open ponds and not roofed or tiled.

3.b. Irrigation Channels

Mountain farming depends highly on the natural resource systems for its sustainability. Water for irrigation is one such important natural resource which is crucial for the development and sustainability of farming systems in these topographically difficult terrains. Water is a scarce commodity in the hilly terrain and water resource management for irrigation thus becomes an important collective responsibility of the people living in these areas. In the absence of sophisticated technology, and the lack of groundwater tapping opportunities as well as the resource scarcity to tap ground water where it is available, gravity channel irrigation system is common in the Himachal, in fact in all mountainous regions all over the world. In Himachal, like in other hill areas of the country, gravity channel irrigation system is practised in almost all areas of the State. However, from the point of view of the management issues that are the focus of this discussion, the gravity irrigation system of Kangra district of the State requires a special mention. Historically, water resource management system in this part of the State, for the irrigation as well as other household purposes, has attracted the attention of many common property resource (CPR) managers as well as researchers. The water resource management in the district and also in other parts of the State, particularly for irrigation, has traditionally been so managed that it secured the participation of all users for maintenance of these systems. Irrigation is done by the small gravity channels that interweave the farming landscape. Irrigation water use rules or customs are well documented in the book of irrigation customs or the *Riwaj-i-Abpashi* (Baker 1995, Chand *et al.* 1991, Thakur 1996).

The small gravity irrigation channels, or the *kuhls* as pointed out above, are constructed along the field bunds. These channels receive water from various natural sources, viz. melting snow, small rivulets, and springs. This mode of irrigation accounts for about 85 per cent of the irrigation in the State. The command area of the *kuhls* depends on the location of the water source and the amount of water in the source. In Himachal, district Kangra accounts for more than 83 per cent of the area under *kuhl* irrigation. Majority of these *kuhls* are managed by the farmers themselves. However, some of the larger *kuhls* are also managed by the Irrigation and Public Health Department of the State Government. While the main management responsibility of managing the private *kuhls* lies with the member farmers in a channel's command area, they may also get some assistance from the government for some major repairs. The *kuhl* management system requires a sound local administrative system so that the formal management rules or the informal arrangements for irrigation water harnessing and distribution can be enforced. The following discusses, mostly based on Thakur (1996) and Thakur *et al.* (1998), the *kuhl* management systems in the region.

3.c Kuhl Administration

The performance efficiency or the success of a *kuhl* depends on its managerial control as well as the voluntary participation of the water users. In the past the economy of the region or for that matter State as a whole was a closed one, with only a few linkages with the outside world. Thus cultural or religious rules, both formal and informal, were very effective in socially binding the people. This arrangement is noted to have worked very well for the management of *kuhls* in the region. Over time, however, these informal binders are seen to lose their effectiveness, and as a result voluntary participation in the resource management is declining. As for example, a few *kuhls* of the region are believed to have failed due to the lack of the people's participation (Sharma *et al.* 1995, Thakur 1996). Negligence on the part of the Panchayat, and members of the *kuhl* committee is also among the reasons for these failures. Historically, the *kuhl* master or the *Kohli* is entrusted with the management of these irrigation channels. A Kohli is a person appointed by the Irrigation Channel Management Committee for smooth functioning of the *kuhls*. Traditionally, the post of Kohli has been an inherited one; thus entrusting a single family with the administration of a *kuhl*. However, in the event of a *kuhl* master or Kohli, showing his inability to continue working on the post, the committee would appoint a new Kohli. In larger *kuhls*, the Kohlies used to have assistants to help in the *kuhl* management and in the water distribution.

The smooth functioning of a *kuhl* is the foremost duty of a Kohli and his assistants, if there are any. They need to survey the condition of the *kuhl* and take appropriate steps for its upkeep. For this purpose, Kohli or his assistants can assign the required jobs or duties to the *kuhl* committee members for smooth running of the *kuhl*. Kohli has also to maintain the traditional sequence of water distribution that depends on the already fixed norms (as prevalent in the area or as mentioned in the book of irrigation customs). He has all the records pertaining to *kuhl* members, and terms and conditions of water rights in the command area of the *kuhl*. *Kuhl* committees mainly are responsible for the management of *kuhls* and for arranging financial and technical assistance from different quarters. In the sphere of management of these irrigation channels, one of the important tasks of the committee is to help the Kohli in conflict resolution; for which various socio-cultural pressures or methods may be used.

From the old times *kuhls* have been associated with the livelihood of the farmers in the region. For long these *kuhls* also were the supplementary sources of drinking water (to *baolies* or *baories*) before the installation of drinking water taps. Even now, the channels serve as an important source of water for other household needs like washing clothes, cleaning utensils, livestock care, etc. (Thakur 1996, Baker 1995, 97, Verma 1998). For the purpose of running the *kuhls*, various operations like the cleaning and deepening of *kuhl* (locally called *khanah*), repairs or construction of channel's retaining wall, watch-and-ward (*honda*) against water theft and damage to *kuhl*, water distribution and conflict resolutions, etc. are carried out. All these operations are important and have their own importance. Thus timely action to complete a function/operation is of utmost importance for the smooth running of the *kuhls*.

Cleaning and deepening of a *kuhl* is the most important, time consuming and a difficult operation (Baker 1995, Thakur 1996, Thakur *et al.* 1998) and it is carried out about two times a year (depending upon the condition of the *kuhl*). These operations are carried first in the secondary channels and then in the main channel. Kohli of a particular *kuhl* plays an important role in organizing *khanah*, in areas where the institution of Kohli is prevalent and respected. In other parts of the State, the task of *kuhl*-cleaning is carried out at the initiative of a local leader, respected elder, at the initiative of the representative of local deity or the temple management committee, and *panchayat* officials or members, etc. The dates for the cleaning and repairs of *kuhls* are set well in advance of the crop planting season. Where Kohli is engaged, he first announces the dates and informs all members in the command area of a *kuhl* to participate in the operation. On the completion of the works needed in the secondary channels, the dates for the main channel are fixed by him. For this purpose, customarily the presence of all *kuhl* members, irrespective of their location in the secondary channel is a must. After this operation or along with it, the repairs or construction of embankments is carried out. Completion of these tasks often leads to a community feast at the *kuhl* site; which is because of the religious sentiments attached to the *kuhl*. Belief is that by worshipping the *kuhl* one can ward off any havoc in the channel during the season.

However, lately it is being noticed that the religious sentimental attachments are getting diluted and that the voluntary participation of the members in the *kuhl* works is declining. Some well-to-do farmers who previously used to be among the first to participate, now lack that enthusiasm. One of the reasons for this state of affairs is the increased involvement of elderly or other male members in off-farm jobs, as a result of which the other members, particularly the female members of the household, are not in a position to take the lead. The out-migration of people for off-farm employment is quite prominent in the region as pointed by the spurt in the figures for the male population of the Neugal river basin which was engaged in non-farm employment. Male out-migration increased by more than 200 per cent in 1991 as compared to the situation in 1961 (Baker 1995). Secondly, because of the increased household incomes the dependence on farm, particularly the traditional system, is undergoing drastic changes. Moreover, some of the farmers have started to bank upon their personal arrangements for irrigation. In general, it is also the result of concentration of females on the farms with the outmigration of the male members. Bounded by the taboos, females are not expected to take part in the *khanah* and *honda* duties. Therefore, those in position to do so will make alternative arrangements for irrigating their lands.

Honda or watch-and-ward is done to check thefts of water and also against any mischief to disrupt the *kuhl* water flow by the members or some other persons. A group of 4-5 volunteer *kuhl* users or *kuhl* members, on the advice of the Kohli, carry out the *honda* duties. It is seen that there is more enthusiasm among the tail-end farmers to do the *honda*, particularly in the peak irrigation season. Watch-and-ward is also done by the individual families whose fields are being irrigated. During this period of farm operations, there occasionally arises the need for conflict resolution as well. Conflicts arise mainly due to the excessive use of water by the upper and mid-stream farmers. Conflicts may also arise because of the mischief by the neighbouring farmer who may divert water to his own field or to the field of his near and dear ones. Sometimes, out of sheer jealousy water to a particular field may be blocked by some miscreants. These actions annoy the aggrieved party and the same results in conflicts over water use which, at times, may take a serious shape. Within a group of water users, conflicts may arise because of the doubts raised about the sincerity and regularity of the *kuhl* management works by a group member. Also, there often are people in the group who have the tendency to free-ride. The conflict resolution, however, is carried out at the Kohli's level in most of the well-managed *kuhls* or at a village level only and rarely is it taken to courts. Kohli may take the help of *kuhl* committee members and the Panchayat in this regard.

3.d. Water Rights and Distribution

Water distribution among the rights holders is the major and most hectic job of the Kohli. Although he is empowered to distribute water in a manner he deems most suitable, it is, however, not always possible for him to exercise this power. Water distribution is done by using a traditional measure known as *thelu*, a wooden device to measure the flow of water through a channel. The device is fixed by the carpenter in the presence of Kohli or his representative and some water users.

Farmers in a command area of a particular *kuhl* also have the rights to draw water from other *kuhls*, although for a limited and specified period only. These special rights are called the *dol* rights. During the period of *dol* rights, no permanent member of a *kuhl* in question has a right to disrupt these rights. Farmers generally have *dol* rights in the mid and downstream *kuhls*. Harvesting of crops in the downstream areas is climatically possible much in advance compared to the position in the upstream areas. Thus farmers in these areas lead the starting of crop operations for the next season. Taking note of this natural climatic advantage, the downstream farmers have been traditionally adjusted for irrigation purposes by way of the *dol* rights; without affecting the rights of the farmers in the upstream areas. This water is mostly used for sowing paddy with improved planting techniques that are more demanding in terms of irrigation. One interesting thing about the maintenance of these rights is that farmers will always use their rights, irrespective of the water requirements of the crops. This is done mainly to maintain the traditional rights lest the members take another view about the water requirements by the right holders. Once the rights are missed it becomes difficult for the farmers to exercise their rights in future.

4. A Synthesis

A particular resource utilization pattern, or a set of patterns for different resources, at a place, develops as a compromise to balance the socio-cultural, economic and ecological conditions governing the resource use. CPRs use and management patterns in Himachal Pradesh seem to be location specific in their management details. However, at a broader level, these are the result of similar resource development and use processes. Thus, one notices differences in the level of people's dependence on forests, pastures, and irrigation water, although the underlying fact remains that CPRs contribute significantly to their household and farm requirements. In fact, these CPRs supplement the otherwise meagre incomes of the subsistence economy of this region. As, for example, the annual direct contribution of CPRs in a study has been estimated to be in the neighbourhood of Rs. 7,000 per farm family, with the grass collection for the farm animals as the main component of this contribution (Vashist *et al.* 1998).

Traditionally, the dependence on CPRs seems to have started as a result of the fewer options for income generation from diversified farm and non-farm activities in the region. The often-talked-about mountain specificities of the hill regions, for long, put constraints on the physical access to areas outside of the region. This, thus, hindered the access to information or new farm or non-farm technology. Further, the socio-cultural setting, where group action, cooperation and respect for resource systems was, in a way, in-built in the local systems, promoted the management of various CPRs for their optimal use under the prevailing socio-cultural and economic decision environments. Thus, labour and capital resource sharing was a common phenomenon. In this regard, it would be appropriate to mention the practice of taking sheep and goats of a village for grazing by a few selected persons from a village. Similarly participation in acts like control of forest fires and management of gravity irrigation channel (*kuhl*) can also be mentioned.

However, the natural resource systems, people's perception of their use patterns and the socio-cultural and economic environments are all dynamic in nature. Thus, with the changes in decision environment the CPRs use and management scenario is bound to change. With the fast increasing human and livestock population, CPRs, particularly forest areas being used as such, are burdened with the increasing and diverse demands. Further, with the relaxation in constraints of physical access to markets and also to most CPRs, these common property resources are no more being taken as the supplementary sources of meeting farm and household requirements. The extractions from these CPRs have gained commercial significance. Market forces, thus, are redesigning common property resources use (Gadgil 1989), particularly lands. A common case is the grazing in pasture lands, where not only the animals from the villages having traditional rights are grazed but also the animals from other villages (often on some mutually agreed upon monetary arrangements). In fact, at times it is not uncommon to see conflicts arising over the allotment of additional grazing permits for the outsider in a traditional grazing area of a village or community, or over the issue of animals being brought from villages at a far-off distance to graze in these common pastures. Market opportunities thus have initiated a shift to increased commercial use of CPRs.

The continuance of traditional common property resource management regimes and their effectiveness in the current socio-economic environment depends crucially on the likelihood of congruence of resource users' goals. The stability of these use patterns, may be in their modified forms, would require the stability of the contextual factors which, however, are fast changing. Thus, a dynamic model of CPRs management would be required. Different experiments are being made to effectively balance the changing goals of resource users and also CPRs' potential to meet these goals. In this regard, the policy emphases on finding ways that would be technologically *feasible*, socially *adoptable* and economically *gainful* (Fiery 1960) are the attempts being made by involving people in various resource development programmes. Social and agroforestry programmes of the 1970s are the noted efforts made in this direction. However, excepting the success stories, people's participation on a continued basis was found lacking in these cases as well. It, thus, becomes important that if promoting resource development and conservation efforts are to be the policy emphases, programmes that weaken people's constraint and strengthen motives that characterize these efforts would be required (Negi 1993). This would require an analysis of interrelations of how societal norms work in these regions, so as to improve our diagnostic framework (Sanwal 1989). Therefore, it is of crucial importance that the resource management strategies hinge on the concept of local people's participation.

Some of the ways to strive for this goal would be to create stakes for the local people in the resource and also to influence resource use through the *push* or *pull* strategies. People do respond to an improved market situation and also to improved household incomes through better management of their resources and through incorporating new farm activities to meet these ends. Push strategies would seek pressure relieving opportunities out of CPR command area. The pull strategies, on the other hand, would focus on employment generation in the command area. Creating stakes in the resource imbibes a sense of belongingness and the same acts as a catalyst for bringing management efficiency. This is an issue of current debate in the field of resource management and opportunities for effective involvement of local people are being sought. However, to further project the importance of local people's participation, particularly in the current changing scenario, it would be worthwhile to emphasize the following from the Rio Declaration: "Human beings are the center of concern for sustainable development. Indigenous people and their communities have a vital role in environmental management and development because of their knowledge and practices". Since resource use patterns are the reflections of people's efforts to balance their varied socio-economic and ecological concerns, their active participation in common pool resources management is crucial.

REFERENCES

Agarwal Chetan and Katar Singh. 1996. "The Village Cooperative Forest Societies in Himachal Pradesh". In: Katar Singh and Vishwa Ballabh (eds.). *Cooperative Management of Natural Resources*. New Delhi: Sage Publications.

Ahluwalia, M.S. 1988. *History of Himachal Pradesh*. Delhi: Intellectual Publishing House.

Anderson, A. 1986. *Report on the Demarcation of Kullu Forests*. Reproduced in 1975. Shimla: Himachal Pradesh Forest Department.

Baker, Mark J. 1995. "The Gravity Flow Irrigation System of Kangra Valley of Himachal Pradesh: contemporary transformations and interactions with farming systems". In: *Proceedings of the International Seminar, "Natural Resources: Management and their Linkages with Farming Systems"*. Nauni-Solan, Department of Social Sciences: Dr. Y.S. Parmar University of Horticulture and Forestry.

Baker, Mark J. 1997. "Common Property Resource Theory and the *Kuhl* Irrigation Systems of Himachal Pradesh, India", *Human Organization*. Vol. 56, No. 2, pp. 199-208.

Berkes, F. *et al.* 1995. *Sustainability of a Mountain Watershed Ecosystem in the Himachal Pradesh Himalaya: Background and Overview*. Technical Report No. 1. Winnipeg: Natural Resources Institute, University of Manitoba.

Bhatia, Anupam. 1997. "Power, Equity, Gender, and Conflicts in Common Property Resources in the Hindu-Kush Himalayas". ICIMOD, Kathmandu (Nepal): *Issues in Mountain Development*. 97/7.

Chand, Ramesh *et al.* 1991. "Impact of Government Assistance on Operation and Maintenance of Rural Development Department *Kuhls* in Solan and Sirmour districts (H.P.)". *(mimeo)* Solan: Dr. Y.S. Parmar University of Horticulture and Forestry.

Chen, Marty. 1988. "Women and Household Livelihood Systems". Paper presented at the IVth National Conference on Women's Studies, Waltair, Andhra Pradesh. New Delhi: Centre for Women's Development Studies.

Chopra, Kanchan, G.K. Kadekodi, and M.N. Murty. 1990. *Participatory Development, People and Common Property Resources*. New Delhi: Sage Publications.

Davidson-Hunt, J. Iain 1995. *The State, the Village and the Commoner: Interactions in the Management of Western Himalayan Commons*. Winnipeg, Manitoba: Natural Resource Institute, University of Manitoba.

Firey, W.W. 1960. *Man, Mind and Land*. Glencoe, Illinois: Free Press.

Gadgil, Madhav. 1989. "Deforestation: Problems and Prospects". *Foundation Day Lecture*. New Delhi: Society for Promotion of Wastelands Development.

GOI (Government of India). 1989. *Van Stithi Per Report*. Dehra Dun: Indian Forest Survey, Ministry of Environment and Forests.

Ham, Laurie. 1995. "Livelihood Security in Mountain Ecosystems: Coping and Adapting in Two Himalayan Villages, India". *Technical Report No. 5*. Winnipeg: Natural Resources Institute, University of Manitoba.

Jodha, N.S. 1992. "Sustainability of Himalayan Forests: Some Perspectives". In: Anil Aggarwal (ed.), *The Price of Forests*. New Delhi: Centre for Science and Environment.

Jodha, N.S. 1992. "Rural Common Property Resources: The missing dimensions of development strategies". *World Bank Discussion Paper. No. 169*, Washington D.C.: The World Bank.

Jodha, N.S. 1986. "Common Property Resources and the Rural Poor in Dry Regions of India". *Economic and Political Weekly*. Vol. 21, (27): 1169-1181.

Joshi, Srinivas. 1986. "Himachal Pradesh—Its Geography and Culture". In: *Agricultural Research and Development in Himachal Pradesh*. Shimla: Government of Himachal Pradesh.

Kaushal, Parvinder and Ram Krishan Gaur. 1998. *Ecological Aspects of Pasture Management in Alpine Zone of Himachal Pradesh*. Regional Centre, National Afforestation and Eco-development Board. Nauni-Solan: Dr. Y.S. Parmar University of Horticulture and Forestry *(mimeo)*.

Khosla, P.K. *et al.* 1992. *Status of Social Forestry in Jammu and Kashmir*. Nauni-Solan: Dr. Y.S. Parmar University of Horticulture and Forestry.

Mitto, H.K. 1978. *Himachal Pradesh*. New Delhi: National Book Trust.

Nagpal, R. 1991. *Status Report on Forestry and Watershed Development — Himachal Pradesh*. Chandigarh: National Bank for Agriculture and Rural Development.

Negi, G.C. 1990. *Livestock Development in Himachal Pradesh*. Palampur: Himachal Pradesh Krishivishva Vidyalaya.

Negi, Y.S., S.C. Tewari, L.R. Sharma, and Manoj Gupta. 1997. *Estimation of Consumption Pattern and Supply of Forest Products in Himachal Pradesh*. Nauni-Solan: Department of Social Sciences, Dr. Y.S. Parmar University of Horticulture and Forestry.

Negi, Y.S. 1993. "The Conditions for Agroforestry Development on Farms in the Western Himalayas of India". Ph.D. dissertation. Berkeley: University of California.

Negi, Y.S., L.R. Sharma and Jagtar Singh. 1986. "Factors Affecting Fuelwood Consumption —A micro level study". *Indian Forester*. Vol. 112, No. 8.

ODA (Overseas Development Administration Report). 1994. *Himachal Pradesh Forestry Project: Socio-economic Setting, Kullu and Mandi Districts*. Vol. 2, Annex. 1. (cited in Ham, 1995).

Raina, K.K. 1996. *Migratorial Grazing in North-Western Himalayan Region: Sustainability Issues and Implications for Migratory Gaddi Shepherds*. Nauni-Solan: Dr. Y.S. Parmar University of Horticulture and Forestry.

Rathore, M.S. 1991. "Livestock Development in Himachal Pradesh: Threat to Sustainable Agriculture". In: *Proceedings of the Seminar on Constraints of Agricultural Development in Hilly Areas*. Palampur: Himachal Pradesh Krishivishva Vidyalaya.

Sanwal, Mukul. 1989. "What We Know About Mountain Development: Common Property, Investment Priorities, and Institutional Arrangements". *Mountain Research and Development*. Vol. 9, No. 1.

Shah, S.L. 1996. *Agricultural Development in Hill Areas - Constraints and Potential*. New Delhi: New Age International (P) Limited, Publishers.

Sharma, L.R. and J.P. Bhati. 1995. "Dependence of Hilly Rural Economy on Common Property Forests: A Study in North West India". *Artha Vikas*. Vol. XXXI (I).

Sharma, R.K., A.K. Sharma and Virender Kumar. 1995. "Water as a Natural Resource and its Linkages with Farm Productivity in H.P." *Proceedings of the International Seminar on Natural Resources: Management and their Linkages with Farming Systems*. Naun-Solan: Department of Social Sciences, Dr. Y.S. Parmar University of Horticulture and Forestry.

Singh, Dalbir. 1995. "Changing Size and Status of Common Property Resources and Ecological Stress in Himachal Pradesh". In: *Proceedings of the International Seminar, Natural Resources: Management and their Linkages with Farming Systems*. Nauni-Solan: Department of Social Sciences, Dr. Y.S. Parmar University of Horticulture and Forestry.

Singh, Katar. 1993. *Managing Common Pool Resources: Principles and Case Studies*. Delhi: Oxford University Press.

Singh, Mian Goverdhan. 1985. *History of Himachal Pradesh*. New Delhi: Yugbodh Publishing House.

Singh, R.C. Pal. 1961. "Chirgaon—A Village Survey". *Census of India*. Vol XX, Part VI, No. 13.

Swarup, R. 1991. *Agricultural Economy of Himalayan Region*. Nainital: Gyanodaya Prakashan.

Thakur, Rajesh K. 1996. "Economics of Hill Farming Systems and their Linkages with Common Property Resources". Ph.D. dissertation. Nauni-Solan: Dr. Y.S. Parmar University of Horticulture and Forestry.

Thakur, R.K., S.C. Tewari and Y.S. Negi. 1998. "Community Participation in the Management of Gravity Irrigation System in Himachal Pradesh". *Journal of Agricultural Development and Policy*. Vol. X, No. 1.

Vashist, G.D., Parkash Mehta and M.S. Pathania. 1998. *Common Property Resources and Rural Poor in Low and Mid-hills of Himachal Pradesh*. Palampur: Department of Agricultural Economics, Himachal Pradesh Krishi Vishvavidyalaya.

Verma, L.R. 1998. *A Glimpse of Indigenous Technology Knowledge for Watershed Management in Upper North-West Himalayas of India*. Watershed Management Technology Center (WATMATEC) of the Dr. Y.S. Parmar University of Horticulture and Forestry, Solan (H.P.), India, and PWMTA Netherlands/FAO (UN), GCP/RAS/161/NET, Kathmandu, Nepal.

4 Commons, Development and the Poor

M.V. Nadkarni

1. The Problem

The Commons in a wider sense cover most of our environment—air, water, oceans, rivers and other inland water bodies, forests, grazing lands and so on. When Hardin (1968) drew attention to the "Tragedy of the Commons", he meant it in this wider sense using the grazing lands only as a symbol. This chapter also keeps mainly the local commons in focus rather than global commons, though some problems are common between the two. For example, the absence of properly defined or recognised property rights was what attracted the attention of Hardin, a condition, resulting in a situation of open access.

All collective or joint use of resources outside the market framework need not necessarily mean open access leading to the tragedy of degradation and decline. Hardin has been criticised by quite a few scholars for having ignored the possibility of community cooperation and management (Ciriacy-Wantrup and Bishop 1975, Bromley and Cernea 1989, Ostrom 1990, Sengupta 1991, Marothia 1993). Instances of community management are being documented increasingly. Jodha (1985a and b), for example, has shown how in the past the user of CPRs was regulated through measures like a grazing tax, livestock-related levies payable during ceremonies, obligatory contribution of labour for digging and desilting water ponds, and penalties for unauthorised use. There are also examples of "sacred groves" maintained and protected through tradition and religious veneration of forests by local communities (Gadgil and Vartak 1976). Such community management in respect of both grazing and irrigation is still prevailing in several villages of Andhra Pradesh (Wade 1988). That the tragedy of the commons could be avoided not only by traditional societies but also in contemporary ones through a "co-operative game" of people contributing to the local economy and welfare of all participants has been demonstrated by cases like Sukhomarji (Chopra, Kadekodi and Murty 1990) and Pani Panchayat (Deshpande and Reddy 1990). A more comprehensive study by Singh (1994) has presented more cases of collective action in India covering irrigation, fisheries, forest management and watershed development.

Unfortunately, however, such examples of community management of local commons are not so usual as one would wish. They became more an exception than a rule by the end of 1970s, though there are now signs of revival thanks to official encouragement under Joint Forest Management and Watershed Development programmes and to the efforts of gifted community leaders, NGOs and the Forest Department. The revival has hardly been adequate enough to meet the biomass needs of local communities or to reverse degradation of forests. There may, of course, be a few cases of success but in a wider desert of the Tragedy of the Commons *a la* Hardin.

It is becoming increasingly evident that larger and stronger forces of economic development are at work promoting a decline of the local commons. The efforts made to restore collective action to manage them are not enough to cope with these forces. This chapter tries to understand the working as well as the impact of these forces on the local commons and their implications for the poor. This leads us, by way of conclusion, to some policy measures to protect the poor and promote a sustainable use of the local commons. We shall also see, at least briefly, if lessons derived from the experiment on local commons can also be used to indicate policies to manage global commons as well, keeping both equity and sustainability in mind.

2. Economic Development and the Local Commons

Both Hardin (1968) and Jodha (1985-a) put emphasis on population growth as being a major factor in the decline of the Commons. The role of population growth comes out conspicuously through pressures on forests for extension of cultivation, which accounts for a major share of the decline in the area of forests during the last few decades in India. However, there is more to it than what appears at first glance. Encroachments into forests for extending cultivation are not so much for producing more food for a larger population as they are for creating a source of livelihood. Even in a situation when the total supply of food is enough to meet the subsistence needs of a population, there can still be a demand for extension of cultivation at the cost of forests when the means of alternative sources of livelihood are not expanding rapidly enough to take the pressure of land.

Moreover, encroachments into the commons like grazing lands and forests for cultivation often characterise initial phases of economic development in the concerned regions, especially when agricultural development takes an extensive character. It becomes more intensive only when further extension of cultivation is not possible or is uneconomical.

TABLE 4.1: **Area of Lands Used as Commons in India**

(Thousand hectares)

S.No.	Land Use	1955-56	1970-71	1995-96
1.	Total Geographical Area	328726	328726	328726
2.	Forests	51343	63917	68829
		(15.6)	(19.4)	(20.6)
3.	Cultivable Waste	21537	17500	14102
		(6.6)	(5.3)	(4.4)
4.	Grazing Lands	11473	13262	11054
	including Permanent Pastures	(3.5)	(4.0)	(3.4)
5.	Fallows	12544	8759	10013
	(other than current)	(3.8)	(2.7)	(3.0)
6.	=(2)+(3)+(4)+(5)	96897	103436	103995
		(29.5)	(31.4)	(31.6)
7.	Barren and	34476	28161	19030
	Uncultivable Waste	(10.5)	(8.6)	(5.8)

Source: *Indian Agriculture in Brief*, respective editions for 1955-56 and 1970-71; Fertiliser Statistics —1996-97 for 1995-96.

Note: Figures in brackets are percentages to total geographical area.

It would be useful to see what has happened at the aggregate level in the country as a whole in the last four decades, in terms of official landuse data. This picture is presented in Table 4.1. Broadly, forests, cultivable waste, grazing lands and fallows other than current fallows could be considered as lands used as CPRs. However, not all forest lands are used as CPRs—certainly not those used as National Parks and Wild Life Sanctuaries. Local communities have a limited access to reserve forests, and greater access to "protected forests" and village forests. The bulk of the forest area comes under the "Reserved" category. The picture we get is somewhat mixed. While the area under forests has increased consistently between 1955-56 and 1970-71, and also between 1970-71 and 1995-96, the areas under cultivable wastes, grazing lands as also under barren and uncultivable wastes have declined consistently in both the periods. Only the area under fallows, other than current, declined in the first period and increased slightly in the second period. Even out of the mixed picture, we get the clear impression that the area under forests has increased at the cost of other lands used as commons. The increase in the forest area is so high that it more than offsets the decline in other categories, and the total of all these categories (excluding the barren lands) has increased in both absolute and relative terms (see No. 6 in Table 4.1). However, an increase in the area under forests mainly in the categories where locals have no or very limited access, at the expense of other commons, is no good news for the local communities. It need not necessarily be good news even to environmentalists, since all the area regarded as under forests officially need not actually be under tree cover. Official statistics are more legalistic than realistic and underestimate the decline in CPRs and the increase in the cultivated area, as we shall presently see.

The micro-level findings, however, offer a more clear picture of the decline in the area under CPRs. In a substantive work involving 82 villages spread over 21 districts of the dry regions of India, Jodha has documented how the decline in the area under CPRs has varied from 31 per cent in Maharashtra to 55 per cent in Rajasthan between early 1950s and early 1980s. The decline has been in both quantity and quality, the latter as seen from the decline in the number of products collected, number of water points or ponds, and number of trees (Jodha 1990, pp. 7-8). Damodaran (1987) has shown how in a Karnataka village, the area under CPRs declined from 526 acres in 1966 to a mere 60 acres in 1985. The bulk of this decline was due to a take-over of sizable land by the Forest Department for commercial plantations. A study of 25 villages in Gujarat by Iyengar (1989) showed that there was a decline in CPRs in both quantity and quality, mainly due to encroachments as well as legal privatisation.

At ISEC, we probed further in this regard first about the discrepancy between official landuse data and actual landuse seen through personal visits and observations in selected villages and, secondly, about the differences in the extent of CPRs as per the level of development of the concerned villages (Nadkarni and Pasha 1991, p. 546). Regarding the first point, after allowing for land in the village owned by those outside the village, the discrepancy between official landuse data and actual landuse as gathered by us was mainly due to private encroachments on public lands, which were yet to be regularised by entering these into official records. The same is likely in the case of macro-level data, involving underestimation of the decline in all CPRs in the official landuse data.

The extent of encroachments was by no means insignificant in the selected villages (see Table 4.2). The encroachments were more in developed villages than in others. On the other hand, the extent of area under CPRs was higher in backward villages than in developed villages. The classification of villages here as per the level of development was based on our judgement based on availability of irrigation and other infrastructure. Most of the encroached areas were not available for community use, as they were put under cultivation of annual crops. A picture is unmistakable wherein with the higher level of development, demand for private property resource increased and the need for CPRs declined resulting in less resistance to privatisation.

TABLE 4.2: **Area under Commons in Selected Villages Classified by Level of Development**

	Type of Villages	Developed	Medium	Backward	All
1.	Number of Villages	6	5	3	14
2.	Geographical Area (hectares)	3788	1812	2353	7953
3.	CPR Area as per our Survey (hectares)	654	336	817	1807
	(3) as % (2)	17.3	18.5	34.7	22.7
4.	Area Encroached for Cultivation (hectares)	360	121	203	684
	(4) as % (2)	9.5	6.7	8.6	8.6

Source: Nadkarni and Pasha 1991 (Table 1 on p. 546).

The decline of area under CPRs in the course of economic development has been documented also in another study at ISEC (Kanbargi and Kanbargi 1991). The authors have observed that, in course of time, a developed and prosperous village witnessed almost a complete disappearance of land under CPRs, and also a similar disappearance of at least absolute poverty. On the other hand, a neighbouring village, which did not so develop, faced a decline neither in CPRs nor in poverty. Both these villages are in a semi-arid district, Tumkur, in Karnataka. The authors have argued that it was poverty which made people depend on CPRs. If development could wipe out poverty, the decline in CPRs which might come side by side need not worry the poor, they felt.

Unfortunately, the story of the decline of CPRs in the course of economic development is not as simple and harmless as in the above case of a prosperous village in Karnataka. It all depends on how this economic development takes place. In many cases, the "development" and also the decline of CPRs takes place through the entry of commercial interests intent upon exploiting forests and other local resources, depriving the local people of their access to their natural resource base considerably. Often, local people have protested against this (Nadkarni, Pasha and Prabhakar 1989: Part I by Nadkarni, Guha 1989). And once they saw a complete breakdown of the system of sustainable use and management of the local resource converting a resource meant almost exclusively for local use into an open access resource, the local people also in despair and desperation started to use the resource recklessly.

The tragedy of the commons here was brought about not because the local people were unwilling to cooperate with each other, but because their cooperative game was disrupted by outside entrants who had no respect for their game. What makes it absolutely unbearable for the locals is that the outside entrants are backed to the hilt by the State. This is what appears to have happened in the Garhwal Himalayas as seen by Guha (1989) and probably in several places elsewhere.

The commercial interests outside may not always act directly, but indirectly through the State. This happened when the Forest Department took over "wastelands", used as commons for grazing and collection of fuel wood by the rural people, to raise commercial plantations to meet the raw material needs of industries. This directly deprived the local people of access to their commons, though the aim was to make a more productive use of wastelands in a market framework. An NGO in Karnataka (Samaja Parivartana Samudaya) led a prolonged struggle against this policy mobilising rural people and public opinion.

In both the above situations—the first marked by "endogenous" development with the local people themselves being agents of development, and the second marked by "exogenous" development with outside commercial interests being the agents of development—a process of commoditisation of a collective resource used earlier outside the market framework takes place. This process converts a public good into a private good. But the decline or the "tragedy" of the commons takes place here not because of the undefined nature of the property rights or because of their use outside the market process, but because of their commoditisation. Its implications for poverty will be analysed in the next Section. Presently, we can look into environmental implications.

Of the two types of developments above, exogenous development seems to involve more environmental problems. The outside commercial interests have normally no stake in the sustainable use of a local resource, as they generally get it at a throw-away price. They exploit it and, once the local resource is exhausted, they go elsewhere for greener pastures. Neither the outside interests nor the State take effective steps for regeneration in such cases, and the resource is degenerated and depleted almost forever. This is how many of our Reserve Forests and bamboo resources were depleted. The same story prevails in fisheries. The unexploited or unharvested fishery resources can be treated as commons. Where they remain local commons, used only by local fishermen through simple country boats and nets to meet only their own needs and local markets, there is no threat of depletion of fisheries. But once outside interests enter with their mechanised boats and trawlers, depletion of fisheries is clearly in sight.

What happens when commons such as forests are encroached upon for cultivation? Such encroachments may be by the locals as well as outsiders.

While normally the encroachment into local commons is by the locals, Reserved Forests may be encroached upon by outsiders, often with the blessings of politicians and the government (Govindaru 1991). Normally, forest lands particularly on hill slopes are not suitable for cultivation. When such lands are cleared of trees and shrubs for cultivation of annual crops, they are instantly exposed to soil erosion leading not only to degradation of such lands but also to silting up of waterways and tanks downstream and consequently to flooding. The negative externalities involved thus are spread out far and wide. The farmers who encroach upon the forests and grazing lands for cultivation put minimal inputs in such lands and hardly undertake soil conservation works, since the land does not belong to them legally as yet, as was seen from a study of such areas in Idukki district of Kerala (Nadkarni and Govindaru 1995). At the same time, it is difficult to grant property rights on all the lands encroached upon in order to give incentives for undertaking soil conservation works and growing tree crops, because such a permissive situation would mean an open invitation to encroach upon and clear more and more forests. It is not easy for State Governments to resolve this dilemma. Usually they wait for a few years and then regularise under public pressure, permitting in the meanwhile all the associated environmental damage.

The declining importance of common lands in supporting rural livelihoods and the increasing demand for their privatisation in the course of economic development both act together and reduce the extent of common lands and also their quality. This can be a worrisome trend because common lands such as forests will continue to be required to serve their ecological functions, which include soil and water conservation, maintenance of biodiversity, prevention of global warming and keeping the oxygen cycle running. The importance of these functions will increase rather than decrease in the course of economic development. To conserve the commons and to continue to enable them to perform their beneficial ecological function, it is necessary to institute a scheme of incentives both for both nations/regions and local people. More of this in our concluding section.

3. Commons and the Poor

The importance of the commons for the poor is now widely taken for granted. Jodha has documented how the poor have gained from CPRs more than the rich in absolute as also in relative terms. Not only have the poor earned a greater proportion of their meagre incomes from CPRs than the non-poor, they have also earned more in rupee terms. The proportion of income earned by the poor ranged from 14 per cent in Maharashtra to 3 per cent in Rajasthan in Jodha's sample villages (Jodha 1990). This would mean that any deprivation of access to commons for the poor leads to their further impoverishment and destitution. The dependence of the poor on nature for their livelihood is very significant in less developed societies. Any degradation of the natural resource base of the economy of the poor would affect them very adversely. This is so not merely in the case of forests, but also in the case of fisheries and such other natural resources. If the poor are deprived of commons in the course of economic development and if they are also not compensated by economic development through new opportunities, then the poor would only be in the proverbial *Trishanku-lok,* neither on the earth nor in the heaven but left precariously hanging in between. If modern economic development bypasses the people who have neither productive assets of their own nor skills to gain from new opportunities, then their being deprived of the commons in addition would be most tragic indeed.

Jodha's prescription in terms of revival and regeneration of the commons as an important component of poverty alleviation programmes would, therefore, sound very apt. The commons would provide them at least that precious little which means a difference between survival and complete collapse. Even granting this, however, it is important to note that there is nothing automatic about benefits from the commons flowing more towards the poor. There are also serious limitations to the role of the commons in alleviating rural poverty, though they have this potential.

In our work at ISEC, we found that the poor gain from the commons more than the rich only in relation to their own meagre incomes, but not in absolute terms. The non-poor happen to gain more from the commons in absolute terms. This was seen from surveys of four villages in a forest region of Uttara Kannada district of Karnataka, and also of villages mostly in semi-arid regions of Karnataka. The income per household received from forests in the forest region in a year was: Rs. 1,058 among agricultural labourers, Rs. 2,853 among poor peasants, Rs. 3,799 among middle peasants, and upwards of Rs. 6,537 in richer classes. In relative terms, however, the poor peasants earned 24.3 per cent of their total income from forests, and the middle and richer peasants earned between 13.7 and 18.1 per cent. But the agricultural labourers earned only 11.9 per cent which was less than in any other class. They earned less in both absolute and relative terms (Nadkarni, Pasha and Prabhakar 1989). Another study at ISEC carried out in 14 villages also confirmed a similar pattern. Though the share of income derived from forests was 10 per cent among the poor and 6.2 per cent among other households; in absolute terms, the former gained only Rs. 794 in a year while the latter got Rs. 1,393 from forests (Pasha 1992).

This happens because there is a complementarity between private agricultural economy and CPRs. Farmers get several agricultural inputs from them such as green manure, fodder, fencing material and even wood for the construction of houses and cowsheds. The more cultivated land a household has, the more it tends to extract from the commons. Where the agrarian structure is unequal, the rich gain more in absolute terms even from CPRs. Even the stock of animals increases in absolute terms with increasing holding size, though animals per unit of land tend to gradually decrease (see Table 4.3).

In spite of this, the significance of the commons is vital for the poor households. They can afford to maintain at least a limited number of livestock mainly because of their access to the commons. In the absence of the commons, they would have to meet themselves even their meagre requirements of fodder and fuelwood from the richer farmers, which would make them dependent on the latter and reduce their bargaining power. Secondly, in the course of commercialisation and general economic development, the richer households begin to depend on their own resources or on the market, for example, purchasing more nutritious fodder from the market and/or getting it from their crop residues. So long as the commons remain, they may continue to rely on them too in addition to their own resources. For example, unproductive cattle remaining with them graze on the commons, while the milch and draught cattle are fed on additional and more nutritious fodder from the market. But the richer rural households do not lose much if the commons are privatised. On the other hand, the poor households have nothing to fall back upon. There is a continuing need to have the revival of the commons as a component in poverty alleviation programmes. It is no use giving cattle, sheep and goat to the poor, unless the village also grows fodder for their maintenance on its common lands.

TABLE 4.3: **Possession of Livestock (cattle, buffaloes and calves) among Rural Households in a Forest Region of Karnataka**

Class of Rural Household	Average size of holding (ha)	Livestock per household (No.)	Livestock per ha (No.)
Landlords	17.6	17.6	1.0
Capitalist Farmers	8.2	9.8	1.2
Middle Peasants	5.5	7.8	1.4
Poor Peasants	1.4	7.2	5.1
Landless agri. labour	nil	1.7	-

Source: Calculated from Table 7.3 (p. 116) and Table 9.1 (p. 142) in Nadkarni, Pasha and Prabhakar 1989.

But because the rich also gain from the commons and try to corner benefits from them, it is necessary to ensure participation of the poor in the management of the commons and give them the right of equitable share in the produce from the commons. This leads us to the next section.

4. Institutionalising the Commons: A Conclusion

The discussion in the preceding two sections leads to two conclusions : (1) There is a tendency for the commons to degrade or decline in the course of economic development, though their ecological functions increase in importance, requiring their conservation; (2) This decline of commons can hit the poor badly as they depend for their survival on them; yet, their revival need not automatically benefit the poor more since the non-poor may corner more benefits from the commons in absolute terms (if not in relative terms). While there is a need for reviving the commons not only on environmental considerations but also in the interest of the poor whom economic development bypasses, it is at the same time necessary to ensure that the poor do indeed benefit at least equitably, if not more, in absolute terms. Any institutional arrangement, therefore, would have to pass the double test of whether it is equitable and oriented to providing greater justice to the poor, and if it promotes ecological functions of the commons and sustainable use.

It is easier to design proper institutional arrangements in the case of common lands and even irrigation tanks and other minor irrigation projects than in the case of other commons like fisheries, groundwater and air. One can think of three institutional alternatives in the case of the former: (1) privatising, (2) State property and management, and (3) collective management. Privatisation of common lands under the tacit support and even encouragement of politicians and State Governments has already been occurring. Evidence from field work has shown that a major part of the encroached lands is under non-poor rather than the poor (Nadkarni *et al.* 1989 : 165; Jodha 1990 : 11). Even if some poor may gain land, the remaining poor would be deprived of access to common lands. Moreover, there are limits to privatising common lands particularly forests, since they have ecological functions which are lost if they are converted as cultivated areas. This is particularly so with conservation of bio-diversity.

Absolute State ownership with complete State management is also subject to severe limitations, as it brings the State in direct conflict with the local people dependent on them for livelihood. Alienation of the local people from participation in managing the Reserve Forests has only led to unsustainable exploitation by them since they did not feel responsible for maintaining them. The same thing happened in the case of irrigation tanks, which were earlier taken care of by the people themselves. When the State Governments took over their management, their maintenance suffered.

This leaves us with the third alternative of collective management by people. Since the legal ownership of common lands vests with the State and it is ultimately the State which has the legal authority either to prevent or regularise encroachment and is responsible for conservation of forests, a joint management with active participation by the people rather than exclusive management by the people alone seems more desirable. The State has to ensure sustainable and equitable use particularly when the people's collective action breaks down; otherwise, it needs to play only a catalytic role and ensure fair play. But this need not reduce the people's responsibility and their role in management.

Within an institutional structure like Joint Forest Management, there need to be institutional devices which ensure the achievement of the goals of management, namely, equity and sustainable use. Though evolving these devices is ultimately left to the good sense of the people themselves, three principles can be set forth. First, limit the total load of exploitation of the produce or benefits from the commons to their regeneration capacity, while taking steps at the same time to increase regeneration and productivity of the commons. In the case of irrigation tanks (and even other sources of irrigation) this principle can be extended to involve maximising the productivity per unit of water, rather than productivity per unit of the cropped land. This is to ensure sustainable use and check profligacy.

The next two principles are for ensuring equity. The first of these is to institute equal right on the produce of the common lands—equal right per household irrespective of the size of land owned or livestock. This principle was implemented in the case of *pani panchayats*, with the households being allowed to have tradeable rights on water. The principle can be extended to cover equal rights to grass too, the households with a surplus allowed to sell to other households within the village or even outside the village depending on the consensus of the people of the village. The principle of equal but tradeable rights on the commons can be extended to cover even global commons like air, with all countries having equal per capita rights on carbon emissions fixed at a certain past year as a base for population. The last clause is to see that there is no incentive to increase population! (CSE 1992).

The third and last principle —to ensure equity and pro-poor bias—is to give priority to the produce which is needed mostly by the poor. Growing eucalyptus on the grazing lands is the very opposite of this principle! Several social forestry projects committed this mistake in the initial years of the programme sponsored by the State Governments. It is necessary to orient the common lands used for grazing to produce more of grass and brush wood used as both animal feed and firewood by the poor, though they can also have some trees scattered here and there but avoiding high density.

However, poverty is too large a phenomenon to be tackled through a revival of CPRs alone. While it can give some opportunity for survival to the poor, poverty needs to be tackled by wider and more ambitious poverty alleviation programmes and also by a strategy of economic development oriented to uplift the poor. Revival of commons can only be a component of this overall strategy, though by no means an insignificant one.

In an economic environment of highly individualistic commercialisation, revival of commons and community management can also mean revival of a communitarian ethos. There should be some secular activities which induce shared interest, collective activity and care involving people irrespective of caste and creed, so that a tradition of interaction between human beings for the common good of all is continued and strengthened. In this respect, the commons have not only an economic and ecological role, but also a political (in a constructive sense) and institutional role.

REFERENCES

Bromley, Daniel W. and Michael M. Cernea. 1989. *The Management of Common Property Resources: Some Conceptual and Operational Fallacies*, World Bank Discussion papers, Washington: The World Bank.

Ciriacy—Wantrup, S.V. and R.C. Bishop. 1975. "Common Property as a Concept in Natural Resources Policy", *Natural Resources Journal*, 15(4): 713-728.

Chopra, L., G.K. Kadekodi and M.N. Murty. 1990. *Participatory Development: An Approach to the Management of Common Property Resources*, New Delhi: Sage.

Centre for Science and Environment (CSE). 1992. "'The CSE Statement on Global Environmental Democracy", *Alternatives* 17 (2) Spring: 261-279.

Damodaran, A. 1987. "Structural Dimensions of Fodder Crisis—A Village Study in Karnataka", *Economic and Political Weekly*, March 28 (Review of Agric.) : A - 16-22.

Deshpande, R.S. and V. Ratna Reddy. 1990. "Social Dynamics and Farmers' Society : A Case Study of Pani Panchayat". *Indian Journal of Agricultural Economics*, 45 (3) July-Sept. pp. 355-361.

Gadgil, Madhav and V.D. Vartak. 1976. "Sacred Groves of Western Ghats of India", *Economic Botany*, 30 : 15-60.

Govindaru, V. 1991. "Policy Environment of Deforestation : Kerala's Experience" presented in the *Seminar on Towards Greening India's Wastelands*, Bangalore : ISEC (Unpublished).

Guha, Ramachandra. 1989. *Unquiet Woods : Ecological Change and Peasant Resistance in the Himalayas*, New Delhi : Oxford University Press.

Hardin, Garret. 1968. "The Tragedy of the Commons", *Science* 162, December 13: 1243-48.

Iyengar, Sudarshan. 1989. "Common Property Land Resources in Gujarat : Some Findings about their Size, Status and Use", *Economic and Political Weekly*, June 2 (Review of Agri.) A - 67-78.

Jodha, N.S. 1985-a. "Population Growth and the Decline of CPRs in Rajasthan, India", *Population and Development Review* 11 (2) : 247-264.

Jodha, N.S. 1985-b. "Market Forces and Erosion of CPR's" presented in *Agricultural Markets in Semi-Arid Tropics*, ICRISAT, Patancheru : 263-277.

Jodha, N.S. 1990. "Rural CPRs : Contribution and Crisis", Foundation Day Lecture, SPWD, New Delhi.

Kanbargi, Shantha and Ramesh Kanbargi. 1991. "Emerging Development and Declining CPRs : Is it Necessarily an Evil? - Some Observations", presented in the *Seminar on Towards Greening India's Wastelands*, Bangalore : ISEC (Unpublished).

Marothia, D.K. 1993. "Property Regimes and Institutional Arrangements: Concepts and Their Relevance in Managing the Village Commons", *Indian Journal of Agricultural Economics*, 48(3): 557-565.

Nadkarni, M.V. and V. Govindaru. 1995. "Nobody's Child : The Economic and Institutional Aspects of Soil Conservation in India", *Journal of Environment and Development* 4, 1 (Winter): 171-183.

Nadkarni, M.V. and Syed Ajmal Pasha. 1991. "Developing Uncultivated Lands - Some Issues from Karnataka Experience', *Indian Journal of Agricultural Economics* 46 (4) October-December : 543-554.

Nadkarni, M.V. with Syed Ajmal Pasha and L S Prabhakar. 1989. *Political Economy of Forest Use and Management*, New Delhi : Sage Publications Pvt. Ltd.

Ostrom, Elinor. 1990. *Governing the Commons : Evolution of Institutions for Collective Action*, Cambridge : Cambridge University Press.

Pasha, Syed Ajmal. 1992. "CPRs and the Rural Poor: A Micro Level Analysis", *Economics and Political Weekly*, 27(46), November 14.

Sengupta, Nirmal. 1991. *Managing Common Property - Irrigation in India and the Philippines*, New Delhi : Sage.

Singh, Katar. 1994. *Managing Common Pool Resources : Principles and Case Studies*, Delhi : Oxford University Press.

Wade, Robert. 1988. *Village Republics : Economic Conditions for Collective Action in South India*, Cambridge (USA) : Cambridge University Press.

5 Integrating Common Pool Resources Management with Rural Development Programmes

Katar Singh

1. Introduction

Rural development policy and programmes in India as also in other developing countries of the world have traditionally been heavily influenced by economic considerations. Increase in income and employment opportunities has been the overriding goal of rural development policy, and public investment and subsidies the major instruments of achieving that goal. The major premise underlying such a policy is that once the necessary capital investment is made in an area, rural development will automatically follow whatever the prevailing socio-cultural environment and natural resource endowment of the area/region. This premise has been belied in India in the sense that even after more than four decades of pursuit of this policy, the quality of life for most of the people in rural areas continues to be poor, that the economic growth has led to deterioration in the quality of natural environment and degradation/depletion of natural resources and that there has been an increase in social and economic disparities among the various regions of the country and between the poor and the rich within the regions giving rise to increasing social conflicts and evils. Certainly, this is not what the planners had expected their plans to lead to. There are many reasons for the hiatus between what was expected of development planning and what, in fact, has been achieved. But one of the major reasons of this is the failure of the planners to integrate ecological, economic and social factors in the development policy and planning.

Of late, there has been a spectacular growth in public awareness about the adverse environmental impacts of economic growth. This has come from increasing air and water pollution, soil erosion, depletion of groundwater aquifers, denudation and degradation of forests, increasing waterlogging and soil salinity in canal command areas, growing desertification and extinction or threat of extinction to many valuable plant and animal species. The growing awareness of and concern over environmental degradation are reflected in many popular movements such as Chipko, Appiko and Narmada Bachao, extensive media coverage of environmental issues and emergence of numerous non-governmental organisations (NGOs) with the avowed objective of environment protection and conservation (Singh 1994, pp. 21-3). A new paradigm of sustainable development is fast emerging which does not favour blind pursuit of economic growth at the cost of environmental degradation. In the Human Development Report of UNDP (1996), per capita income is only one of the many indicators of quality of life. But despite all this, a serious problem that has not yet been adequately addressed is how to reconcile the (conflicting) goals of ecodevelopment and sustenance of the poor who mostly depend on common pool natural resources and environment for their livelihood. By ecodevelopment, we mean environment-friendly economic development, or sustainable development. By a common pool resource (CPR), we mean a natural resource or an environmental amenity that is used in common by an identifiable group of people. In the context of ecodevelopment or sustainable development, an important question that begs an answer is: how can we expect the poor dependent upon CPRs for their livelihood to give up their access to CPRs and cooperate with the government departments in the programmes of ecodevelopment and biodiversity conservation unless they are provided with sustainable alternative means of livelihood? The answer to this question or the key to sustainable development lies in a proper blending of the goals of economic growth and of conservation of natural resources, especially CPRs and environment through a CPR-based development strategy.

In this chapter, we first examine the relationship between economic growth and environment including natural resources. This is followed by a brief account of India's CPRs and bio-diversity including wildlife and then a presentation of a framework for CPR-based development planning and management. Finally we outline the main elements of an institutional mechanism for integrating CPR management and the rural development programmes.

2. Economic Growth and Environment

In simple words, economic growth implies increased per capita availability of goods and services. Production of goods and services requires many inputs/ resources from the Mother Nature, or biosphere such as land, water, air, solar radiation, trees, animals, minerals, fossil fuels, metals, etc. Besides, in the process of production of goods and services, many wastes—solid, liquid and gaseous—are produced. These wastes are dumped into the biosphere. So the Mother Nature serves two important functions in the process of economic growth, namely, providing inputs and assimilating wastes (Fig. 5.1). Since our planet earth (Mother Nature) is finite, closed and non-growing, there is a natural limit to both these critical functions, i.e. the input provisioning and waste assimilating capacities. This means that one cannot go on increasing the production of goods and services using natural resources for ever, i.e. there are ecological/natural limits to economic growth and hence it cannot be sustained forever. Sustainable development requires that in the process of economic growth, we maintain our natural resources and environment intact and use/ harvest only that much quantity which is regenerated naturally, i.e. we live on the "flows" and keep the "stock" of natural resources and environment intact. I would like to add that it is now possible to augment through appropriate management interventions the natural flow/harvest of products of nature.

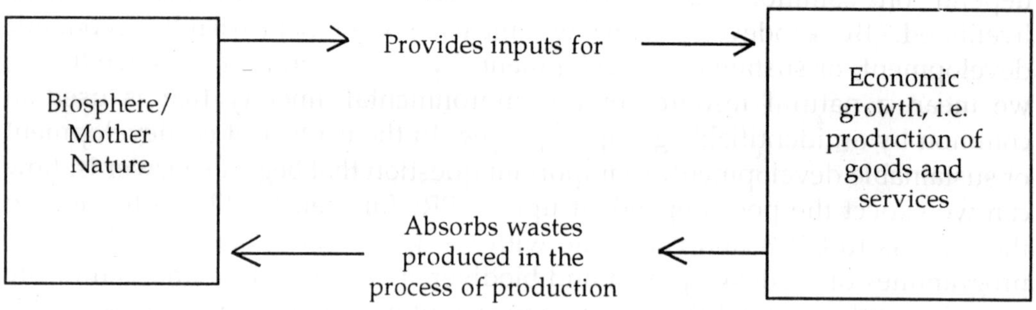

Fig. 5.1: Role of Mother Nature/Environment in Economic Growth

For example, fish catch can be increased sustainably through artificial feeding and breeding, crop yields can be increased sustainably through application of balanced organic and inorganic fertilisers, pesticides and scientific soil and water management and forests can be rejuvenated faster and their natural productivity increased through application of fertilizers and water. Thus, the carrying capacity (in terms of population of living beings) is to some extent amenable to augmentation through technological and managerial interventions. Thus, contrary to what growth maniacs and technocrats believe, there are limits to economic growth, and also contrary to what ecologists assert, the limits are not absolutely rigid; they can be relaxed. Proponents of sustainable development recognise this truth and advocate the middle path between the two extremes represented by technocrats and ecologists.

The middle path permits eco-friendly technological and managerial interventions in the natural resources systems with a view to augmenting their productivity (flows) without any detrimental effects on the resource stocks and the quality of environment. Recent developments of such inputs and practices as biofertilizers, biopesticides, bioenergy, solar energy, organic farming, and so on are examples of the middle path to sustainable agricultural development. However, we have a long (middle) path ahead of us to tread on. In India and other developing countries, the greatest challenge facing technologists and environmentalists is how to reconcile the currently conflicting goals of increasing food production to meet the increasing needs of the rapidly growing population and of keeping the natural resources intact and environment clean (free of pollution).

3. India's Common Pool Resources and Biodiversity

Common pool natural resources in India include such diverse things as Village Panchayat grazing land, privately-owned fallow land, privately-owned cultivated land lying vacant in between two crop seasons, community threshing floors, degraded revenue land, degraded forest land, protected and unclassed forests, village forests and woodlots, land lying alongside railway tracks, roads, water reservoirs, tanks, ponds, lakes, rivers, streams, *nalas*, groundwater basins, marine fisheries, public (state) and community inland fisheries, wildlife and so on. In the Indian context, it is important to note that public land such as the degraded revenue land owned by the State Revenue Departments and degraded forest land owned by the State Forest Departments are also *de facto* CPRs in the sense that they are accessible to and used in common by the villagers in whose (village) jurisdiction they lie. The rights and practices that determine who has access to and can use such public land are generally a matter of convention.

There are no reliable estimates of the extent of natural CPRs available in India. But roughly speaking, all protected, unclassed and degraded forest lands, all degraded revenue land, all surface water resources and most of the groundwater aquifers, and all marine and riverine fishes are *de facto* CPRs. It is estimated that more than 100 million hectares of non-forest land and some 28 million hectares of forest land are CPRs (Singh 1994, pp. 9-11). Given their fairly large extent, CPRs play an important role in India's rural economy as a source of sustenance and income to millions of the rural poor.

India is endowed with fairly good natural resources and an immensely rich biodiversity. It is rated as one of the 12 megadiversity countries in the world accounting for 60-70 per cent of the world's biodiversity. India has six per cent of the world's flowering plant species, 14 per cent of the world's birds, one-third of the world's identified plant species numbering over 45,000 and about 81,000 identified species of animals (World Bank 1996, p.1).

India's natural resources and biodiversity are economically important both nationally and globally. As one of the world's oldest and largest agricultural countries, India has an impressive diversity of crop species and varieties. At least 166 species of crop plants and 320 species of wild relatives of cultivated crops originate in the subcontinent. About 90 per cent of all medicines in India come from plant species, many of which are harvested in the wild. Medicinal plants and other non-timber forest products are particularly important as a source of income and sustenance for the poor tribal population. Natural ecosystems strongly influence natural resources development and management which is important not only for agriculture but also for industrial and municipal development.

Natural resources including environment and biodiversity in India have been under great biotic pressure for decades now. India's high levels of human and domestic animal populations, their high density and rapid growth, high incidence of poverty and high level of illiteracy have all contributed to degradation of natural resources and environment. Many plant and animal species are on the brink of extinction. It is high time that India adopted a responsible national policy of natural resources and biodiversity conservation which is in tandem with its economic and social development policies.

The availability of CPRs, and hence their role, varies widely from region to region in India, depending mainly on the ecological conditions and agricultural systems prevailing there and partly on the present and past land settlement and land tenure systems. These factors affect not only the nature and extent of CPRs but also the broader institutional framework that governs their management and integration with private property resources (PPRs). Arnold and Stewart (1991, pp. 8-11) identify three regions in India which exhibit markedly different patterns of endowment, use and management of common property land and related resources. The regions are: (1) semi-arid and arid regions; (2) hill regions; and (3) forested tribal regions. In the semi-arid and arid regions, CPRs are less in extent than those in wet mountainous areas but are more fully integrated into the agricultural production systems and local institutional frameworks than is the case in other regions. In the hill regions, local people heavily depend for fuelwood, fodder, grazing of animals, green manure, small wood and timber on CPRs of forests that comprise 60 to 80 per cent of the wet forest areas in the Himalaya, Shivaliks, and parts of the Western Ghats. The forested tribal region stretching from West Bengal to Gujarat is characterised by a great variety of forest and land resource use and management systems, and forest communities. Compared to the hilly and semi-arid and arid regions, CPRs are relatively less important as a source of inputs for agriculture in this region but are very important as a source of minor forest produce for sale, and sites for shifting cultivation. Irrespective of their actual use and management, many areas in this region are classified as forest or revenue lands with very limited private or village rights. Therefore, it is necessary to take into account regional variations in the endowment and use of CPRs while planning for their development/restoration, use and management.

4. A Framework for CPR-based Development Planning

Development planning is essentially a two-step process of diagnosis and prescription. In the first step, the system for which a plan is proposed to be formulated is subjected to a diagnostic study aimed at identifying its strengths, weaknesses, opportunities and threats (SWOT). In other words, a SWOT analysis of the system is done. A plan is a blueprint for action aimed at achieving a specified set of objectives set for the system with available means within a stipulated period of time (Singh 1999, pp. 245-261).

4.a A Model for Diagnosis

Many methods/models of diagnostic studies are in vogue these days. We briefly describe here a model that is appropriate for the SWOT analysis of a natural resource system/ecosystem/ protected area (PA). The model is simple enough and can be used by anyone familiar with the ecosystem or PA to sort out the information available, establish relationships among the key variables involved, diagnose what is wrong, and why and offer potential solutions of the problem(s) diagnosed. The model consists of four components, viz. (1) technical and ecological characteristics of the specific resource or ecosystem; (2) decision-making arrangements, i.e. organisations/institutions, rules and traditions that govern the relationships among resource users; (3) economic and socio-cultural attributes of the resource users and patterns of interactions among them and between them and decision makers; and (4) outcomes and consequences of the ecosystem (Singh 1994, pp. 42-47).

Following Oakerson (1986), a diagrammatic representation of the model is given in Fig. 5.2. In the short run, components 1 and 2 are treated as exogenous (given or determined outside the system) and components 3 and 4 as endogenous. In the long run, all the four components of the model are treated as endogenous, i.e. they can all change. The basic relationships among the four components of the model in the short run are shown by the solid lines and in the long run by the broken lines in Figure 5.2. Information about these components and their characteristics is collected through both conventional surveys and non-conventional methods such as Participatory Rural Appraisal (PRA). Some salient features of these components are briefly described in the following paragraphs.

The technical, physical and ecological characteristics of a resource or ecosystem that are relevant for diagnosis include:

(a) type of resource-exhaustible or renewable;
(b) extent/size of the resource;
(c) number of resource users;
(d) possibility of exclusion of illegitimate users and free riders;
(e) divisibility;
(f) physical condition of the resource; and
(g) major climatic parameters of the region.

Organisations and institutions, if any, that have been created to regulate the use of the resource in question should be briefly described and so also the rules, procedures, norms, customs, traditions, etc., that influence individual and collective choices in the use of the resource. Relevant organisations and decision-making rules including government acts at the grassroot level and higher levels (district, state and nation), orders, etc., should also be identified and listed.

Economic and socio-cultural characteristics of resource users such as religion, culture, caste, literacy, size of land holding, income status, settlement pattern (habitat), cooperation, conflicts, reciprocity, etc., should be briefly described. Patterns and frequency of interactions among the resource users and between the resource users and policy/decision makers should also be described. Patterns of interactions are reflected in the ways the individuals choose their strategies and relate to one another in a given situation. Presence or absence of reciprocity among resource users determines whether they will succeed or fail in the joint use of the resource in the larger interest of the community. Absence of reciprocity is reflected in the free-riding behaviour of members of a group and may lead to mutually destructive competition and/or conflict.

Interactions among Components 1, 2 and 3 produce outcomes/consequences that should be evaluated to determine the performance of a given resource management regime/system. The criteria of efficiency, equity and sustainability should be used for evaluating the performance of a management system. The efficiency criterion can be used by asking this question: Is a proposed change in the existing use and management system likely to make a few or most of the members of the group better off without making anyone worse off? If the answer is yes, then the present system is inefficient and the proposed system is more efficient and hence desirable. The equity criterion makes sure that each member of the group contributes his fair

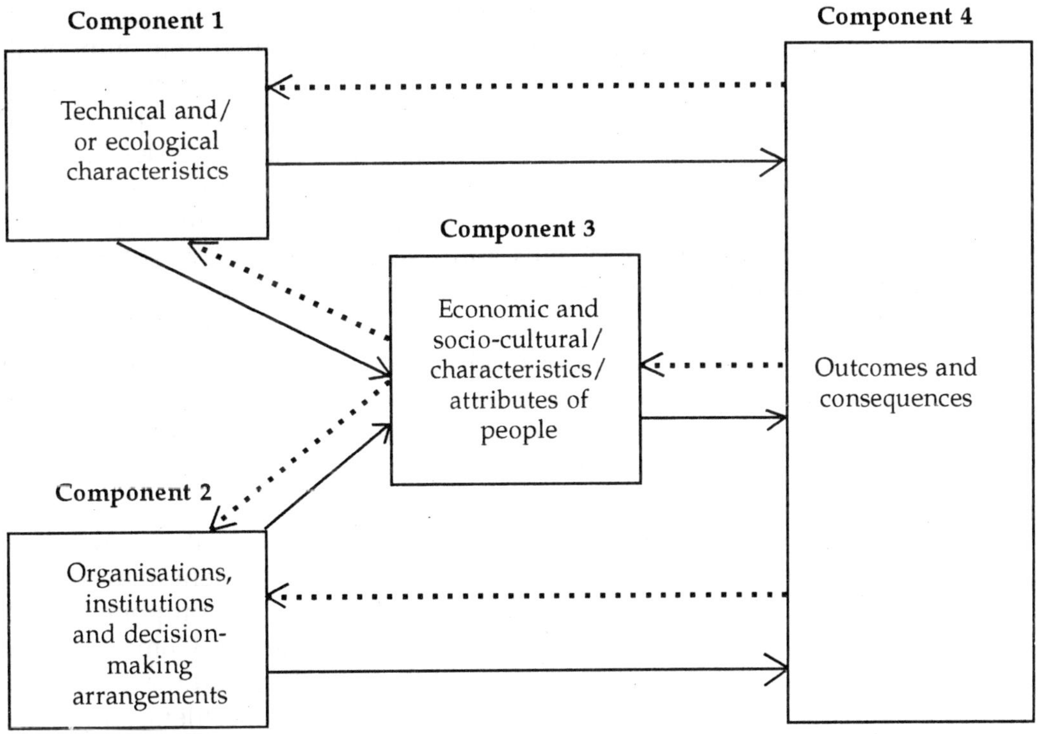

Fig. 5.2: A Diagrammatic Representation of the Oakerson Model (Oakerson 1986)

share to the maintenance/management of CPR and gets returns/rewards commensurate with his contribution. The sustainability criterion makes sure that the existing or enhanced flow of benefits from the CPR can be maintained for ever, i.e. production of goods and services/amenities does not lead to degradation and depletion of natural resources including environment.

We will now discuss how the Oakerson model can be used to diagnose CPR problems and identify their root cause(s). To begin with, we look at the outcome of a particular resource-use regime and evaluate it, using the criteria of efficiency, sustainability and equity discussed in the preceding paragraph. If the outcome passes all these three tests, then we can say that there is no problem and the present management regime is Pareto efficient. But if the outcome is found wanting on one or both the grounds, then we should work backward through the model to trace the cause(s) of the problem. We should ask ourselves questions like these: Is there anything wrong in the prevailing patterns of interaction (Component 3) that might cause the problem? What characteristics of the decision-making environment (Component 2) and the CPR in question contribute to the present patterns of interaction and choice of present resource-use strategies? Is there a mismatch or lack of congruence between the technical and physical attributes of the CPR (Component 1) and the decision-making arrangements or the organisational structure (Component 2)? In particular, we should ask if there are any obstacles or inducements built into the decision-making structure that explain the observed pattern of interaction or whether the difficulty lies at the constitutional choice level, i.e. in the by-laws of the organisation in question, which can be rectified only by an amendment of the by-laws. In the answers to these and similar questions might lie the clues to possible problems and also to their possible solutions.

To find solutions to the problems diagnosed, we will need to work prospectively forward through the model. We can look at Components 1 and 2 and ask ourselves about the kinds of modifications necessary in the physical and technical traits of the CPR in question and in the decision-making arrangements that would produce the desirable pattern of interaction and collective choice strategies and hence desirable outcome. Also, whether the benefits from these modifications would substantially exceed the costs. Answers to the former would need to be empirically substantiated and to the latter could be found by using the technique of social cost-benefit analysis.

In the dynamic version of the model we allow changes in Components 1, 2 and 3 whereas in the static version (short run), we assume that Components 1 and 2 cannot be changed. The static version of the model is good for diagnostic purposes and the dynamic version for studying specific problem situations over a long period of time and evaluating the consequences of various interventions/modifications in the existing system. The dynamic version allows the resource users to learn from the consequences of their collective actions and thereby to modify their strategies so as to produce desirable outcomes in the future. Besides, over time resource users may also modify some of the physical and technical attributes of the CPR through the use of the latest available technologies and also restructure their decision-making arrangements to secure a better match with the modified attributes of CPR. This, in turn, may change their strategies and thereby produce outcomes that are more desirable for the group as a whole.

The Oakerson model could be used by CPR managers to diagnose various problems of protection, conservation, utilisation and management of natural resources and identify practicable alternatives for their resolution. The model has been used extensively by natural resource analysts and managers all over the world (Bromley 1992) and in India (Arnold and Stewart 1991, Marothia 1993, 1996, Singh 1994 and Singh and Ballabh 1996).

4.b. Alternative CPR Management Regimes

A pragmatic CPR management policy should specify a particular management system or a combination of management systems appropriate for fulfilling its goals. *A priori*, any one or a combination of privatisation, nationalisation and collective management (by CPR users) could be used to achieve the goals of a CPR management policy and, theoretically speaking, any one of these three alternative systems could be as good or as bad as any other. In practice, all the three systems co-exist in most situations and there is no single best system of management that will work successfully in all situations and at all times. The choice of a system will depend on the particular resource and setting in question and often requires an interdisciplinary approach, use of traditional knowledge and modern scientific knowledge and consultation with local people and government functionaries. It is not always easy to determine whether a resource would be better managed as a private property, public property, or common property; there are many "grey" areas when it comes to choosing a particular management system. Based on a survey of literature, the following general guidelines/principles could be laid down to help determine an appropriate management system. The guidelines are organised under three heads, namely, privatisation, centralised public management and decentralised collective management (Singh 1994, pp. 314-18).

4.b.1 Privatisation

Privatisation means creating private property rights in CPRs and enforcing them. Privatisation can be accomplished in many different ways such as by enacting laws, issuing government decrees/resolutions, signing voluntary contracts, and so on. The property rights created for the purpose could be conferred on an individual, a group of individuals, a private firm, a cooperative society, or a voluntary agency. Privatisation of CPRs may prove to be an appropriate system if the assignees of property rights are poor, are organised into some formal or non-formal associations, are willing to use CPR in a socially desirable manner and if the government is willing and able to help the assignees with technical information, training and funds.

4.b.2 Centralised Public Management

Under centralised public management or nationalisation, the central government fully owns and manages CPRs directly through one of its departments/agencies. Nationalisation of CPRs has been a policy pursued by numerous developed and developing countries of the world, particularly the socialist countries. The underlying rationale of nationalisation is that a national government can better serve the interest of the people at large, can raise investment funds more easily and has a longer planning horizon and hence, a lower discount rate than individuals. The experience with nationalisation of

CPRs has not been generally good; there have been more failures than successes. However, nationalisation may be an appropriate system if the CPR in question is of strategic importance to the nation, is bound to be overexploited and depleted under the existing system, and if the investment required for its restoration is beyond the capacity of CPR users.

4.b.3 Decentralised Collective Management

An increasing number of scholars now advocate that decentralised collective management of CPRs by their co-users is the most appropriate system. Cases of success in collective management of CPRs by their co-users abound in the literature on CPR management. Collective management is likely to succeed under the following conditions:

(i) If the community of CPR users is small, well-defined, homogeneous, self-conscious, self-governing with political and economic independence to manage the CPR as it sees fit, and organised formally into some association which is headed by a good leader;
(ii) Access to and use of CPRs are both regulated by a set of rules that are compatible with the technical and physical characteristics of the resource and the local setting and that are mutually accepted, enforced and monitored by the CPR users themselves rather than an external superordinate authority;
(iii) Rules for equitable sharing of benefits and costs are incorporated in the bye-laws of the CPR users' association, have a legal back up, are easy to understand and enforce, and are enforced and monitored by the CPR users themselves;
(iv) There exists a system of sanctions against violation of rules and free-riding or shirking that is mutually accepted by all the CPR users and is enforced by them voluntarily;
(v) CPR users have high stakes in the CPR and there is an immmediate threat to their survival if the CPR is degraded or depleted;
(vi) There exists good local leadership and political support to CPR users and their organisation at all levels;
(vii) The government is willing and able to help CPR users with needed funds, technical information, training, provision of basic infrastructure including marketing and processing facilities and facilitating legal and political environment; and
(viii) Last but not the least, expected private benefits to each individual CPR user from collective management not only markedly exceed the expected private costs of his participation in the collective management but also are assured by an honest and benevolent local leader or an

external authority having high credibility among CPR users.

4.c. Implementation and Monitoring

A responsible CPR management policy should provide for effective implementation and regular monitoring of various project activities and establishment of a computerized management information system for the purpose. Some general guidelines for CPR project implementation and monitoring are given below. The guidelines are based on a survey of the literature available on the subject.

1. Prepare a plan for project implementation which should, at the minimum, specify what is to be done, who is to do it, when and where it is to be done and how it is to be done;
2. Provide for the maintenance of a continuing dialogue between natural resource policy-makers and analysts, and for communication and flow of information both ways, from policy-makers to analysts and back to policy-makers;
3. Involve CPR users in implementing and monitoring CPR development projects on a continuing basis which is best done when they are organised into small and homogeneous groups and are properly consciéntised, motivated and empowered through provision of technical information, training and financial incentives;
4. Educate politicians, policy-makers and CPR users and provide them complete and unbiased information about various aspects of CPR management so that they are able to take the right decisions;
5. Blend conventional wisdom with knowledge of modern technologies in designing and implementing CPRM policies;
6. Build up an adequate natural resource data base and set up a computerized Natural Resource Information System (NRIS). The Planning Commission has already sponsored a number of pilot projects in NRIS and has set up an Inter-agency Expert Committee to formulate policies and oversee the implementation of NRIS. This needs to be strengthened and user organisations enabled to have access to and use the NRIS;
7. Keep the formats of monitoring reports simple and their contents brief and precise;
8. Link the monitoring system to the responsibility centres in the project organisation concerned. A responsibility centre is simply a unit of an organisation headed by a responsible manager who is accountable for the work done by his unit. The manager should be provided with the

information that he needs for decision-making, control and remedial action; and

9. Use collegial sanctions against poor work and communicate directly with the area where the bottleneck has occurred.

4.d. Enlisting People's Participation

Local people's participation in planning, implementation and monitoring of development projects is essential for sustainable development. For this to happen, it is essential that people are organised into formal or non-formal groups, conscientised about the need for an all-round balanced development, empowered through education and training and motivated and guided preferably by local NGOs. There are many factors that affect people's participation in collective action of the type required for development. But the most important among them is that the expected private benefits from participation must markedly exceed the expected private costs and that the expected benefits must be assured and equitably distributed among the participants in proportion to their contribution in the form of labour, cash or both. Singh (1992) identifies various factors that affect the people's participation in natural resource management. They include project design, characteristics of the resource, characteristics of local people, type and orientation of project personnel, and institutional arrangements and incentives for the people's participation. The National Forest Policy of 1988 and Resolution of June 1, 1990, of the Government of India (GOI), Ministry of Environment and Forests, provide for the people's participation in the protection and development of forests. Following the GOI Resolution, many state governments have issued similar Resolutions/Orders facilitating the participation of local people in what has come to be known as Joint Forest Management (JFM). There are now umpteen examples of successful JFM in India (Campbell 1992; Singh 1994; Pandey 1992). They include the famous Arabari Experiment in South-West West Bengal and JFM projects experience in Harda Forest Division in Madhya Pradesh. All these experiences show that given the policy/legal back-up and strong motivation and determination on the part of forest officers at all the levels of hierarchy, it is possible to reconcile the apparently conflicting goals of ecodevelopment/biodiversity conservation and local social and economic development.

5. An Institutional Mechanism for Integration

In this section, we briefly describe an institutional mechanism for coordination and integration of CPR management plans with the plans of various government departments engaged in agricultural and rural development.

5.a. Integration at the National Level

Environment/ecology and forestry are on the Concurrent List and agricultural and rural development on the State List of the Constitution of India. This means that policies for the former are made by both the Central and State Governments and for the latter by State Governments. Even in the case of rural development and environment, the Central government plays an important role by way of providing policy guidelines and sponsoring and funding programmes of national importance. So, to be meaningful, the process of integration should start at the Central government level. At the national level, Union Ministries of Environment and Forests, Agriculture and Rural Development are primarily responsible for planning and programming in their respective fields. The Planning Commission also plays an advisory and coordinating role in these exercises. So, the first step in the process of integration is to make a clear policy statement that every agricultural and rural development programme will have an Environmental/Ecological Impact Statement (EIS) built into it and that no programme will be approved for funding until and unless such a statement is incorporated. For overall coordination, guidance and monitoring of the compliance with this requirement, a small Standing Committee of Secretaries representing the Union Ministries concerned and Members incharge of the relevant portfolios in the Planning Commission may be constituted. The Committee may be headed by the Union Minister of Environment and Forests (MOEF)/Vice Chairman, Planning Commission, and the Secretary, Ministry of Environment and Forests, may be its Member-Secretary. The Committee may meet at least once every three months and convene one National Consultation of all the Chief Wildlife Wardens of the states where ecodevelopment projects are underway once every year to review the progress and problems of the projects and chalk out a programme for the coming year. A multidisciplinary cell comprising specialists in forestry, ecology, agriculture, animal husbandry, natural resource environmental economics, sociology, rural development and development planning may be set up within the MOEF to assist the Committee and to provide technical guidance to the participating State Forest Departments on a regular basis. Such an administrative procedure will need to be backed up by an appropriate legislative measure as has been done in the USA under their National Environmental Policy Act of 1969. In India, the Environment (Protection) Act of 1986 provides for such a back-up. Many other countries also have formalised incorporation of EIS in their development programmes.

A typical EIS would include information on the following:

(a) A brief description of the proposed project;
(b) A description of the environmental features likely to be effected by the proposed project;
(c) An analysis of likely environmental consequences of the project;
(d) A description of the measures envisaged to mitigate those consequences; and
(e) A review of the relationships between the project and the existing policy.

Care should be taken that compliance with EIS requirement should not result in unnecessary delays, rigidity and increase in the cost as has been the case in the USA and other developed countries. Preparation of EIS is a technical job which should be done by well-trained ecologists/environmental scientists with the help of and in close cooperation with the project personnel.

5.b. Integration at the State Level

A mechanism similar to the one proposed at the national level will need to be established at the State level. The Standing Committee of Secretaries and members, State Planning Commission concerned may be headed by the Chairman, State Planning Commission. At the State level, besides the rural development programmes with EIS incorporated therein, separate projects for ecodevelopment of PAs may be prepared and launched. In the beginning, a two-day Consultation/Meet of the State level officers may be organised to discuss the rationale of ecodevelopment and determine the roles of various agencies involved in planning and implementation at the State level. The Secretary, Department of Environment/Forestry may convene the meeting and secure a commitment of all the officers concerned with the programme.

5.c. Integration at the Protected Area Level

In the context of CPR-based development and management, PA constitutes the basic planning unit. At the PA level, a Coordination and Monitoring Committee representing the following departments/disciplines may be constituted:

1. President(s) of the Zila Parishad(s) in whose jurisdiction the PA in question lies;
2. District Collector(s) in whose jurisdiction the PA lies;

3. District Head of Department of Agriculture/Soil and Water Conservation;
4. District Head of Department of Rural Development/District Rural Development Agency;
5. District Head of Animal Husbandry Department;
6. Ecologist;
7. Socio-economist/environmental economist;
8. Development Banker; and
9. Field Planning Officer (FPO)

The Committee may be headed by the President, Zila Parishad, or the District Collector and the FPO concerned may be its Member-Secretary. The Committee should be responsible for integrating agricultural/rural development programmes with the ecodevelopment plan of the PA under consideration. Ideally, there should be only one comprehensive integrated plan for overall development of the PA. A format and guidelines for preparing such a plan will need to be developed by the Coordinating and Monitoring Committee. Guidelines prepared by Pabla *et al.* (1994) seem to be an important step forward in this direction. All the funds earmarked for agricultural/rural development, animal husbandry and dairy development, forestry, irrigation, watershed development and infrastructure development in the area should be placed at the disposal of this Committee.

Similar committees may be constituted at the sub-divisional and block levels, if necessary. The sub-divisional level committee may be chaired by the Sub-Divisional Officer and the block level committee by the Block Development Officer concerned and the Assistant Conservator of Forests and the Range Forest Officer concerned may be the Member-Secretary of the Committees respectively.

To begin with, a two-day consultation/meet of all the members of the Committee may be convened to seek their commitment to ecodevelopment and to discuss and evolve a workable procedure for planning, funding, implementing, coordinating and monitoring ecodevelopment plans. The Committee may meet regularly thereafter at least once every three months to review the progress and problems and to ensure smooth implementation of the ecodevelopment plan.

6. Protected Area Approach to Ecodevelopment

The best way to operationalise the CPR-based development strategy is to adopt what is known as the Protected Area (PA) approach. By PAs, we mean areas notified as protected (against human interference) under the Wildlife

(Protection) Act, 1972. The Act provides for the setting up of national parks and wildlife sanctuaries with a view to affording varying degrees of protection to a whole range of animal species. The Act has since been amended in 1982, 1986 and 1991. The 1991 amendment affords protection to scheduled plants and prohibits commercial felling in wildlife sanctuaries.

Duly recognising the importance of and need for PA approach, the Government of India, Ministry of Environment and Forests, has recently launched an Ecodevelopment Project in seven selected PAs in India. The selected PAs are Buxa (West Bengal), Gir (Gujarat), Nagarhole (Karnataka), Palamau (Bihar), Pench (Madhya Pradesh), Periyar (Kerala) and Ranthambhore (Rajasthan). The project is financially supported by the Global Environment Facility (GEF) and the International Development Association (IDA) (World Bank, 1996, pp. i-iii). Earlier, a pilot project titled "Strengthening Wildlife Management and Ecodevelopment Planning Capabilities" was executed by the Wildlife Institute of India, Dehradun, in 10 selected PAs. The project was a collaborative endeavour of the Government of India (Ministry of Environment and Forests) and the United Nations Development Fund (UNDP, 1992). The project envisaged collaboration with various governmental and non-governmental agencies engaged in rural development in the selected PAs. In particular, it was envisaged that the PA authorities would seek functional collaboration with the district-level government departments dealing with income and employment-generating activities, poverty alleviation, dry farming, soil and water conservation, animal husbandry, sericulture, pisciculture, non-conventional energy and rural industries and mobilise and utilise their funds for implementing ecodevelopment projects. The project employed the Protected Area (PA) approach to biodiversity conservation and participatory ecodevelopment in and around PAs as an instrument of achieving the goal of biodiversity conservation.

The PA approach is not new to India. The recorded history of protection of animals, fishes and forests in India dates back to 252 BC, the era of Emperor Ashok (Panwar and Mathur 1992, p. 3). Setting aside sacred (forest) areas as sanctuaries as distinct from exclusive hunting reserves is even older. Article 48-A of the Constitution of India also provides that the state shall endeavour to protect and improve the environment and to safeguard the forest and wildlife of the country. Article 51-A imposes as one of the fundamental duties on every citizen the duty to protect and improve the natural environment including forests, lakes, rivers and wildlife and to have compassion for living creatures. Now, it is proposed under the project to expand and strengthen the PA system and manage it scientifically.

The network of PAs comprising National Parks (NP) and Wildlife Sanctuaries (WLS) has steadily grown from 10 NPs and 127 WLSs covering an area of about 2.50 million ha in 1970 [before the enactment of the Wildlife (Protection) Act 1972] to 75 NPs and 420 WLSs covering about 14 million ha (about 4.3 per cent of India's total area) in 1996. It is planned to expand the PAs further to cover 1,83,574 km^2 (5.6 per cent of India's total geographical area) in keeping with the global trends in wildlife and biodiversity conservation. The project represented an important step forward in that direction.

Funds for ecodevelopment are available from several governmental and non-governmental agencies —both national and international. The major categories of sources of funds for ecodevelopment are: (a) Central and State governments; (b) banks; (c) Indian non-governmental organisations; and (d) international donors. The Central and State Governments provide funds for rural development through budgetary allocations. Banks which provide credit for rural/ecodevelopment comprise: (a) National Bank for Agriculture and Rural Development (NABARD); (b) Cooperative banks —both short-term and long-term structures; (c) Regional Rural Banks (RRBs); and (d) Commercial Banks. Non-governmental sources of funds include public trusts, autonomous societies/foundations, private companies and corporations. The government has been and still is the biggest source of funds for rural development. Banks come next to the government. Contributions of NGOs —both national and international —have been small as compared to those of the government and the banks.

There are dozens of government-sponsored and funded rural development programmes currently underway in India that can be drawn upon for funding CPR-based development projects. What is needed to make this possible is an institutional mechanism to secure and maintain interagency coordination and functional relationship among various departments engaged in rural development on one hand and between governmental and non-governmental organisations on the other.

7. Concluding Remarks

Sustainable or eco-friendly development seems to be a socially more desirable goal of development policy in India than the goal of economic growth and hence it needs to be pursued seriously and vigorously at all levels. In order to incorporate environmental and ecological considerations in development planning, there is need for formulating a comprehensive strategy for CPR-based development planning and management. Initially, such a strategy may be adopted in selected protected areas (PAs) in India, as is being already done now, and lessons learned from those projects may be incorporated in formulating programmes for sustainable development. In the short run, the goals of sustenance of poor people depending on CPRs and of biodiversity conservation are conflicting. But in the long run, it is possible to reconcile these goals through integration of ecodevelopment projects with various ongoing rural development programmes such that the poor are able to benefit from the latter and their dependence on CPRs for their survival is reduced.

The Oakerson model could be used to diagnose the weaknesses in the existing CPR management system(s) and to identify areas for intervention. Using this model, it is possible to formulate CPR- based development projects which would achieve the goal of sustainable development. To make ecodevelopment projects self-sustaining, people's participation in their formulation and implementation is a must. Organising the poor dependent on CPRs around some economically viable activities which assure them substantially high private benefits on a regular basis and conscientising, educating and training them about participatory ecodevelopment and biodiversity conservation seem to be a practical strategy for enlisting the people's participation. A beginning in this direction has already been made in some selected PAs in India. There is need to learn from the experiences of the pilot projects now underway in the selected PAs and scale up and replicate the success stories in other parts of the country. There is no dearth of funds for ecodevelopment purposes. What is needed is a strong political will and a pragmatic national policy for promoting CPR- based rural development and management.

REFERENCES

Arnold, J.E.M. and W.C. Stewart. 1991. "Common Property Resource Management in India", *Tropical Forestry Paper No. 24*, Oxford Forestry Institute, Oxford: Oxford University.

Bromely, D.W. (ed.). 1992. *Making the Commons Work*, San Francisco: ICS Press.

Campbell, J.Y. 1992. "Joint Forest Management in India", *Social Change*, 22(1): 36-54.

Marothia, D.K. 1993. "Property Regimes and Institutional Arrangements: Concepts and their Relevance in Managing the Village Commons, *Indian Journal of Agricultural Economics*, 48, 557-65.

Marothia, D.K. 1996. "Cooperative Management of Nontimber Forest Products: Issues of Property Rights and Institutional Structures", In: R. Rajagopalan (Ed.), *Rediscovering Co-operation: Strategies for Models of Tomorrows* (Vol. 2). Institute of Rural Management, Anand.

Oakerson, Ronald J. 1986. "A Model for the Analysis of Common Property Problems", In: *Proceedings of the Conference on Common Property Resource Management*, Washington, D.C.: National Academy Press.

Pabla, H.S., Sanjeeva Pandey and Ruchi Badola. 1994. "Guidelines for Ecodevelopment Planning", Draft Mimeo, WII-UNDP/FAO Project IND-92/007, Wildlife Institute of India, Dehradun.

Pandey, Sanjeeva. 1992. "Ecodevelopment at its Best: A BMS Experience", *WII Newsletter*, April-June, Vol. 73, No. 2, pp. 29-31.

Panwar, H.S. and V.B. Mathur. 1992. "Protected Area Network in India: A Review", Paper presented at the IV World Congress on National Parks and Protected Areas, February 10-12, Caracas, Venezuela.

Singh, Katar. 1999. *Rural Development: Principles, Policies and Management,* Second Edition, New Delhi: Sage Publications Pvt. Ltd.

Singh, Katar. 1992. "People's Participation in Natural Resource Management", *Workshop Report 8,* Institute of Rural Management, Anand

Singh, Katar. 1994. *Managing Common Pool Resources: Principles and Case Studies,* Delhi: Oxford University Press.

Singh, Katar and Vishwa Ballabh (eds.). 1996. *Co-operative Management of Natural Resources,* New Delhi : Sage Publications Pvt. Ltd..

United Nations Development Programme (UNDP). 1992. *Project of the Government of India: Project Document,* IND/92/007/A/01/99, Strengthening Wildlife Management and Ecodevelopment Planning Capabilities, New Delhi, 28 May 1992 (Confirmed copy).

UNDP 1996. *Human Development Report. 1996,* New York: Oxford University Press.

World Bank. 1996. *Staff Appraisal Report: India Ecodevelopment Project, Report No. 14914-IN,* South Asia Department II, Agriculture and Water Division, Washington, DC: The World Bank.

SECTION 2

WATER RESOURCES, LAND USE AND IRRIGATION SYSTEMS AND INSTITUTIONS

6 Community and Household Water Management: The Key to Environmental Regeneration and Poverty Alleviation

Anil Agarwal and **Sunita Narain**

"Lack of access to even basic necessities like safe drinking water, adequate food and health care means that almost a third of the people in the developing world have a life expectancy of just 40 years. For them, poverty is a denial of the most basic of all human rights: the Right to Life."

Gus Speth, Administrator, United Nations Development Programme.

1. Importance of Environmental Regeneration for Poverty Alleviation

Rural people largely survive within a biomass-based subsistence economy, that is, an economy based on products obtained from plants and animals. Food, fuel, animal feed, building materials like timber and thatch, medicinal herbs and other such needs are largely met through locally available biomass resources.[1]

Environmental degradation, therefore, has a serious impact on the lives of rural people. A large portion of the world's rural poor today live in highly degraded lands in China, South Asia, Africa and Latin America. For such people, improvements in the *Gross Nature Product* are far more important than the *Gross National Product*.[2] In fact, the "economic globalization" process is expected to leave a lot of these people untouched. The climate instability predicted for the 21st century as a result of the greenhouse effect will make life even more difficult for the world's rural poor living in degraded lands.

The 21st century human society will, therefore, have to address itself to the following critical question: Do we forget these marginalized people till they learn to integrate themselves with the world economy or do we do something for them in the meanwhile? The neglect of the marginalized will clearly lead to mass impoverishment and starvation, social violence and wars, and distress migration both within nations and between nations. The 1980s and 1990s have already seen these problems on a massive scale in several parts of the world. The answer to this problem is obvious: *If the market cannot reach the marginalized, we must at least do something to help them to help themselves.* And the best way to do that would be to address the problem of "ecological poverty" that dominates the lives of the rural poor living in degraded lands. (See Fig. 6.1)

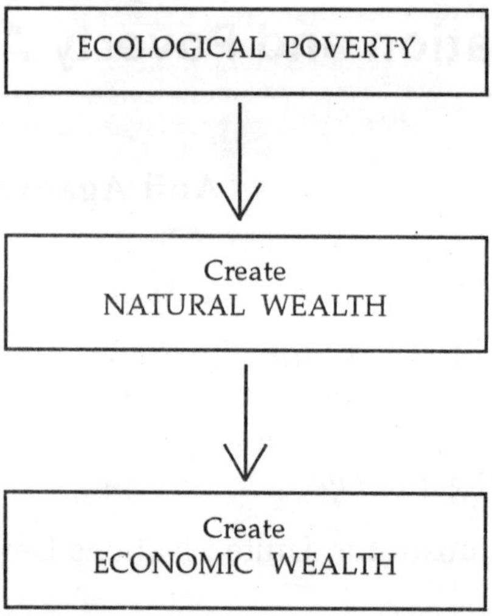

Fig. 6.1: Helping the Poor to Help Themselves

'Ecological poverty' can be described as the lack of an ecologically healthy natural resource base that is needed for a human society's survival and development. High levels of 'ecological poverty' today prevent a large part of the world's poor from helping themselves to improve their economic condition. Healthy lands and ecosystem, when used sustainably, can provide all the wealth that is needed for healthy and dignified lives.

'Ecological poverty' is a different concept from 'economic poverty', which modern economists love to revel in. Economic poverty is measured largely in terms of cash incomes and is almost irrelevant in a biomass-based subsistence economy. The approaches to deal with 'ecological poverty' and 'economic poverty' are also vastly different. While economists normally talk of welfare measures to deal with 'economic poverty', rural practitioners who have tried to deal with 'ecological poverty' talk more of 'institutional, legal and financial empowerment' with a strong emphasis on community-based property rights over ecological resources.

The challenge today lies in empowering and mobilizing the labour of the marginalized billion to get out of their 'ecological poverty', create natural wealth, and develop a robust local economy based on that natural wealth. It means natural resource degradation must stop and natural resource regeneration must start, as soon as possible.

Villages in the developing world are usually highly integrated micro-ecosystems. Indian villages, for example, especially those situated in the semi-arid and sub-humid hill, mountain and plateau regions, are highly integrated agrosylvopastoral systems. In other words, each Indian village has its own croplands, grasslands, and tree or forest lands, and each of these land-use systems interact with each other. Developments in one component invariably impact on the others.[1] (See Fig. 6.2)

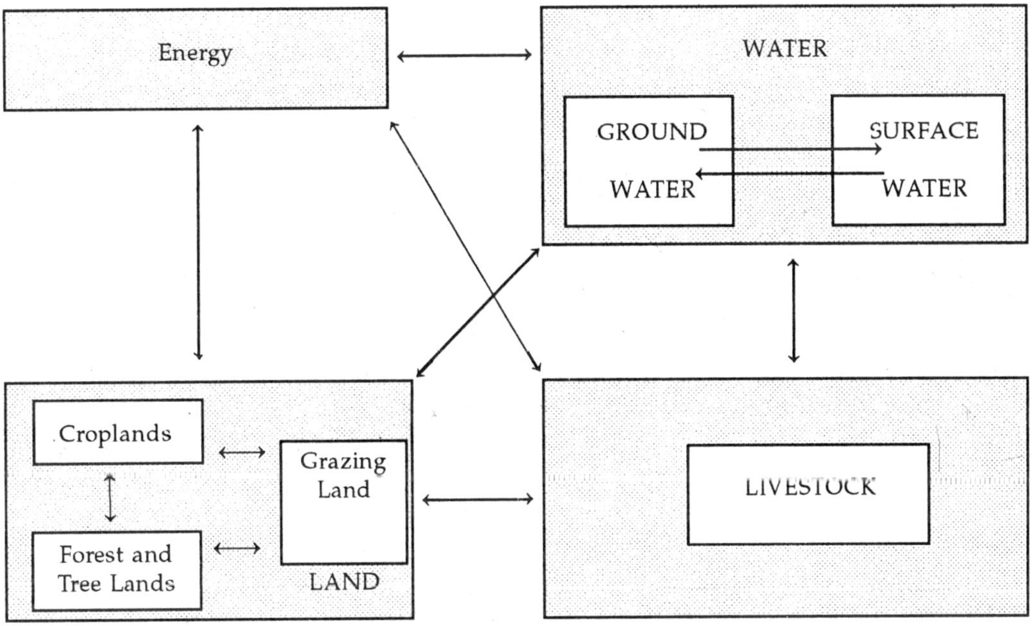

An indian village is a complex land-livestock-vegetation system in which the land sub-system, the water sub-system, the livestock sub-system and the energy sub-system, all interact with each other. The purpose of village ecosystem plans should be to bring about a holistic enrichment of the entire village ecosystem without destroying the synergy between the various sub-systems.

Fig. 6.2: The Complex Indian Village Ecosystem

The entire village ecosystem is often held in fine ecological balance. Trees or forest lands provide firewood. This helps villagers to avoid the burning of cowdung, which is used as manure to maintain the productivity of the croplands. The nutrients are gathered by the cows while grazing in the grasslands. Simultaneously, trees and crops help to complement the grasslands in the supply of animal feed. Grass is generally available from the grasslands during the monsoon period. As grass availability declines with the onset of the dry months, crop residues obtained from croplands and leaf fodder obtained from trees to help animals to tide over the critical scarcity period. This finely tuned system can get easily split apart.

Experience worldwide shows that natural resource regeneration and management demands community participation. Experience in India during the 1970s and 1980s has repeatedly shown an outstanding economic change in rural communities wherever they have organized themselves to regenerate and manage their resource base. There has been absolutely nothing more heartening in the entire world in the last two decades of the environmental movement than the transformation that these communities have been able to achieve. On the other hand, bureaucratic resource management systems have invariably failed or have been totally cost-ineffective, which makes them irrelevant in the world of the poor where financial resources are limited.

This chapter presents four case studies from India of a transformation from a state of ecological poverty to a state of sustainable economic wealth. These case studies are important because they describe experiences which are now several years old and have reached an advanced high level of ecological succession and associated economic impacts. They show that the ecological succession-economic growth is a long continuum with multi-faceted dimensions and strategies. The experiences of Sukhomajri and Ralegan Siddhi villages now span over 20 years, and the work of Tarun Bharat Sangh is now 12-15 years old. The work of the Madhya Pradesh Rajiv Gandhi Watershed Development Mission is only four years old but it is an important case study as it shows that government agencies can learn from NGO experiences of the type described in the first-three case studies and replicate them on a large scale. Finally, this chapter goes on to derive some key conclusions from these case studies.

2. Water as the Key: Four Case Studies

Local water management and rainwater harvesting provide the key to the transformation of the ecological and economic base of villages dependent on a biomass economy. However, this demands a fundamental change in water management strategies. Community control and participation is essential for any strategy that seeks to use and manage local water resources. But, as successful village-level experiments in India show, this participation is not possible unless the institutional framework for natural resource governance is amended.

Over the 1980s, India has seen a number of microexperiences of successful community resource management. These microexperiences are remarkable as they are testimony to the potential of generating wealth and well-being from rainwater harvesting. What is also remarkable is the short time it takes to transform a poverty-stricken, destitute and ecologically devastated village to a rich and green village. This wealth can be used to create more wealth by regularly investing in resource management, thus leading to cyclical system of sustainable growth. The community will also have stake in the good management of the natural resource base as it benefits from its development.

The natural assets that are created as a result of better management of water are quite fragile and, therefore, need to be carefully managed keeping sustainability in mind. This sustainable management of the asset base will be possible only if people are involved in the management of the resource. These examples of community management of natural resources teach us what happens when people are given the right to manage their natural resource base.

2.a. The Sukhomajri Experience

Sukhomajri village has distinction of being the first village in India to be levied income tax on the income it earns from the ecological regeneration of its degraded watershed. This village is near the city of Chandigarh and has been widely hailed in India for its pioneering efforts in microwatershed development.

In the 1970s, Sukhomajri—with a population of 455 in 1976—was like any other village situated in the sub-Himalayan Sivalik foothills: sparsely vegetated, with poor agriculture, and high levels of soil erosion and runoff. Though the annual average rainfall was about 1,137 mm, groundwater was not available at a reasonable depth. Soil erosion and gully formation was steadily leading to a decrease in the farm area. As agriculture was riddled with uncertainty, villagers traditionally kept herds of livestock to minimize risk. They cultivated about 50 ha. of unirrigated land and kept about 411 animals. Subsistence for bare survival was the norm. The open grazing by the livestock suppressed regeneration and kept the surrounding hills and watersheds bare. Barely 5 per cent of the slopes had any vegetative cover.[3]

In 1979, when the nation was facing a severe drought, the villagers built a small tank to capture the rainwater and agreed to protect their watershed in order to ensure that their tank did not get silted up. Since then the villagers have built a few more tanks and have protected the heavily degraded forest that lies within and around the catchment of its minor irrigation tanks.[4] The tanks have helped to increase crop production by nearly three times and the protection of the forest area has greatly increased grass and tree fodder availability. This, in turn, has increased milk production. With growing prosperity, Sukhomajri's economy has undergone a change. The villagers have replaced their thatch-and-mud dwellings with brick-and-cement houses and most of the houses boast of radio sets, electric fans, sewing machines and television sets. "Who could imagine that televisions, tractors and bicycles could be had for mere grass and water?" asks a villager. Annual household income has also increased.

A combination of public, private and community investments and the participatory efforts of the villagers has produced, according to one cost benefit analysis, a rate of return of the order of 19 per cent.[5] The Sukhomajri project proves that it is possible to get sustained development with limited outside financial investments. One of the most impressive savings resulting from the project is in the cost of desilting the Sukhna lake which supplies water to the downstream city of Chandigarh. The inflow of sediment has come down by over 90 per cent. This saves the government Rs. 7.65 million each year in dredging and other costs.[5]

The following economic and ecological changes have taken place in the village over the years:

— Between 1977 and 1986, because of the availability of irrigation water, wheat production increased from 40.6 tonnes in 1977 (with a productivity of 0.68 tonnes per hectare) to 63.6 tonnes in 1986 (with a productivity of 1.43 tonnes per hectare) and maize production increased from 40.9 tonnes in 1977 (with a productivity of 0.61 tonnes per hectare) to 54.3 tonnes in 1986 (with a productivity of 1.22 tonnes per hectare).[6]

— Protection of the watershed has led to increased grass production which steadily went up from 40 kg per hectare in 1976 to 3 tonnes per hectare in 1992. (b) Increased availability of fodder led to a transformation in the livestock composition. The number of goats went down from 246 in 1975 to 10 in 1986 while the number of buffaloes went up from 79 in 1975 to 291 in 1986. (c) This led to increased milk production which increased from 334 litres per day in 1977 to 579 litres per day in 1986.[6]

— Meanwhile, the tree density increased from 13 per hectare in 1976 to 1,292 per hectare in 1992. The 400 hectares Sukhomajri forest today has over 0.3 million highly valuable khair (*Acacia catechu*) trees.[7] Each tree provides about 100 kg of wood which sells at about Rs. 30 per kg. Thus, each tree is worth Rs. 3,000 and the entire forest is worth Rs. 900 million. If the wood is converted into *katha* as a village enterprise, the return from the forest will be even higher because *katha* is a highly valued condiment used with betel leaves. If the forest is harvested on a sustainable basis, say, about 10,000 trees a year with a girth of more than 60 cm, the forest will yield Rs. 30 million annually.[8] If the villagers were to set up a small village enterprise, they can produce and market *katha* directly and hope to earn Rs. 36 million.

— Watershed protection has also resulted in increased production of a highly fibrous grass that is commonly found in the region called *bhabhar* *(Eulialopsis binata)*. This grass provides good fodder when it is young but is also very good pulping material for paper mills when it is mature. This grass was very widely used traditionally to make ropes that were commonly used to make beds across north India. Villagers of Sukhomajri use *bhabhar* both as fodder and for sale to paper mills.

— The economic benefits have been substantial. By the mid-1980s, Sukhomajri had turned from a food-importing village to a food-exporting village.[6] In just five years, from 1979 to 1984, its household income went up from about Rs. 10,000 to Rs. 15,000. It today earns about Rs. 3,50,000 from sale of milk and another Rs. 1,00,000 or so is earned collectively from sale of *bhabhar*.[6] The village has yet to earn anything from the wood in the forest because the Forest Department has not yet decided how it will share the proceeds with the villagers. But, as indicated above, it will run into several crores of rupees.

— A survey conducted in 1998 revealed the following income distribution in the village.[9]

Annual household income	Distribution of households (%)
Less than Rs. 24,000	30.2
Rs. 24,000 - 48,000	41.5
Rs. 48,000 - 96,000	24.5
Rs. 96,000 - 1,92,000	3.8

Note: The survey questionnaire had solicited responses on monthly household income. Converting the monthly into annual household income may result in an overstatement of the annual income as respondents may not be earning the same monthly income round the year. But figures are given above in annual household income merely for comparison with available data on the distribution of annual household income in rural Haryana, the State in which village Sukhomajri is situated.

Source: S.C. Gulati and Suresh Sharma 1998.

This income distribution today matches the income distribution of rural Haryana which is one of the most agriculturally prosperous States of India. A survey conducted by the National Council of Applied Economic Research on income distribution in rural Haryana in 1994 revealed the following figure[10]:

Annual household income	Distribution of households (%)
Less than Rs. 20,000	38.65
Rs. 20,001 - 40,000	32.16
Rs. 40,001 - 62,000	14.46
Rs. 62,001 - 86,000	6.56
Above Rs. 86,000	8.17

Source : S.L. Rao and I. Natarajan, 1996.

A comparison of the two tables shows that Sukhomajri now matches the income distribution in rural Haryana. This is impressive because Haryana is one of the richest States in India which has greatly benefited from the agricultural prosperity created through the Green Revolution.

One simple sign of wealth in rural India is the type of houses that people live in. In 1998, 89 per cent of the households had pucca (brick and mortar) houses and the remaining had semi-pucca houses. There was no household with a kutcha (mud) house.[9]

In Sukhomajri, the main incentive for the villagers to protect their watershed came because of the assurance they got from the Forest Department that they would have the right to the usufruct of the degraded forest land. Earlier, the Forest Department would auction the grass in the degraded watershed to a contractor who in turn would charge the villagers high rates to harvest the grass. The villagers argued that as they were protecting the watershed, they should get the benefits from the increased biomass production and not the contractor. The Forest Department agreed to give the grass rights to the village society as long as the villagers paid the department a royalty equivalent to the average income earned by the department before the villagers started protecting the watershed.

The villagers pay their village society a nominal amount to cut grass in the watershed. A part of this is used to pay the Forest Department and a part is used to generate community resources for the village. If the Forest Department's assurance, however tenuous, was not available, the entire Sukhomajri experiment would collapse overnight.

A crucial role in this entire exercise was played by a village-level institution that was specifically created for the purpose of watershed protection. The Hill Resources Management Society, as this institution is called, consists of one member from each household in the village. It provides a forum for all households to discuss their problems, manage the local environment and maintain discipline amongst their members. The society makes sure that no household grazes its animals in the watershed and in return it has created a framework for a fair distribution amongst all the households of the resources so generated, namely, water, wood and grass. Today, the entire catchment of the tank is green and the village is prosperous and capable of withstanding even serious droughts.

2.b. The Ralegan Siddhi Experience

Ralegan Siddhi is today held up as a model of development. It is a village situated in a drought-prone area of Maharashtra where the annual rainfall ranges from 450 mm to 650 mm only and where the villagers were once not even assured one regular crop.[11] In summer, they would regularly take to the State-sponsored drought relief measures.

In 1975, the village was stricken by poverty. It had hardly one acre of irrigated land per family. Yield was less than 0.75 tonne per ha. Food production was only 30 per cent of the village requirements and some 15-20 per cent of the families were undernourished and most men migrated each year to look for work. The village was in the grip of chronic poverty, moneylenders and countrymade liquor.[12]

Krishna Bhaurao Hazare—a retired driver from the Indian army—began work in the village by constructing storage ponds, reservoirs and gully plugs. Due to the steady percolation of water, the groundwater table began to rise. Simultaneously, government social forestry schemes were utilized to plant 300,000-400,000 trees in and around the village.[13] Because of the increased availability of irrigation water, land that was lying fallow came under cultivation and the total area under farming increased from 630 hectares to 950 hectares.[14] The average yields of millets, sorghum and onion increased substantially.

Every effort was made in the village to ensure equitable access to the resources generated. Water is distributed equitably. As cultivation of sugarcane requires a large quantity of water, it was forbidden in the early years to ensure that the limited amount of water available was distributed equitably to all farming households. Only low water-consuming crops were allowed. All families get water in turn. No farmer will get a second turn of irrigation until all families have been served. Since the commons belong to all, even the landless families—four to five in the village—have a right to the water. Even where individuals have dug wells, they have been persuaded to share water with others.[15] Water conservation efforts resulted in increased availability of groundwater which in turn has facilitated the development of community wells. Water from these wells, supplied at a moderate price, has enabled farmers to grow two to three crops a year including fruits and crops, some of which are exported all the way to Dubai.[11]

Today not a single inhabitant of the village depends on drought relief. Incomes have increased substantially. A 1998 survey revealed the following income distribution.[9] (See Table 6.1).

Even after discounting the discrepancies that may have crept in by converting the monthly household income into annual household income, the current income distribution in Ralegan Siddhi shows considerable wealth when compared to the income distribution estimates of rural Maharashtra prepared by the National Council Applied Economic Research for the year 1994. (See Table 6.2).

By Indian standards, Ralegan Siddhi is a very rich village now. The fact that over a quarter of the households earn nearly haf a million rupees a year has to be seen against the fact that there are only a million households in India—whom the National Council of Applied Economic Research calls the "super rich"—who earn more than a million rupees a year, including estimates of black money. Ralegan Siddhi's income distribution is also much less skewed than that of rural Maharashtra.[10]

TABLE 6.1: **Income Distribution**

Annual household income	Distribution of Households (%)
Less than Rs. 24,000	13
Rs. 24,000 - 48,000	24.1
Rs. 48,000 - 96,000	16.7
Rs. 96,000 - 192,000	9.3
Rs. 192,000 - 300,000	3.7
Rs. 300,000 - 480,000	5.6
Above Rs. 400,000	27.8

Note: The survey questionnaire had solicited responses on the monthly household income. Converting the monthly into annual household income may result in an overstatement of the annual income as respondents may not be earning the same monthly income round the year. But figures given above are of annual household income merely for comparison with the available data on the distribution of annual household income in rural Maharashtra, the State in which village Ralegan Siddhi is situated.

Source : S.C. Gulati and Suresh Sharma, 1998.

TABLE 6.2: **Annual Household Income**

Annual household income	Distribution of households (%)
Less than Rs. 20,000	59.88
Rs. 20,001 - 40,000	28.53
Rs. 40,001 - 62,000	7.05
Rs. 62,001 - 86,000	2.85
Above Rs. 86,000	1.69

Source: S.L. Rao and I. Natarajan, 1996.

Ralegan Siddhi is, in fact, so rich that it has now even got a branch of a major bank in the village itself. The total savings of Ralegan Siddhi villagers alone are reportedly Rs. 30 million. For a village that was less than two decades ago a drunkard's den with a badly degraded environment, this is indeed a miracle.[15]

2.b.1 Institutional Developments

An impressive system of decision making has been created in the village. Some 14 committees operate to ensure people's participation in all decision making. A participatory democratic institution called the Gram Sabha was created to take community decisions. According to the Gandhian philosophy on rural development, the Gram Saha, an assembly of all village adults, should act as the most important forum for collective decision-making in a village just as a nation's parliament collectively decides on the welfare of a nation. If villagers are involved in the planning and decision-making process, they are more open to any changes taking place in the village. The purpose of the Gram Sabha is, therefore, to involve every villager in the development process and exert social pressure wherever required.[1]

Ralegan Siddhi gave considerable importance to the participatory institution of the Gram Sabha in which all villagers could participate rather than the elected Village Council called Gram Panchayat which is a statutory organization under the Constitution of India. In other words, Ralegan has given greater importance to participatory democracy rather than representative democracy.

In Ralegan Siddhi, the Gram Sabha meetings are held periodically. Watershed development activities are undertaken only after they are discussed in the Gram Sabha. Decisions are normally taken by consensus. In case of difference of opinion, the majority opinion becomes acceptable. The decision of the Gram Sabha is final.[15] Once the Gram Sabha has taken a decision, the Gram Panchayat carries out programmes for the village.[15]

In addition to the Panchayat (elected Village Council), there are several registered societies that take care of the various projects and activities of the village. Thse large number of village institutions are quite remarkable for an Indian village. The village has established different organizations to carry out different activities relating to development. All these organizations have been registered as societies. They hold regular meetings according to their own rules and their annual accounts are audited and presented to the Gram Sabha every year and approval of the villagers is obtained. The following societies operate in the village.[15]

- The Sant Yadavbaba Shikshan Prasarak Mandal (Saint Yadavbaba Education Society) monitors educational activities.
- The Vividh Karyakari Society (Multipurpose Cooperative Society) gives assistance and provides guidance to farmers regarding fertilizers, seeds, organic farming, financial assistance, etc.
- The Dairy Development society gives guidance regarding the dairy business.
- Seven cooperative irrigation societies provide water to the farmers from the cooperative wells.
- The Mahila Mandal (Women's Group) attends to the welfare needs of the women.
- The Tarun Mandal (Youth Group) is responsible for the social and cultural activities, including the group marriages.

While these societies operate independently of each other, all of them are responsible to the Gram Sabha, which is the apex body. If any new work is to be undertaken, complete details of how the work is to be executed, what would be its costs and benefits, whether the cost is within the means of the village and is manageable or not, etc., are discussed and a final decision is taken by the Gram Sabha. Unless there is unanimity of opinion, no new work is undertaken.

The Gram Sabha has played an important role in enforcing discipline within the village by exerting social pressure. For instance, as is common in Indian villages, some people had encroached upon government land within the village. The Gram Sabha forced them to vacate these lands so that they could be used for afforestation on a community basis. Some people behaved as despots in the village, did what they liked, and were a law unto themselves. But the united social forces that were created in the village curbed their activities. Some farmers sent their cattle for grazing on the open grasslands. This, too, was stopped to promote ecological regeneration. Since it was the will of the community as expressed and decided in the Gram Sabha, they had to give up or sacrifice their privileges due to public pressure.

In order for democracy to prosper, it is necessary to hold elections. But elections can also lead to divisive tendencies within a village. In Ralegan Siddhi, none of the positions in any of the societies have been contested for the past 20 years. When it is time for elections, the Gram Sabha is convened. In this Gram Sabha, elected representatives to the Panchayat as well as the societies are nominated unanimously. Sometimes there are disagreements which are sorted out mutually by the villagers, taking into consideration the majority opinion. The elections are, therefore, not contested.

In 1994, the village witnessed the creation of the first women's self-help group. "As the village economy has become surplus, we thought about small savings by women to help other women in future. Within three years the village has already seven self-help groups, each of 20 members," says Dillip Gowane who looks after this activity. Every month the members save Rs. 25 to Rs. 100 and they have a collective saving of Rs. 2 lakhs now. From this saving, soft loans (with an interest as low as 2 per cent) are given to women who want to start their own business or for other purposes.

The evolution of village institutions in Ralegan has been an important part of its development. As Hazare puts it, "Institutions were never made but evolved out of need as we wanted to involve all the villagers in different activities."[11]

2.b.2 Development Finances

The financial resources for the transformation of Ralegan have come mainly from the villagers themselves and from government rural development programmes and bank loans.

People's Contribution to Costs of Watershed Development Programme till 1993-94[14]

Total cost of Development Programme till 1993-94	Rs. 74.37 lakhs
Contribution by the people of Ralegan Siddhi	48.43%
Contribution by Rural Development Department	6.74%
Water Conservation Schemes of Government	44.83%

Source : 1. Annasahed Hazare ud, Micro Watershed Development, Mimeo.
2. Anna Hazare 1998, Personal Communication.

At Ralegan Siddhi, self-sufficiency and a spirit of self-dependence has been fostered through *shramdan* (voluntary labour). Each individual contributes one day of *shramdan*, every 15 days. Very poor and very old people are not expected to participate. Poor people are, in fact, paid to do work on community projects. Days for *shramdan* are allocated to each family according to the number of members in the family. When a particular project is taken up, the number of days for *shramdan* are decided according to the amount of labour that will be required for the project.[15]

The villagers perform *shramdan* even for government projects. Therefore, they identify themselves with these projects and remain involved in the maintenance of these projects. The cleanliness of village and community toilets and maintenance of all community structures is done through *shramdan*.[15]

Donations from development agencies or foundations were not accepted in Ralegan Siddhi.[12] But Ralegan did try to take the full benefit of government schemes and loans from banks. The most important contribution has, however, come from the free labour of the villagers, which has accounted for at least Rs. 30 lakhs in the construction of the school building, hostel building, and community wells and watershed development schemes.

The village benefited from government schemes like the watershed development programme of the Soil Conservation Department. About Rs. 22 lakhs were spent on 855 ha. at the rate of Rs. 2,500 per hectare. The Social Forestry Department of the government also did some work in Ralegan. Houses were constructed for the homeless under a scheme of the District Rural Development Agency (DRDA). Solar energy equipment was installed under the government's "Urjagram" (Renewable Energy Villge) project. Because the villagers were eager to learn and were responsive, the Urja Gram Udyog Medha (Rural Energy Development Centre) installed solar panels for heating water. Solar cookers were supplied at subsidised rates. The Council for Public Action and Rural Technology has provided funds for putting up a windmill that is used to pump water. But no special preference or extra allocation was given to Ralegan. It was the coordination between the government agencies and the villagers that made all the benefits more visible in Ralegan whereas in other villages there was improper implementation and, as a result, commensurate benefits did not accrue and were, thus, not visible.[12]

Even in Ralegan, not all government schemes were successful right from the beginning. But the villagers did not abandon any project just because it did not succeed. For instance, afforestation done by the government on one plot did not succeed. The villagers and the Forest Department discussed the problems and tried again on the same plot and succeeded the second time. A percolation tank built by the Minor Irrigation Department in 1972 had failed to store water but the villagers did a proper repair job of it. The farmers also undertook the job of tree plantation all over again after the work done by the Agricultural Department in their fields did not give the desired results. In other words, the villagers made the best out of the numerous government schemes that would have otherwise produced limited results.[12]

Under the leadership of Hazare, the villagers have tried to adopt all possible modern technologies and alternative energy sources, whether it is drip irrigation, solar energy or biogas. Street lights with solar fittings are a common feature. Some 2,000 litres of water in the school hostel are heated by solar panels. The local people are fully trained to maintain the solar panels. The television in the hostel is powered by solar energy. For about 250 students, rice and *dal* (lentils) are cooked in giant solar cookers. Chapatis (bread) are made on large smokeless *chulhas* (wood stoves). Government agencies have several programmes to promote renewable sources of energy which were fully utilized by the villagers of Ralegan.

With the help of a bank loan of Rs. 60 lakhs some 37 ha. of land were brought under drip irrigation, including 14 ha. of *mausambi* (citrus) orchards. Since this water conservation technique is expensive, collective of 28 farmers took a bank loan to install this irrigation system. Between the *mausambi* trees, vegetables are grown ensuring that the village's immediate needs are met.

2.c. The Alwar Experience

Gopalpura is a poor, drought-stricken village, located at the base of the Aravali hills in the State of Rajasthan. The area is semi-arid and over the years deforestation has left it devoid of any vegetation. Water shortages are common and have a deep impact on the lives of the people and their agriculture. In 1986, assisted by the Tarun Bharat Sangh (TBS), a local voluntary agency, the villagers built three small earthen rainwater harvesting structures, locally called *johads*, on their fields and village grazing lands to store monsoon rains, irrigate their fields and increase percolation in the ground to recharge wells. The science of *johads* comes from the traditional knowledge in which village communities built earthen structures across their fields to catch the small rainfall of the region. In the hot, semi-arid and arid regions of Rajasthan, surface water evaporates fast. The *johad* harvests the rain and holds it to improve percolation and recharge. Farmers cultivate on the same moist land after the water has seeped into the soil.[16]

These engineering structures are built across the contour of a slope to arrest rainwater. Sometimes a series of such structures are built to hold the run-off from one structure to another. The region gets roughly 600 mm of rainfall, most of it is distributed in 4-5 rainbreak periods of a few days each and separated by several days.[17]

The effort of Gopalpura has attracted so much attention that within 10 years Tarun Bharat Sangh has been able to build almost 2,500 water conservation structures in over 500 villages of the region. Till 1997-98, the water conservation structures had cost Rs. 15 crores of which 11 crores was contributed by the poor villagers in cash or kind. The voluntary agency follows clear guidelines—while villagers contribute labour and local materials, TBS supplies external resources like cement or diesel for tractors. In each village, detailed discussions are held with the village assembly—the Gram Sabha—to identify the site which receives the maximum run-off, the size of the dam and the beneficiaries. The village assembly also makes rules about the annual repairs, the distribution of water and the management of the watershed. In some villages, in order to protect the watershed of the *johad*, villagers have evolved rules for penalizing cutting of trees and even breaking of leaves.

TABLE 6.3: **Cost Sharing Arrangements of Tarun Bharat Sangh.**[16]

Johad's Name	Village	TBS Contribution	Village Contribution	Total	Villagers Contribution to the total cost (%)
Gopal Johad	Buja	14,510.60	1,76,000.00	1,90,510.60	92%
Chavada Johad	Pathroda	30,483.00	21,156.90	41,639.90	51%
Saankada Johad	Bhavata	15,183.50	60,701.30	75,884.30	80%
Harala Johad	Kakar ke Dhani	17,418.00	29,159.80	46,577.80	63%
Bhajaka/ Natata	Bhajaka/ Natata	83,537.00	96,497.50	1,80,034.50	54%

Source : Anon 1998.

The direct and most dramatic impact of these structures has been to increase the groundwater as well as surface water availability in the region. An evaluation done by the former head of the Department of Civil Engineering at the Indian Institute of Technology, Kanpur, G.D. Agarwal, shows that the rise in the groundwater table was a direct impact of the conservation structures. Agarwal's study which covered 36 villages has made the following interesting conclusions.[17]

— Though all the structures were built by the people themselves without any calculations, essentially on their gut feelings, 36 per cent of them had the right capacity. Only 13 per cent had a capacity which was more than required.

— In 1995 and 1996 when intense rainfall washed away numerous structures designed by government engineers, each one of these structures stood the test.

— The structures have been built at an extremely low cost ranging from a low of Re. 0.2 per cubic metre of storage capacity to a high of Rs. 3 per cubic metre and an average of Re. 0.95 per cubic metre. No engineering organization would be able to build water harvesting structures at this cost.

— The study assessed that about 1,000-1,500 cubic metres of storage capacity would have to be created to support one hectare of cultivated land. This would raise the average groundwater table by about 20 ft.

TABLE 6.4: **Groundwater level in wells of the village Buja before and after Johad[16]**

No.	Total depth of well (in feet) 1988	Water level before Johad	Water level of well after Johad, 1994 (in feet)
1.	81	Dry completely	44.5
2.	73	Dry completely	37
3.	67	3 feet	40.5
4.	55½	4 feet (dry most of the time)	27
5.	81	10 feet	66
6.	69	20 feet	50
7.	43	15 feet	35
8.	83	20 feet	58
9.	80½	19 feet	55
10.	66½	Dry completely	25

Source: AFPRO, 1994, quoted in (1) Anon. 1998.[16]

— In the 36 villages[17], 166 *johads* with a combined storage capacity of 335,000 cubic metres to capture rain running off a combined catchment area of 8,152 ha. and the total cost was Rs. 30,35,202. In these villages, the groundwater table rose from a low of 10 ft up to a high of 24.5 ft. The annual Gross Village Product rose from a low of Rs. 78,648 to a high of Rs. 11,23,857 and the annual per capita income rose from a low Rs. 126 to a high of Rs. 3,585. In order to calculate the increase in the annual Gross Village Product, Agarwal[17] took into account the increase in the value of agricultural produce, increase in milk production and increase in produce from forests before and after the water conservation programme began. Thus, with an investment of Rs. 30,35,202 in water conservation in these 36 villages, the total annual Gross Village Product of these villages combined has gone up by Rs. 1,30,43,721 and the average per capita income has gone up by Rs. 845.

— Agarwal found that not only did these water harvesting structures have a direct impact on the economy of the region, increases in income were strongly correlated with the investments that had been made in *johads*. An investment of Rs. 1,000 on *johads* raises economic production by over Rs. 4,200 per annum.

What is absolutely stunning today is to see the "rebirth" of several rivers in the region. In just three years of making water conservation structures along the dead, dry courses of streams in these hills, the rivers started coming to life. Today, two seasonal dry streams, Arvari and Ruparel, for example, have become perennial rivers whereas these rivers earlier had no flow in them after the monsoons. Both rivers are roughly 90 km long flowing from the Aravali hills through hundreds of villages. Villagers have built over 250-300 *johads* and water conservation structures along the river courses, bringing them literally to life again.[16]

Water has increased agricultural productivity of this extremely impoverished land. Most villagers who earlier used to migrate with their men and women to work as labourers in cities are now returning to till their lands which had been lying fallow for decades. A study has estimated that wheat production with *johad* water had increased 100 per cent.[18] People are still practising subsistence agriculture, but now they have enough to eat and do not have to migrate any more.

2.d. The Madhya Pradesh Experience

This remarkable transformation of rural ecosystems with the people's participation described above has remained isolated and scattered led by remarkable NGO leaders. Government efforts in afforestation and watershed management have never been able to replicate these successes. In most cases, the problem has been that the devolution of power to local communities has been half-hearted and inadequate. People's participation has remained largely stuck in the "you participate in my programme" syndrome.

In Madhya Pradesh, however, the watershed management programme has become an outstanding example in which the government has been able to intervene in a way that promotes public participation in environmental management. Trees are coming up in the district of Jhabua which in the mid-1980s looked like the moonscape. Today, dug wells are literally overflowing with water in a place that was described as chronically drought-prone. Some 149,283 ha. covering 374 villages in Jhabua alone which account for some 22 per cent of the district's land area have been brought under the Rajiv Gandhi Watershed Development Mission (RGWDM).[19]

The State-wide programme had covered 750 milli-watersheds (a milli-watershed covers 5,000-10,000 ha. and consists of several micro-watersheds of 500-1,000 ha.), 7,827 villages, and an area of 3.39 million ha. by end-March, 1998, which is slightly more than one per cent of India's total land area. The total investment in the programme has been of the order of Rs. 300 crores since it began in 1995-96.[20] The cost of treating one hectare has come to be less than Rs. 1,000 which is amazing because even standard afforestation programmes cost more than Rs. 5,000 per hectare.

Deeply inspired by the work of Krishna Bhaurao Hazare in his village Ralegan Siddhi, Digvijay Singh after he became Chief Minister in 1993 decided to launch a similar programme across the State by the name of Rajiv Gandhi Watershed Development Mission. Funds were no problem because the Central Government provides several thousands of crores every year to State Governments for rural employment programmes. The Central Government's guidelines encourage State Governments to use these funds for watershed development but few State Governments actually do so. Digvijay Singh decided to use these funds for an integrated and participatory watershed development programme in the State.[21]

The foundation of any watershed programme is water and soil conservation. In the case of Jhabua it meant arresting the water that falls on the hillslopes and instead of allowing it to run away and carrying away with its precious topsoils, the water is so trained that it percolates into the land and recharges the groundwater wells. Numerous economic and ecological benefits have resulted from this exercise. A study of 18 microwatersheds in Jhabua district revealed that within four years, the following benefits were obtained.[22]

— With increased water availability, the irrigated area increased to 1,115 ha. which is nearly double the irrigated area of 1994-95.
— The flow intensity and duration of natural streams has also increased.
— With increased irrigation, agricultural productivity is increasing.

— Estimates show that over 2 million trees have regenerated.

— The regeneration rate has been far more rapid as compared to lands where only forest protection programmes have been implemented because the water conservation efforts increase soil moisture and, therefore, plant growth. In turn, there is a more rapid increase in economic returns to the poor people involved in watershed management. The biggest and earliest benefit to the local people has come from the rapid regeneration of grass and, therefore, increased fodder availability. Some estimates suggests a 5-6 times increase in grass from the regenerated lands.

TABLE 6.5: **Increased Grass Production and Resulting Incomes in the Hathipahwa Microwatershed**

	1995	1996	1997
Grass Production	160 tonnes	360 tonnes	480 tonnes
Grass value (about Rs. 2,000) per tonne)	Rs. 3.2 lakh	Rs. 7.2 lakh	Rs. 9.75 lakh
Grass Productivity (1)	0.69 tonne per hectare	1.56 tonnes per hectare	2.08 tonnes per hectare
Grass value per household (2)	Rs. 3,048	Rs. 6,957	Rs. 9,286

Notes: (1) The project covered 81.26 ha. of revenue land and 150 ha. of forest land. The entire project area has been used to calculate grass productivity.

(2) The total number of households in the project area is 105.

Source: Data on households and project area provided by the District Collectorate, Jhabua.

— The watershed programme is already having a substantial social impact. Dependence on local moneylenders has gone down. In the 18 microwatersheds studied, loans from moneylenders had gone down by 22 per cent. Grain banks have resulted in increased food security. And distress migration has reduced considerably.[22]

The transformation of Jhabua is a fine example of the results we can expect when a government seriously starts working with the people. The watershed programme in Madhya Pradesh has happened because several tiers of institutions have been created: firstly, at the State level, for policy coordination; secondly, at the district and milli-watershed level, for implementation coordination; and, finally, at the village level to ensure that all villagers acquire an interest in the effort.[1] For example, there were 1,748 women's groups, with

25,506 participants, were created in 374 villages of Jhabua.

TABLE 6.6: **Village-level institutions for the watershed development programme in Jhabua district**[22]

Village-level institution	Number of institutions	Number of participants	Distribution of Participants
User's groups	1,668	13,947	About 7 users' groups per micro-watershed About 8 participants per users' group
Self-help groups	1,256	9,699	About 5 per micro-watershed About 8 participants per self-help group
Women's groups	1,748	25,506	About 7 per micro-watershed About 15 per women's group

Source : Anon 1998.

But most importantly, serious efforts have been made to give local communities power over decision making, and control over resources. For instance, the villagers play an active role in managing the funds meant for the watershed programme. Nearly 80 per cent of the funds for the programme are put in a bank account managed by the Watershed Development Committees made up of village people. The Watershed Development Committee tries to bring together all the important interest groups in the village and thus replicates the concept of the Gram Sabha. Experience has shown that where the WDC has been made in a hurry and all interest groups have not been involved, the watershed programme has proved to be less effective, especially from social and equity considerations.

Till mid-1998, the total expenditure in Jhabua was Rs. 16.48 crores of which Rs. 11.95 crores has been direct investment into watershed development works, mostly spent on employment generation. The project encourages villagers to save and put a part of their wages into a village-level watershed development fund (which will provide villagers with money to maintain their water harvesting structures after the government withdraws after its stipulated period of four years), a village fund (which will provide the village community for village welfare and investment), and women are encouraged to put aside their savings in thrift and credit groups. By mid-1998 the village welfare fund had 0.42 crore, the village watershed development fund which would support maintenance of village watershed structure had Rs. 0.48 crore and the women's groups had total deposits of Rs. 2.44 crores or about 18 per cent of the project expenditure—all this money was saved by the villagers from the wages they had received for the watershed development work. Thus, the project had not only improved the ecology but also the financial security of local villagers.[19]

It is interesting to see the State bureaucracy in a unique mode to work with the people. Now that the groundwater is being recharged, many people fear that the more powerful will begin to exploit it through private tubewells even though recharge is the result of a united community effort. Nowhere in India has bureaucratic regulation of groundwater worked and water tables are falling rapidly everywhere. In Madhya Pradesh, too, the officials now know that their success in Jhabua has brought them to a stage where they have to confront issues of inequity in the water management. In an unprecedented move in favour of community-regulated water management, the officials working with the programme propose to argue that communities who have come together as watershed committees should be given powers to regulate withdrawal of water from their watersheds.

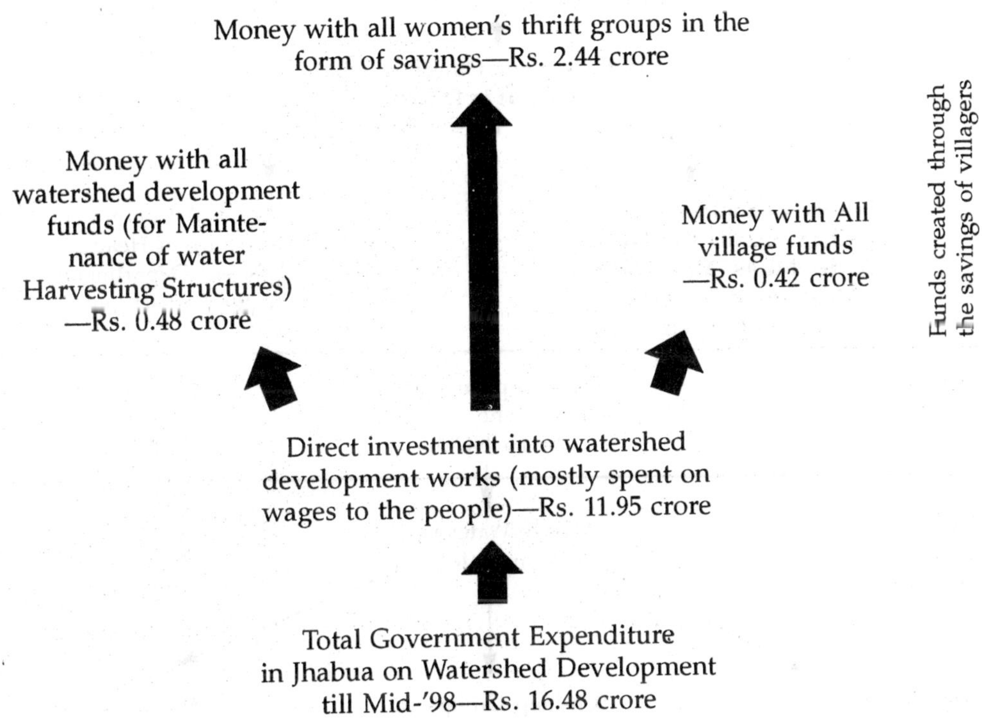

Fig. 6.3: Management of Watershed Development Finances in Jhabua District

Source: Chief Executive Officer, Zilla Panchayat, Jhabua, quoted in Anil Agarwal 1998, The house that Digvijay built, in Down to Earth, Society for Environmental Communications, New Delhi, December 31, p. 35.

Of Rs. 16.48 crore spent on watershed development in Jhabua till mid-1998, a large part has been spent on wages. But out of these wages, people have saved money for village welfare, future maintenance of watershed works and for women's needs.

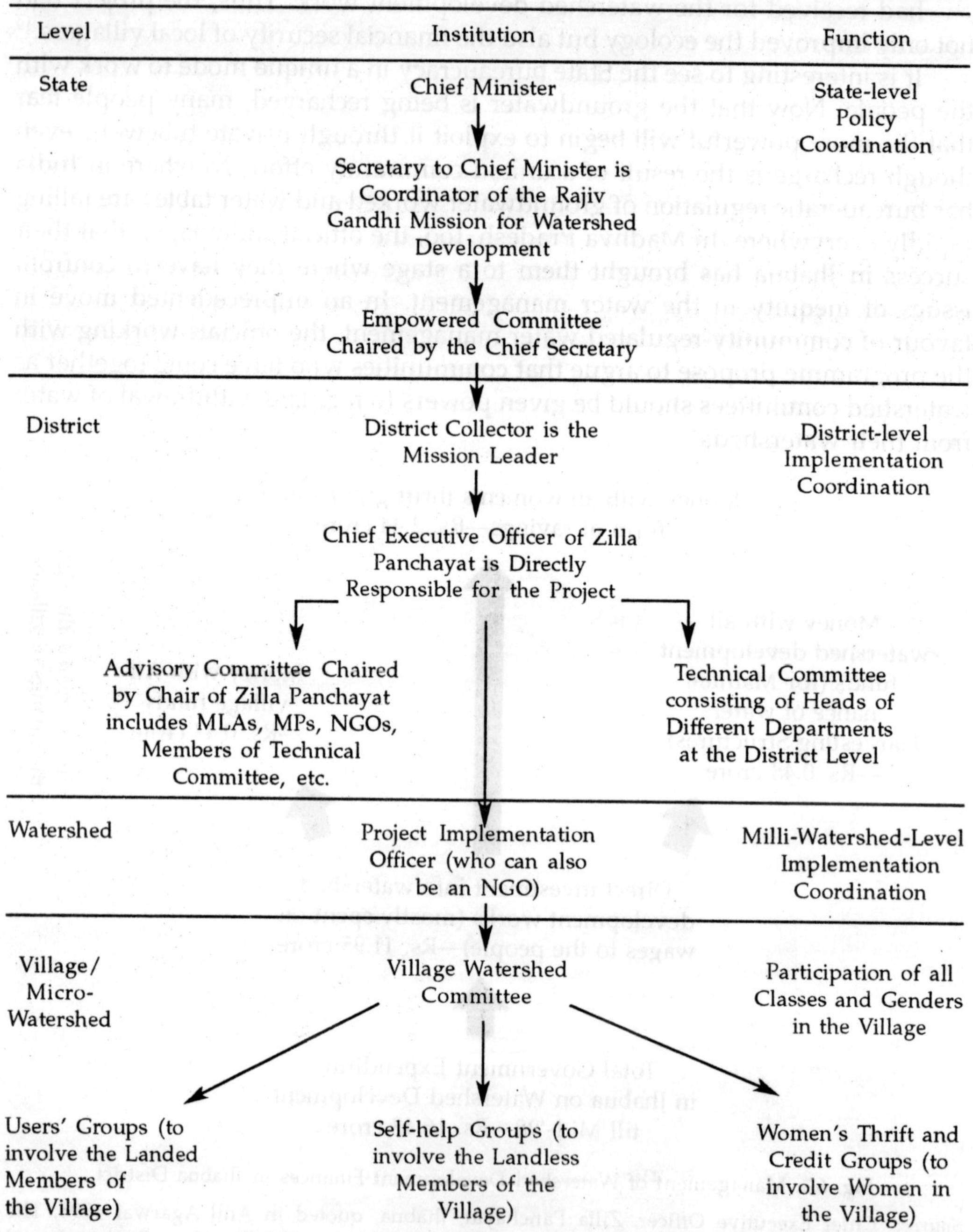

Fig 6.4: Structure of Institutions Created to support a People's Movement to undertake Watershed Development in Madhya Pradesh

Source: Anil Agarwal and Richard Mahapatra, 1999, Madhya Pradesh: Paradise Regained, in Anil Agarwal, Sunita Narain and Srabani Sen (ed). State of India's Environment 1999—Citizens' Fifth Report, Centre or Science and Environment, New Delhi.

The example of Jhabua shows that increasing population pressure does not necessarily result in an irreversible trend towards environmental degradation. It simply means improved environmental management that is usually not possible without the involvement of the people and the government playing a limited but strategic role.

3. The Importance of Rainwater Harvesting

One of the biggest environmental challenges that India faces in the coming decades is that of balancing its increasing demand with the diminishing availability of water. Increases in population coupled with the ongoing processes of industrialization, urbanization and agricultural development are, on the one hand, leading to an ever increasing demand for water and, on the other, a decreased supply of fresh water, especially in the absence of effective mechanisms to regulate pollution. The future scenario is one characterized by overexploitation of water resources, decreased accessibility to clean water, and increased competition for and potential of conflict over water resources.

Major institutional, policy and technological initiatives are required to ensure an efficient, socially equitable and environmentally sustainable management of our water resources.

There is only one source of fresh water and that is precipitation whether it is in the form of snow that makes glaciers or rain which ultimately flows down as streams and rivers and recharges the groundwater.

A major reason for the growing overexploitation of water resources is the current stress on riverwater and groundwater to the neglect of rainwater and floodwater, the availability of which is far greater.

India—one of the wettest countries in the world and yet a country that is facing a growing water shortage—receives 400 million hectare-metres (mham) of precipitation, primarily as rain. But India uses only a small part of it. By 2025 A.D., India is expected to be using 105 mham.[23] If all this water use was to be met from rivers and groundwater systems, riverine ecosystems and groundwater resources will come under extreme stress, as is already being noticed across the country. Rainwater harvesting cannot only provide a source of water to increase water supplies but also involve the public in water management, making water management everybody's business. It will also reduce the current demand on government institutions to meet water needs, reduce the need for government subsidies, and help everyone to internalize the full costs of their water requirements, thus encouraging the public to be more conserving in its water demand. And in rural areas water harvesting should also be seen as part of an integrated programme for sustainable development of land and water resources on a watershed basis whose objective is to improve total biomass output.

Water harvesting and integrated land-water management is not new to India. The art and science of "collecting water where it falls" is ancient but this "dying wisdom" needs to be revived to meet modern freshwater needs adequately, equitably and sustainably and modernized with inputs from science and technology.[24]

Water harvesting means capturing the rain where it falls or capturing the run-off in one's own village or in one's own town. And taking measures to keep that water clean by not allowing dirty activities to take place in the catchment.

Therefore, water harvesting can be undertaken through a variety of ways:

(a) Capturing run-off from rooftops.
(b) Capturing run-off from local catchments.
(c) Capturing seasonal floodwaters from local streams.
(d) Conserving water through watershed management.

These techniques can serve the following purposes:

(a) Provide drinking water.
(b) Provide irrigation water.
(c) Increase groundwater recharge.
(d) Reduce stormwater discharges, urban floods and overloading of sewage treatment plants.
(e) Reduce seawater ingress in coastal areas.

Two major discontinuities have emerged in the management of water since the 19th century. Not only in India but across the world. One, the State has emerged as the major provider of water replacing communities and households as the primary units for provision and management of water. Two, there has been growing reliance on the use of surface and groundwater, while the earlier reliance on rainwater and floodwater has declined, even though rainwater and floodwater are available in much greater abundance than river water or groundwater.

According to one water balance study of India, the country receives 400 mham of rain and snowfall. Another 20 mham come from outside. These 420 mham give us river flows of 180 mham—most of which comes during the rainy season—and another 67 mham as ground water. Thus, river flows and ground water add up to 247 mham of which a substantial amount must flow out to neighbouring countries and to the sea.[23]

But India still has an enormous amount—theoretically as much as 173 mham—an amount which can be captured as rain or as run-off from small catchments in and near villages or towns. Capturing the flood waters of major rivers can further increase water availability. India's projected use of water is 105 mham in 2025 A.D.

Theoretically, the potential of water harvesting in meeting household needs is enormous. Rain captured from 1-2 per cent of India's land can provide India's population of 950 million as much as 100 litres of water per person per day. There is no village in India which cannot meet its drinking water needs through rainwater harvesting.

Despite all official efforts to provide drinking water to India's villages, shortages of drinking water continue to plague India's rural areas. According to the Department of Rural Development, India's efforts to provide drinking water to Indian villages have run into peculiar problems.[25] Even as the government invests in drinking water projects in numerous villages, there are always many left to be covered (see Table 6.7).

TABLE 6.7: **Government's Experience in Providing Drinking Water**

Survey Year	No. of problem villages identified	Villages covered till the next survey	Villages not covered till the next survey
1972	1,50,000	94,000	56,000
1980	2,31,000	1,92,000	39,000
1985	1,61,722	1,61,652	70
1994	1,40,975	1,10,371	30,604
April 1997	61,747	—	—

Why are so many problem villages found at the start of the survey as compared to the number of uncovered villages at the end of the survey period? There could be several reasons:

(a) Corruption, leading to poor projects and data collection.
(b) Lack of people's interest in government projects, leading to poor maintenance of the projects implemented.
(c) Groundwater depletion, leading to new problem villages.
(d) Pollution, leading to new problem villages.
(e) Increased fluoride and arsenic contamination of groundwater leading to new problem villages.

It is obvious that appropriate policies are needed to address both shortage of water and declining quality of water.

What does water harvesting mean in human terms? It means making water everybody's business. Every household becomes involved both in the provision of water and in the protection of water sources. It means making water the subject of a people's movement. It means re-establishing the relationship between people and their environment. It means turning water into a sacred element of nature. It means the empowerment of our urban and rural communities to manage their own affairs with the State playing a critical supportive role and the civil society playing a critical role in encouraging equity and sustainability in the use of water. It means a role for everybody with respect to water.

Water harvesting will bring many benefits:

— Apart from increasing water availability, local water harvesting systems developed by local communities and households will reduce the pressure on the State to provide all the financial resources needed for water supply. As the State is often short of funds, this approach will greatly reduce limitations posed by financial considerations.
— Involving people will also give the people greater ownership over water projects and will probably go a long way towards reducing misuse of government funds.
— Moreover, when communities and households develop their own water supply systems, they also take good care of them—the spectre of unrepaired, broken down systems and wasted funds will haunt us less. Water will also be used more carefully instead of being squandered away as most rich people do.

Therefore, there is eminent sense—ecological, financial and political—in promoting community and household-based water harvesting systems. In catching water where it falls. Water harvesting cannot only meet the people's basic water needs but also improve food and livelihood security.[26]

4. The Way Ahead

But even after their astounding success, the community and NGO-based experiences of Sukhomajri, Ralegan Siddhi and Tarun Bharat Sangh cited above have remained scattered and isolated for a long time. Critics have often used these facts to condemn these examples as irreplicable creations of remarkable individuals who have persevered to bring change. But that is not the correct picture. These examples have remained scattered because the governance system that would foster people's control over natural resources does not exist in the country. The current examples exist despite the system and not because of the system. It, therefore, takes enormous perseverance of an individual to bring change at the micro level. However, if the system of governance enabled local communities to improve and care for their resource base, it would be easier to bring change. The Rajiv Gandhi Watershed Development Mission of the Madhya Pradesh Government has shown that the State can replicate these community-based efforts if there is adequate political will and pressure on the technical and administrative bureaucracy to deliver.

In order to develop a good village-level natural resource management programme, it is essential to develop a conceptual framework that addresses both the private and common property resources of the village, its diverse biomass needs, and the interests and requirements of different socio-economic groups within the village community (See Fig. 6.5).

Such a programme sets into motion a series of ecological successions, beginning with increased quantity and productivity of croplands because of increased water conservation and, hence, availability of irrigated water and leading to increased grass production from the grasslands and slowly increased production of fodder and timber resources from the tree and forest lands. Each of these stages of ecological succession generate their own economic impacts on the village society which slowly unfold in the years to come. (See Fig. 6.6) The ultimate impact of the ecoregeneration on the local economy is hard to predict because it will depend on the local resource endowments, technological interventions and economic strategies chosen.

But it is clear that ecoregeneration will not only have a significant impact on the village economy by increasing local carrying capacity, increased incomes and local employment but, by reducing distress migration, it can also have a significant impact reducing urban poverty and enhancing social development in urban areas, especially if the ecoregeneration is undertaken on a large, regional scale. It should reduce distress urbanization and increase the bargaining capacity of the rural-urban migrant leading to reduced incidence of slums and exploitative practices like child labour (See Fig. 6.7).

The current success stories of village-level resource management teach us that a bundle of policy measures are needed for good natural resource management. These measures include changes in the current institutional, legal and financial framework towards systems that engender community-level, participatory democracy. It is only once this policy package is implemented that these "isolated" microexperiences will bloom into a "million" villages.

From the above experiences we learn that programmes to enhance the Gross Nature Product with equity and sustainability have to be developed at two levels:

4.a. The Conceptual Level

The conceptualization of the programme will have to be developed at the level of the ecosystem so as to develop ecosystem-specific development guidelines. All the four programmes described above fall in semi-arid to sub-humid hill and mountain ranges and plateaus with undulating topography. The technology package of water conservation built on rainwater harvesting combined with composite "village ecosystem" planning and management, which has been employed in the above case studies, will be suitable for similar areas but may not be appropriate for coastal regions or for flood plains. For these ecological regions, other technology packages would have to be developed.

In India, ecological poverty can be found in all the following ecological regions but there are not enough field experiences in all the different regions which can provide us with an anthology of good field practices which are appropriate to all different ecological regions:

Availability of Good Field Experiences in Different Ecological Regions of India

Ecological Region	Traditional dominant land-use component	Field Experiences of ecological succession leading to economic growth
Semi-arid to sub humid hill and plateau regions	Mixed land-use consisting of integrated components of croplands-grasslands-tree and forest lands	Numerous field experiences
Arid regions	Grassland	No noteworthy field experiences
Humid slopes in hill and mountain regions	Forest lands together with shifting cultivation or terraced farming	No noteworthy field experiences
Highly flood-prone plains	Croplands interspersed with wetlands	No noteworthy field experiences

In order to develop good concepts to understand how the poverty-environment interface can be better managed in different ecological regions, the above case studies show that the following approach is the best:

(a) Start with developing an understanding of the traditional natural resource and village ecosystem in the region itself or in similar ecological regions in other parts of the world;

(b) Undertake village-level projects based on community participation to develop field practices which go beyond technological dimensions to include institutional, legal (that is, property rights) and financial dimensions; and,

(c) Develop macro-strategy framework to translate these micro-experiences into macro-programmes.

4.b. The Action Level

The action level will have to be at the level of the human settlement because it is only at that level that people can be involved in ecological enrichment and biomass generation programmes. Without popular participation, environmental regeneration is impossible.

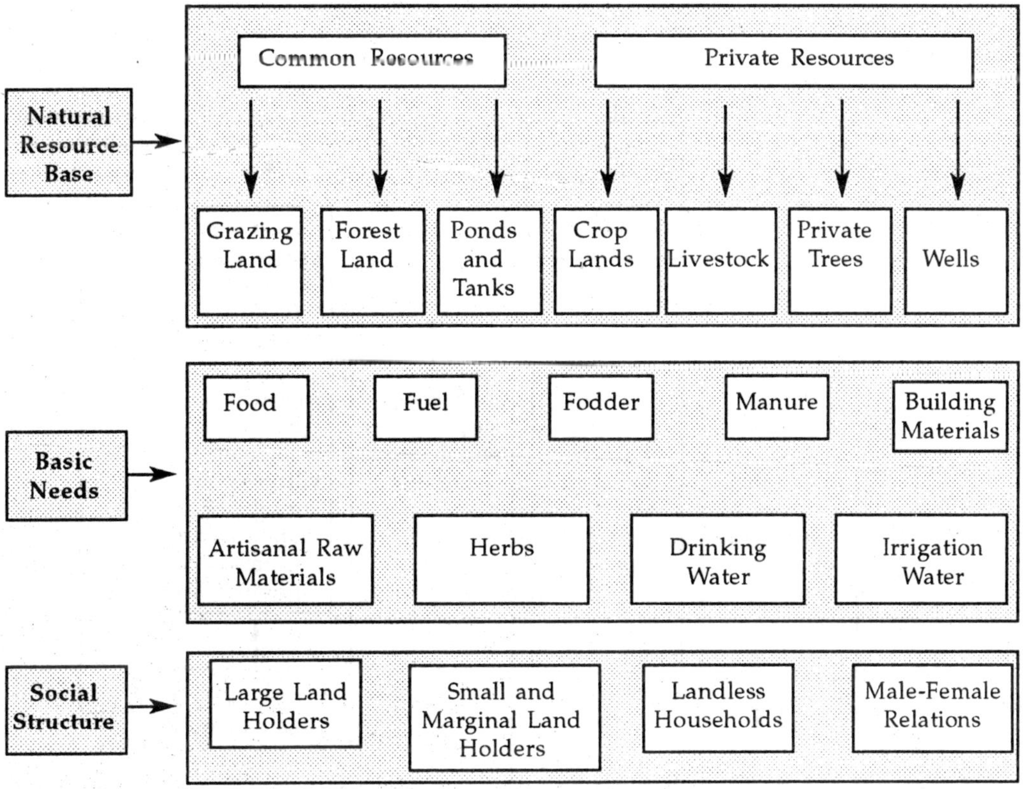

A Village Ecosystem Management and Improvement Plan will have to be developed keeping in mind the natural resource base of the village, its basic needs and its social structure. It is important to take the social structure into account as some groups in the village may depend more on common resources and the village ecosystem improvement plant should be such that it safeguards their access to the commons.

Fig. 6.5: Components of a Village Ecosystem Management and Improvement Plan

At this level, four different actions will have to be undertaken as follows:

4.b.1 Action Point 1: Village Ecosystem Planning

What India desperately needs today is the holistic enrichment of each of its village ecosystems. By holistic we mean an approach in which attempts are made to increase the productivity of all the components of the village ecosystem—from its grazing lands and forest lands to its croplands, water systems and animals—and in a way that this enrichment is sustainable.

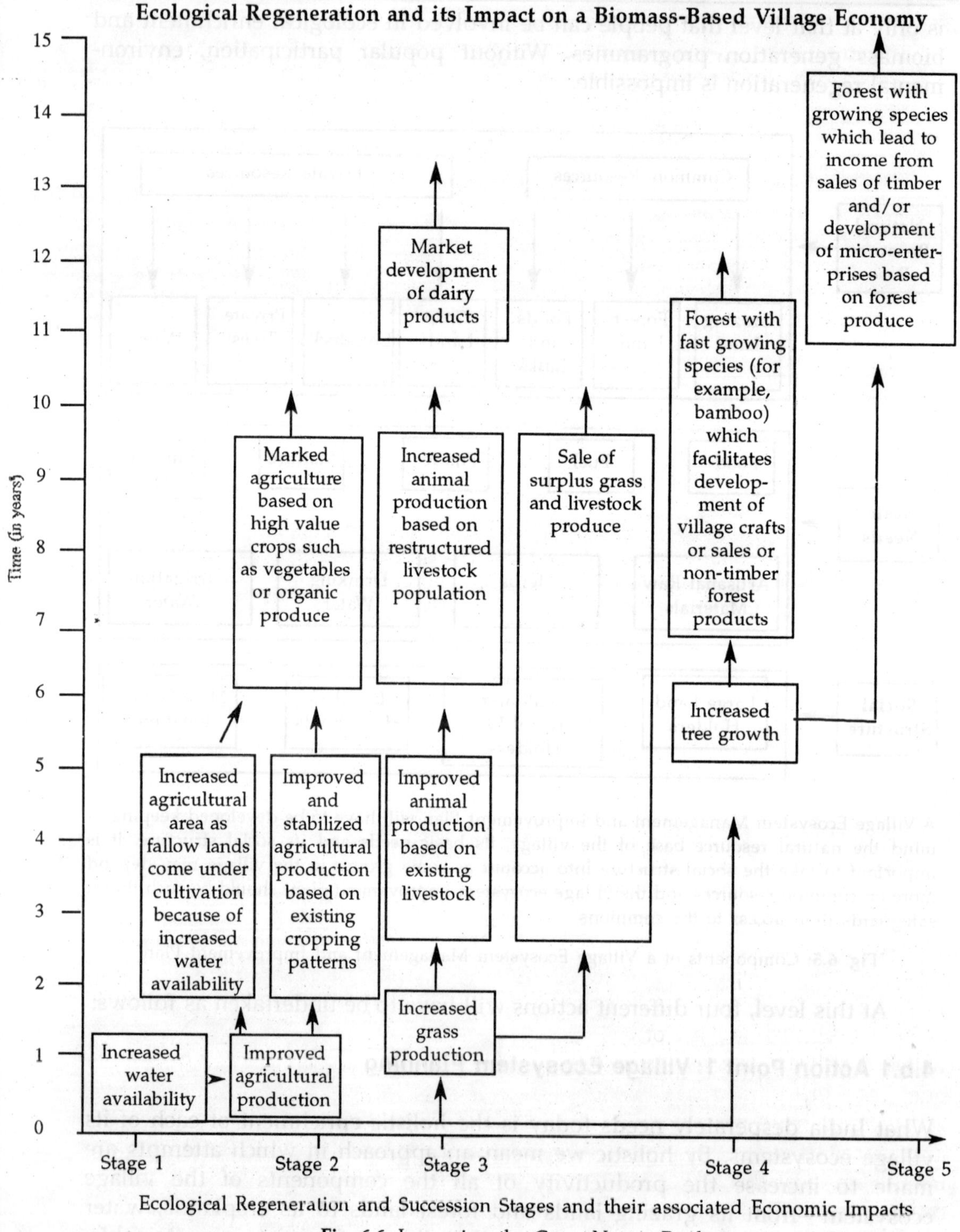

Fig. 6.6: Improving the Gross Nature Product

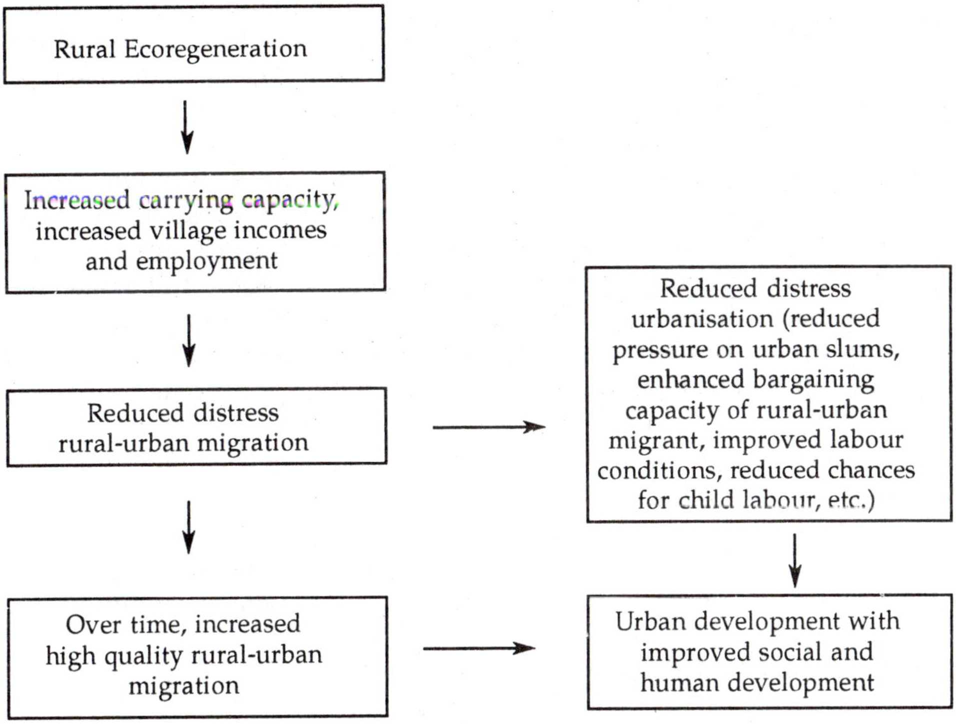

Fig. 6.7: Impact of Rural Ecoregeneration on Urban Poverty and Social Development

Current rural development efforts are extremely fragmented, they focus mostly on agriculture, and often the efforts are contradictory and counter-productive. For instance, government departments which build ponds and tanks do not want to do anything about getting an appropriate land-use implemented in the village to protect the catchment of these tanks. Those who look after animal husbandry or promote dairying operations pay little attention to increasing fodder supply. The only way to end these fragment approaches is to promote integrated village ecosystem planning.

This type of planning can be attempted only at the village-level, village by village, and not at any higher level. There are two important reasons for this. Firstly, there is an enormous diversity in Indian village ecosystems. No entity, even if it be at the level of a district, can plan for each Indian village. Even within one overall ecosystem, village agro-ecosystems can vary greatly from one another. Within the narrow confines of the high Himalaya, village ecosystems have considerable similarities but they also have considerable differences. If we take a village at the bottom of a valley and a village situated up the slope of the same mountain, we will find that their land-use systems differ greatly. Plans for the ecologically-sound development of each of these village ecosystems will necessarily differ and the planning process must be such that it allows for suitable solutions to be found to accommodate these differences. This can be achieved only if the planning is undertaken at the micro-level of a village.

Secondly, the stupendous task of planning for every Indian village can be achieved, rapidly and judiciously, only if it is participatory. It can be assisted by government bureaucracies but cannot be done by it. Despite the fact that migration to towns has led to an erosion in villager's interest in their immediate environment, experience shows that villagers still relate well to their immediate village ecosystem—their croplands, their grazing lands, their tree and forest lands, their animals and their ponds and tanks. And it is at this level, they can act most easily and readily, given the appropriate framework for action.

The most important goals of village ecosystem planning for biomass regeneration will have to be:

(1) enhancement of the total natural resource base of the village ecosystem;
(2) production of basic biomass needs of the village community on a priority basis; and
(3) equity in the distribution of biomass resources.

Thus, any village-level plan to be both sustainable and equitous would have to be a matrix of solutions which keeps in mind the specific natural resource base of the village, its biomass needs and its social structure (See Fig. 6.5).

Moreover, the commons have to be managed as commons by organizing and mobilizing village communities to develop the commons as a community enterprise. This is socially and ecologically a difficult option. This, however, does not mean that it cannot be done. The best efforts in the country to manage the environment show that this is indeed possible but provided the following three principles of control, unity and equity are observed:

1. *The commons must be brought under the control of the village communities.* This will mean divesting government agencies of their control over the common lands through changes in legislation. Though this does not necessarily mean transfer of ownership.
2. *The entire community must be involved in the protection of the commons under its control.* If only a section of the community is involved in the protection of a patch of the commons, then that section of the community must have clear control over a definite patch of the commons. In other words, the legal situation must be clear and whichever group controls a portion of the commons, it must control it

completely and protect it jointly. If only a few members of a group are left to protect a common resource against the wishes of the rest, they will fail. It does not matter whose goat enters the protected patch, the damage will be the same. All have to keep their animals away.

3. *All the members of a group will protect a common resource only if all of them know that they will benefit from the resource equally.*

These principles of *control, unity* and *equity* may sound difficult to implement in practice. But the experiences cited above show that given the right leadership and the suitable legal framework for community action, villagers will come together to protect and manage village resources.

Fig. 6.6 shows that this planning will have to continue for years if the maximum economic advantages of ecological regeneration are to be derived.

4.b.1 Action Point 2: Village Institutions

The obvious conclusion of all these experiences is that each settlement must have an institution of its own which brings its members together to manage its common resources and provides a forum for resolving disputes amongst them. And the extent of natural resources that belong to one settlement should be clearly defined to reduce the chances of inter-settlement tensions.

A village-level institution that can work with a high order of democracy in decision-making as well as discipline within the group members is needed.

In almost all the cases cited above village-level institutions have been created which parallel the concept of a Gram Sabha. Every family in the village is actively involved through this Gram Sabha-like institution in taking decisions of common interest to the village.

Open public forums can work much better than elected councils to bring about good natural resource management and sorting out intra-community differences, especially if properly created and adequately supported by the State, even within the existing circumstances of poverty and inequality. In those areas where inequality is intense, there will definitely be greater difficulties in achieving equity through any public forum that can be created in the existing circumstances but here too clearly the concept of Gram Sabha—which allows everyone to take part in decision-making—will be far better than an elected body.

Gandhiji's concept of village republics works very well for ecological regeneration—each village with an active community forum and an ecosystem of its own to control, manage and share, in which common resources are developed and improved and all get their due benefits. Only this form of decentralized decision-making can match the enormous cultural and biological diversity of Indian villages.

It is absolutely vital that all interest groups—from the landed to the landless and women—play an important role in the affairs of the village community. Experience in India shows that women take an active interest in programmes designed to improve ecological conditions because of their culturally determined role as fuel, fodder and water carriers. Women, of course, will be members of any Gram Sabha but women rarely participate in any institution dominated by men. Therefore, together with the establishment of Gram Sabhas of all adults, separate Sabhas or Mandals could be formed in every village, as a distinct sub-unit of the Gram Sabha, but with clearly and legally defined roles, rights and access to funds. The institutional mechanisms needed to ensure women's participation have to be thought through clearly. It is already clear from all the past experience in India that women's participation will make a crucial difference for ecological regeneration programmes and must be achieved on all counts.

4.b.3 Action Point 3: Enabling Property Rights

This is a very important point. As the village ecosystem will invariably consist of many components that are common property resources, which in many countries are owned by the State, the State will have to create appropriate community-based property rights so that the community can undertake the management of these resources. In each of the cases cited, there were numerous instances where people had to protest against bureaucratic interference. For example, as soon as Tarun Bharat Sangh had built its first *johad* in the village of Gopalpura, the Irrigation Department declared the structure "illegal" under the existing water laws. Under the Rajasthan Drainage Act of 1956, "water resources standing/collected either on private or public land (including groundwater) belong to the Government of Rajasthan." The villagers were asked to "remove" these structures as all drains and small streams are government property. The irrigation agency first argued that a downstream dam would get reduced water because of these village structures. Later it changed its stand to say that these unauthorized structures could get washed away and flood local villages. The next rains, ironically, saw several "official" structures being washed away but not the *johads* built by the people. After a protracted fight, the charges were dropped by the administration. The people refused to allow their *johads* being broken down. Later the rules were amended to allow people's participation in the creation of water conservation structures.

4.b.4 Action Point 4: Village Funds

No village institution can work without money. In the present system, from the

Centre to the State, to the district and finally to the block, finances for community development are controlled by various functionaries and agencies of the government. Ultimately, only a proportion reaches the community and is spent on projects over which it has no control and for which it has not set any priority.

Village institutions can raise substantial sums of money for the common good especially if they can organize their common property resources to reach a high level of productivity.

If used properly, this money can be used further by the village institutions to increase the productivity of the common land and water systems. The commons will support the economic growth of the village through supply of food, fuel, fodder, artisanal raw materials, wood and monetary resources for development. But the village should also save and invest in the ecological improvement of the commons. Then we will see a kind of cyclical growth, pushing the rural economy into an upward spiral.

But to do all this, any village institution will need start-up funds. This is where the role of government funding is crucial. The government ought to provide village institutions directly with financial grants. These grants can be minimal but they should be sufficient to enthuse the people to get the feeling that they can set their own priorities. We have seen that once so enthused, village communities readily put in even free labour to undertake community activities.

To direct people towards specific activities, which the State considers ecologically and scientifically appropriate, a system of matching grants for specific activities could be worked out. So, for instance, if the government wants to promote afforestation in a region, the villages in the region could be given an incentive to plant trees by offering them a matching contribution to the amount they are prepared to spend towards this activity. In other words, the government can still enthuse villagers to move towards priorities set by the nation as a whole. But this approach will also give the villagers a chance to decide.

To sum up, it is possible to deal with the ecological poverty of people living in degraded ecosystems and, thus, put them on the path to sustainable economic development.

NOTES

1. Anil Agarwal and Sunita Narain. 1989. *Towards Green Villages: A Strategy for Environmentally-Sound and Participatory Rural Development*, Centre for Science and Environment, New Delhi.

2. Anil Agarwal. 1985. "Politics of the Environment", in *State of India's Environment 1984-85—The Second Citizens' Report*, Centre for Science and Environment, New Delhi.
3. P.R. Mishra *et al.* 1980. "Operational research project on watershed development for sediment, drought and flood control—Sukhomajri", Central Soil and Water Conservation Research and Training Institute, Chandigarh, *mimeo.*
4. Anil Agarwal and Sunita Narain. 1980. "Strategies for the Involvement of the landless and women in afforestation: Five case studies from India", World Employment Programme, International Labour Office, Geneva, *mimeo.*
5. Kanchan Chopra, Gopal Kedekodi and M.N. Murthy. 1990. *Participatory Development: People and Common Property Resources*, Sage Publications, New Delhi.
6. Madhu Sarin. 1996. *Joint Forest Management: The Haryana Experience*, Centre for Environment Education, Ahmedabad, pp. 2g, 29 and 198; and, Kanchan Chopra *et al.* 1998, *Sukhomajri and Dhamala Watersheds in Haryana: A participatory approach*, Institute of Economic Growth, New Delhi.
7. S.K. Dhar. 1997. "Chief Conservator of Forests, Government of Haryana", *personal communications.*
8. S.K. Mittal. 1998. Principal Scientist, Central Soil and Water Conservation Research and Training Institute, Chandigarh, *Personal Communications.*
9. S.C. Gulati and Suresh Sharma. 1998. "Population Poverty-Environment Interface Case Study of Sukhomajri, Jattamajri, Ralegan Siddhi and Panoli villages", Centre for Science and Environment, New Delhi, *mimeo.*
10. S.L. Rao and I. Natarajan. 1996. *Indian Market Demographics: The Consumer Classes*, Global Business Press/National Council of Applied Economic Research, New Delhi, pp. 49 and 133.
11. Richard Mahapatra. 1997. Field Report on Adarsh Gaon Yojana, Centre for Science and Environment, New Delhi, *mimeo.*
12. Anna Hazare. 1997. *Ralegan Siddhi: A Veritable Transformation*, Ralegan Siddhi Pariwar, Ralegan Siddhi.
13. Kanchan Chopra and D.V. Subba Rao. 1996. "Economic Evaluation of Soil and Water Conservation Programmes in Watersheds", Institute of Economic Growth, Delhi, *mimeo.*
14. Annasaheb Hazare ud, Microwatershed Development, *Mimeo* and, Anna Hazare 1998, *personal communication.*
15. Anna Hazare. 1998. *Personal Communication.*
16. Anon. 1998. *Putting Tradition back into Practice: Johad—Watershed in Alwar District, Rajasthan*, UN-Inter Agency Working Group on Water and Environmental Sanitation, New Delhi.
17. G.D. Agarwal ud, An Engineer's Evaluation of Water Conservation Efforts of Tarun Bharat Sangh in 36 villages of Alwar District, Tarun Bharat Sangh, Alwar, *mimeo.*
18. Anon. 1998. *op. cit.*, p. 17.
19. Anil Agarwal and Richard Mahapatra. 1999. "Madhya Pradesh: Regaining Paradise", in Anil Agarwal, Sunita Narain and Srabani Sen (ed), 1999, *State of India's Environment-1999: Citizens' Fifth Report*, Centre for Science and Environment, New Delhi, pp. 33-53.
20. Richard Mahapatra. 1999. "Success Spreads", in Anil Agarwal, Sunita Narain and Srabani Sen (ed) 1999, *ibid.*, p. 33.
21. Chief Executive Officer. 1998. *Zilla Panchayat*, Jhabua, quoted in Anil Agarwal 1998, The house that Digvijay Built, in *Down to Earth*, Society for Environmental Communications, New Delhi, December 31, p. 35.
22. Anon. 1998. "Rajiv Gandhi Mission for Watershed Development: Key Findings of Intermediate Assessment of Watershed Management Programmes in Jhabua District", Government of Madhya Pradesh, *Mimeo*, quoted in Anil Agarwal, 1999, Economic Gains from Ecological Wealth, in Anil Agarwal, Sunita Narain and Srabani Sen (ed) 1999, *op. cit.*, p. 45.

23. B.N. Nag and G.N. Kathpalia. 1975. "Water Resources of India", in *Water and Human Needs*, Paper presented in the Proceedings of the Second World Congress on Water Resources, Vol. 2, CBIP, New Delhi, quoted in Anil Agarwal, Sunita Narain (ed) 1985, *State of India's Environment 1984-85: Second Citizens' Report*, Centre for Science and Environment, New Delhi.
24. Anil Agarwal, Sunita Narain (ed). 1997. *Dying Wisdom: Rise, Fall and Potential of India's Traditional Water Harvesting Systems, State of India's Environment: A Citizens' Report*, Centre for Science and Environment, New Delhi.
25. N.C. Saxena, Secretary, Department of Rural Development, Government of India, *personal communications*.
26. Anon. 1998. CSE Briefing Paper: Potential of Water Harvesting—Traditions, Technologies, Policies and Social Mobilisation, Centre for Science and Environment, *mimeo*; and, Anon. 1998, Draft Recommendations of the CSE Conference on water harvesting—Technologies, Policies and Social Mobilisation, New Delhi, October 3-5, *mimeo*.

7 Integrated Management of Water and Land for Sustainable Development in Semi-Arid Areas

V. Ballabh and P. Thomas

1. Introduction

For India, a densely populated and biomass-based society, sustainable management of land, water, forests and other natural resources is crucial for the survival of the people. As India faced chronic shortages of biomass, competing claims made on the dwindling resource bases led to social conflicts which, initially localized, developed into powerful environmental movements during the 1970's and 1980's. A positive outcome of these conflicts and discourses on the environmental movement has been the attempts by non-governmental organizations (NGOs) to explore new ways to redeem the health of India's natural resources. In the early 1990's, however, India faced a crisis of balance of payment which shifted attention towards the process of liberalization of the Indian economy. "Faster economic growth" and "exports" have re-emerged as the key words for development. Planners and policy makers in India commonly believe that rapid economic growth would resolve the twin problems of poverty and sustainability.

The purpose of this chapter is to review perspectives on sustainable development, economic growth and their interlinkages. It is argued that the neo-classical economic paradigm of sustainable development suffers from a basic fallacy that natural resources and man-made capitals are completely substitutable. Furthermore, the neo-classical economic paradigm considers physical and technological capital as the only relevant variables for economic growth. Since these assumptions are not correct (other forms of capital such as human capital and social capital are important for growth and development), the strategies based on these assumptions for sustainable development are unlikely to lead to either realistic or desired outcomes. This chapter presents an alternative development strategy, based on microlevel initiatives to manage human aspirations and to build human, social and natural capital stock for sustainable development. Finally, we summarize the discussion and argue that only pragmatic policies and institutions that enhance the people's capacity would lead us toward sustainable development, and prevent a social and ecological breakdown.

2. Sustainable Development

The World Commission on Environment and Development (1987, hereafter the Brundtland Commission) defined sustainable development as development that meets the needs of the present generation without curtailing the capacity of future generations to meet their own needs. Sustainable development as a goal rejects those policies and practices that support current living standards by depleting the production base, including the natural resource base that leaves future generations with poorer prospects than our own (Repetto 1986). There is a general agreement as to the goals of sustainable development. However, considerable differences exist among scholars about the paths to achieve these goals.

The dominant paradigm among the economists is more concerned with the relative scarcity of resources than their absolute scarcity. This paradigm emanates from the work of Solow (1974) and Hartwick (1977). Hartwick (1977) demonstrated that Solow's intergenerational equity of constant consumption could be achieved if all returns from exhaustible resources are invested in reproducible capital. The rule has intuitive appeal in the sense that it implies that all rent (contribution to the production over efficient path of extraction costs) from a resource is invested in reproducible capital. Given that the resource is extracted efficiently and rent is not consumed but added to the capital stock, sustainability would be achieved (Common 1995). These assertions, however, are questionable. Hartwick assumed that man-made capital could completely substitute for natural resources capital.[1] In fact, natural and man-made capital are often complementary to each other, and the past high rates of return on the man-made capital were possible only with unsustainable rates of natural resources utilization and the liquidation of natural capital (Korten 1991-92). The societies driven solely by economic efficiency favour over-capitalization leading to unsustainable use of natural resources; sustainability is replaced with substitutability, and the future is discounted, particularly when it is difficult to know the preference function of future generations (Becker and Ostrom 1995).

Other scholars, particularly ecologists, in contrast, define sustainability in terms of resilience and stability of productive capacity, and treat humans as a part of the biospheric system rather than as a consuming unit. Stability refers to the propensity for a return to an equilibrium level following a disturbance, and resilience system functions in essentially the same manner in the face of a major sock (Conway 1985). The concept of ecological sustainability is imprecise, and *a priori* it is difficult to determine a system's stability and resilience (Common 1995). It is evident that the meaning of sustainability differs and it is a complex and contested concept. It is more important, therefore, to discuss what is being sustained for how long and for whose benefit and at whose cost, over what area and measured by what criteria (Pretty 1995).

While it is difficult to give a precise and workable definition of sustainability, it is possible to weigh up trade off and agree on the criteria for measuring sustainability. For example, practices which reduce soil erosion and distress migration may be considered as more sustainable than those that accentuate these problems. We, therefore, define sustainability as those strategies of managing human affairs and resources which alleviate poverty, reduce social inequality and also restore ecological imbalances.

3. Economic Growth and Sustainable Development

In spite of severe limitations, in the neoclassical economic paradigm, accelerated economic growth and integration of the world economy are presumed to be the keys to human progress. In fact, the Brundtland Commission concluded that "if a large part of the developing world is to avoid economic, social and environmental catastrophe, it is essential that global economic growth be revitalized". The world's economic growth should rise to 5-10 times the current output, and accelerated growth in industrial countries is essential to generate demand for the products of less-developed countries. Thus the Brundtland Commission "fundamentally contradicted its own analysis that growth and over-consumption are the root causes of the problem" (Korten 1991-92). Moreover, focus on rapid economic growth concentrates on physical capital and ignores social capital. Like physical capital, social capital also opens up some opportunities and restricts others. Social capital is created by individuals spending time and effort with other individuals that is otherwise not possible (Ostrom 1994). However, unlike physical capital, which has characteristics of pure private good, social capital is pure public good and, therefore, suffers from "underinvestment" and "free-riding".

The rapid economic growth is neither a prerequisite nor in itself sufficient for human progress, and the conventional approach to measuring human well-being in terms of Gross National Product (GNP) is increasingly being questioned. For example, Sen (1987) argues that "the value of living standards lies in the living, not in the possessing of commodities that have derivatives and varying relevance". Instead, he argues that "well-being" has to do with being well, which at the most elementary level means being able to live long, being well nourished, being healthy and literate and so on, Once the measures such as educational attainment, life expectancy and progress toward the elimination of absolute poverty are also included, the route for social progress does not depend only upon economic growth (Dreze and Sen 1989, Sen 1993). Many countries which have little economic growth (measured in conventional terms) have managed to reduce mortality and increase life expectancy (Dreze and Sen 1989).

> "One economic reason why even very poor countries that are politically inclined to reduce mortality and increase basic education can afford to do so is that services involved are labour intensive and labour is relatively cheap in poor countries. For example, China, Sri Lanka and the State of Kerala in India have been able to provide extensive health care and education services despite modest public budgets. By contrast, many countries have managed to raise GNP or GDP quite rapidly, but have not used resources generated to advance health and education, and as a result the impact on mortality has been rather minimal."

This empirical evidence does not support the idea that for an improvement in the general well-being, rapid economic growth is a necessary condition, as it is generally believed. In fact, Anand and Ravallion (1993) found that the relationship between life expectancy and real per capita income was insignificant once they controlled the incidence of poverty (p. 141). Thus, it is only if growth is "pro poor" that it would promote general well-being. Empirical evidence also supports the idea that regionalized and concentrated economic growth makes development lopsided. The efforts of the past 50 years of industrial development in India have created conditions in which millions of people are migrating under distress and living like refugees on the margins of developed areas. Thus, Gadgil and Guha observe:

> "As the natural world recedes, so shrink the capacities of local ecosystems to support these people. Dams and mines, for instance, have physically displaced millions of peasants and tribals in independent India. Others have fled as forests, and with them, springs, have vanished. These people constitute the ecological refugees who live on the margins of prosperity, as sugarcane harvesters in western Maharashtra or farm labourer in Punjab, as hawkers and domestic servants of Patna or Hyderabad. As many as one-third of the Indian population live today as displaceds, with little that they can freely pick up from natural world, but not much money to buy the commodities that the shops are brimming with either." (Gadgil and Guha 1995, p. 4).

As India pursues faster her economic growth through those strategies which promote exports, the pressure on natural resources would build up on forests, fish, water, leather and textiles. The impact of the export of natural resources would be felt more by those living at the margins, either through diversions of resources traditionally used by them, or through pollution-related damage (Kurien 1993)[2]. One way to reduce pressures on the natural resources is to shift development strategies from the current macro perspective, in terms of trade, export and integration with world economy, to a micro level, restoring the productive potential of land, water springs and forests through an integrated management of all natural resources. For this to succeed, the ecological restoration and economic growth are to be embedded with the people's life-supporting system. This is not an impossible task. However, it is slow and painful but sustainable as the following case study demonstrates. The strategy has the potential to reverse the trend of distress migration and prevent millions of people from becoming *"migrant coolies"*.

4. Path to Sustainable Development: The Shankerpura Experiment

4.a. The Setting

The village of Shankarpura is located in the eastern part of the Panchmahals district of Gujarat State (India). It is a typical village of the semi-arid tropics. The topography of the village is undulating with steep slopes in certain pockets and plain lands in low-lying areas. Agro-climatically, the village falls in the semi-arid tropical area of western India. Demographically, it is in the tribal belt which stretches across the Indian States of Rajasthan, Gujarat and Madhya Pradesh. There are 200 households in the village, and all of them belong to the *Bhil* tribe.

Geographically, the northern and eastern portions of the Panchmahals district are covered by hills and forests, intercepted by cultivated plains in villages situated in river valleys. The soils of these areas are shallow, hilly, full of rocky tracks, and interspersed with deep black soil in the valleys. The normal annual rainfall in this part of the district is about 800 mm., though with very high variability. Since the eastern part is highly undulating, much of the rainfall is lost as runoff. The groundwater in this area accumulates only in cracks and fissures. The rocks are found in the basement beneath the younger alluvial and sedimentary formations, which constitute the principal aquifers (GOG 1982). The topography in the western part of the district is flat, punctuated in isolated places with hills, very fertile soil with a slightly higher annual rainfall than that found in the northern and eastern parts of the district (GOG 1982).

In the undulating topography of the Panchmahals, forests have an important role in reducing soil erosion and preventing the washing away of the vital top soil. Thereby the forest maintains soil fertility. The following is a vivid description of the forests in the Panchmahals district made by a Chief Conservator of Forests:

> "The west, though well wooded, has a few forest trees and the east, except for fruit trees in fields and some stony hill lands in the remoter villages, is bare of timber. In the center, the Godhra woodlands stretch over undulation plains, the side of small granite hills and those in Halol partly over the plains, partly over the rocky uplands, and partly on the slopes of the Pavagad hills" (Patel 1972).

At the turn of the century, however, the district had rich forest resources, covering about 40 per cent of the area. Some parts had dense forests, even as recent as independence. According to the *Imperial Gazetteer*, some of the erstwhile princely States of the district were almost 100 per cent forested.[3] In contrast are the adverse consequences of deforestation—erosion of top soil, reduction in fertility and decline in productivity. The process of deforestation has been similar to what happened to forests in other parts of India. The government policies not only commercialized forest products and intensified resource use but also alienated human beings from the forest (Gadgil and Guha 1995, Guha 1989). As a result, the tribal community which had been a hunter and gatherer community was forced to become an agricultural one (Ahmed 1994). However, increasing population and reduction of fertility due to soil erosion meant that the agricultural sector could not sustain the livelihood of the people. As a consequence, "to keep the household going', a large majority of the people from this part had to migrate to other parts of the State (Thomas and Ballabh 1995).

While resource degradation and poverty mark the landscape in the Panchmahals, one also comes across islands where this trend has been reversed. Part of Dahod and Jhalod talukas of the district are a case in point, where an NGO, the Sadguru water and Development Foundation (SWDF) has been working since 1974.[4] The heterogeneity of the resource base in such regions demands that any development intervention take into account the location-specific nature of the resource condition in the area, and the people's understanding of the management of the resources. The basic approach adopted by SWDF is to improve the livelihood of the people through an integrated management of the natural resources. The interventions made by SWDF in Shankerpura villages in Panchmahals district, and the changes that have taken place, are discussed in the following section.

4.b. Cooperative Lift Irrigation Scheme

A series of visits to Shankerpura made it obvious to SWDF that the irrigation potential of water stored in the village tank was tremendous. However, the proper utilization of this valuable resource required water to be lifted from tanks, located in the valley, to the settlements and cultivated areas located at a higher elevation on steep slopes. Initial discussions were met with skepticism and apprehension, not so much about the potential of the project as the motivation of the agency.[5] However once actual physical construction work commenced, the apprehension and suspicion gradually waned, and in 1976 the villagers agreed to draw up a cooperative lift irrigation scheme.

The scheme cost Rs. 3,36,000 and covered a designed net command of 300 acres. It has 150 members. Water is lifted 140 feet to the main distribution chamber, and then on to the 16 outlet points. The water is taken from the tank to the main distribution chamber through an underground pipeline. From there it is distributed by gravitational flow. So as to ensure the required flow to the farmers fields, only selected outlets are operated on a particular day. Usually four outlets operate at a time. The operation of the outlet points is fixed in advance. So is the price of watering. In the winter (November-March) of 1994-95, the irrigation charge was Rs. 200 per acre, per irrigation. The recovery of past dues before the next watering is mandatory. Equality and fairness in the distribution of water are ensured by the management committee, operating through the distributors.

SWDF provided a package of services which included an investment fund, execution of scheme, initial operations, maintenance fund, and support for agriculture extension. In the initial phase, SWDF also provided managerial support in identifying young, energetic people for the post of secretary, operators and distributors; SWDF trained them, and paid their salaries. However, today all management functions are looked after by the management committee, chosen from and by the villagers. At present it has a secretary, an operator, four water distributors (seasonal), and a watchman on its payroll, all of them being paid from the revenues of the Cooperative.

The day-to-day management is carried out by an elected/selected management committee consisting of 11 members. The management committee decides the prices, distribution system, receiving of dues and conflict resolution. The social structure in the village as well as the customs among the tribe also help in resolving disputes and conflicts. *Traditionally, within the Bhil community, decisions are taken by consensus, rather than by majority of votes, and discussions and negotiations continue until a consensus is reached* (Verma 1978, italics our emphasis). The monitoring and enforcement costs are reduced substantially once the decisions are made by general consensus, and a commitment to follow the rules obtains (Ostrom 1990).

The population of Shankerpura is dispersed in small hamlets of a few families each, called *falias*. Almost all the *falias* are represented in the Cooperative Lift Irrigation Society. The criteria for the choice of the individuals, however, are the moral qualities of the person. Individuals chosen as the chairman and vice-chairman have to be well respected for their qualities and character (Singh 1987). It appears that social acceptance, more than competence, counts in the selection of members of the management committee.

Overall, the Cooperative Lift Irrigation Scheme is functioning well and it is financially self-sustaining. Starting from a net irrigated command area of 90 acres in 1976-77, it reached 300 acres in 1982-83. In more recent times, its command has shrunk to about 170 acres, primarily because many farmers have constructed their own wells within the command of the Scheme, in the construction of which the income generated from increased agricultural productivity was a major contributing factor. In addition, irrigation has also led to the appreciation of the value of land. This phenomenon of sharp appreciation, in turn, raises the socio-economic status of the landowner and also improves his creditworthiness for both institutional and non-institutional finance. The social status in such a situation of an owner of one to two acres goes up very high and he becomes a respectable member of the society by virtue of the high value of his irrigated land (SWDF 1995).[6]

4.c. Soil and Water Conservation

The Gujarat Government initiated soil conservation programmes in the Panchmahals district in 1960 (Patel 1972). These included (i) contour bunding, (ii) afforestation, (iii) reclamation of land, (iv) *nala*-plugging, (v) *Kotar* reclamation and terracing. However, many of these structures were not protected and were washed away (Shylendra 1994).

In Shankerpura also, contour bunding was done some thirty years ago. These structures are protected, maintained and strengthened by the people. Irrigation (through the Lift Scheme) improved the productivity of the farmers of Shankerpura village land and, therefore, they do not migrate for searching employment. In order to further enhance water harvesting, SWDF constructed six check dams. It has helped in two ways: (i) water recharge in the surrounding area has increased and this has provided impetus to farmers to construct private wells for irrigation purposes, and (ii) some farmers directly lift water with portable pumps, which, in turn, increases the area under irrigation. The Cooperative Lift Scheme and the construction of check dams together have provided incentives for private investment.

4.d. Farm Forestry

Farm forestry in Shankerpura which had over 200 acres of private land was started in 1982 as a part of the overall watershed development programme. Tree plantations were done mostly on bunds, private inferior lands, field strips.

SWDF consciously chooses to work on private wasteland for two reasons: (i) large scope, and (ii) it avoids transaction costs associated with the working of community land and, in the case of forest land, it avoids obtaining permission from the Forest Departments. In the initial stages only eucalyptus was planted but now a number of other species, including fruit trees, are promoted, Still, farmers continue to prefer eucalyptus in this area, as it is a fast-growing species.

The benefits of tree-growing in Shankerpura have been investigated by a number of researchers (Balooni and Singh 1994, Conroy 1991, Grant 1989, Sharma *et al.* 1991, and Thomas and Ballabh 1995). One of the villagers captured the transformation brought about by tree-growing in the cryptic remark, *shanti che* (there is peace). He elaborated this notion of "peace" as the qualitative change in the condition of a household's existence, where the basic needs are met without too much struggle, where people enjoy a certain degree of confidence that in an emergency they have an asset to fall back upon, and need no longer run from one door to another pleading for loans. One of the manifestations of this transformation, as already noted, is the dramatic decline in the proportion of people who migrate in search of casual wage employment: earlier about 75-80 per cent of the households depended on migration, whereas now only about 5-10 per cent need to resort to migration. Grant (1989) reports a similar impact of SWDF's social forestry programme on migration. *In the 11 villages she studied, the reduction in migration was found to be 80 per cent* (italics our emphasis). A recent study of a nearby village where SWDF has made intervention in a part of the village suggests that the number of persons per household migrating has declined significantly and female migration has almost completely vanished in the areas where SWDF makes intervention; in other areas it continues either at the same level or has increased (Shylendra and Rani 1998).

It is the scarcity year that tests the robustness of the survival mechanism of a community. In this, Shankerpura has now a different story to tell. During the scarcity of 1992, for example, very few villagers had to leave the village in search of employment; most survived with income from the sale of trees. Coping with emergencies, be it drought, illness, or any other calamity, often involves the sale of assets. Conroy (1991) found that during the drought of 1989 in this region "trees were the main assets sold, both in terms of the number of families selling them, and in terms of the mean income obtained," underlining one of the important uses of trees, namely, as insurance substitutes. Moreover, it was observed that "partly because of the trees and partly because of other improvements to their standard of living, other less favoured insurance substitutes, such as land sales and seasonal migration, appear to have largely ceased" (1991:29, 36).

One of the surest indicators of whether the improvement in the quality of life will be sustained or not is the changes that take place in the asset structure of the household. To the extent that one of the prime avenues of utilization of income from trees has been in productivity-enhancing investments (construction of wells, purchase of oil engines, purchase of livestock, development of land, etc.), tree-growing has certainly led to the consolidation of the production base (Table 7.1). The table also shows that the income from trees has been used to meet a number of household needs like buying food and clothing, education of children, purchase of medicine, purchase of jewelry, and conducting marriages. Balooni and Singh (1994) estimated the per acre per annum financial rate of return to be 33 per cent.

TABLE 7.1: **Utilisation Pattern of Income accruing from the Sale of Trees**

Various uses	Number of respondents* reporting the use
Purchase of livestock:	
Bullocks	20
Others (cows, goats, etc.)	8
Construction of wells	3
Construction of houses	4
Repayment of debts	5
Purchase of jewelry	5
Releasing of mortgaged land/jewelry	3
Purchase of fertiliser/seeds	4
Purchase of clothes	11
Cash gifts/bride wealth in marriages	10
Children's education	8
Medical expenses	4
Purchase of food items	11

*Total number of respondents in the sample = 30.

Adapted from Conroy (1991:18).

In assessing the benefits of the farm forestry programme, we cannot ignore the environmental consequences of the choice of a particular species, in the farm forestry programme of Shankerpura, the species planted is mainly eucalyptus. But its cultivation has been criticized on the grounds that it led to a reduction of the acreage under food crops, and that it promoted the environmentally undesirable monoculture of eucalyptus. The case against eucalyptus has been most vigorously argued by Shiva and Bandhopadhya (1985), who claim that "eucalyptus plantations in dry lands drain the soil of its fertility and moisture. . ." (They) are thus ecologically incompatible with farm forestry, since they act as sink, not as a source of nutrients and moisture. Similarly Saxena (1994) has concluded that the benefit cost ratio of eucalyptus plantations on bunds reduces from 9.2 to just 2.0 if one takes account of the crop losses due to plantation.

The experience of Shankerpura tree-growers, however, does not corroborate these findings. According to the growers, the cultivated area does not decrease due to eucalyptus plantation since the plantation is done on wasteland. Neither do they perceive losses due to plantation of eucalyptus on bunds. On the contrary, as one of the farmers remarked to us, because the bunds are raised after the eucalyptus are planted, they reduce soil erosion during the rainy season. This, in turn, improves the productivity of the nearby land.

4.e. The Changes

In any attempt at assessing the change of particular strategies, two points need to be kept in mind. One is the difficulty in establishing the causal link between a particular outcome and its cause when more than one factor is at work. In the case of the changes that have taken place in Shankerpura, for instance, one can identify different causes—government-sponsored tribal development programmes, SWDF-initiated watershed development, irrigation and forestry development programmes.

The other point is the tendency to confine impact analysis exclusively to quantifiable variables, to the neglect of often more significant qualitative changes in the life of the community. This limitation is evident in the indicators used in Table 7.2. They do not capture adequately the full significance of the phrase used by a villager to describe the change in his life, *shanti che* (there is peace). The peace referred to here is more than the contentment derived from material possessions; it also stands for the confidence and assurance that come from the knowledge that now they possess the capacity to cope with emergencies on their own, without having to enter into exploitative debt relations; that in order to "keep the household going," they no longer need to assume the socially looked-down-upon occupation of a *migrant coolie*. The criteria used in Table 7.2 to assess the changes brought about in Shankerpura are, therefore, to be considered as indicative rather than exhaustive (see Table 7.2).

TABLE 7.2: **Developmental Interventions and Socio-economic Change in Shankerpura**

Indicators	Before (1976)	After (1993)
I. On-farm Changes		
Cropping intensity	Wet season only	Wet+winter seasons Summer (partial)
Cropping pattern	Maize+pigeon pea; minor oilseeds	Maize+pigeon pea wheat+gram mixed with mustard (winter) onions (summer)
Land under any kind of use (ha).	328	568
All kinds of wasteland (ha). (grazing land, etc.)	260	20
II. Changes in Levels of Living		
Availability of foodgrains for home consumption		
— Normal year	4 months	8-10 months
— Scarcity year	Less than one month	4-5 months
Two full meals a day (% households)	20	80
Hand-pumps for drinking water	Nil	6
New houses constructed out of own wood	Nil	160
III. Changes in the Asset Structure and Occupational Pattern		
Land development measure (land levelling terracing, etc.) (Ha)	Nil	240
Land under irrigation (Ha)	Nil	260
No. of families having access to irrigation	Nil	200 (lift irrigation, portable pumps, private wells)
No. of private wells	2	80
Water harvesting structures		
— check dams	Nil	6
— coop. lift irrigation	Nil	1
No. of trees/plants in the village (approx.)	100	600 thousands
Occupation	Agri.+seasonal migration for wage labour	Cultivation
Dependence on seasonal migration	75%	5%normal year 10% in scarcity year
Educated persons serving outside	4	70
No. of teachers	1	14

Source: Thomas and Ballabh 1995.

The changes, grouped into on-farm changes, changes in the levels of living, asset structure and occupational patterns, have been subjected to "before" and "after" analysis. The indicators of on-arm changes point to the improvement in the primary source of livelihood of the population, viz. agriculture, be it in terms of improvement in the cropping intensity, the capacity to grow new and more crops, or the extent to which hitherto unutilized land is brought under cultivation. Thus, for instance, compared to the 260 ha of land that remained unused in 1976, by 1993 all but 20 ha was brought into cultivation.

The improvement in the livelihood base is reflected in the changes in the standards of living. The ability to secure two square meals a day remains one of the most revealing indexes of a household's living condition, and the data point to a substantial improvement in this. The phenomenal increase in the quality of the housing in the village is closely related to the farm forestry programme launched in 1982. SWDF records show that the cost of wood used in house construction is in the region of Rs. 20,000-30,000 per house.

The extent to which the above improvement are sustainable depends on the changes that have taken place in the means of production. The data on the improvements in the three key resources—land, water and trees—show that significant investments have been made in the consolidation of these resources. In this, trees hold a pre-eminent position, since they have become one of the major sources of income and an important insurance substitute.

The changes in the occupational pattern to which the data point are another proof of the improvement that has been brought about in the resource base of the village. The fact that the percentage of the labour force dependent on migrant labour has come down from 75 per cent to 5 per cent proves that the productivity of the land and other resources has been restored to a degree that the village is able to feed its people, and its people need no longer wander around in the cities and prosperous villages of south Gujarat to eke out a living. All these are different facets of the changes captured in the expression, *shanti che*.

4.f. Why does Shankerpura Succeed?

The transformation of Shankerpura consequent upon the intervention by SWDF holds important lessons for any programme aimed at reversing the degradation of resources and immiserisation of people. The factors that contributed to the intervention being an effective instrument of change are likely to be critical reconditions if similar interventions are made to achieve their objectives.

The aim of SWDF was not just growing trees *per se*, nor constructing a lift irrigation scheme. The overarching concern in all its programmes has been to improve the living conditions of the tribal communities, in strengthening the livelihood system in these villages. To the extent that this could not be achieved without improving the natural resource base, and the management of these resources, attention had to be paid to the development of water and trees, the two most crucial resources for the people in the area. Hence the priorities set for watershed development in general, and irrigation and farm forestry in particular, are to be viewed as essential components of a broader programme aimed at strengthening the livelihood system in these villages. This integrated approach and holistic understanding of the needs of the village community are put forward by Thomas and Ballabh (1995) as one of the explanations as to why tree-growing in Shankerpura did not end up as another instance of giving in to the departmental compulsions of meeting the targets, as has happened in so many cases, and instead led to the programme being accepted by the people and becoming an effective path to development and change.

If a programme were to be effective, the people's participation was essential. In order to elicit participation, people had to be first convinced of the utility and feasibility of the Shankerpura. In this, the proper sequencing, in terms of both the type of activity and the scale of activity, was of extreme importance. The compulsions to leave the village in search of wage labour could not be removed by a measure like tree-growing, whose benefits would take 4-5 years to appear. Meeting the need for food and other basic needs of day-to-day existence could not wait for the trees to grow. In other words, there had to be some source of income to meet these needs, and hence attention had to be paid to agriculture even before tree-growing. For agriculture to be a viable proposition in a rain-fed area, water is critical. In order to guarantee this, the first intervention had to be in irrigation. Whether the decision to start with the construction of the lift irrigation scheme was the outcome of a clear understanding of these causal linkages or an expression of blind faith in the success formula of the green revolution is a moot point. The important point is that beginning with irrigation and land development, which led to cultivation being accepted as a more satisfactory and rewarding option to eking out one's living through migration, increased the capacity of the people to take up a profitable but long-gestation programme like tree-growing.

Sequencing in terms of scale of operation was also important. For a tribal community of first generation settlers, new to working with modern technologies like lift irrigation and intensive cultivation, to be willing to undertake big, risky schemes like lift irrigation, the confidence in their carrying capacity as well as their conviction in the utility of the project had to be built up through smaller, less risky initial intervention. This is precisely the approach that SWDF adopted in their intervention in Shankerpura.

The presence of a mechanism to bear the high transaction costs in the initial stages of any major intervention was another factor that determined the success or failure of an intervention. For a scheme to take off, heavy demands will be made on the organisational skills, negotiating skills, as well as capital. Despite not possessing these capabilities at the start, if the tribal community in Shankerpura was able to go ahead with different programmes, it was largely on account of the presence of SWDF which supplied the capabilities that were absent in the beginning. These included technical expertise required for the installation and maintenance of irrigation equipments, organisational input to promote sustainable people's organisation, liaisoning with various government departments for critical inputs such as electrical power, licence to lift water from the tank, saplings for forestry programmes, and so on. While intervening in the social process and designing of people's organization, for example, Cooperative Lift Irrigation Society, SWDF consciously used internal tribal leadership to frame rules and norms for sharing resources, particularly irrigation water from the lift. This gave social respectability to SWDF in the area.

5. Summary and Conclusions

Brundtland Commission defined sustainable development as development that meets the need of present generation without curtailing the capacity of future generations to meet their own needs. It was suggested that the rapid economic growth was essential for sustainable development. However, the meaning of sustainable development is complex and contested by scholars of different backgrounds. While it is difficult to precisely define the meaning of sustainable development, it is possible to weigh up trade off and agree on measuring criteria of sustainability. The development practices and interventions, which reduce soil erosion and distress migration, improve the people's capabilities to cope with adverse climatic catastrophe and, therefore, may be considered as sustainable than those practices which accentuate these problems.

The strategies of sustainable development have been demonstrated through a case study of Shankerpura village located in the semi-arid areas of Gujarat. Until twenty years ago, the village displayed all the features of acute poverty and degradation of resource-base and immiserisation of people. But SWDF's development intervention on sustainable lines could restore the livelihood system of the people which would enable them to support themselves even during scarcities.

The overarching concern of SWDF in all its programmes has been to improve the living conditions of the tribal communities and strengthen the livelihood system in these villages. The factors which contributed to the success of Shankerpura include sequencing of programmes, presence of SWDF to bear the transaction cost in the initial stages and development institutions which enabled people to evolve rules and norms for sharing resources and resolving conflicts. Many villages in the tribal belt of India stretching from Rajasthan in the west to West Bengal in the east exhibit features similar to those of Shankerpura. The livelihood systems in these villages have also become fragile and unsustainable due to degradation of the resource base. It is in the context of this scenario that the transformation brought about in Shankerpura is to be viewed. What the Shankerpura experiment demonstrates is the possibility of triggering off similar transformations in these areas and communities and similar regions of other parts of the world. In the success of Shankerpura, SWDF played a crucial role in organizing people, capacity building, and bearing the transaction costs associates with uncertainty of technology, negotiation with government, and organization. If sustainability is to be achieved, many more efforts would be required for building collectives among villagers and generating capacities among people to redeem the health of natural resources. Wisdom lies in correcting those institutional anomalies which hinder or restrict growth of such processes.

NOTES

1. Hartwick used the Cobb-Douglas production function, which assumes that resources are perfectly substitutable throughout production possibility frontiers.
2. *cf.* Gadgil and Guha 1995.
3. According to government records, the district has 25 per cent geographical area under forests (see CMIE 1993; GOG 1982). At present, however, much of this is barren rocks and denuded land.
4. When SWDF began work in Shankerpura it did not have a known strategy for intervention. However, the success led SWDF to design a strategy for land, water and forest development with the underlying premise that if the rains were harvested, stored and utilized properly, land productivity could be restored. Since then, SWDF has intervened in more than 250 villages. See Singh and Shah (1994) for details.
5. These apprehensions were removed through constant dialogue with community leaders, and by involving them at every stage of decision-making and project implementation (Singh 1987).
6. The external environment the Shankerpura lift irrigation cooperative faced was quite hostile; the society had to pay fixed yearly charges for electricity even when it did not run due to insufficient water in the tank. In normal years it runs approximately 100 days, and during drought sometimes not even for a single day, but the society had to pay for the whole year under a flat tariff rate. SWDF persuaded the State Government, and it has now shifted to meter-based pricing since 1995.

REFERENCES

Anand, S. and Martin Ravallion. 1993. "Human Development in Poor Countries: On the Role of Private Income and Public Services." *Journal of Economic Perspectives* 7(1): 133-50.

Ahmed, S. 1994. "The Forests of Mahudi: Historical Change and People's Perceptions." *Rural Livelihood Systems and Sustainable Resources Management in Semi-Arid Areas of India.* Interim Report, Institute of Rural Management, Anand.

Becker, C. Dustin and Elinor Ostrom. 1995. "Human Ecology and Resource Sustainability: The Importance of Institutional Diversity." *Annual Review of Ecological Systems* 26: 113-33.

Balooni, K. and Katar Singh. 1994. "Economics of Farm Forestry: A Case Study in Shankerpura Village, district Panchmahals, Gujarat." Working Paper #61. IRMA, Anand.

CMIE. 1993. *Economic Intelligence Services.* Bombay: Centre for Monitoring Indian Economy.

Common, M. 1995. *Sustainability and Policy-Limits to Economics,* Cambridge: Cambridge University Press.

Conroy, C. 1991. "The Contribution of Farm Forestry to Rural Livelihoods: A Case Study from Eastern Gujarat." ODA (mimeo).

Conway, R.R. 1985. "Agroecosystem Analysis." *Agricultural Administration* 20; 31-55.

Dreze, J. and Amartya K. Sen. 1989. *Hunger and Public Action.* Oxford: Clarendon Press.

Gadgil, M. and R. Guha. 1995. *Ecology and Equity: The Use and Abuse of Nature in Contemporary India.* London and New York: Routledge.

GOG. 1982. *Statistical Atlas of Gujarat: Resource Profile, Volume I.* Gandhinagar: Bureau of Economics and Statistics, Government of Gujarat.

Grant, N. 1989. *A Study of the Impact of the Sadguru Water and Development Foundation's Social Forestry Programme on Women.* Dahod, Panchmahals: SWDF.

Guha, R. 1989. *The Unquiet Woods: Ecological Change and Peasants Resistance in the Himalayas.* Berkeley: University of California Press.

Hartwick, J.M. 1977. "Intergenerational Equity and the Investing of Rents from Exhaustible Resources." *American Economic Review* 67(5): 972-74.

Korten, D.C. 1991-92. "Sustainable Development." *World Policy Journal* 9:157-90.

Kurien, J. 1993. "Ruining the Commons: Overfishing and Fishworks' Actions in South India." *The Ecologist* 23(1): 5-12.

Ostrom, Elinor. 1990. *Governing the Commons: The Evolution of Institutions for Collective Action.* New York: Cambridge University Press.

Ostrom, Elinor. 1994. "Constitution Social Capital and Collective Action." *Journal of Theoretical Politics* 6(4): 527-62.

Patel, G.D. 1972. *Gujarat State Gazetteers—Panchmahals District.* Ahmedabad: Government of Gujarat.

Pretty, N. Jules. 1995. *Regenerating Agriculture: Policies and Practice for Sustainability and Self-Reliance,* London: Earthscan Publications Ltd.

Repetto, R. 1986. *World Enough and Time.* New Haven: Yale University Press.

Saxena, N.C. 1994. *India's Eucalyptus Craze—The God That Failed.* New Delhi: Sage Publication Pvt. Ltd.

Sen, Amartya. 1987. "The Standard of Living." The Tanner Lectures, Cambridge: Cambridge University Press.

Sen, Amartya. 1993. "Economic Regress—Concept and Features," In: *Proceedings of the World Bank Annual Conference on Development Economics,* pp. 315-33.

Sharma, K.C., V. Ballabh and Ajay Pandey. 1991. "An Analysis of Farm Forestry in Gujarat," In: N.C. Saxena and V. Ballabh, *Farm Forestry in South Asia,* New Delhi: Sage Publications Pvt. Ltd..

Shiva, V. and J. Bandhopadhyay. 1985. *Ecological Audit of Eucalyptus Cultivation.* Dehradun: English Book Depot.

Shylendra, H.S. 1994. "External Interventions and Livelihood in Mahudi." In *Rural Live-lihood Systems and Sustainable Resources Management in Semi-Arid Areas of India,* Interim Report, Institute of Rural Management, Anand.

Shylendra, H.S. and Uma Rani. 1998. "Sustainable Rural Livelihood and Natural Resources Management in the Context of Growing Occupational Diversification and Rural-Urban

Linkages", Paper prepared for the RLS Research Forum Meet, Institute of Rural Management, Anand, Feb 10-13.

Solow, R.M. 1974. "Intergenerational Equity and Exhaustible Resources". *Review of Economic Studies Symposium*, 29-46.

Singh, Katar and Tushaar Shah. 1994. "Managing Water and Land Resources: Lessons and Experience of NM Sadgure Water and Development Foundation." Paper presented at the workshop on NGO's Experience in Managing Water and Land Resources held at Udaipur, February 3-5, 1994.

Singh, K.K. 1987. "Tribal Lift Irrigation Cooperative Societies: The Sadguru Water and Development Foundation, Dahod, Gujarat." Agriculture and Rural Development Area, Administrative Staff College of India, Hyderabad (mimeo).

SWDF. 1995. *Annual Report*. Dahod Panchamahals: NM Sadguru Water and Development Foundation.

Thomas, P. and V. Ballabh. 1995. "Forestry and Economic Development: Lessons from the Tribal Belt of Eastern Gujarat." Paper presented in the National Seminar on Linkages between Forests and Other Sectors of Indian Economy, Indian Institute of Forest Management, Bhopal, 5-6 June, 1995.

Verma, S.C. 1978. *The Bhil Kills*. Delhi: Kunj Publishing House.

World Commission on Environment and Development. 1987. *Our Common Future* (The Brundtland Report). Oxford: Oxford University Press.

8 Improved Water Management through Farmers' Participation

I.C. Mahapatra and **R.K. Rajput**

Water is the key input for enhancing and sustaining agricultural production. In the post-independence era in India, growth in agricultural production has gone hand in hand with the expansion of irrigation. In many areas, expansion of irrigation has also provided a basis for the growth of investment in off-farm related agro-industries and distribution facilities. The performance of many irrigation systems in terms of efficiency, equity, cost recovery and accountability has often been poor. Further, the pace of irrigation development has slowed down due to rising costs, time lag, problems of operation and maintenance, spread of water logging, salinity, etc. Due to an ever increasing demand for water to meet the diverse needs of burgeoning population, agricultural and economic developments coupled with large-scale unabated pollution of fresh water (both surface and groundwater), the quantum of fresh water availability is getting scarcer with every passing day and also becoming costlier to harness. Fresh water is now becoming a finite commodity and it can no longer be treated as a renewable resource. The foregoing facts would make it necessary to improve efficiency of the existing irrigation systems if crop yields are to be increased as needed in the future. This would include improving timeliness of irrigation deliveries to farmers, saving of water through greater efficiencies in conveyance and ensuring that the saved water is redistributed to be used effectively, reducing losses from waterlogging and salinity.

Thus far, in India, like many other countries of the world, the goverment has a strong presence in the construction of infrastructure and management of irrigation water resources. However, the poor performance of the irrigation systems as enunciated above has led to the realization for increased participation of beneficiaries, the farmers, in the management of irrigation at different levels. In this chapter, an attempt has been made to briefly trace the progress of water resource development, its impact on agricultural production, possible reasons for the low performance of irrigation projects and prospects of farmers' participation in irrigation management for improving the efficiency of irrigation systems.

1. Water Resources of India

India receives about 400 M ha.m. precipitation annually—about 300 M ha.m. in the four monsoon months and the remaining 100 M ha. m. in the other eight months. The occurrence of rainfall is highly variable both in time and space. Of the average rainfall, 188 M ha.m. is the surface water of river basins in the country, 60 per cent of which is contributed by the Ganga, Brahmaputra and Mahanadi systems (Mohile and Goel 1995). The utilizable surface water is estimated to be 68.9 M ha.m. per year. The other reliable source of water is groundwater. It is a dynamic system and is a renewable resource being replenished annually. The total annual replenishable groundwater has been estimated as 43.2 M ha.m. (CGWB 1995). After making a provision of 7.1 M ha.m. for domestic, industrial and other uses, the available groundwater resource for irrigation is 36.1 M ha.m. of which the utilizable quantity is 32.5 M ha.m.

The National Commission on Agriculture (1976) has estimated the ultimate irrigation potential to be 113.5 M ha., 58.5 M ha. through major and medium irrigation projects and 55.0 M ha. from minor irrigation schemes. Of the latter, 40 M ha. was estimated to be from groundwater exploitation. As per the latest estimate, groundwater resource for irrigation is 64 M ha. (CGWB, 1995). Further, the national perspective envisages an additional benefit of 25 M ha. through surface storage and inter-basin transfer of river waters. Thus, the ultimate irrigation potential gets upgraded to around 164 M ha. India's irrigation potential in 1950-51 was only 22.6 M ha. and it has created an irrigation potential of 90 M ha. by the end of 1995-96, i.e. four times in 45 years. The creation of irrigation potential through major and medium projects has slowed down considerably owing to higher cost, reduced availability of good sites for construction of dams, problems in operation and maintenance, etc. However, the priority, at present, is to harness the irrigation potential through minor irrigation schemes. It is estimated that even after achieving the full irrigation potential, nearly 30 per cent of the cultivated area will remain rain-fed.

2. Gap in Utilization of Created Irrigation Potential

Not all the irrigation potential is being effectively utilized and the gap in all the irrigation systems is increasing. Prior to the Sixth Five Year Plan (1980-85), the utilization of irrigation potential developed through minor irrigation schemes was considered to be 100 per cent which was not correct. Accordingly, from the

Sixth Plan onwards, separate reckoning of unutilized irrigation potential has been made for minor irrigation schemes as well. At the end of the Seventh Five Year Plan (1985-90), the gap in the utilization of irrigation potential was of the order of 7.9 M ha. which further increased to 8.7 M ha. by 1993-94, 4.6 M ha. in major and medium irrigation projects and 4.1 M ha. in minor irrigation schemes. The gap in the utilization in major and medium irrigation projects has been due to non-development of the command area, adoption of cropping pattern in favour of high water requiring crops and excess use of irrigation water in the head reaches by the farmers. In the minor irrigation schemes, the gap has obviously resulted from the lack of energization of tube-wells, frequent load-shedding, inadequate and untimely availability of diesel for running of pumps, etc. To help narrow down the gap in the utilization of created irrigation potential, a centrally sponsored command area development authority (CADA) has been under implementation since 1974-75 in selected irrigation commands. The functions of CADA are:

(i) Modernization and efficient operation of the irrigation system and development of main drainage beyond 5-8 ha block,
(ii) Construction of field channels,
(iii) Land shaping and levelling ,
(iv) Lining of field channels,
(v) Adoption and enforcement of suitable cropping patterns,
(vi) Preparation of plans and making arrangements for input supply,
(vii) Strengthening of existing extension, training and demonstration programmes, and
(viii) Development of ancillary activities like credit, marketing and processing facilities, animal husbandry, farm forestry, etc.

Because of administrative flaws in the organizational set-up and inadequate financial and technical support, the expected output from the CADA programme has remained far from satisfactory. Many of CADAs have been closed on account of poor performance. In spite of the national scenario on the availability of groundwater being favourable, there are pockets in certain areas in the country that face scarcity of water. This is because the groundwater development over different parts of the country is not uniform, being quite intensive in some areas resulting in over-exploitation leading to a fall in water levels and even salinity ingress in coastal areas. The declining water levels have resulted in failure of wells/tube-wells leading to higher cost of pumping. Out of 4,272 blocks in the country (except Andhra Pradesh, Gujarat and Maharashtra where groundwater resource assessment has been carried out on the basis of mandals, talukas and watersheds, respectively), 231 blocks have been categorized as "over-exploited", i.e. stage of groundwater development exceeds the annual replenishable limit and 107 blocks are "dark", i.e. the stage of groundwater development is more than 85 per cent (CGWB, 1995). Besides, out of 1,104 mandals in A.P., six mandals have been categorized as over-exploited and 24 as dark. Similarly, out of 184 talukas in Gujarat, 12 are over-exploited and 14 are dark. In Maharashtra, out of 1,503 watersheds, 13 are dark. The National Water Policy adopted by the Government of India (1987) enunciates that exploitation of groundwater resources should be so regulated as not to exceed the recharge posibilities as also to ensure social equity. Further, the conjunctive use of groundwater with surface water should be envisaged right from the project planning stage for best advantage to the region and nation.

3. Impact of Irrigation on Agricultural Development

It has been an established fact that progress in agricultural production has largely been incidental to the availability of irrigation water. Even future gains will continue to be determined by appropriate development and utilization of the country's water resources. There has been a growing awareness about environmental security which in turn is linked with proper use of our water resources. The country has been able to create the largest irrigation infrastructure in the world and has surpassed even China. It is recognized that irrigation has subscribed to the resilience of Indian agriculture. Development of irrigation has been an important factor in the continuation of the Green Revolution initiated during mid 60s. The irrigated area under foodgrains which averaged 19.6 per cent during the quinquennium 1961-65 increased to 30.6 per cent during 1981-85 and to 37.6 per cent during 1991-95. The deep troughs and peaks in the foodgrain production in the 50s and 60s have been narrowed down to a great extent. Irrigation has, therefore, brought about not only enhancement in production but also stability. Continuous food security has been the hallmark of irrigated agriculture in India. Increase in foodgrain production has been phenomenal since it increased from 50.8 mt in 1950-51 to 199.3 mt during 1996-97. The irrigated areas contributed nearly 60 per cent of gross foodgrain production. Among the non-foodgrain crops, appreciable gains in production have been obtained in rapeseed and mustard, sunflower, soybean sugarcane, potato and cotton (Table 8.1).

The increase in the production in foodgrains, groundnut and cotton has been largely due to technology advancement during the period whereas sunflower and soybean production increased due to an expansion in area. Increased growth in production of sugarcane, potato, rapeseed and mustard crops was due to both area expansion and partly due to improved technology adoption.

Development of irrigation has not been an unmixed blessing. In majority of the irrigation projects (major and medium), there has been development of twin maladies of waterlogging and salinity. These problems have fast appeared in projects located in arid and semi-arid regions, the situation being grim in projects located in vertisols of central and south india which are potentially saline soils. The major contributing factors to the rise in the water table are seepage from canals, excessive application of water in the fields and operation loss in canals .

TABLE 8.1: **All India Compound Growth Rates of Principal Crops during 1967-68 to 1996-97 (per cent per annum).**

Base TE 1981-82=100

Crop	Area	Production	Yield
Rice	0.63	2.86	2.29
Wheat	1.52	4.68	3.11
All cereals	0.01	2.89	2.41
All pulses	0.16	0.94	0.76
Total foodgrains	0.04	2.62	2.19
Groundnut	0.49	1.73	1.2
Rapeseed and mustard	2.64	5.58	2.87
Sunflower	13.80	12.87	0.82
Soybean	23.39	25.13	1.41
All oilseeds	1.38	3.63	1.73
Sugarcane	1.77	3.12	1.33
Cotton	0.09	2.89	2.80
Potato	3.39	6.01	2.53

Source: GOI, Ministry of Agriculture (1998): *Agric. Statistics at a Glance.*

4. Institutional Changes for Improving Performance of Irrigation Systems

The rapid development of irrigated agriculture during the past four decades has been achieved with very little change in the institutional setting for agriculture. This slow rate in the institutional change cannot keep pace with the dramatic change in policies, the reduced profitability of foodgrains based agriculture, the rapid increase in competition for scarce water and other resources. Experience during the 60s and 70s, the world over, clearly points to the need for improvement in the farm water management status as a primary means to better the performance of irrigation systems. In the South and South East Asia also it has been demonstrated that irrigation systems can substantially benefit from improved water allocation and distribution methods at the main-system level (Bhuiyan, 1982). Irrigation system management efforts should take a holistic view of the problems existing at all levels of the system.

Transferring responsibility for operation and maintenance of increasingly larger portions of irrigation systems to water users seems to be an attractive solution. Whatever little effort has been made in this direction in India, the technical concerns of government agencies still outweigh the interests of farmers. It will be a major challenge for Irrigation Departments to actually transform themselves from this rather paternalistic mindset to respond effectively to more democratic institutions, i.e. Water Users Associations, Water Cooperatives, etc. Realizing this, the Government of India adopted a National Water Policy in 1987 which envisages that farmers should be associated with all facets of irrigation water management including utilization of created irrigation potential, equitable distribution of water at farm level, operation and maintenance of irrigation system, recovery of irrigation cess, resolution of water-related conflicts. Besides, they can help member farmers in obtaining the needed inputs timely and at competitive prices for irrigated agriculture with the sole objective to improve the efficiency of water use in the command.

Irrigation being a State subject, the efforts being made by different States in India are variable because of varying traditions of States, their interests and needs. As a result, there is a great deal of variability in the approaches to dissolution and participation in irrigation. To facilitate farmers' participation in irrigation water management, the Government of India issued detailed guidelines to all State Governments (Pathak 1991) clearly enunciating the necessity of involving farmers, objectives of farmers' participation, area of operation and methodology, membership, duties and responsibilities, advantages and incentives to the farmers, training, etc. The Union Ministry of Water Resources funds the farmers' associations formed at minor levels for taking over the management of water distribution on a matching basis—50 per cent of cost of management subsidy at the rate of Rs. 100 per ha. for the first two years and Rs. 75 per ha for the third year.

Although in India there are success stories of farmers' associations involved in taking up responsibilities relating to irrigation water management in the commands, these are only scattered and isolated. Examples of some of these associations are as under:

4.a. Phad System

This system is prevalent in Nasik and Dhule districts of Maharashtra. These organizations are over 200 years old and with 4 to 92 ha. command area under different weirs on the tributaries of river Tapi. The contiguous fields are grouped to form a *Phad* for growing a specific crop for better post-sowing management. The crops to be grown in different *Phads* are decided by the farmers concerned well in advance of the rainy season. The sequence of irrigation within and between the *Phads* is from head to tail. Actual water application on the farm is carried out by the watermen, who are appointed on a year-to-year basis and not by land owners or any other member of their families. The maintenance and repairs of the weir structure is the responsibility of the government whereas the canal system is maintained by the irrigators themselves. For management of irrigation under the command of each weir an elected Panch Committee functions.

4.b. Mohini Water Cooperative Society (MWCS)

This society was registered in September, 1978, and started work in 1979 with its headquarters at village Mohini of Chorasi taluka in district Surat (Gujarat). The society draws irrigation water from Bhestan minor of Kakrapar canal system.The gross command area (GCA) covered under the charge of the society is 525 ha with culturable command area (CCA) of about 487 ha. The main objectives of MWCS are :

(i) To promote the spirit of cooperation and self-reliance,
(ii) To purchase water in bulk and distribute it among its members, equitably,
(iii) To operate and maintain canal system in the area of its jurisdiction,
(iv) To arrange for on-farm development (OFD) works for efficient water use on the farm,
(v) To educate farmers in improved farm water management and agronomic practices,
(vi) To arrange for supply of agricultural inputs and agricultural equipments on competitive rates, and
(vii) To collect irrigation charges and other dues from the farmers and pay them to the government in time.

Initially, MWCS had a membership of 145 which increased gradually to 239 in 1989-90. Besides the president (Pramukh), there are nine members in the management committee (MC) of the society. One-third of the members of MC retire by rotation every year and are replaced by elected/selected members. The management committee is assisted by a team of six salaried staff in the discharge of responsibilities of the society including water distribution maintenance of records, accounts, etc.

The Irrigation Department releases water in the minor as per the requirement of the society on a consolidated indent basis and charges on volume basis of Rs. 30 per 10 lakh litres which includes local cess of Rs. 5

payable by the society to the government. MWCS supply irrigation water to member farmers on the rates fixed by the Gujarat Government on flat area actually irrigated. The difference between the water charges realized by the society and those paid to the government is substantial. Normally, the repair and maintenance charges are met out of the society's net profits from the sale of water but if the expenditure exceeds the amount available, the balance is recovered from the members. The society has generated a good amount of reserve fund and has also been paying dividends to the members.

MWCS has purchased a tractor which is made available to the members on custom hire service. The agricultural inputs, viz. fertilizers, chemicals, seeds, etc., could be purchased from the Farmers' Service Cooperative Society located in the village on competitive rates. At the time of formation of MWCS, the area under sugarcane was planned to be only 18 per cent which quickly increased to about 92 per cent owing to greater profitability.

After the establishment of MWCS and measures adopted for improved water management on the field, the area irrigated has increased by 100 per cent which is a great achievement in terms of both efficient water use and additional production from the command area. Besides, the irrigated agency is saving recurring expenditure on operation, maintenance and repairs of the canal system covering the area assigned to MWCS. The society has a provision in its by-laws for both incentives and disincentives to members for good or bad cooperative behaviour. The success of the society may also be attributed to greater equity in water use, there being practically no conflicts for water among the member farmers.

4.c. Shri Datta Cooperative Water Management Society

This society was established on minor 7 of Mula Right Bank Canal at village Chanda, about 40 km from Ahmednagar (Maharashtra). The culturable command area of the minor is 361 ha serviced by 13 outlets. The society is registered under the Cooperative Society Act with 200 member farmers. A private organization, Centre for Applied System Analysis in Development (CASAD) of Pune, actively assisted in the establishment of the society and took over two years in convincing both, officials of the Irrigation Department and the beneficiary farmers about the need and benefit of such society. Prior to the handing over of the minor to the society, the Irrigation Department arranged for repair and maintenance of the minor's physical infrastructure and now contributes a grant of Rs. 10,000 annually for the maintenance of the minor. The society also got 50 per cent of the cost of management, subsidy from the Government of India through CADA for three Years at the rate of Rs. 100 per hectare in the first two years and at Rs. 75 per hectare in the third year.

The irrigation water at the minor's head is made available by the irrigation agency regularly in all three crop seasons—four to five times in each season, for four days at a time—thus ensuring adequate water supply on time. The Irrigation Department charges for water supply on a volume basis crop season-wise at negotiated rates, Kharif—Rs. 10, Rabi—Rs. 15 and summer—Rs. 37.5 per 1,000 cubic metre of water. The society collects the water fee from farmers in advance at Rs. 50 ha in Kharif, Rs. 75 ha in Rabi and Rs. 150 ha in summer besides a service charge of Rs. 25 per ha annually. There are no overdues.

Earlier, farmers were growing only foodgrains because of uncertainty of water supply but have now diversified the cropping in favour of sunflower, groundnut, sorghum and to some extent sugarcane with assured water supply in the minor. Besides, water distribution, the society maintains the irrigation channels.

The Irrigation Department saves on maintenance cost and gets all water dues in time. Since water is charged on the quantum used by the farmers, it is not wasted and more land is irrigated. Due to certainty in water supply on time and in adequate quantity, there are practically no conflicts amongst the farmers. There is also substantial improvement in water use efficiency, and equity in water use.

4.d. Lower Bhavani Project—Thindal Distributary (Tamil Nadu)

In a cooperative effort of a different kind, a group endeavour of the farmers of the Thindal Distributary has resulted in equitable distribution of water to all their fields. Seventy two farmers owning about 70 ha area are assured of their due share in 2.8 cusecs (79.2 lps) water. Two stone-lined channels take off from the division box at different levels provided with proportionate vents. The irrigation channels have been constructed by the farmers under the supervision of the irrigation agency, i.e. CADA. The Irrigation community organizers (fresh engineering graduates) who are stationed in the village have played a challenging role in convincing the farmers of the benefits of cooperative effort in irrigation water management related issues. Consequently, many conflicts have been resolved amicably and utilization has increased by 30 per cent with the same amount of water. Problems of maintenance have also reduced to a minimum.

4.e. Water Users Associations in Kerala

There are 10 completed irrigation projects in Kerala under CADA. About 2,000 societies have been registered covering nearly all outlets and the registration is under the Scientific and Charitable Societies Act of Kerala. The main purpose of the primary association is to distribute water and maintain water courses below the outlet. CADA is also promoting group farming since the farm holding size is very small. Group farming includes common provision of seeds, fertilizers, nursery, night patrol of fields, plant protection, transportation etc.

4.f. Paliganj Distributary (Bihar)

An action research programme (ARP) was initiated by the Water and Land Management Institute (WALMI), Patna, with the support of United States Agency for International Development (USAID) in 1988 at the Paliganj distributary of the sone Irrigation Project to improve the performance of the canal network in respect of productivity and profitability of irrigated agriculture. This distributary diverts water directly from the Patna canal in the eastern Sone system. The gross command area (GCA) of the distributary is 14,867 ha with a CCA of 12,197 ha. During Kharif, the main crop is rice whereas in Rabi wheat is largely grown. Almost no crop is grown during the summer season since the canal is closed for maintenance. Water distribution follows the *satta* system whereby farmers make requests, called *satta* for water. Below each outlet, one farmer acts as a *sattadar* and manages distribution of water below the outlet—the Irrigation agency is responsible for delivering water to the outlet. Water courses are constructed and maintained by the farmers whereas the water charges are collected by the revenue wing of the Irrigation Department with the help of the *sattadar*. After identifying the major problems of water distribution, the farmers with the help of an ARP team devised innovations—first clearing obstructions from the channels and then adopting 10-day rotation for the irrigation. Before the ARP, the tail end (30.7 per cent CCA) hardly received 10-12 per cent of the water diverted into the canal but after three years of ARP and the farmers committee's plan, the tail-end received 18 per cent of water. This was due to a relative decline in water diverted into the head and middle section blocks. Between 1990 and 1993, the area irrigated by the Paliganj distributary during the Kharif season rose from 3,614 ha in 1990 to 4,350 ha in 1992 and 1993 (Vermillion and Brewer 1996). Encouraged by these results, the Government of Bihar has initiated large-scale Participatory Irrigation Management (PIM) programme in 20 distributaries of different irrigation projects. The proposal aims at :

(i) Transfer of full operation and maintenance (O&M) responsibility to WUAs.
(ii) Create WUAs at village level and distributary level up to 15,000 ha.
(iii) Require WUAs to collect irrigation fee and retain 70 per cent of the fee collected for the Association's functioning and deposit 30 per cent of the amount with the Water Resources Department.

5. On-Farm Water Management Research Pilot Project (ICAR)

In order to evaluate the adaptability of improved water management practices developed on the experimental stations of ICAR Coordinated Project for Research on Water Management, an on-farm water management (OFWM) research was conducted in selected irrigation commands in collaboration with the Union Ministry of Water Resources and State departments of water resources/irrigation on farmers' fields. The irrigation commands where OFWM studies were conducted were : (1) Hirakud (Orissa), (2) Ukai-Kakrapar (Gujarat), (3) Gandak (Bihar), (4) Sharda canals (U.P.), (5) Chalakudy (Kerala), (6) Lower Bhavani (Tamil Nadu), (7) Mula (Maharashtra), (8) Malprabha (Karnataka), (9) Ravi-Tawi (J.K.), (10) J.L.N. lift irrigation (Haryana). Before initiating technology interventions, a detailed bench-mark diagnostic survey based on a stratified sampling procedure was conducted to identify the major problems of water management and other production factors. These studies, *inter alia,* aimed at studying the methodology and strategies for farmers' involvement at the farm level. The study unit was a hydraulic unit—a distributary or two to three minors of a distributary. The farmers in the command area of the distributary/minors were advised to form registered societies for help in water management and related operations. Water managenent constraints and other related production factors were then prioritized to decide implementation of the most important two or three interventions to relieve the constraints for improved water use and enhanced crop production and productivity in the distributary/minors command. The results revealed that there was water economy vis-a-vis higher water use efficiency in the system. The saved water was diverted in the command of the same minor or in the adjoining minor to increase area under irrigation. With improved irrigation scheduling in rice in OFWM studies in Ukai-Kakrapar irrigation project, the saved water in the upper reaches of the minor increased the irrigated area at the tail-end by 15 per cent. In the Sharada canal command at Pantnagar (U.P.), removal of water congestion by providing surface drainage and channelization of excess water to natural drainge system along with adoption of other improved practices increased yields of rice, wheat and sugarcane crops by about 40 per cent in a period of four years (Rajput 1994). Likewise, in other commands where OFWM studies were made, positive improvements were observed in the efficiency of water use. Over and above, the farmers were convinced about the beneficial impact of interventions in crop production, economy in water use and increase in their incomes.

5.a. Privatization in Irrigation Management

Along with on-farm water management through participation of farmers, the

Union Ministry of Water Resources has proposed private sector participation in irrigation and multi-purpose projects on the Build, Own and Operate (BOO) or Build, Own and Lease (BOL) basis. Already there have been some initiatives towards limited private sector participation in A.P., Maharashtra, Gujarat, M.P. and Karnataka. Privatization may require changes in water rights so that operating companies may charge for their services as wholesalers of water to individuals or group of water users.

6. Lessons and Implications

From the foregoing presentation of farmers' association in water management, the following lessons may be useful :

6.a. Resistance to Change

Both the irrigation agency and the farmers are apprehensive about any change in the existing practice of management of irrigation water in the command areas. Often the Irrigation Department is not prepared to share its powers with the farmers. The field functionaries of the Irrigation Department have to defend the existing system of water management and cannot find fault in it for obvious reasons. Nor can they encourage farmers in sharing the responsibility of water management due to fear of losing job opportunity, career advancement, etc. On their side, the farmers question, in what way WUAs would be better organized than the departmentally managed system and beneficial to them? A prerequisite for the farmers' association in water management is that the economic gains of irrigated agriculture must be visible and substantial. Thus far, the State has been planning and constructing the irrigation projects and also controlling all the operations of water distribution, maintenance, etc., whereas the farmers were not required to put any effort and hence they have little incentive for any collective action in improving water management. Oftentimes, the physical system below the minor and laterals is unsatisfactory and hence the farmers are reluctant to take over such responsibilities of an undependable, unreliable and failing system.

6.b. Legal Limitation and Policy Changes

The pace of formation of water users' associations has been somewhat satisfactory in the States of Gujarat, Maharashtra, Tamil Nadu but in Punjab, Haryana, West Bengal, Rajasthan, Orissa and Karnataka the irrigation Acts being old, farmers have not been provided participation in irrigation water management and hence legal flaws in establishing these associations. Appropriate amendments have thus to be made in the irrigation Acts.

While it is in the farmers' interest to increase farm productivity through irrigation, some of the water management policies of the government may conflict with the farmers' interests. For example, farmers may be less concerned about increasing production of less remunerative and risky crops such as foodgrains, oilseeds, etc., whereas the government want their higher production.

6.c. Assured Water Supply at the Head of Hydraulic Unit

The crux of a successful water users' association is assured supply of water at the right time and in requisite quantity by the Irrigation Department. This imposes greater responsibility on the latter to maintain the system upstream in a perfectly fit condition to convey water up to the point of diversion in the minor. It is essential that the department assures seasonwise quantum of water and this fact is clearly brought out in the memorandum of understanding with the farmers.

6.d. Financial Assistance, Incentives and Disincentives

It has been observed that often there is a longer gestation period in WUAs becoming self-sustaining. The Union Ministry of Water Resources is funding on a matching basis 50 per cent of the cost of management subsidy through CADA for a period of three years for Farmers' Association formed to shoulder responsibility of management of water at the minor level. It is felt necessary in many cases that this subsidy is allowed for at least five years.

To encourage cooperative behaviour and to restrain non cooperative behaviour on the part of the members of the Association, WUA should have provision for incentives and dis-incentives as existing in MWCS. Those who pay the water charges and other dues to the Association before the due date may be allowed some discount whereas some penalty may be imposed on the defaulters. A heavy penalty may be imposed on the members who deliberately waste water or indulge in unauthorized irrigation or such other malpractice.

6.e. Involvement of Voluntary Agencies and Scientific Organizations

Convincing farmers to form Water Users Association/Co-operative Society for sharing responsibility of water management to improve performance of an irrigation project is a ticklish and time consuming job. It is beyond the reach of the field functionaries of the Irrigation Department to accomplish this task due to many reasons. Experience of Shri Datta Cooperative Water Management Society, Action Research Programme in Paliganj Distributary, On Farm Water Management Research Pilot Project of ICAR in different irrigation commands and many other cases has revealed the urgent need for an external voluntary agency to help in the establishment of WUAs through a continuous dialogue with the irrigation agency and the farmers. Also these agencies can help in the training of farmers in improved water management and agronomic practices for higher agricultural production and efficient water use including equitable distribution. Voluntary organizations may act as a catalytic agent in the efforts of organizing farmers and also of social and attitudinal change in bringing about harmonius interaction between the farmers and the irrigation agency and also between technology and social institutions.

6.f. Training in Field Water Management

Training of farmers, members of management committees and the managerial staff of WUAs on various facets of field water management including irrigation scheduling, measurement of water, OFD works, rights, duties and responsibilities of the individuals concerned is very essential and has to be pursued vigorously. This could be done by the staff of the Irrigation Agency alone or in association with the voluntary/private organizations.

6.g. Extent of Farmers' Participation

Organizing farmers and entrusting them the responsibility of water management and maintenance of the entire project would be ideal but in the case of large irrigation projects the problems of water flow in main/branch canals, maintenance and repairs of large irrigation infrastructures, water measurements, etc., require higher engineering skills and expertise which are beyond the comprehension of farmers/groups. WUAs can function efficiently and economically, if their areas are small and compact, viz. an outlet, minor or at the most a distributary command. When WUAs have gained adequate experience and have successfuly worked up to distributary level, the responsibility of water management in the project command could be entrusted to them leaving the highly skilled jobs to the irrigation engineers.

6.h. Identification of Leadership

Experience of some of the successful farmers associations indicates that a purposeful group on a sustainable basis depends, to a large extent, on the quality and devotion of the leaders managing the society. In the case of MWCS, its President (Pramukh) was elected and reelected year after year for a period of 10 years continuously. It is, therefore, necessary to identify, the devoted farmers who command respect, and authority due to their moral/social standings in the society and to persuade them to lead in the formation of

WUAs and later to manage them so that the latter may fulfil the set objectives.

7. Conclusions

In India, irrigation is a State subject and with highly variable agroclimatic situations, it may not be possible to propose a single model for irrigation institution applicable to all irrigation commands. The institutional framework must reflect the complexity of the social, political, cultural and economic conditions of each State. One thing, however, seems certain, the change is coming and it cannot be resisted any longer. It is incumbent on policy makers and planners to understand the forces affecting irrigated agriculture, identify appropriate goals and policies, institutions and strategies required to achieve them, and guide their implementation, while being prepared to adjust to new issues that were not foreseen.

REFERENCES

Bhuian, S.I. 1982. *Irrigation System Management Research and selected methodological issues.* Irri. Res. Paper Series No. pp. 9. IRRI, Manila, Philippines.

CGWB. 1995. *Strategy for Groundwater Development.* Background note for the colloquium organized by WAPCOS, New Delhi, pp. 26.

Govt. of India, Min Agric. 1998. *Agricultural Statistics at a Glance.* Pub. Dte Economics and Statistics, Dept Agric and Coop. New Delhi.

Govt. of India, Min Finance. 1995. *Economic Survey for 1994-95,* Pub. Economic Div. Min. Fin., New Delhi.

Govt. of India, National Commission on Agric. 1976. *NCA Report on Resources Development.* Part V, pp. 344.

Govt. of India, Planning Comm. 1989. *Report of Working Group on Irrigated Agricultural Production for the formulation of Eighth Five Year Plan.* Planning Comm., New Delhi.

Govt. of India, Planning Comm. 1992. *Eighth Five Year Plan Document 1992-97,* Planning Comm., New Delhi.

Govt. of India, Min Water Resources. 1987. *National Water Policy,* Min. of Water Resources, New Delhi.

Pathak, R.S. 1991. *Farmers Participation in Irrigation Management.* Pub. Min. Water Resources CAD Div., New Delhi

Mohile, A.D. and P.D. Goel. 1995. Paper presented in National Symp. on *Managing Water Resources for Sustainable Agric and Environment.* Indian Soc. Water Management, GAU Navsari Oct. 5-7.

Rajput, R.K. 1994. *Annual Report on Farm Water Management,* Research-collaborative project for 1993-94. Dte. Water Management Res. (ICAR), Rahuri, Maharashtra.

Rajput, R.K. 1995. "Strategies for Improving Water Management in Structural Reforms and the Fertilizer Sector". *Proc. FAI Seminar 1995,* pp. S iii-2/1-14.

Rajput, R.K. and M.C. Agarwal. 1984. *Irrigation and Drainage in 2000 AD.* Proc. National Symp. Agronomy in 2000 AD looking ahead. Indian Soc. Agron. pp. 71-97. New Delhi.

Vermillion, D.L. And J.D. Brewer. 1996. *Participatory Action Research to Improve Irrigation Operations: Examples from Indonesia and India.* Proc. ICID/FAO Workshop on Irrigation scheduling: from theory to practice, Rome 1995 pp. 241 -249.

WALMI, Patna. 1997. *Half Yearly Report (April-Sept, 1996) on Implementation of PIM in Bihar.* Patna (Bihar): Water and Land Management Institute.

Note:

1. India's Irrigation Projects are classified on the basis of their culturable command area (CCA) as major with >10,000 ha medium 2,000-10,000 ha and minor<2,000 ha.
2. The hydraulic units in an irrigation system are designated on the basis of the stream flow in litres per second (lps) at the point of diversion as:

Outlet/Water Course	-	< 50 lps
Sub-minor	-	50 - 200 lps
Minor	-	200 - 1000 lps
Distributory	-	1000 - 5000 lps
Branch Canal	-	5000 - 50,000 lps
Main Canal	-	> 50,000 lps

9 Sustaining Tamil Nadu's Tanks: A Review of Issues and Approaches

**Tushaar Shah, R. Seenivasan,
C.R. Shanmugam and M.P. Vasimalai**

1. Introduction: History and Context

Andhra Pradesh, Karnataka and Tamil Nadu have around 150,000 tanks. Tamil Nadu itself was estimated to have 39,200 in the early 1980's; of these some 9,000 were system tanks, 10,000 were so-called ex-Zamin[2] tanks. In both these categories are included large tanks, and most of these are now controlled by the PWD; in addition, some 20,000 tanks with an *ayacut* area smaller than 40 ha. are under the control of Panchayats (in fact, of Panchayat Unions) and are, therefore, commonly referred to as Panchayat tanks.

Tanks are, however disappearing fast throughout South India, and most of the remaining have long since fallen into disrepair. A recent estimate places the actual population of tanks in Tamil Nadu at 34,000, the remaining 5,000+ have just disappeared over the past 15 or so years because of a variety of reasons: many have just disappeared after decades of siltation and encroachment; rapid urbanization has taken the toll of many; many in the urban fringes have been given away, often by the government agencies themselves, to create housing colonies. All over South India, tanks are losing ground as flow-irrigation systems; and their share has been increasingly captured by irrigation from wells and tubewells. During the 1980's, for example, the area irrigated by tanks in Tamil Nadu—as a proportion of total area irrigated—declined from 33 per cent to 26 per cent; and the share of well-irrigated areas has increased from 34 per cent to 41 per cent (PRADAN 1996:5.1). In Andhra Pradesh, similarly, tank's share in irrigated areas declined from 40 per cent during the 1950s to 20 per cent in the 1980's; while, over the same period, the share of wells and tubewells increased from just over 10 per cent to over 40 per cent (PRADAN, 1996.)

Yet, /as they have always/ been tanks still continue to be an important and valuable component of South Indian socio-ecology, and they can be even more important and valuable if only they are restored to their original performance potential and then managed more diligently. Their sustained decline has been a general source of concern for the government as well as social observers and activists. A number of initiatives have been made to arrest and, if possible, reverse this trend. However, continued degeneration of tanks despite them suggests that these interventions are either ill-conceived or are inadequate. This suggests need for superior analyses than have been used so far to design interventions, of why tanks are declining, and how best to raise their productivity. Regardless of whether current interventions succeed or not, reflective planning and execution of each such attempt has lessons to offer and new questions to ask about the tank resource and the problems encountered in ensuring its sustainable use: What historical processes explain the decline of tanks to their present state? Are tanks as valuable in today's context as they were several hundred years ago? What are their economics? Or, indeed, how does one study the *real* economics of the tanks? What are the productivity, equity and sustainability issues involved in the existing institutions of tank management? And what might be the most effective approaches to making tank complexes more productive, equitable and sustainable?

In these field notes, we explore some of these issues—and the explorations into these issue by others who are far more knowledgeable on the tanks and their context. The notes are based on a brief spell of field work we did which included visits to a sample of tanks in Madurai and Ramnathapuram districts of Tamil Nadu, discussions with PRADAN professionals and participation in a day-long workshop at ISEC, Bangalore, preparatory to the launch of PRADAN's tank management activity in Karnataka. An attempt has also been made to review some past and upcoming literature, especially where it contributes to sharpening the learning from the field work.

Tanks are an ancient resource and, therefore, understanding their present state necessarily entails explorations in the history of the region, of the socio-political and ecological context in which tanks came into existence and were managed over the centuries. Luckily, the history of South Indian tanks has been rather well documented and analysed by a number of scholars like Vani, David Mosse and others based on a huge body of oral history, archival records, inscriptions and scriptures. A powerful notion that has swayed the discussion on South Indian tanks is about the centuries-old tradition of management, repair and maintenance (*kudimaramat)* by local communities which enjoyed unrestricted ownership and use rights over these. Under the Colonial Rule, the government took over the larger tanks and handed these to the Public Works Department apparently for maintenance but actually to raise revenue. With this gradually, local communities got (or felt) disenfranchised and increasingly began ignoring their traditionally assumed responsibility of maintenance and repair. With this went the traditional structure of rights and obligations that were enforced by local authority and which sustained these institutions. Over tens of recent decades, this has meant insignificant investment in repairs and maintenance; and excessive focus, in such little repair and maintenance that does occur, on tank bunds and masonry structures and neglect of catchment areas, supply channels and surplus courses. Fragmented responsibilities amongst different government departments[3], heavy encroachment on supply channels, catchments, water spread areas have been the other major contributory factors that explain the decline of tanks (PRADAN 1996). And since the break-down of local community management is the root cause of the decline in tanks, the argument runs, it will not do to just undertake a one-time rehabilitation to bring tanks into pin-up condition since they will soon be in need of another rehabilitation unless the root cause of their decline is fixed in the first place. Thus it is asserted, approaches to restore tanks to their old glory need to first undo the damage done by the colonial administration to the traditional institution of local community management of tanks.[4]

A natural corollary of this reasoning is that upgrading tank productivity on a sustained basis entails organizing tank users and vesting in them powers, responsibilities and rewards of a superior management regime. At this juncture, then, the discussion on tank irrigation improvement merges into the wider discourse on Irrigation Management Transfer that has dominated the debate on improving the performance of public irrigation systems in general. We return to this debate many times in the course of these field notes, but presently, we review some unique features of Tamil Nadu's tank complexes that distinguish them from tanks elsewhere in the country.

2. Some Unique features of South Indian Tanks

Most States in India have tanks, though not quite as many, as densely concentrated and as central to local socio-ecologies as in South India. However, what uniquely distinguishes South Indian tanks from tanks elsewhere is that the bulk of the former obtain in chain-like cascades. Tanks here are commonly understood as system tanks, chain of tanks and solitary isolated tanks. System tanks have a perennial water source such as a large reservoir or a river from which they receive water besides their catchment.[5] They always occur in a chain that so links each other that surplus water from the upper tanks forms the inflow into lower tanks. They are larger, somewhat better maintained and are able to offer better irrigation because they store more water. Chains of tanks are generally located in a watershed where tanks have hydraulic linkages through supply and/or drainage channels, receiving and passing on surplus water to each other. Tank chains may occur in system tank areas or in rainfed areas. (See, eg. figures 11.2 and 11.3)

Farmers in the command of system tanks are invariably better off compared to those in the command of isolated Panchayat tanks or rain-fed chains of tanks. As a result, the former are more difficult to organize and involve in a programme of rehabilitation compared to farmers in the command of smaller tanks. As a result, after trying working with system tanks, PRADAN programme now focuses on Panchayat tanks. Despite local control and management, Panchayat tanks are as badly maintained as PWD tanks. A Panchayat has several hamlets, and tanks typically serve a part of one or two hamlets. For many years, Tamil Nadu did not have elected Panchayats, and even now that they have them, the Panchayat governance does not effectively reach the hamlet level systems; so it just auctions out the fishing rights and lets the *ayacut* farmers manage the tanks as they see fit.

Linking the tanks in a chain is a supply channel (*Varattu Voikkal*); often there is a network of supply channels woven around a main supply channel (*Kalanikarai*) that may serve 40-60 tanks and small drinking water ponds locally called *oorani*'s before emptying into a river or a big tank. Originally, many of these supply channels were probably improvisations over natural gullies and nallas. However the British recognized the primacy of these channels in enhancing the vigour and productivity of the tank systems, and invested in systematizing them, improving realigning and redesigning the channels to maximize the harvesting and storage of rainfall precipitation. The *Varattu Voikkal* and *Kalankarai* are probably far more important to Tamil Nadu's aquatic environment than many other components of tank systems. In fact, the lack of maintenance, cleaning and desilting of these probably cause far more damage than of tanks.

The key function that these channels perform is of collecting into a growingly thick flow numerous tiny bodies of water which otherwise would get dissipated and lost mostly by evaporation. When in service condition, supply channels are quite deep minimizing the lateral contact of the flowing water with sunrays as well as the earth thereby cutting evaporation as well as seepage losses. When the supply channels get silted up, they become wide and shallow streams allowing maximum losses through both evaporation and seepage. In the worst scenario, after years of disrepair, road construction, stream diversion by farmers and so on, segments of what once used to be supply channels just disappear. The rain water that earlier underwent consolidation through numerous facilitating grooves in the form of channels now gets spread thin over a vast surface and evaporates before contributing much even to groundwater recharge, leave alone tanks and *ooranis*.

Another important problem in restoring tanks to their original productive potential is widespread encroachment[6] typically of the *poromboke* (public land in the water-spread area) and the supply channels but often of the tank bund itself; this is also the most difficult to handle. In some of the tanks taken up for rehabilitation by PRADAN, 20-60 per cent of the tankbed is encroached (PRADAN 1996: 2.1). Encroachments involve people from all socio-economic categories; but these are typically farmers with lands near the *porombokes*. All encroachments are difficult to deal with; but this is particularly true when the culprits are the local bigwig, the resourceful and the well-connected who are able to browbeat the local protesters as well as government functionaries. Moreover, the procedures used by the revenue department to clear encroachments are also tardy and unhelpful. When encroachments are noticed, the illegal occupant is given a B-memo and a penal levy of land revenue is imposed on him by the Village Administrative Officer. The penal levy is so small that it is usually quite profitable to pay it and continually enjoy the usufruct over the land through unauthorized cultivation (PRADAN, 1996: 2.2).[7]

Encroachers' interests are markedly different from those of the *ayacutdaars*. Encroachers on the supply channels are not affected by tank storage downstream and encroachers on the *porombokes* have a strong interest in breaching the bund and minimizing the storage to prevent submergence of the standing crops. There is also the invidious psychology of encroachment—once an encroachment goes unnoticed and unpunished, it has a chain effect. In one of the PRADAN-adopted tanks, one farmer on the border of the foreshore encroached into the *poromboke* and when nobody bothered to have him cleared out, neighbouring farmers followed suit. Eventually, even farmers away from the foreshore—and some in the *ayacut*—encroached. As a result, of the total waterspread area of 14.93 acres, 8.95 (or, some 60 per cent) got encroached, making rehabilitation wellnigh impossible (PRADAN 1996: 2.3). In PRADAN's scheme of things, a major role of Water Users Associations (WUAs) is to use local social pressure to prevent future encroachments and clear past ones because the law seldom takes its normal course, and when it does, it is too tardy and long even if it works at all. Planting a row of trees separating the *poromboke* from the *patta* lands is often an effective way of checking encroachments in the tank bed, provided the trees are allowed to survive.

3. Tank Management Issues

3.a. Tanks and Social Change

From the viewpoint of the design of social and management interventions, tanks are best viewed as socio-technical systems. The social interaction around tanks is a story of continuity and change. Age-old traditions form the basis of several management rules used in tank operation and use today. However, these are not static. Changing social and power equations keep reshaping the norms and are instrumental in deciding what can be done and what cannot.

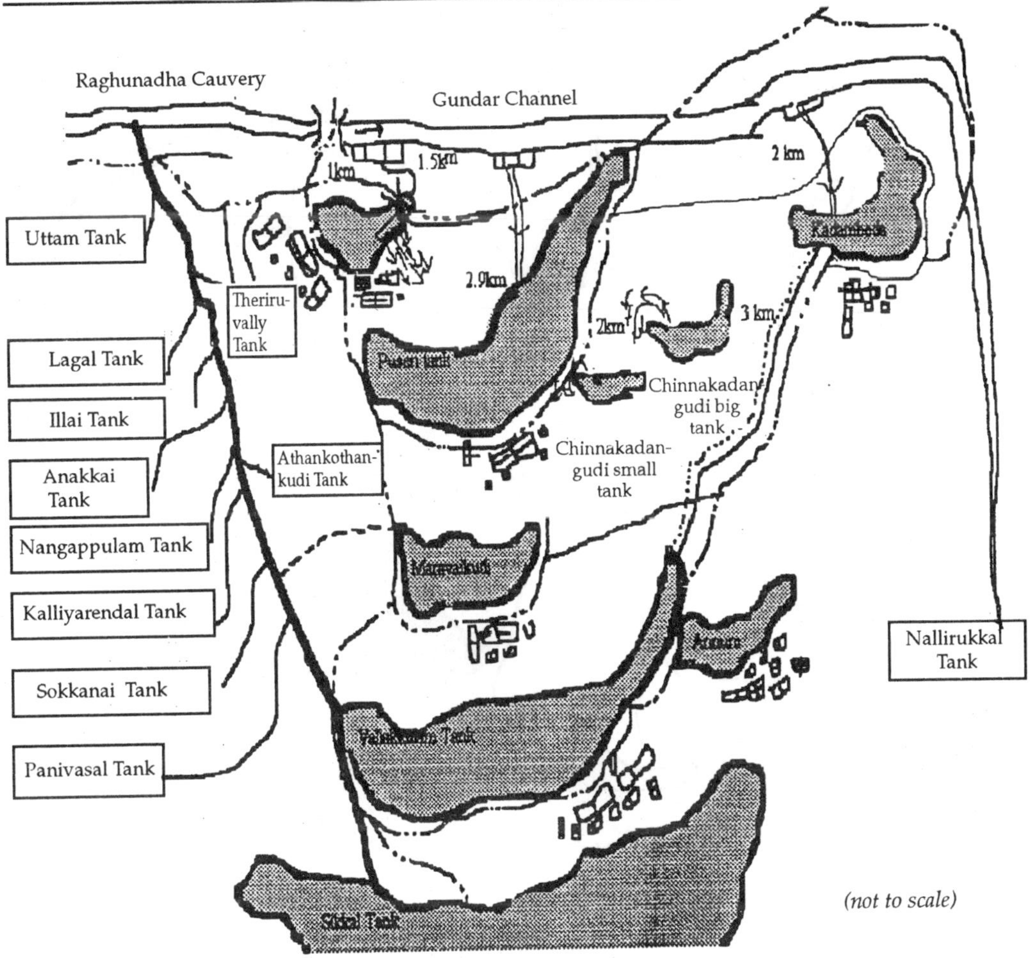

Fig. 9.1: Vallakkulam Tank Chain and Supply

Gripping stories of social upheavals and change affecting local communities are an important element of the tank folklore in every village. In some older tanks, these span decades or even centuries; in some others, the stories are of recent origin. We came across some of these during our field work, and these highlighted how tanks were central to the historical evolution of communities to their present state. A backward community of some 40 Pallar families we met in the command of the Thattanenanthal tank in Kelakodumalur village of Mudhukulathur block had fled their native village some 30 years ago because of a feud with Thevars that ended up in an open and violent conflict. They came here and settled as the tenants of a Muslim landlord to rebuild their lives and property. Gradually, little by little, they began buying land; even today, some of them are tenants; however, it is only a

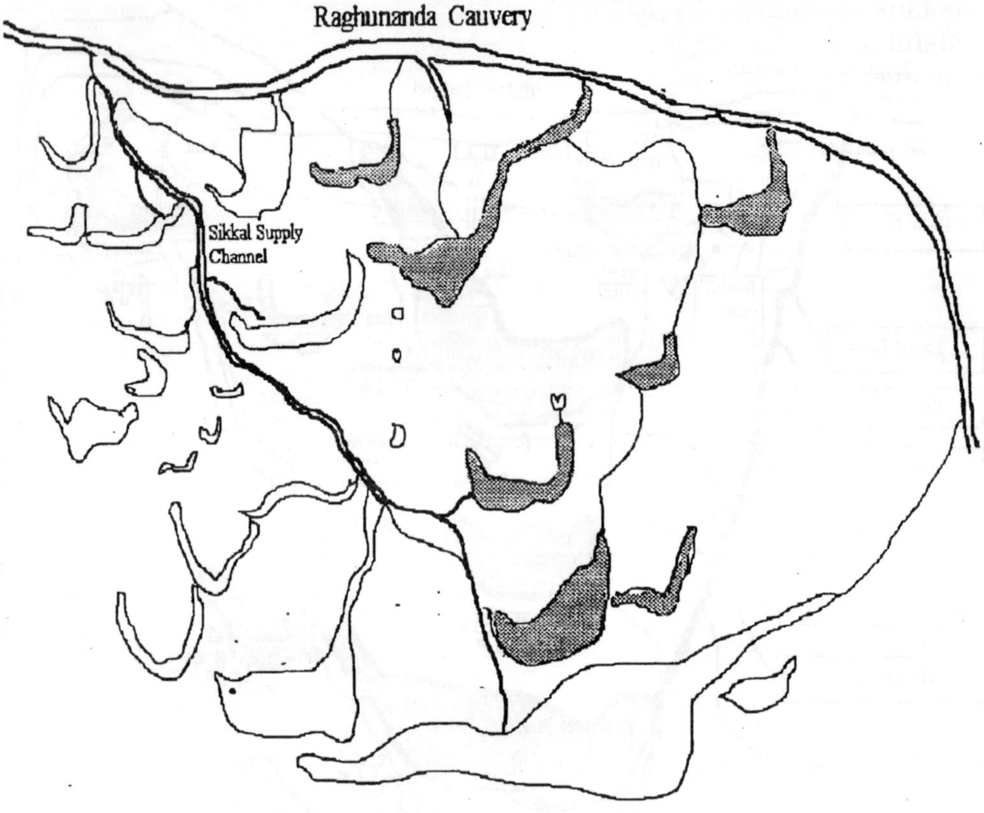

CHAIN OF TANKS

1. Theriruveli Small Tank 2. Puseri Tank 3. Kadambodai
4. Chinnakadangudi big tank 5. Chinnakangudi small tank
6. Maravaikudi 7. Vallakkulam 8. Annuni

Fig. 9.2: Chain of Tanks-Palar Basin Ramanathapuram District

matter of time before they end up as owners. The Pallars we met were still extremely poor and resourceless, but the tank was the centre of their socio-economic progress. And any intervention designed to strengthen their livelihoods could not possibly overlook the tank and its possibilities.

In Ponnakaneri, we found a similarly backward group of families which had pulled itself up by bootstraps. These were Udayar Christian families who were tenants of a Muslim landlord around the 1960s. But, unlike the Pallars we met in Kelakodumalur, these were forward-looking progressive people, so they gradually bought up their lands and are now a prosperous looking lot. Their thatched roofs have been replaced by smart looking pucca houses; farm productivity is high; they make intensive use of inputs and take a cotton-chilli crop and millets and coriander that follow paddy using groundwater irrigation.

The tank is again at the centre of their story of renewal. The community was grateful to PRADAN for all it did to their tank and were asking for more and were ever so willing to pitch in with their share.

3.b. Drinking Water

In many villages, we met groups of women to explore if they had a viewpoint on tanks—on any aspect of it. As it turned out, the groups had little to interest them, even to crib. Many were off-hand about irrigation tanks, even in villages where these were extensively used for bathing and washing. This was probably because the primacy of irrgation use of irrigation tanks has remained largely unquestioned. In Ponnakaneri, however, menfolk were vociferous in demanding steps in the part of the irrigation tank used by women and children for bathing and washing— women stood far away and nodded appreciatively.

However, what women and men were equally emphatic about was in demanding an array of improvements in *ooranis*—small, deep perennial ponds used by the whole village for fetching drinking water. *Ooranis* were top priority, not only for women but also for men. They made many recommendations about what PRADAN/DHAN could do to help; a common recommendation was for building steps so that women and girls could easily go to the water and fill up their pots. Another was to deepen the *oorani* so that it would store and retain more water throughout the year. Yet one more was to build fencing around the *oorani* to keep the cattle and goats from entering it.

In Cheyyamangalam village, PRADAN supported the village to construct an *oorani* at a cost of Rs. 1.4 lakh against an estimate of Rs. 1.1 lakh; 33 per cent was contributed by the people in the form of labour and material, and 67 per cent by the government. The village took up the work with great enthusiasm because it was widely needed. They put their heart and mind into it and built an ornate *oorani* using guidance available in the Hindu scriptures. They made a big fuss about the types of trees to be planted on the *oorani* bunds, the order in which they are to be planted and so on. The *oorani* was built in the centre of an irrigation tank so that the input of water was not a problem. The village contributed a total of 1,000 mandays of work. The women we met were proud of the *oorani* but wanted it fenced to eliminate the entry of cattle and goats into the area. This was intriguing, because *ooranis* as well as cattle have been there for ages and fencing of *ooranis* has never been a custom. The most likely explanation is that, with growing literacy and education, village women's preferences and conceptions of hygiene have changed, they have become more conscious of the quality of drinking water and have developed a new resentment to cattle sharing their drinking water source. Popular demands for fencing *ooranis* are beginning to find sympathetic ears in the government, and it may not be long before someone comes up with an. "*oorani* Fencing

Programme".

In Ponnakaneri as well as Pooseri, *oorani* was high priority for men, and their concern for both hygiene and their women was clear. In Ponnakaneri, there was a proper *Varattu Voikkal* for the *oorani* itself, drawn from a bigger *Kalankarai,* a kilometre upstream; this ensured ample inflow during the monsoon and beyond. The *oorani* was deep; even in early April, it had some 8 feet of water at the centre. Then, two open filter wells were built in two corners of the pond; women and small girls fetched water from these rather than directly from tanks. Even in the wells, the water was white opaque and thick instead of transparent. The farmers assured us the water was of highest quality and most suitable for human consumption. While we merrily drank the *oorani* water in preference to the sterile water with us, the white gravy passed off as nutritious drinking water continued to be bothersome. Pooseri was one up; its dynamic and patronizing Panchayat President took great pride in "his" *oorani* which PRADAN helped deepen and almost seemed to imply that PRADAN's work had gained in fame because of Pooseri's *oorani*. Pooseri has also made two filter wells which pass water through 3-4 filterings before it comes into the wells. Besides, the village has a huge desalination plant with a capacity of 15,000 litres/day at an average direct cost (which did not include overheads and the salary of government staff who operate the plant) of Rs. 2.50/litre!

Pooseri and Ponnakaneri were, however, exceptions that proved the general rule that the problem of supplying drinking water fit for human consumption is assuming the proportions of a crisis in these parts of Tamil Nadu. Elsewhere, we kept encountering the thick white gravy in *oorani* after *oorani*. Nowhere, however, did we find the women unduly, bothered about this. Just off the Thattanenthel tank outside Kelakodumalur village, we had a free-flowing discussion with a group of women on the thick white gravy in their *ooranis*. They were bothered enough to treat the white, gravy water from the *ooranis* so that it became crystal clear and transparent, but curiously, also said that the white colour of the water was guarantee of its safety. Three technologies are used to treat the thick white gravy to produce clear drinking water: one part saline ground water added to 9 parts white gravy yield clear water; a stone found 20 km away is soaked in water and ground in a white powder which when mixed with white gravy *ooranis* yields crystal clear water in a few minutes as the white substance settles at the bottom. Yet another technology involves lining the inside wall of the pot with a commonly found herb that separates the white substance and causes it to settle at the bottom of the pot.

3.c. Ayacut, Non-Ayacut, Poromboke and Foreshore

A peculiarity of the Tamil Nadu tanks is the relationship between the *ayacut,* non-*ayacut* lands, *poromboke* and the tank—foreshores. In Tamil Nadu, most tanks are vast and shallow bodies or water during the monsoon which soon reduce to long thin alleys filled with water. In areas with a flat topography, the tank bund is low and long, it is often no more than 5-6 feet above the sill level but several kilometres long. In April, by which time tanks are all but empty, in better maintained tanks, one finds a long thin strip of water along the bund. In the poorly maintained tanks, it is difficult to tell the *ayacut* from the tank foreshores. In most tanks, *patta* lands (that is, privately owned farm lands) are at a stone's throw from the bund; in small tanks, *poromboke* (that is, the government owned land that is supposed to constitute better part of the submergence area) is enclosed within a few tens of metres from the tank itself. Naturally, post-monsoon, a very large proportion of the tank foreshores, that is, all of *poromboke* and a good deal of the adjoining *patta* lands, are submerged, ruling out farming in the *patta* lands adjacent to the foreshores. But this sumergence probably helps induce moisture in top soils and recharge groundwater. Moreover, some amount of submergence can probably be of great value for growing paddy. But in the course of our fieldwork, we did not have an opportunity to talk to many farmers owning farmlands in tank foreshores about this and the alternative opportunities available to them for productive use of their land. One impression we formed was that their owners were very likely the worst off amongst the farmers around the tanks; tanks above them treat them as "dry lands" not eligible for flow irrigation; and tanks below them treat them as part of the foreshores. These lands are supposed to hold water for the *ayacut* farmers for 2-3 months, but they have no irrigation rights over the water they hold except through wells![8] But the productivity of wells in tank commands seem to vary. In hard-rock areas—that constitute 70 per cent Tamil Nadu's land surface—groundwater recharge tends to be limited; where recharges rates are good, groundwater tends to be saline. Finally, well-ownership tends to be limited and skewed in commands of many tanks. As a result, benefits from groundwater recharge through tanks are often cornered by the well-off *ayacutdaars*.

We had an opportunity to participate in an interesting discussion with farmer leaders of Pooseri village in Ramnad about tank irrigation rights. Subramaniam, the firebrand President of Pooseri Village Panchayat was emphatic that the tank was meant for the *ayacutdaars;* tank-foreshore farmers cannot get water even if suplus; if the tank has surplus water, the *ayacutdaars,* might condescend to provide some to non-*ayacutdaars* for appropriate consideration; "... but it must never be forgotten that the tank is meant for the *ayacut...*" The only way non-*ayacutdaars* can get into the *ayacut* is by buying land in the *ayacut* if someone would sell. And that sellers are far fewer than buyers—and are far less eager to sell than buyers are to buy—is evident in the variations in land prices. In Pooseri, according to Subramaniam, *ayacut* land, depending upon its location and fertility, commands a market price of Rs. 80,000-100,000; non-*ayacut* lands sell for Rs. 5,000-10,000/acre; and *patta* land in the water-spread area goes abegging for a measly Rs. 3,000-5,000/acre. Our assessment is that the *ayacut* land is heavily overvalued in comparison to the present value of the future net cash inflows it promises to offer. This is because few *ayacutdaars* are willing to sell and. The market is thus starved and the market land values, therefore, contain large monopoly premia.

BOX I
Patterns of Land Ownership and Equity in Access to Tank Resources

In a discussion with a group of 20-25 tank farmers in Ponnekaneri, it was suggested that concentrating tank benefits on *Ayacutdaars* was functional, and not necessarily inequitable since almost everyone owned small pieces of land in *ayacut*, dry lands as well as foreshores. If this is indeed a general situation, then probably equity issues are less important.

Surprisingly little information is available on what proportion of landowners own only dry lands; if the proportion is small, then, the case for vesting tank rights in *ayacutdaars* makes sense. Subramanian, president of Pooseri Panchayat in Ramnad, suggested that there are farmers who have only dry lands. And from what the Madurai Federation leaders we met at the outskirts of Vellinipatti village suggested, it does not look as though the intersection between *ayacutdaars* and dryland owners is very large, at least in Kottampatti area of Madurai. In fact, they suggested that there is an exclusive group of households who own only *ayacut* lands; another which owns only dry lands; yet another which owns some of both; and yet another which owns no land. If this is indeed the general situation, there are important issues of equity and income distribution in tank-based irrigation that need to be addressed.

There is nevertheless a built-in inequality in the tank irrigation system which might be even more oppressive and difficult to escape than the over-flogged inequities of groundwater irrigation. A resource poor farmer without access to groundwater has many options besides rain-fed farming: he can buy pump irrigation, he can wait and save to by a pump and make a bore; even the government has recognized this inequity and created a range of schemes and policies to deal with it. But for someone who inherits a piece of land in non-*ayacut*, or worse, water-spread area of a Ramnad tank—little can help except perhaps a well and a pump.

In Tamil Nadu, the *poromboke* lands are probably as large as the tank *ayacuts*. In some ways, this is a great waste in a region with high population density where land is in such a short supply. The only use of *poromboke* land is to hold water for 4-6 months; the *patta* lands in the tank foreshores which also do this at least get cropped after the tank gets emptied; but the *poromboke* lands just stand there doing nothing for better part of every year. And with continuous inflow of slit, these are no doubt very productive lands. Equally, being overlain by the hard, impermeable silt-pan, they are limited in their capacity for groundwater recharge although they hold a large amount of water for a good part of the year. It is not surprising then that the Forest Department was tempted to raise social forestry plantations on these lands. It is also not surprising that *patta* holders have an irresistible temptation to encroach upon these and privatize them. This makes periodic desilting of tank beds a particularly attractive proposition: first, desilting deepens the tank bed near the bund, helping it to store a larger quantum of water in a smaller surface area second, desilting removes the impermeable hard silt-pan making tanks more valuable for groundwater recharge.

Several things can be done with *poromboke* lands as part of a tank rehabilitation programme, and PRADAN's tank programme leans heavily on the possibilities offered by the *porombokes* for resource generation. Desilting the *poromboke* lands and deepening them can enhance groundwater recharge and create a perennial water body below the sill level of tanks that can be tapped by lifting devices. It can also serve as a perennial fishing tank. But doing all these would mean entirely new ways of managing the tank.

Areas in tank *ayacuts* are generally referred to as "wet lands"; those outside them are referred to as "dry lands". Wet lands are eligible for flow irrgation of paddy crops, dry lands are not, and may get residual flow irrigation for cotton or other dry crops during the second season but only in years of surplus water. Dry lands are typically the tank-foreshore lands beyond the *porombokes*. These are at the far end of the tail of the upper tank and in the submergence area of the lower tank; the upper tank treats them as dry lands; for the lower tank, they are not part of the *ayacut* and therefore not eligible to water rights, even though, curiously, some of these are the closest to the tank. This marginalization of the so-called dry lands in tank *ayacuts* is an age-old phenomenon.[9] As a result, chances are high that beginning with the lands near the sluice gates to the end of the dry land, the land ownership pattern reflects the class and caste inequalities of the Tamil village. The direction of the causal relationship may, however, be more complex; it is as much likely that the strong and better-off have over the centuries cornered the lands in the head of the *ayacut* pushing the less well-off and lower caste farmers to the dry lands as the possibility that those who happened to own lands at the head over the generations became well-off and strong compared to those who happened to own the dry lands.

Some suggested that most farmers owned land in *ayacut*, water spread area as well as in the non-*ayacut* dry lands. But this does not seem to be the general case. In Pooseri village of Mudukulathur block, we raised this issue with a group of 8-10 village leaders. According to them, land holdings in the non-*ayacut* and the waterspread areaq tend to be larger than in the *ayacuts;* but it is not common that many farmers own parcels of land in the *ayacut*, waterspread area and dry lands. A land holding survey conducted by PRADAN staff showed the average land holdings in *ayacut* smaller than in dry lands in Pooseri.[10]

3.d. Dilemmas in Conceptualizing Local Organizations

Discussions on local/community management of tanks hovers around the *ayacutdaars* as the primary or even the only stake-holders. Thus, while the tank is recognized as a common property of the village community as a whole, programmes to promote community management are commonly based on entrusting tank management rights and responsibility to the exclusive group of *ayacutdaars*. This is not unique to Tamil Nadu; elsewhere, too, farmers in the command area are viewed as the natural candidates for management turn-over. However, in Tamil Nadu as elsewhere tanks have several interested user groups besides *ayacut* farmers who get flow irrigation; these include well-irrigators in and around the tankbed and the submergence area, fish-farmers, silt-users, cattle-keepers, domestic water users, tank-foreshore tree growers. Since entrusting tank management responsibility to a particular group automatically implies vesting rights, rewards, benefits and incentives to it as the "residual claimant", the decision about which group should manage the tank raises both the question of productivity and sustainability, as well as of equity.

This poses important operational questions for action organizations, As PRADAN (1996) argues: "Historically, tanks were the property owned by the village community as a whole...social system...did not provide titles of land ownership to anyone. But now that individual ownership of land is legitimized and legalized, it becomes difficult to identify the "village community" which was in existence 200 years back". Further, "the question of *'to whom'* can be modified slightly to identify the *'best person or body to whom'* tanks can be turned over". Of the two possible groups, viz. *ayacutdaars* and other including the landless, PRADAN argues that "out of these groups, *ayacutdaars* qualify better because they have a greater stake in proper upkeep, maintenance and management of tanks". But then ask, "...socio-economically, is it right to return a (public) resource to a relatively better-off group of people—land owners—as compared to landless people of the village?" (*ibid.*)

Despite such ethical dilemmas, seldom does the approach to tank rehabilitation adopted by government as well as NGOs in Tamil Nadu and elsewhere accord the same—often, any—role or status to other stake-holders as they do to the *ayacutdaars*. As a result associations are formed mostly of *ayacut* farmers although fish-farmers (or, fishing contractors) probably make—or can in many tank systems make—more money and pay more money for the use of the tanks. There are also likely to be conflicts of interest amongst different stake-holder groups but, commonly, the interests of the *ayacut* farmers are given primacy and this, in some ways, implies that tanks are viewed primarily as flow irrigation systems—which is clearly a limited view of tanks—rather than multi-purpose socio-ecological structures. As Ambler (1993) (cited in Shanmugam and Vasimalai (1996)) points out: "Tanks need to be thought of in terms of a wide complex of natural resources, physical facilities, landuse patterns and managerial institutions. The tank is not simply an irrigation system that starts from the reservoir down. It is also a collection point for run-off from the catchment area, a pond for pisciculture, a source of silt for fertilization and construction material, a recharge structure for local groundwater, a location for cultivation on common lands, a source of drinking water for the livestock, and finally, an irrigation system for crops...it is useful to think of *tank complexes* (italics added) rather than tanks, which too often connote only the direct surface irrigation aspects of these systems". Ideally, any effort toward improved management of tanks should yield an all-round increase in these various benefits of a "tank complex"; however, these may accrue only if the tanks are managed as tank complexes and not simply as flow irrigation systems, as is likely if tanks are managed by *ayacutdaars*.

Experience in other parts of the country seems to suggest that in the absence of tight, well-defined ownership and management control trade-offs involved amongst alternative patterns of use of tank resources tend to get settled in favour of benefits to which users assign primacy. In fluoride-infested areas of North Gujarat where tanks are made essentially to recharge groundwater, farmers sink a cluster of percolation wells inside the tank to ensure that " seepage losses" are maximized and that the tank fills up twice, thrice or even more often during a monsoon season to produce maximum recharge in the upper aquifers from where they can draw fluoride-free water for drinking (Shah 1998). In Alwar district of Northen Rajasthan where farmers grow wheat, millets and mustard using soil moisture and supplementary well-irrigation, tanks are managed for what is locally called "inundation irrigation". Its aim is to submerge as large areas as possible under a thin sheet of tank water to maximize storage and retention of soil moisture. To achieve this, tank storage is emptied in one spell around the middle of September, and the water released spreads over an area often twice the command area which remains submerged in 1-2 feet of water for 25-40 days. Tank bed areas, which consist of private land holdings, are sown with crops as soon as the tank is emptied; and the lands below the bund are sown as soon as they dry up (Shah and Raju,

1998). Elsewhere in Rajasthan, where groundwater is good and soils highly permeable, well owners in and around tank-beds and command areas virtually transform the tank into a large source of groundwater recharge, as they seem to do in many parts of Karnataka. Here, groundwater irrigation as a "tank derivative" is considered more valuable than undependable flow irrigation from tanks. In many arid and semi-arid regions, erstwhile irrigation tanks are now found more useful for their contribution to groundwater recharge, and in this use, releasing water for flow irrigation is often considered inferior than leaving the water to recharge the aquifers. In Anantpur district of Andhra Pradesh, an NGO called Chaitanya has successfully persuaded farmers to close the sluices of 20 or more tanks to use them solely for groundwater recharge (Shanmugam, pers. comm.)[11]. Using tanks as fishing reservoirs would mean maximizing the period of the year over which standing water body is retained. And as pure wealth generation mechanisms, it might be best to lift tank water through pumps, provide pipe irrigation at Rs. 40/hour like private water sellers do. This diverse way of viewing tanks has not been thought about sufficiently. There is no doubt powerful synergy to be harnessed between various uses. Conjunctive use of ground and surface water in tank areas can produce larger overall benefits compared to using tanks exclusively for flow irrigation or recharge. Similarly, irrigation use need not come in the way of pisciculture use; and all these in turn may have nor conflict with other valuable benefits tanks can offer. The point is the transition to any improved tank management regime should be based on a reasonable chance that this synergy will be exploited to the full, and the benefits so produced would be widely shared.

4. Issues in Tank Rehabilitation

4.a. Tank-Bed Desilting

Technically, rehabilitation means restoring tanks to their original design conditions and performance. This would invlove desilting tank bed, desilting supply channels that bring water into the tank from the catchment, repairing or replacing sluices and sluice gates, fixing breaches in the bunds and cleaning main canals. While desilting and cleaning supply channels, repairing breaches in tank bunds, fixing sluices and gates and rebuilding wasteweir are obviously beneficial and non-controversial the same cannot be said about tank-bed desilting which, some believe, is the costliest and fuzziest component of rehabilitation. PRADAN's rehabilitation works on supply channel desilting has shown dramatic increases in inflows into the tank. Farmers know the criticality of keeping the supply channel clean, but still they seldom take the trouble to desilt it on their own. Often, upstream farmers divert the channel to their fields or wells, and it remains so diverted for years since nobody cares to find out. Restoring these is probably the most productive and needed part of tank rehabilitation in Tamil Nadu.[12]

Desilting of tank bads, in contrast is widely considerd impractical as well as prohibitively expensive. Large-scale tank desiltation projects also have another problem; they offer huge opportunities for corruption by contractors expecially in the large-scale earthwork invloved[13]. As a consequence, to minimize corruption, the government policy has banned tank-bed desilting; where desilting is allowed, the government does not permit shifting silt over a long distance; so silt has to be deposited either on the bund or in the tank-bed away from the bund. PRADAN has also got some tank-bed desilting done under government supported programmes; and as a rule, the silt excavated has been used to raise bunds. Beside such "rent seeking" another problem with tank rehabilitation programmes has been that these always tend to go overboard on construction. Under one such project during mid-1970's for rehabilitation of some large tanks including tank-bed desilting, the per hectare costs were so high that in subsequent tank rehabilitation projects, the cost/ha was brought down from over Rs. 28,000 to just over Rs. 11,000 by eliminating the lining of field channels and bed-desilting.

BOX 2
Rehabilitation of Thattanenthal Tank

Thattanenthal tank is a relatively small tank with a bund length of barely 1 km. Its registered command is all of 13 acres although the actual area commanded is close to 25 acres. PRADAN's intervention has resulted in the repair of the tank bund, some bed-desiltation, the construction of a proper sluice and the installation of a community well to provide supplementary irrigation once the tank gets emptied. Farmers we met were happy and grateful to PRADAN. Much as we probed, however, there was no firm indication about additional irrigation resources created; the quality of irrigation has improved, no doubt, with the new sluice, water control was easier; with the desilted tank storage would also increase in a good year, the community tubewell at a cost of Rs. 1.2 lakh (of which Rs. 75,000 was contributed by the government and Rs. 45,000 by the community) was a clear benefit; users paid a dry rent of Rs. 10/hour that paid for Rs. 600/month operator salary, the cost of oil and repair and maintenance. The Tank Association paid for half a litre of diesel/day to pump water for domestic use outside the irrigation season. Since groundwater throughout Ramnad is saline, the community well is of limited use for drinking. Still some people prefer to drink well water rather than use the *oorani* water, which was thick white gravy.

Decades ago, automatic annual tank desilting done by farmers was related with the utilization pattern of bullock power. During the off season, when bullocks were idle but still needed to be fed, their traction power was consigned to low-urgency uses, and one of these was of hauling silt from the tank-bed to the fields. Bullocks thus provided a low opportunity cost fertilizer to the fields and kept the tanks desilted. With the rise of tractors and decline of bullock power in agriculture, the cost of transporting silt to the fields has increased manifold, as a result, this tradition of automatic desilting by private farmers has all but disappeared except in dry areas with black cotton soil where there is still some private demand for silt. Apparently, private demand for silt also remains high in some parts of Karnataka,[14] but the fertilizer value of silt too has been declining with the declining in the vegetative cover on the catchment areas. As a result, farmers no longer place the same value on the silt as they did earlier.

4.b. Mechanical Bed Desiltation

Kolar is one of the four districts of Karnataka with highest concentration of tanks as well as borewells. Sanjay Dasgupta, a district collector, decided to try desilting tank-beds using heavy earth-movers and diggers from Bharat Earth Movers Limited. He tried it on 10 tanks and found the results strikingly beneficial. He found the positive impact of desiltation on well recharge extending to a radius of up to 5 km; in some tanks water tables rose by 150-200 feet from 400 feet or more. An independent study by Chandrakant and Arun (1998) also indicated that the desiltation of the Mutthur tank increased the yield of dug wells of different types from around 500 gallons/hour to 808 gallons/hour, of dug-cum borewells from 1,000 gallons to 4,000 gallons, and of borewells from 1,000 to 1,350 gallons/hour.

Chandrakant and Arun (1998) found mechanical desiltation economically viable; the cost/acre in the command area was Rs. 5,961; the direct benefit was Rs. 3,900/ year; and direct and indirect benefit was Rs. 7,647/acre per year. Borewell owners were naturally very happy; however, mechanical desiltation costs were around Rs. 1 lakh/acre to start with. Over 80 per cent of the cost was for transporting the silt. In later tanks, a demand emerged for silt; farmers queued up with bullock-carts and tractor trolleys to transport the silt to their fields. In some other places, non-agricultural demand for silt has reduced the cost of desiltation; in Mutthur tank in Kolar, Chandrakant pointed out that the demand from brick makers for silt ensured that the tank got regularly desilted to the great benefit of tank irrigators and borewell owners. Demand for silt even at zero price thus reduces the desiltation costs drastically. However, still later, the demand for silt began to slacken. Farmers found that the silt added little productivity to their fields because the catchment areas were neglected.

Dasgupta, however, believed that mechanical desilting of tank beds offered a quick and large-scale answer to the problem of declining tank productivity. His main worry was that the density of wells in and around tanks increased proportionately to capture the increasing groundwater recharge; and, therefore, some kind of social control over borewell making is essential to make desilting tank beds socially worthwhile. In contrast, Chandrakant's analysis seemed to suggest that if tanks are viewed as well recharge structures, an appropriate measure of the cost of desiltation is cost/well recharged which was as low as Rs. 4,000/well in the desilted Mutthur tank in Kolar.

BOX 3

Muscle versus Machine Labour in Tank Desiltation: PRADAN Experience

Based on its experience with dozens of tanks, PRADAN has come to the conclusion that desilting tank-beds using human labour is impractical and prohibitively costly. A typical labourer can excavate 1.5 cum of silt/day; a JCB can do 90-100 cum in an hour. One tractor can take 4 bullock-cart loads of silt for transport; and a tractor can do 6-8 trips in an hour while a bullock-cart can barely do two. A bullock-cart hired for a day costs Rs. 160-180; a tractor costs Rs. 700-800 but does 24-30 times the work. A labourer is paid Rs. 50/day; a JCT costs Rs. 600/hour but can do more work in 1 hour than 100 workers do in a day. Most importantly, labour is not available in the numbers needed; and the speed of execution is critical since the work has to be completed within 2-3 months. All in all then, although desirable, the idea of desilting tank-beds using human and bullock labour appeals as practical or viable neither to PRADAN nor to the farmers.

The investments that mechanical desiltation requires are of a far higher order than ever made so far. In fact, even in Karnataka, tanks have been all but neglected by the government policy which has devoted the bulk of the resources to major irrigation projects. Thippaiya, for example, estimated that of the total of Rs. 6,900 odd crores invested in irrigation since the First Five Year Plan, just above Rs. 725 crores have gone to minor irrigation; and what tanks have received is a fraction of the minor irrigation budget. Similarly, Gram Vikas, a Karnataka based NGO, dispatched a group of over 200 women to study the problems besetting tanks in Kolar. The women's analysis indicated that the main problem that needed to be tackled is not tank-bed siltation but cleaning of weeds in the tanks and the repair of waste weirs. Based on this analysis, Gram Vikas has asked NABARD to provide Rs. 5 crores to rehabilitate 200 tanks at an average cost of Rs. 5 lakh/tank.

Another argument against a tank restoration policy that advocates caution against excessive reliance on bed desiltation is that other factors are of greater importance in explaining decline of tanks. Thippaiya argued that tank decline can be explained in terms of three classes of factors: (a) problems in the catchment areas; (b) factors that have reduced tank storage, including bed siltation; and (c) problems with the structures built on the tank including tank bund, sluices, sluice gates, etc. He argued that research showed that in Karnataka, siltation of the tank-beds seems to contribute only 42 per cent of the decline in tank storage; encroachment on tank-beds explains 27 per cent of the decline and borewells in and around tanks explain the balance of the decline in tank storage. This confirmed Dasgupta's apprehension that merely desilting the tank-beds without controlling the groundwater pumping in the tank areas may not be of much help.

The main lesson from the discussion on Karnataka tanks was that while the State irrigation policy was busy building big dams and major canal systems, farmers have been devising their own private strategies to make tanks subservient to their needs. Since the government has been ignoring their repair and maintenance, farmers have reduced their dependence on tanks for irrigation; instead, they have reduced irrigation tanks to recharge tanks and captured their benefits by sinking private borewells. According to Thippaiya's analysis, 44 per cent of all borewells in Karnataka are in or around tanks. Then, despite their supposedly harmful impacts on groundwater recharge from tanks, in the catchment areas of tanks, farmers have grown big mango plantations, a trend which has also caught on rapidly in parts of Madurai district and is transforming, in some fundamental ways, the socio-ecology of tanks.

4.c. Poromboke Plantations

Porombokes, the public lands that form part of the submergence area of each tank, are an important and potentially productive resources. *Porombokes* are also large compared to the *ayacut* lands; in an undulating terrain, the ratio of *ayacut* to *poromboke* tends to be 1:0.20; but in flat lands, it is often as high as 1:1. *Porombokes* are often highly fertile lands and, therefore, tempting to encroachers. People generally find it useful to plant trees on the border of the *poromboke* and *patta* lands so that encroachments get noticed. In recent decades, plantation work in the water-spread area has attracted greater attention. Under the SIDA supported social forestry project, Tamil Nadu Forest Department had also created tank foreshore plantations. There exist detailed rules about where tree plantations can be undertaken between the three levels of water identified: Full Tank Level (FTL) for which the tank is designed; Maximum Water Level (MWL) and Tank Bund Level (TBL). FTL is the closest to the bund followed by MWL and then TBL. According to government rules, trees can be planted up to Tank Bund Level; but in many tanks private *patta* lands extend right up to the FTL and even beyond; as a result the Forest Department has planted trees right up to the FTL.

The arguments for and against such zealous plantation work are many: it makes it impossible for tractors or bullok-carts to enter the tank-bed to remove the silt; then, many people believe that leaves and branches falling into the tank reduce the irrigation quality of tank water. Finally, it is alleged by the antagonists that trees lose water through evapo-transpiration (ET). Actual evidence on the pros and cons of tree plantation on foreshores is, however, mixed: it has been claimed that leaves and branches actually enhance the fertilizer value of water, and that the saving of evaporation losses due to crown cover of trees is often larger than the ET losses due to trees. Above all, plantations in the foreshores can potentially be a good source of financial resources for tank maintenance and repair work. Be that as it may, tank foreshore social forestry plantations create a political economy of their own. When the trees grow up, they are valuable capital, and being public property, they are not protected; so everyone tends to have a field day. Instead, PRADAN argues, if the Tank Farmers Association is given ownership of these plantations, it will not only guard them but also create resources to manage the tanks properly.

Subramanian, President of Pooseri Panchayat in Ramnad, was definitely in favour of a tree plantation in the water-spread area. Pooseri has some of it created by the Social Forestry Project, and so has Kadambankulam, the tank which bought a tank-fill from Mudukulathur mega-tank. Here, every ten years, the plantation is harvested; 70 per cent of the net revenue goes to the Panchayat: 30 per cent goes to the Forest Department. Because elected Panchayats were not in place until recently, nobody cared to claim the Panchayat share in many villages. In Kadambankulam, for example, they harvested the plantation last year and in the absence of the Panchayat, the Tank Association claimed Rs. 20,000 share and added it to the hamlet fund. In an informal debate on the pros and cons of foreshore plantation, Subramanian, in his inimitably authoritarian style, put paid to the scholarly debate on the impact of tank-bed plantations; trees attract birds in large numbers; these provide manure; leaves also add the nutritive value of tank water. And trees provide the much needed revenue to the Panchayat. The case against tank-foreshore tree-plantation dismissed. Period.

4.d. Encroachments

Getting old encroachments cleared is amongst the most vexing and intricate problems in initiating tank rehabilitation. This was nowhere more evident than in our field visit to Mudukulathur block of Ramnad district where PRADAN has initiated a collaborative project with the PWD-WRO to rehabilitate a chain of tanks. The major element of the project includes formation of Tank Associations, repair of sluices, construction of surplus weir, desilting of the supply channels and desilting of *ooranis*. We visited Therurivalli and Pooseri villages which depend upon two of this chain of tanks. Therrivalli tank receives water from two supply channels both off-taking from a main supply channel emerging from river Vaighai. However, in recent years, the tank has been receiving very little water because of heavy siltation of the supply channels. In course of their planning work, PRADAN figured out that the left (longer) supply channel which, many claim, was the main supply channel, cannot be rehabilitated because it has the wrong gradient. The bed level of the tank is higher than the level of the channel; so when the tank gets full, water flows back into the main channel through the left channel. That means that the Therurivalli tank can be rehabilitated only by working on the shorter right channel.

The problem in proceeding with this is that around 200 m of this 1 km channel is encroached upon by a past president of the Panchayat who is both resourceful and politically well-connected. And there is no point in beginning the desilting from the main channel end unless the encroachment is cleared (see Box 4). The Public Works Department-Water Resource Organization(PWD-WRO) Executive Engineer, whom we met, was aware of the problem and was confident that the Revenue Department could get the land vacated if it was a case of unauthorized encroachment. His apprehension was that it might be "authorized" encroachment; during his tenure as the President, the ex-President might have got the land records changed and got the *poromboke* converted as *patta* in his name. In such a case, it would be extremely difficult to reclaim the channel. Some frustrated old farmers said: "If one man can hold the rehabilitation of the village tank to ransom, there is no use of the tank... then PRADAN should help cut up the tank-bed into pieces and allot one to each family in the village....and we will also build our homes there...what is the point of wasting so much land under the tank if it is never going to get full...." One of them also obliquely suggested that there was more encroachment of the *poromoboke* in the water-spread area by people who had built houses; and these encroachers were in league with the ex-President. They were interested that some more houses are built so that they have society and so that the old encroachment is hidden by the new one.

4.e. Water Markets

Pump irrigation markets are common and extensive in many parts of Tamil Nadu. But in Ramnad, tank water markets are common too; and these have a very different dynamic. And as we figured in our visit to Pooseri—and form detailed and painstaking field research done by Martin Selvaraj for PRADAN—

the interplay of tank water markets and pump irrigation markets gives birth to a deadly dynamic that sometimes leaves the non-*ayacut* farmers with the wrong end of the stick.[15]

Ayacutdaars in Tami Nadu do not pay a separate irrigation fee to the government—irrigation fees are built into the land revenue which, for tank *ayacut* lands, is over twice as high as for the water-spread area and the dry lands. The rate levied is for owning the *ayacut* land and not for the irrigation service. In tanks like Therurivalli, *ayacutdaars* may not have irrigated their fields with tank water in a decade; but they keep paying irrigation fees. However, the implicit water charge is around Rs. 40-50 acre, so it is largely a non-issue. But in years of good monsoon, when the tank has good store of water, it is common for *ayacutdaars* to sell water to non-*ayacutdaars* for the second crop; and this gets commonly done at Rs. 150-200/ha. for irrigation of chilli or cotton crops.

BOX 4

Encroachment on Therurivalli Supply Channel

While we were on the Therurivalli tank bund, a group of 15-20 farmers collected and ended up in a highly animated discussion on the need to remove the encroachment. Everyone present was bitter about the encroachment and wanted it removed as soon as possible so that the tank regains its usefulness. However, the village people felt unable to take the wily ex-President on. Someone had complained to the Revenue Department some years ago; and their staff had come to resurvey the area. But the ex-President chased them away each time either by bribing them or by using his clout. Some village people had also gone to persuade him to remove the encroachment on the *poromboke* land, but he drove them away effortlessly. The tank that serves 150 families of the village will have to wait for rehabilitation until a way is found to retrieve the supply channel because the other side of the channel is a *pucca* road. All that is needed for the supply channel is a 6-foot-wide strip of 200 metres; but it may take many months—even many, many years—before the village lays its hands on that land.

Martin Selvaraj, who did fieldwork in Pooseri and thereabouts, however, concluded that tank water pricing policy is also influenced by the pump irrigation markets. Pooseri had over a dozen borewells, half electrified and half with diesel pumps. After the first paddy crop is harvested, these pump owners get into the act and sell considerable amounts of pump irrigation for the second crop. With the tank full of water, the pump irrigation sellers faced bleak business prospects, and their worst fears came true with the Tank Association selling water at Rs. 40/wetting/acre whereas irrigating with pumps would cost many times more. Electric pump owners of Pooseri charged Rs.15-20/hour according to the President and Rs. 25-30/hour according to Martin Selvaraj, diesel pump owners charged Rs. 30/hour according to the President (and Rs. 40/hour according to Selvaraj). Wetting an acre takes 10-12 hours; which means a cost of Rs. 200-500/wetting/acre. The pump owners so priced out of the Pooseri water market brought subtle pressure on the Association to create a level playing field and, according to Selvaraj, when tank irrigation rates were raised to Rs. 200/wetting, pump irrigation sellers bounced back into the business. Pump owners' pressure worked because they included the President of the Panchayat, presidents of the Tank Associations and other local bigwig.[16,17]

Selvaraj also suggests that pump irrigation sellers use ingenious ways to consummate their market power. Diesel pump owners are more inflexible in their water prices than electric pump owners. This is because the electric pump owners can play around with both the price and the size of the flow. If a buyer bargains for a lower price/hour, electric pump owners agree nonchalantly, and then cut the flow to a half or 2/3rd so that wetting the acre takes that much longer and he gets the same—or even higher—rate for wetting an acre. For diesel pumps this is difficult to do—their owners have to worry about fuel efficiency which the electric pump owners paying zero power tariff do not have to worry about.

According to Selvaraj, the rise of well irrigation and groundwater markets has reduced farmer dependence on tanks and encouraged them to neglet the maintenance of field channels. Especially, with electricity available at zero cost, owners of electric pumps co-operate even less in supply channel maintenance. As a result, these have lost width and depth and got silted up. In Vandaga Solan Kanmoi, Selvaraj found that farmers in the north sluice who had no wells were dependent solely on the tank and, therefore, cleaned their supply channel regularly, but farmers in the south sluice who had their wells were supremely indifferent to the tank and had stopped cleaning supply channels. Seenivasan, PRADAN'S tank programme leader, suggested that if the wells became unproductive or were to be banished, farmers' attitude towards tanks would radically change for the better. Else he thinks, in many parts of Tamil Nadu, tanks must go the Karnataka way. And the real challenge before tank rehabilitation programmes is: how to keep the farmers from "sawing off the limb they sit on as degradation of the tank will ultimately affect their well yield" (Ambler 1993).

While *ayacutdaars* selling water to non-*ayacutdaars* of the same tank and making some money on the side is common enough, even inter-tank water sales are not uncommon especially when large and "well-channelled" tanks—such as Mudukulathur tank—are surrounded by a number of smaller tanks.

The Mudukulathur tank management committee this year sold water to several smaller surrounding tanks. We visited Kadambankulam Tank Association which purchased a tank-fill from Mudukulathur. Mudukulathur let water out of their sluice into the *ayacut* and at some point, the water was directed to a supply channel linked to the receiving tank. Mudukulathur first asked for Rs. 15,000 for the tank-fill, but Kadambankulam drove a hard bargain and finally settled the price of the tank-fill at Rs. 7,000. It was some kind of a Pareto-improvement for Mudukulathur; their water-surplus after harvesting a full crop of paddy was embarrassing and wasteful; and for Kadambankulam, irrigation for 110 acres of paddy (70 in the *ayacut* and 50 outside) for Rs. 7,000, and still having plenty of water to grow fish looked like a deal. The Kadambankulam Association raised Rs. 200/acre from the *ayacutdaars* to pay off the Mudukuluthur tank management committee.[18]

Markets for tank water are extensive in Ramnad district. Mosse (1997b: 18) writes: "Conditions of scarcity and surplus (of tank water) are the result of locally specific factors of rainfall, hydrology and cropping patterns. In response to this, a market has emerged in which water is transferred and sold (as well as gifted) between connected villages. Most (73 per cent) of the sandy soil villages included in this study had purchased or sold (given or received) water, often several times, over the past 15 years. Inter-village transactions involving irrigation water are more important in years of shortage prompted by the risk of loss of paddy crop. These transactions often bring into play complex negotiations within and between villages mediated by men of power and influence."

Prices paid and received for such tank water transactions appear to be high reflecting the scarcity value of water in tank-dependent farming systems. Mosse (1997b) collected and analysed information on 57 inter-village tank water transactions. In 1991, villages of Cakkur located at the tail-end of a chain forked out Rs. 50,000 for a tank-fill; the sum was mobilised by pawning jewellery and by charging individual wet-land farmers. Not all of them paid, however, since many raised their crop without additional water, others paid based on use. Villagers of Kotikarai paid Rs. 20,000 for one foot of water to Ciriyur tank which also sold a half-foot to Illandakarai village for Rs. 14,000, and charged their wet-land farmers Rs. 800/acre for chilli and cotton to collect the sum. Most water transfers involved adjacent villages; but in some, water was transferred through a complex network of channels, occasionally through an intermediary tank.

4.f. Groundwater Recharge and Conjunctive Use of Tank and Groundwater

Groundwater recharge is often counted as an even more valuable benefit compared to direct flow irrigation provided by tanks. This is, however, not true about much of Ramnad where groundwater is saline. Unlike much of Tamil Nadu, a good deal of Ramnad has alluvium, well-suited for recharge; the problem is not hard rock, but all the fresh water recharge that takes place is not able to help reduce salinity in groundwater. Well irrigation is still used, but only sparingly, to provide crop-saving supplemental irrigation to cotton and chilli both of which can tolerate some salinity. We found the same was the case in Thattanendhal where wells were 120-150 feet deep and the groundwater was saline. It could be used for one or two waterings, but farmers would not risk their land with exclusive groundwater irrigation of paddy. One would have thought that shallow wells would be able to tap the tank water seepage at shallow depths as a North Gujarat, but this does not seem to be the case here. The moment good water enters the ground, it becomes saline. And deeper wells do not seem to help either. In Ponnakaneri, wells were 250-300 feet deep and used 7.5-8 hp submersible motors on their pumps; yet they pumped saline groundwater which could not be used to irrigate paddy except for the final one or two wettings.

In contrast to Ramnad, in the neighbouring Madurai district (especially Kottampatti area that we visited), well-recharge is amongst the most valued uses of irrigation tanks. This is also the case in most of Karnataka as was pointed out by a number of researchers who participated in the Bangalore workshop[19]. Thippaiya (1998), for instance, showed that nearly half of the borewells in Karnataka—and borewells came in a big way only with the onset of the 1980's—are sited in or around tanks. These have direct hydraulic links with the tank; as the tank fills, it recharges wells in a radius of 1-5 km. Well recharge by tanks is often a better indicator of farmer prosperity than the size of their land holding. Chandrakant and Arun (1998)[20] suggest that grape cultivation, the most lucrative farming enterprise, is pursued in Karnataka by farmers who have abundantly tank-recharged wells rather than farmers who are wealthy or have large land holdings. Over the past 50 years, Thippaiya (1998) argues, the area irrigated by wells has increased rapidly while the area irrigated by tanks has declined to nearly half; this is a trend opposite to what we found in Tamil Nadu where the area actually irrigated is far greater than the registered *ayacut*.

Where conjunctive use of tank and well irrigation is possible and popular, well owners have a decisive advantage over non-well owners. Even in villages like Pooseri in Ramnad, where well irrigation can be a micro supplement to tank irrigation or soil moisture, well owners command substantial monopoly power as pump irrigation service providers. But where conjunctive use is the rule, well owners' writ runs large, and truly deprived are those who, for some reason, cannot even purchase pump irrigation, as the following extract (Table 9.1) from a PRADAN study shows.

BOX 5
Tank Water Sale in Pooseri

In Pooseri, Subramanian, the Panchayat President, and other leaders—all of them *ayacutdaars*—explained their water demand management strategy with great flourish. With a very good monsoon, the Pooseri tank was awash with water this year; so after the paddy crop was harvested, the Tank Association and the Panchayat called a meeting of the Village Council in which it was decided to provide water to the non-*ayacutdaars* at Rs. 40/wetting/acre. So many dry-land owners planted chilli or cotton or both. However, as the water level in the tank began to drop, the President decided to raise the price to Rs. 75/wetting, then to Rs. 150/wetting/acre and finally, to an astounding Rs. 200/wettig/acre. This looked like a particularly smart—almost devious—way of monopoly rent extraction; raise the price in direct proportion to the helplessness of the buyer!

Subramanian, however, asserted that this was an effective strategy for achieving another goal critical to the village community: of ensuring that the dead storage of water in the tank lasts for 2-3 months longer than in usual years. And this objective was served through his pricing policy because at Rs. 75/wetting, 150 acres were watered; but when the price was raised to Rs. 200/wetting, over half of the earlier irrigators dropped out—perhaps with strikingly deleterious implications for their crop yields. But by cutting the water demand as the year progressed, the wily President did achieve his demand management goal.

TABLE 9.1: **Impact of Quality Conjunctive Use on Crop Yields in a Tank Command**

	Well-owning ayacutdaars	*Well-Water Buying ayacutdaars*	*Tank ayacutdaars*
a. No. of farmers	7	21	12
b. area cultivated (ha)	8.27	4.05	3.09
c. Water released through sluices (cm)	42.34	64.56	65.66
d. Well water used (cm)	57.04	21.16	00.00
e. No. of well irrigations	4-9	1-6	0
f. Total water use (cm)	100.84	87.08	67.12
g. Crop yield (kg/ha)	3705-4817	1482-3385	741-1853

Soruce: PRADAN 1996: 4.4.

Conjunctive use of well and tank water has a dramatic effect on the productivity of tank *ayacut* lands. Farmers who depend exclusively on tank irrigation get 20-50 per cent of paddy yields/ha compared to *ayacutdaars* who own wells. Those who are fortunate enough to be able to buy well irrigation are somewhat better off, but due to their inability to get well irrigation at crucial stages of crop growth—initial tillering, flowering and earhead formation—these farmers cannot get the best results possible. Well-owners in the tank *ayacut* are the best off; they take best crops because of complete control they have over water applications; they are able to optimize on irrigation costs, using low-cost tank water when it suits them and supplementing it with costly well water only in times of moisture stress; they also make a packet by selling water to other farmers within and outside the *ayacut*. Indirectly, the table also suggests that well-owners are typically large *ayacutdaars*; an average well owner owns over 1 ha. under paddy in the *ayacut*; water buyers and farmers exclusively dependent on tank irrigation have 0.2-0.25 ha. within the *ayacut* (PRADAN 1996: 4.3).

Well-irrigation in tank commands has positive as well as negative effects. Well irrigation promotes conjunctive use, helps enhanced recharge, controls water logging, and helps aquifers store rain water more efficiently. However, as Ambler (1993) has argued, well-owners tend always to be lukewarm about tank maintenance and rehabilitation because their dependence on tank storage is limited; and their myopia and inability to forge collective action on tank maintenance keeps them from recognizing that as tanks decline, their wells must decline, too. Well owners have the passport to privatize the common property tank water and it has been suggested that one way to alter the behaviour of well-owning *ayacutdaars* is to view the groundwater in the *ayacuts* as common property. However, this can be operationlized only if private wells are banned and groundwater is extracted only through community wells. (PRADAN 1996: 4.6). Ambler (1993) suggests exploring legislation that makes the groundwater under the *ayacut* the property of the *ayacutdaars* rather than private farmers; cutting off credit, power and well-deepening subsidies for wells in the *ayacuts* or making these available to *ayacutdaars'* associations rather than individual farmers, or empowering local bodies to license and tax well owners in *ayacuts*. "With the technology available for groundwater extraction today, ignoring the need for building institutions to manage groundwater in the *ayacuts* is surely to slowly bleed the tanks to death..." (Ambler 1993).

5. PRADAN's Tank Programme

5.a. Objectives, Organization, Strategy

PRADAN's tank programme aims to promote a proactive tank management regime designed to preserve and restore tanks, and use their potential for productivity and efficiency. In particular, it has averred: "(The) operation of a common property resource like an irrigation tank calls for cooperative action on the part of all those who would benefit from it. The focus of operation shall be on equity and efficiency. Translated into practical terms, (the goal) will be the economic use of water with the least loss during its conveyance from the tank storage to the root zone of the standing crops in the *ayacut* and its equitable distribution to all the land holdings..." (PRADAN 1996:7.1). This might seem like a tight—even if somewhat narrow—definition of a tank management goal, in comparison, for example to Ambler's (1993) exhortation to manage it as a tank complex with multiple benefits to multiple user groups. Implicit in the PRADAN statement is the conception of the tank essentially as a flow-irrigation system; the central efficiency concern is of optimizing the use of tank storage in its irrigation use in the *ayacut; ayacutdaars* are viewed as the sole or primary claimants over the tank storage; and equity in distribution within the *ayacut* is given primacy.

The approach evolved by PRADAN for reviving and conserving tanks has five elements: (i) restoring local management by farmer's organizations at the tank and district levels; (ii) adopting a watershed or cascade approach to tank rehabilitation involving the whole chain or system of tanks rather than isolated tanks; (iii) vesting usufructory rights on *porombokes* and tank bunds to WUAs to generate resources and incentives for maintenance and repair; (iv) using a mix of human and machine labour for tank desilting, supply-channel excavation and raising the bunds; and (v) changing government policies, as for example vis-a-vis encroachment, to facilitate people's management (PRADAN 1996).

PRADAN's tank programme already has some 160 tanks in its ambit at various stages; the pace of the programme has just begun picking up and three more Tank Farmers' Federations (TFF) are on the anvil; and PRADAN hopes that its tank programme will reach out to some 500 tanks by the turn of the millennium. On all these 160 tanks, PRADAN has formed tank farmers' associations. In Madurai and Ramnad, these are formed into District Federations whose primary role is to lobby for government funds, receive these and distribute these to the primary associations[21]. At the intermediate levels, there are informal associations of tanks in a chain. In Madurai, we visited the TFF based at Kottampatti, and two of its Tank Associations and interacted with the leaders of these as well as local associations. Starting in 1992, PRADAN's Madurai initiative first worked with system tanks but then also began to work with rain-fed tanks. Fortyone Tank Associations have been formed and 37 tanks have been renovated in Kottampatti block, four more in East Madurai and one in Mellur.

The Madurai Federation was formed in 1996, and since then, a division of labour between the Federation and the PRADAN team has gradually been evolving with the Federation taking greater responsibility for identifying new

BOX 6
Empowered Tank Communities

In Mysore, the colonial government tried to restore tanks to local management through a Tank Panchayat regulation at the beginning of the century. The Tank Panchayat was nothing but the WUA of today. However, from the power it conferred upon Tank Panchayats, it seems the government meant business. For example, the Tank Panchayat was to control funds derived from: (a) fines and payments from ryots; (b) proceeds from the sale of fishing rights in the tank; (c) rent from short-term cultivation in tank beds or material cut in the tank bed or on its bund; (d) grants or loans from government for tank maintenance and improvement. The Tank Panchayat experiment failed to take off for whatever reasons which are not clear (Ambler, 1993). However, few efforts to entrust tank management to local organizations today bestow so much power and resources into them as the Tank Panchayat Regulation of Karnataka did nearly 90 years ago. Similarly Malony and Raju (1994, cited in PRADAN, 1996) have written about inscriptions showing that local bodies could exercise full control, without any State involvement, on construction of tanks, sale of tanks, sale of shares in tanks, purchase of water from other villages, sale of fishing rights, and excavation of field channels for diverting river water.

tanks for renovation, organizing Tank Associations, and supervision and monitoring of the renovation work. PRADAN provides technical support and general oversight to the entire programme; but a critical role that the Federation was to take over which PRADAN still has to perform is of funds mobilization through the DRDA. In actuality, thus PRADAN evolves technical plans, formulates estimates and presents proposals to the DRDA. A good deal of follow-up is needed to get these cleared, and PRADAN has been able to succeed in tapping DRDA resources primarily because some collectors have seen the importance and usefulness of their work much better than others. As a result, like with the present Collector, PRADAN proposals get cleared straight at the Collector's level cutting through the DRDA's red tape. However, it is an open question as to how far will the Federations themselves succeed in linking up with the government agencies and mobilize funds on their own. In the 27 tanks renovated by December, 1996 in the Madurai Federation, there were a total of 890 *ayacutdaars* owning a total of 657.8 acres of *ayacut* land at a total cost of Rs. 28 lakhs of which Rs. 6.7 lakhs was mobilized from the DRDA for tank rehabilitation work. An additional Rs. 16.83 lakhs was raised from the DRDA for community wells. Farmer contribution has been extremely variable and has ranged from a minimum of Rs. 200/acre to Rs. 4,000/acre. Moreover, the Tank Associations have not been able to compel all their members to contribute.[22]

Tank Associations as well as Federations have formal byelaws, Federations are registererd under the Societies Act; Associations are registered with the Federation. Each Tank Association has one vote in electing a member of the Federation Board (which is called the Executive Committee); elected EC members then elect from among themselves a secretary, a treasurer and a president. Normally, the three office-bearers are supposed to meet every week; and the full board once a month. At present , the process of electing boards at the level of the Tank Association as well as the Federation Board is informally vague so that most likely the most vocal and aggressive—rather than the most competent and committed—probably get into these positions. The Madurai Federation board has already run into some problems—the President collected some donations for the Federation but has not turned in the money. He is engaged in a local feud and has been trying hard to use his presidential powers to get one up on his rivals. The rest of the Board is after him but the President has proved elusive.

BOX 7

Tank Farmers' Federations

The Madurai Federation has three staff members excluding the Managing Director who is a PRADAN staffer. Their salaries are paid by PRADAN for the first year, from then on, the Federation is supposed to pay their salaries. The Federation's principal source of income is an entry fee of Rs. 100 and an annual contribution of Rs. 200 made by each of the Tank Associations. But this offers it a very limited income; even if the Madurai TFA has 300 Tank Associations, its income will be limited to Rs. 60,000/year, and not much can be done with such limited resources. The Federation leaders have been trying to raise resources by collecting donations, but it is not clear how far they can go on this route. In some ways, it is PRADAN's strategy to keep the Federation in moderate poverty and power and make the Tank Association strong. For the present, however, it is not clear how well this will eventually work out.

5.b. Impact of PRADAN's Work

The core of PRADAN's work on tanks in Madurai so far has been renovation which involves several or all of the five works: (i) desilting of the tank bed; (ii) raising and repairing the bund; (iii) repairing or rebuilding sluices;

(iv) repairing of building a waste-weir, and (v) building a community irrigation well.

Desilting of the tank bed is done by using a combination of machine and human labour. Using machine labour for desilting is controversial; the wisdom of desilting tank-beds itself has been questioned by many. However, after visiting a renovated tank in Madurai, the idea of desilting small tanks did appear worth a thought, if not outright appealing. In terms of the value farmers attached to increased groundwater recharge as the benefit farmers sought from tank-bed desilting, the parts of Madurai district on the border of Trichi seemed similar to much of Karnataka and, in some ways, even Rajasthan. This was evident in the Athiyakulum tank in Vellinipatti village where we talked to a group of *ayacutdaars*. The tank has a water-spread area of 14.8 acres and an *ayacut* of 16 acres owned by 14 *ayacutdaars*. As part of the renovation, the tank was desilted, bunds were raised to a height of over 3 metres against the regulation 1.8 metres; a new sluice was constructed and some repairs were done on the waste weir. Unfortunately, the last three years have been of drought in these parts; as a result, the real impact of renovation was yet to be seen. Even so, the farmers asserted that what little water the tank could collect has recharged 16-20 wells in a radius of around 1 km. The owners of 4 wells with electric pumps in the *ayacut* were of course supremely happy with PRADAN. Pre-renovation, these wells had water at 40+ feet; and they could be pumped intermittently for spells of half to one hour; now, they can run their pumps 24 hours. The wells were owned by kinship groups; as a result, there was no water market. The only *ayacutdaar* without his own well had leased out his land. The wells were the mainstay of farming; they were used to irrigate a little—a total of about 2 acres—of paddy in the *ayacut*, but they were used a good deal to provide weekly watering during summers to the coconut and mango plantations that have come up in the *ayacut* and in some dry land.

The Vellinipatti tank scene in Madurai was quite different from what we had seen in Ramnad. Here, paddy had a lower profile in the cropping pattern even within the tank *ayacuts;* there was a good deal of mango, tamarind, coconut plantation in the *ayacut* as well as in the dry lands. The difference between wet and dry lands was thin in both physical sense and the social one. And the groundwater recharge was given a lot more value by farmers than in Ramnad. The scene here was more like in Karnataka. Accordng to Seenivasan, the leader of PRADAN's tank programme, and many farmers we talked to plantations and orchards were 35-40 years old in the area; earlier, the agriculture here too was paddy-centric. The rise of the plantation activity in the dry lands has fundamentally altered the disadvantaged position of dry land owners. Plantations are lucrative and need relatively little irrigation, as a result, the dry lands are acquiring the same economic value in these parts as *ayacut* lands. Some of the Federation members and leaders we met at Vellinipatti suggested that the dry-land market prices in these parts was Rs. 1 lakh/acre; and *ayacut* land prices too were the same; and dry land holdings are commonly larger than *ayacut* holdings. Some 40 years ago, before the plantation wave began, dry lands sold at Rs. 2,000/acre when *ayacut* land was still valued at Rs. 60,000-70,000/acre. This is the situation that obtains in Ramnad today! But the plantation-based spurt in dry land productivity and value is apparently limited to the Kottampatti Panchayat Union area, elsewhere, the plantation wave is less extensive.

BOX 8
Informal Cooperation: Vellinipatti

There is a supply channel that feeds around 10 small and medium-sized tanks in the village. Even before the PRADAN intervention, there has been a tradition of cleaning the channel annually through chaotic informal cooperation. Not all farmers join in the effort all the time; but somehow, enough is done to ensure that tanks get filled. Farmers who have grown a nursery or have puddled their fields are most hard up about the tank filling up; so with the onset of the first rain, their anxiety drives them along the supply channel often right to the off-take point at the source river/stream; they begin working and gradually some others join them along. In an average year, farmer participation would be 20-60 per cent. Most farmers in Vellinipatti are *ayacutdaars* in several tanks and this paves the way for strong commonality of interest in keeping the common supply channel in working condition.

Amongst the Madurai TFA and WUA leaders we met at Vellinipatti, there was also a more active assertion of rights over the trees in the water-spread area. According to law, these belong to the government, and the BDO's permission is necessary before *ayacutdaars* can use these. The *ayacutdaars* of Vellinipatti, however, have been merrily selling *acacia juliflora* lots in the foreshores to raise revenue for common purposes. They are also resourceful in multiplying their funds. For instance, Attiakulam tank farmers raised some money (Rs. 5,000) through the sale of juliflora trees from the water-spread area and auctioned them through an auction chit. The tank farmers themselves formed into an auction chit group on the lines of many others that operate in the village.[23] In these chit funds, they auction lots of sums like Rs. 100-200 for a period of 3 months to the highest discount bidder and sometimes, discounts bid on small amounts for 3 months are as high as 30-40 per cent. As the size of the lot increases, the repayment period also increases and the implicit interest rate declines to the standard 2-2.5 per cent a month common in the informal credit market. For a 3-month chit of Rs. 200, the bid may go down to as low as Rs. 120; but for a Rs. 1,000 chit for the same period, it may go to only Rs. 900 or thereabouts. Attiakulam group used auction chit to multiply the revenue from julifora and eventually used that money to contribute to the *ayacutdaars'* 25 per cent share in the tank renovation programme while the rest was provided by the DRDA. They also used Rs. 3,000 to bribe some Revenue Department officials to get encroachment in their water-spread area vacated.

Attiakulam is part of a 7-tank chain. The next lower tank, fancily called Kumar Samudram, had an *ayacut* of 31 acres which also got renovated with PRADAN's assistance. In fact, PRADAN began working here because in 1993, they had landed up here to find a group of farmers trying to fix a seemingly impossible breach in the tank bund, PRADAN offered to help redo the whole tank if the farmers formed into an association, and contributed money and labour. The farmers promptly agreed; and PRADAN got the tank desilted, bund raised, a sluice built and the waste weir redone with DRDA funds. In addition, PRADAN also helped build a huge open well in the tank bed fitted with a diesel pump; and farmers put a 400 metre pipeline to take well water to their fields with their own money.

The total project cost was Rs. 4 lakhs including 25 per cent farmers monetary and labour contribution. The cost per *ayacut* acre came to Rs. 13,000 which seems high even by government standards, but more than half of this cost was for the community well and the pipeline. For the well and the pipeline, farmers raised contributions, not all paid up; only owners of some 20 acres did. Now that the well has been gushing water, the rest of the farmers want in, but the original investors would have no part of it; they have already pumped the well for over 2,000 hours and irrigated nearly 60 acre crops with the help of the well, and have probably recovered the bulk of their investment in the well. The well is fitted with a 8 hp diesel pump that, being new, uses just around 0.85 litre of diesel/hour. They charge Rs. 20/hour to cover Rs. 5/hour for the operator, Rs. 5 for the maintenance fund and Rs. 10 towards the cost of diesel and oil. Like the Attiakulam Tank Association which has a cash balance of Rs. 20,000, Kumar Samudram Association too is cash rich—it has Rs. 30,000 in a fixed deposit and Rs. 12,000 in savings account.

Unlike in many Ramnad tanks—such as Pooseri, where all households of the village are enlisted as members—Tank Associations in Kottampatti have only *ayacutdaars* as members; the farmers were absolutely clear that the *ayacutdaars* have the sole and exclusive use rights over tank as well as the water-spread *poromboke.* Dry land farmers can get flow irrigation but only from waste weirs; they can never be allowed to irrigate through sluices. And although there is theft of juliflora trees by others, especially poor women, by and large, common property rights[24] are fairly well-defended. It is also perhaps because of wide acceptance of the *ayacutdaars'* exclusive flow irrigation rights over the tank that some minimum maintenance of tanks as well as supply channels seems to get done.

We explored with a group of Federation and Association leaders in Vellinipatti the role the Associations and the Federation now play and the role they should seek to play. For most rehabilitation was the prime one-point agenda; in this, the role of the Associations and the Federation is to minimize leakage of funds, self-execute all the works, and do quality execution; that done, there was some confusion about what these bodies might do. With some probing, following elements of an agenda emerged:

— undertake annual maintenance of tanks, structures and supply channels;
— establish and protect usufruct on tank foreshore, harness these resources and apply them to tank productivity programmes;
— regularly maintain sluices and masonry joints;
— plant and protect trees along tank bunds to raise resources; and strengthen the bund.

The leaders' expectations from the Federation seemed far too high compared to its present role, resource-base and capacity. They wanted the Federation to undertake input supply activity as well as provide output marketing support as also to lobby and get electricity connections for the community wells. More perceptive of them, however, suggested that, before everything else, the Federation needs to become strong and stand on its own feet. Today, it is but a shadow of PRADAN and has neither the energy nor resources to do things on its own. They wanted PRADAN to help in making the Federation strong and independent. One of them ardently requested PRADAN to give the Federation Rs. 40-50 lakhs to use as bridge finance; at present, DRDA approvals take enormous time; after approvals, release of funds takes months. The Federation has no drive to form new Associations if it cannot initiate renovation work expeditiously; so if the Federation has its own capital, it can undertake the work while DRDA takes its own sweet time to process the proposal; and get reimbursed once the DRDA funds get released. Another equally bold suggestion was to provide the Federation with a JCB or a bulldozer or better still, a Pokeline. The Federation can undertake works for the Associations on a direct cost recovery basis; and some other means have to be found to cover the depreciation and interest cost on the machine. They suggested that, to sustain the momentum, the Federation needs to rapidly expand its membership, resources and outreach for which a new programme and strategy need to be devised for the Federation.

We had a few other opportunities to explore the impact of PRADAN's rehabilitation work outside Kottampatti, except in Ponnakaneri which has a

Tank Farmer's Association of 120 members. Of these, only 110 were *ayacut* farmers; 10 were owners of dry lands which get flow irrigation in years of good monsoon. Some landless were the members of the Association too; they undertook farming either on fixed rental (at Rs. 1,000-2,000/acre) depending upon the quality of land) or on crop-share basis on 50:50 rate (although the crop share they claim is 60-70 per cent because they invest heavily in fertilizer and other inputs). All these contributed money as well as labour in PRADAN-supported tank rehabilitation.

In Ponnakaneri, PRADAN's tank intervention included the construction of three pucca sluices followed by a fourth that the Association constructed from its own resources; desilting of the supply channel; desilting of the tank-bed, and the construction of a pucca surplus weir. We asked a group of 30 odd-members who collected to talk to us to rank each of these in order of the scale of their impacts, and the ranking was as follows:

Rank Intervention	Impact
1. Surplus weir	Spared the hassle of building earthen structure; increased storage
2. Construction of pucca sluices	Offered greater control over water release
3. Desilting of the supply channel	Increased the inflow to the tank
4. Desilting of the tank-bed	Increased the storage.

In the *oorani*, of course, they found the deepening of its bed extremely beneficial since it made the pond a perennial source of drinking water supply which they needed most. However, their ranking of irrigation tank interventions was interesting and counter-intuitive; tank-bed desilting, widely talked about as the panacea of tanks, was quite low; what mattered to them more were the relatively inexpensive changes such as pucca sluices, overflow weir and desilting of the *Varattu Voikkal*. If this is the experience of many tanks, then PRADAN's tank programme probably has a potentially robust design-concept, after all![25]

In the irrigation tank, rehabilitation brought in its wake acceptance of new norms and practices, and the resurrection of some forgotten ones. Each of the four sluices is now in charge of a sluice manager appointed by the village community which, in Ponnakaneri, is the WUA. His job is to open and close sluices so as to minimize wastage of water. Only day irrigation is practised; in the evening, all sluices are closed. This was not possible earlier since in the absence of a *pucca* sluice gate, closing the sluice was a hassle but now, this is regularly done. Even after rehabilitation, in best of years only two tank waterings are possible; in a below normal season, only one irrigation may be feasible. At such times, the community meets, takes stock of the situation, and decides on the proportion of the *ayacut* that can be reasonably irrigated; and the proportion so arrived at is applied to all owners of *ayacut* land. If 50 per cent irrigation is possible, then 50 per cent of everyone's land in the *ayacut* is irrigated. Irrigating the entire command takes 7-10 days. When the tank is full, water is released during the day until all the *ayacut* land is wetted. As water begins receding, it is released to each plot on demand.

In Ponnakaneri, tank irrigation productivity appeared to be quite high on the margin. Since tank irrigation is used during the monsoon, it essentially becomes supplemental to rain; the bulk of the water requirement of the crop is met by the rain in a normal year; at such times, two wettings with tank water are sufficient to take a good crop of paddy 20-25 bags of 65kg/acre. Well irrigation is needed and given only in a below-normal north-eastern monsoon year.

If Ponnakaneri was an indicator of what one generally finds in Ramnad, it appeared that *ayacutdaars* are well-organized for tank management even without PRADAN's help. This was evident in the presence of basic operational rules for tank management even before rehabilitation which only helped strengthen these further. Thus, first wetting for paddy is done for all *ayacut* lands together, but for the second wetting, each farmer places a separate request with the sluice-in-charge appointed by the *ayacutdaar* community; and he irrigates each plot based on an indent to ensure efficient use of water. Here also, the *ayacutdaars* sit together and decide what proportion of the *ayacut* can be irrigated in times of water shortages and applies that proportion to each *ayacutdaar's* land. In Pooseri, similarly, the Panchayat President decided that lift irrigation from dead storage can be done only by manual lift. In Kadambankulam tank, *ayacutdaars* decided that water was not enough for all to take a second crop, so no one would grow a second crop and they would raise fish instead. Some 10-15 *ayacutdaars* wanted to grow chilli but were persuaded against it. In Mudukulathur tank, a tank management committee of *ayacutdaars* consummates deals on tank water sales. Thus, the *ayacutdaars* are a strong, well-organized interest group that defends its rights from the non-*ayacutdaars* and organizes functionally efficient use of water.

An important issue that came up in a focussed discussion with Ponnekaneri farmers was the development of Tank Associations as robust member organizations. After all, tanks are central to the socio-economic lives of Ramnad villages; and if Tank Associations get a really meaty agenda and execute it well, they can become central to village life. Our limited exposure suggested that although Tank Associations have a lot of goodwill, their presence in the tank political economy is yet to grow to a significant extent. Their most valued work in many areas is still in *ooranis*, and considering the acuteness of the drinking water problems in Ramnad, this is nothing to scoff at but it certainly does not get WUAs and TFAs a big foothold in the powerful tank political economy which is strongly dominated by the local bigwig. In fact, one got the impression that the really powerful considered the tank affairs to be far too important to be entrusted solely to the Tank Association. In Pooseri, it appeared that the powerful Panchayat President handed down his tank management policies to the Tank Association. Even as we entered the village, he pointed out two labourers manually lifting dead-storage tank water from a channel below the silt level to a raised channel and asserted: "you see, *my* policy this year is to ensure that water stays in the tank for 2-3 months longer . . . so *I* have banned the lifting of water from dead storage by machine power . . . . anyone who wants to irrigate can hire men and lift the water manually . . . no engines . . . this is *my* policy . . ." This was not necessarily bad; the Panchayat President was articulate, able and enthusiastic; but he made no secret of the fact that the TFA was merely an adjunct to the Panchayat created to keep PRADAN in good humour.[26] From what he said, it also looked as though the *oorani* was his personal project. Subramanian's plan was to use the *oorani* to raise fish. Having decided the policy, he intends to appoint the TA as the managing agent responsible to execute the policy. In return, 70 per cent of the net revenue (expected to be Rs. 60,000-70,000 a year) will go to TA and 30 per cent to the Panchayat. A major challenge for PRADAN is not just to form TAs and TFAs but help them become strategic players in the tank political economies.

6. Concluding Remarks

6.a. PRADAN's Action and Research Agenda

6.a.1 Programme Strategy and Underlying Assumptions

The challenges facing PRADAN's tank programme are as great as its promise. And since no one has successfully demonstrated a workable method of achieving sustainable tank rehabilitation, the project has great learning value and is, therefore, best managed as a "learning system" as PRADAN is already doing. The project's action agenda and its learning agenda must, therefore, move in tandem with each other. In ensuring this, the PRADAN team will have to creatively manage two opposing demands; its action agenda will demand a clear operational strategy with only limited room for questioning and experimenting; and its learning agenda will demand that the project team is willing—nay, insistent—on questioning everything it does, including its own strategy.

To an outsider, the key strategic elements of PRADAN's tank programme are:

— create a Water User Organization at the tank level and help it emerge as the engine for sustainable operation of tank systems at a significantly higher plain of performance than they have so far;
— use technical rehabilitation of the tank along with the establishment of a community well where appropriate as the key trigger to introduce a new tank management regime;
— in order to avert the danger of atrophy in the new tank management regime, ensure that the tank level WUA is vested with strong common property interests in tank conservation by concentrating management rights, responsibilities and rewards in a clearly defined body of registered *ayacutdaars*;
— create new sources of on-going resource generation for sustained investment in maintenance and repair of the tank complex—essentially, through giving the WUAs rights over plantations in the water-spread area;
— create upper tier organizations as co-ordinating structures which lobby with government agencies for resources and favourable policies.

As an initial operating strategy, this is probably as good as any. However, its eventual success will critically depend upon the assumption on which each strategy element is based. And the central contribution that the tank project's research agenda can make is to constantly check the veracity and appropriateness of these assumptions and help formulate superior assumption and improved strategy.[27] For example, the assumptions underlying the present strategy are: (a) weakening of traditional community organizations for tank management is the prime cause of degeneration of tanks; and that modern WUAs can simulate the same authority structures and collective behaviour in today's conditions; (b) one-time tank rehabilitation with external assistance will produce a powerful enough stimulus to install a distinctly superior sustainable tank management regime; (c) *ayacutdaars'* associations bestowed with common property rights over the productive value of the entire tank complex will create powerful incentives for them for sustainable tank management as also contest others' claims to the tank as the village common property; (d) upper tier tank farmer organizations would be able to help sustain and.expand the movement by mobilizing resources, resolving internal conflicts, and generally providing overall stewardship to the tank regeneration movement.

6.a.2 Promoting New Thinking and Innovation

PRADAN's current thinking and strategizing seems to imply that the systems and institutions farmers have evolved over centuries of adaptation are proven by the test of time and are close to ideal in today's conditions. This probably explains why experiments with farming systems other than paddy-based have received little attention; it also explains the strong belief that *ayacutdaars*—who have traditionally held water rights—are the best group to be entrusted with sustainable tank management; it also explains the dominant idiom underlying the project strategy that making community management work on tanks through *ayacutdaars'* associations is the only institutional alternative that is available.

This thinking is probably right, and eventually, perhaps, it may well have the best chance of working. But then, this is also the dominant thinking underlying government attempts to rehabilitate tanks under the World Bank and EC programmes. The role a reflective NGO like PRADAN-DHAN Foundation can play in such situations is not just doing tank rehabilitation better—and in a more participatory manner—than government does; an equally important role it can play is to promote new thinking and experimentation on the side while pursuing a programme of action based on received wisdom. And in playing such a role, PRADAN's tank research programme can be an invaluable aid, provided the tank team is willing and prepared to nurture an open and reflective stance towards the key assumptions underlying its programme. Is the traditional use of tanks their best use in today's context? Can we think of alternative ways of using the tank resource that is more attractive and sensible? Would the *ayacutdaar* associations happily undertaking the rehabilitation of tanks with PRADAN's assistance be also willing and able to impose a new tank management regime? Are farming systems other than the paddy-dominated ones possible in tank commands? If they are, what are their economics? And how best to experiment with them with farmer participation? Does it make sense, in certain situations, to think of a more "inclusive" tank organization like in Ponnekaneri? How might it work? Is it possible to create incentives and authority structures under which a tank-chain organization might be encouraged to manage the entire chain as a socio-technical system? Are there ways to monitor and regulate well-irrigation in tank commands through local action? Is it possible to introduce market-like processes in tank management? While it is standard for local organizations as well as government to give away fishing rights to contractors based on open auctions, how might auctioning overall tank management contract work? What might be the productivity, equity and sustainability implications of such an institutional arrangement? What would be the implications of banning flow irrigation from tanks and converting them into lift irrigation tanks *a la* Egyptian *mescos* in the Aswan dam? All these—and several other such questions—might be important on the research agenda of an NGO that considers it its function to promote innovative thinking and experimentation on tank management.

6.a.3 Tank Farmer Organizations

As its programme evolves, PRADAN/DHAN Foundation will also feel the need to work on the design of tank farmer organizations at the village, chain and district levels so that these can serve as an appropriate vehicle for sustainable tank management. Historical studies show that traditional community management of tanks entailed considerable use of local power and political processes that involved caste and kinship affiliations, temple authority as well as feudal rights. Even today, we can see the glimpses of these in the way tanks are managed and rights over them are negotiated. The dynamic of the WUAs will, however, be substantially different from that which energized traditional tank management institutions; and the way they are envisaged and designed will have a great impact on their future effectiveness. As the agency that promotes these organizations, then, one of the crucial concerns of PRADAN/DHAN Foundation will be to concentrate a good deal of its learning energy and resources on the design of WUAs and, in doing this, a central task will be to constantly probe and reappraise its own design objectives and how best these fit in with the objectives of the members and leaders of WUAs. India's vast experience in farmer organizations shows one result with a remarkable consistency: they seldom amount to much if all they have to pursue is their promoter's goals; but they become self-energizing the moment they assume a purpose their members value, either as individuals or as a collectivity.

Based on the study of farmers organizations in a number of sectors, Shah (1996) has suggested that promotional agencies can influence the design of farmer organizations they promote by helping them: (a) acquire a purpose central to their members, and over time, to enhance the centrality of their purpose to their members; (b) develop an "operating system" which includes resources, management systems, rules, norms, etc., capable of serving their purpose; (c) evolve a system of governance whose central behavioural tendency is to cohere around member interests and concerns; and (d) constantly evolve ways of securing, nurturing and retaining member allegiance so that the organization can get their willing compliance on their common agenda (Shah 1996:241-280). Our belief is that by constantly exploring these questions vis-a-vis WUAs and TFAs—and by searching innovative new answers to them—the tank programme can build robust tank farmer organizations that will yield sustainable, productive and equitable tank irrigation systems *in the process* of pursuing the agenda important and valuable to their members.

6.a.4 Contending with the Challenge of Rising Well Irrigation

Dominant thinking on the history of tanks suggests that the breakdown of community management is the principal reason behind the decline of tanks in South India. In the course of our fieldwork, however, it seemed that decline of tanks is a complex phenomenon and a lot of factors seem to be at play. The rise of the modern groundwater technology seems to be the most important one in many areas of Southern India. Traditional tank irrigation institutions and methods are probably quite unsuitable for modern intensive crop farming which often requires controlled irrigation regime. In Karnataka, for instance, we were told that farmers who undertook lucrative grape orchards were not the biggest or the richest but the owners of productive wells. Well irrigation is also convenient; it gives farmers independence; it imposes no need for collective management or rule making and enforcement; the fast and progressive farmers among the community need not wait for the rest to take to new crops and technologies if they have access to groundwater; above all, the uniform tendency of South Indian States—especially tank-intensive Tamil Nadu, Karnataka and Andhra Pradesh—to pursue the cheap electricity policy for agriculture has made the privatization of tank water through tubewells not only easy but extremely cheap. In point of fact, it might not be far-fetched to argue that cheap electricity to agriculture has proved to be the enemy No. 1 of South India's tanks. And if organizations like PRADAN are to take to policy advocacy in a big way, rationalizing electricity pricing for agriculture should be top on their agenda; such a policy not only ruins electricity industry, and groundwater resources but, in this specific context, also the legacy of tanks. The catch is, if NGOs like PRADAN take to advocacy on such issues, and begin to succeed, they may soon begin losing farmer support.

Even if electricity pricing policies do get rationalized—as they are likely to at least in Andhra Pradesh, what with its CM's gutsy restructuring of the AP Electricity Board—chances are that borewells in tank complexes will continue to remain popular despite the high costs of groundwater irrigation because of the control and quality they offer in irrigation. However, establishing a more sustainable regime of conjunctive management of ground and surface water might become much more possible and easy with electricity priced at cost rather than when it is free.

NOTES

1. These field notes are based on a richly guided tour of several villages of Ramnad and Madurai districts organized by PRADAN/DHAN Foundation, Madurai. Tushaar Shah's field work and subsequent research and writing were supported under *Irrigation Against Rural Poverty* Research Programme supported by the International Development Enterprises, New Delhi, and the Ford Foundation, New Delhi. The work by Shanmugam, Sreenivasan and Vasimalai is supported by a Ford Foundation research grant to PRADAN. The authors gratefully acknowledge the financial support that made this work possible.
2. Apparently because they were built by erstwhile overlords during the rule of Pandyans, Cholas and Sethupatis.

3 Fragmentation of control over the tank and associated components has been an important historical reason for the decline of tanks. The Forest Department looks after foreshore plantations; Fisheries Department sells fishing contracts; PWD's writ runs large on tank-bed, bunds and canals, Revenue Department collects irrigation charges, and agriculture department undertakes on farm development (OFD) works. In the process, traditional roles have been marginalized; *neerkattis* who kept a watch over encroachments in the tank bunds, supply channels, and water spread areas in the tanks of Andhra Pradesh are a disempowered lot today (Ambler 1993).

4 Some scholars, notably David Mosse (nd, 1997a, 1997b) have challenged this notion and advocated a more nuanced understanding of the historical evolution of tank management through the colonial and pre-colonial times and suggested that tanks have been in a state of disrepair as far back as written history can take us:, "Indeed, the descriptions of silted tanks, broken sluices, encroached channels and so forth in the 1890's differ remarkably little from those in the 1990's. Detailed tank-by-tank surveys available for areas of late nineteenth century Sivagangai dispel the notion that tank systems were better off in Zamindari areas because these had been spared the atomising influence of direct state control under Ryotwari revenue settlement". (Mosse 1997b:10). Mosse has argued that the traditional community management of tanks as common property systems "in terms of sets of rules and cooperative equilibrium outcomes internally sustained by a structure of incentives" (1997a)—and the somewhat simplistic ideas of reinventing such management—is a figment of the imagination of the Colonial rule just as the concept of the traditional Indian village community is. Mosse has argued for a "reconception of common property which recognizes symbolic as well as material interests and resources". In his work, "Tamil tank systems are viewed not only as sources of irrigation water but as forming part of a village 'public domain' through which social relations are articulated, reproduced and challenged."

An alternative—and equally plausible—explanation of tank decline might be offered in terms of the viability and suitability of tanks as flow irrigation devices in today's context. In many ways, in a land-hungry region, tanks are supremely inefficient as water conservation and storage structures: they use up nearly as much land in water-spread as they manage to irrigate; for every hectare of the area they command, they need several that can serve as free catchment. Compared to groundwater aquifers, the storage efficiency of tanks is low since they lose a great deal of water through evaporation. Even in financial terms, constructing tanks costs as much per hectare of command area as large irrigation projects. After all this, the quality of flow irrigation they provide is poor compared to wells. Thus, a radical argument could well be that tanks are of interest because we have inherited them; in regions which do not have them, it is seldom suggested that tanks should be built in large numbers. Scholars have suggested the possibility of a direct relationship between tank development and population density (Rao 1998). At very low levels of population density, tanks did not make sense because favourable land : man ratio ensured adequate food supply from rainfed farming. As population density increased, in some regions suitable for it, tanks began to make sense and, therefore, they got built in large numbers. Today, in most of South India, population density has increased far beyond the level where tanks make sense : the high demand for land, development of alternative irrigation sources, rise of modern HYV technologies—all these necessitate a re-examination of the role of tanks in their traditional form. Else, the tendency for tanks to decline will inexorably continue unless radically new uses that are far more attractive are found for them.

5. If the rivers are wild and non-perennial, the system tanks depending on them are known as Rainfed System Tanks. When tanks get their supplies from canals, they provide assured irrigation. But serveral hundred tank systems in the Madurai area fed by wild rivers like Raghunatha Cauvery, or Narayana Cauvery, or Gundaru are rainfed tank systems. System tanks vary greatly in size, but all are, as a rule, maintained by the PWD.

6. Encroachment is commonly used to mean unauthorised occupation and use of public or common lands. In Tamilnadu context, unauthorised irrigation with tank water invites the same penal action as in the case of encroachment. The irrigation rights of the *ayacutdaars* over the tank storage are so widely accepted that others using tank water for irrigation is treated in the same way as unauthorised encroachment (PRADAN 1996: 2.4).
7. Encroachments are often difficult to deal with even through the normal process of law because the difficulties are genuine. According to Mosse (1997b: p. 9); "Watercourses in this (Ramnad) ecology have not followed unchanging channels. Flood flows breach or extend channels, cause diversions, establish new courses, or obliterate old ones. Such changes have for long provided focused opportunities for villages to reconstruct past landscapes and redefine antecedent natural or customary water flow to their advantage." And futher, "... Court case 'exhibits' are full of competing 'natural histories' of rivers, channels and other water-worn courses and features. They show that the meaning and purpose of any tank structure was not fixed, but defined by conflicting representations of landscape, An embankment from one point of view could be channel obstruction from another, a breach could be seen as a supply channel or river course. As endless appeals and reversals of judgements show, in arbitrating between competing definitions and in passing judgement on the customary or *mamul* water flow, the courts in fact struggled hopelessly to look into an enduring set of rights and an endlessly changing hydrology."
8. A PRADAN colleague suggested that submergence of the *patta* land is not much of an issue in Ramnad; some submergence does occur, but it is not detrimental to their owners; in other districts with red soils, submergence area is restricted to the *porombokes*; and *patta* land seldom gets submerged. This might be true in a year of below normal rainfall, but one would expect the *patta* land in the tank foreshores to get sumerged in a year of normal or above normal monsoon when tanks would receive and store a lot more water for a longer period than they normally do.
9. It would be interesting to see how this system of tank water rights would fit with the doctrine of riparian rights. Quoting a judicial decision, Shanmugam (1998) writes. "Riparian owners have a natural right, incident to the ownership of land abutting upon the stream." He further asserts, "A riparian owner has a right to use the water of a stream which flows past his land equally with other riparian owners and to have the water come to his undiminished inflow, quantity or quality and to go beyond his land without obstruction. This right of the riparian owner is subject to the right of the lower riparian for water to flow in the customary manner down to him. However, as the law of the land stands, the lower riparian owner does not have a right to inundate or submerge the land of the upper riparian by obstructing or building a dam or a bund across." The construction of a tank to irrigate an *ayacut* does precisely this in violating the riparian rights of upstream landowners whose lands are inundated in tank water and who, to top it, are also denied access to the use of such water as inundate their lands.
10. In general, land holdings in the *ayacuts* tend to be smaller than in dry lands; this was the case in Pooseri; but it is also true elsewhere in Tamil Nadu. At the national level too, we find holdings in dry areas to be larger than in irrigated areas. This trend seems to change where tanks are used primarily to recharge private irrigation wells as in Karnataka. A survey of two villages in Kolar district of Karnataka by Chandrakant *et al.* (1998) showed that there was no discernible pattern in the land-holding size of well owners within and outside tank commands.
11. A recent finding by Rao (1998) reports on this initiative by the Society for Promotion of Wastelands Development (SPWD) and Chaitanya to convert traditional flow irrigation tanks into percolation tanks. In these, with farmers' participation, sluice gates are closed; and water is allowed to recharge the aquifers. Anyone who wants to irrigate has to pump out the water. Water rates are fixed on an hourly basis. In the villages of Chilamattur mandal, Rs. 5/hour are charged for the first crop; and Rs. 10/hour and Rs. 15/hour are

charged respectively for the second and third crops. Impressionistic analysis by Rao suggests stupendous benefits from conversion of irrigation tanks into percolation tanks: in village Adepalli in Chilamattur block, in Rabi 1993 before the tank-conversion, 5 borewells irrigated 23 acres in the command area (total income: Rs. 79,000) and 4 borewells irrigated 21 acres (total income: Rs. 48,700); after conversion a year later, in Rabi 1994, the same five borewells irrigated 37.5 acres in the command (Total income Rs. 1,41,000) and 30 acres in the catchment area (Total income Rs. 83,100). This is a very rough analysis; Rao does not take into account the gains from flow irrigation in Kharif 1993; even so, the impact of conversion on Rabi irrigation seems dramatic, what is more, it is doubtful if even tanks several times larger generate as much money by way of irrigation fees as probably these converted percolation tanks do.

12. In his earlier work with the PWD several years ago, Prof Shanmugam got one such channel fixed and the tank had 20 day's additional irrigation water supply.
13. The government seems to assume that by squeezing the rate for earthwork, it would reduce the scope for swindling by contractors. As a result, while CPWD rates for earthwork are Rs. 26 cum, Tamil Nadu State Government's rate is Rs. 15/cum. However, money gets swindled in earthwork not so much by over-pricing but by over-reporting the work done. The problems of measuring the actual quantum of work raise the transaction cost of monitoring it even compared to brick and masonry work where work done can be measured. So the government tends to minimize earthwork contracts.
14. PRADAN continues to believe, however, that even in Tamil Nadu, ingenious ways can and need to be devised to undertake low-cost tank desiltation by harnessing people power. The first step, in their scheme of things, is to demonstrate the benefits of modest desilting (by making pits adjoining the bund) in terms of long-term storage of water, pisciculture, and of groundwater recharge, especially to well-owners. PRADAN also suggests experiments with low-cost desilting programmes of *ayacutdaars* in collaboration with dry-land farmers with the former seeking improved water storage and the latter in need of silt for fertilizing their lands. They also suggest that in districts like Ramnad, where farmers are unemployed half the year, giving them wage-work can be a good way to get tanks desilted.
15. In Pooseri, however, the dynamic was complex. Here, the non-registered *ayacut* is even larger than the registered *ayacut*; over the years, the *ayacutdaar* community has legitimized tank irrigation by unregistered *ayacut* which receives flow irrigation without any extra fee. The area beyond this "deemed-registered" *ayacut* is irrigated in good years after recovering an additional fee by the village association.
16. Groundwater markets in tank commands have received increasing attention from social science researchers over the past decade. Field surveys conducted by Palanisami (1989) in Ramnad led him to conclude that well owners—who were just 15 per cent to the total farmers in the commands of his sample tanks—claimed some 38 per cent of non-well owners's farm incomes through water sales for his sample of tanks. He also concluded that water sellers' profits are maximum when wells have around 4.6 m water and they are able to pump for around 10 hours/day. Even at high water prices, water buyers are well off with purchased well irrigation since the net return on irrigation varied from Rs. 15-204/ hour of well irrigation.
17. There are villages like Thoori where Tank Associations charge a water fee for the last three irrigations, but this is different from Pooseri where the fee is levied primarily for generating resources for village development, for desilting supply channels and maintaining tank bunds.
18. Why did they not charge the non *ayacutdaars*? Because they own most of the non-*ayacut* lands, so there was no need to raise a separate bill on non-*ayacut* lands. Whoever pushed this logic must have had more non-*ayacut* land.
19. Even in Tamil Nadu, groundwater recharge from surface water bodies is considered important. In point of fact, while irrigation tanks are falling into disrepair, many

government departments have been busy building percolation ponds to increase recharge. By 1987-88, for instance, the agricultural engineering department had built 4,798 percolation ponds and the PWD had contributed 1,226 ponds. All these were justified on the beneficial impact they produced on wells in their neighbourhood, especially downstream. A study by Thiruvenkataswamy and Shaktivadivel (1989) of 7 such ponds from Dharmapuri, Salem and North Arcot concluded that "the yield of wells around the pond increased significantly compared to those situated outside the zone of influence.

20. The increase in the yeld varies with the distance at which the well is situated at the downstream side of the pond and the type and extent of geologic formation. The study also found that the zone of influence extends from 1.65-2.803 km on the downstream side; that some 60 per cent of the water stored in the pond percolates to the groundwater, while 3-16 per cent is lost by evaporation.
21. In specific terms, primary functions of the Tank Farmers' Federation are : (i) promote local management of tanks and facilitate turnover; (ii) to mobilize resources for conservation of tanks, (iii) to collaborate with government agencies and research institutions to improve tank-fed agriculture; (iv) to consider the strategic approach to tank system development at sub-watershed/district level; [v] demonstrate people's initiatives in conserving tanks and providing livelihood to farmers in fragile agro-climatic environments; [vi] to give shape to grasroots democracy by occupying space at the district level; and [vii] to legitimize WUAs and integrate them within Panchayat system (Shanmugam and Vasimalai 1996).
22. These details are for the associations formed by PRADAN before 1996; these exclude the District Farmers' Federation at Madurai.
23. We explored whether tank chits are common, but the farmers said they were not. In Vellinipatti, there are a total of 6 auction chit groups in addition to 2 tanks chits. But the idea seems worthwhile as a way to strengthen the resources of the tank associations.
24. In many tank foreshores, where tree plantations are raised by the Forest Department, the *ayacutdaars* have no legal rights over the trees. However, partly because of the traditional acceptance of *ayacutdaars* as the sole claimants over tank resources and partly because *ayacutdaars* offer some measure of protection to the plantations in the mistaken belief that they belong to them, they presume and claim common property rights over them. One of PRADAN's arguments is that if these rights are legitimized, foreshore plantations would be protected even better and the resource paucity that explains poor tank maintenance would be overcome.
25. The SPWD-Chaitanya programme on tanks in Anantapur gave last priority to tank-bed desiltation; it is by far the mot expensive component; and they found other improvements tend to produce larger benefits. Repair of feeder channels and rectification of problems in the catchment areas, repair of bunds, sluices and surplus-weirs, repair of water supply channels, etc., are given high priority compared to desilting of tank-beds. And these cost just around Rs. 3,000-4,000/ha. Besides, for conversion of irrigation tanks into percolation tanks, they have found it more useful to deepen the tank near the bunds to minimize evaporation losses (Rao 1998).
26. PRADAN field managers, however, felt that TFA leaders, though quiet, are together more powerful than the Panchayat president and would not let his writ run large on tank matters; and that Mr. Subramanian's influence in water-related matters in the village is at best limited. Moreover, they pointed out, although the Panchayat president has co-opted the *oorani* as his pet project, it is he who blocked government funds for an *oorani* in one of the hamlets falling within his Panchayat itself!
27. That a radically different reasoning can be advanced to explain the decline in tanks is indicated in Rao (1988) which raises a basic doubt about the viability of traditional tank irrigation technology in today's context: "With the increase in population and overall economic activities, the demand for land has been growing. In semi-arid conditions, to

irrigate one hectare, tanks need an average of 0.8 ha for storage and two-three hectares for catchment area. If the catchment area is under tree or green cover, the tanks are very effective. Once the green cover is removed, there is a marked decline in the effectiveness of tanks. Under present circumstances, such inefficient land utilization is unacceptable. Further, efficiency in water use is very low in the tank technology. A lot of water is lost in the transition and evaporation. Economy in the water application is hardly practised. Further, tanks can provide irrigation to just one crop per year. To meet growing demand for food and other raw materials, the cropping intensity, especially under irrigation conditions, has to be increased." Because of all these reasons, according to Rao, managing tanks as they have been for centuries is no longer sensible; and alternative ways of using and managing tanks, more suitable to today's conditions, are necessary.

REFERENCES

Ambler, John. 1993. "Financial and Institutional Challenges for Tank Sustainability: Some Historical Lessons", Keynote address delivered at the "Think Tank Seminar" organized by Madras: Anna University, August 12.

Ananda, K.K., M.S. Shyamasundar, M.G. Chandrakanth. 1998. "Tanks and Wells in Karnataka: Challenges and Opportunities for Development". Paper for the Consultative Workshop on Renovation of Rain-fed Irrigation Tanks with Farmers' Involvement in Karnataka held at ISEC, Bangalore, on April 4, 1998.

Chandrakanth, M.G. and V. Arun. 1998. "Externalities in Groundwater Irrigation in Hard Rock Areas", *Indian Journal of Agricultural Economics*, Vol. 52, No. 4, October-December.

Dasgupta, Sanjoy. 1998. "Project Tank: Tank Action for a New Kolar", Paper for the Consultative Workshop on Renovation of Rain-fed Irrigation Tanks with Farmers' Involvement in Karnataka held at ISEC, Bangalore, on April 4, 1998.

Malony, Clarence and K.V. Raju. 1994. *Managing Irrigation Together: Practice and Policy in India*, New Delhi: Sage Publications.

Mosse, David (nd.). "The Ideology and Politics of Community Management in Tank Irrigation Development in South India: Village Institutions, Resources and Power", Swansea: University of Wales (unpublished manuscript).

Mosse, David (nd). "Local Institutions and Power: The History and Practice of Community Management in the Development of Tank Irrigation Systems in South India", Swansea: University of Wales (unpublished manuscript).

Mosse, David. 1997a. "The Symbolic Making of a Common Property Resource: History, Ecology and Locality in a Tank-irrigated Landscape in South India", *Development and Change*, Vol. 28, Number 3.

Mosse, David. 1997b. "Ecological Zones and the Culture of Collective Action: The History and Social Organisation of a Tank Irrigation System in Tamil Nadu", *South Indian Studies*, 3, January-June, 1-88.

Palanisami, K. 1989. "Hydro-Economic Interaction and Groundwater Market in Tank Irrigated Area". Paper presented to the Workshop on Groundwater Management held at the Institute of Rural Management, Anand, January 30-February 1, 1989.

PRADAN. 1996. "Resource Management of Minor Irrigation Tanks and Panchayat Raj" In: *Proceedings of the Seminar on Conservation and Development of Tank Irrigation for Livelihood Promotion*, held at Madurai on July 12.

PRADAN. 1998. *Rebuilding Irrigation Tanks: Master Plan for Irrigation Tank Renovation and Management in the Plain Mandals of Visakhapatnam District*, Madurai: PRADAN.

Rao, G. Bhaskara. 1998. "Harvesting Water: Irrigation Tanks in Anantapur", *Wasteland News*, Vol. XIII, No. 3.

Selvaraj, S. Martin. 1998a. "Rehabilitation of Traditional Drinking Water Bodies in Ramanathapuram District of Tamil Nadu", Madurai: PRADAN, unpublished manuscript.

Selvaraj, S. Martin. 1998b. "Muthukulathur Periya Kanmoi Tank irrigation: A Case Study", Madurai: PRADAN, unpublished manuscript.

Selvaraj, S. Martin. 1998c. "A Note on the Present Status of Pooseri Tank Irrigation System", Madurai: PRADAN, unpublished manuscript.

Selvaraj, S. Martin. 1998d. "A Study Report on Theriruvali Cinnakanmoi (Small) Tank Irrigation", Madurai: PRADAN, unpublished manuscript.

Selvaraj, S. Martin. 1998e. "Tank Irrigation Under Kottampatti block: A Baseline Survey", Madurai: PRADAN, unpublished manuscript.

Shah, Tushaar. 1996. *Catalyzing Cooperation: Design and Management of Self-governing Organizations*, New Delhi: Sage Publications.

Shah, Tushaar. 1998. "The Deepening Divide: Diverse Responses to the Challenge of Groundwater Depletion in Gujarat", Anand: The Policy School Project.

Shah, Tushaar and K.V. Raju. 1998. "Rajasthan Minor Irrigation Tank Rehabilitation Project: Socio-Ecological and Organizational Assessment, Anand: The Policy School Project.

Shanmugham, C.R. and R. Saktivadivel. 1988. *An Action Research Study on Modernising a Tank Irrigation System in Tamil Nadu*, Madras: Centre for Water Resources, Anna University.

Shanmugham, C.R. 1998. "Water Rights: A Concept Note", Madurai: PRADAN.

Shanmugham, C.R. and M.P. Vasimalai. 1996. "Tank Irrigation Technology: Relevance and Modelling for Other Countries", In: *Proceeding of the Seminar on Conservation and Development of Tank Irrigation for Livelihood Promotion*, PRADAN held at Madurai, July 12.

Steen, Folke. 1995. "Conflicts over Natural Resources in South India in a Political Economy Perspective", Paper for the Third Conference of the Nordic Association for South Asian Studies, Oslo, Norway, 18-22 May.

Thippaiya, P. 1998. "Status of Tank Irrigation in Karnataka", Paper for the "Consultative Workshop on Renovation of Rain-fed Irrigation Tanks with Farmers' Involvement in Karnataka", held at ISEC, Bangalore, on April 4, 1998.

Thiruvenkataswamy, K.R. and R. Saktivadivel. 1989. *An Investigation in Groundwater Recharge due to Percolation Ponds*, Madras: Anna University.

Vani, M.S. 1992. *Role of Panchayat Institutions in Irrigation Management: Law and Policy*, Delhi: Indian Law Institute.

10 Management of Common Pool Irrigation Tanks of Southern India

K. Palanisami and **R. Balasubramanian**

1. Introduction

Irrigation tanks are typically common property resources in India which are mostly distributed in the southern States, viz. Andhra Pradesh, Karnataka and Tamil Nadu, accounting for about one-third of the total irrigated area in these States. Tamil Nadu State alone has about 39,000 irrigation tanks with varying sizes and types with an irrigation potential of about one million ha (Govt. of Tamil Nadu 1995). The tanks are classified into system tanks and non-system/rain-fed tanks. The system tanks receive supplemental water from major streams or reservoirs in addition to the yield of their own catchment area whereas non-system/rain-fed tanks depend on the rainfall in their own catchment area and are not connected to major streams/reservoirs. The tanks are also classified into Panchayat Union (PU), Public Works Department (PWD) and *Ex-zamin* tanks based upon the management authority structures. PU tanks have a command area less than 40 ha, and are under the control of village communities and PWD tanks have a command area of more than 40 ha and major maintenance works are attended by the PWD. *Ex-zamin* tanks were constructed by *zamindars* (landlords) during the British administration. *Zamindars* ensured the proper maintenance of the tanks and channels, since they reaped the benefits of farming in large areas. However, when the British introduced the ryotwari system in 1886, these tanks—based on their size of the command area—were brought under the administrative control of either Public Works Department or vested with the villagers themselves. Since the local bodies did not have qualified engineers and the duties of the *ayacutdars* were not clearly mentioned, the system of the farmers themselves taking up maintenance work known as *Kudimaramathu* works slowly declined. Consequently tanks were silted up, and supply and distribution channels were choked. This led to deterioration of the tank irrigation system which has been a subject of considerable discussion, at least since the middle of the nineteenth century.

The Report of the Public Works Commission of 1852 stated that there was not much of voluntary community labour involved in tank maintenance, and it reported that in all districts labour was more or less forced to work. In fact an Act was passed, namely, the Madras Compulsory Labour Act of 1858 (or what is known as the *Kudimaramath* Act), with a view to legalizing compulsory labour for certain aspects of maintenance, and also to penalize the non-performance of *kudimaramath* labour. The entire administration of the Act of levying and collection of fines was left to the irrigation panchayats. The Famine Commission of 1878 brought to light quite forcefully the deteriorating conditions of tanks and advocated a systematic policy of maintenance. One of the most important recommendations of the Commission was the creation of tank restoration policies (Janakarajan 1993). After the abolition of the *zamindari* system by the State Government in 1957, they were transferred to the Panchayat Union and PWD based upon the sizes of command areas (Palanisami and Easter 1984, 1987).

Most of the tanks in Tamil Nadu and elsewhere (see Marothia 1992, 1997) have further degraded in the post-independence era into open access resources due to weak property relations or resource use ownership, institutional arrangements and breakdown of the local authority system. Encroachment, privatization and government appropriation of the tanks have been the main outcome of the failure of the local authority system to enforce the institutional arrangements for managing tanks under the common pool resource management regime. As a result, the net area irrigated by the tanks declined from 33 per cent in 1960-61 to 22 per cent in 1990-91 (Table 10.1) in Tamil Nadu. It is, therefore, important to examine the causes of degradation of tanks in Tamil Nadu and suggest institutional structures for their restoration. This chapter, using the results of the recently concluded study in Tamil Nadu, outlines the current status of the common property irrigation tanks in Tamil Nadu with needed policies for the future management of these neglected Common Pool Resources (CPRs) (Palanisami, Balasubramanian and Ali 1997).

2. Objectives and Data Base

The detailed study was undertaken in the State during 1993-96 with the objectives of: (a) enumerating the actual number of tanks in operation in selected districts, (b) to study the pattern and extent of resource mobilization from tank usufructs, (c) to compare the performance of the tanks managed by the PUs and PWD, and (d) to suggest policy alternatives for better management of the tank irrigation systems.

TABLE 10.1. **Per Cent Share of Different Sources of Irrigation in Tamil Nadu**

	Source	1960-61	1970-71	1980-81	1990-91
India	Canals	42.05	41.28	39.40	35.63
	Tanks	18.50	13.22	8.24	6.84
	Wells	29.56	38.22	45.70	51.04
	Others	9.89	7.28	6.66	6.49
	All	100	100	100	100
Tamil Nadu	Canals	35.80	33.90	32.70	32.40
	Tanks	38.00	34.50	32.10	22.38
	Wells	24.20	29.80	33.80	44.61
	Others	2.00	1.80	1.40	0.61
	All	100	100	100	100

Source: *Tamil Nadu—An Economic Appraisal* (Various issues).

To give adequate representation to all tank locations, Tamil Nadu State has been divided into three regions, viz. north, central and south, and the districts were classified into tank-intensive and less-tank-intensive districts. The northern (undivided North Arcot and Chengalpattu districts) and southern (Tirunelveli and Sivagangai districts) districts are tank-intensive, while the central districts (Coimbatore, Erode, Salem and Thanjavur districts) are less-tank-intensive. Enumeration of tanks has been undertaken in each of the eight sample districts, where 50 per cent of the total number of taluks were randomly selected and from each of these taluks one block was randomly selected. In the selected blocks, all the tanks were enumerated covering 2,708 tanks in all. The second phase of the study has included the collection of detailed information on resource mobilization for tank maintenance, tank performance and irrigation management at tank level covering 690 tanks in all the eight (four tank-intensive and four less-tank-intensive) districts. Both survey method and interviews were used to collect the relevant information. All the tank-level data related to the five years' average from 1989-90 to 1993-94.

3. Degradation of Tanks

Several factors such as encroachment, siltation, poor organization and management by the farmers, poor operation and maintenance budget from the government and growth of wells in the tank command contributed for the gradual degradation of the tanks.

In the tank-intensive region (where the major source of irrigation is tanks), the percentage of defunct tanks was marginally higher among the PWD tanks which was about 2.62 per cent of the total number of PWD tanks enumerated, while the percentage of the defunct PU tanks was only 1.21 per cent. In the less-tank-intensive region (where the major source of irrigation is canals and wells), the percentage of defunct tanks was higher among the PU tanks (76 per cent) as compared to PWD tanks (64 per cent). The main reasons for the higher percentage of tanks going defunct in the less-tank-intensive districts were the predominance of well irrigation resulting in the disintegration of irrigation institutions, urbanization, government takeover and conversion of those tanks close to the cities for public use, encroachments in tankbeds, heavy siltation, etc.

In most of these districts tanks are merely functioning as percolation ponds—even in some of the large tanks with proper tank structures for adequate water storage and direct irrigation, the farmers do not open the sluices for irrigation and allow the tank water fully for recharging the wells for three important reasons: (a) wells are already in large numbers in these tank commands mostly owned by farmers having more acreage which amount to on an average one well per cultivator and hence the farmers are not willing to use tank water for direct irrigation as this may lead to disputes and inefficient water use; (b) tank irrigation is not a dependable source in many years, due to poor storage and irrigation structures like sluices, channels, etc., were under disrepair; and (c) free electricity is available, so well irrigation is more efficient for cultivating commercial crops than using tank water in specific periods which may lead to drainage problems and thus crop restrictions.

The well density was, in general, higher in defunct tanks than in functioning tanks. Poor tank water supply has probably resulted in comparatively more investment in wells which has finally resulted in poor functioning of tanks, due to less interest of the well owners in tank maintenance. Like most other Common Pool Resources (CPRs), tanks are also victims of the "tragedy of the commons". All these problems arise mainly from a tendency on the part of the users to shirk their responsibility to contribute to the repair and maintenance of the tanks and to their protection and management. In other words, tank users do not cooperate with one another to maintain them in good condition. This non-cooperative behaviour of the farmers might be due to: (a) farmers believe that their private marginal costs (cash plus labour for repair and maintenance) will exceed the private marginal benefits they could receive from cooperating in repairing and maintaining tanks, and (b) each farmer feels that his/her contribution would have an insignificant impact on the overall the tank performance (Singh 1997).

The key difference between common pool and open access resources is that, with increased scarcity, open access leads to increased resource depletion, while a well-functioning CPR tends towards ecologically and socially sustainable resource base. Increased scarcity in a CPR creates an intensive desire for stronger property rights and resource mobilization. In the case of tanks, the resource is owned in common but is open-access to everyone due to lack of appropriate property rights structures, institutional arrangements and authority systems. Further, the uncertainty associated with tank water availability has become the basis for resource mobilization among the tank farmers. To this end, we now discuss the resource mobilization in less-tanks intensive and tank-intensive regions respectively.

4. Resource Mobilization in Less-tank-intensive Region

Out of the total of 690 tanks selected for the tank-level study, 124 tanks were in less-tank-intensive districts. Of these, the tank-level survey could be taken up only in 56 tanks in Salem district, since in other districts, viz. Coimbatore, Erode and Thanjavur, most of the sample tanks selected for the study were completely defunct and hence no meaningful data collection work on resource mobilization and tank performance could be taken up. Out of the 56 tanks, 31 were PWD tanks and 25 were PU tanks. The mean command area of the PWD tanks was 92.56 ha and that of PU tanks was 18.52 ha. The mean annual rainfall (recorded in the nearest rain-gauge station) was about 800 mm in both PU and PWD tanks. The number of tank-fillings was marginally higher at 1.34 in PWD tanks than in PU tanks which had about 1.22 fillings in a year. The operation and maintenance expenditure was significantly higher in PU tanks which was about Rs. 228 per ha while the corresponding figures for PWD tanks was only Rs. 62.50 per ha of the command area. The revenue mobilized was also significantly higher in PU tanks which was Rs. 82.60 per ha of the command area, out of which more than 95 per cent was from social forestry plantations. The revenue mobilization from social forestry was much higher than the revenue mobilization from the tanks in the tank-intensive districts as there is a possibility that massive social forestry may boost up the total revenue mobilization from trees. The revenue mobilized from PWD tanks was very meagre at Rs. 3.00 per ha which came solely from social forestry. There was no fishery income in both PU and PWD tanks. The well density (i.e. number of wells per hectare of the tank command area) was higher in PU tanks (1.56 wells/ha) compared to PWD tanks (0.63 wells/ha). The tank performance (i.e. actual area irrigated to the total command area) was around 43 per cent in both PU and PWD tanks .

5. Resource Mobilization in Tank-intensive Region

As much as 31 per cent of the PWD tanks had informal Water Users'

Organization (WUO), whereas only 14 per cent of the PU tanks had informal WUO. The functions of these organizations include the appointment of "neerkattis" (common waterman), organizing and coordinating tank maintenance works (mainly cleaning supply channels and main canals), resource mobilization for tank maintenance, lobbying with government departments for better maintenance of tank structures, etc. (Table 10.2).

TABLE 10..2: **Frequency Distribution of Sample Tanks based on Informal Water Users' Organization**

Tank type	Water Users' Organization	
	Present	Absent
PU	55 (14.20)	332 (85.80)
PWD	55 (31.30)	121 (68.80)

Note: Figures in parentheses are percentages to total number of tanks.

The well density (number of wells per ha of command area) was relatively higher in the PU tanks (0.53) than in the PWD tanks (0.32), and these were not statistically different. The reasons for the higher number of wells in the PU tanks are that the duration of water supply is comparatively lesser in the PU tanks and that the water availability per ha of the command area is also lesser in the PU tanks.

5.a. Operation and Maintenance Expenditure

The total outlay on operation and maintenance expenditure at State level at current prices has increased from about Rs. 12.50 to Rs. 77.40 million during the period 1978-79 to 1994-95. It is also clear that though the nominal outlay (at current prices) per ha of the command area has increased more than sixfold, from Rs. 26 to Rs. 161 per ha, the real outlay (at constant prices) has not shown significant increase, it has hovered around Rs. 33 to Rs. 43 per ha (Table 10.3). The data for the sample tanks for the period 1989-90 to 1993-94 indicates that the average expenditure on operation and maintenance was about Rs.55/year/ha for the PU tanks and Rs.78/year/ha for the PWD tanks.

5.2 Productive Activities and Flow of Resources

Resources for the overall tank management by the farmers and tank management authorities are mobilized through individual contributions as well as through common sources related to tank. More commonly, the resources mobilized in the recent years can be grouped under forestry, fishery and other resources. The other contributions included the water users' association (subscription fees), direct labour contribution for tank maintenance works, commission from the social forestry contractors, and other minor sources such as grazing lease, duck and goat rearing in the command areas (after harvest).

TABLE 10.3: **Operation and Maintenance Expenditure on Tanks in Tamil Nadu**

Year	Maintenance & Repair outlay (Rs. in millions)	Nominal outlay (Rs./ha)	Real outlay (Rs./ha) at 1980-81 prices
1978-79	12.471	25.98	33.35
1979-80	12.991	27.06	30.17
1980-81	16.005	33.34	33.34
1981-82	15.281	31.83	28.86
1982-83	17.764	37.00	31.09
1983-84	15.567	32.43	25.16
1984-85	15.915	33.15	23.92
1985-86	23.744	49.47	33.13
1986-87	23.465	48.89	30.69
1987-88	35.483	73.92	42.68
1988-89	32.087	66.85	35.82
1989-90	32.073	66.82	33.16
1990-91	32.436	67.58	30.35
1991-92	49.720	103.58	42.27
1992-93	52.780	110.00	—
1993-94	74.165	155.00	—
1994-95	77.430	161.31	—

Source: Notes on the funds required for M & R for minor irrigation works—revised estimate, CE (MI), Chepauk, Chennai.

The social forestry project was launched in Tamil Nadu in 1981 with the Swedish International Development Authority's (SIDA) assistance. More than 80 per cent of the social forestry has been established in tank foreshores and bunds and has become an integral part of the tank systems in recent years. A total of 12,000 Panchayats out of the 12,612 Panchayats in the State have benefited from this project. But the share amount has so far been paid only to 2,055 Panchayats. It was found out that the social forestry plantations are organized and planted by the government agencies and the revenue from these plantations is shared by the Department of Forestry and the Panchayats in the ratio of 40:60.

Historically, the rights to fishery benefits were vested with the respective local village panchayats. Privatizing of fishery rights of community resource often creates conflicts between the owners (Panchayats) and fishermen (Marothia 1997). However, there was no organized set-up to culture fish or plant trees to increase the revenue of the village/tank. Only after the launching of the social forestry project in 1981 and establishment of Fish Farmers' Development Agency (FFDA) in 1982 there has been an organized way of promotion, maintenance and harvesting and sharing of the benefits of fishery in the tank system.

But, the fishery resource is most often managed by the village communities and most of the revenue from fisheries goes into the maintenance of tanks as well as for village festivals. The other sources of revenue for tanks such as grazing contracts, subscription fee for the Water Users' Organization, etc., are negligible. In most cases, the fisheries were auctioned by the farmers themselves, after paying a meagre amount as "fishery revenue" (just as land revenue) to the Revenue Department. In cases where the PWD/PU authorities auctioned the fishery, the farmers (through the Water Users' Organization) take the auction at a very low bid and then re-auction the same for a significantly higher amount. In all such cases, the actual share of the PU/Revenue Department was less than 10 per cent of what the village community gets from re-auctioning.

Out of the total number of 69 tanks in which fishery was present, the fishes were allowed for free consumption by the villagers in about 53 per cent of the tanks. Out of a total of 37 tanks where fishes were auctioned, the entire revenue was spent for temple repairs and/or celebrating the village festivals in as much as 80 per cent of the tanks. The fishery revenue was received by the tank management authorities (PU/PWD) only in 13 per cent of the tanks, where the fishery was directly auctioned by these authorities; only in 6.7 per cent of the PU tanks, the fishery revenue was utilized by the village community for tank maintenance (Table 10.4). The revenue mobilized per ha of the command area was lower in the case of PU tanks (Rs. 9.00 per year) as compared to PWD tanks (Rs. 14.00 per year). This might be due to the higher expenditure on operation and maintenance by the PU which in turn reduces the necessity for resource mobilization by the farmers.

6. Performance of Tanks

Performance of tanks is generally measured as the ratio of the actual area irrigated by tank to the total command area. This definition, however, does not purely reflect the actual tank performance since the wells in the tank command also contribute to tank performance both as a supple-menting source in the wet season and as a sole source of irrigation during the dry season. However, data

TABLE 10.4: **Frequency Distribution of Tanks based on Utilization of Funds mobilized from Tank Usufructs**

Tank type	Purpose for which the funds were utilized		
	Temple maintenance/ festival	Paid to PU/Revenue Department/Fishery Department	Spent for tank maintenance
PU	46	8	4
	(80.00)	(13.33)	(6.67)
PWD	2	23	—
	(9.38)	(90.65)	—

Note: Figures in parentheses are percentages to the total number of tanks.

on the area irrigated exclusively by wells and tanks are not available from the village records. Also the higher number of wells reflects the water uncertainty in the tank water supply and the farmers' ability to cope with the deficit supply compared to tanks with adequate supplies whose dependence on wells will be comparatively less. Hence, comparing the tanks with the existing wells would be misleading. Therefore, the tank performance was redefined by excluding the probable area accounted for by the wells above the threshold level (i.e. the sample mean of well density) in the tank command and the adjusted tank performance was calculated for each tank.

Classification of the parameters influencing tank performance under different levels of tank performance reveals that there is a negative relationship between revenue mobilized and tank performance (Table 10.5).

The revenue mobilized per ha of the command area is found to be higher in tanks with poor performance. The revenue mobilization was Rs. 28 per ha in PU tanks and Rs. 68.80 per ha in PWD tanks with the performance index less than 25 per cent. The revenue mobilization is about Rs. 8.25 to Rs. 9.45 in tanks (both PU and PWD) with the performance index between 50 and 100 per cent. The major reasons for the negative relationship between revenue mobilization and tank performance might be the higher density of wells and low rainfall which are the two important factors restricting the tank performance.

7. Policies for Development Planning of Tanks

The most challenging planning issue in managing the tanks over the next several years will be that of designing the appropriate management policies for restoring and improving the productivity of these tanks. The policies that may be relevant in this context are discussed below.

TABLE 10.5: **Parameters Influencing Tank Performance under Different Levels of Adjusted Tank Performance**

Tank type	Adjusted tank performance (%)	O&M expenditure (Rs./ha/year)	Farmers' participation (man-days/ha/year)	Revenue mobilized (Rs./ha/year)	Well density (wells/ha)	Rainfall (mm)	Duration of tank supply (months)
PU	<25	73.80	9.50	28.00	1.30	710	3.00
	25-50	12.07	8.80	0.60	1.00	853	3.00
	50-100	154.00	14.00	8.25	0.30	1089	3.00
	>100	24.00	0.00	0.00	0.00	N.A.	3.65
PWD	<25	28.50	21.00	68.80	1.25	437	1.5
	25-50	108.00	14.50	61.30	1.00	494	3.40
	50-100	73.20	6.80	9.45	0.30	936	4.14
	>100	No tanks under this category					

7.a. Investment for Improving the Water Storage Capacity of the Tanks

Tank rehabilitation options that restore the original standards should be given priority in the tank-intensive regions covering both PU and PWD tanks. Desilting is an important option. However, it was observed, that in a 10-year cycle, only in 3 years, the tanks get full storage, in five years deficit storage and in two years the tanks fail (Palanisami and Flinn 1988). Hence, desilting the tank fully will not be economical, as the benefits due to desilting will be in three years only, when tanks get full supply. Also, disposal of the entire desilted material is difficult, as the fertile silt is found only in the top (0.4 metre) layers. Therefore, full-scale desilting may not be warranted. Considering the high cost of Rs. 120/m^3 of desilting, partial desilting that helps to restore original (10 per cent) dead storage could be attempted as part of tank rehabilitation options as this will help increase non-irrigation benefits of tank water particularly in the non-tank-irrigation season. Also recharging of wells will be improved. Partial desilting can be done nearer the lower sluice as well as around the periphery of the tank water spread area.

7.b. Management of Tanks as Percolation Ponds

The well density was relatively higher at 0.53 per ha of the command area of the PU tanks, as compared to only 0.32 in the PWD tanks. Where water supply is quite scarce, the density of wells is very high and in such situations, similar tanks could be easily converted into percolation tanks with the main aim of recharging wells, providing water to other village needs. This will help the tank farmer to go for non-rice crops in the command. Government/panchayats should make a list of such tanks and persuade the farmers to use the tank water in a more productive way (Palanisami and Easter 1991).

7.c. Crop Diversification

Farmers in a few water scarcity tanks have already been adopting the crop diversification strategy involving groundnut, pulses, cotton and other crops and this practice should be extended to tanks whose water storage is 50-60 per cent. Hence, by using 50 per cent tank storage, the entire command area can be covered with non-rice crops. Extension efforts and marketing support to farmers should be strengthened to introduce crop diversification particularly in the wet season. Crop demonstrations by the Department of Agriculture should help speed up the process.

7.d. Community Wells and Water Users' Associations

Groundwater supplementation is gaining momentum and the rice yield response to groundwater use is positive and encouraging. Hence, groundwater supplementation should be encouraged through easier credit facilities to small and marginal farmers who represent about 80 per cent of the farmers in the tank command and only about 15 per cent of the farmers own wells and they belong mainly to larger farmer categories. Provision of community wells will also benefit a group of farmers, in a cost effective manner as the cost of irrigation is Rs. 4/hour under community wells compared to Rs. 12/hour under private wells, provided the community wells are better managed by the WUO. Through commercial banks, NABARD can help provide loans to farmers in the tank command on easier terms of repayment and interest (Palanisami and Flinn 1989).

Though most of the tanks have informal WUO, only in 31 per cent of the PWD tanks and 14 per cent of the PU tanks, the WUOs were found to be active. The extent of revenue mobilization was found to be positively correlated with the presence of water users' organizations. This would serve as an important policy guideline for improving resource mobilization through farmers' cooperation. Water Users' Organizations proved to be useful in distribution/ management of tank supplies as well as mobilizing resources at tank level. The existing informal WUO should be given incentives by the Government/PU in such a way that they become formal and are able to generate more resources for tank management. This will help work out a linkage between the elected Panchayats and WUO in sharing the benefits.

7.e. Revival of Labour Sharing Arrangements

Resource mobilization from tank usufructs including labour contribution for tank maintenance works was significantly higher in PU tanks than in PWD tanks in both head and tail reaches of the chains. This gives some hope for the revival of *Kudimaramath*. Further, given the significant contribution of social forestry plantations in the resource mobilization from tanks and also to make a compromise with those who argue against tree plantations, at least the foreshore areas of the tanks shall be allowed for tree growing, which will mitigate the problem of encroachment, besides preventing soil erosion and siltation.

7.f. Fisheries

Efforts should be made to augment some minimum tank storage for a specific period which can facilitate fishery development in the tank. One way of approaching this is the partial desilting near the lower sluices, which can maintain the (10 per cent) dead storage. This storage will also help the groundwater recharges even when the tanks are dry before the tank season is over. The Panchayats or PWD can take initiatives in this direction to mobilize the fishery resources.

7.g. Legal Measures

A tank enumeration survey revealed that a higher proportion of tanks in less-tank intensive (western and central) districts have gone defunct than in tank-intensive districts (southern and northern districts). Legal measures such as eviction of the encroachers and prevention of polluting industries near the tanks should be strengthened in order to prevent more tanks to go defunct. Local Panchayats should be given powers to implement these measures. Also, the Government should stop for encroachment of the tankbed by its departments in the name of city expansion.

8. Conclusion

In India, most of the common pool resources (CPRs) such as irrigation tanks have over time degraded into open access. Encroachment, siltation, government appropriation, privatization through increased investment in wells, poor budget allocation for maintenance works by the Government and weak farmers' organizations have contributed to the failure of tanks. Management of CPRs on a sustainable basis largely depends on designing the appropriate policies for tank management. These policies broadly include investment, management and legal aspects.

In the case of the investment option to increase the tank storage capacity, partial desilting that helps to restore the original (10 per cent) dead storage is recommended. The management options include conversion of defunct tanks as well as those tanks where well density is high into percolation ponds. Also, to meet the water shortages, crop diversification strategy involving groundnut, pulses, cotton and other crops should be recommended. Extension efforts and marketing support to farmers should be strengthened to introduce crop diversification particularly in the wet season. Crop demonstrations by the Department of Agriculture should help speed up the process. Groundwater supplementation should be encouraged through easier credit facilities to small and marginal farmers who represent about 80 per cent of the farmers in the tank command. Currently, only about 15 per cent of the farmers own wells, that too belong mainly to larger farmer categories. Provision of community wells will also benefit a group of farmers in a cost-effective manner. Water Users' Organizations have proved to be useful in distribution/management of the tank supplies as well as mobilizing resources at tank level. The existing informal WUO should be given incentives by the Government/PU in such a way that they become formal and are able to generate more resources for tank management. This will help work out a linkage between the elected Panchayats and WUO in sharing the benefits. The legal measures include eviction of encroachers and prevention of polluting industries near the tanks. Local Panchayats should be given powers to implement these measures. The Government should take necessary measures to ensure that the tank beds are not encroached for the expansion of cities.

REFERENCES

Department of Statistics. 1995. "Season and Crop Report of Tamil Nadu", Government of Tamil Nadu, Chennai.

Evaluation and Applied Research Department. "Tamil Nadu-An Economic Appraisal" various years, Government of Tamil Nadu, Chennai.

Janakarajan, S. 1993. "In Search of Tanks : Some Hidden Facts", *Econ. and Polit. Weekly*, 28 (26): A53-A60.

Marothia, D.K. 1992. "Village Irrigation Tanks: Institutional Design for Sustainable Resource Use". *Agricultural Situation in India*. 47(6): 479-87.

Marothia, D.K. 1997. "Institutional Arrangements for Common Village Ponds", in *Natural Resource Economics: Theory and Application in India*, In: John M. Kerr, Dinesh. K. Marothia, Katar Singh, C. Ramasamy and William R. Bently, (eds.), New Delhi: Oxford & IBH Publishing Co. Pvt. Ltd.

Palanisami, K. and K. William Easter. 1984. "Tank Irrigation in India and Thailand : Problems and Prospects", London: Irrigation Management Network, Agricultural Administration Unit, Overseas Development Institute, November.

Palanisami, K. and K. William Easter. 1987. "Small-Scale Surface (Tank) Irrigation in Asia", *Water Resources Research*, 23 (5) : pp. 774-780.

Palanisami, K. and K. William Easter. 1991. "Hydro-Economic Interaction between Tank and Well Water", *Indian Journal of Agric. Economics*, 46 (2) :174-179.

Palanisami, K. and J.C. Flinn. 1988. "Evaluating the Performance of Tank Irrigation Systems", *Agric. Systems*, 28 :161-177.

Palanisami, K. and J.C. Flinn. 1989. "Impact of Varying Water Supply on Input Use and Yields of Tank-Irrigated Rice", *Agric. Water Management*, 15: 347-359.

Palanisami, K., R. Balasubramanian and A. Mohamed Ali. 1997. *Present Status and Future Strategies of Tank Irrigation in Tamil Nadu*, Water Technology Centre, Coimbatore: TNAU Press.

Singh, K. 1997. "Property Rights and Tenures in Natural Resources", In: John M. Kerr, Dinesh. K. Marothia, Katar Singh, C. Ramasamy and William R. Bently (eds.), *Natural Resource Economics: Theory and Application in India*, New Delhi: Oxford & IBH Publishing Co. Pvt. Ltd.

11 Groundwater Management: Problems and Opportunities

P.K. Joshi

Historically. groundwater is an important source of irrigation in India. Its contribution in enhancing agricultural production was better realized during the green revolution period. However, in the race for increasing agricultural production, its over-exploitation and mismanagement resulted in several environmental-related problems, for example, fall and rise in the watertable, groundwater pollution, etc. These problems are now bothering agricultural scientists, policy makers and environmentalists that any threat to this important resource will adversely affect the pace of agricultural development in the country. The environment-related problems are more pronounced in the favourable and high-growth regions in the country. The undesirable trend of groundwater management is to be checked through appropriate technology and/or policy interventions. This chapter highlights the environment-related problems of groundwater development, and proposes appropriate technologies and policy options to revert the diseconomies resulting from the mismanagement of the groundwater. More specifically, the chapter addresses three issues pertaining to the externalities related with the groundwater. These are: (i) review the fluctuations in the groundwater level in the most critical regions of the country, (ii) assess the implications of externalities related with the groundwater management, (iii) propose appropriate technology and policy options to improve the groundwater status.

1. Groundwater Development

Indian agriculture received highest priority in irrigation development in successive Five Year Plans. The irrigated area increased from about 20 million ha. in 1950-51 to 51.5 million ha. in 1993-94. With the advent of new agricultural technology in mid 1960s, several incentives (like electrification, bank credit, etc.) were given to the groundwater development.

The area under groundwater irrigation, which was less than 6 million ha. in 1959-51, went up to 18 million ha. in 1980-81 to 28 million ha. in 1993-94. More than half of the total irrigated area is through groundwater. The share of groundwater in total irrigated area increased from 30 per cent in 1960-61 to 54 per cent in 1993-94 (Table 11.1). Most of the groundwater development came through private investment. The area under groundwater is increasing progressively as this is the most reliable and cost-effective source of irrigation.

TABLE 11.1: Source-wise Irrigated Area (per cent)

Year	Canal	Tanks	Wells	Other
1950-51	40	17	29	14
1960-61	42	18	30	10
1970-71	41	13	38	7
1975-76	40	11	42	7
1980-81	39	8	46	7
1985-86	39	7	49	6
1990-91	36	6	51	6
1993-94	33	6	54	7

Source: Government of India (1997).

2. Emerging Problems of Groundwater Management

There are two distinct problems, which are threatening the sustainability of the agricultural systems. These are (i) declining watertable and (ii) rising watertable. often difined as waterlogging. The present section addresses both these complex problems in the context of agriculture and related activities.

2.a. Declining Groundwater Table

2.a.1. Magnitude of the Problem

One of the major concerns that attracted the attention of researchers and policy makers in recent years was the over exploitation of groundwater in the regions endowed with good quality water. The problem is more pronounced and largely confined in the rice-wheat based cropping systems in the Indo-Gangetic plains, and some sugarcane-growing regions in the western and southern parts of India.

In Haryana, it is reported that the problems was too acute, and the watertable in good aquifer regions has declined to between 1-83 cm during the past one decade, and is posing a serious threat to the agricultural economy of Haryana. The worst hit districts in Haryana are Karnal, Kurukshetra, Kaithal, Ambala, where the number of tubewells has increased manifold during the past three decades. The watertable in these districts declined at the rate of 12-33 cm per year (Singh *et al.* 1997). The watertable in Kurukshetra declined from 8.21 metres in June, 1980, to 14.50 metres in June, 1990. In Karnal district, it came down from 6.4 metres in 1980 to about 9 metres in 1990 (Sharma, Gajja and Shah 1995). The Haryana State Minor irrigation and Tubewell Corporation, which regularly monitors the status of watertable, reported that the falling watertable is witnessed in all the districts endowed withgood quality water.

In Punjab, the situation is worst than in Haryana. The official estimates revealed that the watertable in the State is lowering at a rate of 20 cm per year. It is reported that the annual ground water draft insix districts. namely, Kapurthala, Ludhiana, Patiala, Amritsar, Sangrur and Jallandhar, has exceeded the annual recharge (Bathla 1997). Sidhu and Dhillon (1997) assessed the fall in the watertable in different districts during 1984-94, and reported that the decline was about 5.1 metres in Sangrur, 4.8 metres in Patiala, 4.5 metres in the paddy-growing regions of Ferozepur and Faridkot districts, and 2.5 metres in Jallandhar district. The total availability of water resources in the State was estimated at 3.13 million ha-metres, out of which underground water accounted for about 54 per cent, and the remaining accounted for the surface water. The demand for water in 1991-92 was estimated at 35.50 million ha-metres, leading to a net deficit of 1.27 million ha-metres. The area under the watertable depth less than 5 metres has declined from 37.5 per cent in 1973 to only 18.3 per cent in 1994, which clearly indicated over exploitation of the groundwater.

In Uttar Pradesh, the traditional well irrigation methods were also replaced by the electric-operated tubewells, which resulted in a decline in the groundwater in defferent agro-ecological regions of the State. Tewari and Singh (1997) estimated that the groundwater recharge was far below the net draft with the expansion of high water requirement crops like rice and sugarcane, and the mushrooming growth of electric-run tubewells. It was noted that there was a differential pattern of decline in the watertable in various agro-ecological regions between 1982-83 and 1993-94. The fall in the watertable during these periods was from 8.9 to 9.12 metres in western Uttar Pradesh. from 5.08 to 6.58 metres in central Uttar Pradesh, from 7.52 to 9.27 metres in the Bundelkhand region, and from 4.48 to 5.64 metres in eastern Uttar Pradesh.

The problems of declining groundwater is also reported from other parts of the country (for example, Gujarat, Maharashtra, Andhra Pradesh and Tamil Nadu) where agriculture is rapidly intensifying. Satyasai and Viswanathan (1997) have observed that the watertable in Anant purdistrict of Andhra

Pradesh has been receding at a fast rate. It was reported that dugwells, which were the important source of irrigation in the region, became dry, and the farmers chased the groundwater initially by deepening the wells, and later adopted the borewell technology coupled with high-power submersible pumpsets which further led to over exploitation of the groundwater. Similarly, because of heavy pumping in parts of Tamil Nadu, the water level dropped by as much as 25-30 metres in a decade. With particular reference to western Tamil Nadu. Ramasamy and Sekar (1997) have noted that the groundwater level kept falling over the years till it reached the threshold of irreversibility in certain pockets of Coimbatore region. In Gujarat, decline of the watertable of 2-3.5 metres per year in the confined aquifers of south Mehsana and 0.5 metre per year in east Mehsana was noted (Moench and Kumar 1997). Unconfined watertable declined in parts of Banaskantha districts have averaged 1-2 metres per annum.

The above information on the declining status of the groundwater level in the green revolution and other intensifying belts is alarming. Such trends are to be checked and reversed for sustainable agricultural production.

2.a.2 *Factors Responsible for Declining Watertable*

A number of factors are responsible for the receding groundwater level. These include:

- Huge subsidies on the electricity to extract groundwater for irrigation;
- No additional (marginal) private cost of extracting additional quantity of water because of flat electricity charges;
- Inadequate availability of canal water for high water requirement crops;
- Change in the cropping pattern in favour of high water requirement crops (for example, rice and sugarcane) in the low rainfall areas; and
- No State regulation for the use of groundwater resource.

It is noted that electric-run pumps and tubewells are excessively used to exploit the groundwater resource. A fairly large amount (18 per cent) of the electricity in rural areas is consumed for agricultural operations. In order to encourage groundwater use, the subsidy element on electricity consumption in Indian agriculture rose from Rs. 3.53 billion in 1980-81 to Rs. 14.57 billion in 1986-87 (Gulati 1989). The present subsidy status on electricity in agriculture may be worst as many State governments, under political compulsions, wave off power tariff in agriculture. Bulk of the electricity is used for operating tubewells to extract groundwater. There is no State regulation for the use of this common property resource. Consequently, groundwater levels are drastically falling in most intensively cropped areas of the country as withdrawals exceed recharge (Vohra 1987).

Rice cultivation has also led to on excessive mining of groundwater. Due to higher profitability from the crop and yield stability, rice is grown widely even in the non-traditional areas, like Punjab, Haryana and parts of western Uttar Pradesh. In order to meet the water requirement of the crop, in areas of inadequate canal water supplies or in low rainfall regions, the farmers were forced to depend upon groundwater as it was cheap, reliable, and meets the demand. The net result was overdraft of groundwater compared with recharge through rainfall.

2.b. Rising Groundwater Table

2.b.1 Magnitude of the Problem

The other serious problems is related with the rising groundwater level which is leading to soil salinity and waterlogging. It is often observed in areas where canal water is introduced without appropriate drainage system, and where either groundwater is brackish or good quality groundwater is not used. It has been estimated that the rate of rise in the watertable in the poor water quality areas of Haryana is of the order of 0.15-1.00 metre per year (FAO 1985). It has also been reported that high groundwater levels already account for about 0.4 million ha. in Haryana. It is apprehended that up to 1.5 to 2.0 million ha. may be affected by high water levels, waterlogging and, in the long run, by soil salinity in Haryana (Gangwar and Toorn 1987). It is observed that in the poor quality groundwater regions, the watertable has risen at the rate of 3 to 10 metres during the last three decades in around 40,000 ha. (Patel and Panghal 1997).

The saline water belt of Punjab also shows similar trends. The problem of rising watertable is becoming serious in Faridkot, Ferozepur and certain pockets of Bhatinda district (Sidhu and Dhillon 1997). The area under watertable depth less than 10 metres has been increasing over time in these districts. The rise in the watertable has been found to be more than 7 metres during 1973-83 and more than 4 metres during 1983-93. In a specific case study in the Muktsar block of Faridkot district, it was observed that the watertable rose from 17 to 2 metres between 1970 and 1990 (Khepar and Kausal 1991).

Rising watertable is mostly observed in many of the surface irrigation projects. For example, waterlogging in the Sharda Sahayak Irrigation Project is reported to be 50,000 ha., in the Indira Gandhi Canal Project it was estimated to be about 29,000 ha., and in the Kakarpar irrigation project 8,000 ha. At the aggregate level in the country, the estimated area under waterlogging has been estimated to be in the range of 2.45-3.53 million ha.

2.b.2 *Factors Responsible for Rising Watertable*

A large number of causative factors are responsible for the rising watertable. The important reasons for deteriorating soil environment due to rising watertable are:

— higher seepage losses from canal;
— poor operation and maintenance of canal networks;
— introduction of canal irrigation in marginal lands;
— mismanagement and over-use of canal water;
— high subsidy on canal water charges;
— higher acreage allocation in favour of rice and sugarcane; and
— poor groundwater quality.

Some other location-specific reasons observed are poor drainage porosity of soil, lack of drainage outlet, presence of shallow hard pan below soil surface, saline groundwater, etc.

3. Consequences of the Problems

The declining stock and deteriorating quality of the most important natural resource, (i.e. groundwater,) is a loss to the society. Declining watertable reduces tubewell discharge, which affects the command area of a tubewell, hence the cost of irrigation. While the command area is positively related with the discharge, the cost is negatively related. Although the cost of extracting groundwater is never reflected in the private cost of irrigation because farmers are paying flat rates for electricity to operate tubewells and their marginal cost of extracting groundwater is zero (Dhawan1986), the private cost is unaffected, while the social cost will rise with progressive pumping. Nonetheless, the lower discharge rate affects the overall irrigation efficiency in the farm with additional time needed to irrigate the same area. Joshi and Tyagi (1991) estimated the change in the social cost of groundwater extraction in 1980 and 1990. It was found that the cost increased from Rs. 2.15 per hour in 1980 to Rs. 4.27 per hour in 1990. It will definitely increase the subsidies on electricity and adversely affect the social profitability.

Unlike overextraction of groundwater in good quality areas, the poor quality groundwater areas are witnessing continuous rise in the watertable. The problem is taking a serious turn in terms of loss in production and decline in farm income (Joshi *et al.*1997). Gangwar and Toorn (1987) have estimated a loss of Rs. 26.8 crores due to rise in poor quality water in Haryana during 1982, and predicted the loss to rise to a high level of Rs. 71.9 crores in 2000 AD. Depending on some specific assumptions, investment requirement was estimated, which ranged from Rs. 450 crores to Rs. 530 crores to reclaim and prevent the losses due to the problem.

Another problem, which is expected to adversely affect the society, is related with equity. It is expected that in the absence of suitable measures, where the watertable is declining, a stage will soon be reached when shallow tubewells will be ineffective. Eventually, to harvest groundwater, farmers will have to go for deep tubewells. The deep tubewell technology is costly and beyond the reach of a small farmer. Aslo, unlike a shallow tubewell, the deep tubewell technology is uneconomic for smaller areas. It is feared that with the continuous decline in the watertable, the small and less resource endowed farmers will not be in a position to install deep tubewell and will be dictated by the large farmers. Consequently, the small farmers will have to pay much higher irrigation charges and adjust agricultural operations according to the availability of water. It will certainly increase the cost and severely affect and small farmers and production in the long run.

In areas where the watertable is rising, the worst affected group is small and marginal farmers. The crop yields are adversely affected. In many instances, small and marginal farmers have to abandon crop production activity because of negative returns (Joshi and Jha 1991). Such a situation is leading to income disparities.

4. Measures to Improve Groundwater Management

4.a. Technology Options

A number of technology options are available to improve the groundwater status. Important ones are given below:

4.a.1 *Water Saving Devices*

Irrigation water use efficiency can be increased substantially by using drip or sprinkler irrigation systems. The irrigation efficiency of drip and sprinkler methods are 90 and 85 per cent, respectively, which is 70 per cent with surface irrigation method with proper levelling (Tyagi, Joshi and Svendsen 1995). Field experiments have proved that the sprinkler and drip irrigation systems can save water up to 30 and 50-70 per cent, respectively (Srivanappan 1994), increase crop yields and improve the quality of the crop (Garg and Aggarwal 1996). Satyasai and Viswanathan (1997) estimated that water saving through these techniques varied from 25 to 66 per cent depending upon the crop. The extent of water saving was more than one-third even in the water-intensive crops like sugarcane, and 60 per cent in the case of mulberry. It was further reported that the impact on yield varied from 3 per cent in mulberry to 25 per cent in cotton with drip irrigation, and 46 per cent in potato with sprinkler irrigation. The advantage of these irrigation systems has remained unexploited due to high initial investments, and lack of knowledge about the real economics. The government is giving huge subsidies on these irrigation systems to popularize them and encourage farmers to efficiently use the scarce water resource. These irrigation systems are equally effective in declining and rising groundwater environments.

4.a.2 *Crop Diversification*

Rice and sugarcane are prominent crops, which require high water, and lead to externalities. Crop diversification through those crops, which require less water, may contribute significantly in enhancing the sustainability of the production system. In this context, legumes can play an important role. Legumes complement cereals in both production and consumption. In the production process, legumes improve soil fertility status, require less water than cereals, and their rotation with cereals help control diseases and pests. However, the profitability of legumes is too low in comparison with rice and other high and medium water requirement crops. Joshi *et al.* (1997) monitored the profitability and other indicators and assessed the trade-off. Examining the trade-off values for shifting rice by pigeonpea, it was observed that farmers would lose about 49 per cent profit. The region had to sacrifice 76 per cent of foodgrain production; and 57 per cent of fixed resources would remain idle. However, on the positive side, the region would save about 95 per cent of the groundwater, and 65 per cent of nitrogenous fertilizer. Similarly, assessing the trade-off between wheat and chickpea, it was noted that farmers would lose about 19 per cent profit. The region would sacrifice about 64 per cent foodgrain production, and about 49 per cent fixed resources would remain idle. On the gain side, cultivation of chickpea would save about 85 per cent of groundwater, and 73 per cent of nitrogenous fertilizer.

To replace rice, the production technology of competing crops will have to be upgraded. In order to compete with rice, the yield of maize should be increased by 70 per cent that of green gram by 130 per cent, pigeonpea by 169 per cent, cotton and groundnut by 47 per cent (Johl 1984). Though these crops yield less they also require less water for irrigation. These crops which can substitute rice should receive high research priority to increase their yield potential for realizing higher profits.

4.a.3 *Sub-surface Drainage*

In the rising watertable regions, provision of sub-surface drainage is sound enough to be a feasible technology option. Sub-surface drainage removes excess water from the root zone. The cost of sub-surface drainage depends upon several factors: depth and spacing of drains, type of drainage material, soil type, area under drainage, and wages of labourers. The cost of installing sub-surface drainage in Haryana was Rs. 10.700 per hectare during 1989-90. For Gujarat, it ranged from Rs. 9,710 to Rs. 13,500 per hectare (Joshi, Tyagi, Svendsen 1995). Investment on drainage for saline-waterlogged soils was found financially feasible (Joshi *et al.* 1987; Datta and de Jong, 1991). The internal rate of return under farmers resource endowments was 13.3 per cent, with benefit-cost ratio at 1.26. The scientific frontier of managing saline waterlogged soil was considerably high, where the cost-benefit ratio was as high as 3.99.

4.b. Policy Intervention

(i) *Irrigation price policy:* The existing price policies related with irrigation are not compatible with the recommended sustainable measures. Water rates for canal irrigation are too low in relation to the operation and maintenance cost and to the benefits derived from the irrigation. The low canal water charges encourage farmers to over-irrigate the fields, which result in a gradual rise in the watertable. This is what happens in many major and medium irrigation projects.

Similarly, the power tariffs are too low, in many cases totally exempted, for extracting groundwater. The low or zero and flat power tariff encourage farmers to overexploit groundwater as there is no incentive to save the water. The incentive is to increase use of water. This has resulted in rapidly declining groundwater in many good aquifer ragions.

These policies which are designed on political logic, not on economic and ecological considerations, need to be changed. These have to be rationalized. Pricing of canal water, and power tariff for groundwater extraction should be designed in such a way that they maximize production and also conserve and protect the scarce water resources. Appropriate price policy for irrigation (both canal and groundwater) to a large extent can solve the problem of both rising and declining watertable. The need is to design such policies, and educate farmers about its beneficial effects.

(ii) *Subsidies on water saving devices:* It was mentioned earlier that sprinkler and drip irrigation systems save a lot of irrigation water and increase irrigation efficiency. The Government of India has already extended huge subsidies, as high as 75 per cent (in some States it is even more), on the use of the water-saving devices. These are not widely adopted despite their benefits due to the simultaneous encouragement by the government in the form of incentives to use more water for irrigation through high subsidies on canal water and power rates to use of groundwater. The need is to withdraw subsidies from all kinds of technologies, which encourage farmers to over-use irrigation, and transfer that to the water-saving devices. It is equally important to expand the manufacturing capacities of sprinkler and drip irrigation systems to meet the growing demand as well as to keep the prices under check so that the full benefit of the financial incentives could be passed to the farmers (Marothia 1997). Such a mechanism will increase production, improve irrigation efficiency, which will save the water resource, and substantially increase the system efficiency.

4.c. Institutional Arrangements

Management of groundwater calls for collective action. Although a lot has been proposed on institutional arrangements for managing natural resources, limited is available with respect to groundwater use. Reforms are, therefore, needed to develop organizations/institutions in the affected areas to solve the emerging threat to the productive agriculture system. Location specific models should be developed for the judicious use of groundwater. The models may include assessing various partners in building new institutions like participation of cooperatives, NGOs, corporations, etc. Collective action by resource users is required to adopt the technical components with well-designed institutional structures relating to decision-making arrangements and patterns of interactions (Marothia 1996). The new institutions, which encourage farmers for collective action on the use of groundwater, must be complemented by the government support in the form of developing strong programmes on education, credit and markets.

Marothia (1997) argued that the traditional property rights structure dominated by private property rights need serious rethinking for a judicious use of groundwater. Ownership of groundwater is tied with ownership of land in India and landowners have the right to extract groundwater beyond any time limit, till it is available.

4.d. Legislative Measures

At present there is no legislation on the use of groundwater. One good decision was taken by the government that no credit would be given for installing a tubewell where the watertable is characterized in the dark zone. Such an initiative is welcome. However, there is no restriction on private investment in installing a tubewell even in the dark zones. There is an urgent need to introduce a legislation which restricts over-use of groundwater where it has fallen to a critical level.

5. Conclusions

This chapter addresses the following issues related with the mismanagement of groundwater in different parts of the country:

1. The groundwater is falling at a very fast rate in favourable, high-growth and intensive agricultural regions. The problem is more pronounced in Punjab, Haryana and Uttar Pradesh where groundwater quality is good.
2. Fast increasing area under high water requirement crop, like rice and sugarcane, in relatively less rainfall regions, is the main cause of overexploitation of groundwater. The flat rates and low or no electricity charges are other important reasons for overexploitation of the groundwater.
3. In poor groundwater regions, the watertable is rising which is causing waterlogging and soil salinity. The problem is worsening at an alarming pace in the surface-irrigated areas where adequate drainage is not provided.
4. Defective irrigation pricing policy is the main cause of both rise and fall of the groundwatertable. Pricing of both canal water and power tariff are not decided on economic and ecological considerations. These are determined on political considerations, which result in a very high social cost.
5. The implications of groundwater mismanagement are an increase in the irrigation cost, decline in productivity, and widening income disparities.
6. Technological and policy options are available but they need implementation. Among the technological options, sub-surface drainage and water-saving irrigation methods (like drip and sprinkler systems) are feasible and cost-effective means to control rise in the watertable. To prevent the fall in the watertable, as also encourage water-saving irrigation systems, crop diversification through low water requirement crops can be introduced. The problem with low-water-requirement crops, for example legumes, is their low profitability. The need is to step up their production potential in favourable and high-growth regions.
7. Appropriate policies can play a significant role in controlling diseconomies related with groundwater. One, there is need to appropriately determine irrigation pricing policy. It should be so designed that economic and ecological objectives are met. An appropriate irrigation pricing policy will encourage farmers to judiciously and rationally use groundwater. Two, there is need to withdraw all subsidies from canal water charges, and power tariff, and transfer them to water-saving irrigation systems. Such a move will

encourage farmers to save irrigation water, use it judiciously and rationally, and maximize their profits.

8. There is need to educate farmers about the beneficial effects of collective action in using groundwater. The role of cooperatives or any group-oriented system will be an effective way to control externalities related with groundwater. It is necessary because action of an individual farmer will be ineffective, only group action can be effective and result oriented.
9. There is need to introduce some effective legislation to control over-exploitation or mismanagement of groundwater, at least in the critical regions.
10. More investment should be allocated to water management research with special emphasis on water-saving methods, crop diversification and institutional arrangements.

REFERENCES

Bathla, Seema. 1997. "Groundwater sustainability: A case study of Ludhiana district". *Indian Journal of Agricultural Economics* 52(3), p. 546.

Data, K.K. and de Jong, C. 1991. *The effect of sub-surface drainage on the farm economy.* Wageningen: International Institute for Land Reclamation and Improvement.

Dhawan, B.D. 1986. "Irrigation and water management in India: perception of problems and their resolution". *Indian Journal of Agrlcultural Economics* 41(3).

Food and Agriculture Organization (FAO). 1985. Studies for the use of saline water in command areas of irrigation projects, *Haryana Technical Report*, Rome: United Nations Development Program.

Gangwar, A.C. and Toorn, W.H., van don. 1987. "The economics of adverse groundwater conditions in Haryana State". *Indian Journal of Agricultural Economics* 42(2).

Garg, S.P. and Aggarwal, Deepak. 1996. "Sprinkler and drip irrigation system for efficient use of water resources in developing countries". In: *Proceedings of the All India Seminar on Modern Irrigation Techniques*, Bangalore, June 26-27, pp. 63-68.

Government of India. 1997. *Statistical Abstract of India,* Vol. I, Central Statistical Organization, Ministry of Planning and Program Implementation. New Delhi: Government of India.

Gulati, Ashok. 1989. "Input subsidies in Indian agriculture: A statewise analysis". *Economic and Political Weekly* 24(25), June 24.

Johl, S.S. 1984. "Some determinants of agricultural growth and development in India". *Indian Journal of Agricultural Economics* 39(3).

Joshi, P.K., M. Asokan, K.K. Datta and P. Kumar, 1997. "Socio-economic constraints in legumes production in the rice-wheat based cropping system". In: *Proceedings of the Workshop on Legumes in Rice-Wheat Cropping System of the Indo-Gangetic Plains: Constraints and Opportunities,* 15-17 Oct 1997, ICRISAT. Patnacheru 502 324. Andhra Pradesh, India: International Crops Research Institute for the Semi-Arid Tropics.

Joshi, P.K., B.L. Gajja and Jai Singh, 1997. "Adverse effects of land degradation on agricultural economy: Some evidences from saline and waterlogged areas", pp. 193-199. In: Agarwal, Anil (ed.), *The Challenge of the Balance,* New Delhi: Centre for Science and Environment.

Joshi, P.K. and D. Jha, 1991. "Farm-level effects of soil degradation in Sharda Sahayak Irrigation

Project". *Working Paper,* Washington, D.C. USA: International Food Policy Research Institute.

Joshi, P.K., O.P. Singh, K.V.G.K. Rao and K.N. Singh, 1987. "Sub-surface drainage for salinity control: An economic analysis". *Indian Journal of Agricultural Economics* 42(2). pp. 198-205.

Joshi, P.K., and N.K. Tyagi, 1991. "Sustainability of existing farming system in Punjab and Haryana: Some issues on groundwater use". *Indian Journal of Agricultural Economics* 46(3), pp. 412-421.

Joshi, P.K, N.K. Tyagi and Mark Svendsen, 1995. "Salt-affected and waterlogged soils in India: A review", pp. 225-240. In: Svendsen, Mark and Gulati, Ashok (eds), *Strategic Change in Indian Irrigation,* New Delhi: Macmillan India Ltd.

Khepar, S.D. and M.P. Kausal, 1991. "Conjunctive use of water resources", Paper submitted to the Indian Society of Agricultural Engineering, New Delhi.

Marothia, D.K. 1996. "Designing institutions for self-governing system of common pool resources". Agro-Climatic Regional Planning Unit of Planning Commission (ARPU), Government of India. *Technical Paper No. 25* ACRPU, Ahmedabad.

Marothia, D.K. 1997. "Agricultural technology and environmental quality: an institutional perspective". *Indian Journai of Agricultural Economics* 52(3), pp. 473-487.

Moench, Marcus and Dinesh Kumar, 1997. "Distinction between efficiency and sustainability: the role of energy proces in groundwater management", pp. 305-309. In: Anil Agarwal (ed.), *The Challenge of the Balance,* New Delhi: Centre for Science and Environment.

Patel, R.K. and B.S. Panghal, 1997. "Impact of technology on environment and sustainability in Haryana". *Indian Journal of Agricultural Economics* 52(3), p. 552.

Ramasamy, C. and C. Sekar, 1997. "Groundwater exploitation and its impact on environment in Western Tamil Nadu", pp. 310-315. In: Agarwal, Anil (ed.), *The Challenge of the Balance,* New Delhi: Centre for Science and Environment.

Satyasai, K.J.S. and K.U. Viswanathan, 1997. "Evaluation of alternative water management strategies for water scarce areas". *Indian Journal of Agricultural Economics* 52(3), pp. 499-507.

Sharma, Vijay Paul, B.L. Gajja and Deepak Shah. 1995. "Managing land and water resources for sustainable agricultural development: issues and options". *Artha Vijnana* 37(1), pp. 46-65.

Sidhu, R.S. and M.S. Dhillon, 1997. "Land and water resources in Punjab: their degradation and technologies for sustainable use". *Indian Journal of Agricultural Economics* 52(3), pp. 508-18.

Singh, Jai, V.K. Singh, K.K. Kundu, 1997. "Modern technology vis-a-vis environmental degradation a case of rice-wheat cropping system". *Indian Journal of Agricultural Economics* 52(3), p. 553.

Srivanappan, R.K. 1994. "Water management: thrust on irrigation harvesting". *The Hindu Survey of Indian Agriculture,* Madras.

Tewari, Laxmi and A.K. Singh. 1997. "Nature and extent of Groundwater resource scenario due to technological change in Uttar Pradesh". *Indian Journal of Agruculturai Economics* 52(3), p. 554.

Tyagi, N.K., P.K. Joshi and Mark Svendsen. 1995. "Cost-effectiveness of salinity-mitigation measures", pp. 252-271. In: Svendsen, Mark and Gulati, Ashok (eds), *Strategic Change in Indian Irrigation,* New Delhi: Macmillan India Ltd.

Vohra. B.B. 1987. *Case of Natural Resources—still an Area of Great Neglect,* p. 4. Second Mandyan Chatrapathy Rajmannar Memorial Oration on Environment, Bangalore, 31 Dec.

12 Groundwater Resources : Looming Crisis

M.S. Rathore

1. Emerging Threats

A large proportion of the world's population relies on groundwater as a primary source for drinking and domestic use. It is far more reliable as a source of supply than surface water and, if protected, can provide high quality potable water. But it is an often unnoticed and unacknowledged cornerstone in the foundation of rational economic and environmental systems. The social, economic and environmental values associated with groundwater are often unrecognised (Marcus 1992, 1994).

Groundwater is the primary buffer against drought. Areas with access to groundwater irrigation achieve higher agricultural yields. If climatic variability increases, because of global climatic change, the buffering value of groundwater will be a particularly important factor determining the society's ability to meet the basic food security, drinking water supply and environmental needs. Groundwater is thus central to meeting large-scale needs for food security and urban drinking water supply. Indian agriculture is highly dependent on groundwater, as of the 35 per cent of the irrigated area of India, 53 per cent is irrigated from groundwater sources (Table 12.1 & 12.2).

However, groundwater resources are endangered due to overuse in many regions. In the arid and hard-rock regions groundwater extraction often exceeds sustainable limits. Dropping water tables, deteriorating quality, and increasing pollution are evident in such areas. The poor, whose ability to invest in new wells or in deepening of existing wells is limited, are generally the worst affected by these problems. Dropping water tables have major implications in terms of higher energy consumption. Equally important to the role groundwater plays as a critical source of water supply for agricultural and municipal uses are the more subtle roles related to poverty alleviation, health and social vulnerability.

TABLE 12.1: **Net and Gross Irrigated Area—India and Rajasthan**

('000 ha.)

Area	Year	Net Irrigated Area	Gross Irrigated Area	Per cent of Sown Net	Per cent of Sown Gross
INDIA					
	1970-71	31103	38195	22.17	23.04
	1980-81	38720	49775	27.66	28.83
	1990-91	48023	63204	33.61	34.03
	1992-93	50101	66144	36.16	35.66
RAJASTHAN					
	1970-71	2132	2453	14.05	14.66
	1980-81	2983	3749	19.54	21.61
	1990-91	4471	5486	26.40	27.20
	1992-93	5232	6361	31.57	32.33

Source: CMIE—Agriculture, September, 1998, Bombay.

TABLE 12.2: **Area Irrigated by Sources of Irrigation in India**

(area in '000 ha.)

Year	Canals	Tanks	Wells: Tube-well	Wells: Others	Total	Other Sources	Total Net Irrigated Area
1970-71	12838	4112	4461	7426	11887	2266	31103
	(41.3)	(13.2)	(14.3)	(23.9)	(38.2)	(7.3)	(100.0)
1980-81	15292	3182	9531	8164	17695	2551	38720
	(39.5)	(8.2)	(24.6)	(21.1)	(45.7)	(6.6)	(100.0)
1990-91	17453	2944	14257	10437	24694	2932	48023
	(36.3)	(6.1)	(29.7)	(21.7)	(51.4)	(6.1)	(100.0)
1992-93	17084	3243	15824	10714	26538	3236	51001
	(34.1)	(6.5)	(31.6)	(21.4)	(52.9)	(6.5)	(100.0)

Access to groundwater is, perhaps, the most critical factor enabling much of the rural population to maintain a sustainable livelihood.

Assured water supplies greatly reduce the risks poor farmers face when investing in agricultural inputs, such as seed and fertilisers. This enables them to greatly increase yields, income levels, saving and capital formation. Similar benefits occur where health is concerned. Groundwater is generally less vulnerable to pollution than surface water. It is also often available quite near the points of use. Poor sections of the population largely depend on groundwater resources. Groundwater is also important from the environmental point of view. It is the primary source of base-flow in many streams and rivers, besides it is also a major source of water for many surface vegetation communities, water-related eco-systems and is critical to the maintenance of most wetlands.

The multiple roles groundwater plays in meeting the needs of society and the natural environment are threatened in many parts of the world. A massive increase in the extraction has led to falling water table and, in some cases, an irreversible depletion or damage to the aquifers. Improper water uses are leading to a gradual increase in the pollutants and contaminants resulting in health and environmental hazards.

The proximate causes of groundwater depletion and pollution are rooted in the population growth, economic expansion and spread of energized pumping technology.[1] There has been a massive expansion in the pumping capacity over the past five decades in most parts of India.

The groundwater extraction rate is exceeding the sustainable yield, that is, the level at which draft and recharge are balanced. If the groundwater extraction rate continues to be the same, over long run, it can lead to economic exhaustion of the groundwater resources. Simple indicators, such as long-term water level declines and increases in the salinity, pathogens or key pollutants are the important signals of the need for management. In this chapter an attempt has been made to highlight the emerging groundwater crisis in Rajasthan and a few measures recommended to deal with the emerging problem of depleting groundwater.

2. Water Resources in Rajasthan

Rajasthan has already crossed the phase of groundwater "development" and has entered the phase of groundwater "management" (Shah 1997), that is, from a stage in which maximizing the benefits of groundwater was a priority to a stage in which the costs of groundwater overuse have to be minimized. A majority of the traditional groundwater irrigation districts in Rajasthan have already reached an over-development stage, in terms of water use ranging between 70-100 per cent of the potential (Table 12.3). They are facing a serious threat of over-exploitation and all the externalities associated with it.

Groundwater contributes significantly to the irrigated area of the State. The percentage share of groundwater in the total irrigated area increased from 57.9 in 1960-61 to 66.9 in 1995-96 (Table 12.4). Over 80 per cent of the drinking water needs are also met from groundwater. There has been phenomenal growth in the number of wells, tubewells, diesel and electric pumpsets (Table 12.5). The agricultural input subsidy policy of the government, particularly the subsidized electricity supply, has led to a faster increase in the number of

TABLE 12.3: **Categorization of Districts by Status of Groundwater (1984-97)**

Safe	Semi-Critical	Critical
	Ajmer	Alwar
Barmer	Bundi	Jaipur
Jaisalmer	Chittorgarh	Dausa
Bikaner	Churu	Baran
Ganganagar	Dholpur	
Hanumangarh	Dungarpur	Jodhpur
	Jhalawar	Nagaur
Banswara	Kota	Sikar
Bhilwara	Pali	Jhunjhunu
	Rajsamand	Jalore
(7)	Tonk	(9)
	Sawai Madhopur	
	Sirohi*	
	Udaipur*	
	Bharatpur**	
	(15)	

Note: *Being hard-rock areas and due to below normal rainfall of 1996 they have slided to the critical stage.

**In safe category as per data, but being in the saline area, it has been placed in the semi-critical category.

Source: Groundwater Department, Government of Rajasthan, Jaipur.

tubewells and electrified wells. This is an important factor contributing to the emergence of the problem of over-development.

Groundwater resources in Rajasthan are showing increasing signs of degradation, as can be seen in Map 12.1, which depicts the water level changes between the years 1984 and 1997. The most affected are the central and eastern parts of the State. The net result has been the creation of overdraft condition across large areas accompanied by a significant decline in the water levels. Between 1984 and 1994, there has been a decline of 3 to 10 metres in the groundwater throughout central and eastern Rajasthan (Govt. of Rajasthan).

Besides the alarming problem of groundwater depletion in the State the other important problem is the difference between regions and areas in terms of availability and quality of groundwater. Groundwater quality has been a serious problem in many parts of Rajasthan. High concentration of fluorides, nitrates and salinity are common occurrences. All these seriously affect the health of rural population and act as serious constraints in the regional economic growth in the State (Rathore 1996, 1997).

TABLE 12.4: **Net Area Irrigated by Source of Irrigation in Rajasthan (1970-71—1995-96)**

(area in '000 ha)

Source	Yearwise Net Area Irrigated				
	1960-61	1970-71	1980-81	1990-91	1995-96
Canals	535	865	941	1354	1497
	(30.5)	(35.3)	(31.5)	(34.7)	(28.6)
Tanks	166	290	112	184	189
	(9.5)	(11.8)	(3.8)	(4.7)	(3.6)
Wells: (i) Tubewells	—	8	212	—	703
		(0.3)	(7.1)		(13.4)
(ii) Wells	1014	1266	1662	—	2797
	(57.9)	(51.6)	(55.7)		(53.5)
(iii) Total	1014	1274	1874	2341	3500
Wells	(57.9)	(51.9)	(62.8)	(59.9)	(66.9)
Other	37	24	56	25	50
Sources	(2.1)	(1.0)	(1.9)	(0.7)	(0.9)
Total Net	1752	2453	2983	3904	5232
Irrigated Area	(100.0)	(100.0)	(100.0)	(100.0)	(100.0)
Total Gross Irrigated Area	—	2453	3749	—	6361

Source: *Agriculture in Rajasthan—A Statistical Handbook,* Deptt. of Agriculture, GoR, 1989 & 1998.

TABLE 12.5: **Growth in the Number of Wells in Rajasthan**

	1956-57	1983-84	1993-94	1994-95
Number of Wells				
In Use	509242	815761	961448	975664
Out of Use		224795	294380	295912
Total		1040556	1258528	1271576
Electrified Wells	342	255942	452044	502310
Tube-wells		46233		104842
Oil pumpset/engines	1317	178378	329390	340683
Sprinkler Sets	—		19557	32045

Source: (i) *Vital Agricultural Statistics - 1995*, GoR.
(ii) *Agriculture in Rajasthan—A Statistical Handbook.*

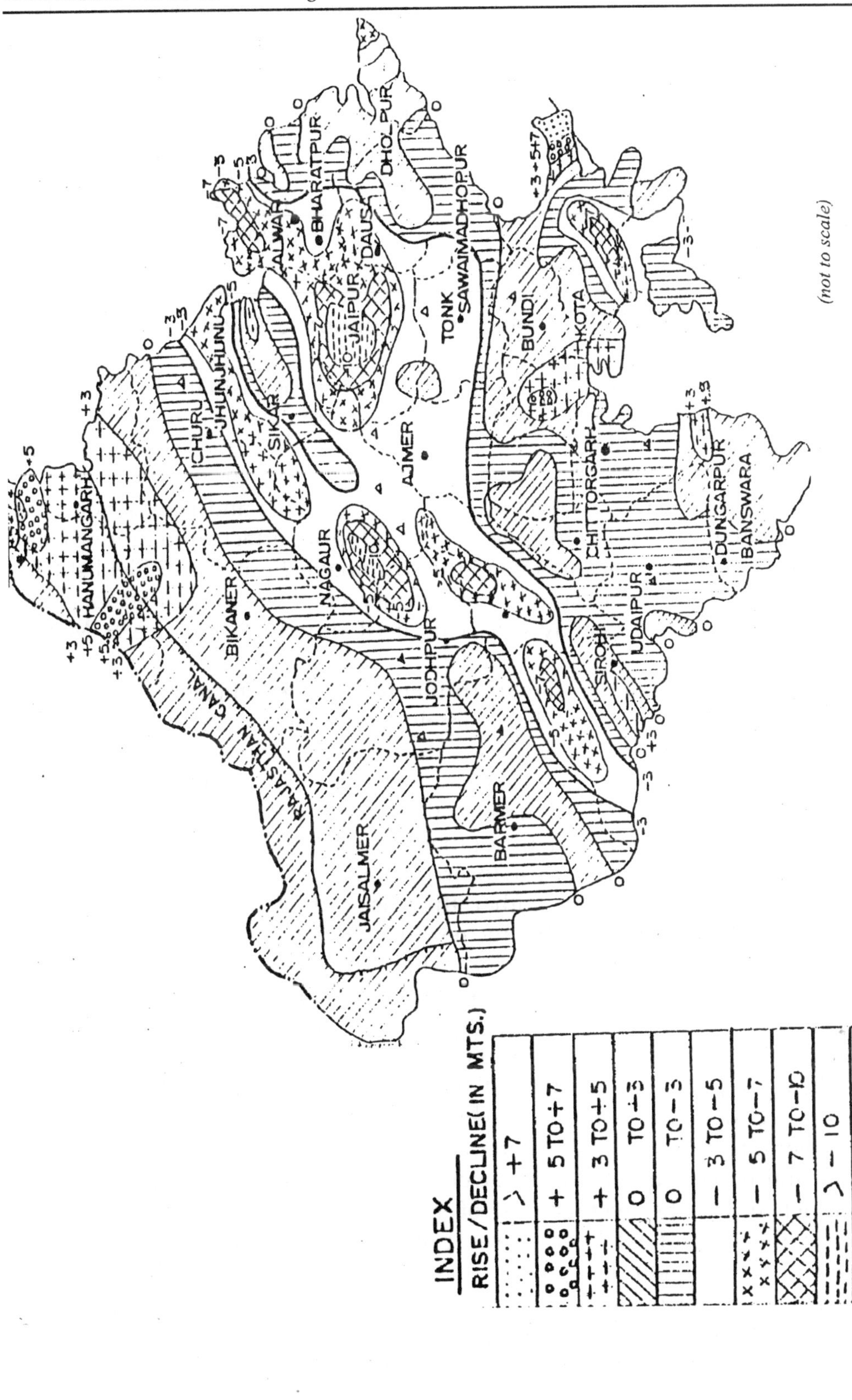

Map 12.1: Profile of Groundwater Resources in Rajasthan

3. Suggested Interventions

There are three complementary rather than alternative options to deal with Rajasthan's alarming groundwater situation. These include management of groundwater (i) as an economic good, (ii) legal and regulatory provisions, and (iii) as a community resource. May be that each of these provisions may not work if applied independently, and a solution to the problems may lie in using all the three together.

3.a. Management of Groundwater: As an Economic Good

Groundwater for irrigation is valued very high in Rajasthan. Most farmers depend on groundwater for cultivating rabi crops. Access to groundwater enhances the land value manifold. Reddy (1996) using the hedonic pricing method estimated the value of irrigation of about Rs. 40,000 per hectare of which 50 per cent was considered as the cost of water and transaction costs involved in obtaining water. In spite of this high price attached to groundwater it is being overextracted, even beyond the sustainable limit. Why? Field studies show that it is the myopic nature of the farmer—he lives in the present rather than in the future and heavily discounts it (Reddy 1996; Rathore & Mathur 1998).

The market is one of the instruments for the efficient allocation of resources. Use of resource/good can largely be regulated in the desired manner by appropriate market interventions. However, the market can play only a limited role in the case of natural resources, especially in the case of water because of the institutional and market failure (Reddy *et al*. 1997). Nevertheless, price, as a market instrument to regulate demand, is, directly or indirectly, being tried in the case of water use for irrigation. But it is considered as part of the larger agricultural policy, rather than as part of a policy designed for management of water as an economic resource. In the case of surface irrigation, water is priced according to its use. The existing tariffs are ineffective in encouraging an efficient use or conservation of water. When groundwater is privately managed through wells/tubewells using animal, diesel or electric power, no direct price control is possible except through electricity rates and diesel prices which influence the cost of irrigation for the farmer. In fact, energy price intervention is a weak instrument.

Power rates charged to the agricultural sector are highly subsidized, as the agricultural power tariff is much lower than the non-agricultural tariff and is also much below the average cost of generation and transmission. Let us examine the case of whether power policy as an instrument for checking groundwater exploitation can be an effective instrument. Presently the Government of Rajasthan is charging a flat rate, varying according to the capacity of the machine. There is no connection of these charges to the area irrigated or the amount of water lifted. Farmers have no incentive to conserve/ economize use of water. However, the price of electricity can be fixed on the following two basis: First, to charge a price for power that is based on its cost of generation and distribution; second, to fix a power tariff based on the price of diesel, as the existing technology of diesel pumps and diesel-operated generators can be substituted for electricity. However, in the given socio-political milieu it is very difficult to change the electricity tariffs, as the adjoining States are supplying it free of cost under their political commitment to the people.

The present tariff has failed to check the groundwater depletion to the desired level as the demand for electricity is determined by several factors, such as availability of groundwater, size of farm, cropping pattern, diesel price, standby arrangements in which farmers ensure diesel pumps are available when electricity supplies are limited, creditworthiness, etc. Also, as there is a tendency among the farmers to switch from electric to diesel pumps, and from low-value crops to high-value crops to counter the rise in electricity tariff and regulate limited supply, it seems clear that none of the two criteria for determining agricultural power tariffs listed above will have much influence on the groundwater extraction decisions of the farmers. Rather, it will adversely affect small and marginal farmers, as they do not have the capacity to switch from electricity to diesel pumps. More importantly, the issue is a political one and is likely to be tackled only at that level. Hence, it can be concluded that groundwater over-exploitation cannot be addressed effectively via power tariff policy (Saleth 1997, Narayanamoorty 1997, Moench 1995).

In Rajasthan a subsidy was used as an economic instrument to promote water-saving technology, particularly sprinklers for irrigation. As intended, it emerged as a powerful instrument in boosting the adoption of sprinklers in the early eighties. The main objective was to save the groundwater. But the results have been quite the opposite. The water table has continuously gone down, both because of an increase in the area under cultivation and due to the tremendous number of pumps installed. Hence, there is a need to search for alternative policy options/instruments whereby farmers could be induced to reduce extraction of groundwater.

The above observations are applicable only to areas where the switch to diesel pumps is technically and economically feasible. In the case of hard rock and deep groundwater areas, using a diesel pump is either a more costly option or a technically infeasible option. In these areas electrical pumps are likely to be used, and so a higher electricity tariff can definitely have an effect on the extraction rates. Still, there are cases where farmers opt for the more costly option of using diesel-operated generators, as in the case of rich farmers in Churu district of Rajasthan.

Presently, the State Government is adopting a policy of power rationing. This is a response to the overall shortage of power and is unrelated to the water management strategy. Let us examine how far this has been effective in controlling groundwater use. Power rationing can definitely reduce power consumption and water withdrawal. This helps in achieving the dual objectives of sustainability and efficiency in water use. However, power rationing makes the diesel pumpset option quite attractive and leads to groundwater depletion, the degree of depletion depending upon the hydrology of the region.

Power tariff coupled with power rationing cannot be an effective instrument for simultaneously achieving the three policy goals—equity, efficiency and sustainability.

A sound agricultural price policy along with other marketing measures seems to have worked in influencing groundwater use indirectly via a change in the economics of cropping in favour of the water-saving crops. This instrument, if used with water saving as its prime objective, can definitely help in improving the groundwater problems of the State.

3.b. Management of Groundwater: Legal and Regulatory Provisions

The second option to deal with the problem of groundwater overdevelopment is the legal option of changing the existing water laws. While enacting any law, firstly, a case has to be prepared to guarantee social justice, particularly to the poor households. Secondly, if the State is to use the law to regulate the use of water resources, it should be made clear how the people can use the law to make the State more accountable and efficient? This is particularly important because the popular impression is that the State itself is instrumental in bringing about a massive depletion of the water resources through inappropriate forest and irrigation policies and also in creating great inequalities in the distribution of water (Singh 1992). As in the case of large canals the control over water resources is taken away from the people compared to the type of control they have over tanks or wells. What is being noticed in the case of government-operated schemes is that the resource is inequitably distributed and rich/powerful interests have gained more control while the poor have been left out.

The attack on current groundwater rules focuses on their inefficiency. The absolute ownership privilege fails to give groundwater users good signals of the true costs and benefits of the water they are pumping. Singh (1992) argues that there are three sources of poor signalling under absolute ownership: (i) the common pool externality, (ii) the public good nature of pumping lifts, and (iii) the lack of means to transfer water claims.

Groundwater is a "common pool" resource under the absolute ownership rule, meaning that the common supply is exploited by independent individuals. Each unit of water pumped in excess of re-charge has a scarcity cost because it depletes future supplies. The absolute owners do not, however, suffer the scarcity cost of their own pumping, since future scarcity will be shared by all users of the common pool. Because it is imposed by the pumper on third parties (neighbouring pumpers), the scarcity cost is called an "external" cost of pumping. Since the absolute owner will not pay the cost, a pumper who is economically "rational" will not count it as a cost. Each plumber, then, treats the stock as though it were not scarce, or as though it had zero price, with the result that the resource is inefficiently owner-used. Lifts are allowed to increase at an inefficiently rapid rate, and distribution of water among the competing users will be inefficient because the right to use water is not transferable (Singh 1992).

The absolute ownership gives the landowner, firstly, a claim on all income that can be created by the use of the water beneath his or her land, so long as there is water beneath the land. Also under absolute ownership, a landowner has complete discretion about when to irrigate, what lands to irrigate, and how intensively to irrigate. The flexibility that comes with this discretion may itself be very valuable in adjusting to any changes in the prices and weather conditions. On the cost side, the absolute owner lacks the authority to guarantee that water will be available in the future for irrigation.

On the cost side, the landowner is exposed to the costs of the depletion of the stock by other landowners. An alternative rule must offer farmer's incomes net of costs at least as great as these expected under absolute ownership. Since by presumption the resource is being operated inefficiently, a more "efficient" rule would improve the net benefits to the irrigation farmers unless water is put to alternative uses of higher returns.

Thirdly, absolute ownership gives landowners a real property right that could not be taken away by State action without the payment of compensation.

The public good problem requires a collective solution, while the disregard of future scarcity costs may be internalized either by privatization or by regulation. The regulation should take care of the following: (a) it should be cost effective, so that irrigators follow voluntarily; (b) if private benefits are large enough to encourage conservation practices at the limit of existing technology, voluntary compliance would be consistent with full provision of the public good; and (c) regulation should retain the flexibility of irrigators to adjust to climate and price changes.

However, no property system should be adopted which injures the interests of the parties who are powerful enough, through their command over economic, social or political factors, to keep it from being adopted. Therefore, regulations should provide incentives to poor farmers to organize and protect their future interests.

The basic issue involved in the water law is that of rights, i.e. what kind of rights the people have, and what are the rights of the State. The question of the State's accountability to the people, and the people's accountability to each other and to the State cannot be worked out unless we are clear about the legal framework of rights in water. It has been observed in India, as well as in other parts of the world, that in the absence of clearly defined water rights many irrigation schemes have failed to function desirably (Gerbrandy & Hoogendam 1996, Nederlof & Wayjen 1996). Likewise, in the case of Rajasthan, the groundwater rights should be clearly defined before enacting any additional laws to regulate groundwater use.

The present position of the laws applicable in case of groundwater is as follows: According to the Easement Act of 1882, a person has no natural or customary right over groundwater, whether collected in a well, or passing through springs or flowing in an undefined course. Any diminution of such water by neighbours, therefore, gives ground for action under the Easement Act. However, rights to groundwater belong to the landowner, since it forms part of the dominant heritage. Land ownership, in turn, is governed by the tenancy laws of the State and there is no mention and limitation on the use of groundwater. The consequence of such a legal framework is that only landowners can own groundwater. The ultimate result is over-exploitation of groundwater. It is very clear in the case of the groundwater laws that rights of the landowners are at present absolute, while the State has no rights whatsoever. It is only in the case of public wells or tubewells that the State has the right to regulate use.

Considering that water is a vital resource for life, being deprived of it is simply a violation of a fundamental human right. Therefore, the important issue is prioritization of water use, for example, giving precedence to drinking/domestic uses over agricultural and industrial uses. In fact, prioritization of water use must be a central concern for water legislation. Law is a double-edged instrument. It can be used to cut or heal, to exploit or to liberate, both by the State and by the people. So far both the State and the people have failed to behave in a manner that ensures sustainable management of the resource. Furthermore, the likely outcome of the intended groundwater legislation is questionable on many counts particularly in execution of the law.[2]

Many scholars and policy makers believe that the right to groundwater should be that of use and not of ownership (Vaidyanathan 1996). If ownership has to be decided, it could be with the State, but with use rights going to the community. This community can be a village or number of villages situated in a hydrogeological zone. In addition, the regulatory rights should be transferred to the community. The State should facilitate the functioning of the community and the efforts to harness and conserve water resources by providing technical and financial inputs for monitoring groundwater and the status of water balance in the zone. It would require some special efforts to organize communities around water resources in such a manner.

4. Community Participation

The other alternative is community participation in the management of groundwater resources. Traditionally, individuals have considered water fetched from wells located on their lands as private property. Since society has sanctioned such treatment, it seems very difficult to change such *de facto* property rights very quickly. It is often argued that the enactment of a groundwater law to abolish private property rights to water can change the situation. On the other hand, refuting this argument, others argue that in order to enforce such a law the State would have to post agents, thereby adding one more class of "rent seekers" to the existing system and no guarantee of better control over the depletion of the resource. This group sees better community controlled water resource management as a more pragmatic approach.

The problems with community participation are: (i) the process is too slow to be applied widely and the notion of community participation is poorly defined; (ii) community-based activities often depend on the driving force of one charismatic person or a small group of motivated people and, in spite of the good intentions of such people, partisan politics have often interfered; and (iii) sometimes even the community participation projects become manipulative. For such reasons, most of the cooperatives and community development experiments of the 1950's and 1960's ended in failure.

The other negative outcomes of participation can be that it is possible that participation will bring about the development of the "participating elite" in a community and, therefore, contribute to inequality. There is always a political dimension to participation since it is tied to changes in the control of resources. Regardless of the intentions of those who administer programmes, it is even possible that political demands can lead to violence.

In spite of these negative factors, community participation remains an important factor in addressing groundwater management issues. User group management of natural resources has always existed in some form in India. Recently successful efforts have been made by a number of NGOs to establish that they can even work today under changed environment and natural resources can be better managed by user-groups (Moench 1992).

4.a. Management of Groundwater: As a Community Resource

The large body of theoretical and empirical literature deals with the distinction between Common Property Resources (CPRs) and Open Access Resources (OARs)[3] and it largely cites the example of land resources and little about water resources. Within water resources it is mostly the surface water resources, such as lakes, rivers, ponds, etc. The issues related to groundwater are largely unattended. Groundwater resources basically are Common Pool Resources (CPR) and have open access but because of their physical location, i.e. beneath land, presently access is restricted by the ownership of land, which is mostly private. Hence, it is governed by a property regime and contradicts the principal of open access. It does not strictly adhere to the definition of CPR where the physical boundaries, ownership and controls are clearly defined or identifiable. In a strict sense it does not exclude the non-owners of land or non-members of the group from any claims to the use of the resource.[4]

In the case of CPRs there exists common property rights, the user is part of a community and there are practical rules to co-ordinate resource utilization. There is a certain community-based authority to enforce rules and define the contexts in which conventions and contracts are to be negotiated. The authority system and the cooperative ethics provide the users assurance about the expected behaviour of other users, enable coordination and minimize free riding (Runge 1992). The assurance problem, that is, the uncertainty about the expected actions of others, can be minimized by the community institutions if there exist homogeneity of interests among the users and a strong regulatory machanism. Increasing heterogeneity of the community makes cooperation increasingly difficult. State intervention aimed at the economic development of rural areas by way of asset distribution and conservation and management of natural resources has mostly added to increasing community heterogeneite and breaking up of traditional CPR management institutions.

On the other hand an OAR is not governed by an enforceable property regime, there is no restriction on the entry of resource appropriators. In India, more often than not, State property resources have become *de facto* private or open access resources due to the State's failure to enforce property rights for various reasons, such as high transaction costs, corruption in enforcement agencies and lack of political will (Jodha 1992, Shanmugaratnam 1996). In the case of groundwater resources the problem of 'The Tragedy of the Commons" (Hardin 1968) or "Prisoner's dilemma game" referencing to individual strategies regardless of the expected actions of others in the use of common resources are also not strictly applicable as it fails to take into account the effects of non-separable externalities on private costs (Runge 1981, 1992).

Development policies and demographic and technological changes have contributed to the trend of privatization of land and agricultural expansion in most parts of India (Shanmugaratnam 1996). Availability of water for irrigation from underground and surface sources has dramatized this trend. The high variability in the annual rainfall in arid and semi-arid areas creates further dependence on groundwater which is unequally located under ground and is unequally accessible to holdings of different sizes and location. Consequently the gains of groundwater are unequally shared by the society. It has also led to the breakdown of traditional common property resources management institutions.

The issues of how best to govern natural resources used by many individuals in common are no more settled as some writings about the "tragedy of the commons" recommended that "the State" control most natural resources to prevent their destruction, while others recommend that privatizing those resources will resolve the problem. What one can observe is that neither the State nor the market is uniformly successful in enabling individuals to sustain a long-term, productive use of natural resource systems. It may also be that we do not have the necessary intellectual tools or models to understand the array of problems that are associated with governing and managing natural resource systems and the reasons why some institutions seem to work in some settings and not others.

Hardin gave the expression "the tragedy of the commons" which has come to symbolize the degradation of the environment to be expected whenever many individuals use a scarce resource in common. Hardin's model has often been formalized as a prisoner's dilemma game. It fascinated many scholars as it challenged the paradigm that rational human beings can achieve rational results and came out with the paradigm that individually rational strategies lead to collectively irrational outcomes. Later on a closely related view of the difficulty of getting individuals to pursue their joint welfare, as contrasted to individual welfare, was developed by Olson (1965) in *The Logic of Collective Action: Public Goods and the Theory of Groups.* Olson specifically set out to challenge the grand optimism expressed in group theory: that individuals with common interests would voluntarily act so as to try to further those interests. He also challenged the presumption that the possibility of a benefit for a group would be sufficient to generate collective action to achieve that benefit. The argument rests largely on the premise that one who cannot be excluded from obtaining the benefits of a collective good has little incentive to contribute voluntarily to the provision of that good.

The tragedy of the commons, the prisoner's dilemma, and the logic of collective action are closely related concepts in the models that have defined the accepted way of viewing many problems that individuals face when attempting to achieve a collective benefit. At the heart of each of these models is the "free-rider" problem. Whenever one person cannot be excluded from the benefits that others provide, each person is motivated not to contribute to the joint effort, but to free-ride on the efforts of others. If all participants choose to free-ride, the collective benefit will not be produced. The temptation to free-ride, however, may dominate the division process, and thus all will end up where no one wanted to be. Alternatively, some may provide while others may free-ride, leading to less than the optimal level of provision of the collective benefit. These models are thus extremely useful for explaining how perfectly rational individuals can produce, under some circumstances, outcomes that are not "rational" when viewed from the perspective of all those involved.

The similarity between the many individuals jointly using a resource in a natural setting and the many individuals jointly producing a sub-optimal result in the model has been used to convey a sense that further similarities are present. By referring to natural settings as "tragedies of the commons", "collective-action problems", "prisoner's dilemmas", "open-access resources", or even "common-property resources", the observer frequently wishes to invoke an image of helpless individuals caught in an inexorable process of destroying their own resources (Ostrom 1990).

Most writers on CPRs argued that because of the tragedy of commons, environmental problems cannot be solved through cooperation and the rationale for government with major coercive power is overwhelming (Ophula 1973, Heilbroner 1974, Carruthers & Stoner 1981).

The presumption that a strong external input is necessary to avoid tragedies of the commons leads to recommendations that central governments control most natural resource systems. Different authors have endorsed this view with variations on the extent of the control or nature of control. The policy advice to centralize the control and regulation of natural resources, such as grazing lands, forests, and fisheries, has been followed extensively, particularly in the developing countries.

Other policy analysts, influenced by the same models, have used equally strong terms in calling for the imposition of private property rights whenever resources are owned in common (Demsetz 1967, Johnson 1972, Smith 1981, Welch 1983, Smith 1988) suggest that "the only way to avoid the tragedy of the commons in natural resources and wildlife is to end the common property system by creating a system of private property rights". Welch asserted that privatization of the commons was the optimal solution for all common-pool problems. His major concern was how to impose private ownership when those currently using a commons were unwilling to change to a set of private rights to the commons. Ostrom (1990) argues that private rights are possible in case of land resources but difficult to define in regard to water resources.

Both centralization advocates and privatization advocates accept as a central tenet that institutional changes must come from outside and be imposed on the individuals affected. Despite sharing a faith in the necessity and efficacy of "the State" to change institutions as to increase efficiency, the institutional changes they recommended could hardly be further apart.

Ostrom argues that "getting the institutions right" is a difficult, time-consuming, conflict invoking process. It is a process that requires reliable information about time and place variables as well as a broad repertoire of culturally acceptable rules. New institutional arrangements do not work in field as they do in abstract models unless the models are well specified and empirically valid and the participants in a field setting understand how to make the new rules work.

Many successful CPR institutions are a rich mixture of "private-like" and "public-like" institutions defying classification in a sterile dichotomy. By "successful" Ostrom means institutions that enable individuals to achieve productive outcomes in a situation where temptations to free-ride and shirk are ever present.

Common property resource management provides a complex system of rules and conventions regulating individual rights to a variety of natural resources including grazing lands, forests and water. Although management of resources as common property has proved to be a stable form of resource management in some traditional societies, the combination of population growth, technology change, climate and political forces has destabilized many existing common property management institutions. Much of the current literature on CPRs leads to a general, but false, conclusion that common property is universally mismanaged. In the context of poverty, natural resource dependency and resulting uncertainties, incentive structures are created that may make common property a comparatively rational solution to certain problems of resource management. Researchers and planners have often called for the imposition of private property rights. However, perhaps in most cases, private rights have failed to stop overuse when implemented, and in many cases may have contributed to an even more rapid degradation of resources and increased inequality in an already unequal distribution.

The role of village-level conventions, including common property institutions, to reinforce expectations of collective behaviour leading to a critical mass of individuals to adopt such a solution to groundwater use as a cooperative strategy is the ultimate solution. If the user group functions optimally, common property institutions can lead to equilibrium outcomes in which each individual is assured that a critical mass of others will cooperate, so that they too will have an incentive to do so. Of course, common property institutions do not always provide this assurance. If the State recognizes these institutions and gives them the authority to manage groundwater resources, the chances are good that these will work efficiently.

Sugden (1986) has argued that the more homogeneous a community is, the more likely it is that the outcomes will be optimal. Conversely, the more heterogeneous it is, the more difficult coordination becomes. As the heterogeneity of the group increases, and as the resource constraints facing it become more severe, common property rules may become increasingly difficult to maintain (Johnson & Libecap 1982). A heterogeneous community will require more enforcement of agreements. The enforcement may emerge from inside the group or be imposed from outside. The key element determining the success or failure of institutions is, therefore, the extent to which they foster coordinated expectations in relation to a particular physical and social environment. The fairness implicit in joint access may prove a highly assuring feature of common property agreements. Frequently, the relative benefits accruing to individual members of the group are somewhat less than under a system of exclusive use right. If some assurance regarding the actions of others is provided, via an institutional rule, it is possible to achieve the desired goal of the group even though the benefit to the individual may be lower.

Cooperative solutions are most likely to succeed where the locus of decision-making is a relatively small, cohesive body. However, individuals who have high discount rates and little mutual trust tend to act independently, rarely communicate well and are often unwilling to enter into binding agreements for monitoring and enforcement. Overall, they are unlikely to choose jointly beneficial strategies unless such strategies happen to be their dominant strategies.

Groundwater in Rajasthan is drawn by digging wells and tubewells owned under joint or individual private ownership mostly by landowners. There is little homogeneity in asset ownership, caste, class and access to the resources, and yet the chance of coming together to form management systems where everyone can benefit is strong, as there is a strong trade-off in favour of joining. There is a recognition that acting independently will aggravate the crisis situation, and may even force people to migrate or depend on unirrigated crops and non-farm enterprises. Both heterogeneity of group members and variation in availability of groundwater need serious consideration in order to determine the level of organization. It seems feasible to form a group at the village level and also a higher level group of villages at river and groundwater basin level (Rathore 1996, 1997).

5. River Basin Approach

A river basin is a surface hydrological boundary having an integrated drainage system. A river basin is a functional unit established by physical relationship for the purpose of water resource management (both surface and ground) where activities in one part can indicate a chain of environmental impacts affecting other parts of the basin. It is the combination of soil, water and vegetation based activities which affect the sustainability of resource use in a basin. Impacts on one resource invariably affect the status of others, suggesting that externalities of this type are generally non-separable. There are several cases where surface water is treated as a common property resource and collectively managed successfully. However, in the case of the groundwater situation, the idea of the "tragedy of the commons" applies all too well. Groundwater is perceived as private property rather than as a common pool resource even though the externalities in groundwater use are fairly widely understood. Too many well owners "ride free", overly concerned with their own benefit. These multiple individual actions have contributed collectively to the continuous depletion of the groundwater resource. The problem comes from the fact that individual wells tap water from what is physically a common pool. Unless groundwater is perceived in this way, as a "public good", the problem cannot be resolved.

In order to develop cooperative institutions around groundwater it is important to ask the following questions: (i) What economic incentives do the well owners have to participate? (ii) How do these incentives vary with the size of landholding? (iii) What social and cultural attributes are correlated with cooperation or defection?

The collective consequences of individual behaviour, if properly understood by well owners and the local population in general, may generate enough pressure to enable people to organize around groundwater issues. However, unless there is a situation in which there is little loss to individual well owners and there is a benefit to all other community members, it will be very difficult to ensure cooperation. There are a number of actions that can be taken to assure widespread access to any benefits. For example, it is possible to ensure the same or higher level of returns from the land with less consumption of water by adopting technologies that support the efficient use of water and its conservation or by changing the cropping pattern and irrigation practices. With this goal in mind, the government can extend support with a technology package, price incentives, sprinkler and other such water saving devices, and prompt and appropriate extension services. The activities planned under various government programmes to improve replenishment of groundwater, such as watershed development, land development, soil conservation and afforestation can be carried out at a much lower cost if a cooperative institution is already in place.

The lessons learnt from the watershed programme implementation within Rajasthan, as well as in other Indian States, can be helpful in planning the formation of such institutions. A large number of NGOs working in the rural areas can be involved in the formation of these groups and in creating awareness among people of the groundwater problems. Rather than thinking of groundwater based collective action institutions as solutions to the regular public good problem, it is perhaps more appropriate to think of such institutions as a bundle of opportunities that solve different problems for different individuals but that link the success of the individual to the survival of the group as a whole.

Finally, it seems that village resources can be managed in an efficient and sustainable manner only if the single village panchayat can be revived. This panchayat needs to be focused on the developmental problems of the village and have an equal participation by all sections of the community, and it needs to be as free of political ideology as possible.

To summarize, to initiate efforts to control the groundwater disaster the following steps are required:

(i) define water rights in the State in such a way that use rights are held by the community rather than individuals (community resource);
(ii) provide legal support to new institutions and organizations to manage groundwater resources;
(iii) organize a social movement around water by creating mass awareness among all sections of society and forming groups at the village level;
(iv) adopt the river basin as the basis of planning for sustainable management of all natural resources including water;
(v) evaluate the impact of economic policies that may encourage excess groundwater extraction particularly the agricultural input and output policies; and
(vi) use price policy and subsidy instruments to conserve groundwater.

NOTES

1. The falling of the groundwater levels by 5-10m in India is usually explained as a result of the increased number of tubewells and/or energized pumping technology. Contrary to this Reddy (1989) argues that the decline is the product of destruction of indigenous water harnessing systems, disbanding of organisations concern with indigenous management systems of natural resources, etc. Refuting the argument that the groundwater decline is the result of the increased number of tubewells and energized pumpsets, he argues that the tubewell came onto the scene at the time when groundwater levels had already fallen beyond the reach of dug wells.
2. To deal with the fast-depleting groundwater table all over Rajasthan, the State Government during January, 1998 circulated a draft groundwater legislation for public debate and discussion. Several rounds of meetings, seminars, discussions were organised seeking participation of politicians, stakeholders, NGO's, government officials and academicians.
3. For a detailed discussion on the subject see Ostrom (1990).
4. For definition and theoretical discussion on CPRs and OARs see Ciriacy-Wantrup and Bishop (1975), Veeman (1978), Bromley & Cernea (1989), Runge (1981), Provencher and Burt (1994), Shanmugaratnam (1994), Marothia (1995, 1997a, b), Bromley (1992), Ostrom (1980), Marothia, 1997-b.

REFERENCES

Bromley, D.W. 1992. "The Commons, Common Property and Environmental Policy" *Environmental & Resource Economic*, Vol. 2, pp. 1-17.

Bromley, D.W. and M.M. Cernea. 1989. *The Management of Common Property Natural Resources: Some Conceptual and Operational Fallacies*, World Bank Discussion Papers No. 57,

Washington, D.C.: The World Bank.

Carruthers, I and R. Stoner. 1981. "Economic Aspects of Policy Issues in Groundwater Development", World Bank Staff Working Paper No. 496, Washington, D.C.

Ciriacy-Wantrup, S.V. and R.C. Bishop. 1975. "Common Property" as a concept in Natural Resource Policy", *Natural Resource Journal*, Vol. 15, pp. 713-27.

Demsetz, H. 1967. "Towards a Theory of Property Rights" *American Economic Review*, Vol. 62, pp 347-59.

Gerbrandy, G. and P. Hoogendam, 1996. "The Materialization of Water Rights: Hydraulic Property in the Extension of Rehabilitation of two Irrigation Systems in Bolivia", In: Diemer, G. and F.P. Huibers (eds.), *Crops, People and Irrigation*, Intermediate Technology Pub., U.K.

Government of Rajasthan, "Water Resources Planning Study", Draft Report, October, 1997.

Hardin, G. 1968. "The Tragedy of the Commons", *Science*, Vol. 162, pp. 1243-8.

Heilbroner, R.L. 1974. *An Inquiry Into the Human Prospect*, New York: Norton.

Jodha, N.S. 1992. "Common Property Resource—A missing Dimension of Development Strategies", World Bank Discussion Paper No. 169, Washington, D.C.

Johnson, R.N. and G.D. Libecap, 1982. "Contracting Problems and Regulation: The Case of the Fishery", *American Economic Review*, 72: 005-22.

Johnson, O.E.G. 1972. "Economic Analysis, the Legal Framework and Land Tenure Systems" *Journal of Law and Economics*, Vol. 15, pp. 259-76.

Marothia, D.K. 1995. "Urban Lake Pollution : Issues of Property Rights and Institutional, Arrangements", Paper Presented to the Beijer Research Seminar organised by the Beijer Institute—the International Institute of Ecological Economics, the Royal Swedish Academy of Sciences, Stockholm, Sweden, held at Kota Kinabalu, Malaysia, May 16-19, 1995.

Marothra, D.K. 1997. "Property Rights, Externalities and Environmental Pollution", In: Anil Agrawal (ed.), *The Challenge of the Balance—Environmental Economics in India*, C.S.E, New Delhi, pp. 290-298.

Marothia, D.K. 1997. "Agricultural Technology and Environmental Quality: An Institutional Perspective: Keynote Paper", *Indian Journal of Agricultural Economics*, Vol. 52, No. 3, July-Sept. pp. 473-487.

Moench, M. 1992. "Chasing the Water Table: Equity and Sustainability in Groundwater Management", *Economic and Political Weekly*, Dec. 19-26, 1992, pp. A171-A177.

Moench, M. 1994. "Approaches to Groundwater Management : To Control or Enable", *Economic and Political Weekly*, Agricultural Review, September 24, pp. A 135 - A 146.

Moench, M. (ed.). 1995. *Electricity Prices : A Tool for Groundwater Management in India*, VIKSAT, Ahmedabad.

Narayanamoorthy, A. 1997. "Impact of Electricity Tariff Policies on the Use of Electricity and Groundwater", *Artha Vijnana*, Vol. 39, No. 3, Sept. 1997, pp. 323-340.

Nederlof, M. and E.V. Wayjen. 1996. "Religion and Local Water Rights Versus Land Owners and State: Irrigation in Izucar de Matamoros (West Bank)", In: Diemer, G. and F.P. Huibers (eds.), *Crops, People and Irrigation*, Intermediate Technology Pub., U.K.

Olsen, M. 1965. *The Logic of Collective Action: Public Goods and the Theory of Groups*, Cambridge, Mass: Harvard University Press.

Oplus, W. 1973. "Leviathan or Oblivion", In: H.E. Daly (ed.) *Toward a Steady State Economy*, pp. 215-30. San Francisco: Freeman.

Ostrom, E. 1990. *Governing the Commons—The Evolution of Institutions for Collective Action*, Cambridge: Cambridge University Press, U.S.A.

Provencher, B. and O. Burt. 1994. "A Private Property Rights Regime for the Commons: The Case for Groundwater", *Amer. J. Agri. Eco.*, 76 (November 1994): 875-888.

Rathore, M.S. 1996. "Community - based Management of Handpumps in Rajasthan—A Search for an Alternative", Workshop Report No. 24, Institute of Development Studies, Jaipur.

Rathore, M.S. 1997. "Strategies for Managing Drinking Water Crisis in Rajasthan", Working Paper No. 086, IDS, Jaipur, 1997.

Rathore, M.S. and R.M. Mathur. 1998. "Local Strategies for Water Management and Conservation—A Study of Semi-Arid and Arid Areas". Project Report, Jaipur: Institute of Development Studies.

Reddy, V.R. 1996. "A Study of Willingness and Ability to Pay for Water", Project Report, Jaipur: Institute of Development Studies.

Reddy, V.R. *et al.* 1997. "User Valuation of Renewable Natural Resources", Project Report, Jaipur: Institute of Development Studies.

Reddy, S.T.S. 1989. "Declining Groundwater Levels in India", *Water Resources Development*, Vol. 5, No. 3, September 1989.

Runge, C.F. 1981. "Common Property Externalities: Isolation, Assurance and Resource Depletion in a Traditional Grazing Context", *American Journal of Agricultural Economics*, Vol. 63, pp. 595-606.

Runge, C.F. 1992. "Common Property and Collective Action in Economic Development", in Daniel W. Bromley (ed.) *Making the Commons Work,* California: ICS Press, pp. 17-39.

Saleth, R.M. 1997. "Power Tariff Policy for Groundwater Regulation: Efficiency, Equity and Sustainability", *Artha Vijnana,* Vol. 39, No. 3, Sept. 1997, pp. 312-322.

Shah, T. 1977. "Groundwater in Rajasthan: Situation Analysis", Policy School, Anand (Unpublished).

Shanmugaratnam, N. 1994. "The Natural Resource Management Problem in Arid Areas", NORAGRIC Occasional Paper Series C—Development, Environment, No. 13, Norway: Agricultural University of Norway.

Shanmugaratnam, N. 1996. "Nationalization, Privatization and the Dilemmas of Common Properly Management in Western Rajasthan", *The Journal of Development Studies,* Vol. 33, No. 2, pp. 163-187.

Singh, C. 1992. *Water Rights,* Vol. 1, New Delhi: Indian Law Institute.

Smith, R.J. 1981. "Resolving the Tragedy of the Commons by Creating Private Property Rights in Wildlife", *CATO Journal,* Vol. 1, pp. 439-68.

Smith, R.T. 1988. *Trading Water: An Economic and Legal Framework for Water Marketing,* Washington, D.C: Council of State Policy & Planning Agencies.

Sugden, R. 1984. "Reciprocity: The Supply of Public Goods Through Voluntary Contributions", *Economic Journal,* 94: 772-87.

Sugden, R. 1986. *The Economics of Rights,* Co-operation, and Welfare, Oxford: Blackwell.

Vaidyanathan, A. 1996. "Depletion of Groundwater: Some Issues", *Indian Journal of Agricultural Economics,* Vol. 5, No. 1 and 2 January-June pp. 184-192.

Veenam, T. 1978. "Water Policy and Water Institutions in Northern India: The case of groundwater rights" *Natural Resources Journal,* Vol. 18, No. 3, pp. 569-587.

Welch, W.P. 1983. "The Political Feasibility of Full Ownership Property Rights: The Cases of Pollution and Fisheries", *Policy Science,* Vol. 16, pp. 165-180.

13 Managing Groundwater Resource on Deccan Plateau: Pani Panchayat as an Institution of Collective Action

R.S. Deshpande and **Amalendu Jyotishi**

1. Introduction

Irrigation development in India has been under discussion for the last decade and the issues debated cover broadly three aspects. First, the controversy regarding big dams vs. small dams, and the associated environmental cost dominated the central stage. Narmada and Tehri projects offered the necessary empirical base for the debate. Rehabilitation of dam oustees also became a dominant issue during this period (Paranjapye 1988, 1990, Dhawan 1997). Second, the debate also initiated discussion on the alternative development path. Efficiency of water use or costs of and returns to the investment in irrigation were the core themes of the second set of issues (Key *et al.* 1997; Svendsen and Gulati 1995). Third set of issues it related to the use and exploitation of groundwater in India and emergence of water markets in some of the States (Shah 1993 and Dhawan 1986). Even though all these issues had water as a focal point, in any such context use of surface water and groundwater has to be treated differently because of the institutional peculiarities. Major part of the surface water irrigation avenues are controlled and the returns harnessed by the State. But the legal status of groundwater has always stayed a pondering point. It is often treated as a common property resource but in view of its placement and access many times, it should be taken as an open access resource. This is mainly because it can be privatised as soon as it is captured and thus until it is actually exploited it can come under the open access category. Under the British and Indian law until recently sinking a well or bore hole was the sole right of the land-owners (Shah 1989). But, recently distance and licensing norms have been adopted by the groundwater control authorities, cooperatives and banks. However, circumvention of these requirements has been quite easy. Well interference has, therefore, been a common phenomenon especially so in the groundwater scarce regions.

Estimates of irrigation potential in India have put the groundwater potential in area terms at about three-fourth of that of the surface irrigation. These estimates, however, are static in nature and both under surface and groundwater irrigation, the potential will depend on the development of the recharge or catchment area. Of the 47.5 million ha. metres of India's known groundwater potential about 18 million ha. metres is being used (Shah 1989). Across the country there are wide variations in the availability and use of groundwater. Especially some of the States could take better advantage of the availability of groundwater irrigation potential but in certain other areas it is essential to step up its use. In some States the availability of groundwater is in peril both due to well interference and depletion of recharge zone. Table 10.1 shows the status of groundwater development in India. It can be seen from the table that the States falling on the Deccan plateau have faced over-exploitation of groundwater apart from having low recharge possibilities.

The Deccan plateau is characterized as the core hard rock region of the country. Among the specificities of this region four issues assume importance in the context of irrigation. Firstly, the aquifer characteristics of the hard rock region do not promise larger storage. The porosity and permeability are the major problems. During the post-"Bagh Bed" times (Upper Cretaceous to Eocene) vast areas in peninsular India were covered by lava flows as a result of fissure eruptions through the earth's crust. These lava flow from flat-topped plateau are composed of several flows and are having a dominantly basaltic composition (Dhokrikar 1991). It is argued that the very nature of rock formation may not result in larger groundwater availability. Secondly, the recharge zones have been shrinking at a fast rate due to inhabitation, deforestation and infrastructural development. There have been some attempts in the State of Karnataka (World Bank tank project) and Maharashtra (percolation tanks construction during the post-1972 drought) to extend and revitalise the recharge zones. These are sporadic and insufficient attempts. Thirdly, the harnessing of surface water on the Deccan plains has not been very easy nor economical. Per unit investment (per hectare of irrigated area) in surface irrigation as well as the maintenance cost of surface irrigation schemes are among the highest for the States falling on Deccan plateau (CMIE 1996). In addition to this, the efficiency in the use of surface water has also been in peril in the States falling on Deccan plateau. Lastly, the access to groundwater is dictated by the availability of the financial resources as well as the least aquifer interference. But unfortunately conditions to meet these requisites are not in favourable in Deccan region.

TABLE 13.1: **Status of Groundwater Development in India**

	Stage of Groundwater Development (Percentage utilised)		
	Area Approach	Volumetric Approach	Potential in Million Hect. Metres
States with more than 50 per cent utilization			
Uttar Pradesh	134	29	8.05
Tripura	120	2	0.06
Gujarat	108	25	2.26
Haryana	97	70	0.85
Punjab	92	82	1.80
Rajasthan	91	30	1.62
Bihar	86	21	3.38
Tamil Nadu	84	37	3.33
Maharashtra	77	19	4.25
Andhra Pradesh	74	20	4.34
Madhya Pradesh	56	8	5.99
Orissa	56	5	2.33
Karnataka	51	14	1.41
States with less than 50 per cent utilization			
West Bengal	46	30	2.07
Kerala	39	13	0.76
Himachal Pradesh	33	24	0.04
Assam	30	1	2.35

Source: Vishwa Ballabh and Tushar Shah (1989).

Given this background a search for proper institutional alternatives to facilitate use and access to groundwater was an inevitable outcome. Property rights are treated as guiding incentive to achieve greater internalization of externalities, but in such cases property rights have to be well defined. It cannot straightaway be assumed that the markets operate efficiently and have no distribution bottlenecks. This is more difficult in the case of groundwater exploitation for various institutional problems. Development of groundwater markets as it happened in Gujarat is one alternative institutional emergence (Shah 1993, Ruth 1996). Water markets provide most promising institutional alternative which works in a situation facing water scarcity or difficulty in access. It is also noted that water markets improve the productivity of small and marginal farmers. But Ruth (1996) did not conclude on a positive note about the working of water markets in Pakistan. She called for strategies to improve equity of access to groundwater and noted unreliability of access even to the purchased tube-well water for more than half of the water buyers in the study area (Ruth 1996). Moral norms and cooperation have been taken as other alternatives. Economic theory explicates that interaction takes place between self-interested individuals with given preferences. Things do get complicated when the homogeneity assumption is relaxed and preferences may differ between sub-groups. If collective actions have to be more successful, Baland and Platteau (1996) enlist four conditions based on criteria namely, pay-off structure, interest in cooperation, not discharged by bad experience and avoid free riding (Baland and Platteau 1996). In the Indian context, Deshpande and Reddy (1990) have enlisted certain criteria for collective action which can be viewed as the institutional norms that lead people to come together bounded by the moral exchange. Thus, under the situation of groundwater scarcity, credit bottlenecks, well interference, inefficiency in water use, low income and employment levels, it becomes necessary to search for an institutional alternative to overcome these problems.

In this chapter we intend to analyse the logic of collective action through an empirical example of institutional alternative. Following the pioneering work of Mancur Olson, on collective action a good number of models viewing collective action in managing commons have come up.[1] In the background of the process of collective action in the Indian context we intend to analyse here the experiment of Pani Panchayat, an informal group irrigation scheme operating in one of the drought prone talukas of Maharashtra. We conclude the paper on a note bringing together the findings in terms of norms of collective action.

2. Management of CPRs and Pani Panchayat: An exercise towards reflection

We look at the theories of access and utilization of CPRs in order to analyse one such experiment in the real world. The issue in this case (and many other also) is how best to limit the use of natural resources (groundwater in our case) so as to ensure their long-term economic viability. For long, the attempts in academic circle were restricted to two divergent prescriptions for managing and governing the natural resources. One recommendation was that the State control of natural resources is essential to prevent their destruction, whereas the other recommendation advocated that privatizing these resources will solve the problem and the market will take care of the externalities. But it is generally observed in the real world that neither State nor market is uniformly successful in the sustainable and productive use of natural resources. One cause may be the absence of complete understanding of the institution involved in the individual sphere which resembles neither State nor market to govern some resource system. Another cause is that resources like groundwater are not characterized as to fall into the specific form of public good or private good. Thus, for any empirical study it is essential to understand the institutions involved in the sharing, governing and managing these resources. In making any prescription our kit bag of institutional forms contains depressingly a few items; in fact, it contains just two: common and individual. We have a situation analogues to one we had in the 1950s, when all goods were divided into two types—private and public. But the space between these two type of goods was soon filled in with an infinity of intermediate forms. It is only fair that we fill up thc comparable space in the property institution continuum (Marothia 1989). In this context it needs to be analysed how an intermediate institution emerges and functions for the group.

2.a. Specificity and Divergence

To understand the opportunities and constraints that individuals using a property-rights regime face, one also needs to distinguish between type of resources. Common Pool Resources (CPRs) are natural or man-made resources sufficiently large that it is costly to exclude users from obtaining subtractable resource units. For relatively small CPRs, a single family or small production unit may be technically able to enclose the entire resource and exclude others at low cost. For large and amorphous resources it is extremely difficult, both technically and economically, to exclude potential beneficiaries from obtaining benefits from them. The costs of exclusion are affected by the size and type of the resource system's natural boundaries and the technology available to enclose it. Entry and exit rules also affect the operational patterns of exclusion.

Failure to make the distinction between the subtractability of the resource units and the jointness of the resource system has contributed to the confusion about the attributes of CPRs. CPRs and collective (public) goods share one major attribute (jointness) and differ in regard to a second (subtractability). The relatively high cost of achieving physical exclusion is an attribute of both collective goods and CPRs. The theoretical literature focussing specifically on the problem of free riders is relevant to the analysis of both collective goods and CPRs because the problem of free-riding stems entirely from the difficulties of excluding beneficiaries from resources. In order to understand the common property regimes our basket contains a few theoretical prescriptions of which four important models are : (i) Hardin's model explicating the tragedy of common, (ii) the game of prisoner's dilemma, (iii) problem of assurance and (iv) the logic of collective action. All these have only a partial application as far as groundwater exploitation is concerned.

The emergence of Pani Panchayat as an institution for management of groundwater is not a case of conflict but a cooperative action within the beneficiary group (though conflict may be there with other institutions). Here the case is not that an individual rationality will lead to the tragedy of the commons (depletion of groundwater in our case). The cooperation here can be understood from the assurance problem where choices are inter-dependent. The game here is not one of conflict like the prisoner's dilemma. It is a cooperative game because there is no dominant strategy for either individual. Hence, agreement once made contains no incentive to defect, the agents gain adhering to the rules. The problem is assurance regarding the other's intended action. The agents must correlate their expectations and cooperate through some rules which assures a resultant collective action. This theoretical setting comes close to the base of efforts towards Pani Panchayat.

The assurance problem provides a formal way of looking at inter-dependence and uncertainty associated with non-separable externalities. By providing securities of expectation, or assurance, reliable institutions are endogenous responses to the uncertainty of social and economic interaction. Pani Panchayat was formulated in the background of and in response to the drought of 1972-73. However, enforcement from outside is a second order solution, if these cooperative strategies are ineffective. Gram Gaurav Pratisthan (GGP) was an outcome of this. The inferior outcomes of CPRs do not necessarily arise from the strict dominance of independent individual strategy. Rather, depletion of CPRs results from the inability of interdependent individuals to coordinate their actions. Factors like population growth, technological change, and climate changes make such coordinated action more difficult than in more static settings.

Private property regimes fail as a solution for the CPR, because they do not solve the problem of assurance. Such assurance may require a decentralized approach to institutional building based on the institutional norms and conventions of traditional cultures. Cooperative solutions are more likely to succeed where the locus of decision making is relatively small and it is a cohesive body. GGP ensured this while forming Pani Panchayat societies. The process is such, not because of the "size of the group" *per se*, but because assurance about the actions of others is largely a matter of information conveyed via transactions and communication. Information, organized as a set of rules, reduces uncertainty. The free flow of information and cooperative institutions which promote it, are most likely to occur at a relatively decentralized level (Runge, 1981). Keeping the above theoretical background we propose to analyse the experiment of Pani Panchayat in Purandhar taluka of Pune district in Maharashtra.

3. Nature Objectives and Functioning

The movement named "Pani Panchayat" was started on the background of the severe drought of 1972-73 in the State of Maharashtra. During the drought year a forum of industrial technologists was organized under the leadership of Shri Vilasrao Salunke to suggest ways and methods to deal with the drought. The usual metal-breaking work was being followed for over years, which was not only strenuous but had little linkage with drought proofing on a long-term basis. Working with the Forum and the severity of the drought left an indelible mark on the young mind of Shri Salunke. The theme of Pani Panchayat germinated in his mind at that time.

As a first step, in the process he registered a trust under the name Gram Gaurav Pratishthan (GGP), the year was 1974. As an initial step GGP took on lease a 16 ha. plot of land on a long-term basis at Naigaon in Saswad taluka for the work. Objectives of the GGP were as follows:

1. "To provide initially relief to the farmers of Purandhar taluka by improving their economic conditions and to remove the cause of recurring droughts.
2. To create facilities to raise their social and economic conditions to attain welfare of the people in this taluka.
3. To conduct research studies in socio-economic conditions, so that the urban interest is in linked with the process of creating integrated rural development.
4. To do all such lawful things as are conducive or incidental to the attainment of all the above aims and objectives" (GGP 1983).

The initial work started at the Naigaon plot of GGP. This is part of a 200 acre micro-watershed where water can be impounded into a small percolation tank. Along with the construction of the tank, the soil and water conservation treatments were started in the catchment areas. These included levelling contour bunding, contour ploughing, vegetative bunding and forming waterways. Out of these 16 ha, 9.60 ha were brought under protective irrigation, 2.40 ha under afforestation and the remaining 4 ha., under the percolation tank as well as other structures. The experiment proved to be a good success.

The experience of the Naigaon farm from 1974 to 1979 and a continuous thinking about the GGP's objective gave rise to certain principles in water-sharing. Shri Salunke brooded over the idea of starting a farmer's cooperative life irrigation scheme with the initiative coming from them. He did not have to wait long. The initial schemes started at Naigaon itself. Seven basic guidelines were formulated. These were:

1. "GGP would help in formulating a group lift irrigation scheme of cohesive groups. Individual schemes will not be taken.
2. The sharing of water would be on the basis of the number of members in the family and not in proportion to the land owned by them. Every household would get water rights to the maximum of 2.5 acres with an allocation of 0.5 acre per capita. The land in excess shall remain under rain-fed conditions. This particular clause incorporated the principle of equity in water sharing.
3. The beneficiary shall not have exclusive rights to irrigation. These will not be attached to the land. If the land is sold, water rights shall revert back to the Trust.
4. All the members would contribute 20 per cent of the capital cost in cash initially, the balance 80 per cent would be provided by GGP in the form of interest free loan (wherever subsidy was not available) or 50 per cent would be met from government subsidy and the remaining 30 per cent would be given by GGP as interest free loan.
5. The landless labourers can also share water on the basis of which they could enter into informal contracts for cultivating other's land.
6. High water consuming crops like sugarcane, banana and paddy will not be included in the cropping pattern of the beneficiaries. These crops will distort the equity of water sharing across crops.
7. The project would be entirely administered by the beneficiaries with the help of "Panch Committee" from among themselves." (GGP 1983 and Kolhe *et al.* 1986)

With these principles and the administration left to the beneficiaries, the first scheme started functioning in 1979 itself. The functional steps in the Pani Panchayat scheme are simple and easy to operate. Once the beneficiaries decide to form a lift irrigation society, they must prepare the documents required for operating the society. These include the record of rights, cropping pattern, no dues certificate from bank/village accountant and a consent letter. An account will be opened in the bank jointly with a representative of GGP and Gat Pramukh (group incharge). A *Panch* Committee will be formed which will acquire the necessary land for pump house, pipelines, etc. A *sevak* (worker) would be appointed by GGP to operationalize water distribution according to the fixed time-table given by the *Panch* Committee. The Committee will resolve the difficulties, problems and tensions amongst the beneficiaries. The *Panch* Committee is expected to ensure recovery of *Pani Patti* (water charges fixed on crop/acreage basis) and the contribution towards the loan of GGP.

The formation of a new scheme involves a meeting of the beneficiaries with a GGP representative at the initiative of beneficiaries. This is followed by selection of the group and survey of the area. It also includes checking the preferences of individual beneficiaries and their inclinations. This is followed by a technical survey which GGP undertakes with the help of technicians. A meeting of the beneficiaries is called in the presence of a representative from GGP to finalize the capital requirements, mutual share and preparation of the documents. Record of rights is checked including the encumbrances and individual shares in terms of capital and benefits are finalized. The next step involves obtaining various sanctions, certificates and electricity from the State Government.

While understanding the dynamics of Pani Panchayat we have to go beyond the work of Hardin, for it is essential to begin to specify the conditions that are conducive to the emergence of coordinated, rather than independent, actions by the individual users of a CPR. Ostrom (1992) gives us the conditions conducive for the emergence of collective action. He also specified the set of variables that influence the stability of such institutions.[2] Individuals will tend to switch from independent strategies for exploring CPR to more costly, coordinated strategies when they share a common understanding that:

(i) Continuance of their independent strategies will seriously harm an important resource for their survival.
(ii) Coordinated strategies exist that effectively reduce the risk of serious harm to CPR.
(iii) Most of the other appropriators from CPR can be counted on to change strategies if they promise to do so.
(iv) The cost of decision-making about future coordinated strategies is less than the benefits to be derived from the adoption of the cooperated strategies.

It is interesting that all the criteria get satisfied under GGP's experiment of Pani Panchayat.

3.a. Pani Panchayat's Approach to Development of Agriculture

Distribution of water on a most rational basis is the core of the problem of irrigated agriculture. In a drought-prone area, protective irrigation is the major strategy for drought proofing. If irrigation is provided, it is most likely used for commercial crops like sugarcane, banana, vegetables, etc., and the water-starved part of the drought-prone economy continues as it is. The entire process leads to the spread of a large quantity of irrigation water (thereby the investment) on small area base and in the hands of a few families.

Pani Panchayat's approach to agricultural development has six important factors, as can be seen from their operations. Firstly, the economic use of irrigation water is on the priority list of Pani Panchayat. Mostly, the irrigated areas have to face this acute problem. Major irrigation command areas of Maharashtra and other States bore an ample proof for this. (Mitra 1987, Deshpande and Ramakrishna 1987, Deshpande and Reddy 1990). Secondly, the equitable distribution of benefits across farm families helps in establishing a just society. Family instead of area, as the distributional weight, helps to correct the distortions caused by ill distribution of land. Thirdly, the insistence on the cropping pattern emerging out of self-imposed regulations does not allow uneconomic use of land by a few farmers. This also stops the process of land degradation due to heavy irrigation in drought-prone areas. Fourthly, the scheme is initiated by farmers themselves and hence, the process of development begins at their doorsteps, instead of coming from above. This helps in true participation of the people in their own development. Operationalization of the scheme fosters community spirit, the villages come together to help their other activities also. Fifthly, the scheme is handed over to the *Gat Pramukh* (Team leader) and the Panchayat, GGP withdraws from its operationalization. This gives the beneficiaries a good management experience. Lastly, the scheme has a focus on improvement of agriculture in a chronically drought-prone region but, the philosophy and approach is directed towards building economically independent social groups, directing their own development path.

3.b. Interaction with Government Agencies

Pani Panchayat schemes involved interaction with the State Government right from its inception. Over the years of the operations, different schemes have been on the path of seeking total cooperation on the part of the government (represented by bureaucracy) and also sometimes long-drawn conflicts. There are four distinct phases at which the participants of Pani Panchayat have to deal with the government officers at different levels. First, the revenue authorities of the block, represented either by Tahsildar or Village Accountant. They have to be approached for record of rights as well as while laying the pipeline. Second, while getting the permission to form a lift irrigation society, the government has a parallel programme existing and the regulations are not as stringent as those of Pani Panchayat. Therefore, there is a possibility of getting attracted to government-initiated lift irrigation programme. Third and the most crucial, interface with the government comes while obtaining permission of the Executive Engineer, Department of Irrigation. Robert Wade has written quite pointedly about the functioning of this department (Wade, 1979). Lastly, the real problem in lift irrigation scheme lies with the provision of electricity. The Maharashtra State Electricity Board (MSEB) has to be approached to provide the necessary connections. Initially for a few schemes electricity was available and the functioning was quite smooth. But in the later phase the farmers and GGP had to undergo severe hardships to obtain proper electricity connections. The undue delay on the part of MSEB staggered the project implementation. The farmers had invested after borrowing, which caused accumulation of interest. An agitation was called by GGP and a good number of persons were jailed. It was only at the intervention of the then Chairman of NABARD that the electricity connection was given. But by then the damage had already been done to the movement, which had picked up in the early eighties. The initiative was curbed to a large extent and the schemes were not coming with the same enthusiasm. Added to this, the government initiated parallel schemes which obviously did not have the principle and philosophy of Pani Panchayat. Thus a good movement was discouraged by State efforts.

3.c. Impact Assessment of the Programme

Pani Panchayat is directly a crop economy oriented scheme and hence its impact can be easily assessed by ascertaining the incremental crop economy parameters. The impact needs to be interpreted as the impact of institutional intervention in using groundwater. We had selected two schemes near Dhalewadi, both belonged to weaker sections of the society. Another scheme totally managed by women at Rajuri was also taken up for study.[3] The fourth scheme was selected from Shindewadi which included a mixed strata of the society. This gave us a good cross-section of the schemes. All the schemes had started before 1986 and hence their impact parameters have completely stabilized. We selected 50 beneficiaries from among the four schemes and 25 non-beneficiaries. All the impact parameters about the four schemes have almost similar behaviour and, therefore, we decided to combine them for the present purpose.

The cropping pattern of beneficiaries as well as non-beneficiaries is largely dominated by cereals and millets. But when we came to irrigated crops, we found that the beneficiaries devote larger area share to cereals and millets whereas, non-beneficiaries concentrate on cash crops. The composition of cash crops in the group of beneficiaries as well as non-beneficiaries is different. Only one farmer among the beneficiaries cultivated sugarcane. The beneficiary group has 58.9 per cent of land under rain-fed conditions as against 64.3 per cent of the non-beneficiaries (Table 13.2 and 13.3).

We have presented the gross value of output of the main products as well as by-products in Table 13.4. The average gross value of production of a beneficiary group is larger than that of the non-beneficiary group. The difference can be clearly felt in the case of cereals, millets, pulses and other crops. For the cash crop as well as oilseeds the non-beneficiaries seem to be having an upper edge.

TABLE 13.2: **Cropping Pattern of Irrigated Crops (per cent to gross cropped area)**

	Beneficiary				Non-Beneficiary			
	Up to 2 ha.	2 to 4 ha.	Above 4 ha.	All groups	Up to 2 ha.	2 to 4 ha.	Above 4 ha.	All groups
Cereals	38.05	27.96	17.55	22.92	12.74	4.74	19.79	12.65
Cash Crops	18.29	12.04	12.01	12.88	16.98	2.26	25.14	15.21
Pulses	4.71	6.37	0.74	2.66	3.40	1.81	2.31	2.54
Oilseeds	5.03	0.47	0.99	1.42	0.00	0.00	0.00	0.00
Others	0.70	2.34	0.88	1.21	1.35	1.35	0.00	0.90
GIA	20.99	27.32	45.28	93.59	8.93	2.25	11.46	22.64
GIA as/to GCA	66.78	49.18	32.17	41.10	34.47	10.16	47.24	31.31

Note: GIA—Gross Irrigated Area. GCA: Gross Cropped Area.

TABLE 13.3: **Cropping Pattern of Rain-fed Crops (per cent to gross cropped area)**

	Beneficiary				Non-Beneficiary			
	Up to 2 ha.	2 to 4 ha.	Above 4 ha.	All groups	Up to 2 ha.	2 to 4 ha.	Above 4 ha.	All groups
Cereals	25.71	42.39	61.86	52.13	54.96	79.81	46.17	59.38
Cash Crops	0.00	2.25	0.14	0.64	1.35	0.90	0.00	0.76
Pulses	2.29	2.93	4.83	4.02	6.18	8.58	6.60	7.05
Oilseeds	1.91	2.88	0.85	1.49	2.51	1.35	0.00	1.31
Others	3.31	0.36	0.14	0.63	0.54	0.00	0.00	0.19
RFA	10.44	28.23	95.48	134.15	16.98	19.90	12.80	49.68
RFA as/to GCA	33.22	50.82	67.83	58.90	65.53	89.84	52.76	68.69

Note: RFA—Rain-fed Area. GCA: Gross Cropped Area.

Gross value of output brings prosperity to the farm family. This, at times, gets reflected in terms of asset holding as well as borrowing (credits and its repayment). It may be noted that the asset value of the beneficiary group is generally higher as compared to non-beneficiaries. The value of non-farm assets of the non-beneficiaries is slightly higher than that of the benficiaries. On the other hand, in the entire operation of Pani Panchayat credit and its repayment

TABLE 13.4: **Productivity Per Hectare across Crops Groups—Beneficiaries and Non-Beneficiaries**

(in qtls.)

	Beneficiary				Non-Beneficiary			
	Up to 2 ha.	2 to 4 ha.	Above 4 ha.	All groups	Up to 2 ha.	2 to 4 ha.	Above 4 ha.	All groups
Cereals	9.76	7.31	4.13	5.52	5.36	2.66	4.44	4.12
Cash Crops	305.18	128.09	188.09	197.70	130.33	95.00	108.52	116.67
Pulses	11.84	6.83	4.24	6.22	31.05	1.63	2.31	1.64
Oilseeds	8.58	8.60	2.50	6.20	10.68	3.33	0.00	8.36
Others	9.84	97.67	129.86	82.36	15.61	6.67	0.00	12.22

TABLE 13.5: **Gross Value of Main Products and By-Products Per Hectare.**

	Beneficiary				Non-Beneficiary			
	Up to 2 ha.	2 to 4 ha.	Above 4 ha.	All groups	Up to 2 ha.	2 to 4 ha.	Above 4 ha.	All groups
Gross Value of Main Products								
Cereals & Millets	2818.11	2141.12	1123.64	1555.00	1451.88	759.57	1218.75	1133.46
Cash Crops	29054.78	14982.37	11261.99	17210.30	17094.74	9464.29	16147.54	16132.03
Pulses	5179.55	2633.46	2568.88	2968.44	766.13	666.00	996.84	824.94
Oilseeds	5084.86	6241.94	1807.69	4125.25	8095.38	3333.33	0.00	6591.58
Others	975.40	10691.18	14717.74	8090.24	4823.53	3333.33	0.00	4125.00
Gross Value of By-Products								
Cereals & Millets	644.81	638.61	526.21	565.82	404.79	266.85	546.88	399.31
Cash Crops	89.57	17.63	11.70	27.77	431.58	0.00	81.97	220.78
Pulses	0.00	0.00	17.22	6.88	12.10	0.00	0.00	3.69
Oilseeds	550.46	80.65	0.00	203.31	461.51	0.00	0.00	315.79
Others	476.19	129.41	403.23	28.57	147.06	0.00	0.00	78.13
Gross Value of Main Products	7866.66	4413.18	2935.19	3961.44	4481.91	1090.83	4796.22	3557.09
Gross Value of By-Products	484.79	456.81	424.41	435.40	369.95	221.48	366.19	323.43
Total Gross Value of Production	8351.45	4869.99	3359.60	4396.85	4851.86	1312.30	5162.30	3880.52

have a vital role. Thus, it is not surprising that the outstanding credit of beneficiaries was observed as larger than that of non-beneficiaries. Beneficiaries have borrowed from both institutional and non-institutional sources. The amount borrowed per household in the beneficiary group is Rs. 11,136 as against Rs. 5,506 of the non-beneficiary group.

Thus, in aggregate we find that the Pani Panchayat scheme has created a six-fold impact as follows on the group of beneficiaries. Firstly, the beneficiaries depict a clear optimum use of the land resources, though the cropping intensity is low. The share of crops and crop groups in the case of beneficiaries shows a judicious combination. The non-beneficiary group seems to be inclined more to commercial cropping. Secondly, the input intensity on the beneficiary farm is generally lower as compared to non-beneficiaries, but when we looked further into productivity of crops, this again reflects optimised pattern of inputs. Thirdly, technologically beneficiary farmers are advanced as compared to non-beneficiaries which should be inferred from the low input-high productivity combination. Fourthly, the productivities of almost all the crops on the beneficiary farms are higher as compared to non-beneficiaries. Consequently the group of beneficiaries also enjoy higher gross value of output per hectare. Higher gross value of output also acts as a correcting factor towards equity because the small farm households show higher productivity. Fifthly, the crop economy of the beneficiary household seems to be better managed with low input intensity and high output as compared to non-beneficiaries. Lastly, the credit taken for the lift irrigation schemes shows a slightly higher burden on the beneficiaries but their repayment performance to GGP as well as other financial institutions was satisfactory.

3.d. Role in Social Action Modalities and Sustenance

Pani Panchayats are resource-based organizations which were conceived and initiated by GGP. The first difficulty, any such society faces, is about sharing of resources and especially when the resource is in the group of Common Property Resources (CPRs). The usual dilemma between personal gains vis-a-vis social gains is faced and always the decision is heavily in favour of private profits. In the process, the weaker sections of the society get further pushed down increasing inequality. The only way to come out of the embroiled situation is to provoke the partners in the society to share the resources in the most economic way. Pani Panchayat could succeed in this objective.

The basic philosophy of Pani Panchayat is to share water on certain commonly agreed principles. These principles foster the people's participation in three different ways. Firstly, everyone in the group shares the concern about the principles laid down. Therefore, it is only rarely that one comes across the violations of the regulations. Secondly, the scheme is operated on a horizontal basis rather than vertical administrative principles. This binds the partners into a theme for mutual development. Thirdly, GGP's help is always available on a large number of technical and other matters. This forges a tie between the nodal agency and the scheme.

The theoretical framework was developed by Olson in "The logic of collective action" in order to view the difficulty in getting individuals to pursue their joint welfare, as compared to individual welfare. Olson challenged the argument that the collective or group interest is aggregation of individual interests. He argued:

> "Unless the number of individuals is quite small, or unless there is a coercion or some other device to make individuals act in their common interest, *rational, self-interested individuals will not act to achieve their common or group interest*" (Olson 1965).

Individual interests are satisfied through a complex set of voluntary exchanges. Agreement and stability between individuals will occur when there are no further gains to be made from exchanges. Thus, individuals will agree to observe the rules of group membership if the net benefits of doing so outweigh the costs. From the experience of Pani Panchayat it is obvious that the beneficiary group gained more than the non-beneficiaries in all respects, including production, productivity and technology.

The tregedy of commons, prisoner's dilemma, assurance problem, and the logic of collective action are closely related concepts in the models that have defined the accepted way of giving many problems that individuals face when attempting to achieve collective benefits. At the heart of each of these models is the free-rider problem (Ostrom 1990).

The Pani Panchayat movement had faced rough weather some time back and the speed of its spread had slowed down. Among the many factors there were three important ones responsible for this situation. First, the parallel lift irrigation schemes promoted through government programmes. This scheme also had the advantage of subsidy. It would, therefore, be natural for the rich elements of the society to take advantage of such a scheme, rather than forming a group on the basis of the Pani Panchayat principles. These principles would not serve the interests of those who are influential in society and consequently with the government. Secondly, the scheme involves curbing private profits and use -rights of a group and promoting the same in the weaker sections. Any such social engineering approach has met with difficulties because of the neglect of the interests of "haves". Pani Panchayat was not an exception to this. There are certain examples where outside elements have taken interest in blocking the spread of the schemes. Lastly, a resource-based scheme cannot remain unaffected by politicization. In Maharashtra, irrigation availability has a close relationship with politicization through the social prestige. Pani Panchayats and the area around could not stay out of local politicization. Fortunately, this process did not influence the working of Pani Panchayat itself.

4. Conclusion

The property right paradigm predicted in strictly individual strategies misdiagnoses the CPR problem. By failing to recognize the endogenous character of property institutions caused by interdependent of choices, it supports solutions which may be poorly suited to traditions of CPR-based societies. By seeking institutional rules imposed and enforced from outside, it has promoted costly, top-heavy institutional regimes which restrict the potential for collective action. The strict dominance of individual strategy leaves no place for such solutions. This, however, is not an argument against private property rights. Such rights may be entirely appropriate as an institutional form, especially in societies based on the law of contract. But they are not the only institutional alternatives nor the best in all circumstances.

It is often found that private property is not a viable institutional alternative, and common property regimes have deteriorated. In those instances where open access prevails, it can be re-established through standard approach, to improve incomes, to enhance equity, and to sustain the resource base. The search for appropriate institutional responses must respect both the tradition (in a limited sense) and the constraints on need in a specific choice environment. In our case the groundwater management through Pani Panchayat is such an institution, which suggests some alternative pathway of management of CPRs through assurance of collective action.

NOTES

1. Good reviews of these are available even in the Indian context. For details see Singh 1996 and Marothia 1989.
2. For details see Ostrom in Bromley edited, *Making the Common Work: Theory, Practice and Policy*, 1992.
3. These are named as 1. Bapdeo, 2. Indira, 3. Mhasoba and 4. Dr. Ambedkar lift irrigation schemes.

REFERENCES

Baland, Jean-Marie and Jean-Philippe Platteau. 1996. *Halting Degradation of Natural Resources*, Oxford: FAO and Clarendon Press.

Ballabh, Vishwa. 1989. *Efficiency and Equity in Groundwater Use and Management*, Workshop Report No. 38, Anand: Institute of Rural Management.

Braden, John B. 1985. "Uncertainty and Open Access: Implications from the Repeated Prisoner's Dilemma Game". *The American Journal of Agricultural Economics*, Vol. 67, No. 3.

Bromley, Daniel W. 1992. "The Commons, Property, and Common Property Regimes" In: Daniel W. Bromley (ed.), *Making the Commons Works: Theory, Practice and Policy*, California:

Institute for Contemporary Studies.

Center for Monitoring Indian Economy (CMIE). 1996. *India's Agricultural Sector,* Mumbai.

Chandrakanth, M.G. and V. Arun. 1997. "Externalities in Groundwater Irrigation in Hard Rock Areas", *Indian Journal of Agricultural Economics,* Vol. 52, No. 4.

Deshpande, R.S. 1990. "Agro-Ecological Problems of Command Areas" In: H. Ramachandran (ed.), *Environmental Issues in Agricultural Development,* New Delhi: Concept Publishing Company.

Deshpande, R.S. 1993. *Impact of Non-Governmental Organization on Agricultural Development,* Mimeograph Series No. 36, Gokhale Institute of Politics.

Deshpande, R.S. and K.S. Ramakrishna. 1987. *Impact Study of Krishnaraja Sagar—Report on Farm Economy,* Research Report, ISEC, Bangalore: Nagarabhavi.

Deshpande, R.S. and V.R. Reddy. 1990. "Social Dynamics and Farmer's Society: A Study of Pani Panchayat", *Indian Journal of Agricultural Economics,* Vol. 45, No. 3.

Dhawan, B.D. 1997. "India's Irrigation Sector: Myths and Realities", Presidential Address to the Indian Society of Agricultural Economics, Panthnagar.

—— 1986. *Economics of Groundwater Irrigation in Hard Rock Regions,* New Delhi: Agricole.

Dhokarikar, B.G. 1991. *Groundwater Resource Development in Basaltic Rock Terrain of Maharashtra,* Pune: Water Industry Publications.

Field, Barry C. 1985. "The Optimal Commons" in *American Journal of Agricultural Economics,* Vol. 67, No. 3.

Key, Merlin, Tom Franks and Laurence Smith (ed.). 1997. *Water Economics, Management and Demand, International Commission on Irrigation and Drainage,* London: E and FN Spon.

Kolhe, A.K., N.R. Paranjape, A.K. Gupte and M.D. Sathe. 1986. *Pani Panchayat: An Overview,* Pune: Development Group.

Marothia, Dinesh. 1989. Resource Ownership and Human Interaction: A Theoretical Exposition, *Anals of Arid Zone,* Vol. 28, No. 3&4.

Marothia, Dinesh. 1993. "Property Regimes and Institutional Arrangements: Concepts and their Relevance in Managing the Village Commons", *Indian Journal of Agricultural Economics,* Vol. 48, No. 3.

Mitra, Ashok, K. 1987. "Planning and Management of Surface Irrigation in Drought Prone Areas", Pune: Gokhale Institute of Politics and Economics.

Oakerson, Ronald J. 1992. "Analysing the Commons: A Framework", In: Daniel W. Bromley (ed.), *Making the Commons Work: Theory, Practice and Policy,* California: Institute for Contemporary Studies.

Olson, Mancur. 1971. *The Logic of Collective Action, Public Goods and the Theory of Groups,* Mass: Harvard University Press, U.S.A., (fifth printing, 1994).

Ostrom, Elinor. 1990. *Governing the Commons, The Evolution of Institutions for Collective Action,* New York: CUP.

Ostrom, Elinor. 1992. "The Rudiments of a Theory of the Origins, Survival and Performance of Common Property Institutions", In: Daniel W. Bromley (ed.), *Making the Commons Work: Theory, Practice and Policy,* California: Institute for Contemporary Studies.

Paranjpye, Vijay. 1988. *Evaluating the Tehri Dam,* New Delhi: Indian National Trust for Art and Cultural Heritage.

Paranjpye, Vijay. 1990. *High Dams on Narmada,* New Delhi: Indian National Trust for Art and Cultural Heritage.

Runge, C. Ford. 1981. "Common Property Externalities: Isolation, Assurance and Resource Depletion in a Traditional Grating Context", *American Journal of Agricultural Economics,* Vol. 63, No. 4, November.

Runge, C. Ford. 1992. "Common Property and Collective Action in Economic Development", In: Daniel W. Bromley (ed.), *Making the Commons Work: Theory, Practice and Policy,* California: Institute for Contemporary Studies.

Runge C. Ford. 1985. "The Innovation of Rules and the Structure of Incentives in Open Access Resources", *American Journal of Agricultural Economics*, Vol. 67, May.

Ruth, Meinzen-Dick. 1996. *Groundwater Markets in Pakistan: Participation and Productivity*, Research Report 105, Washington: International Food Policy Research Institute.

Shah, Tushar. 1989. *Efficiency and Equity Impacts of Groundwater Markets: A Review of Issues, Evidence and Policies*, Research Paper 8, Institute of Rural Management, Anand.

Shah, Tushar. 1993. *Groundwater Markets and Irrigation Development*, New Delhi: Oxford University Press.

Singh, Katar. 1994. *Managing Common Pool Resources: Principles and Case Studies*, New Delhi: Oxford University Press.

Svendsen, Mark and Ashok Gulati (ed.). 1995. *Strategic Change in Indian Irrigation*, New Delhi: Macmillan.

Tilley, Marcia L. 1984. "Strategic Interdependence in models of Property Rights", *American Journal of Agricultural Economics*, Vol. 66, No. 5.

Wade, Robert. 1979. "The Social Responses to Irrigation: An Indian Case Study", *Journal of Development Studies*, Vol. 16, No. 1.

SECTION 3

DEGRADED LANDS AND FRAMING OF INSTITUTIONAL CHOICES

14 Common Property Land Resources in India: Some Issues in Regeneration and Management

Sudarshan Iyengar and **Nimisha Shukla**

1. Introduction

Common Property Land Resources (CPLRs)[1] have come into focus during the recent past with regard to two major concerns. One, the institutional arrangements, which facilitated sustainable and controlled use of CPLRs in the rural areas of developing economies for the past many centuries and in the process provided significant support to the poor and marginalized households not owning private land, are breaking down very fast. The Government programmes' limited success in covering the marginalized rural poor households and providing them with effective income earning alternatives has increased the vulnerability of the poor especially in the arid and semi-arid regions. The second concern relates to the shrinking size of CPLRs. Apart from providing livelihood support to the poor, it is believed that the CPLRs also perform several useful ecological functions. Quick and significant reduction in the extent of CPLRs largely due to privatization has brought down the ratio of uncultivated land to cultivated land. Thus, due to severe degradation and privatization of commons, the health of both the ecology of the region and that of the poor households dependent upon CPLRs is supposed to be in serious jeopardy. It is being argued that regeneration of degraded CPLRs would not only improve the performance of ecological-environmental variables, but also provide fresh income-earning opportunities to the rural poor households.

The above arguments are, however, accompanied by some problems. One, the identification and quantification of region specific adverse impacts of degrading CPLRs on the ecology and environment are yet to take place adequately. Two, there are problems with respect to actual availability of CPLRs and their current status and use at the village level. In fact, the available uncultivated land which essentially qualifies to be CPLRs are not really common property resources which have clearly identified exclusive user groups. Most of the areas are either open access land over which there are no exclusive rights or they have been privatized. The conversion of CPLRs into open access lands or private lands indicate the erosion and extinction of institutional arrangements. It would be difficult to introduce plans for land regeneration for such open access areas. In this context, questions raised by Thimmaiah (1997) about the state of degraded lands, dynamics of degradation of common land in different situations, the kind of efforts that have been successful in restoring their productivity, the kind of institutional arrangements needed for sustainable regeneration, etc., become relevant. Fortunately, scholars have sought answers to some of the questions raised. In this chapter an attempt is made to continue to address some of the questions raised above by reviewing critically some of the evidences provided and experiments documented in the literature. The purpose is to assess the reality at the ground level and examine the scope of achieving the twin objectives of restoring the environmental health of CPLRs and provide income-earning opportunities to the poor through the experiments that have taken place to manage CPLRs. In Section II, the size, status and dependence on CPLRs is reviewed. One of the most important changes taking place in the rural areas is the privatization of CPLRs both legally and illegally. We have examined and analysed this aspect in Section III. There have been a number of experiments both in forest and in CPLRs involving the stake holders giving rise to new institutional configurations and management practices. A review of some of the experiments is undertaken in Section IV. The problems and prospects of regeneration of CPLRs are also examined in the light of the reviews undertaken in the section.

2. CPLRs: Some Evidence on Size, Dependence and Status

The pioneering work in the area of studying CPLRs was undertaken by Jodha in the early 1980s. He was driven to this research by the survival capacity of the population in rural Tanzania during the severe drought of 1980 (Jodha 1995). He then conducted research in 80 villages in 21 arid and semi-arid districts spread over seven States in India. He pointed out that the land reforms that were effected in Rajasthan had led to the breaking down of customary arrangements and conventions, which led to a rise in the desertification of the area. This was a serious development since the objective of the land reform was to redistribute the land in favour of the poor. The poor who had significant and substantial stakes in CPLRs, which were governed within the framework of the common property management, found that when they were given private land ownership, its productivity was declining. Jodha also found that in the post-independence era, new markets opened for some of the CPLR products resulting in over- or un-sustainable exploitation of the resources. (Jodha 1982, 85a, 85b, 86, 90 and 96). His studies revealed that CPLRs had contributed significantly towards employment and income of the poor. Income per household ranged between Rs. 530 and Rs. 830 in different areas. During the Sixth Five Year Plan period (1980-85), households earning less than Rs. 4,800 were considered the poorest of the poor among those who lived below the poverty line income, which was Rs. 6,400 under the Integrated Rural Development Programme (IRDP). The implication was that the poorest households in the early 1980s earned between 11 and 17 per cent of the total income from CPLRs. Jodha's major concern was that with the area and productivity of CPLRs falling, the poor would be left without effective alternatives because the anti-poverty programmes such as the IRDP had not done well.

2.a. Dependence on CPLRs including Forests

Several studies followed Jodha's. A somewhat comprehensive study of a State was attempted by Iyengar (1989, 1997). It examined the incidence and intensity of problems relating to CPLRs in 25 villages in Gujarat. The area under forest was excluded from the analysis. It was observed that as compared to the non-drought areas, the size of CPLRs was higher in the drought areas. Although the area under non-cultivated land had not significantly altered between 1961-62 and 1990-91, the area under Gaucher or grazing land had declined. At the village level, the recorded area under uncultivated land also showed a decline. Dependence on CPLRs for survival was higher in the drought-prone areas, but in all other areas the dependence was largely limited to grazing and fuelwood. The study also observed that as the prospects for agriculture improved by way of an increase in irrigation, the dependence of people on CPLRs, including that of the poor, declined. The composition of livestock also changed in favour of buffaloes, which are stall-fed. It was difficult to establish unequivocally whether the poor were affected more adversely due to decline in CPLRs.

Chen (1989) in her study of a semi-arid village near the saline coastal region of Ahmedabad district recorded relatively a large number of uses of CPLRs. She noted a shrink in CPLRs from about 225 ha. in the 1960s to 130 ha. in 1987—a loss of about 33 per cent. She enumerated all commons including water bodies and identified seven types, which included permanent pastures (grazing land), village forests (effectively belonging to the Forest Department), village tanks, Panchayat well, river, Panchayat trees and private property land, wells and trees, fallow, threshing grounds, etc. (seasonal CPLRs). She also listed types of trees and grasses available and their uses as fuel, fodder, food and others. She reported that fuel and fodder were the main items, which people got from CPLRs. In her paper there was no attempt to estimate money income and its contribution to total income. An important point that emerged from the paper relating to access was that although in principle, all villagers, as citizens of the village, should have had unrestricted access, there were in actual practice several restrictions. The locally powerful forces either privatized or disallowed the not-so-powerful.

While Iyengar and Chen had largely concentrated on non-forest CPLRs, many scholars treat forests as CPLRs as well. In fact, only when dependence on forest is considered, various activities of collection, consumption and sale of forest-based produce appear to fetch some income to the poor households. Thus, in this review we include the studies which have tried to work out dependence of people on forest for income. Lal (1987) in his study of 13 villages of five tehsils in Gujarat has estimated the contribution of non-timber forest produce (NTFP). Based on the data collected from 582 households, he has concluded that 18.2 per cent of all the households did not depend on CPLRs at all for earning cash income; 59.2 per cent were able to earn cash from collection of NTFP ranging between Rs. 20 and Rs. 500; 22.6 per cent earned income between Rs. 500 and Rs. 1,000; 4 per cent earned between Rs. 1,001 and Rs. 3,800. The average earning per household was Rs. 129. Considering Rs. 6,400 annual income per household for those living below poverty line, the share of NTFP worked out to a little above 2 per cent.

J.P. Singh et al. (1988) have examined the dependence of rural households on forest and forest produce. In a study conducted in five villages of Cuttack tehsil in Orissa, they have shown that for 4.4 households forest was the main source of income. For about 44 per cent, forest-based occupations were secondary. In all, 76 per cent households were dependent on forest for firewood and despite commercialization of construction material, 10 per cent households depended exclusively on forest for it. They have not given any figures for cash incomes from forest-based activities.

Marothia (1994) in his study of Bastar district found that about 20 per cent houses, income and employment were generated through collection of non-timber forest products. In another study of three tribal villages of Raipur district Marothia and Gauraha have shown that almost 100 per cent people are engaged in the collection of non-water forest products and earn more than 50 per cent of their total earnings through marketing of NTFPs.

Sarabhai *et al.* (1991) in their study of four villages in Rajpipla tehsil of Bharuch district in Gujarat have found that in three villages where the dependence on forest was substantial, forest produce contributed 38.5 to 46.3 per cent to the total village income. 48 per cent of the income accruing from the forest-based activities were from fodder and fuel.

Chopra, Kadekodi and Murty (1990) in their study of seven States, found a decline in the CPLRs area during 1970-71 to 1986-87, ranging from 4 per cent in Maharashtra to 30 per cent in Haryana (with the exception of Himachal

Pradesh, which is known to have protected forests). According to Kadekodi, the decrease in the CPLRs[2] area of arid and semi-arid States is more significant (Kadekodi 1997). However, the all India level CPLR areas seem to remained more or less the same. Chopra and Gulati (1997) have studied the size of CPLRs in western Rajasthan and found a decline in the CPLRs area from 60.5 per cent in 1951-52 to 45.1 per cent in 1977-78.

Pasha's study (1992) of 14 villages of Karnataka showed that CPLRs came down from 35.6 per cent to 23.7 per cent of total geographical area during the 1980s. The share of income derived from CPLRs ranged between 10 per cent among the poor households and 6.2 per cent in the case of non-poor households. In absolute terms it was Rs. 794 and Rs. 1,392 respectively. Nadkarni (1997), quoting a 1989 study of four villages of Uttar Kannada district in Karnataka, says that even though the poor gain more than the rich in relative terms (24.3 and 18.1 per cent of the total income respectively), in absolute terms the poor realized less income. Poor farmers earned Rs. 2,583 per household and rich farmers earned Rs. 6,537 from forest. It should be mentioned that 67 per cent of the total cost was accounted for the imputed cost of fodder through open grazing. It was as high as 89 per cent in the case of poor farmers.

Tony Beck (1994) has studied three villages in West Bengal with agriculture as the main source of income. According to his estimates, the average annual income for a household from all sources was Rs. 4,000 and the common property resources (in this study the water bodies were also included) contributed between Rs. 782 and Rs. 1,195. Thus, the share was significant at 19 to 29 per cent. Beck goes on to argue that his findings match well those of Jodha's and it was only unfortunate that more studies in West Bengal were not taken up on the issue.

Although some evidence is found in most of the inquiries on the dependence on the CPLRs for livelihood among most households in general and poor households in particular, the range varies substantially. It may be observed that the items considered by different scholars under CPLRs differ. For instance, Pasha, Nadkarni and others, Lal, Singh and others and Sarabhai *et al.* have worked out the contribution from CPLRs including forest. Tony Beck includes water bodies also and thus estimates contributions from CPRs rather than CPLRs with or without forests. It is only Jodha's work which considers CPLRs in arid and semi-arid regions of the country. However, he does not specify anywhere whether all types of the forest land were included. He has included community forestry area. Iyengar had consciously excluded forest area and found relatively insignificant dependence on CPLRs for items other than fodder and fuelwood even among the poor in arid and semi-arid villages in Gujarat. The reason to exclude forests was that in case of forests, the control is clear. The Forest Department is the owner and manager of forest land. Conservation and protection efforts are part of the department's plans. It is a

CPLR with completely different characteristics.

2.b. Recent Evidence

It is feared that due to continuing degradation of the non-forest CPLRs, the levels of dependence and contribution may have dipped further. In order to ascertain the recent situation, a few village studies were undertaken by the post-graduate students of the Economics Department of the Gujarat Vidyapith, Ahmedabad, during 1996-97. In all 15 villages were studied of which 11 were from south Gujarat, 2 from central Gujarat and one each from south coastal belt and north Gujarat. A study of a minimum of 30 households was taken up in each village. The households were selected on the basis of the economic activities of the head of the household. The categories were marginal, small and medium and large farmers; agricultural labourer, artisan and animal husbandry. In 11 out of 15 villages, the area under gaucher and fallow land declined. In most villages, gaucher area was either encroached upon or was allotted to Scheduled Caste and Tribe households under the Indira Awas Yojna, a Government of India's housing scheme for the poor. In a semi-arid village Mota Gorayya, soil from gaucher was appropriated by large farmers for improving the fertility of their privately owned land.

Dependence on CPLRs was also studied in depth. In an earlier article by Iyengar (1989), it was shown that the dependence was relatively limited and the main items were fuelwood and fodder. The situation has not altered much in the 1990s. It has been shown that the share of the monetized value of CPLRs in the consumption expenditure of the households studied in selected villages by the students was in the range of 0.1 to 11.4 per cent in the case of farm households and between 1.06 and 22.14 per cent in the case of non-farm households. The most important item was fuelwood and the non-farm households, i.e. the landless, animal herdsmen and artisans relied more on the supply of fuelwood from CPLRs. It becomes further clear when one looks at the share of fuelwood in the total CPLRs valuation. It was 5.5 to 60 per cent in the case of farm households and 18.9 to 90 per cent in the case of non-farm households. Iyengar (1989) had reported that in agriculturally developed regions where CPLRs have shrunk in size, the households showed a tendency to shift to substitutes such as dung (inferior substitute), kerosene, gobar gas, and Liquefied Petroleum Gas (LPG). Even the landless households reported use of kerosene stoves and kerosene for cooking. In the villages studied in the 1990s, it came out that the farm households were increasingly shifting to the substitutes. This has to do with affordability and improved availability. Gobar gas is being popularized by the government under various schemes which have a substantial subsidy component and the LPG is becoming more accessible with improved road network and public and private transport facilities. The net result is that the dependence on CPLRs for fuelwood appears to be going down.

Four villages of Chikhli tehsil of Valsad district out of the 15 studied have good forest and vegetative cover but showed negligible share of CPLRs in the total income of the households. Value of the items from CPLRs (including monetized value of water for irrigation drawn from common source) was 5.3 per cent of the total income of the farm households and one per cent of the non-farm (landless and others) households. The average share per household was 2.9 per cent. Interestingly, forest was the main source of income. Of the CPLRs' income 64.5 per cent came from wood and 18.7 per cent from leaves (Tendu leaves sold for bidi rolling and Khakhra for leaf cups). The wood was mainly sold in the market. The share of the monetized value of CPLRs in the total consumption expenditure was 0.9 per cent in the case of farm families and 0.2 per cent for non-farm families. Thus, even the recent evidence shows a relatively lower dependence on CPLRs even if one includes the income from forests. A qualification here would be necessary, that in the four villages studied, the average annual rainfall is more than 1,500 mm and the extent of irrigation ranged from 7 to 45 per cent. Thus the agriculture prospects were generally good. In the villages where the agricultural prospects are not good, people are likely to depend more on the forest produce, but then as shown by Nadkarni and others, the absolute income is low. In arid and semi-arid regions, the income was significant in the past, but since the 1970s, it appears to have gone down considerably because of the degraded status.

2.c. Deteriorating Status of CPLRs

Most scholars have also expressed concern about the deteriorating status of CPLRs. We have already noted that Jodha, way back in 1982, had raised an alarm with respect to the desertification of land in Rajasthan. The environmentalists have also begun to raise the issue of degrading and degenerating status of commons. Anil Agrawal and the team members in their pioneering work, *State of India's Environment, First Citizen's Report,* have reported exploitative use of forests and other natural resources (Centre for Science and Environment, 1982). Elsewhere he has said that in various parts of India, the resources have been depleted and miseries of the poor have increased significantly (Agrawal 1985). D. Nagabrahmam and D. Sambrani (1983) had also reported that the decreasing size of CPRs of land, forest and water have resulted in miseries and drudgery of women, since they have to travel many kilometres to collect fuelwood, fodder and water. Marothia (1989) made similar observations about fuelwood, fodder and small timber scarcity and suggested measures to mitigate drudgery of rural women.[3]

Iyengar (1989) also reported degradation of CPLRs in Gujarat. Tree species having good timber value were perceived to be disappearing in most of the dry areas. Similarly, the productivity of grass in grazing and other wastelands was perceived to be declining. It was not possible to quantify, but the village elders were asked to communicate their impressions about the change in the status of CPLRs over a 25-year period. In arid and semi-arid villages, which lacked irrigation facilities, people reported relatively heavy loss of tree cover and grass production. They attributed this to an increase in human and livestock pressure, breakdown of conventions and laxity on the part of the regulating authorities.

While the social scientists have been able to describe the degrading status of CPLRs in terms of impressions and perceptions of the people living in the study areas or by using certain indicators, which help in approximating the extent of degradation, the ecological implications of the degradation of CPLRs are yet to be worked out in detail at micro levels. Except for Jodha, who argues that because of degradation of CPRs and their privatization in arid Rajasthan, the regular agriculture has suffered because the changes in CPLR's status has unleashed the desertification process. At the macro level, the quantification of degradation of CPLRs has been attempted by some. Most estimates are available at all-India level and CPLRs are variously defined. Thus, whenever a proportion is mentioned, one has to be careful to ascertain the total from which the proportion has been worked out. Kadekodi (1997) has discussed elaborately the issues involved in estimating the wastelands in India. The problem, of course, starts with the definition of wastelands, which mainly form CPLRs in the country. Three different definitions are in use. One is based on land productivity, second on ecological characteristics and the third on both. The Technical Group of the National Wasteland Development Board (NWDB) in its Report of 1986 defined wastelands as follows: "Wastelands mean degraded lands which can be brought under vegetative cover, with a reasonable effort and which are currently lying as underutilized and land which is deteriorating for lack of appropriate water and soil management or on account of natural causes." (Quoted in Kadekodi 1997). This definition is based on both land productivity and ecological characteristics. Using these different definitions for estimation of wastelands have their own problems. Since the definitions are not coterminous with the landuse classification of the agricultural department of the government, the total count under various estimates is not available. Scientists have tried to build robust estimates based on samples. However, non-availability of complete toposheets and minimal topographic information make the estimation exercise difficult and erroneous (Kadekodi 1997, Ch. 2).

Yet several macro level estimates are available. The landuse statistics of the government is one. They give an estimate of the uncultivated land by the legal class of ownership. Bagchi and Philip have estimated the extent of wastelands in the States covering the 1978-1988 period and based on the landuse classification of the government. They arrived at a figure of 82.17 million ha. of non-forest wastelands (Kadekodi 1997, Table 2.4). However, there are serious problems with government classification and estimates and hence one cannot rely on it for planning especially at the lower levels (Iyengar, 1998). Some other macro estimates of the wastelands are also given by Kadekodi (1997, Ch. 2). In 1989, National Remote Sensing Agency (NRSA) estimated wastelands based on remote sensing and ground truthing. Based on detailed satellite mapping of 146 districts of the country, NRSA arrived at an estimate of 129.57 million ha. of wastelands of which 93.69 million ha. were non-forest areas. Bansal (1990), came out with a figure of 162.9 million ha. of total wasteland in India. (The total geographical area in India is 329 million ha). Another FAO/UNDP study quotes an estimate of 83.4 million ha. of which 43.6 million ha. was due to wind and water erosion. In yet another estimate by the Indian Council of Forestry and Education the total wind and water eroded area in 1995 was 150 million ha. Kadekodi reports that NWDB also had estimates for saline/alkaline lands, wind eroded area and water eroded area separately. He goes on to say that while it was important to understand different kinds of degradations and their impact on the livelihood, the estimates produced by various scientists and agencies do not really go into the desired depth in finding out the actual environmental impacts. Estimating changes in land productivity by itself would not adequately capture the full environmental effect (Kadekodi 1997, Ch. 2).

There are some studies which bring out the ecological implications of degradation. For instance, scientists have conducted some studies in the Banni grassland area in Kachch district in Gujarat and have found that the grasslands have been seriously degraded affecting the ecology of the region. Tracing the factors responsible for degradation, Dixit (1997) quotes various scholars and lists the factors. The major factors enumerated are the invasion of prosopis juliflora, an exotic vegetation, damming up of rivers, regular droughts, overgrazing and salinity ingression. As a combined effect of these factors, the grasslands in Banni have declined at an unprecedented rate of 3,039 ha. per year. In 1980 the total area under grasslands was 101099 ha.

Scientists with the help of remote-sensing techniques are in a better position to assess the status of the wastelands (however defined). The estimates produced by the remote sensing scientists may go on improving the precision and perhaps they will also be able to provide the status of land at more and more micro levels. An important point that is missing in the analysis is regarding the use of CPLRs people are making at village level. Such information is critical for planning for regeneration and management. If one agrees that the old community regulated institutions about the access and use of CPLRs have broken down, it should be necessary to examine what obtains at the village level. The *de facto* status of CPLRs at village is examined in the following section.

3. CPLRs Management : *de jure & de factor*

In the Indian context, the ownership, use and regulation of CPLRs have changed significantly over time. Before the British, the King or the State was the ultimate owner of all land, but individuals enjoyed ownership rights on the cultivable lands. The uncultivable lands were used and regulated by communities. The State hardly interfered. During the British period, the government became the owner of all land resources in the country. Farm lands that were owned and operated by individuals with exclusive property rights continued to be under the control of individuals. The uncultivated lands were brought under State regulation. The Forest and Revenue departments came into existence. Community's control over the uncultivated lands was lost legally. In independent India the British system has more or less continued. However, several reforms were introduced in the laws relating to ownership and operation with an objective to accomplish more egalitarian distribution of land benefiting the tenants and poor landless genre. Thus, the privately owned land is regulated by different land revenue codes designed at State levels.

All the land area in a village not privately owned falls in the public domain. Most parts of land in the public domain form CPLRs. The land in the public domain at the village level is regulated by the Village Panchayat (village level local body), the Revenue Department and the Forest Department. All land is essentially owned by the Revenue Department of the State. It hands over the regulation rights over the grazing land and land for specified purposes to the Village Panchayat. The area that is notified as forest is transferred to the Forest Department, which also becomes the owner. It is altogether a different matter that the department has recognized and approved certain customary rights of the local population. These rights are slowly being extinguished because of fast disappearing forest cover. It may be useful at this stage to understand the landuse and regulation in the country with the example of a particular State.

Gujarat State has a vast area, which is not under cultivation. Almost half of the State's total reporting area is uncultivated on record. Substantial portions of land are lying unused. However, the exact size and status of the uncultivated land are not clearly known. It must be clarified once again for the purpose of understanding that the phrase "common property land resources" (CPLRs) are not really common property in the sense in which the term is used in social science literature. Historically, village communities in the rural areas had fairly well-defined collective property rights, which facilitated its use and regulation. Similarly, forests were most of the time the property of either the State or the tribes who regulated its use. Under the Moghal and the British rules, the total landmass of the State came to be vested with the government and hence the State. Two departments—revenue and forest—became the virtual proprietors. In independent India, the introduction of the Panchayati Raj system transferred certain use and regulation rights to the village Panchayats. Further, there is the Agriculture Department which can influence landuse through its policy regimes. Cultivable land, however, is owned under the private property regime. Thus, presently, four departments are involved in the use and regulation of land in the State and the types of land they regulate are given below (see Table).

Department	Type of Land	Type of Controls
Forest	Protected Areas Reserve Forests Other forests	Proprietorship, Management, Use Regulation, Control over access
Revenue	Barren and Uncultivable Area under non-agri. use, cultivable waste	Proprietorship, Use regulation
Panchayat	Gauchar and other permanent pastures	Use regulation
Agriculture	Land under cultivation of which net area sown, current fallow and other fallow	Indirect regulation

Over a period of time, the control and use regulations are effectively carried out only by the Forest Department. There too, it should be noted that the control is effectively utilized over the stock and not the flow. The land area under forest is closely guarded and protected. Laxity is found in regulating and conserving the forest products—major as well as minor. It should also be mentioned that in some places even the stock, i.e. the forest land, is also not regulated effectively because there are instances of encroachments[4].

The Agriculture Department exercises hardly any influence over the landuse. At best, with its policy instruments it is able to influence the cropping pattern in the private lands. Most of the landmass is thus left with the Revenue Department. Here again the department has not been able to regulate effectively the use of land under its control. Similar is the case of the Panchayat land. As part of the democratic decentralization, some land was given to the village-level institution, namely, the Panchayat, by the Revenue Department, but it too has by and large failed to promote its sustainable use. As a result of the massive failure on the part of the State as well as the local institution, two types of major developments have taken place:

1. The common property land resources (CPLRs) have turned into open access thereby leading to the tragedy of commons (overuse and abuse).
2. Legal and illegal privatization of land under revenue and Forest Departments of the governments and the Panchayats has taken place.

3.a. Privatization of CPLRs

The privatization of CPLRs is taking place because the pressure of population in the rural areas has increased highly, the regulatory mechanisms have become permissive and the State has taken a conscious decision to distribute uncultivated open access lands to socio-economically weaker households in the villages. The Forest Department, because of its effective presence at the ground level, is aware of the nature and extent of encroachments whereas the Revenue Department does not even have any clear picture about it. The policy decisions to turn the wastelands into productive land areas do not take off from the ground in a big way mainly because the planning agencies are hardly aware of the ground realities. Many studies have tried to quantify the magnitude of the encroachment on revenue and Panchayat lands. Iyengar had reported in his study in 1989 that out of 25 villages, in 12 villages various types of encroachments were made by individuals and institutions. Following were the types of encroachments:

(a) Removal of soil from grazing and other public land (private farmers and potters);
(b) Encroachment on grazing and other public land including forest for cultivation (farmers);
(c) Encroachment for non-agricultural uses (individuals for residential and other purposes, cooperatives and private industry);
(d) Encroachment of public land adjacent to the land allotted by the government, i.e. cultivating more area than allotted by the government (both by individuals who were allotted land and by those who leased it from the actual allottees).

It is difficult to get the estimates about the encroachments especially when one inquires as part of a research study. People are suspicious and curious and hence do not report the correct figures, though, in some cases, people are more candid. The range of encroachment is high. In the study villages (Iyengar 1989), where CPLRs were large, the encroachment ranged from 10 to 50 per cent. Chen (1989) reported engineered privatization of government agricultural land in her study village by feudal landlords. The possession was taken (encroachment) and then the regularization took place. The area involved was sizable. About 60 ha. were encroached and privatized. This was 5 per cent of the total geographical area of the village and about 25 per cent of the total CPLRs as estimated by Chen.

Nadkarni and Pasha (1992) have also estimated the encroachments in 14 villages in Karnataka. They verified the recorded status of uncultivated lands (UCLs) by talking to the people in the 14 villages and found that the encroachment explained the difference between the recorded size of (UCLs) and the size found on the ground. 24 per cent of all the (UCLs) were found to be encroached. Interestingly, they have observed that even this was an underreporting. Further, more developed the villages agriculturally, the higher was the extent of encroachment. Nadkarni and Pasha argue that the rural elite are responsible for this land hunger. We differ somewhat over this perception. The present author and the Gujarat Vidyapith students have found that even the poor and landless are equally eager to encroach once they are sure that the land productivity is good if put to use for crop cultivation. Thus, the extent of encroachment is influenced by the productivity potential and the pressure felt (due to rise in the family size). The economic status of the encroacher is relatively less important.

Evidence of privatization was also found in the 1990s when 15 villages were studied by the Gujarat Vidyapith students. In three villages, the Panchayat had allotted a part of grazing land for Indira Awas Yojna, a housing scheme for the poor and socially backward families. In five villages, the Panchayat had allotted land to the Forest Department for social forestry. Importantly, the general experience has been that the Forest Department does not return the land after the afforestation is over and further, the benefits flowing out of the tree-growing activity are not shared with the residents of the village. There is a strong resentment about this among the villagers. In seven villages, people had encroached the gauchar and wastelands for cultivation. In four villages people have encroached the clear felled forest land for cultivation of crops.

In some parts of Saurashtra and the Kachch region in Gujarat, the pressure on land has increased significantly also because of the income accruals from the non-farm activities. In Bhavnagar district, for instance, a large number of working members from the farm families have diversified into diamond cutting and polishing. Since the 1980s, scope for enterprise and employment in the diamond industry has increased enormously. As a result of this activity, farm families belonging to Patel and Ahir communities have experienced substantial rise in the household incomes. Even the Scheduled Caste population has benefited to some extent. There are no survey-based estimates for the observations made, but, in the process of conducting some other studies in the area, some reliable information was available on the subject. The surplus in the incomes is being used for improving the productivity of land, first by exploiting groundwater facility and then by extending the area under cultivation. Since cultivable land is limited, the extension in cultivation is attempted by illegal occupation of CPLRs adjacent to the private farmlands and at times also on lands that are located at a distance. Unlike most encroachments where CPLR is just brought under the plough along with the regularly cultivated land, CPLRs that are being encroached for the past 10 years or so are being systematically reclaimed. The reclamation generally takes three to four years. In the first year, silt from the tank or riverbed is spread on the highly eroded land in the summer months. During the monsoon, the encroached land is sown which helps in binding the soil. During the second year, more silt is spread and a grain crop such as sorghum or millet is sown. In the third year, with or without irrigation, groundnut, wheat or other high-value crops are grown. Thus, by about four to five years, land becomes reasonably productive. Since the regulation from the Revenue Department is weak, the land is eventually privatized. This process is taking place on a substantial scale. It is not necessary that only large and resourceful farmers are engaged in this, even the small holders are found to privatize CPLRs in this manner. It must be noted that such a process is on in cases where the farmers are enterprising and have non-agricultural income to generate the capital needed for investment in land.

The Government of Gujarat as a matter of policy has distributed parts of CPLRs and the land acquired under the Land Ceiling Act twice in 1960 and in 1976[5]. A total of 100,000 ha., which was one per cent of the total cultivated area in the State was on record released under the ceiling. However, the actual possession could be only on 56,000 ha. The land parcels allotted to the landless poor were small. The average size of the parcel was 2.5 ha. By 1985, 22,277 holdings were allotted to the landless (Sharma 1993). The fertility of most of the land was below average and the allottees were not able to make investments necessary to improve the productivity. In 76 per cent of the land released as per the 1960 Act and 31 per cent of the land released after 1976 revision were brought under regular cultivation. The government allotment of land whether CPLRs or private for redistributive purposes has had a very modest success. Sharma has pointed out that the government should integrate the efforts of various departments, organize technical guidance and improve the access to more investible resources. When farmers take the initiative on their own to privatize or reclaim land, the improvement in productivity appears to be better. It is very likely that people tend to encroach land for cultivation which is potentially promising. One is reminded of Vinoba's Bhoodan Movement of the 1950s, in which landlords donated least productive or unproductive land parcels.

3.b. Privatization and Encroachments

All evidence gathered above as part of the research studies offers proof about the incidence of privatization of CPLRs, but the exact figure has not been available. It becomes known only when a concrete scheme is launched to develop CPLRs with or without participation of the local community. The experience of NGOs in this respect is illustrative. After the formation of the National Wasteland Development Board, and the Society for the Promotion of

Wasteland Development (SPWD), an NGO, many regional NGOs tried to launch CPLRs development schemes and had to face mostly illegal privatization of CPLRs when they identified plots with survey numbers and went to the location for possession. Aga Khan Rural Support Programme's (AKRSP - India) executives, while implementing the natural resource development programme in Junagadh district in Gujarat during the late 1980s, were shocked to find encroachments on the survey numbers allotted to them for development by the revenue officials. The executives then decided to test check a few more villages. Thus, in all they made a thorough check in 20 villages in three tehsils of the district. While there were inter-village variations—no encroachment (one village) to 100 per cent (two villages), the actual CPLRs were 28 per cent short of the recorded size (Oza 1989). AKRSP's second team working in Bharuch district found that in nine villages encroachments in CPLRs including forests were 65 per cent (Shankar Narayan 1989).

Some official evidence of encroachments are also available. In the Gujarat Government's Development Commissioner's office, there is an official whose office compiles the records of encroachment on the Panchayat lands all over the State. Obviously, the official recording is far below the actual encroachments as is evident from the AKRSP data. However, in December 1988, the size of officially recorded encroachments all over Gujarat was 7,454 ha. The number of encroachments was 22,658 (Gauri Kumar 1989). Thus, on an average each encroachment had an area of 0.33 ha. In 1991, the total area under all grazing and pasture lands was about 0.85 million ha. This land is generally under the Panchayat's control. The Development Commissioner's office records encroachments on this land. Relating the data that has been collated at the State level in 1989, one can see that the recorded encroachment was about 0.9 per cent of the total land in the category. If we take the AKRSP estimates of 28 per cent the actual area encroached in the villages of Junagadh district and 65 per cent in Bharuch, it is very clear that the official recording is highly inaccurate.

Encroachment in the forest area is another type which is significant in size. Very often deforested and degraded forest lands are brought under cultivation by the tribal families who do not own or control any productive assets including land necessary for survival. This problem is serious in Gujarat. Two voluntary organisations working in the tribal areas of Gujarat have raised the issue significantly. Both the organizations have pointed out that the tribal population growing in number faces a severe shortage of cultivable land. The tribal families have no option but to take up cultivation of the degraded forest land (ARCH-Vahini 1993 and DISHA 1994). The Government of India's Ministry of Environment and Forest had to release 60,000 ha. of forest land for cultivation. The land released was brought under cultivation before 1980. Between 1980 and 1998, still more area would have been encroached about which there are no published statistics (the Forest Department may have the data). If effective alternative means for livelihood are not offered to the resourceless poor in the rural areas in general and in tribal areas in particular, the area under forest and other CPLRs is likely to be under severe stress and ultimately be lost to crop cultivation and thus, privatization (Iyengar 1998).

From the above analysis it may be inferred that privatization of CPLRs for cultivation appears to be quite substantial and hence, the scope for restoring the productivity of CPLRs through collective efforts may be somewhat limited. However, in the recent past, the government departments, especially the Forest Department and NGOs have tried to improve the status of CPLRs by trying various organisational forms involving relatively poor and backward sections of the population in selected villages all over the country. The efforts are reviewed in the following section.

4. Regeneration and Management of CPLRs

It has been observed in the earlier sections that most researchers treat forests as part of CPLRs. Forests as such may not be classified under CPLRs because the State Forest Departments are the owner of the forest land. The Forest Conservation Act, 1980, which confers on the Centre the right to permit or withdraw permission to convert forest land for non-forest use, makes the right of the Centre amply clear. People living in and around the forest area have certain rights relating to collection and use of material such as fuel, fodder, passage, water and other NTFPs. But the Forest Department has all the power to take away any and all of these rights. For example, in the sanctuary areas, the passage rights also cease. In the CPLRs literature, the experiments conducted by the Forest Department involving the people around have been documented as the collective development of CPLRs and the success stories or otherwise have been used to draw lessons for CPLRs as a whole. In our opinion, this is not correct.

4.a. Joint Forest Management

In the case of forest resource there is a principal owner. This is true even in the case of Joint Forest Management (JFM). People are at best involved as partners (most would not like to be this generous about the people's status in JFM) without any ownership rights over the assets (forest land in this case) of the partnership concern. The department is the sole owner. It is willing to enter into a contract with a group of individuals who may be living as a community in villages adjacent to forests. The dominant purpose still is protection and not conservation. Since the department has failed to fully protect forests through policing, it is now inclined to involve the local people in the management. The rights granted under the agreement of JFM relate to the usufruct rights over the produce in the forest which may include timber, a major forest produce. The forests under JFM do not become community forests as it happens in the case of Van Panchayats in U.P. (Singh 1994) nor are they community owned as they used to be in the distant past before the British. Van Panchayats may deserve to be treated as CPLRs and not as the reserved and protected forests. However, after the 1976 amendments in the rules, one will not be very sure about treating them as community owned (Singh 1994). The experiments of JFM conducted in 16 States from December, 1988, onwards, have covered mostly the degraded and protected forests (Kadekodi 1997, Table 5.3A pp 5.10 - 5.11). Only one State, Orissa, has tried JFM in the reserved forest area. None of the State Forest Departments has tried any sanctuary and/or national park area for JFM. The department is not willing to enter into partnership with people and turn forests into CPLRs where the standing forests are in good condition. Most of the areas where it has tried to involve people are clear felled and degraded. The regeneration efforts have to be made afresh. These are also the areas where the department is certain that it will be very difficult for it to regenerate vegetation on its own and provide protection once the regeneration efforts begin.

Interestingly, Kadekodi (1997) has recorded that JFM has been adopted as a strategy by the Forest Departments in 16 States, which have more than three-fourths of the forest area of the country. More than 10,000 forest protection groups (FPGs) have been formed which protect over 1.5 million ha. of forest land. This would imply that each FPG on an average is involved in protecting 150 ha. of forest land. The country in 1993-94 had 68.42 million ha. of forest land. Thus, FPGs are active in 2.2 per cent of the total forest land in the country. If we assume that each FPG represents one village, the coverage here too works out to 2 per cent (assuming that the country has 500,000 villages). Kadekodi, based on the success of Arabari and Bankura districts in West Bengal, Sukhomajri in Haryana and some experiments in Orissa and Bihar, appears optimistic about the success of JFM on a large scale. Singh (1994) has earlier observed that JFM is a potentially sound strategy for the regeneration of degraded forest land, but the success stories in West Bengal were made possible because of a strong political will that helped change the attitude of the forest officials down the line. He only hopes that it can be replicated in other States as well. Vijaylaxmi and Parikh (1997) have listed various conditions for the success of JFM strategy in the country. They do not comment conclusively about JFM experiments. Recording the merits and demerits of an experiment in Harda division in Madhya Pradesh, they observe that because of JFM, grazing management improved, villagewise eco-development programme could be planned and people's needs for fuel and fodder could be given priority. The limitations were that there were no powers to the forest protection committee, selection of beneficiaries was crucial and the links between the protection committee and other village-level bodies were not clear.

None of the major reviews on JFM seems to explicitly recognize a crucial fact that the resource in question is essentially owned and regulated by the State. It is not at the disposal of the community with an exclusive right over it, and thereby excluding all other users including the State or the department. In the case of forests, the State, through its executive organ, the Forest Department, has the right to choose the beneficiaries to which it may grant certain use rights. It also reserves the right to withdraw the benefits extended. The Forest Department on its own managed and regulated forests and their use. Problems began when it was realized that it had failed to protect the forests effectively. Since independence deforestation and degradation set in fast and in about 25 to 30 years, a substantial part of the prime forest cover was lost. The area under forests got degraded first because of laxity in regulation[6] and second because of the tremendous pressure of the fast-growing population. The second reason, although often advanced by the Forest Department as the most important, is weak. Quoting a recent NCAER study by I. Natrajan, Anil Agrawal (1998) in *Down to Earth* argues that the fuelwood crisis which was supposed to destroy whatever forests most of the States had did not actually do so mainly because the bulk of supply never came from the forests. It was a myth that was created which not only led to the strengthening of the policing powers of the Forest Department but also led to the introduction of exotic fast-growing fuelwood yielding species that did not necessarily suit all the regions.

The problem of the Forest Department is thus essentially a problem of failure in implementing a centralized regulation policy. This cannot be compared to the ethical codes evolved by the communities over a long period of time for the use of collectively owned common property resources and which are far more binding on the members in regulating their use. The Forest Department has thought of decentralizing the regulatory mechanism and try and involve local people at the former's conditions. Essentially, it is not an equal partnership between people and forest officials. As stated, the department reserves the right to withdraw any powers and rights granted to the protection committee or the groups. Even in selecting members of the committee and the group, the department officials have a better say. People are junior partners or associates in this game. JFM may have led to regeneration of degraded forest lands in some States, but how sustainable it would be in the long run and how effectively it can be replicable everywhere in the country under the present framework is a moot point.

4.b. Management of CPLRs—Van Panchayat Model

A somewhat better experiment is that of the Van Panchayats (VPs) of the Uttar

Pradesh Hill regions. They in the past did qualify to be CPLRs because people had significant control over its management and appropriation of produce. Singh (1994) has shown that the autonomy of VPs has eroded substantially between 1931 when the institution came into existence and 1976 when critical revisions were made in the rules by the government. The forests were CPLRs in the real sense of the term where people's collectives owned and managed forests in the U.P. hills. The British took total control over the ownership and management and evicted people completely. After persistent protests by people, the Van Panchayat scheme was introduced in 1931. VPs had substantial autonomy in forming rules relating to use, appropriation and regulation. Most of them were taken away by the 1976 amendments. In the present form VPs cannot now take any independent decision. They have to seek approval of either the Deputy Commissioner (Collector) or the Divisional Forest Officer (DFO). (Singh 1994 Table 11.3). A further revision in VP rules was also in the offing in 1989. However, the final authority of the government officers over VP's decisions were not altered in any significant way (Singh 1994).

Despite significant curbs in the control over the forests vested with VPs, people have expressed their desire to continue with them. Even in 1989, Singh has recorded that there were at least 842 VPs in the Nainital and Ranikhet sub-divisions. In all of Uttarakhand, 4,645 Van Panchayats were there in 1997 (Kadekodi 1997). In an indepth study of Parwara Van Panchayat, Singh has reported that all sample respondents realized the importance of the VP forest as an indispensable source of firewood, fodder, small wood and timber. They also reported an understanding about the relationship between forest and agriculture and forest and animal husbandry (Singh 1994). Their response to a proposition of handing over all the forests to the Van Panchayats for management was interesting and suggestive. People plainly refused. The main argument was that VP forests could be managed only because the forests were relatively open access areas and the pressure on VPs could be deflected over to the non-VP forests in the areas adjacent to the VP forests. If all the forests were handed over to VPs for protection, the VP forests would also disappear. The expression used was *Jangal ki chori har koi karta hai,* meaning everybody steals from forest (Singh 1994). In fact, the study also reveals that over time VPs are under pressure and there are instances of encroachment, theft and breach of rules in a number of VPs.

In its present form, VPs may be viewed as a variant of JFM. They have certain features such as powers to fine, distribution of forest produce, management of accumulated surpluses, etc., which may be adopted under JFM with appropriate changes suiting local conditions. After the 1976 amendments (and even if the 1989 revisions in rules are accepted), VPs are essentially under the total control of the government's two officers, Collector and Divisional

Forest Officer (DFO). Thus, as in the case of JFM, here too, the issue is one of decentralizing the management of the centralized set of rules set to suit the interests of the State and not necessarily to hand over a common resource to people for use and management and to this extent it would not be appropriate to classify VP forests under CPLRs.

We began by saying that CPLRs have drawn attention for two main reasons. One because under the control of people as collectives, it helped the poor households in generating substantial incomes and two, it provided sound ecological services. In JFM and VP schemes, scope of regeneration is found to be somewhat satisfactory in a large number of cases thereby nearly achieving the objective of ecological services, the evidence relating to the augmentation of income of the poor households in the communities involved does not come out so very clearly. Grazing seems to be fairly better regulated and the situation of firewood seems to have improved, but the income from other produce from the land or forest doesn't seem to have improved. Thus, even if the forests are considered CPLRs, under the present type of management regimes (JFM and VP models), the scope for forests becoming a resource base for lifting the households above the poverty line appears to be extremely limited.

4.c. Non-forest Land for Forest Development

Let us now take a look at some experiments, which have tried to improve the productivity of these non-forest open access uncultivated land through different approaches. A significant experiment relates to exclusive involvement of women in the degraded land regeneration programme in Gujarat. The well-known organization, Self Employed Women's Association's (SEWA) Nursery raising programme is spread in eight rural districts and the city of Ahmedabad. A total of 3,647 women are directly engaged in the forestry-related activities that began in 1988, with as many as 1,400 or 38 per cent in one district, Banaskantha, an arid region (Nanavati 1997). Although the exact nature of the programme in each of the blocks or districts is not very clear in the article, women seem to be engaged in nursery growing, sapling plantation and fodder farming. In 350 ha. of land women reportedly grew fodder. Under the DWCRA (Development of Women and Children in Rural Areas) programme of the government's rural development department, women have formed groups and the government has leased wasteland for one to five years. On this land women grow seedlings and supply these to the Forest Department. This obviously is a good step towards regeneration of degraded forest. However, Nanavati points out a number of problems in the scheme. To begin with, the lease period of one to five years was found to be insufficient. The Forest Department has not provided any technical support or guidance to women in nursery growing and sapling raising. Third, water for irrigating the seedlings was a critical input and in the design of the scheme it was totally ignored. The most important problem was about the economics of the scheme. The cost norms set by the District Rural Development Agency (DRDA), which is responsible for sanctioning and implementing the scheme, had prescribed cost norms that were a decade old. Further, the returns realized by women were not significant at all. It has been argued that on an average the Forest Department paid 50 paise for a sapling, which is not sufficient to meet the cost leave alone eke out a living. The cost of raising a sapling was Re. 1.25. It is suggested that the Forest Department pay a minimum of Re 1.25 per sapling. Unless an economic price was paid, it was not possible to undertake nursery growing as an economically viable activity.

One is inclined to believe that the SEWA experiment may be fairly successful in regenerating the land, which the women use for nursery raising and fodder farming, but how effectively regeneration takes place in the forest areas where the saplings are planted by the Forest Department may need some assessment. Second, details regarding the extent of income, which the women earn from the nursery related activities, are not available in the article. One can get an idea that it may not be enough to earn a living solely out of it because the rates offered by the Forest Department for the saplings were very low and did not meet even the cost of raising them. The issue of earning is also important because women's time would have alternative uses. One would like to know whether, in the absence of nursery activities, women would have gone to the forests for NTFP collection including firewood and fodder and how much money that activity would have fetched? From the presentation, it appears that the opportunity cost of labour in the NTFP collection or other alternative occupations (theoretically including the value for leisure if one preferred it in the absence of any other work) was even less than the nursery activity because women did get involved in nursery raising. The programme has the potential to achieve the twin objective of regeneration of degraded land and providing a living for the poor, but evidently, a lot more effort is needed to make it a success.

The remaining experiments may be classified into certain types of institutional arrangements within which the open access lands were converted into CPLRs. The major types are:

1. Granting land lease to individuals or Tree Patta Scheme.
2. Formation of cooperatives for CPLR development.
3. Formation of village level groups for governing commons or other institutional innovations,

4.d. Tree Pattas and CPLRs Development

The literature suggests that the tree patta scheme has been implemented mainly in three States—Uttar Pradesh, Karnataka and West Bengal. In Uttar Pradesh and Karnataka respectively degraded wasteland and degraded forest land were leased (patta) to the poor households for raising trees. The area ranged between 0.2 and 0.8 ha. per household. In U.P., 59,410 pattas were given covering an area of 19,267 ha. On an average a household got 0.32 ha.

Lease-holders were supposed to grow trees and enjoy the produce. The land was allotted by the Revenue Department, the finance was to come from the Rural Development Department and the technical guidance was to come from the Forest Department. It did not happen and the experiment failed (Vijaylaxmi and Parikh 1997). In Karnataka, the degraded forest lands were allotted and were planted with trees. The poor households were supposed to protect the plants and grow them into trees. The Forest Department would cut the trees on maturity and pass on a part of the proceeds realized. In addition, a patta-owning household was to be given Rs. 500 a year for maintenance until maturity. The poor mostly used it for grazing and hardly protected the plantations. They also used it as collateral with the banks and tried to improve their private agriculture. They made no investment in the allotted land because they were not certain whether they would get a fair share from the proceedings in the end.

In West Bengal the patta land consisted of both agricultural and non-agricultural land. The former was acquired mostly under the Estate Acquisition Act and the Land Ceilings Act. Singh (1994) has given some estimates about the total land that was distributed up to December, 1988. According to him, a total of 349,000 ha. of land were distributed to the landless under the Patta scheme. This amounted to 30 per cent of the total area available including the acquired agricultural land. The problem in allotting land to more landless was that most of the lands acquired under the above two Acts was subjected to court injunctions. West Bengal's Patta scheme was essentially a scheme for bringing more area under agriculture with an objective of land redistribution in favour of the landless. Singh's study indicates that the experiment of granting land patta to the landless for cultivation had a very limited success as far as improving agriculture was concerned. In his words, "the productivity of CPLs which were highly degraded has been restored, if not improved". (Singh 1994). When data for crop yields for four years were compared it was found that the average productivity of patta land was very low compared to the owned land. As a result most of the patta lands were left fallow. Only those landless who did not have any other alternative ploughed the land and harvested whatever they could.

In the second stage, the Government of West Bengal launched the social forestry scheme for the patta lands. Singh has studied Nepura village in Midnapur district in this context and reports that irrespective of the knowledge of the economics of eucalyptus plantations, the patta holders were happy with whatever income they got from the plantation because (a) in the absence of the eucalyptus plantation, the patta yielded nothing, and (b) the income was a windfall as they had planted without any expectations of income (Singh 1994). Interestingly, Singh goes on to conclude that the West Bengal model was good and worth emulating all over the country with some modifications such as sound technical back up by the Forest Department, etc. What he perhaps overlooked was that of the total land that was pooled together (thus he calls it Common Pool Lands—CPLs), about 44 per cent was under private cultivation with farmers who were either big or estate owners. Once acquired it would have gone out of cultivation until the lease holders cultivated or grew trees on them. With about 16 per cent of land under court injunctions, and a significantly more land yet to be distributed (only 30 per cent in all could be distributed), the macro cost-benefit may not turn out to be favourable. Secondly, the country as a whole saw the rise and fall of eucalyptus and hence any mono plantation may have serious problems. The moment we have tree plantations in the patta lands all sorts of problems ranging from technical guidance to the financial support, etc., will crop up and our experience is far from satisfactory in handling them well. Therefore, State-backed privatization is likely to have serious limitations.

4.e. Cooperatives and CPLRs Development

The second type of arrangement has been the formation of cooperatives for the use of land. First of the two types of cooperatives is a cooperative of individuals for collective farming purpose. The Gambhira Cooperative Farming Society was registered in 1953. Interestingly, 176 poor farmers in four villages—Gambhira, Kathiakhad, Nanisherdi and Bilpad of Borsad tehsil in Kheda district—were initially allotted individually an acre of land in the bed of Mahi river. The farmers could not make much use of the private allotments as the river-bed land was saline and relatively unproductive and they did not have enough resources to reclaim the productivity. A Gandhian social worker, Chhaganbhai Patel, organized the farmers into a cooperative and suggested collective farming. The experiment was highly successful (Singh 1994). The cooperative is still working in 1998 after more than 45 years. The main reasons attributed for the success are the exceptionally able and good leadership, dedicated employees who worked at low wages and socially homogeneous groups (the lessees are mainly Baraiya). The leadership was provided by Chhaganbhai Patel who passed away only in 1997. This is a case where the degraded CPLR was improved and in the process the poor earned a decent livelihood out of it. Such a success story is rare and efforts need to be made to replicate it.

The second type of cooperative is the Tree Growers' Cooperative (TGC) at the village level. The idea was born in 1986 in response to a request from the National Dairy Development Board (NDDB) to the National Wasteland Development Board (NWDB) to help in developing an institutional mechanism for regenerating degraded common land to meet fuelwood and fodder deficits in the villages (Vijaylaxmi and Parikh 1997). Over time, it was felt that the formation and development of TGCs needed some technical guidance on a continued basis and hence a federation of TGCs was constituted in 1988 as Rashtriya Vriksha Mitra Sahayog Limited. It was renamed as National Tree Grower Cooperative Federation (NTGCF) in 1990. By 1996, there were 366 TGCs in six States with 28,377 members. TGCs covered an area of 5,797 ha. with plantation of approximately seven million trees. On an average each TGC has 77 members and it covers an area of about 16 ha. with more than 19,000 trees. In such a short time, this appears to be an impressive achievement.

There are two TGC case studies available. One in Karnataka and the second in Gujarat. It would be difficult to say anything conclusively about the entire experiment of 366 TGCs based on these two cases. However, the cases do provide useful insights into their working and performance. Both the cases appear highly successful. (Reddy *et al.* 1997; Saxena and Agarwal 1997). A detailed economic analysis of the cases shows a great potential for economic viability of TGCs. The Mallanahally case from Karnataka provides rich details about the socio-economic setting and participation processes among the residents (Reddy *et al.* 1997). Though the Sarnal village case of Gujarat does not contain the socio-economic analysis in detail, it provides a lot of input-output analysis. From both the cases it appears that when a majority among the village community decides to exercise restraint on access and use of one part of the common land, the productivity of that part can be improved significantly. However, the critical issue is who takes the decision? In the case of Mallanahally, all 66 households were members of TGC. In the case of Sarnal we have no idea how many out of 300 households were members. There is some grey area here in regard to the long-term sustainability of the experiment.

It is clear from the Mallanahally case and it may also hold true for Sarnal that the areas allotted to TGCs were relatively a small portion of the total common land in the village. In Mallanahally, for instance, out of 227 ha. of common land, 20 ha. or 8.8 per cent was leased to TGC. It would be extremely important to know the pattern in all TGC villages. As long as the land leased to TGC is a small portion of the total common land of the village, the villagers may not object and may abstain from freely accessing it. If the total common land is limited, the residents are likely to resist allotment to TGC. This was evident in another case in Gujarat. In Aslali village in Gujarat, villagers had agreed to allotment of land for social forestry from the commons. While a majority approved the allotment, a few belonging to the Rabari and Bharwad (cattle herders) communities strongly resented and had complained about the scarcity of grazing land (Singh 1994). Unless the village as a whole makes a unanimous decision to allot land for a special purpose in which the access and use are regulated, there is likely to be resistance form some quarters. The lower the size of the common land in the village, the higher may be the resistance. Further, we have shown in the previous section that at the village level the actual availability is a problem because of encroachments. In Mallanahally, it is reported that the land was leased out by the Forest Department (Reddy *et al.* 1997). In Sarnal, it was leased by the Revenue Department. In the former case the process of allotment is easy once the Forest Department decides. In the latter case both decision making and actual lease would be extremely time-consuming and difficult unless of course a lot of influential forces were creating pressures at appropriate levels. There are instances when for the release of a small piece of revenue wasteland the Minister had to be approached. Incidentally, this leads us to an important question which is not answered adequately in the case studies. By whom and how were the initiatives taken for the formation of TGCs in the six States? If the milk producers' federations took the initiative then it has a different set of implications. In which type of villages the milk unions will have influence over people? Would they be able to influence people in all villages? Which other alternative organization would be able to influence and convince people? Has any NGO tried the experiment? These questions are yet to be answered. Under such circumstances it may be said that although TGCs may hold the key to improve the status of some parts of CPLRs and provide support to the poor, its replication on a large scale may face rough weather.

4.f. Other Institutional Innovations and CPLR Development

Before we discuss other institutional innovations in CPLRs' development and their potential for replication, it may be useful to clarify a point. The Forest Departments at the State and the Centre have indeed been more innovative than any other department with regard to protection and improvement of land under their jurisdiction (with or without the World Bank aid). We have already mentioned a few cases in the analysis made in the previous sections. However, we do not intend to make an exhaustive list of all innovative schemes which the Forest Department may have tried over years. For instance, there are experiments such as social forestry, village woodlot schemes, eco-development projects for the national parks and protected areas and others. Substantial critical literature is available on most of these experiments. We are interested more in the possibilities of tackling the common lands that are under revenue and Panchayat departments and are *de facto* open access areas and therefore highly degraded. We believe that there are a large number of institutional innovations in conserving CPLRs in the country and it will not be possible to make an exhaustive review of all. Further, many historical institutional arrangements may still be surviving under relatively favourable circumstances or because of the sheer grit of communities in maintaining the traditions amidst pressures from all sides (Bishnois from Rajasthan are a case in point).

One of the interesting and successful experiments in regeneration of wastelands has been undertaken in six villages of Udaipur district in Rajasthan by an NGO named Ubeshwar Vikas Mandal (UVM). The experiment has been well-documented by Chopra and Gulati (1997). UVM started by making villagers to agree to protect a 20 ha. private pasture land in 1985. The results were so encouraging that people from neighbouring villages agreed to come forward to regenerate their totally degraded wastelands. The activity was then expanded to 600 ha. during the next year involving four villages. The programme was converted into a micro watershed development programme in which the Forest Department also came forward with sound support. Soil and water conservation, improved animal husbandry and agricultural practices were part of the programme. The programme was implemented by mobilizing people and creating new community facilities. A large community-based pasture and an open well community lift irrigation scheme were started. More importantly, mutual labour aid for private land development was introduced and self-help groups for savings among women were formed. The success story is well known all over. Two important factors that made this possible were the desperation on the part of the people to do something as they were trapped in a worst possible situation and two, the experience of UVM organisers in working with the communities in these villages for more than 15 years.

The second interesting experiment is located in Bihar, another relatively underdeveloped State. The experiment is known as Chakriya Vikas Pranali (CVP)—cyclic system of development. Kadekodi (1997) has documented this experiment. It started in 1986 in Bhusaria village of Palamau district and by 1997 the CVP experiment had spread to 40 villages. "CVP seeks to blend modern science and technology with traditional wisdom in order to promote multi-layered, multi-cropping based on the compatibility of different plant species. It seeks to optimize sustainable management and use of the entire natural resource base of the village which includes land, water, vegetation, sunshine, air and human resources." (Kadekodi 1997). It pools the private and public wastelands together for development. The landowners and landless workers receive 30 per cent of the produce each, 30 per cent is used for capital investment and the remaining 10 per cent is used for village welfare fund (Vijaylaxmi and Parikh 1997).

In the recent past some industrial houses have also taken up the development of common lands in a number of villages. Kadekodi (1997) has documented IFFCO's sponsored wasteland development experience in 26 villages in four districts of eastern Uttar Pradesh. IFFCO organized the villagers into cooperatives and set up nurseries. This was followed by tree plantation. The members of cooperatives provided protection. The experiment has been successful. IFFCO has made a total investment of Rs. 8 crores for the experiment and it has set up an apex Indian Farm Forestry Development Cooperative (IFFDC).

Another important experiment is taking place all over the country. In Gujarat, NGOs are involved in it in a big way. It is the participatory watershed development programme of the government of India—Units of 500 ha. are formed for development and Rs. 4,000 are made available for the treatment of one ha. On the watershed principles, planning for 500 ha. micro watersheds are prepared and implemented. NGOs are invited to take responsibility of one or more micro watersheds. They are supposed to undertake entry point activities in selected micro watershed villages for which a separate fund is allocated. A Watershed Development Team (WDT) has to be constituted by the NGO which is to be made responsible for planning and implementation. The first phase of the programme launched in April, 1995, is planned to be completed in March, 1999. The results are encouraging. The most important feature of the programme is the development of both private and public land and water resources within a micro watershed. It is an integrated natural resource management programme. There have been such experiments earlier on a pilot basis. Sukhomajri in the Shivalik Hills in Haryana, Mittemari project and MYRADA's experiment in Karnataka are well known watershed-based natural resource regeneration experiments. With the National Watershed Development Programme, the scaling up has been achieved.

One of the important specific problems in implementing the watershed programme relates to the difficulty in actually treating the common land. In two workshops organized by the Development Support Centre and Gujarat Institute of Development Research, both based in Ahmedabad, in 1997 and 1998 respectively, NGOs brought up the issue of the treatment of common land in the micro watersheds. Encroachment on the common land was the major issue. Second, people's readiness to work on the common land was also less. Although not admitted categorically by NGOs, the problems faced in treating the common land are either being neglected, i.e. the commons are bypassed or a cursory treatment is given which may not be sustainable. One will have to wait for more evidence in future to say anything more concretely.

4.g. Scope for Sustainable Regeneration of CPLRs

We have perhaps covered a large variety of experiments being undertaken for the regeneration of the degraded CPLRs in the country. A dominant thesis is of protection which is on the top of the agenda of the Forest Department and those who support environment protection at any cost. We have seen that in most land regeneration programmes land under the Forest Department is involved and also it is the department which comes forward with greater initiative. In most such experiments we are also told that the scope for providing a reasonable living standard from the existing forest-based activities, innovative or traditional, autocratic or participatory, for the poor households is somewhat limited. If the situation has to improve, the entire framework of planning may have to be altered. It may be necessary that forests need to be protected and preserved for environmental sustainability, but people will have to be involved in such attempts by putting the resource under the community's control. The department will have to play a consultant's role by providing technical guidance and scientific innovations generating in the formal institutions. If one allows for protection thesis alone, the Forest Department will become more powerful and chances are that it will alienate people completely creating severe conflicts.

Second, the problem of encroachment has to be faced squarely. As mentioned earlier, in the areas where the scope for agriculture is good and will improve with better irrigation facilities, etc., there will be pressure for privatization for agriculture. The population is increasing and even in arid and semi-arid regions the pressure is immense (Iyengar 1997). Thus, even there with the improvement in agricultural productivity, people will convert CPLRs into private properties. This would be true even in cases where certain innovative experiments in developing CPLRs may get initiated. For instance, in the UVM villages in Udaipur, if CPLRs' productivity improves significantly and the land becomes suitable for agriculture in the coming five to ten years, the same members of UVM's CPLR development group will not hesitate to privatize it for cultivation of crops. In the CVP experiment in Bihar, private and public lands have been pooled and the produce is appropriated individually which has features of private gains for initiatives. Perhaps, this may also be one of the reasons for its success. We have observed that in Saurashtra farmers have financed reclamation of hitherto unproductive land into good agriculture land from the financial resources mobilized from the savings generated out of non-agricultural activities. Interestingly, development of non-agricultural activity may not only ease the burden on agriculture temporarily, but it may also lead to its development in a subsequent stage. The State need not really think of distributing land to the poor for private cultivation without assessing the demand for it. Unless there is a cooperative effort such as the one at Gambhira in Gujarat, poor generally will fail to cope with the allotted land parcels. In cases where they encroach land either in forest or non-forest areas, they are certain about the prospects for agriculture in those land parcels using the means they can employ on them. The government should view such cases and either try to provide alternative land or non-land based occupations, if the encroached lands happen to be in ecologically fragile zones and where agriculture is not suitable, or alternatively regularize the encroachments. It is here where the experiments such as the ones undertaken by UVM in Udaipur and Chakriya Vikas Pranali in Bihar need to be encouraged. Unless people are clearly demonstrated that the value addition in the activities undertaken on CPLRs is larger than private crop cultivation, there would not be any incentive to come together and convert open access areas into CPLRs.

The National Watershed Development Programme is also a sound alternative to improve the status of degraded lands in the country and in the process provide better income earning opportunities to the poor. However, the functional relationships between the common land and the private lands need to be established clearly. There is an area of conflict here which will have to be resolved. An encroachment on the common land by one or more individuals may disturb the agriculture of a number of individuals owning and operating private agricultural lands. While the latter group may be willing to undertake soil and water conservation measures in the public land to improve the productivity in their private farms, the encroachers may take objection. Here too, the conflict resolution will have to take place considering who the encroachers are. If they are poor, the community may have to think about an alternative enterprise or some way of compensation. These are the real difficult situations. The involvement of NGOs in the process may help. There is a view that Gram Panchayats with the 73rd and 74th (Constitution) amendments should play a more decisive role in development interventions, but one has to be wary because the Panchayats may become partisan. Here NGOs or people's voluntary organisations may act as countervailing powers.

It is true that there are no very clear solutions and plurality of interventions and innovations will have to be encouraged. However, it is important to understand that the institutions around CPLRs were formed over a long period of time and involved considerable ethical codes. The traditional institutions may have broken down because the pressures generated could not be withstood by the ethical codes and also that the ethics or values may have changed over time. In order to have a sustainable management of natural resources in the public domain which are becoming scarce, the societies will have to evolve new ethical codes. Then alone new institutional arrangements may come up and CPLRs may be revived. Otherwise, it is going to be either privatization or State control one way or the other. Most of the experiments that we have viewed have elements of innovative management in either form, i.e. privatization or State control, but hardly any one of them reflects the evolution and acceptance of sound normative parameters.

NOTES

1. CPLRs here refer to land areas that are officially not under cultivation. They include forest and open access wastelands also. We have not restricted CPLRs by property regimes. For details regarding definition and interpretation refer, Katar Singh, 1994.
2. It should be clarified here that Kadekodi *et al.* have used different and specific definitions for CPLRs, whereas our reference is generally to the uncultivated areas excluding forest unless specified.
3. Based on a study conducted in two villages of Chattisgarh region. Marothia and Nandi (1994) indicated that due to shrinking of CPLRs the villagers collected inferior fuel material and the quality of wood purchased had also increased significantly and thereby increased in expenditure on fuelwood. The scarcity of fuelwood can be mitigated through afforesting wastelands (Marothia 1988).
4. Although encroachment is to be interpreted as illegal occupation, people's act may not necessarily be unjustified. In Gujarat, for instance, substantial area in forests is encroached by tribals who do not have any worthwhile alternatives for earning livelihood. The issue has been taken up by a few voluntary organizations who have organized struggle and won the battle with the Ministry of Environment and Forest, Government of India, by getting the land released for private cultivation.
5. In 1960, when Gujarat State was formed, the Land Ceiling Act was enacted on September 20. The ceiling was set in the range of 23 to 53 ha. per family (Joshi in Usha Sharma 1993). Sharma's study showed that out of an estimated 80,000 ha. of ceiling land available, only 18,605 ha. could be declared and the acquisition could take place on 18,095 ha. Out of this land 14,784 persons were redistributed 17,937 ha. Thus, each person was on an average allotted 1.21 ha. A revision of this Act was passed again in 1976 (although Indira Gandhi had suggested to reduce the ceilings as part of her Congress Party's Ten Point Economic Programme in 1968), in which the ceiling was reduced to 12 to 22 ha. and a liberal provision was made that the father could allot land to each adult son, area not exceeding the ceiling. That is each son could be allotted 12 to 22 ha. of land. A total of 81,250 ha. of land was released as a result. This was much higher than the area released in the 1960 Act. Thus, in all, from about 10 million ha. of land under cultivation, a total of 100,000 ha. or only one per cent could be released.
6. The laxity in the implementation of regulations has been due to various factors. Political interference, unusual increase in the demand for wood in the growing economy leading to irregular practices, etc., led to fast deterioration of forests. It has also been forcefully and convincingly argued that the initial institutional arrangements in which people managed by forests were more sustainable but the department systematically removed people and their involvement in the resource management and use.

REFERENCES

Agrawal, Anil. 1985. "Human-Nature Interactions in a Third World Country", *Partnership in Progress: Water*, Issue No. 15, June 1987, Calcutta: Lutheran World Services (India).

Agrawal, Anil. 1998. "False Predictions", *Down to Earth*, May 31. pp. 29-41.

ARCH-Vahini. 1993. *Forest Preservation: Which Way to Go?* Mangrol, Rajpipla (Mimeo).

Beck Tony. 1994. "Common Property Resource access by poor and class conflict in West Bengal", in *Economic and Political Weekly*. Jan. 22, 1994.

Centre for Science and Environment. 1982. *The State of India's Environment, 1982: The First Citizens' Report,* New Delhi: CSC.

Chen, Marty. 1989. "Size, Status and Use of Common Property Resources: A Case Study of Devdholera Village in Ahmedabad District, Gujarat", in *Status of Common Property Land Resources (CPR-LAND) in Gujarat and Problems of Their Development,* Ahmedabad: Gujarat Institute of Area Planning, (Mimeograph) pp. 123-134.

Chopra, Kanchan, Kadekodi, Gopal K. and M.N. Murty 1989. "People's Participation and Common Property Resources" in *Economic and Political Weekly.* December 23-30, A 189-195.

Chopra, Kanchan, and S.C. Gulati 1997. "Institutions for Management of Common Property Land Resources and Migration: A Study in Rajasthan", In: Jyoti Parikh and Sudhakar Reddy (eds.), *Sustainable Regeneration of Degraded Lands.* New Delhi: Tata McGraw Hill Publishing Company Limited, pp. 257 - 278.

DISHA. 1994. *A Report on Developing Initiatives for Social and Human Actions* (DISHA), January 1993 to August 1994, Ahmedabad.

Dixit, A.M. 1997. "Ecological Degradation of Common Property Land Resources: Problems and Prospects" In: Jyoti Parikh and Sudhakar Reddy (eds.), *Sustainable Regeneration of Degraded Lands.* New Delhi: Tata McGraw Hill Publishing Company Limited, pp. 91-103.

Gauri Kumar. 1989. "Availability of Panchayat Grazing Land for Development", in *Status of Common Property Land Resources (CPR-LAND) in Gujarat and Problems of Their Development,* Gujarat Institute of Area Planning, Ahmedabad, 1989 (Mimeograph) pp. 14-20.

Iyengar Sudarshan. 1989. "Common Property Land Resources in Gujarat: Some Findings about their Size, Status, and Use", in *Economic and Political Weekly,* 24 June, A.67-77.

Iyengar Sudarshan. 1997. "Common Property Land Resources in Gujarat: Some Issues in Size, Status and Use", In: Jyoti Parikh and Sudhakar Reddy (eds.), *Sustainable Regeneration of Degraded Lands.* New Delhi: Tata McGraw Hill Publishing Company Limited, pp. 57-76.

Iyengar Sudarshan. 1998. "Land Use Statistics: Implications for Environmental Data Base", Gujarat Institute of Development Research, Ahmedabad. *Working Paper No. 97,* March.

Jodha, N.S. 1982. "The Role of Administration in Desertification : Land Tenure as a Factor in Historical Ecology of Western Rajasthan", In: Spooner Brian, and Mann H.S. (eds.), *Diversification in Development: Dry Land Ecology and Social Perspective,* New Delhi: Academic Press.

Jodha, N.S. 1985a. "Population Growth and Decline of Common Property Resources in Rajasthan, India", in *Population and Development Review,* 11 (2).

Jodha, N.S. 1985b. "Market Forces and Erosion of Common Property Resources", in *Agricultural Markets in Semi-arid Tropics, Proceedings of an International Workshop,* October 24-28, 1983. International Crop Research Institute for Semi-Arid Tropics (ICRISAT), Patancheru (AP) India.

Jodha, N.S. 1986. "CPLRs and Rural Poor in Dry Regions of India". *Economic and Political Weekly,* 21(27), July 1986.

Jodha, N.S. 1990. "Rural Common Property Resources Contributions and Crisis", *Economic and Political Weekly,* June 30, pp. 65-78.

Jodha, N.S. 1995. *Sustainable Development in Fragile Environments,* Ahmedabad: Centre for Environment Education.

Jodha, N.S. 1996. "Property Rights and Development", in Hanna, Susan S., Carl Folke, Karl-Goran Maler (eds.) *Rights To Nature.* U.S.A.: Island Press, pp. 205-220.

Kadekodi, Gopal K. 1997. *Regeneration of Degraded and Waste Lands - A Status Report on Data Gaps, Valuation, Implementation and Monitoring,* New Delhi: Institute of Economic Growth, (mimeograph).

Kadekodi, Gopal K., Chopra Kanchan and M.N. Murty. 1989. "People's Participation and Common Property Resources", presented in *Economic and Political Weekly,* December 23-30, A 189-195.

Lal, R.B. 1987. *Role of MFP in Tribal Life and Culture*, Ahmedabad: Tribal Research Center. Gujarat Vidyapith.

Marothia, D.K. 1989. "Socio-Economic Rationales of Wasteland Afforestation", *Journal of Tropical Forestry* 5 (Oct.-Dec.) pp. 334-350.

Marothia, D.K. 1988. "Afforestation of Bhata Soils: Socio-Economics and Management Aspects", *Indian Journal of Agricultural Economics*, 43(3), pp. 305-309.

Marothia, D.K. 1994. *Decentralized Planning for Bastar District: An ACRP Approach*, Planning Commission (GOI) Project, IGAU, Raipur, May, pp. 1-119.

Marothia, D.K. and A.K. Gauraha 1992. "Marketing of Denationalized Minor Forest Products in Tribal Economy", *Indian Journal of Agricultural Marketing*, 6(2), pp. 84-91.

Marothia, D.K. and D. Nandi 1994. "Degraded Lands, Agroforestry and Energy Needs: Issues and Development Strategies", In: Punjab Singh, P.S. Pathak and M.M. Roy (eds.) (1994) *Agroforestry System for Sustainable Landuse*, New Delhi: Oxford & IBH.

Nadkarni, M.V. 1997. "Poverty, Dependence on Common Property Land Resources and Economic Development" In: Jyoti Parikh and Sudhakar Reddy (eds.) *Sustainable Regeneration of Degraded Lands*. New Delhi: Tata McGraw Hill Publishing Company Limited, pp. 81-90.

Nadkarni, M.V. and S.A. Pasha 1992. "Developing Uncultivated Lands : Some Issues from Karnataka's Experience in Social Forestry", *Indian Journal of Agricultural Economics*, 46 (4).

Nagabrahmam, D. and D. Sambrani 1983. "Women's Drudgery in Firewood Collection", *Economic and Political Weekly*, 18(1&2).

Nanavati, R. 1997. "Feminise Our Forests," In: Jyoti Parikh and Sudhakar Reddy (eds.) *Sustainable Regeneration of Degraded Lands*. New Delhi: Tata McGraw Hill Publishing Company Limited, pp. 219-228.

Oza, Apoorva. 1989. "Availability of CPR at Micro Level : Case Studies of Junagadh Programme Area of AKRSP (INDIA)", in *Status of Common Property Land Resources (CPR-LAND) in Gujarat and Problems of Their Development*, Ahmedabad: Gujarat Institute of Area Planning, (Mimeograph). pp. 71-84.

Pasha, S. A. 1992. "CPRs and Rural Poor in a Micro Level Analysis", *Economic and Political Weekly*, Vol. 27 (46).

Reddy, Sudhakar, Jyoti Parikh and Kirit Parikh. 1997. "Role of Cooperatives in the Utilization of Common Property Resources:A Stakeholder Perspective," In: Jyoti Parikh and Sudhakar Reddy (eds.) *Sustainable Regeneration of Degraded Lands*. New Delhi: Tata McGraw Hill Publishing Company Limited, pp. 279-294.

Sarabhai, K.V., Seema Bhatt and G. Raju. 1991. *People's Involvement in Wildlife Management: An Approach to Joint Sanctuary Management of the Shoolpaneshwar Wildlife Sanctuary, Gujarat*, Ahmedabad: Nehru Foundation.

Saxena, Rakesh and Rajesh Agrawal. 1997. "An Appropriate Socio-Eco-Environmental Accounting Framework Proposed for Tree Growers' Cooperatives with a case study," In: Jyoti Parikh and Sudhakar Reddy (eds.), *Sustainable Regeneration of Degraded Lands*. New Delhi: Tata McGraw Hill Publishing Company Limited, pp. 137-166.

Shankar Narayan. 1989. "Availability of CPR at Micro Level : Case Studies of Bharuch", in *Status of Common Property Land Resources (CPR-LAND) in Gujarat and Problems of Their Development*, Ahmedabad: Gujarat Institute of Area Planning, (Mimeograph). pp. 85-93.

Sharma, Usha. 1993. "Economic Status of the Beneficiaries of Land under the Gujarat Agriculture Land Ceiling Act". (in Gujarati), 'Ahmedabad: Sardar Patel Institute of Economics and Social Research.

Singh, J.P., M.L. Chakravarty, H.N. Atibudhi '"Economic independence on forests by rural households: a study in Cuttack district, Orissa". *Indian Journal of Agriculture Economics*, Vol. XLIII, No. 3 (Conference papers abstracts).

Singh, Katar. 1994. *Managing Common Pool Resources: Principles and Case Studies*. Delhi: Oxford University Press.

Thimmaiah, G. 1997. "Foreword", In: Jyoti Parikh and Sudhakar Reddy (eds.) *Sustainable Regeneration of Degraded Lands*. New Delhi: Tata McGraw Hill Publishing Company Limited, p v.

Vijay Laxmi and Jyoti Parikh. 1997. "Land Regeneration Programmes: Lessons from Successes and Failures", In: Jyoti Parikh and Sudhakar Reddy (eds.) *Sustainable Regeneration of Degraded Lands*. New Delhi: Tata McGraw Hill Publishing Company Limited, pp. 13-42.

15 Greening the Wastelands: Experiences from the Tree Growers' Cooperatives Project

V.K. Misra

1. Introduction

Traditional institutions for the management of natural resources were evolved by the people at the grassroots on the principles of social justice and equity. These institutions used to function on the basis of unwritten bylaws and were managed by trusted and impartial leadership. During the colonial rule, management of natural resources was centralized, resulting in alienation and gradual collapse of these traditional institutions. The forests were seen as a source of revenue. The results were socially as well as ecologically disastrous. Unfortunately, there was no change in the governance of forests even after independence. With growing pressure of population, absence of people's institutions and inability of the forest cadres to identify themselves with the people within and around forests, we have reached the brink of ecological disaster. The programmes initiated after independence like Van Mahotsav and Social Forestry proved to be unsustainable due to lack of people's participation, as they were not considered their programmes. By mid-eighties, the need for involving people in natural resource management was realized. Efforts were made to find institutional alternatives as a result of which different institutional modes like Forest Protection Committees, Joint Forest Management Programme, Tree Growers' Cooperatives and of late Watershed Associations are being tried in different parts of the country involving forest and non-forest community lands.

The India demonstrated political will to rehabilitate wastelands of the country by creating the National Wastelands Development Board (NWDB) under the aegis of the then newly created Ministry for Environment and Forests. The mandate for the NWDB was to formulate, support and monitor development of five million hectares of wastelands every year mainly through revegetation. The task was massive and resource inadequate, yet some progress was made especially in associating NGOs and testing various institutional models at the grassroots for the management and sustainable utilization of village commons. The gain was mostly in terms of "changed attitudes" towards resource regeneration than the area of wasteland rehabilitated. It was more clear than ever to the bureaucracy that the centralise management of commons by the government departments is impractical and unsustainable, hence more emphasis has to be laid on developing appropriate institutional models which could be created and owned by the people at the grassroots for sustainable management of natural resources. Accordingly, informal village forests protection committees, joint forest management programmes through village-level associations or cooperatives and several other forms of institutional structures were promoted and tested.

2. Genesis of the Project

During 1985, newly created National Wasteland Development Board (NWDB), in its search for institutional alternatives to enhance people's participation in resource regeneration and management, considered whether the principles of Anand Pattern Cooperatives promoted by the National Dairy Development Board (NDDB) in the milk and oilseeds sector can be adapted for wastelands development. At the request of NWDB, a pilot project on Tree Growers' Cooperatives (TGCP) was initiated by NDDB in 1986 in Andhra Pradesh, Karnataka, Orissa, Rajasthan and Gujarat with a budgetary provision of Rs. 50 million for a period of five years. It was an experiment to find out whether this institutional model would prove to be effective in involving people for the development of wastelands. Two years after the initiation of the pilot project, it was realized that instead of NDDB implementing the project, an apex organization of Tree Growers' Cooperatives should do it, hence a Multi-State Cooperative under the name of Rashtriya Vriksha Mitra Sahayog Limited, renamed as National Tree Growers' Cooperative Federation Limited (NTGCFL) in 1990 was promoted by NDDB in 1988, and was entrusted with the responsibility of implementing the pilot project.

A little after the initiation of the pilot project, there were pressures to expand it to a mega project because the Canadian International Development Agency (CIDA) and the Swedish International Development Authority (SIDA) were keen to support it. The Swedish assistance (Rs. 245 million) is in Rajasthan and Orissa from 1991 and the Canadian assistance (Rs. 400 million) is in Gujarat, Andhra Pradesh and Karnataka since 1993. NDDB started supporting the project in Uttar Pradesh Hills from 1992 (Rs. 30 million). The process of expansion is still continuing. Phase-I of the SIDA and EIDA assistance has been concluded. So far more than 500 village-level tree growers' cooperatives have been organized and 15,000 ha. of highly degraded revenue wasteland has been rejuvenated. Recently, the project has initiated to support village-level institutions other than cooperatives for natural resource regeneration and also adopts the watershed mode for regeneration.

2.a. Genesis of Common Land Encroachment

India adopted the policy of land reforms in the early fifties when the Land Ceiling Acts and Zamindari Abolition Act came into force. This was done to minimize disparities between haves and have-nots.

However, the ever present lust for land in human beings prompts them to discover ways and means to acquire what was lost and continue to struggle for more. During the past 40 years, massive land reforms have taken place but side by side massive encroachment of State-owned land has also been in progress due to political patronage and administrative laxity. The encroachments have been regularized and the politicians have often given promises on the eve of elections for regularization of encroachments.

A survey by the National Tree Growers' Cooperation Federation Limited (NTGCF), an apex organization of the village-level Tree Growers' Cooperative in six States of India, reveals a massive encroachment of the cultivable portion of revenue wastelands and degraded forest land adjacent to privately owned marginal/sub-marginal lands and thus, reconfirm the earlier findings (Jodha 1986) about the decline of 41.55 per cent in the area of village commons over a period of 30 years, i.e. 1950-52–1980-87. Similar studies carried out by Iyengar (1988) and Gadgil (1985) also confirm the trend, which could be due to encroachment and policy of the State Government to distribute common land to the landless. The pace of encroachment generally increases a little before elections under the patronage of politicians.

It has been observed that the encroached land away from the cultivated area is initially used for herding animals, tree plantation or as a threshing site or for grazing of animals so that the encroachers could gradually establish their ownership over a period of time while playing safe by not making any significant investment on the encroached land. The illegal occupation of land continues for several years unreported or unrecorded after which it is regularized with the help of political pressure and bribe.

2.b. Privatization of Commons and Encroachments

Under poverty alleviation programmes and in the name of social justice, a large area of common land has been privatized. In numerous cases common grazing land, revenue wastelands, forest land and panchayat land has been allotted to the so-called weaker sections of the society for cultivation or for the construction of houses. There are several instances where panchayat land reclaimed or cultivable revenue wasteland has been allotted to the landless often belonging to other villages. They seldom use such land for any productive purpose due to financial constraints and threats/non-cooperation from the village under whose revenue area the land is located. If the allottees are from the same village and are unable to cultivate the allotted land due to financial constraints, they take loans from the rich/farmers or the moneylenders and allow them to use their lands on unwritten mutually agreed terms and conditions. Generally, the land allotment certificate is handed over to the loan-giver as a surety and also to avoid further loans on the same land. The moneylender then starts encroaching on the panchayat or revenue wasteland adjoining hypothecated land and prefers to pay penalty from time to time so that his name is entered into the revenue records. After a few years, there is a possibility of the encroached land being allotted to the encroacher while he continues to enjoy the benefits of the land allotted to a poor person who is unable to repay the loan. Most such land allotted by the government under land distribution programmes is lying unutilized and cannot be rolled back due to a number of reasons such as lack of financial support, highly degraded nature, remoteness, grazing problem, etc. It is also very difficult to unite the land allottees to develop it through collective action because they are suspicious of losing their lands, which is often fragmented, and the allottees cannot afford heavy investments on land development. The owner being too poor cannot wait for a long time for income from trees or any other such crop venture, which has a long gestation period and attracts the restrictive Tree Felling Act.

In the heavily populated States like Bihar, West Bengal, Uttar Pradesh, Punjab, Haryana, etc. there are virtually no village commons. The question is where do the landless go for meeting their needs of fuelwood and fodder? What does the future hold for them?

2.c. Voluntary Surrender

It would not be an exaggeration to assume that there is no village in the country where land encroachment has not taken place. The extent may differ depending upon a host of facilitating or discouraging factors. In the initial years of project implementation, NTGCF relied on the revenue records obtained from the district/State revenue offices. The cooperatives were organized assuming that the land is vacant and under the ownership of the Revenue Department.

However in a good number of cases, after TGCS was organized it was realized that the land is encroached. Since encroachers are the residents of the village and also members of the cooperative, it is a difficult situation in which neither the interest of TGCS can be sacrificed nor of the individual member. Therefore the only option is to persuade him or through "social pressure". However if the encroachment is old, and is regularly under cultivation, this option also may not work.

In Gujarat in a good number of villages where TGCS have been organized the encroached land has been abandoned in favour of TGCS due to social pressure and persuasion by project staff.

2.d. Conflict Resolution

It has been observed that one and all use the common land lying in a degraded State under the centralized control of the State and even by the adjoining villages. However, when the land is leased to TGCS, the villagers who are members of the TGCS become rightful owners of the same land of which they were illegal users before the land was leased to TGCS. With a sense of ownership they start resisting grazing or trespassing by the neighbouring villages. This often creates social tension, resulting in violence and litigation.

In a typical example of a village in Jaipur district of Rajasthan, where a TGCS was organized by NTGCF, the leased land was used for grazing by an adjoining village as well, as a short route to a patch of forest land where grass growth was better. However, after the TGCS was organized and land was leased, the cooperative members objected to animals of the other village crossing through their territory where trees and grass were planted during the rainy season. This led to social tension between the two villages and subsequent destruction of several thousand newly planted saplings during a night assault followed by criminal and revenue cases filed by TGCS village wholeheartedly contributing cash for meeting the expanses of the legal proceedings. After a lapse of three years, the intelligent chairman of the TGCS approached the Forest Department officials and persuaded them to plant trees in the portion where the neighbouring village used to take the animals for grazing. Once the area was planted and protected by the Forest Department, the conflict automatically got resolved because for the fear of getting booked under the Forest Conservation Act. They stopped grazing. Later the TGCS village won the court cases and both the villages had a conciliatory meeting to cooperate with each other.

In another village Vatra in Kheda district of Gujarat, where 80 ha. of revenue wasteland was leased to TGCS, 20 ha. was put back to open access for grazing under the directions of the district administration because there was political pressure exerted by a strong group of nomads who were residents of the same village and were major users of the entire area of the common land for grazing a large herd of animals owned by them. The district administration took this action on the plea that the available common grazing land was too small (10 ha.) for a large herd of animals in the village. However, they did not accept the argument of TGCS members that only 10-12 families in 350 households village owned 60 per cent livestock hence there was no justification for reverting 20 ha. of revenue wastelands leased to TGCS to open access land. Later, when nomads tried to create further problems by letting loose a large herd of animals into TGCS plantation, the entire village resolved to find them a sum of Rs.3,500 which was promptly paid by the culprits with an oath not to repeat such illegal acts again.

In the village Poli of Shrikalashasti Mandal of Chittoor district of Andhra Pradesh, where over 40 ha. of revenue wastelands having shrub jungle were leased to TGCS a few opinion leaders were able to convince the entire village to go against their own TGCS, as land was fit for cultivation and they were allured with the possibilities of land being allotted to landless who were in a good majority in the village. The TGCS in Poli which was registered during 1987 has remained defunct, and it is interesting to note that no portion of the land leased to TGCS has yet been allotted to any individual and people have preferred to wait for it than to revive the TGCS as individual ownership is always more tempting than collective ownership.

In Karnataka, where land encroachment is rampant and strongly motivated by the political parties, ecologically precarious rocky areas and hill slopes with small patches of land having some soil depth in the midst of rocks are encroached and cultivated in a manner that results into accelerated soil erosion. The rush for encroachment of better quality land is too much and very little area of such land is let unencroached. During 1988-89 when the project was initiated in Kolar, more than 150 villages had an adequate (more than 40 ha) area of wastelands to facilitate organization of TGCS. However, awaiting the government support in terms of land lease, the pace of the project was extremely slow and only 35-40 cooperatives could be organized during the past eight years. Now, when the government support is available, the land identified in potential villages has already been encroached. In Haleupparahalli, a TGCS was organized in 1992 and 40 ha. of C&D class land was leased. A large number of armed people belonging to the so-called Dalit group raided the plantation area destroying more than 25,000 three-year-old trees. It is reported that the local upcoming leaders assured the people who committed this ecological crime that the land would eventually be allotted to them if such a pressure is continued and plantation is not allowed to grow.

The management committee members of the cooperatives who tried to seek police protection were discouraged and even their complaint was not registered. Such inaction on the part of the district administration made TGCS members in other nearby villages suspicious of the safety of their plantation.

2.e. Lack of Inter-Departmental Coordination

In a good number of cases where a portion of common land under the control of the Revenue Department was leased to the TGCS the same was later found to be a reserved forest land or degraded revenue wasteland having a suffix "jungle" which attracts the Forest Conservation Act and such land can be leased only with permission from the Central Ministry of Environment & Forests.

In Orissa, where revenue wasteland is termed as *Patra Jungle, Jungle II Mela* or *Chhota Jungle*, large areas of which are available in different districts in a highly degraded State, cannot be leased to TGCS as the term "jungle" attracts the Forest Conservation Act. The Central Ministry of Environment and Forests would see no reason in supporting grassroots organizations to green such parched lands with collective efforts by leasing or renting on a long-term basis. At least 15 TGCS in Orissa which were granted planting permission on jungle category revenue wastelands have been informed by the State Government that land lease is possible only with the permission of the Central Ministry of Environment and Forests, which has already promptly rejected the applications of three TGCS. Under the TGCP a large sum of project funds has been spent on soil and water conservation and tree, grass plantations which cannot be legally harvested by the cooperatives in the absence of a formal lease deed. The members of the TGCS who participated to regenerate the wasteland are unable to enjoy their share. Any further delay may create social unrest and destroy the cooperatives as well as plantations, which have been an excellent mix of natural regeneration and planted vegetation over a period of ten years.

In Rajasthan, in Thali village of Jaipur district, some 30 ha. of highly degraded land was leased to TGCS by the district administration with the understanding that the leased land was a revenue wasteland falling under Barani III category (uncultivable). After the TGCS planted some area, the Forest Department discovered that the leased land was a reserve forestland hence the lease order issued by the district authority was null and void. In spite of efforts made by the NTGCF and the villagers, the State administration pleaded helplessness and eventually TGCS could not function in the absence of land lease. The trees planted by TGCS members were destroyed in subsequent years and the process of land degradation resumed.

In Karnataka, during 1989-90, more than a dozen tree-growers' cooperatives organized in Kolar district were given planting permission on C & D class land which later turned out to be *gomal* land (village grazing land). In spite of the fact that a large sum of the project fund has been spent on greening such land and villagers have done an excellent job of restoring a highly degraded land to a state of productivity, the State Government is dilly-dallying about leasing such land on the pretext that it could create a precedence which is against the policy of the government to lease common grazing lands. Interestingly, the same government also has a policy to restore wastelands to a productive State through people's participation.

In Gujarat, where the State Land Development Corporation claims to have reclaimed a large area of uncultivable revenue wastelands, it has been delaying the handing over of the so-called reclaimed land to the district administration for years. As a result, the reclaimed land has degraded to its original condition. Leasing such lands to TGCS for the purpose of plantation and conservation needs waiver of a huge amount of money by the State that the Gujarat Land Development Corporation may have spent more than a decade ago on its reclamation. The matter has been under consideration for the past ten years and it may take a few more years before the land is leased to TGCS.

Updating of land records, reclassification of various categories of land from time to time and reconciliation of ownership of land between the departments is very critical to the wasteland development programme in India. Department of Land Resource in the Ministry of Rural Development Govt. of India should create a data base on law revenues and develop a system of survey and land capability classification from time to time for sake of efficient implementation of the wastelands development programme.

2.f. Procedural Bottlenecks

Having no idea of the procedural complexities, the first TGCS in Gujarat was organized where ceremonial plantation of trees was done by the invited dignitaries on a piece of common grazing land in Amrapura village in Kheda district on the basis of verbal permission given by the district authorities. However, after the inaugural function was over, the collector warned the project staff against their offence of trespassing over government property without prior written permission. This was their first lesson in land related matters. Since then many valuable lessons have been learned in this regard.

In all the States, the ownership of common land is mainly with two departments, the forest and the revenue. It was a lucky coincidence that NTGCF did not negotiate for degraded forest lands as custodial approach of the Forest Department may not have allowed degraded forest lands to be leased to TGCS and progress of the project could have been insignificant even after a lapse of 10 years. Participation of TGCS in the joint forest programmes has also been practically nil due to lack of interest of the forest cadres who often feel such programmes are an unnecessary abrogation of authority and the area of operation. However in recent past the change in the attitude of forest cadres is visitors and tree growers cooperatives are also being involved in Joint Forest Management Programme. Yet there are other problems to be resolved.

The terms and conditions of the joint forest management programme go against the underlying principles of sustainability and conservation when the Forest Department insists on 50 per cent sharing of the sale proceeds of mature trees. This condition provides for clear-felling of the forest regenerated with people's participation. Efforts of NTGCF in negotiating a modified joint forest management programme in which only 10-15 per cent of the trees could be harvested by the local community to meet their needs followed by replanting of the harvested area in the very next season have failed due to lack of interest of the Forest Department.

So far as the revenue wastelands are concerned, the procedure for leasing them to TGCS or any other such institution is complex and time-consuming. After a lapse of six-eight years, the efforts of NTGCF have resulted in decentralization of the land-leasing authority from the State Cabinet to the District Collector, framing of suitable terms and conditions of lease and simplification of procedures. As a result, land leases orders, which used to take as long as four-five years, now take only five-six months.

2.g. Terms and Conditions of Land Lease

The terms and conditions of land lease differ from State to State. In Gujarat and Orissa, the period for which land has been leased to TGCS is only 15 years whereas it is 30 years in Andhra Pradesh, 20 years in Rajasthan, 25 years in Karnataka and 30 years in Uttar Pradesh.

In Gujarat, four major departments i.e. Revenue, Agriculture, Irrigation and Narmada Irrigation Project, are involved in dealing with land lease applications. At taluka level, four revenue officials and at the district level, three revenue officials deal with such files. Thereafter, they go to the Agriculture and Irrigation Department for certification that the land proposed to be leased is not cultivable. After each one of them clears a file, it is sent to the Revenue Secretary of the State for final approval. The maximum time taken so far to lease land to TGCS is five years and the minimum one year depending on the attitude and efficiency of the officers dealing with such cases, political atmosphere of the State and the number of objections/queries raised by each department. In other States where similar complicated procedures existed earlier, the State Government has now authorized district collectors to lease uncultivable revenue wastelands to TGCS without referring the matter to the Revenue Secretary of the State or the State Cabinet. In such States, the time taken to lease land to TGCS is now three-six months or even less (See Fig. 15.1).

The period of lease also varies from State to State depending on the attitude of the bureaucracy. Most States have either deferred lease fee or imposed a nominal fee of Re. 1 per acre per year. Some State Governments have been specific in imposing a condition that the cooperative should have membership of SC/ST marginal farmers/landless labour and widows. It is interesting to note that under the State control, access to such land is open to all sections of the community but when a village institution proposes to manage it, the State expects the benefits to be restricted only to socio-economically weaker or downtrodden class. Such restrictions are impractical for both the

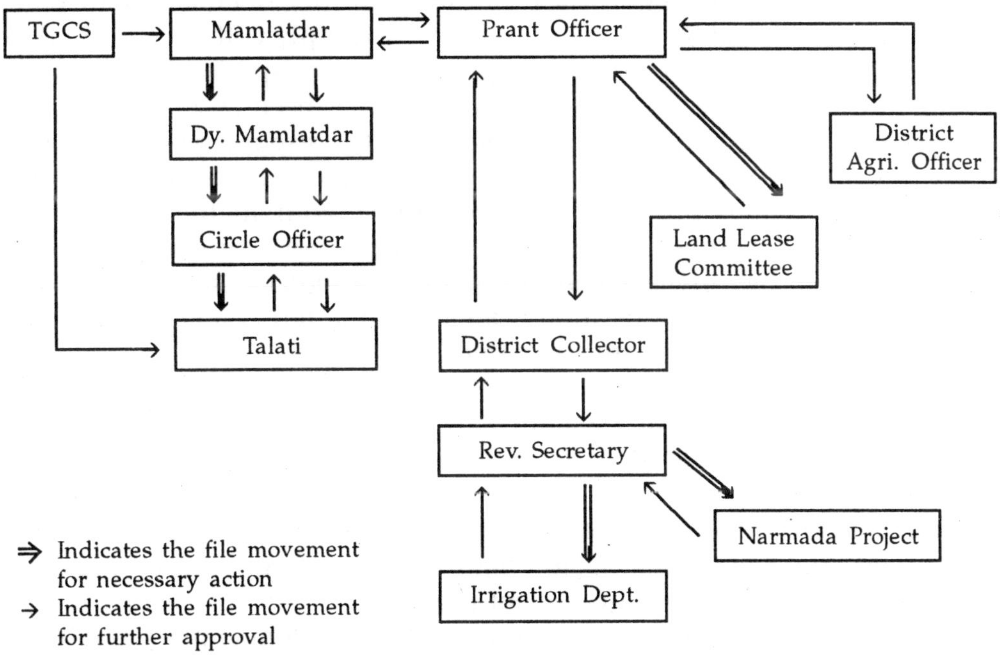

Fig. 15.1: Movement of Land Lease File—Gujarat

management of village commons and cooperatives.

In Gujarat, one of the conditions of land lease is that for the first seven years no rent shall be charged. After that it would be half of the assessed prevailing rate and after 15 years at the full prevailing rate which works out to approximately Rs. 1,000 to 1,500 per ha. per year and Rs. 1,000 to 2,000 per ha. per year respectively. Charging such an exorbitant amount of lease fee the Govt. would in fact penalize a TGCS for their hard work and for back rolling highly degraded land to a State of productivity!

In Orissa, the government has imposed a condition that the leased land should not be planted with any such vegetation as would change the character of revenue wasteland into "jungle" land. It also adds that only such species should be planted on the leased land, which do not compel the Revenue Department to renew lease beyond 15 years.

The first condition has been imposed mainly to avoid a revenue land being declared jungle land by the territorial Forest Department. Once it is done, the State Government practically loses control over such lands. However, while imposing such an impractical condition the fact is ignored that most degraded lands still have good rootstock and with protection by the local people, natural regeneration would take place and transform the area into something similar to a natural forest within eight to ten years. If the above condition is to be fulfilled, the root stock would have to be uprooted and alien species will have to be planted to avoid changing the character of the degraded land into a forest land which would lead to ecological disaster. To comply with second condition community has to plant only fast growing alien species which is also ecologically as well as economically unsound. It has been observed that short-term tenurial security often leads to depletion of the resource and its utilization in an unsustainable manner. It only serves bureaucratic convenience. Such terms and conditions are neither in confirmity with to the policy of the Central/State Government on conservation nor promotes people's participation in the management of natural resources. In view of these experiences the following the modifications in the terms and conditions for land lease/tenurial security are suggested.

— Tenure should be at least for 30 years with clear-cut provisions for extension provided there is no breach of any of the conditions of the land lease.
— State Government should not charge any lease fee because, for similar work, the government would have to incur a huge sum of money and yet there would be management problems.
— Community organization should have full freedom to plant and harvest the produce.
— Leasing process should be simple and expeditious.
— Government should not impose restrictions on the membership of TGCS, as one of the conditions for lease is that they are unrealistic and impractical. A common resource has to be managed as a common resource in a real sense without any bias towards caste/creed or financial status.
— Provision for increasing lease fee from nominal to market rate after a few years or during extended lease period would be a disincentive to the community for developing a degraded resource. Since TGCS are not likely to generate a lot of cash and seem to be content largely with the output in kind, such levies would result in clear-felling of some area for generating cash income, a part of which would be utilized for the payment of lease fee. In the process, it would set a precedence for getting into cash flow system at the expense of sustainability of regenerated resources.

The prerequisites for the success of a Tree Growers' Cooperative are availability of wasteland in compact block, felt need for an institutional structure for the management of the common resource in a sustainable manner so as to meet village biomass needs, elements of collective action compact and homogeneous village with less socio-political frictions. Despite the multitude of problems that hindered the project, the results so far have proved the capacity of the rural people in establishing and managing the Tree Growers' Cooperatives, developing norms for regeneration, protection and sustainable utilization of bio-mass from the village commons. The members of the cooperative have also demonstrated their cost effective managerial capacity, innovative ideas in dispute resolution, benefit sharing and techniques of soil and water conservation and plant protraction. The myth that resource management, institutional development and forestry are the jobs to be performed by people trained in management institutes has been broken by the effort of the village-level cooperatives. This part of the chapter outlines the myriad benefits derived by these communities from their regenerated wastelands. During the past 10 years, villages where Tree Growers' Cooperatives have been organized have experienced significant ecological and socio-economic transformations as discussed below.

3. Ecological Security

3.a. Natural Regeneration

In the initial years of the project, the potential of natural regeneration was ignored. The work plan for the common resource plantation was prepared and implemented without considering the extent of rootstock, its compatibility with the species proposed to be planted and adequate time for the rootstock to regenerate. Subsequently, the strategy has been corrected. The trees have a clear policy of facilitating natural regeneration and undertaking plantation of compatible species only in blank patches.

Generally, the land leased to TGCS has very scanty vegetation comprising rootstock of trees, grasses and weeds. After the land is closed to grazing and biotic interference reduce to minimum, the lower vegetation, i.e. grasses, weeds, etc., come up first followed by bushes and trees resulting in manifold increase in the number of species within a period of five to six years.

The extent of natural regeneration as is clear from the data in Table 15.1 varies across project States, which is due to complex edaphic, climatic and biotic factors.

3.b. Improvement in Wildlife

In almost all locations, an appreciable improvement in the vegetation cover on the wastelands leased to TGCS has provided congenial environment for accelerated reproduction of wildlife. Though it has not been possible to systematically monitor and document such improvements in different project areas, following are the observations of the villagers:

TABLE 15.1: **Statewise Status of TGCS Organization, Natural Resource Regeneration and Biodiversity Conservation (1995-96)**

State	No. of TGCS	Area of wasteland leased (ha.)	Area under natural regene-ration (ha.)	% area under natural Regene-ration	Av. No. of species before protection and plantation	Av. No. of species after pro-tection/ plantation
Andhra Pradesh	39	835	300	36	17	199
Gujarat	43	1264	33	3	14	108
Karnataka	26	610	160	26	18	96
Rajasthan	86	2104	443	21	6	121
Orissa	32	1317	600	46	11	74
Total	226	6130	1536	25	13	120

Source: Reports from the Spearhead Teams of NTGCF.

1. Increase in the population of Neel Gai (bluebull), jackals, jeraks, hares, birds and snakes in Gujarat and Rajasthan.
2. Increase in the population of wild animals like jackals, foxes, bears, chital, wild boars, etc., in Orissa. Villagers feel that plantation of an appropriate vegetation in TGCS land on which herbivores survive would reduce crop damage.
3. Increase in the population of snakes, birds, wild boars due to TGCS plantation in Karnataka and Andhra Pradesh.
4. Reduction in the damage to food crops growing in the adjacent private cultivation area by birds, as more insects and grass seeds are now available in TGCS plantation where birds are nesting.
5. Significant increase in the population of earthworms in TGCS plantation areas during the monsoon and post-monsoon seasons, resulting in improvement in soil fertility and porosity.

In this context, NTGC has initiated an Environment Education programme in TGCS villages to sensitise adults and children about the relationship and impact of resource regeneration and wildlife on the quality of life of the rural poor as a result of which wanton killing of snake/birds and other animals has decreased.

3.c. Edaphic and Hydrological Improvements

Since its inception, the project has promoted conservation of soil and water by creating low-cost structures like check dams, gully plugs, spillovers, stone pitching in small gullies. Saucer pans around planted seedlings, crescent bunds and staggered trenches on the hill slopes that have been found quite effective in retaining soil and water due to which the processes of regeneration have accelerated. The level of water in the wells in villages has gone up as a result of water harvesting structures in TGCS plantation. The extent of soil erosion in private wastelands adjacent to TGCS plantation especially in ravenous areas has been significantly reduced due to vegetal cover. Convinced by the usefulness of soil and water conservation measures, some farmers have started constructing these structures on their farmlands also.

Though it has not been possible to assess the exact quantity of soil and water conserved due to these measures, farmers' assessment is very positive and encouraging.

The improvement in the fertility status of the soils in a TGCS plantation over a short period of three-four years, a result of cumulative effect of improved vegetation and soil and water conservation, as compared to open access land adjoining it, is clear from the data in Table 15.2.

TABLE 15.2: **Nutritional Status, pH and EC of the Soil Samples drawn from the Plantation Area of Sarnal TGCS**

Samples	Nitrogen (Kg/ha.)	Phosphorus (Kg/ha.)	Potash (Kg/ha.)	PH	EC Mhos
Plantation area					
Sample # 1	321.15	12.88	436.03	8.25	0.18
Sample # 2	389.01	10.62	519.77	8.27	0.17
Sample # 3	353.92	8.12	413.20	8.20	0.18
Open access wasteland	278.51	8.90	390.93	8.42	0.17

Source: Reports from the Spearhead Teams of NTGCF (Saxena & Agrawal 1996).

3.d. Biomass Production

The revenue wastelands being leased to the Tree Growers' Cooperatives are highly degraded falling under land capability class below 4 or 5. Due to overgrazing and neglect, the vegetation is very scanty comprising coarse grass, thorny bushes and weeds, which are non-browsable. Within a period of five to six years, the biomass yield from such land improved significantly as a result of protection, plantation and conservation measures.

The data presented in Table 15.3 gives a clear idea of tree biomass yield in Sarnal (Gujarat) TGCS where plantation work was initiated in 1987 on an area of 28.87 ha. and subsequently completed over a period of three years. An area of 6.13 ha. was earmarked for natural regeneration. The first biomass

TABLE 15.3: **Biomass Assessment of Plantation by the Sarnal TGCS in Gujarat**

Tree Species	Area Planted (ha.)	Total Green Wt. (tons)	
		1993	1995
Ailanthus excelsa (Arduso)	0.24	5.00	53.00
Acacia nilotica (Desi Babul)	10.15	445.60	1809.00
Prosopis juliflora (Ganda Babul)	14.32	451.10	950.10
Pithecolobium dulcee (Goras amli)	—	—	0.50
Pongamia pinnata (Karanj)	—	—	27.80
Azadirachta indica (Neem)	1.78	46.30	347.40
Prosopis cineraria (Samda)	0.75	7.40	25.80
Dalbergia sissoo (Sissoo)	0.30	24.50	31.50
Leucaena Leucocephala (Subabul)	0.46	10.00	15.10
Cassia siamea (Kasid)	0.52	10.40	32.90
Dednrocalamus strictus (Bamboo)	—	—	46.80
Moringa olifera (Saragwa)	—	—	4.00
Barkhada	—	—	2.60
Acacia Senegal (Goidia)	—	—	17.60
Parkinsonia aculeata (Ram Babul)	0.27	0.30	1.80
Dicrostachys cineraria (Velantr)	—	—	4.20
Bombax ceiba (Semal)	—	—	10.00
Acacia totilis (Israeli Babul)	0.04	1.00	2.90
Albizzia lebbeck (Sirus)	0.02	0.30	—
Ficus bengalensis (Banyan)	0.01	0.10	—
Ficus religiosa (Pipal)	0.01	0.10	—
Total	**28.87**	**1002.10**	**3383.50**

(i) Green weight (1993) 34.71 t/ ha. of Planted area (28.87 ha.)
28.62 t/ ha. of Allotted area (35.0 ha.)

(ii) Green weight (1995) 117.2 t/ ha. of Planted area
96.7 t /ha. of Allotted area

Note: Sarnal TGCS was registered in 1987 when plantation and protection was initiated on 10 ha. of ravenous land. Remaining area was planted in subsequent years.

assessment made during 1993 recorded a biomass yield of 33.6-t. ha.1 (a total of 1,177 tons). The assessment made during 1995 recorded a total biomass yield of 96.7 ha.1 (a total of 3,385 tons) from the entire area of 35.00 ha. This biomass yield is only of standing form and does not include vegetation on the floor of plantation which is roughly estimated at 5 to 10 t ha.1 on green basis. Thus, within a short period of eight years, the biomass yield has risen from almost zero level to more than 100 T./ha. in a highly ravinous and unproductive land.

In order to document such improvements, the members of TGCS have been trained in simple techniques of biomass assessment, which could be helpful in maintaining the natural resource accounting system to be introduced soon in the member cooperatives for them to manage the resource sustainable.

3.e. Conservation of Biodiversity

In most TGCS plantations, a large number of species of trees, grasses, bushes and shrubs are reappearing including a variety of medicinal plants considered endangered. In order to conserve bio-diversity of such useful plants, TGCS members are being trained in the identification, collection and propagation of medicinal plants. Training camps are also being organised to revive traditional health care system based on medicinal herbs. In Bhal region of Gujarat, where Guggul (*Commiphora wighttii*) used to grow in abundance some 40-50 years ago and has become extinct now, TGCS are making efforts to revive it by planting cuttings on the leased land an on farm boundaries. Similarly in Kola (Karnataka), Angul (Orissa) and Ajmer (Rajasthan) propagation of important medicinal herbs like Ashwagandha (*Widhania somnifera*), Sarpagandha (*Rauivolfia serpentina*) and Gokhru (*Tribulus terrestris*) has been taken up by the cooperatives. Efforts are also being made to explore feasibility of growing short duration high yielding medicinal plants on the farmers' fields along with food/cash crops for sale to pharmaceuticals firms. Establishment of small herbal garden at the village level has also been initiated in order to produce planting material to meet the growing needs of member cooperatives.

3.f. Expansion of Resource Base

Production enhancement through conservation and plantation measures amounts to vertical expansion of the resource base.

Soil and water conservation measures taken in TGCS plantation have decreased soil erosion and improved the moisture status of adjoining private wastelands. The protection provided by the community to TGCS plantation and fear of sanctions against trespassers/poachers reduces grazing menace. Landowners understand that with conservation measures, productivity of the resource can be improved as done in the TGCS plantation area, which has even more degraded than the private wastelands. Therefore, considerable area of privately owned wastelands or marginally productive land located around TGCS sites gradually come under cultivation resulting in lateral as well as vertical expansion of the resource base.

The data collected on the area of private wastelands adjoining TGCS plantation brought under cultivation and the number of farmers benefited in some villages in Gujarat is presented in Table 15.4.

TABLE 15.4: **Area of Private Marginal/Degraded Land brought under Cultivation due to the Initiative of Tree Growers' Cooperatives**

TGCS Name	Area brought under cultivation (ha.)	Families benefited (no.)
Tansia	12.00	10
Nani Bhadol	11.00	8
Vansia	10.20	13
Himmatpura	5.10	8
Dungripura (I)	3.40	6
Total	41.70	45

4. Socio-Economic Gains

With the expansion of the resource base, many social and economic benefits start flowing to the village as discussed below.

4.a. Social Gains

Organization of a cooperative on the commons requires that people have to arrive at a consensus, which needs socio-political realignment and mutual cooperation. It requires forgoing their rights of grazing on the common land proposed for regeneration through TGCS. It also requires perseverance and patience, as restoration of resource to a productive State is a time-consuming process. The major social benefits of a Tree Growers' Cooperative so evolved are:

1. Presence of an institution to deal with the sustainable management of village commons along with managerial, technical competencies of the communities.
2. Settlement of social conflicts related to resource utilization and land encroachment.
3. Enhanced mutual cooperation and collective action for the revival of ecological processes contributing to ecological and social security of rural community, evolution of rules, regulations and sanctions for collective action which spread spatially and functionally.
4. Improved confidence level of the resource poor and women.
5. Reduction in drudgery and improved quality of life due to energy and employment generation.
6. Improved understanding of rural community about the need to match

population with resource capacity.

7. Development of leadership from amongst resourceless and marginal farmers who are major users of the resource.
8. Improved developmental communication as a result of contacts with the field staff of interaction with the visitors and travel to other TGCS villages/project areas.
9. Nested institutions like village assembly, village council, mechanisms for conflict resolution, transparent decision making that have applicability in other spheres of village life.

4.b. Economic Gains

Regeneration of even highly degraded common lands provide some economic benefits to the rural community in various forms as discussed below. In addition to the first layer externalities like increased water table, improvements in adjoining private wastelands/marginally productive lands, etc.

4.c. Employment Generation

Organization of the TGCS creates appreciable employment opportunities for the rural poor who are engaged in land development, soil and water conservation, and plantation and after-care on the common land. It reduces seasonal migration of landless, expansion of slums in urban areas and associated social problems. The wage rate fixed by TGCS is not only higher than the prevailing rates but no differentiation is made between male and female labour. The data presented in Table 15.5 gives an idea of employment generated by the land and plantation-related activities of TGCS.

4.d. Benefits in Kind – Vegetation

Protection, conservation and plantation work on the leased land improves biomes production which is made available to TGCS members at a reasonable price or in lieu of labour. These benefits flow in the form of fodder, grasses for rope-making or thatching fuelwood and small timber, small fruits, berries and vegetables.

Enhanced availability of these products reduces drudgery and generates savings. In several TGCS villages, collection of *Acacia* pods, *Salvadora* seeds, Aromatic/Medicinal plants, Neem seeds, Tamarind, etc. from the trees growing in and around the village has been initiated resulting in employment generation and availability of cash to meet family needs during the lean periods of agricultural activity.

The data in Table 15.6 gives an idea of different kinds of produce, quantity,

TABLE 15.5: **Average Yearwise Employment Generation Per TGCS Per Year Through Wasteland Development in Different States**

State	Year 1	Year 2	Year 3	Year 4	Year 5
			Employment (days)		
Gujarat	5488	9811	4173	2742	3417
Karnataka	7396	7168	1537	1137	995
Rajasthan	291	3060	73	264	0
Orissa	1158	6995	2464	168	0

TABLE 15.6: **Quantity and Value of Non-Timber Tree Produce and Grass collected and sold by Some TGCS in Different States (1995-96)**

State	Produce	Quantity	Rate (Rs. Per Unit)	Amount (Rs.)
		GUJARAT		
Sarnal	Firewood (tons)	331.09	0.57	189.183
	Fodder (tons)	178.00	0.11	19.58
	Neem seeds (tons)	6.40	1.50	9.6
	Eucalyptus Poles (no.)	388	41.80	14128.4
	Bamboo (no.)	s479	67.00	32093.00
Navagambara	Eucalyptus Poles (No.)	8	126.00	1008.00
	Firewood (tons)	42560	0.40	17024.0
Gangadia	Fodder (tons)	280.640	0.25	70.16
		ANDHRA PRADESH		
Guttakindapalli. T	Fodder (bundles)	1600	2.00	3200.00
Chennappagarip alle	Fodder (bundles)	1600	2.66	4256.00
	Tamarind (tons)	19.723	7.80	153.84
		KARNATAKA		
Mallanahally	Eucalyptus Trees (No.)	219.2	680.00	149056.00
Donimadugu	Firewood, (Tractor-load)	1	640.00	640.00
		RAJASTHAN		
Ugariawas	Castor Seeds (kg.)	30	12.00	360.00
	Grass Seeds (kg.)	12	20.00	420.00
	Munj Grass (kg.)	50	3.00	150.00
	Kati Seeds (kg.)	3	5.00	15.00
Mandiani	Munj grass (kg.)	30	2.25	67.50
	Natural grass (kg.)	376	0.78	293.28
	Tree logs (no.)	10	50.00	500.00

4.e. Energy Conservation

Under the project, a number of TGCS in different States have taken up the programmes of popularizing fuel-efficient smokeless chulhas and family biogas plants as an energy conservation measure. The amount of fuelwood saving by using smokeless chulhas is 17 to 34 per cent resulting in saving of a substantial amount of money. It also reduces the pace of deforestation, drudgery of women, and helps ecology and environment.

5. Conclusion

The policies and extension of support from the government in making common resource accessible to the rural institutions and making land-related rules and regulations and procedures/simple and farmers friendly would accelerate the pace and expansion of the project to replicate its processes, which have proved to be effective.

Establishment of TGCS in a Mega Tree Growers' Cooperatives Project funded by the Canadian International Development Agency (CIDA) and the Swedish International Development Agency (SIDA) through the National Tree Growers' Cooperative Federation has set an example of decentralized management of natural resources specifically village commons in a sustainable manner. The project has attempted to enhance ecological and socio-economic security of rural communities thereby improving the quality of their life. Involvement of the cities in planning, implementation, monitoring and evaluation of the project (which has become their project) has been the main strength of the project leading to its success. Though the influence of politicization and administrative constraints have affected the pace of the project considerably, there has been a general appreciation that the approaches and processes adopted by the project have contributed to its productivity and the institutional development.

REFERENCES

Gadgil, M. 1985. "Towards Ecological History of India". *Economics and Political Weekly*, Vol. 20 (45-47).

Iyengar, S. 1998. *Common Property Land Resources in Gujarat: Some Findings about their Size; Status and Use*, The Gujarat Institute of Area Planning, Gota, Ahemadabad, Gujarat.

Jodha, N.S. 1985. "Population Growth and the Decline of Common Property Resources in Rajasthan, India". *Population and Development Review*, Vol. 11(2).

Jodha, N.S. 1986. "Common Property Resources and Rural Poor in Dry Region of India". *Economic and Political Weekly*. Vol. 21(27).

Jodha, N.S. 1992. "Common Property Resources: A Missing Dimension of Development Strategies", *World Bank Discussion Paper 169*, Washington, D.C.: The World Bank.

Misra, V.K. 1996. "Decentralised Management of Natural Resources : Some Recent Experiences and Emerging Issues", Paper presented at the International Workshop on Shared Resource Management in South Asia—The Next Step, Institute of Rural Management, Anand (IRMA), Gujarat, India.

Saxena, R. and Rajesh Agarwal. 1996. "An Appropriate Socio-Eco-Environmental Accounting Framework", Prepared for National Tree Growers' Cooperative Federation Limited with A Case Study. Unpublished Reports of Spear Head Teams. NTGCF, Anand.

16 Socio-economic Impact of Joint Management of Common Lands in the Aravallis of Haryana

Jagdeesh C. Kalla and **R.N. Kaul**

1. The Genesis

Biotic and abiotic pressures disproportionate to the natural regenerating capability have been mainly responsible for the degradation of the natural resource base in almost all developing countries. Lack of alternatives, deteriorating socio-economic conditions, multiple allocations (mining and quarrying) of natural resources, policy of subsidisation of a particular use, have been major distortants conducive to degradation of a natural resource mix. Sensing this preponderant tendency, rural societies in Medieval India evolved institutions called Panchayats for regulated use of natural resources especially under a common property regime (Marothia 1989). Over time Panchayats evolved codes of conduct for regulation of access and use of natural resources through a mix of prohibitive, punitive, legal, social, moral, ethical and financial measures mainly through informal social arrangements. With the advent of the British, the management system of natural resources, especially forests (Sinha 1994) underwent a change in their control environments. This resulted in a collapse of authority of Panchayats (Jodha 1982, Bhoria and Bajaj 1993). The post-independence period has been marked by the reorientation of Panchayats mainly as a political and not socio-economic entity.

Haryana was formed in 1966. The Aravallis which stretch over 625 kms, from Palanpur in Gujarat up to Delhi, pass through five districts, viz. Faridabad, Gurgaon, Rewari, Mahendragarh and Bhiwani, covering almost 1,460 km^2 (Annon 1989) in this State. In the past few decades, the Aravalli hills have witnessed an alarming rate of depletion of vegetal cover due to continuation of biotic and abiotic interferences. In Haryana, the Aravallis comprise almost entirely of village common lands. The landless and marginal farm families have traditionally been dependent on the common lands for their basic needs of fuelwood, fodder and other usufruct.

In order to arrest the pace of degradation, a plan was submitted by the Forest Department of Haryana to the European Union. The project covered 30,600 ha of common lands spread over 293 hilly villages of the five districts in southern Haryana. For the purpose of actual treatment, the common lands were classified into three models. While Model I constituted the denuded area with a soil depth exceeding 60 cms, Model II included areas with less than 60 cms of soil depth and Model III represented areas with a considerable root stock of surviving natural woody vegetation. For each of the three models, a site-specific package of soil preparation and vegetation was adopted (Annon 1989). The extent of area rehabilitated till 1996 is summarised in Annexure I. The project has been primarily of eight-year duration (1990-98). The output-mix from the rehabilitation of common lands in Haryana include fuel, fodder, other minor forest products, enhancement of water retention capacities, protection of soils from erosion and qualitative upgradation of farm and flora. The socio-economic benefits include improvement in the levels of living, redistribution of income, increase in employment, educational benefits, livestock productivity and others. This chapter is an attempt to analyse the socio-economic impact of joint management of common lands in the Aravallis of Haryana.

2. The Premise of People's Participation and Institutional Set-up

One of the most important premises of the project was that of proactive people's participation which in turn was based on the following assumptions.

(i) The project would reinforce the existing structure of traditional authority.
(ii) This authority would result in increased participatory improvement of community.
(iii) Community would eventually be free from external dependence (including government), in framing a set of rules and norms of cooperation commensurate with the felt needs of the community.
(iv) Satisfaction of the felt needs would be designed for low (information sharing and consultations), medium (decision-making and initiation of group action) and high (sharing of benefits on an equitable and sustained basis) strata of participatory management.
(v) Rules and regulations would be applied to the nature of all group participants (passive, hesitant, active and passive).

(vi) In due course of time, catalytic leadership and pressure groups would be formed to watch adherence to rules and allow for flexibility to cope with situations attributable to time (Chopra and Kadekodi 1992).

(vii) The participatory process would enhance local participation in the selection of specie-mix, swift action against deviates damaging the output from the portion of land taken up for treatment.

(viii) The stake holder would be able to qualify tangible (fuel, fodder, fruits, medicine, game) and non-tangible (improved soil structure, water connection) benefits by comparing these with price indices of regulations (labour, inconvenience, benefits forgone, regulations).

3. Institutionalisation of the Project

3.a. The Village Forest Committee

The revival of the common property land resources (CPLRs) in the Aravallis started with the constitution of Village Forest Committees (VFCs). Formation of VFCs is a sensitive and time consuming process with attendant requirement of new skills in social management for the personnel of the Forest Department. This also involved ensuring active participation of women in VFCs. In each village a body of 9-13 members with a Sarpanch as the head was formed. The other members included the Forest Ranger, Forest Protection Guard, at least three women members residing in the village, and representatives of the scheduled castes and tribes if any. VFC is an Executive Committee of the Panchayat. In order to incorporate the interest of all members of the community in the project, all male and female members eligible by virtue of their certified residence in village to be members of Panchayat are deemed to be members of the General Council to which VFC reports. VFCs meet at least thrice a year for the purpose of taking policy decisions on the use of common lands and distribution of the benefits. The project staff, who are also members of VFCs, assist the VFC Chairman by providing a member-secretary who assists the Sarpanch in convening the meeting and keeping the records.

The first step following the constitution of a VFC was an agreement between the villagers and the project authorities on a system of sharing the benefits emanating from the management and protection activities. The issue of sharing these benefits contained in the agreement was of paramount importance. It ensured that all villagers will have an equal right to collect fruits, flowers, deadwood, leaf fodder and cutting and carrying of grasses free of charge. At each thinning and final felling, the community could collect fuel wood, poles and small timber at the rates and prices determined by VFC/ Panchayat

3.b. The Participatory Management Strategy

The project was formulated on the premise that persuasion alone would not motivate and induce communities to participate for managing and maintaining CPLRs for the sake of their eco-restoration only. Thus strategies for managing and maintaining CPLRs in a way that would ensure continuation of immediate benefits from CPLRs right from the beginning were worked out and implemented. Further, benefits sacrificed would need to be compensated monetarily or non-monetarily. The visible and short-run gains as per the participants rankings turned out to be grass production followed by fuel. Accordingly silvi-pastoral and horti-pastoral technologies were adopted. This, however, was preceded by several preparatory steps.

3.b.1 Participatory Micro Planning

Using participatory rural appraisal (PRA) techniques micro plans of all 293 villages were prepared. The community took active part in deciding about the location of area to be allotted for planting trees and seeding with grasses and legumes. The order of preference of specie in order of priority is expressed by the stakeholders.

3.b.2 Monitoring and Evaluation

For proper monitoring and evaluation and for providing the feed-back for mid-course correction, a system of village file records was developed. Copies of these files are maintained at the Sub-Divisional, Divisional and Project Directors Offices. These files contain copies of proceedings of each VFC meeting along with the action taken on the points emerging therefrom. Village files give a complete physical and developmental profile of the villages. These files are regularly updated and serve as important instruments for programme evaluation.

3.c. Compensatory Measures

Majority of the community in the project area is made up of small and landless farm families which cannot forgo the benefits (opportunity of grazing animals or collection of fuel wood) today for the promised ones six years hence, let alone a share in the revenue from the trees grown on a 20-year rotation. The loss of taking away some common lands needed to be compensated. The project thus instituted two novel approaches, viz. Incentive Scheme as a form of community benefits for creating community assets and Plantation Employment Scheme for individual members besides Mahila Nursery and

Saving Bank Account Schemes for the womenfolk exclusively.

3.c.1 The Incentive Scheme

This scheme was designed and implemented in order to strengthen VFCs, and simultaneously ensure active participation of communities for the protection of freshly planted area and protection of area from biotic interferences. The scheme was based on the calculation of sucess index of biomass (Mukherjee 1993). Under this scheme, the villages would qualify for an incentive of cash of Rs. 250 per ha in the first year followed by Rs. 200 per ha for the second and Rs. 150 per ha for the third year, if a VFC achieves an establishment and growth success index of 60. This applied to both plantation and vegetative rehabilitation. Under the joint management of VFCs and project, the funds were invested to create self-sustaining social assets [purchase of utensils for community use, repairs of school buildings, common water resources, fans for schools, construction of *chaupal* (meeting place), construction of roads, etc.]. There is now a growing interest in using this money for the community's good as revolving funds related to money earning activities like sewing machines, carpentry shops, machine repair shops, etc.

3.c.2 Employment Scheme

In most of the Aravalli villages the communities depending upon agriculture could not be provided employment of 180 days in a given year. Unless complemented by livestock-related activities, the families remained unemployed or ungainfully employed during the March-June period. The project, therefore, decided to hire mainly landless and small farm families on the going government rates of Rs. 45 per day, which was upward revised from time to time, in plantation, nursery and other forest-related activities in CPLRs covered under the project. This has occupied an important place in the pattern of accrual of family incomes of landless labourers and small farm families.

3.c.3 Mahila Nurseries (Women's Nurseries)

Commensurate with the multiple roles (household chores, child care, livestock production activities, farm and non-farm wage labour, gathering of forest product, etc.) that women play in rural households in the Aravalli project area, a Mahila Nursery programme was initiated in the Aravalli project as one of the gender-related, group incentives. In all forest project nursery work is invariably carried out by women (Rawat and Bedi 1996). But strict and fixed schedules in the Government-run nurseries frequently increase the drudgery, workload and often clash with household chores and child care. In the Aravalli project, the women groups headed by a leader were organised to produce seedlings. Initially, material (seeds and polythene bags) were provided by the project and water either privately or community-owned was used to raise a nursery with a buyback arrangement on an individual seedling basis. The revenue so generated by the group was eventually be divided according to the work put in by the group including its leader.

3.c.4 Saving Bank Accounts

In order that women in homes have some financial empowerment, the project initiated an individual incentives scheme of saving bank account to meet family contingencies arising out of needs which may be perceived as redundant by the head of the family, or the family just does not have cash to fall back upon. The women groups through this programme were encouraged to participate in the Government of India's *Mahila Samridhi Yojana* whereby an amount of Rs. 300 deposited for 12 months would get Rs. 75 as extraordinary interest. This was tied with the programme to enhance empowerment of the women in the project area.

3.c.5 Other Women-Related Programmes

In order to develop and strengthen linkages of the womenfolk with the project activities, some programmes under the head "Women in Development" (WID) were initiated. These are:

— Introduction and popularisation of fuel-efficient stoves (*Van Jyoti chullas*) by women extension workers trained and hired for the purpose.
— Opening of women's centres for training of women in forest-related and other household crafts.
— Grass Seed Collection by women which is bought by the project at the going market rates for such seeds of grasses and trees.
— Mahila Melas organised by the project and VFC where audio-visual material pertaining to various aspects of the project are displayed for women exclusively.

4. Impact Analysis of Eco-Rehabilitation of CPLRs

A two-pronged approach was adopted to evaluate this project. While a macro analysis adopting the rate-of-return approach examined the overall financial viability of the project, the micro aspects bearing directly on the lives of inhabitants were examined with the help of a socio-economic survey conducted in selected villages in the project.

4.a. The Macro Indicators

In order to arrive at the net inflows, the rehabilitation component—"Minor" work—of the project was subjected to a financial analysis (Galastro 1996). The cash flow streams were computed for planning a horizon of 21 years for each of the three models. The basic data on expenditure and income flows could be estimated for a period of 6 years (1990-96). While the expenditure was available from the budgets and expenditure accounts, benefits were estimated using constant (standing) prices for the goods produced by plantation. The projections for streams were computed modelwise on the basis of expected future production with a horizon of 20 years of planning. A sensitivity analysis was also carried out under three different scenarios (Base case, Pessimistic, i.e. 10 per cent decline in inflow and Optimistic, i.e. 10 per cent enhancement in net flows) to test the sensitivity of the financial indicators in relation to possible future fluctuations in the inflows. Three indicators, viz. Financial Internal Rate of Return (FIRR), Net Present Value (NPV) and Benefit-Cost Ratios (BCR) were employed for the purpose. For discounting, two rates (5 per cent and 10 per cent) were used (Table 16.1).

TABLE 16.1: **Financial Indicators for Evaluation of Eco-Rehabilitation of Aravalli Project.**

Attribute	Benefit cost ratio		Net present value		Financial Internal rate of return(%)
	5% discount	10% discount	5% discount	10% discount	
Base	1.17	0.71	74.93	-96.39	(7) 8
Pessimistic	1.06	0.64	24.85	-120.09	(6) 7
Optimistic	1.05	0.78	125.81	-72.69	(8) 10

The results show that the values of FIRR were 8 per cent in the Base Case, 7 per cent for the Pessimistic Scenario and 10 per cent in the Optimistic Scenario. These values point in the direction of financial viability from the point of view of CPLR users mainly. Application of a higher rate of discount points to less than unitary B-C ratio and naturally negative quantities of NPV of the project. The results amply demonstrated that in the light of socio-economic desirability of the project, the lower rates of discounts alone would favour financial attractiveness of investment in natural resource development (Kula 1984, Harou 1985, Marothia 1988, Lober and Gracy 1997). Despite the inherent viability, the macro analysis does tend to gloss over the structural weakness, the interpersonal distribution of benefits and the impact of the project activities on household levels. The household level studies have been conducted from time to time to fill the critical gap in the socio-economic fabric at the households levels (Sharma 1993, Bokil 1993, Daulay 1994 and Kalla 1996). In the section that follows, the results of household surveys giving information about the socio-economic impact indicators are discussed.

4.b. Micro Indicators

Any impact analysis would lose its relevance if it does not have a "with" and "without" situation. Unfortunately, there was no benchmark survey done at the beginning of the project. Alternatively a proxy for "without" situation by selecting villages which were away from the project area, were socio-economically homogeneous to the project villages and did not come under the ambit of the project activities, were collected (Annexure II). The indicators selected against which the impact was measured included :

— Level of living
— Employment situation
— Livestock productivity
— Availability of fodder and soil from CPLRs
— Extent of common lands, ratio of persons to CPLRs
— Benefits of fuel wood availability from CPRLs
— Income augmentation from CPLRs
— Habitat improvement
— Educational benefits of CPLRs using groups
— Women-specific programmes
— Institution building

4.b.1 Level of Living

Any programme which has the potential to uplift the standard of living would essentially involve an enlargement in the scope of consumption. Essentially, if the productivity of natural resources under the Common Property Regimes is increased, the crucial dependence on the natural resource productivity would have a relevance of considerable importance. In the present context, four non-fodder product-mixes from the common lands of Haryana, viz. fuel, fruits, vegetables, medicinal and other plants, were considered. The results are presented in Table 16.3. These reveal that during 1996-97, families from both project and non-project villages accounted for well over 60 per cent of the total value of consumption attributes forests. It thus seems that irrespective of categories of families based on the size of holding, the consumptive dependence of families for fuel is mainly conditioned by fuel production in common lands. Similarly fruits and vegetables mainly for home consumption were harvested from common lands. The fruits, vegetables, medicinal and others (gums, dyes) were harvested mainly by landless and small farm families. In terms of absolute values, almost all categories realised much higher values of product-mix from forests in the Project than in the Non-project villages. Similar trends were discernible for the value of forest product as a

TABLE 16.2: **Market Value of Consumption (Rs.) of Non-Fodder Forest Products from Common Lands in Project (P) and Non Project (NP) Villages in Haryana (1996-97)**

Attributes of Family	Sample charac-teristic	Forest Products						Total Annual consumption Expenditure	% of total consump-tion
		Fuel	Fruits	Vegetables	Medicinal	Others	Totals		
Landless	P	3019.83 (65.25)	873.85 (18.88)	349.10 (7.54)	289.18 (6.25)	96.12 (2.08)	4628.08 (100.00)	24967.00	18.53
	NP	772.03 (72.69)	264.24 (10.83)	216.91 (8.90)	165.30 (6.78)	24.10 (0.98)	2437.58 (100.00)	33030.00	7.38
Small	P	3393.74 (72.86)	672.54 (14.44)	308.97 (6.63)	201.07 (4.33)	81.22 (1.74)	4657.54	31874.00	14.61
	NP	1667.94 (68.32)	456.50 (18.70)	208.17 (8.54)	97.63 (3.99)	11.12 (0.45)	2441.36	56357.60	4.33
Medium	P	3497.58 (68.93)	1299.17 (25.60)	150.34 (2.96)	178.23 (3.51)	Neg.	5074.11 (100.00)	44954.00	11.28
	NP	2403.37 (77.74)	558.01 (18.05)	78.91 (2.55)	51.27 (1.66)	Neg.	3091.56 (100.00)	55248.00	5.59
Large	P	2650.03 (77.19)	782.95 (22.81)	Neg.	Neg.	Neg.	3432.98	50189.00	6.84
	NP	1620.39 (76.94)	485.71 (23.06)	Neg.	Neg.	Neg.	2106.10	53374.80	3.95
Overall	P	3127.48 (70.30)	907.13 (19.14)	202.10 (4.06)	167.13 (3.52)	44.34 (0.94)	4448.18	34490.00	12.89
	NP	1744.50 (72.75)	441.12 (18.39)	125.99 (5.25)	78.55 (3.29)	7.55 (0.32)	2397.71	59824.40	4.08

Note: Values in brackets are percent distribution of each group with respect to total.

proportion of total annual consumption expenditure per family. The results revealed that due to community protection in the project common lands, the productivity-linked consumption of non-grass forest product-mix was higher in the project villages.

The Proportion of incomes spent for consumption determines the level of living. A Higher proportion of the incomes spent mainly on consumption in general marks the lower level of living. The results of average and marginal propensities of consumption for the different categories of sample families from amongst the project and non-project villages are set out in Table 16.3.

TABLE 16.3: **Propensities of Consumption for Sample Households (1996-97)**

Attributes	Average Propensities		Marginal Propensities	
	Project	Non-Project	Project	Non-Project
Landless	0.4379	0.9422	0.1751	0.7948
Marginal	0.4324	0.9447	0.1967	0.5118
Small	0.3874	0.8991	0.0800	0.6219
Large	0.3335	0.5163	0.0832	0.2132
Overall	0.3474	0.4538	0.1809	0.2539

The results reveal that the proportion of income spent on consumption varied inversely with the size of holdings. Thus while the landless and marginal families, on an average, spent as high as 44 per cent of their income on consumption; the same registered a decline of about 39 per cent for small and 33 per cent for large sample farms. Overall the sample families from the project villages spent about 35 per cent of this income on consumption. Comparatively landless sample families in the non-project villages spent almost 94 per cent of their income on consumption which while varying inversely with the size of holding, was reduced to about 52 per cent for large farms. The overall average for these families was about 45 per cent. Other things remaining constant, a lesser proportion of larger income allocations for consumption shows that households in the project villages have a tendency to go for higher standards of living than their counterparts in the non-project villages.

From the marginal propensities it can be seen that while the project sample families would spend from 17 to 8 per cent of their incremental incomes, the same would be true at higher levels ranging from 79 per cent for the landless to 21 per cent for the large sample families. The results amply demonstrate that while, on an average, a lower proportion of the current and incremental income was allocated for consumption by the project sample families, the same was substantially higher for non-project families.

4.b.2 Income Accruals

The level of consumption has a direct and crucial bearing upon the level of income accruals. The data collected from various farm and non-farm sources for the sample families in both project and non-project villages are set out in Table 16.4.

A perusal of Table 16.4 would reveal that the sample households belonging to all households excepting large ones had larger accruals of annual incomes than their non-project counterparts. The composition of income revealed that this difference in the project families was largely attributable to wage income accruals from the project work. The project also contributed indirectly by a quick turnover of sales of animals because of abundant availability of fodder. Another noteworthy thing was the tendency of mitigating inter-category inequality by favouring mainly the landless and small families from the project villages. Finally, the income-generating capacity of the project activities could attract a large number of persons from non-farm but eco-unfriendly activities of mining and quarrying in the Aravallis.

4.b.3 Distributional Impact on Income Accruals

The cumulative frequency method was employed to generate Gini Concentration Ratios (GR) for all components of income for the sample families from the project and non-project villages. The results (Table 16.5) reveal that in the case of landless families the reduction in the source-wise income inequality was reduced by project wages (GR= 0.18). Similar situations were obtainable in the case of marginal and small families (GR=0.38 and 0.29 respectively). Consequently, for all the 112 sample observations, project wages directly contributed to the income equalisation process. Similarly, livestock incomes, which were derived indirectly in a significant manner owing to the availability of green fodder supply for more than 7 months for all of the sample households from the project sites without increasing any expenditure excepting efforts of collection of fodder, were another source of inducing egalitarianism in the accruals of family income. It can thus be concluded that inter category imbalances in the income accrual processes were considerably reduced by the project wages and fodder availability from the project sites.

4.b.4 Pattern of fuel supplies

Source-wise supply of fuel to meet the requirements of different household categories was compared temporally as well as spatially (Table 16.6). Comparing temporally from the base year of 1990-91, the common lands provided 35 per cent of (879 MT) the fuel to the households in the project

TABLE 16.4: **Source-wise Accruals of Gross Receipts per Sample Household in Project (P) and Non-Project (NP) Villages (1996-97)**

Activity	Household Categories (in %)									
	Landless		Small		Medium		Large		Average	
	P n=48	NP n=25	P n=13	NP n=15	P n=23	NP n=20	P n=15	NP n=10	P n=112	NP n=70
Crops	2.93	2.57	25.62	36.38	44.64	35.78	50.76	50.15	37.50	31.23
Milk and Milk Products	29.98	59.94	27.68	40.17	22.37	34.98	18.81	17.97	23.15	38.27
Sale of Livestock										
Buffaloes	2.69	—	5.93	—	7.34	—	5.51	10.22	5.73	2.56
Cows	9.82	—	2.05	—	2.31	—	5.53	—	4.60	—
Goats & Youngstock	11.84	4.01	0.61	5.19	3.02	4.67	1.03	3.14	3.09	4.25
Wage Incomes										
Farm	13.89	16.80	10.40	1.24	4.92	—	2.43	—	6.28	4.52
Non-farm	13.67	10.26	8.08	6.81	3.53	7.11	2.54	—	5.46	5.21
Project	15.16	—	7.79	—	2.73	—	1.43	—	4.77	—
Services	—	5.72	10.76	10.21	6.11	—	5.88	15.16	6.07	12.31
Business	—	—	0.90	—	3.03	18.12	6.05	3.36	3.36	1.65
Total Accruals	100	100.00	100.00	100.00	100.00	100.00	100.00	100.00	100.00	100.00

TABLE 16.5: **Distributional Impact on Project on Income Accruals (1996-97)**

(Gini Concentration Ratios)

Income Components	Family Groups				
	Landless	Marginal	Small	Large	Overall
Crops	—	0.4814	0.4109	0.1082	0.5838
Farm wages	0.3618	0.3905	0.3617	0.2103	0.5094
Non-farm Wages	0.4201	0.4366	0.4106	0.2011	0.3515
Project Wages	0.1801	0.3816	0.2916	—	0.2502
Livestock Income	0.4709	0.4138	0.2348	0.1559	0.3802
Total Income	0.3471	0.3378	0.2724	0.1293	0.3942

TABLE 16.6: **Impact of Aravalli Project on Pattern of Fuel Supply in Project and Non-Project Villages (1990-97)**

Source	Family Attributes	Annual Supply (MT)	Source of Supply (%)				
			Common lands	Crop Residues	Cow Dung	Farm Tree	Other
Project Bench	Landless	879	35.01	50.18	8.17	—	6.64
Mark	Small	958	20.89	46.53	22.35	1.80	8.43
(1990-91)	Medium	1012	19.12	41.24	29.01	0.89	9.74
	Large	1631	2.34	22.16	40.47	21.78	13.25
	Overall	1120	19.34	40.03	25.00	6.12	9.51
Survey (Project	Landless	1102	48.97	49.92	1.11	—	—
Village	Small	1407	37.85	45.39	10.19	1.91	4.75
(1996-97)	Medium	1470	41.13	40.09	10.51	2.17	6.10
	Large	1985	33.14	21.26	40.81	14.16	20.63
	Overall	1491	32.77	39.14	18.16	4.56	7.87
Survey (Non-	Landless	976	26.91	61.01	7.91	—	—
Project)	Small	1405	11.87	55.07	45.37	—	—
(1996-97)	Medium	1439	12.76	50.11	47.11	—	—
	Large	1928	5.91	30.08	40.03	2.17	2.77
	Overall	1437	14.36	49.07	32.19	0.54	3.77

villages. During 1996-97, the demand rose to about 1,102 MT. But the per cent contribution increased (49 per cent) to meet the enhanced demand for fuel. Spatially, the landless households in the non-project villages could muster 976

T of fuel with only 27 per cent contribution from the common lands. For small farm families, the absolute as well as relative shares of fuel supply were being increasingly met by common lands. In spatial terms the sample/households from the non-project villages could meet only 11 per cent of the fuel requirements as against 38 per cent of an almost identical amount in the case of small households from the project. Large households had predominantly used cowdung and self-raised fuel on farms in all three situations.

The results pointedly reveal a decline in the use of crop residues and cowdung in the project area by landless and small households resulting in an improved bargaining of wage earners on working for large and medium households. The results conclusively show that the improved fuel productivity in community protected CPLRs mitigated economic and social hardships.

4.b.5 Fodder Supplies

One of the avowed objectives of the project was to regulate biotic interference caused by free access to grazing in common lands. The community protected lands had a short-run objective to provide cut-and-carry fodder free as a compensation for the abandoned practice of free grazing. In bench-mark surveys the sample project villages and the non-project villages, crop residues accounted for about 70 per cent of the total supply and the untreated common lands could provide not more than 10-12 per cent of the fodder supplies (Table 16.7). Farm trees as a top feed catered for insignificant supplies (6 per cent in bench mark in the year 1990-91 and 2 per cent in the non-project village in 1996-97). The other sources included either borrowing on a kind repayment basis by the landless and small farmers or purchasing from the fodder markets by medium and large families. Compared to this, in the project villages, the increased demand for fodder was increasingly met by an enhanced contribution from common lands. This is especially true for the landless and small livestock owners who over time switched significantly from goats and sheep to buffaloes and cows. Crop residues still formed the important component but their reduced contributions in the project villages resulted in a reduction of bonded dependence of the landless with medium and large farms and in their relative enhancement in the wage bargaining processes. It can thus be inferred that common lands in the project villages have brought in significant changes by way of increased supplies of fodder on a regular basis. Finally, the ease in and certainty of the spots have resulted in the reduction of time spent mainly by women and children in collecting fodder to 2 hours from about 9 hours to collect the same amount of fodder in the non-project sample villages.

TABLE 16.7: **Impact of Aravalli Project on Fodder Supply in Project and Non-Project Villages (1990-97)**

Source	Family Attributes	Annual Supply (MT)	Source of Supply (%)			
			Common lands	Crop Residues	Farm Trees	Other
Project Bench Mark (1990-91)	Landless	2826	8.43	90.17	—	2.40
	Small	3608	10.21	87.01	—	2.69
	Medium	3767	13.21	65.14	4.38	17.27
	Large	5438	10.5	30.08	7.62	5.19
	Overall	3909.85	10.55	68.10	6.00	15.35
Survey (Project Village (1996-97)	Landless	4810.40	25.60	73.32	—	1.08
	Small	3521.21	17.24	72.38	6.40	4.03
	Medium	5011.10	18.48	64.51	—	16.01
	Large	5111.21	4.16	50.11	13.44	32.29
	Overall	4613.63	16.37	65.08	4.91	13.64
Survey (Non Project) (1996-97)	Landless	1117.15	18.58	81.15	—	0.37
	Small	1102.03	11.95	80.13	—	7.93
	Medium	1311.01	9.51	75.21	3.16	12.12
	Large	1404.41	10.21	70.11	7.34	4.24
	Overall	4934.60	12.56	76.40	2.60	11.40

4.b.6 Livestock Productivity

One of the direct benefits of the certainty in the availability of green fodder for more than seven months in a year was reflected in the composition of the livestock holdings in favour of buffaloes even by the landless and small households (Table 16.8) besides the increase in the production of milk and milk products, meat and quicker turnover of livestock marketing. It may be noted that the livestock feeding schedules for animals in the project and non-project villages had only one difference. Whereas the animals in non-project villages were maintained on a mix of dry fodder and a small supplement of green fodder in two major monsoon months, the similar animals were fed green fodder with an assured supply for over seven months in the project villages. This resulted in cost reduction as well as value addition due to increased production. The net joint effect of the green fodder resulted in a 15-20 per cent increase in the benefits for buffaloes and cows in the project area. This benefit again registered a gain of 14 to 17 per cent for buffaloes and cows and 48.2 per cent for camels and goats (Table 16.9). Barring large households which did not

TABLE 16.8: **Livestock Holding per Family in Project (P) and Non-Project (NP) Sample Households (1996-97)**

Family Attributes	"P" "NP"	Buffaloes (No.)	Cows (No.)	Goat & Sheep (No.)	Herd Average Size (No).
Landless	P	1.14	0.16	1.10	.086
	NP	0.92	0.20	2.32	
Small	P	1.25	0.75	2.35	.404
	NP	1.60	0.55	4.85	
Medium	P	2.00	1.11	0.93	.112
	NP	2.20	0.60	2.07	
Large	P	3.21	1.50	0.57	
	NP	3.00	1.10	—	
All	P	1.64	0.71	1.30	.126
	NP	1.69	0.51	2.66	

TABLE 16.9: **Estimation of Percent Net Benefits of Livestock Productivity from Common Lands in Project (P) and Non-Project (NP) Villages in Haryana (1996-97)**

Animals	P and NP sample	Family Attributes									
		Landless		Marginal		Small		Large		Overall	
		%B	D	% B	D	% B	D	% B	D	%B	D
Buffaloes	P	60	20	31	14	19	10	—	—	27.5	11.0
	NP	40		17		9		—	—	16.50	
Cows	P	65	15	30	17	19	2	—	—	28.50	8.50
	NP	50		13		7		—	—	00	
Camels	P	40	10	19	8	12	7	—	—	17.75	6.25
	NP	30		11		5		—	—	11.50	
Goats	P	60	5	15	2	10	2	—	—	21.25	2.25
	NP	55		13		8		—	—	19.00	
Overall	P	56.25	12.50	23.75	10.25	15.00	5.25	—	—	23.75	7.00
	NP	43.75		17.50		9.75		—	—	16.75	

(1) "P" and "NP" stand respectively for Project and Non-Project villages. (2) "B" stands for benefits measured in monetary terms. (3) "D" stands for difference of benefits between Project and Non-Project samples.

participate in fodder harvesting from the common lands, the net returns accruable to the assured availability of green fodder resulted in the correction of skewedness in the income accruals and employment for the womenfolk. For the landless and small households perhaps were socially unconstrained to work in common for collection of green fodder. The results conclusively revealed that the fodder component mainly contributed to provided the acceptance of the total package of rehabilitation programme in the sample villages.

4.b.7 Employment Generation

One of the major objectives of the project was to provide gainful and eco-friendly employment to the otherwise unemployed or ungainfully employed (in mining and quarrying) persons in the villages situated in the vicinity of the Aravalli. The employment constituted soil working, plantation, upkeep, protection and nursery raising. On an average, one hectare of plantation was found to generate 365 labour days in a financial year in Model I and 340 labour days in Model II. Thus a hectare of plantation would provide employment to one person for almost whole of the year, in the sample villages. For a specific work plan (Table 16.10), the total labour employment in 1992-93 of the project was about 11,000 labour days, which registered continuous increase by about 421 labour days in 1993-94 and about 1,712 labour days in 1994-95 on the base year. The increment was, however, reduced to around 105 in 1995-96. It can thus be seen that the employment on labour days in the project villages, although substantial, suffered from fluctuations in demand for labour in the project work. One of the major achievements of the project nevertheless was a pronounced accent on providing almost 32-39 per cent of the total employment for women. Thus while in the initial year for every two men only one woman found employment, in the subsequent years, the man-woman employment ratio registered a downward trend of 1.94:1 (1993-94), 1.53:1 (1994-95) and 1.93:1 (1995-96). At the prevailing rate of wages paid, the project work created gainful employment of about 47,000 labour days injecting a net inflow of Rs. 15 lakhs in the economy of the sample villages. Of the total wage earning families belonging to landless, marginal and, to some extent, small-land-owning households, the preference for alternative employment of working in mines and quarries was considerably scaled down by women and men over 50 years of age. A good number of widows and destitutes were working at nurseries almost the year round. There was a noticeable preference for working in the project-related activities to ward off fear of contracting tuberculosis by the male family members. It must, however, be mentioned that in the fast expanding economy notably in the Gurgaon-Faridabad-Sohna region, mining still continues to be an attractive source of employment. Similarly, modernisation and intensification of agriculture in the Narnaul-Rewari-Dadri region may substantially curtail availability of labour for the village community projects.

TABLE 16.10: **Employment Generation (Labour Days) in the Project Villages (1992-96)**

Year	No. of Labour Days Generated						
	Males	Females	Total	F-M Ratio	Female (% to total)	Wage Rates (Rs.)	Value Rs. Lakh
1992-93	7391.7	3609.0	10998.9	1:2.05	32.81	34.75	3.82
1993-94	7528.3	3879.0	11421.8	1:1.94	33.96	39.00	3.82
1994-95	8714.3	5708.8	14323.4	1:1.53	39.86	40.00	4.46
1995-96	7085.0	4083.6	11105.9	1:1.73	36.77	45.00	5.00

4.b.8 Women-Specific Benefits

The major premise of the project was perceived importance of woman as a major use of forest output-mix, viz. fodder and fuel. The premise that any policy which took care of mitigating the hardship faced by women would have enhanced the level of community participation. This gave rise to tailoring of some of the components of the programme which would mitigate the hardships of working women who gather fuel, fodder and others. Simultaneously the skill development programme which may or may not have a direct bearing upon interaction with forest was planned. As a result (Table 16.11), the harvesting of green fodder alone benefited 12 per cent of the households, (mainly landless and small ones). The post-establishment harvest of perennial grasses resulted in one-and-a-half time increase in the fodder harvest, which in turn benefited 45 per cent, 48 per cent, 52 per cent and 63 per cent of households respectively in the years following 1993-94. One of the most significant developments resulted in a four-fold decline in the time of collection of fodder and a three-fold decline in the collection of dead and dry branches of trees including *Prosopis juliflora* for fuel.

TABLE 16.11: **Specific Benefits emanating to Sample Villages from Aravalli Project (1992-96)**

Year	Grass Seeds (kgs)	Area Sown with Grasses (ha)	Grasses Harvested Headloads (30 kgs)	No. of Household Benefited	Total No. of Household	% Household Benefited
1992-93	—	158	3069	375	3131	11.98
1993-94	421	455	4450	1400	3131	44.71
1994-95	833	343	61658	1518	3131	48.48
1995-96	278	190	84914	1650	3131	52.70
1996-97	980	300	100000	2000	3131	63.88

Other women-specific benefits (Table 16.12) emanating from the programme were the formation of women's groups to start *Mahila Nurseries* which would raise the plants to be purchased by the department only in 1995-96. Only 3 such groups were formed in 3 sample villages out of a total of 14 villages which could raise and sell about 2 million seedlings worth Rs. 77,000. In most of the sample villages, the reasons for such lack of enthusiasm included lack of sufficient efforts on the part of the project staff to identify such groups, lack of willingness necessitated by non-availability of free time, lack of awareness on the part of the womenfolk for such work possibilities and lack of water availability for raising seedlings in most of the sample villages.

Women extension workers (WEWs) were appointed in each of the sample villages to train women for skill development like tailoring, nursery seedling raising, embroidery and basket-making. They were entrusted with the responsibility of motivating as well as monitoring, the progress of this subprogramme called "Women in Development" (WID). The activities included establishment of training centres, manufacture and use of *Van Jyoti Chulhas* for economising use of biomass and opening up of saving accounts by women for inculcation of saving habits and benefits. Most of the VEWs were attached with VFCs and were engaged in non-specific work besides the specific target-oriented works. It has to be recognised that motivation of women for such work under the existing socio-economic milieu is a difficult task. But signs of gradual improvement in the women participants of this programme has been visible.

TABLE 16.12: **Other Women-Specific Benefits emanating to Sample Villages from Aravalli Project (1992-96)**

Year	Mahila Nurseries				Women Extension workers (No.)	Village Women Centres (No.)	Saving Accts. (No.)	Vanjyoti Chullas (No.)
	No.	Beneficiaries (No.)	Plants raised (No.)	Payment Made (No.)				
1992-93	—	—	—	—	—	—	—	—
1993-94	—	—	—	—	12	2	29	54
1994-95	—	—	—	—	12	5	190	251
1995-96	6	10	2.10	77500	12	9	403	536

4.b.9 Incentive Scheme

The incentive scheme was introduced in 1993-94 by the project to motivate the whole community to protect plantations and natural vegetation in the project area, besides meeting their immediate requirements. The yearly distribution of incentive money (Table 16.13) received was determined by the success Index (Rawat and Bedi 1996). The scheme was envisaged for any given village and the quantum of funds was proportional to the plantation area in each village. The funds were deposited in a bank account which was jointly sponsored by the concerned Chairperson (Sarpanch) and DFO. The amount was spent as per the advice of the VFC for creation of common social assets.

TABLE 16.13: **Impact of Incentives Scheme in Sample Villages of Aravalli Project (1993-96)**

Year	Incentive Money (Rs. Lakh)	No. of Villages	Purposes*						
			I	II	III	IV	V	VI	VII
1993-94	2.15	11	2	3	—	—	—	1	1
1994-95	2.68	12	1	1	—	—	—	1	2
1995-96	1.49	8	—	—	1	2	2	1	2

*I — Water Resource Development (repair of well, mechanisation, water tank repair, tank deepening, water courses repairs).

II — Consumer Durable (utensils for community use, tent, school fan, furniture, cots in community halls, sewing machines.

III — Civil Works (school, panchayat, roads and other community building repair).

IV — Socio-Religious Assets (temple repairs, religious ceremonies, cultural organizational assistance).

V — Agricultural Resource Development (bunding, soil conservation work)

VI — Miscellaneous (community animal sheds, others).

VII — Unspent Money.

Since the inception of the scheme, except for one village all sample villages qualified for at least one-time payment of incentive money. Five sample villages were consistent performers to qualify for incentives for all three years. Three villages qualified for 2 instalments of incentive money and one village qualified only once. The results show that despite the fluctuations in the incentive money receipts, most sample villages participated in protecting plantations and vegetation.

The incentive money was most commonly spent for the creation of either consumer durables of common utility (purchase of big utensils, electrical installations and purchase of fans for schools, construction of public .places, animal shelters), civil works (matching contribution for construction of approach road, water tank for drinking water supplies, class-rooms), water resource development (deepening of wells, cleaning and repairs of tanks) and others.

Some of the constraints in motivating villagers through the innovative incentive approach in creation of social assets as opined by surveyed responses include :

(i) Lack of understanding of village households.
(ii) Administrative delays in reimbursements by the department.
(iii) Assets created had graded access owing to the socio-economic stratification of villages.
(iv) Insufficiency of incentive money vis-a-vis total requirement.
(v) Possible negative impact of discontinuance beyond three years of community protection of plantations.

4.b.10 Habitat Improvement

Provision and protection of forest cover by village communities was instrumental in revival of natural bio-diversity. Consequently almost extinct plant species owing to exploitative use got naturally regenerated. Most notably, the revival of adequate plant densities of *Solanum nigram, Tribulus terrestris, Tinospora cordifolia, Citrullus colocynthis, Commiphora weighti, Xanthium strumarium, Clerodendron multiforum, Justicea vasica, Centella asiatica, Ricicus communis, Withania somnifera, Viola cineraria, Aloe barbadensis, Balanites roxburghri Musuna proriens, Rorippa indica, Fumria indica, Argemone mexicana, Omcimum sanctum* and many others were identified by women and elderly respondents in the sample villages.

For the wildlife regeneration the sample families were canvassed with a sighting responses of wildlife (Table 16.14). The results revealed that habitat improvement during the last eight years due to community protection had resulted in high sighting frequencies of rabbits, hyenas, blue bulls and porcupine. The animals which were ascribed to medium sighting responses included sand grouse, antelopes, wild boars and monitor lizard. A moderate increase was registered for sand grouse, bar headed gease, ruddy shell drake, teal, pochard and panther. The decline was registered for only chinkara and hare.

As against this the non-project households could not report vegetative nor wildlife elements in their common lands. Community protection and management of common lands have, therefore, reversed the trend of loss of bio-diversity through a significant habitat improvement.

5. Educational Benefits

The State of Haryana had 36.1 per cent of the total literacy rate (1981) mostly concentrated in the non-Aravalli region. The Mewat region having a predominant share of villages had only 21.8 per cent literacy level. A survey of

TABLE 16.14: **Habitat Improvement-Incidence of Wildlife Sighting Responses in Sample Village (1996-97)**

Animal/Birds	Sighting Response of Sample Families				
	Decline	Moderate Increase	Medium Increase	High Increase	Very high Increase
(A) BIRDS AND DUCKS					
1. Sand Grouse	—	*	*	—	—
2. Bar headed Gease	—	*	—	—	—
3. Grey leg Gease	*	—	—	—	—
4. Ruddy shell Drake	—	*	—	—	—
5. Teats	—	*	—	—	—
6. Rosy Pahican	—	—	—	—	—
7. Flemming Gouse	—	—	—	—	—
8. Pochard	—	*	—	—	—
(B) ANIMALS					
9. Hyena	—	—	—	*	—
10. Blue Bull	—	—	—	*	—
11. Chinkara	*	—	—	—	—
12. Wolf	—	—	*	—	—
13. Jackal	—	—	*	*	—
14. Hare	*	—	—	—	—
15. Porcupine	—	—	—	*	—
16. Wild Boar	—	—	*	—	—
17. Panther	—	*	—	—	—
18. Rabits	—	—	—	—	—
19. Fox	—	—	—	—	—
20. Antelopes	—	*	*	—	—
(C) REPTILES					
21. Monitor Lizard	—	*	*	—	—

* Represents disgust sighting responses.

- No response.

the households in 1996-97 revealed that the literacy figure for the male heads of the households was 57 per cent as against 5 per cent for the female counterparts. There has been a significant difference in the pattern of literacy as to levels between the various categories of families depending on the size of farm. The low levels of literacy in the Mewat region could be traditionally attributed to apathy toward education, employment of female and male children from the age of 6 years in the household chores including tending of younger children when parents are away on work (females), fuel and fodder picking and livestock grazing (both females and males) and for wages during intercultural operations on other farms (females). The results have obviously yielded lower rates of literacy in the Aravalli region.

Since the inception of the project, the scene has shown perceptible signs of improvement with 75 per cent of the male children literate. The skewness in the female child education (45 per cent) still persists. The augmentation of biomass through the rehabilitation programme has led to a considerable reduction in the domestic employment of the male child.

TABLE 16.15: **Enrolment of Children in Schools in Sample Villages (1996-97)**

Year	Children	Particulars of Enrolment (Nos.)		
		Beginning of session	Closure of session	Dropouts
1991-92	Male	2075	2029	41
	Female	1245	1220	25
	Total	3315	2152	66
1992-93	Male	2083	2038	45
	Female	1164	1126	38
	Total	3247	3214	83
1993-94	Male	2041	1989	52
	Female	1207	1162	45
	Total	3248	3151	97
1994-95	Male	2105	2027	78
	Female	1234	1175	59
	Total	3339	3202	137
1995-96	Male	2087	2010	77
	Female	1307	1228	79
	Total	3394	3238	156

The female child is still employed in household chores but she is at least partially relieved of fuel, fodder and grazing-related activities. The enrolment figures of both male and female children has stabilized around 3,228 with 2:1 female : male ratio and considerably less male dropouts (Table 16.15). Almost all sample families in the sample villages preferred to send their children to school, for broadening their mental outlook especially of male children. The womenfolk in the sample families specifically used child-free afternoons to concentrate on domestic chores, siesta, sewing or any artistic work. In the sample villages, there has been a steady albeit lesser than male counterpart growth in the enrolment of girls due to the social stigmas, including the custom of girls not being encouraged to study. Many Meo children were sent to non-formal *Madarsas* for Qoranic education only.

During the investigation, however, there was a constant refrain in the sample families about the future of educated males and specially female children. Meaningful infrastructural development, curriculum involving hands-on experience in skill development, training of teachers and constant evaluation of education programmes may, therefore, be needed to reap the harvest of child labour released owing to implementation of the programme.

Another matter which merits attention pertains to the attendance of the school-going children. The results of a survey (Table 16.16) revealed that the absence from school was more predominant among the girl students than among the boys. The fluctuations in the attendance were attributable, according to a sample household, to sickness, household chores, festivals and absence of teachers in that order. Needless, therefore, to conclude that the full utilization of this released force of future would be fruitful if proper planning of education on the lines of vocational education is put in proper perspective.

TABLE 16.16: **Distribution of Attendance in Schools in Sample Villages (1996-97)**

Year	Children	Attendance in schools			
		70 per cent and above	69-40 per cent	40-11 per cent	10-0 per cent
1991-92	Male	52.90	38.81	6.27	2.02
	Female	38.72	21.27	37.81	2.00
	Total	37.01	29.23	30.77	1.99
1992-93	Male	59.24	27.23	11.36	2.16
	Female	37.37	17.19	42.18	3.26
	Total	49.41	21.36	28.21	1.02
1993-94	Male	63.10	21.23	13.12	2.55
	Female	36.02	32.13	28.12	3.73
	Total	54.18	20.52	22.31	2.99
1994-95	Male	60.18	28.03	8.08	3.71
	Female	24.25	44.16	26.81	4.78
	Total	41.27	39.28	15.35	4.10
1995-96	Male	61.31	10.34	22.31	6.04
	Female	28.11	19.02	48.28	4.59
	Total	42.59	20.34	32.44	4.63

6. Conclusion and Policy Implications

An attempt to analyse and evaluate the socio-economic impact of the Aravalli project revealed that:

(i) The decades of misuse of natural resources in the Aravalli hills has put the resource productivity of the common lands in complete jeopardy. The growing human and animal populations find it difficult to sustain themselves. Further, unrestricted and uninterrupted use of natural resources is going to accelerate the degradation process.

(ii) The intervention model devised by the Aravalli of the Forest Department, Haryana was mainly based on the premise of compensation of the benefits forgone because of social protection of common lands from all kinds of biotic interference in the form of regulated access to the output-mix, employment on forestry-related jobs, women-specific nursery programme with buyback arrange-ments, and the group incentive for higher survival of plantations, in terms of helping rural societies create socio-economic assets, through recently developed institutions.

(iii) The social content of the programme also included an important component, viz. women-in-development including popularization of smokeless hearths, skill development and health and hygiene.

(iv) The macro analysis of the project revealed sufficient financial resilience to attract favourable rates of return. The micro analysis of 14 villages in representative villages revealed that the programme has significantly altered the income accruals for their more egalitarian distribution. This, in turn, has started showing an impact upon the standard of living. The regulated access has registered impressive productivity gains to meet the growing demands for fuel and fodder. Fodder availability has in turn altered the livestock composition in favour of animals with higher productivity. Besides, free and ensured availability of green fodder from the programme has enabled even the landless and small household realize higher incomes.

(v) The social benefits of this programme include the awareness of women groups of their contribution in the eco-rehabilitation of the region. One of the most important social benefits is the freedom of the child labour from the grind of household and production chores which, in turn, has been mainly responsible for the increase in the enrolment in schools.

(vi) The ecological benefits include re-emergence of almost extinct medicinal, aromatic and other edible flora and varied fauna in the protected common lands spelling a healthy growth in bio-diversity for their future, more gainful use.

(vii) The institutional benefits mainly include formation of 293 village bodies which, through participatory management, would eventually regulate the productive and consumptive utilization of resource-mix generated in these common lands.

While the project has, by and large, successfully compensated for the benefits forgone owing to regularization of access, some of the issues emanating out of this project merit mention. These are as follows:

(i) Goat has been replaced by buffalo and cow, thus pushing up the price of goat meat and other products beyond the reach of average consumers.
(ii) The distribution of permanent assets owing to incentives provided by the project has been conditioned by the social and caste dominance of the villages. This has led to discontent among the socially disadvantaged groups and may accentuate inequalities of resource control.
(iii) Women-specific benefits are far more sporadic and have yet to assume the size of a movement to make a lasting dent in the problems related to the socio-economic status of women.
(iv) There is considerable uncertainty of the continuance of this project if EU withdraws by 1998. In the light of the benefits that have already accrued from the project and the quantum of people's participation generated VFCs need to be strengthened by financial tie-ups with programmes/schemes overseen by the District Rural Development Agency (DRDA) so that this programme of proven socio-economic relevance does not suffer due to financial problems after the withdrawal of the project.
(v) Even though the project has succeeded in generating palpable ecological and economic benefits for the community through their active participation, there is need of continuous monitoring and evaluation of the outcome of the project.

The question now arises whether withdrawal of these forms of investments at this stage of the project development is advisable. The answer is no because sustainability and irreversibility of such projects are intimately linked with sustained employment generation or developing alternative sources of livelihood in order to satisfy the basic needs of those dependent on CPRS, particularly for the poor and the landless. Further strengthening of village level institutions is also essential to increase their competence to match the challenge of managing the CPRs viz., to regulate community's usufruct rights in consonance with the productivity of CPRs.

Kaul (1999) has emphasized "the short-and long-term objectives of sustainable development of CPRs are not attainable if we look at the problem from only a technical perspective. The growth in demands for common land produce is directly linked to human and livestock numbers. The current pressures are due both to ignorance and the need for survival. The demands of human and livestock populations on the common lands need to be regulated through developing alternative sources of livelihood and the means to meet the subsistence needs of the population. Unless a holistic view of village development is taken of which common land is a small part, the common lands will continue to be vulnerable. The human and behavioral dimensions are equally important as they provide a framework within which change and development take place. Therefore development and sustainable management of common lands cannot be achieved in isolation; its development and management should be seen within a public policy framework of integrated village development, which is unfortunately absent".

Acknowledgements

The authors are grateful to Shri J.P.L. Srivastava, CCF and Project Director, for providing access to the relevant literature without which preparation of this paper would not have been possible.

REFERENCES

Annon. 1989. "Eco-Rehabilitation of Aravallis", CEU Report Mimeo.

Bajaj, Manjula. 1992. "Natural Regeneration Vs. Afforestation: An examination of the potential for natural regeneration with community participation". In: Anil Agrawal (Ed.). *The Price of Forest*, New Delhi: Centre for Science and Environment, pp. 234-47.

Bhoria, K.S. and B. Bajaj. 1993. *Haryana District Gazetteers*, Gurgaon, Haryana Gazetteer Organization, Revenue Department, Chandigarh. p. 960.

Bokil, M.L. 1993. *A study on the utilization of Common Lands and the Impact of Aravalli Project.* Gurgaon: Haryana Forest Department, 1-35.

Chopra, Kanchan and Gopal Kadikodi. 1992. "Some Issues in Evaluation and Replication of Participatory Institutions", In: Anil Agrawal (Ed.). *The Price of Forests,* New Delhi: Centre for Science and Environment, pp. 260-71.

Daulay, H.S. 1994. *A Comparative Study of Livestock and Fodder Resources of Aravalli Project,* Gurgaon: Haryana Forest Department, 1-31.

Galastro, Vincenzo 1996. "Rehabilitation of Common Lands in the Aravalli Hills", *Haryana Mission Interim Report Aravalli Project,* Gurgaon: Department of Forests, pp. 1-35. 5

Hardin, G. 1968. "The Tragedy of the Commons". *Science,* 162:(1243-48).

Harou, P.A. 1985. "On a Social Discount Rate for Forestry". *Canadian Journal of Forestry Research* 15:927-34.

Jodha, N.S. 1982. *Decline of Common Property Resources of Western Rajasthan: Micro level evidence, Economics Program,* ICRISAT, Patancheru P.O., A.P., pp. 1-25 (Mimeo).

Kalla, Jagdeesh C. 1996. *Socio-economic Analysis of Joint Forest Management of Common Lands in the Aravallis of Haryana*, Gurgaon, Haryana: 1-65.

Kula, G. 1984. "Derivation of social time preference rates for USA and Canada", *Quarterly Journal of Economics*. 99:873-82.

Kaul, R.N. 1999. "Aravalli Project : Its impacts and future prospects". *Annals of Arid Zone* (in press).

Lober, D. and C.P. Gracy. 1997. "Allocation of Natural Resources Over Time: Risk, Uncertainty and Discount Rates in Natural Resources". In: John M. Kerr, D.K. Marothia, Katar Singh, C. Ramasamy and W.R. Bentley (Eds.). *Natural Resource Economics: Theory and Application in India*, New Delhi: Oxford and IBH Publishing Co. Pvt. Ltd.

Marothia, D.K. 1988. "Afforestation of Bhata Soils: Socio-Economic and Management Aspects". *Indian Journal of Agricultural Economics*, 43:305-309.

Marothia, D.K. 1989. "Resource Ownership and Human Interaction: A Theoretical Exposition". *Annals of Arid Zone*, 28:165-80.

Mukherji, B.K. 1993. *Monitoring and Evaluation Manual for the Haryana Aravallis*, Aravalli Project, Gurgaon: Haryana Forest Department, p. 127 (Mimeo).

Rawat, J.K. and Harinder Bedi. 1996. *Women and the Commons. Towards sustainability in the Haryana Aravallis*. Aravalli Project, Forest Department, Government of Haryana :1-52.

Sharma, R.D. 1993. *Energy Consumption Surveys in the Aravalli Project Area*. Gurgaon: Haryana Forest Department: 1-42.

Sinha, M.D. 1994. "Rehabilitation of Common Lands in the Aravalli Hills, Haryana: Micro Planning", *Proc. of Workshop on Eco-restoration of the Aravalli*, 23-24, Feb.1994. Aravalli Project, Gurgaon: Haryana Forest Department, p. 41.

ANNEXURE-I

Model-wise Distribution of Area Rehabilitation(ha) in Aravalli Project (1990-96)

Year	Model I	Model II	Model III	Total
1990-91	—	—	—	—
1991-92	1885	2266	899	5050
1992-93	2714	3160	526	6400
1993-94	2800	3400	400	6400
1994-95	2893	3107	400	6400
1995-96	1606	2721	2023	6350
Total	11898	14650	4048	30600

**Source*: J.K. Rawat and Harvinder Bedi. 1996. *Women and the Commons: Towards Sustainability in the Haryana Aravallis.* Aravalli Project Forest Department, Government of Haryana, p. 5.

ANNEXURE-II

Project and Non-Project Villages in Five Forest Divisions in Haryana Aravallis (1996-97)

Division	Sub Div./Unit	Selected Villages	
		Project Villages	Non-Project Villages
Sohna	Sohna Nuh Gurgaon Raipur	Baganki Sonkh Ghairatpur Khod	Gangoli
Ferozpur Jhirka	Firozpur Jhirka Ballabhgarh Punhana	Ghatasamsabas Mohammadpur Bas Lakarpur	Sidhrawat
Narnaul	Nangalchaudhry Narnaul Nizampur	Sayyad Alipur Musnota Kamania	Faizlipur
Dadri	Dadri Mahendragarh	— Nangalmala Zerpur	Nimbahera
Rewari	Rewari Khol	Rajgarh Khaleta Manethi	Navdi

17 Fuelwood Production Through Wasteland Development: Some Policy Issues

N.C. Saxena

1. Implications of Fuelwood Scarcity

Fuelwood for cooking continues to be a basic need for many rural families in India. Together with other non-commercial sources of energy such as dung and agricultural waste and wood meets 95 per cent of the fuel needs of rural areas. Of these, the use of dung and agricultural waste as fuel is widespread in the agriculturally prosperous regions with fertile soils and controlled irrigation, such as Punjab, Haryana, U.P. and north Bihar, but wood is the main domestic fuel in less endowed and poorer regions. In 1991-92, 59.2 per cent of the total fuel needs in the rural areas and 35.5 per cent in the urban areas were being met from wood. Roughly, 80 per cent of the rural fuelwood is gathered, and only 20 per cent of this comes from own farms (Saxena 1997).

In the last two decades the share of firewood in fuel consumption has gone up significantly for two reasons: first, the dwarf varieties have yielded much less agricultural residues than before, and secondly, because the per capita population of cattle has declined as a result of the fall in the area under pastures. This should cause concern, for more wood means more collection, leading to an acceleration in the denudation of tree cover.

It is estimated that the average number of hours spent on gathering biomass is about two hours per day per household. If only 50 per cent of the rural families are assumed to be involved in this activity, the total labour spent is 50 million × 2/24 = 4 million man-years. Such human effort for gathering may increase with declining supply and has important social and economic consequences for women and children, the principal gatherers. Self-employment of this magnitude is, however, distress employment, as it is at the cost of their health and children's education, and when it brings cash through headloading (fuelwood collection by the poor from public lands and carrying it on their heads to the nearest market), it leads to environmental damage. In many regions with good forests, headloading has emerged as an important profession in the past 15 years; and a significant number of households have headloading as their major occupation, for lack of an alternative employment.

Because of shortage of wood, in some areas rural people, instead of going up the energy ladder to modern fuels, are coming down the energy ladder to bushes, leaves and twigs. This use of inferior fuels for cooking has implications for the quality of their life, as these inferior fuels do not burn well and produce a lot of smoke. This causes eye and lung diseases among women who spend long hours in close proximity to their hearths. And prolonged exposure to smoke and soot, aggravated by ill-designed hearths and stoves, lack of cooking space, improper outlets for smoke from the kitchen, shortage of rooms and overcrowding cause heart ailments and chronic bronchitis. Carbon monoxide as an important constituent of the smoke, reduces the haemoglobin content of the blood and increases the risks of anaemia particularly among the rural poor, illiterate and malnourished women.

2. Regional Variation

Despite the fact that degradation of forest lands has continued unabated, and social forestry on community lands has not been a viable programme, fuelwood prices in India after 1987 have not gone up in real terms for two reasons. First, farmers in the commercialised and surplus regions of India have produced a great deal of eucalyptus wood in the past 10 years, which had to be sold as fuelwood, being surplus after meeting the needs of poles and pulpwood. Second, the greatest potential for supply of fuelwood at a little opportunity cost is through shrubs, such as prosopis. In the prosopis-abundant districts, its sale has emerged as a cottage industry for the poor, specially for women and children. However, these positive developments, though unconnected with government policies, still leave out a large proportion of the rural population for whom fuelwood is scarce.

As a consequence, to speak of a "fuelwood problem" for the entire country is somewhat misleading. Land production capabilities and access to biomass vary from region to region and this has an impact on whether energy for cooking is a problem for people in the rural areas. One way to classify regions with respect to fuelwood availability could be :

1. Regions with proximity to forests,
2. Fertile and irrigated cultivated lands,
3. Areas with access to prosopis shrubs,
4. Areas where farm forestry has been a success,
5. Areas where dung must be returned to fields for maintaining

productivity.

Fuelwood is an acute problem more in the last type of region, which may cover roughly half of India's geographical area. In forest regions, the issue is not of physical scarcity but of lack of incomes, which pushes the poor in headloading. In regions 2 and 4, there would be a class dimension too, that is, the poor and landless may face shortages, even when it is not an issue for the surplus farmers. Even if the poor have land, their immediate preoccupation is the quick solutions to desperate food and income deficits, and they cannot be expected to use their lands for production of fuelwood. For the poor, shortage of fuel does not generally feature high among their priorities, for if they are short on fuel, they are most likely to be even more deficit in incomes, cash and food supplies. The poor would certainly like better opportunities for gathering of twigs and branches, not because they burn it all, but these get sold and bring the much needed cash to the family. Thus the earlier social forestry projects, in focussing only on fuelwood, proved insufficient in defining what is needed at the farm household level.

Probably the most seriously affected region in India from the point of view of demand for fuelwood and fodder is the Deccan Plateau, and western India. In this dry region with little groundwater, people have used up most of the woody materials either for construction or as fuel, and they are now dependent on straw and shrubs as fuel. Typically these regions have poor agricultural production, which may be partially caused by the diversion of agricultural residues and dung for cooking. These regions along with uplands, therefore, deserve topmost priority in fuelwood production schemes.

3. Land Availability

Two self-explanatory facts about wood need to be stated here, as they have policy implications for production of fuelwood. First, wood is a heterogeneous product. Even a single species, such as eucalyptus, can be sawn for timber, or used as pulpwood and poles, or as fuelwood. These products are processed differently, are sold by different traders, and fetch different prices, being the highest for timber and lowest for fuelwood. Generally fallen wood, smaller pieces, twigs, wood shavings, saw dust, bark and roots which cannot be used elsewhere are used as fuelwood. Thus fuelwood is an inferior form of wood and often a byproduct. Land capable of producing superior wood should not be used for fuelwood, unless equity and sustainability considerations dictate otherwise. Second, wood as a form of biomass is grown on land and, therefore, any plan to grow more wood must answer the fundamental questions: on what kind of land, who owns or controls that land, and what will motivate the owner to use that land for growing wood.

Of the total 305 mha area of the country, for which records are available, 41 mha is under permanent snow, mountains, rocks, desert, rivers, towns, roads, etc., and is, therefore, not available for vegetation. Of the remaining 264 mha, 142 mha is under crops. Cultivated lands, and farm bunds and boundaries, are almost entirely privately owned, and access to them is predetermined by ownership. Although much of this land is owned by large farmers, resource-poor farmers with some land are numerous. They include small and marginal farmers generally, some larger but still poor farmers in dry, infertile areas, and the landless poor to whom 5 to 6 mha of degraded land has been allotted in the past two decades.

Public wastelands are of three types: degraded forests; wastes which are owned by the Government but are used by the community; and grazing lands which are vested in village bodies. The last two are also referred to as revenue wastelands, as their management is with the Revenue Departments. It is estimated that of the 55 mha of uncultivated non-forest lands, some 20 mha, consisting of fallows, groves and owned/allotted/encroached land, are now under private control, whereas the rest 35 mha is still under the control of the Revenue Department. Out of this, perhaps 60 per cent, that is, 12 mha private and 21 mha with the Revenue Department would be available for tree planting.

The magnitude of degraded land available and suitable for growing trees and where trees are not now growing may be classified as given in Table 17.1.

TABLE 17.1: **Ownership of Degraded Land Available for Tree Growing (mha)**

Category of Culturable Land	Total Area	Available for Trees (for new plantation)	Private	Forest Deptt	Revenue/ Other Deptt.
Cultivated	142	13	13	—	—
Forest	67	36	—	36	—
Uncultivated/ non-forest	55	33	12	—	21
Strips (farm bunds, road-sides, etc.)	Already included in the above	2	1	—	1
Total	264	84	26	36	22

Source: Chambers, Saxena and Shah (1989).

Thus it is clear that the major potential is private, revenue and forest lands totalling 84 mha. Assuming an average low productivity of 2 mT per ha per year of fuelwood (besides poles, timber, etc.) from all types of wastelands, it could lead to an additional production of 168 million tonnes, which will totally wipe out the deficit for fuelwood, besides creating decentralised employment for the poorest.

Why has this biological potential not been achieved? What have been the main constraints on afforestation of the three categories of lands? Which policies need to be modified? What would be the impact of the new recommended strategy on availability of fuelwood? We discuss these issues below for each category of land.

Output from tree planting projects depends on many factors, soil, climate and moisture, species, technology and protection being among the most important. Not all, however, can be controlled or predicted. Because they vary, especially survival and protection, output from similar lands can vary by a factor of as much as 10. Of these factors, protection appears to be the most important. On private lands it is usually moderate to good, but on public lands lack of protection is often a major weakness. Improvements (as suggested in later sections) are feasible but, to be realistic, the best producitivity and sustainability would be on private farms.

4. Wood from Farm Forestry

The salient features of the farm forestry programme in the period 1976-88 were:

— More trees were planted in commercialised and surplus-producing agrarian regions than in subsistence-oriented eastern States, despite the fact that rainfall and soil conditions were more favourable to trees in the east rather than in the low rainfall (but irrigated) north-west India.

— Eucalyptus was the most favoured tree with farmers as it grew straight, had a small crown, which allowed more trees to be planted per unit of area, and caused little shading when planted on field boundaries. It did not attract birds, was non-browsable, hence easy to protect, and yielded straight poles which were perceived to have a good market. Eucalyptus accounted for 71.6 per cent of all seedlings distributed under farm forestry.

— Eucalyptus was planted more for sale as small timber, poles or pulpwood, than for use as fuelwood, although because of glut conditions it was often sold as fuel to brick kilns and fuelwood depots.

And finally, farmers' enthusiasm to plant eucalyptus declined after 1988, as the tree failed to generate the kind of returns farmers were expecting from its sale. The disenchantment with eucalyptus was because of the poor quality of the produce which was good only for fuelwood, lack of sufficient demand for poles and, therefore, steep decline in prices, trees causing loss of agricultural production, and problems in marketing of trees. Even when the eucalyptus trees gained girth, timber from them was found to be far inferior in quality and durability to other timbers, and hence fetched a lower price. Ultimately, much of eucalyptus wood is now being sold as fuelwood at less than the expected price. Farmers' produce as fuelwood competes with wood supplies from government, and with coal and petroleum products. These commodities have administered prices. In relation to fuelwood, the price of kerosene declined by 17 per cent, and of LPG gas by 100 per cent during 1970-84 in India. It also competes with supplies of fuelwood brought to the market by the gatherers from public lands. In forest areas, fuelwood is sold from forest depots at subsidised rates and i.e. because of this fuelwood prices have remained low after 1985. Thus farmers could not get the expected price for their output, and further planting of the eucalyptus declined after 1988.

Subsidies exist not only for pulpwood supply to industries, but also for supply of fuelwood from government forests, and this reduces the incentive for farmers to produce fuelwood. For instance, fuelwood markets and marketing in Orissa are quite complex. A three-tier price system exists—heavily subsidised price applicable to rural people for their own use, administered price paid and charged by the Orissa Forest Corporation, and free market price. The situation is complicated further by a multiple supply system: headloaders, merchants, contractors and the Corporation.

One effect of the subsidised prices is to create a very-low-cost source of supply of wood available for use as fuelwood; priced at well below the cost of replacement of growing stock through investment in plantations. As long as this source is available, growers are unlikely to be able to sell their trees to middlemen as fuelwood at a price that would be commen-surate with the costs they have incurred.

The low value of fuelwood also means that in most situations it is likely to be a less profitable crop for farmers than the growing of trees for sale of poles, construction timber and fruit. Moreover, farmers are least concerned with the national objective of supplying fuelwood to the poor. Instead, they would like to maximise returns on their labour and land and, therefore, will like to produce higher-value-tree products for sale, and continue gathering low-value fuelwood from public lands.

5. Farm Trees in Backward Regions

As compared to agriculturally prosperous regions where farm forestry succeeded, the agrarian structure of the eastern and tribal India is characterised by heavy dependence on grain production, smaller holdings, low overall incomes, a less marketed surplus, imperfect credit markets, more dependence on the village merchant for marketing the small surplus, inter-locked credit and output markets, less monetisation, less diversity of rural incomes, greater debt bondage, a less developed infrastructure for the supply of agricultural inputs, greater insecurity of land tenure, and on the whole, poor human capital as far as enterprise is concerned. These conditions can at best promote low-intensity tree-growing strategies for home consumption, and are not conducive to market-oriented high-intensity tree planting.

Subsistence regions do not accept cash crops easily, and when these are introduced indiscriminately, poor farmers may be harmed rather than helped. For instance, in Rajasthan, where there is no paper mill or other large buyer of eucalyptus, and poles are generally imported from Haryana, small farmers found that there were no buyers for eucalyptus trees, and hence they suffered losses from planting eucalyptus, whereas the large farmers with 10,000 or more trees to sell had to locate buyers in other States through newspaper advertisements. Cases of distress sales by the poor peasants to contractors at throwaway prices a few years before the crop matures are reported from other States too. In West Bengal the poor farmers sold their trees to a village school teacher at about 30 to 50 per cent of the price which the school teacher obtained. A case study of district Midnapur, West Bengal, described how two middlemen of the village cheated the tree growers and offered them very low prices. Even the supply of farm inputs, irrigation water, crop loan and other services by the Village Council were given to those who sold their trees to these two middlemen. It may be speculated that such cases would be more common in regions where credit and output markets are inter-locked.

Tree-growing has been constrained in the monocropped millet-growing peninsular India by a number of factors. First, much of the peninsular India is semi-arid, characterised by intense competition for moisture between crops and trees. Unlike *khejri* (*Prosopis cineraria*) in Rajasthan's arid zone, suitable species which may have strong complementary effects between crops and trees are still to be identified for the region. Second, young trees require protection from cattle, especially in the fallow season, when the village livestock is let loose to browse agricultural residues and stubble. During these months in a monocropped village cattle is generally not accompanied by a herder. Semi-arid areas have villages spread over a large area in which individual fields may be far away from village huts, making protection further problematic.

On the other hand, in irrigated villages a tradition is slowly emerging of herding cattle during the cropping seasons. Despite ecological necessity and the easy availability of marginal and degraded lands, protection of young seedlings is difficult in monocropped villages compared with irrigated villages. Thus, unlike annual crops in which crop decisions are autonomous of similar decisions by other families, a farmer's decision to plant trees has to take into account herding practices of the village, availability of irrigation for double cropping, distance of the fields from his hut, and the cropping pattern of other farmers. Conditions prevailing outside the farm become as important as simple costs and benefits from the preferred landuse options.

Third, most of India's forests are located in areas of backward agriculture. Villages in this region of low productivity often have vast, though degraded, open-access lands. Unlike annual crops which are grown on private lands, trees also occur on forest and other public lands. Open access to public lands may vastly reduce the cost of obtaining tree goods for a gatherer, which may work to the disadvantage of a grower. Thus, the concept of trees as a free good to be obtained from public lands inhibits investment of personal labour, land and capital in tree planting. Proximity to forest lands affects private tree growing in other ways too. State often restricts farmers' right to freely harvest the trees on private land in the interest of either conservation or of checking theft from forest lands. These create rigidities in the free flow of products, and increase differences in the prices obtained by different farmers for a similar product. This, combined with differences in yield from farm to farm, may make planning of likely incomes from trees extremely difficult for a farmer.

Lastly, if similar products are raised on forest lands, which are marketed through the State machinery, farmers may find it difficult to compete with the State and get a remunerative price, particularly because the traders may be less interested in buying from dispersed producers, and may prefer to deal with the centralised bureaucracy. Evaluation of the Orissa Social Forestry Project noted that raising of eucalyptus on forest lands by the Forest Department was one of the reasons why farmers did not feel attracted to grow commercial trees on their plots.

The above factors have limited the spread of market-oriented farm forestry to the subsistence regions. A different approach—as suggested below—is required, which would be in harmony with the ecological characteristics of these regions.

6. Suggested Interventions on Farm Lands

6.a. Commercial Regions

The agrarian conditions which prompted farmers to plant eucalyptus in the first place (such as labour shortage, absentee landlordism, etc.) are still present. Farmers are keen to experiment and many have shifted to *poplar* in the north-west, teak and *jatropha* in the west and horticulture elsewhere. Some 18,000 farmers in the north-west India have planted 18 million poplar trees and are supplying raw material to 200-odd plywood industries in the region. This shows that there is plenty of unrealised potential for farm trees.

In regions facing a glut of eucalyptus wood it is possible to provide succour to the farmers to some extent by removing market constraints. First, a great source of market imperfections in wood markets is the legal and procedural framework which makes cutting and selling privately-owned trees difficult, irksome and complicated, besides being unremu-nerative. A study by the Indian Institute of Management, Ahmedabad (IIM, 1993) of charcoal makers in Gujarat showed that a simple operation of converting prosopis into charcoal, which can give employment to thousands of people, requires several permissions. Harvesting, conversion and transportation are all subjected to departmental controls involving cumbersome and time-consuming procedures. Therefore these restrictive laws could be abolished. Second, the government could stop subsidies on government supply of wood to industries, thereby forcing industry to buy from the farmers at a remunerative price. Third, it could also initiate schemes for linking farmers with industries, in ways similar to the linking of poplar-growing farmers with a Swedish match factory in north India. Fourth, improvement in extension could result in production of thicker logs suitable for sawing. Fifth, new uses of wood could be promoted such as utilising wood for power generation through gasifiers. Sixth and last, research is needed to identify other short-rotation, high-value species besides eucalyptus which suit farmers' requirements of planting on marginal lands and bunds.

While planning for wood production on farms in commercial regions, one must keep in mind the likely requirement of marketed wood. A World Bank report (World Bank 1993), quoting FAO figures, states that the total extraction of wood in India in 1988 was 264 million cum, of which 240 million cum was consumed as fuelwood. Thus, of the total wood consumption in the country, only 10 per cent is industrial wood. Most fuelwood is collected for both consumption and sale. The gatherers can always beat the producers over the pricing of fuelwood; the producers would be price-takers, rather than price-makers. This means that the market price of fuelwood would always be lower than its social cost for replacement of growing stock through investments in plantations. Therefore the market price of fuelwood does not make its production on farms an attractive financial proposition in countries with large open-access lands and widespread poverty. Further, the entire arable land in the green revolution areas is devoted to high-cost commercial farming. Thus the opportunity cost of diverting land to tree crops is very high, which is not likely to be compensated by returns from growing fuelwood. If farmers are to grow pulpwood and industrial wood on their farms, which fetch better prices, these species should not be grown on forest lands, otherwise a glut situation cannot be avoided. Thus we recommend that subsistence and consumption should be met from forest and common lands, and the market demand by and large from private lands.

Therefore it appears that the measures suggested in this section, though important in themselves, may not help revive the interest of farmers in trees in commercial regions to the same extent as existed during the first phase of the programme. As such, if farmers took to tree planting on a large scale, problems of a glut in the market might arise again. And this fear has greatly reduced the popularity of growing eucalyptus as a cash crop. One could also argue that the State should not encourage diversion of area from annual crops to perennial crops, which demand less labour. The main compulsion of farmers in these areas, which pushed them away from agriculture, was the desire to minimise labour and supervision costs. Therefore, although landuse in India will continue to be decided by the farmers, nothing should be done by the State which increases rural unemployment. There are better social returns in promoting agroforestry models in the rainfed or semi-arid regions, which contain most of India's wastelands.

6.b. Subsistence Regions

For promoting indigenous agro-forestry models in rice and millet-growing regions a great deal of research needs to be done to identify species which complement agricultural production, as farmers' primary landuse continues to be crop production. Thus the objective should change from "how can farmers be persuaded to grow trees" to "in what manner technology can help in increasing overall production from marginal lands by meeting farmers' priorities?" Ultimately the programme must improve the productivity of degraded private lands, if it is to be sustained over a long period. There are some known indigenous practices, which use trees to improve land productivity. Similar practices have to be introduced extensively in these regions. For instance, the most commonly noticed tree in the arid districts of western Rajasthan is *Prosopis cineraria*, which is a multi-purpose tree, providing fodder, mulch and even food (its leaves are eaten). Every part of this tree is used by farmers. It is planted on both field boundaries and in the fields themselves. And apart from improving soil fertility, it also binds the soil, decreases the velocity of hot summer winds, and provides shade to livestock and birds in the summer months.

In Thanjavur and Tiruchirapalli districts of Tamil Nadu, *Acacia nilotica* tree is cultivated on the rice bunds. It grows rapidly, as it is water tolerant, and benefits from fertiliser and irrigation applied to the field crops. In the summer months farmers pay a nominal sum to herd owners to pen their animals in their fields. The goats relish the tender shoots of *Acacia nilotica* and crop stubbles. In return, the farmer's fields are manured by the animals. Thus the traditional system involves sufficient ecological and economic interaction between the tree, crop and animal components.

It is difficult to rehabilitate degraded lands without introducing moisture conservation and water harvesting measures. These measures are needed for all rainfed areas put to biomass production. The soil conservation technology in India has so far focussed primarily on structural works for controlling and disposing of run-off rather than capturing the maximum amount of moisture in the soil and retaining it for as long as possible to support crop growth. It has been found to be better to adopt *in situ* moisture conservation practices through planting of suitable grasses and trees which may also provide sufficient protection against erosion.

Equally important are institutional constraints in watershed management programmes. Studies of similar other programmes show that planning, organisation and management have been issues of major concern in all projects. In particular, the impact of watershed treatments has been impaired by poor coordination between line agencies, and there has been a marked absence of land user participation in treatment planning and implementation.

Unfortunately, watershed approach and agroforestry research for different agro-ecological regions has so far remained a neglected discipline. Due to a tradition of competition for land between the Agriculture and Forest Departments, both have viewed agroforestry with suspicion. The Forest Department has even gone to the extent of banning agroforestry on forest lands by law!

Growing trees on private wastelands (as opposed to good quality land, which can support more labour-intensive annual crops) is both socially and economically a desirable activity. This could substantially enhance the incomes of farmers, in addition to producing the much needed biomass and giving a cover to barren lands. Therefore the emphasis should change from production of wood on good quality lands to rehabilitation of degraded lands. This would require a great thrust in research, as species complementary to crop production for each eco-region are yet to be discovered. Commercial production of wood will perhaps continue on the lands of absentee and large farmers in the green revolution areas to meet the industrial demand, which forms only a small proportion of the total wood consumption in the country. But the attention of the government and donor agencies should shift now to wasteland development and complementary agroforestry in millet and paddy-growing rainfed regions of India.

7. Village Commons and Revenue Lands

Village commons, roadsides, tank foreshores, and other such open-access lands have been the traditional sources of fuelwood for the rural people. But due to lack of management and interest from all concerned these are today in a deteriorated condition. Often these degraded lands offer only woody shrubs and weeds, such as prosopis (*Prosopis juliflora*) and lantana (*Lantana camara*).

These are not favoured species, because of the presence of thorns in the case of prosopis and low calorific value in the case of lantana. Yet the absence of commercial interest in these species helps the poor in their access to such shrubs.

Fuelwood plantations on village and farm lands were undertaken as a result of the recommendations of the National Commission on Agriculture (NCA) 1976. On the whole social forestry did succeed in increasing the availability of wood, albeit for a short period. This temporary success was due to the popularity of farm forestry in commercial regions during the early period of the programme. Sustainability of tree planting on village lands after the first harvest, with some exceptions, remained doubtful. Briefly the shortcomings in the programme were:

— Local people were not involved leading to high mortality.
— There was no continuity in the management and control of thousands of scattered pieces of planted village lands creating enormous problems of protection.
— Village Panchayats perceived the woodlots as sources of communal income, rather than as sources of fuelwood to meet village needs. The nature of species was also such that if tempted the Panchayats to sell them in the markets, rather than distribute in the village.
— Panchayats are political organisations and could not enforce the discipline required for managing plantations. Continued involvement of the Forest Department in the initial years discourages local bodies from taking over; and encourages them to opt for extending Forest Department management. Besides, control carries with it financial responsibilities which Panchayats have difficulty in meeting—as a minimum hiring watchers to protect the woodlot.
— Projects were designed around the ultimate felling of the planted trees, and degradation often set in after the trees were harvested.
— The targeted area under village lands could not be made available for afforestation because of encroachment, competition from other departments, land being too degraded, competition from grazing and other existing local uses and poor productivity.
— Projects failed to define, establish and publicise the rights to the trees and the procedures for marketing and allocating benefits. The shares which would go to the individuals, village, Panchayat and the Forest Department were not clearly laid down. Insecurity about benefits led to indifference on behalf of the people.

Besides, the poor do not budget for fuel for cooking. As they need regular supplies of small quantities, sources which produce only at the infrequent intervals provided by the harvesting of woodlots are likely to be of only limited value to subsistence users. In general, the woodlot planting, therefore, created a resource which was unlikely to make a significant contribution towards meeting local needs of the poor.

8. Suggested Interventions on Revenue and Village Lands

The present practice of "taking over" common lands by the Forest Department should be stopped, or drastically reduced to experimental projects. Funds for afforestation should either be transferred to the village community or to the Panchayat. If village organisations are able to control and spend funds right from the beginning of community forestry projects, they would take an active part in decision-making and management, and there would be better chances of the resource being sustained over a long period. The role of the Forest Department would then have been mainly extension and technical support.

Where Panchayats represent several villages, single-village organisations, as sub-units of Panchayats, should be created, if the land in question is appurtenant to one village only. If many villages are sharing a resource, conflict management may be difficult.

Model afforestation schemes should be prepared for implementation by the Panchayats. These should be widely circulated, and the panchayats should be encouraged to apply for funds for their subunits. Such Panchayats as are capable of looking after plantations should be given funds in the first instance. Their example and good work should then be publicised so as to encourage many others to take advantage of the schemes.

Generally only a small area is available in a village. The entire area of the village is then taken up by the Forest Department for afforestation in a single year, because of administrative convenience, rather than afforest only a small part of many villages. This has then caused hardship to those whose livestock depended on the commons for grazing. If afforestation is left to the Panchayat, it would take up only a small proportion of the total available area, and thus plenty of area would be left to be used by the poor for grazing.

People's wishes should be the guiding principle in species selection. There is a good case for non-rotational "low" market value trees and shrubs in community plantations, so as to reduce problems in protection and later in distribution. This is in sharp contrast to individual-oriented schemes on private lands where one should give priority to multiple use and income-oriented trees. This distinction needs to be kept in mind while planning location, species-mix and ownership of nurseries.

In ex-ryotwari States, transfer of revenue lands to Panchayats has still not been done, which makes it problematic to the Village Panchayats to 'own up' efforts on such lands.

Lastly, most degraded land is in States where water is a scarce resource, and, therefore, only strategies based on watershed approach are likely to succeed. These have their own problems, of lack of coordination, and lack of adequate interest from senior officers of State Governments. Most watershed funds from the Government of India are treated as a "milking cow" by the field machinery.

9. Fuelwood from Forest Lands

As Table 17.1 shows, India has 36 mha of degraded forest lands. Hence the main responsibility of meeting fuelwood needs has to come from forest lands. There is plenty of sunshine, and adequate rainfall in most parts of the country, due to which trees can grow fairly fast. There are also sufficient funds for the forestry sector, at least since 1988, thanks to assistance from multilateral and bilateral donor agencies. And notwith-standing failures, funding for this sector has continued on a liberal scale.

Fund availability for forest lands had become quite precarious during the Social Forestry phase. As State funds got locked to meet the matching contributions required for external assistance for projects on non-forest lands, forest lands were starved of funds, with several adverse effects. The neglect of forest lands hurt forest dwellers and tribals, and they had to travel even greater distances to collect fuelwood. This reduced timber supplies to the markets, resulting in price escalation, which further increased smuggling from forest lands. Price increases for both timber and fuelwood have been highest during the period 1975-85, as compared to either before 1975 or after 1985.

The favourable biological potential and availability of financial support are buttressed by a change after 1988 in the policy framework governing the management of forest lands, which is more conducive to sustained development of fuelwood resources than the previous policies. According to the new Policy, the requirements of fuelwood, fodder and small timber of the tribals and other villagers living in and near the forest are now to be treated as the first charge on forest produce. Equity and environmental considerations will be given more importance than mere earning of revenues.

Therefore social forestry concepts should be extended to reserved and protected forest lands by changing the nature of species from teak, eucalyptus and pine to usufruct and fuelwood-based trees. These should be supplemented with shrubs and bushes to yield fuelwood and fodder in the shortest possible time. This would strengthen access of the poor and women to forests specially if species suitable for individual gathering by households are also planted, and benefits would be directly appropriated by the poor.

An area of confusion as regards forest lands has been as to what constitutes fuelwood species. There are two divergent perspectives. According to foresters, fuelwood is obtained by felling trees having a high calorific value, or as a by-product from lops and tops of timber trees. Casuarina and eucalyptus, therefore, seem perfectly justified on public lands. But the poor obtain fuelwood from twigs and branches of living trees, and not by felling trees, and often get little from the felling of so-called fuelwood trees. Casuarina and eucalyptus may be justified on farm lands, if they improve farm incomes on a sustainable basis. But these hardly serve the poor, when raised on public lands.

A further advantage of planting "trees of the poor" (which are essentially employment augmenting trees, as they require labour for gathering and collection, as opposed to trees which are clear-felled) on forest and village lands is the likelihood of improved cooperation. People are reluctant to protect trees which are to be auctioned or felled, to the benefit of the government, contractors and forest staff. They are much more likely to collaborate in protection of trees from which they, much more than others, are in a position to benefit. Protection by the people and greening of degraded forests through regeneration (as opposed to artificial planting) would reduce the overall cost of afforestation, so that more degraded area could be taken up for fuelwood production.

Another way of looking at this issue of afforestation on forest lands is to opt for species which have high proportions of branches and twigs relative to stem wood. Given the inefficiency of administration and "soft" character of the political system, one could generalise that of a tree the stem goes to the rich and the towns, and only the branches and twigs go to the poor.

While barren forests with little root stock may be afforested with usufruct-based species, degraded forests with some root stock are best brought to vegetation with natural regeneration. This requires working with the people through participatory methods. Natural regeneration is less costly, and is more amenable to Joint Forest Management (JFM) techniques, as people can contribute their labour to protection, but have little capital for afforestation. Though the regenerating species, such as sal and teak, may not be short gestation fuelwood species, even these species with appropriate changes in silviculture can contribute to the people's livelihood through NTFPs, and other forms of gatherable biomass. Here again fuelwood may be at best a byproduct of forest protection, which may give other benefits to the people by way of stabilisation of water regime, NTFPs and grasses. However, JFM has itself run into problems in many States because of lack of institutional support from government and lack of enthusiasm on the part of field staff. These problems require a separate paper and are not being discussed here.

10. Summing Up

Up to the beginning of the 1970's, India's forest policy did not give adequate importance to fuelwood supplies. How does then one explain the "discovery" of a fuelwood crisis by the policy makers in the mid-1970s? There could be two explanations: one, the oil crisis of the early 1970s led the developing countries to a general re-assessment of their energy options in favour of bio-fuels. Second, deforestation, land degradation and other ecological consequences were linked in the minds of policy makers with an insatiable demand for fuel gathering by the rural people. This put increased pressure on the reserved forests, and hence, in order to reduce this pressure, fuelwood production had to be increased. It was also assumed that planting of trees through the social forestry programmes on non-forest lands was the most appropriate response to deal with fuelwood shortage.

Over the past decade, understanding of the ways in which rural people use trees and forests has improved considerably. For instance, urban and rural fuelwood problems are completely distinct, and require different solutions. The urban demand is best met by freeing markets from bureaucratic distortions and let the producers find fuelwood prices attractive enough to invest their labour and land in its production. The rural poor, on the other hand, would like better opportunities for gathering of twigs and branches, not because they burn it all, but because these get sold and bring the much-needed cash to the family.

Although social forestry projects were designed to produce fuelwood, in actual practice market-oriented trees were planted which did nothing to improve the consumption of fuelwood by the rural poor. The main product of community and farm forestry was eucalyptus poles, which could never reach the rural poor. Then, half of social forestry has been on private lands. As fuelwood was not seen as income generating, farmers preferred income giving trees, and continued to collect twigs and branches from public lands as before because farmers are least interested in using their scarce resources of land and capital to generate a low-value product they could collect. And it was unfair to load social concerns on farmers if they saw no economic returns.

As regards forest lands, the field staff have not yet accepted the fact that these lands are meant, according to the current Forest Policy, for meeting subsistence needs of the poor. Their mindset is still influenced by the social forestry philosophy—give fuelwood to the people from other sources so that the pressure on forests is reduced.

What policy prescriptions follow from the above analysis? First, a distinction must be made between fuelwood from logs and fuelwood from twigs and branches. The former, even if produced on public lands, is out of the reach of the rural poor, as it gets marketed, and at best helps the urban poor. The rural poor have access to only twigs and branches, which require the labour-intensive process of collection and do not attract the contractor's greed. Second, such material is best made available to the poor through shrubs and bushes, and not from large trees whose value lies in their stem. Third, as fuelwood shortages are not high on the priority list of the forest dwellers, the objective of degraded forests should be not only to produce twigs and branches, but also to generate self-employment for the poor through the gathering of consumption goods like minor forest products, wild fruits and mulch. Fourth, the concept of social forestry must be extended to reserve forest lands, where usufruct-based trees would be planted along with short gestation grasses, shrubs and bushes. Fifth, barren wastelands should be utilised for fuelwood plantations of suitable species, such as prosopis, so as to increase the availability of fuelwood in the shortest possible time and with little investment. Sixth, farm forestry should be geared to meet the farmers' priorities, rather than national priorities. And last, for both degraded private lands and forest lands, fuelwood production cannot be the primary objective of management. Reclamation of revenue lands is beset with many other problems, and in any case, except in isolated cases, such lands are best brought to vegetation through a watershed approach, which may involve all the three categories of land. On the whole there is no escape from making land regeneration the primary objective of government policy, rather than production of fuelwood.

One of the banes of planning in India has been that at a particular time there is one fashionable idea and it is sought to be imposed over the entire State/country ignoring agro-ecological diversities and location and ownership specificity. Thus the earliest forestry projects emphasised fuelwood and fodder, and it was believed that these were the real priorities of the rural poor everywhere, although later research showed that the problem was more complex, and required varied approach. Some years later farm forestry became a name of the game, and every district was given ambitious targets in seedling distribution, ignoring the constraints imposed by the specificity of farming systems. This resulted in reporting of bogus figures to show unrealisable targets. Now JFM rules the roost. Perhaps, after five years, it would be realised that structural conditions do not suit the JFM approach everywhere in the country, unless radical changes are introduced in several policies. The disadvantages of this kind of uniformity in policy prescription are many and wellknown. Even today there would be areas where social forestry concept is relevant or where the cheapest way of producing wood would be via the farm forestry. However, these programmes get a low priority by way of international funding when compared to JFM for which high targets are set in all the villages ignoring both the capacity of the Forest Department to build up and respond to local institutions, and the need to simultaneously introduce several reforms in rights and privileges over forests, policies and laws pertaining to NTFPs, Working Plans, silvi-cultural arrangements, etc., so essential for the success of the JFM approach.

Indifference to introducing such reforms could be because of many reasons. Firstly, State Governments treat JFM as another programme, which they think can be implemented without making any changes in other sectoral programmes. JFM, however, requires a paradigm shift and will be successful only when radical changes are introduced. Secondly, field officials are willing to entrust protection to the communities, but hesitate to involve themselves in the management and control of government forests. Unless serious efforts are made to trust the communities with control functions, people's efforts to protect may not be sustained for long. Thirdly, government resolutions tend to overprescribe what communities may or may not do, leaving little flexibility for them to adjust to the local situations. Fourthly, the main support to JFM has so far come from the environmentalists, academicians, NGOs, and external agencies in India. While their support is crucial in documenting the dynamics of community behaviour in different ecological conditions and throwing up of policy issues, the hold of this class of people on the instruments of policy formulation is rather weak. In addition to the forest bureaucracy which is often hostile to the idea of empowering the people, politicians too have not put JFM high on their agenda. They see greater political advantage in espousing schemes which bring individual benefits.

Despite these serious constraints, the success of JFM would have been more widespread if the scheme was linked with other afforestation programmes, on farm lands, village lands, and forest lands. Failure to take an integrated view of land management may perhaps be the biggest stumbling block to increasing land productivity.

REFERENCES

Chambers, Robert, N. C. Saxena and Tushaar Shah. 1989. *To the Hands of the Poor: Water and Trees*, New Delhi: Oxford and IBH and Intermediate Technology, London.

IIM. 1993. *Charcoal Production from Prosopis*. Ahmedabad: Indian Institute of Management.

Saxena, N.C. 1997. *The Woodfuel Scenario and Policy Issues in India*, Bangkok: FAO.

World Bank. 1993. *India: Policies and Issues in Forest Sector Development*, Report No. 10965, Washington.

18 Common Pool Degraded Lands: Technological and Institutional Options

P.S. Pathak

Land degradation is a growing problem. It is a direct consequence of the ever-increasing population pressure (both human and livestock), and over-exploitation of the natural resources (deforestation, mismanaged irrigation, unwise landuse and land cover, intensive agriculture, etc.) in the absence of effective village institutions. In India, out of 328.7 million ha geographical area, about 200 million ha are degraded in one or the other form. While there is a growing effort to crop more area for increasing food production, vast tracts of highly productive land are rendered useless due to flooding and secondary salinization. At present, the country is self-sufficient in food production but there is a huge deficit in forage and firewood production. Agroforestry, being an age-old farming system, has been recognized as the potential technology to meet these challenges (Pathak and Dagar 1998b). Land degradation is a symptom and energy scarcity is the result of unwise landuse management of forests and agriculture for which agroforestry is considered to be an effective means to provide bioremediation along with promises for meeting the challenge. One could also consider agroforestry as a compromise to meet the economic requirements of food, wood and fodder production along with soil conservation/amelioration and an efficient nutrient use on the presently degraded lands before they reach the point of no return.

This chapter is an attempt to analyze the problems of common pool degraded lands in general and wasted lands in particular and to project the potentials of new agroforestry models in meeting the rural energy needs. In this chapter these rural energy needs incorporate the biomass requirements to meet the demand for forage and firewood that are in deficit supply. This chapter also suggests agroforestry models for degraded lands (common pool and other privately owned) and prepare a balance-sheet for meeting these challenges. Besides, the potential of agroforestry for bioremediation of the polluted and problem sites is also recognized to reclaim the area for productive use. This chapter further intends to provide connectivity to the presently disjointed issues of land degradation, agroforestry and rural energy needs, resource, practice and product. In other words, it tries to retrace the traditional pathways which assured conservation, production and sustainability and make full use of the modern technology to meet the increasing employment needs and environmental concerns under effective institutional arrangements for resource conservation, production and marketing.

1. Land Degradation and its Extent

The increasing human activities on the limited land resources accelerate erosion which rapidly depletes the productive capacity of soil causing eutrophication and pollution of natural waters (Lal, 1988). Abrol and Sehgal (1992) observed that the socioeconomic and ecological consequences of land degradation are far-reaching affecting over 50 per cent of the total geographical area of the country. Thus, land degradation reduces the overall capacity of resource potential.

It is estimated that more than 5,000 mt of top soil is being eroded every year of which about 1,600 mt (30 per cent of the total eroded area) is permanently lost to the sea in India (Dhruvnarayana and Ram Babu, 1983). In India 200 m ha of the 328 m ha geographical area are degraded in one or the other way and about 6,600 mt of soil is displaced and carried to the oceans annually (Sehgal *et al.* 1990 a).

Abrol and Sehgal (1992) opined that of the total 187.7 m ha area under wastelands, 15.1 m ha faces very high severity and 127 m ha, high severity indicating need for immediate steps to check further degradation. Out of this area, water erosion affects the largest proportion followed by salinization and terrain deformation (Table 18.1). It is noteworthy that ravines encroach 8,000 ha area of table lands annually. The annual soil loss is estimated at 16.4 t/ha along with 5.7-8.4 mt of nutrients. Problems of alkalinity and salinity are alarming and are on the rise. Besides these, about 50 m ha area is degraded due to mining activity. The extent of degraded forests in the country is itself more than 40 m ha of which most of the area is under dry deciduous forest type of vegetation with less than 10 per cent canopy cover.

2. Degraded Lands and their Ecoregional Perspectives

The main forces responsible for land degradation are the unwise use of land resources coupled with the human and animal population pressure where the interplay of aridity poses a great barrier to the recovery of the land. In the States with arid and semi-arid regions the maximum area under waste-lands

TABLE 18.1: **Land Degradation Problems in India**

	Particulars	Area in m ha (1984-85)
1.	Geographical area	328.7
2.	Area subject to water and wind erosion	162.4
3.	Total drought-prone area	260.00
4.	Special land degradation problems:	
	Waterlogged area	11.6
	Salt-affected soils	10.1
	Ravines	4.0
	Shifting cultivation	9.0
	Average annual area affected by shifting cultivation	1.00
	Riverine torrents	2.73
	Average annual encroachment of table lands by ravines	8,000 ha
	Total of special problem areas	29.22
5.	Total problem area	200
6.	Average annual soil loss per ha (ICAR)	16.4 t
7.	Average annual loss of plant nutrients	5.7-8.4 mt.

(after Pachuari and Sridharan 1998).

is in Rajasthan followed by Madhya Pradesh and Maharashtra where the animal population is also very high. Misra (1987) considers that the desertification of modern times as we see is not due to any climatic shift but is man-made. The grazing lands in almost all parts of the country have to support the animals beyond their carrying capacity. Repeated grazing/brousing by the animals hardly leaves any vegetational elements to survive unless specially protected. The repeated biomass removal exhausts the stored food of the root stock and gets decimated. Savannas thus pass through steppe into deserts.

The area of different types of non-forest wastelands in different States shows maximum area in the dry parts of the country. In the arid regions of Rajasthan and Haryana the maximum land degradation was due to wind erosion compared to water erosion. The States with more area under water erosion have the problems of saline-alkali lands (Bhumbla and Khare 1984).

3. Technological Options for Improvement of Degraded Lands

Improvement of degraded lands implies restoration or reclamation or rehabilitation (Pathak and Dagar 1998). All the efforts aim at upgrading the productive capacity of land with sufficient conservation value. Search for applicable technologies to provide a cover without much external energy input and use of perennial species in place of annuals is sought for. Most of the degraded lands in tropical zones are poor in their organic matter content and the major nutrients. Physical limitations are also present in many a cases. The IUCN guidelines for the restoration of degraded ecosystems define restoration as a process of bringing a degraded ecosystem or landscape back to some prescribed, productive condition—in short a process of revitalization (Lamb, 1988).

Redevelopment is a multicomponent process by which a degraded ecosystem is managed so that the process of degradation is halted to achieve sustainability and enhanced optimal use. Redevelopment can be achieved by change in substratum through amendments, treatments or assisting the process of natural regeneration or protecting it for ecological succession. But biomass addition, production and optimization are needed to speed up the process. Agroforestry is considered as the most applicable alternative to manage the degraded lands in a holistic perspective, since it is based on soil-plant-animal-man interaction and homeostasis.

4. Agroforestry

Agroforestry has attracted considerable attention during the past two decades. It is a collective term used for all the landuse systems and practices in which woody perennials are deliberately grown on the same land management unit as crops and/or animals, either in some form of spatial arrangement or in a time sequence and in which there is a significant interaction between the woody perennials and the crops or animals. In other words, it is a land management system that optimizes overall gains from a farming system through the integration of trees. It capitalizes on the complimentarity of the components in the system. Multiple cropping is a prerequisite where biological and economic interactions exist in a time sequence in an agroforestry system. Thus, agroforestry is a form of multiplc cropping which satisfies three basic conditions: (1) there exist at least two plant species that interact biologically, (2) at least one of the plant species is woody perennial and (3) at least one of the plant species is managed for forage (annual or perennial) crop production.

People's perceptions about agroforestry are varied based on their objectives and knowledge (Pathak and Dagar 1998a). Some such agroforestry options for degraded lands are presented in Table 18.2.

Agroforestry helps resource regeneration in terms of profile recharge, biomass optimization and effective land cover. It is an effective technology to treat the problems of soil fertility decline.

TABLE 18.2: **Agroforestry Systems for Degraded Lands**

Dry	Moist
1. Silvipastoral in place of natural savanna on degraded forest lands	1. Energy farms for high economic output of biomass to meet fodder and firewood needs
2. Horti-silvipastoral systems on marginal agricultural lands	2. Silvipastoral with species diversity and intensive management
3. Agri-silvicultural use of rainfed farming areas	3. Agri-silvicultural with perennial crop species
4. Multi-tree-stylo combinations to derive nursing effect from legume and short rotation tree species	4. Tree-crop mixture for higher biomass production and nutrient turnover
5. Farm boundary planting with crop lands to get improved microenvironment	5. Fruit trees on farm boundary mixed with fast-growing MPTS
6. MPTS mixtures around homestead for shade, fruit, feed, microenvironment	6. MPTS around homestead for fruits like *Artocarpus heterophyllus, Arecanut, Coconut* and others.
7. Suitable Species	
Acacia albida, A. farnesiana, A. tortilis, A. nilotica, Albizia amara, Azadirachta indica, Dalbergia sissoo, Hardwickia binata, Leucaena leucocephala, Melia azaderach, Pongamia pinnata, Prosopis cineraria, Prosopis juliflora	*Acacia auriculiformis, A. decurrens, A. mangium, A. nilotica, Albizia falcataria, A. lebbeck, A. procera, Areca catechu, Calliandra calothyrsus, Casuarina oligodon, Cocos nucifera, Gliricidia sepium, Gmelina arborea, Leucaena leucocephala, Melia azaderach, Morus alba, Populus deltoides, Sesbania spp.*

(modified from Singh *et al.*, 1994)

The prevalent agroforestry practices in different regions of the country indicate the larger area suitable for agro-silvopastoral landuse with occasional horti-pastoral and agri-horticultural systems. Silvipastoral and agrihorti-cultural systems have a high potential for resource generation for arid and semi arid regions. The problem soil regions need special emphasis of species and plantation technologies (Singh and Pathak 1998). Similarly, the humid and tropical regions have high potential for agri-silvicultural and block plantations activities. Coastal areas with the plantations of *Casuarina equisetifolia*, Cashew and *Acacia mangium* conserve the site along with its use for higher biomass production.

Nitrogen fixing species, such as *Acacia mangium, Erythrina poeppigiana, Alnus acuminata, Casuarina littoralis,* are commonly occurring on acid soils and have undergone selection for strains of *Rhizobium* (or *Brady rhizobium*) and *Frankia* that are effective under acidic conditions. Their effectiveness appears to be due to increased tolerance of Al, Mn imported by rhizosphere organisms or complexing agents, and the enhanced Ca, Mo and P nutrition created by mycorrhizae and increased nutrient availability in the rhizosphere.

4.a. Prominent Applicable Agroforestry Options/Models

Considering the potentials of agroforestry for reclamation and utilization of degraded lands applicable models need to be implemented. The process needs a strong base of manpower, money and the applicable technology. The basic need on these lands is arresting erosion and assisting conservation of moisture and nutrients. For this process, after applying the soil conservation practices, seeding of grasses and legumes and planting multipurpose trees is the only alternative. Such easy-to-establish and fast-growing species provide cover to the soil surface and their organic interactions improve the soil environment for sustaining higher production. Depending upon the land type, the techniques are termed as energy plantation, silvipastoral system, agrosilvopastoral system, agrisilvicultural system, hortipastoral system, agrihorticultural system, field boundary planting, homestead gardens, etc. which are all the components of agroforestry systems. These practices specific to each type of land have a high potential for reclamation and improved productivity. Major techniques and species for each type of land are as under:

4.a.1 Silvipastoral Systems on Dry Degraded Lands

The silvipastoral technique involves planting of multipurpose trees in the existing pastures/grazing lands or planting such multipurpose trees on wastelands or denuded lands followed by sowing/planting grasses, legumes or cereals in between the lines of trees. It could be achieved through new planting or regeneration of old stock through assistance and management for desired production. During the initial years of tree establishment and growth, varying from 3-5 years depending upon whether the species, the grasses and legumes are harvested as hay and afterwards the area is maintained either as seasonal hay plot followed by aftermath grazing by animals or grazing the animals as per the carrying capacity of the land in a rotational or deferred rotational grazing system. This technique looks very simple but the land area, soil type, topography, natural vegetation, local socioeconomic status of the population, animal pressure, rainfall, temperature and wind are some of the very important factors which ultimately determine its success.

On a sloppy and uneven topography the rainwater harvesting technique with a watershed management approach becomes the pre-requisite for providing the ideal soil moisture status to the soil and checking erosion and loss of nutrients. The small staggered contour bunds, trenches and intermittent pitting is essential to provide this effect and channelize the water on one side for slow disposal and storage. This is followed by digging 45 cm^3 pits at a spacing of 3 x 3 or 3 x 4 or 4 x 5 m. With the onset of the monsoon, the tree seedlings are planted in these pits after applying 100 g mixture of urea, single superphosphate and potash in a ratio of 1:4:1 with 10 g BHC around the seedling to protect it from termites. The space between these seedlings is sown with the seeds of adaptable grasses and legumes in alternate lines. The small seeds are either pelleted with soil and fertilizers mixture or is sown with a small dose of super phosphate and urea. The grass and legume lines are at a distance of 0.5 m. If grass seedlings/rootslips are available, their planting in line provides good establishment. This method becomes more successful when we can assure land preparation and some early weed control to save the grass seedlings from competition from the seasonal herbaceous vegetation.

Another technique involving surface seeding of legumes, viz. *Stylosanthes hamata* and *Macroptilium atropurpureum,* at a line spacing of 1 m, on the trench mounds, contours, around the pits and earth deposits of cattle-proof trenches helps early colonization, growth and formation of a compact mat which protects soil from erosion and provides a good association with native grasses suppressing most of the seasonal weeds. While sowing, the seeds are mixed with single super phosphate at the rate of 40 kg phosphorus/ha. This method has given better results on very poor undulating sites and even in ravinous areas.

In the first year a top dressing of 25-30 kg/ha of nitrogen during early August gives a boost to grass production. The grasses and legumes are harvested during November in the first year when the legumes have shed their seeds. In the subsequent years the harvesting could be done twice depending upon the area. The trees when they form a good canopy after 5-7 years are ready for lopping during the dry season to provide additional forage and also reduce canopy cover to provide optimum light for the grass growth. Choice of species of grasses, legumes and trees and their characteristics are discussed by Pathak and Roy (1994).

Forage Production: Depending upon the land capability, soil type and its fertility, forage production keeps rising from the first year and peaks in the second or third year. Production during the first year could vary from 0.5-2.5 t/ha depending upon the establishment. It has been observed with *Leucaena* and grasses like *Cenchrus citiaris* and *Chrysopogon fulvus* that the forage production of 7.87 and 7.38 t/ha could be easily harvested. In another study in the second year of establishment, 7.18 t/ha production of *Sehima nervosum* under *A. tortilis* was also observed. Further, Muthana and Shankarnarayan (1978) did not observe statistically significant differences between the production under the canopy of different trees. The maximum forage yield of 2.3 t/ha under *P. cineraria* was observed in the arid regions. Under ravine conditions a mixture of *C. ciliaris* and *D. annulatum* gave an yield of 2.5 t/ha (Prajapati 1979). On class

V and VI wastelands at Dehradun *C. fulvus* under *D. sissoo* yielded 10.55 t/ha. Thus, depending upon the soil moisture and nutrients the yield differences from 2 to 10 t/ha/yr could be obtained from the grasses.

Firewood: On most of the short rotation species on degraded lands at a cycle of 10 years one could expect from 4-6 t/ha/year firewood production at a tree density of 500 plants/ha. In many trees annual lopping at 6-7 years has been found to give 2.3-3.5 t/ha fodder and 4.5-6.5 t/ha firewood. Thus, combining the forage and top feed yield it could easily produce 5.3-9.5 t/ha forage and 5 t/ha firewood or 10-14.5 t/ha total biomass. This points to the possibility of producing 10/t/ha/year in a climatic and edaphic condition of a semi-arid region with <900 mm rainfall.

Grazing: It is possible to graze the stubble after grass harvest in the 4th year between December to June. It was found that the animals not only maintained their body weight but showed growth without any additional concentrate or salt. The growth and production of grasses during the next monsoon were found to be normal. The leaf litter of trees, legume component in the pasture and occasional tree leaf provided the balanced ration.

Seed Production: The production of grass, legume and tree seeds is a profitable enterprise, besides on slightly better sites in a rotation of 5-6 years at the time of system renovation a crop of pigeon pea or cowpea could be obtained. Even in the first year in between the lines of grasses the cowpea could be sown. Good production of these crops has been obtained in many situations (Deb Roy *et al.*, 1978, Muthana and Shankarnarayan 1978).

4.a.2 Hortipastoral System

Dryland fruit crops like *Zizyphus mauratiana*, custard apple, *Emblica officinalis* along with grasses and legumes when grown as hortipasture provide early income from fruits, firewood from prunings (Ber) and forage from grasses and legumes. These systems have been found to provide an annual forage yield of 4-6 t/ha besides the fruits. Legume association of *Stylosanthes hamata* provides a nursing effect and helps higher fruit production.

4.a.3 Agrihorticultural Systems on Marginal Croplands

Fruit trees when grown with crops in dry degraded croplands assure a favourable microclimate. In a study involving *Zizyphus mauratiana* with mung bean, the yield reduction in a subnormal rainfall year was 44.2 per cent and 23.4 per cent for grain and dry fodder in intercropping compared to 51.1 per cent and 42.7 per cent in sole crop situation respectively (Gupta and Sharma 1994).

The system inventory also showed that it could provide round-the-year supply of fodder for 5 goats/sheep and fuelwood for the family of four members besides an efficient nutrient cycling and increasing economic stability. In the normal year annual fuelwood yield was 1.26 t/ha with 4878 kcal/kg energy value.

4.a.4 Agrisilvicultural Systems on Marginal Croplands

Rainfed marginal croplands are often leased out to the landless or used carelessly resulting in poor yield and land degradation. Agrisilviculture provides most viable alternative assuring economic and environmental upliftments. In rainfed croplands species like *Acacia nilotica* and *Prosopis cineraria* grow naturally or they are maintained purposefully in the arid and semi-arid regions. Many species, viz *Azadirachta indica, Albizia lebbeck, Ailanthus excelsa,* are retained on the field bunds. Srivastava (1994) reported maximum biomass productivity by *A. nilotica* (2.7 t/ha/yr) compared to *Eucalyptus* hybrid (0.7 t/ha/yr) on vertisols at 520 mm rainfall. Compared to monocrops of rainfed grain crops, the agrisilviculture produced double per year in terms of fodder, grain, firewood, timber converted in sorghum grain equivalents. Maximum production was observed in the alley cropping system of *Leucaena* and Sorghum Sunflower being 3.1-2.3 t/ha sorghum grain equivalent. This practice also left the soil more fertile compared to grain cropping. Agrisilviculture also allowed more efficient moisture utilization. This practice bridges the gap in demand and supply of forage and firewood and reduces pressure on common lands.

4.a.5 Energy Farming

Biomass is the cheapest source of renewable energy which can be produced on degraded lands by plantation of choicest species of fast-growing multipurpose trees. Many species are acknowledged for higher productivity on degraded lands, viz *Leucaena leucocephala, Eucalyptus* hybrid, *Casuarina equisetifolia, Prosopis juliflora, Gliricidia sepium, Acacia auriculiformis, Calliandra calothyrsus,* etc. Peak productivity of 75t/ha/yr at a five year rotation has been recorded by Pathak *et al.* (1985) on the canal banks by *Leucaena leucocephala.* On dry degraded lands and roadsides it has given 24 t/ha/yr in a semi-arid condition. *Eucalyptus* hybrid production ranges from 3-7 cu m/ha/yr which has been raised up to 20 cu m /ha/yr by properly selected clones and has a potential to reach up to 30 cu m/ha/yr. Such high yields of monocrops at a shorter rotation can also exhaust the soil fertility for which proper strategy of legume intercropping or crop mixtures is essential.

4.b. Techniques and Choice of Species for Different Types of Degraded Lands

4.b.1 Waterlogged Areas

Mechanical : Creating drainage facilities, levelling, bunding and lining of canals for checking seepage.
Biological : Crops : High-yielding paddy followed by berseem or any other forage legume (in case of seasonally waterlogged areas). Area not to be left fallow for long.
Trees: Eucalyptus robusta, E. hybrid, Casuarina equisetifolia, Pterospermum acerifolium, Sesbania sesban, S. macrocarpa, S. aculeata, S. rostrata, Terminalia arjuna, Acacia nilotica etc.
Grasses: Brachiaria mutica, B. brazantha, Echinochloa colona, Iseilema laxum, etc.

Most of the salt-affected areas are also prone to waterlogging. In such a saline waterlogged soil, complex problems operate where management of water holds the key for their reclamation. Even the salt tolerant plants are badly damaged when waterlogging comes together. Halophytic species of grasses, shrubs and trees have the capacity to tolerate such situations. Many tree species have potentiality to work as biopumps to reclaim such sites and provide the wood and other products from these wasted lands.

Salinity and waterlogging are taken as a combined environmental feature where the number of days excessive water is available is combined with salinity. Kuligod *et al.* (1994) found that *A. nilotica* was better suited at >500 SEWN. They noted that *A. nilotica, Sesbania grandiflora* and *Dalbergia sissoo* had bio-ameliorative effects under saline conditions. It helped increase organic carbon and decrease salinity and exchangeable sodium percentage under tree cover in just two years.

Trees and grasses when used for bio-drainageability in the irrigation commands, control seepage. Species like *Acacia nilotica* and *Dalbergia sissoo* account for 86 per cent and 84 per cent interception in seepage respectively. Trees interplanted with napier grass were more efficient in intercepting seepage (Patil *et al.*, 1994).

4.b.2 Banjar and Fallow Lands

Mechanical : Proper levelling and drainage in watershed concept to ensure application of water and nutrients. Breaking hard pan of calcium carbonate nodules.
Amendments : As per the soil analysis reports applying gypsum/pyrite/lime/organic manure to balance the nutrients or some essential nutrients through

fertilizers.

Biological Crops : If cultivable, sowing *Sesbania aculeata* or *S. macrocarpa* or sun hemp for green manuring and after 45-60 days mixing with soil followed by flooding. This is to be followed by crops like berseem, barley and paddy/maize-pigeon pea rotations.

Trees : Acacia nilotica, Albizia lebbeck, A. amara, A. procera, Dalbergia sissoo, Leucaena leucocephala, Hardwickia binata, Melia azedarach, Azadirachta indica, Bamboo, etc.

Grasses and Legumes : Cenchrus ciliaris, C. setigerus, Chrysopogon fulvus, Sehima nervosum, Panicum maximum, Pennisetum pedicellatum, P. polystachyon, Stylosanthes hamata, S. guianensis, Macroptelium atropurpureum, etc.

4.b.3 Usar/Saline Sodic Lands

Mechanical : Scrapping surface salts, flushing with water to wash excess salts, impounding water to leach the injurious salts, trenching and flushing to remove surface salts, providing sub-surface drainage, pumping water to lower the water table, deep ploughing/breaking deep hard pan layer to remove hard pan.

Amendments : Chemicals like gypsum, pyrite, sulphur, organic materials like FYM, growing green manuring crops, adding crop residues, etc.

Biological : Crops : Paddy followed by berseem or barley and subsequently paddy-wheat rotation.

Trees: Acacia nilotica, A. tortilis, Prosopis juliflora, Casuarina equisetifolia, Azadirachta indica, Sesbania sesban, etc.

Grasses and Legumes: Brachiaria mutica, Bothriochloa intermedia, Panicum maximum, Dichanthium annulatum, Desmanthes virgatus, Stylosanthes hamata, etc.

4.b.4 Ravine Lands

Mechanical : Depending upon the suitability for a specific purpose, the shallow ravines could be bulldozed, levelled and bunded to grow crops while the medium and deep ravines should be given mild soil and water conservation treatment for covering it by trees, grasses and legumes. Proper grassed waterways and drainage is essential to stop further soil erosion.

Biological : Crops : Leguminous crops providing early cover like Cow pea, Field bean along with Sorghum and Pigeon pea should be grown to afford quick land cover. Depending upon the irrigation potential the crops like barley, wheat, oat or berseem could also be taken in winters.

Trees : Acacia nilotica, A. tortilis, A. farnesiana, Prosopis juliflora, Dichrostachys cinerea, Albizia lebbeck, etc.

Grasses and Legumes : Cenchrus ciliaris, C. setigerus, Dichanthium annulatum,

Bothriochloa intermedia, Stylosanthes hamata, Macroptilium atropurpureum, etc.

4.b.5 Mine Spoils

Mining is a major economic activity. In the process, soil debris and stones pile around causing environmental problems in many parts of the country. The exposed mine overburden is unfertile parent rock material. Different types of mining activities leave different problems of soil management, viz coal-mines, limestone mines, copper mines, etc. Mechanical and biological means are used simultaneously to attend to the problems of land degradation. Jha and Singh (1994) have remarked that the mine spoils are often a physically, nutritionally and microbiologically recalcitrant medium for plant growth. The spoiled physical structure of soil with reduced waterholding capacity, deficiency of organic matter, deficiency of major nutrients, preponderance of micro nutrients/toxic chemicals, acidity/alkalinity/sodicity restrict vegetation growth. Natural recovery is very slow and needs assistance for its speedy recovery. In the development of a degraded land, normally three approaches could be adopted, viz. natural (successional or ecological), assisted ecological and intensive management. The three approaches follow the external input and recovery time in an inverse proportion. A blend of the three in a watershed is more desirable to provide land cover based on its capability. In a case study of a coal mining area at Sigrauli, Jha and Singh (1991) have observed a positive correlation between root biomass and soil carbon biomass which increased with the age of spoil. With ageing the coarse fragments decreased, total soil nitrogen, mineral nitrogen, sodium bicarbonate, extractable phosphorus and potash increased but even after 20 years, they were found lower than the forest soils.

The recovery of soil nitrogen was 0.0012 per cent per year. The biomass carbon nitrogen and phosphorus are taken as indices of soil redevelopment and soil microbial biomass plays a key role in the establishment of nutrient cycling (Srivastava *et al.* 1989).

Grasses and legumes provide early colonization of the site. Species like *Stylosanthes hamata, Clitoria ternata, Macroptilium atropurpureum* produced poor root/shoot ratio but were desirable as colonizer and nitrogen fixer species. Grasses, viz. *Bothriochloa intermedia, B. pertusa, Cenchrus setigerus* and *Chrysopogon fulvus* were early to colonize with high production but poor root/shoot ratio.

4.b.6 Weed Infested Degraded Lands

In Asia, *Imperata* grasslands cover 35 m ha area (4 per cent of the total land area). Indonesia and India are the countries with the largest area of such grassland (8.5 and 8 m ha respectively).

Based on the present land cover, Sri Lanka tops with 23 per cent area followed by the Philippines (17 per cent) (Garrity *et al.* 1997). These grasslands result due to post-fallowing poor regeneration of natural forests or land abandonment after a few productive years of cropping under slash-and-burn agriculture. It has been concluded that integrated strategies are needed to manage *Imperata*, i.e. improving soil fertility, maximizing shade, judicious use of herbicides, etc. Agroforestry is considered as most viable alternative for successful conversion of *Imperata* lands since it results in reduced carbohydrate storage, reduced rhizome and tuber-bulb production, reduced shoot dry weight, increased susceptibility to competition and herbicides and decreased vigour/regeneration (Mac Dicken *et al.* 1997). Tree fallows with fast-growing species, viz. *Acacia mangium*, *A. auriculiformis*, *Sesbania sesban*, *Leucaena leucocephala*, *Crotolaria*, *Mucuna* and *Pueraria* have the potential to effectively cover and reclaim the area of this noxious weed. In a study comparing different woody and herbaceous plants, Akobundu (1995) has observed that after 52 weeks of planting, *Imperata* was completely eradicated under *Gliricidia sepium*, *Leucaena leucocephala* and *Chromolaena oderata*.

Tree establishment after an intensive mechanical site preparation and fertilization controlled *Imperata* by 98.8 per cent under *Gmelina arborea* compared to 47.05 per cent under *Paraserianthes falcataria*. It also reflects the role of relative shade cast since the *G. arborea* is a broad-leaved tree compared to *P. falcataria*, a leaflet tree.

4.b.7 Acid Soils

Around 100 m ha or more out of 329 m ha in India are considered to face the problem of soil acidity. An earlier estimate shows 48-49 m ha under acid soils out of which 25 m ha show pH below 5.5 while 23 m ha have pH between 5.6-6.5. Maximum area under acid soils is in Kerala, H.P., Assam and NEH Region and Orissa (78 per cent). About 20 m ha in Assam and NE States and 15.5 m ha in J&K are under acid soils followed by Orissa (12.5 m ha). Large areas of tropical lands are acidic and infertile as a result of natural or anthropogenic processes.

Generally trees are more tolerant to higher H+ concentration along with high levels of Al, Mn, and other material ions than the crop plants. Mostly trees are adapted to grow at low fertility levels. Their adaptation includes slow or moderate growth rate over a protracted growth season, ability to exploit large soil volume, a rhizosphere effect enhancing nutrient availability, external and internal nutrient cycling systems and high nutrient use efficiency. Plants have a mechanism to either avoid or tolerate the high soil acidity or may have both the strategies (Fisher and Juno 1994).

4.c. Soil Productivity

After six years of silvipasture establishment the nutrients like nitrogen, phosphorus, organic carbon and potash have been found to increase in time even when grasses were harvested and removed every year (Singh *et al.* 1977). Misra *et al.* (1982) have also observed an improvement in the soil physical properties, pH, nitrogen and organic carbon with four years of silvipasture plantation on a calcareous soil. Thus, the poor soils on the wastelands could restore their fertility under such systems. In another study it has been found that the initial organic matter, available nitrogen, phosphorus and field capacity of 0.32 per cent, 131 kg/ha, 6.2 kg/ha and 11 per cent were changed to 0.78 per cent, 267 kg/ha, 15.5 kg/ha and 15.5 per cent respectively over a period of 10 years. It has been observed that compared to pasture development, silvipastoral systems provided faster recoverey to the degraded soil.

4.d. Agroforestry—A Bioremediation Technique for Degraded and Polluted Habitats

Many trees used in tropical and sub-tropical agroforestry are leguminous and have rhizobial associations helping to fix nitrogen in variable amounts. In temperate zones actinorhizal trees perform the same function in association with *Frankia*. In function *Frankia-actinorhizal symbiosis* is similar to that of *rhizobium*-legume symbiosis.

Nitrogen fixation in trees needs formation of root nodules in association with symbiotic micro-organisms. The micro-organism responsible is *rhizobium* in Leguminosae and Ulmaceae and actinomycetes of genus *Frankia* in all other nodulating families (Brewbaker *et al.* 1990). These micro-organisms could be either slow-growing (Bradyrhizobium) or fast-growing (rhizobium) and have specificity with tree species (Danso *et al.* 1992).

Studies on strain specificity of tree species have shown some of the trees as highly specific while others are promiscuous. Sanginga *et al.* (1991) have found that in *Gliricidia sepium*, the same provenance showed variation in nitrogen fixation between 20-129 mg/plant at 14 weeks after planting due to inoculation with different strains of rhizobium.

Phosphorus is required for the energy transformation from host to the symbiont during nitrogen fixation. Thus, phosphorus-rich soils support higher nitrogen fixation. In such a situation mycorrhizal association with rhizobium is sought for to improve the supply of P in the systems. Nitrogen rich soils reduce the efficiency of symbiosis. This is because plants save their energy from nitrogen fixation efforts. Sanginga *et al.* (1988) have observed in *Leucaena leucocephala* that the nitrogen fixation was reduced by 50 per cent at 40 kg

N/ha in the soils. This raises a question about the temporal dimensions of symbiosis and nitrogen fixation in an ageing plantation or a forest where litter and live root dynamics continuously enriches the substratum.

4.e. Economics of Degraded Land Reclamation through Agroforestry

Degraded land reclamation involves investments in conservation of resources, treatment/amendment and production. Often large degraded areas have the problem of ownership. Investment decisions are difficult to make when they are common property resource and there is a lack of social institution. In such situations the joint resource management institution strategies like Joint Forest Management could succeed. The other problem is related to the financial investments for production and conservation-related programmes. In the case of degraded lands both of these are interrelated but if we aim at investments in soil and water conservation or drainage or tank maintenance, investors find it difficult to decide in view of the long-term payoffs and non-monetary returns on the investment (Kerr 1997). While privately owned resources when managed have prospects of improvement and appreciation, the common property resources are highly susceptible to degradation due to poor responsibility sharing. In such a situation, institutional arrangements to suit the local, regional problems and policies are called for to protect and improve the degraded resources. The production-related activities have a direct economic impact and can be analysed in monetary terms when the ownership is individual or societal compared to those functions of environmental conservation where the benefits are social and non-monetary and where any loss has been prevented. Price tagging of such natural resource inventories has a spatial and temporal dimension.

Considering even these, production from degraded lands has been subjected to financial analysis. Abrol and Joshi (1984) have reported a B/C ratio of 1.63 for *Acacia nilotica* plantation on saline sodic soils compared to 1.29 with crop cultivation.

In the case of arid zone afforestation Das *et al.* (1984) have reported a peak B/C ratio (4.42) of *Mateera* cultivation followed by silvipastoral farming with *Prosopis juliflora* (2.36) and *Albizia lebbeck* (2.19). In an earlier study on the tree vs. annual crop cultivation on arid lands, Gupta and Mohan (1982) have reported the merit of silvipastoral and hortipastoral systems indicating its high B/C ratio with a higher employment potential besides the environmental amelioration as a bonus.

In another study on the sub-Himalayan bouldary degraded lands Dhruvanarayana and Ram Babu (1984) have reported a peak B/C value of 3.43 under *Acacia catechu* plantation with Bhabar grass (Table 18.3). In the case of ravines they have observed that silvipasture or silviculture of fast-growing species was the best option with a peak B/C ratio of 1.90.

Dhruvanarayan and Ram Babu (1990) while comparing different landuses have observed that on good lands hortipastoral systems gave a peak B/C ratio of 3.21 while on highly degraded lands silvipastoral systems gave 1.79. Thus, a higher B/C ratio was the function of proper landuse on a specific habitat. In a highly degraded rocky gravelly or ravinous area in the central Indian semi-arid zone, silvipastoral, energy plantations and hortipastoral systems provided the most viable option of landuse and land cover. In several studies Pathak (1991), Pathak and Khan (1990, 1992), Pathak *et al.* (1995) have reported a very high B/C ratio and IRR on energy plantations and silvipastoral systems (Table 18.3). At a 12-year cycle, the B/C ratio of 1.45 and IRR of 21.95 per cent at 15 per cent discounting were found to make it a bankable project. Besides, the other benefits of environmental gains were a bonus.

TABLE 18.3: **Comparative Economics of Establishment of Silvipastoral Farms on Degraded Lands in Central India**

Project Time Years	B/C ratio	DF %	IRR %	Reference
10	2.56	11	—	Singh & Reddy (1986)
10	1.68	20	34.0	
10	1.21	20-30	21.21*	NWDB (1987)
10	1.05	20-30	12.67**	"
10	1.05	20-30	10.99***	"
10	1.16	20-30	17.64****	"
12	1.83	8	—	Pathak & Khan (1992)
12	1.71	10	18.16	"
12	1.60	12	19.89	"
12	1.45	15	21.95	"
12	1.32	18	24.12	"
12	1.25	20	25.63	"
12	0.97	30	29.06	"

* Plain to moderate areas, ** Hilly and undulation areas, *** Revenous areas and **** Desert areas.

The initial cost of wasteland reclamation is high but if phased-out agri-silviculture is adopted, returns are substantially higher after a four year period. Chemical alternatives are not very useful. Returns are higher if a part of land is kept for fuelwood production.

4.b.8 Environmental Issues: Carbon Sequestration

Biomass production increase through different innovations has the implication for the fixation of CO_2 from the atmosphere. Gupta and Rao (1994) have opined that a continuous increase in the CO_2 levels of the atmosphere leading to global warming has serious implications for agriculture and environment. The tropical soils are largely carbon depleted and have a high potential to act as a sink for this additional carbon. They state that the present stock of carbon in the Indian soils (24.3 Pg) can be increased to 34.9 Pg. Thus, there is a potential of 10.6 Pg for sequestering additional carbon. They advocate that grasses and trees planted on the degraded lands have a potential of sequestering 1.9 Pg in seven years as against emission of 2.27 Pg in the same period thus slowing down the warming. Thus, biomass production optimization through multispecies stands in agroforestry should be the priority for sustaining the system and continuously improving the environment.

5. Resource Needs from Degraded Lands

5.a. Fuelwood

Eckholm (1975) has stated that no less than one-and-a-half-billion people in the developing countries derive at least 90 per cent of their energy requirements from wood and charcoal. Another billion people meet atleast 50 per cent of their energy needs this way. Indeed, it has been estimated that at least half of the timber cut in the world still serves its original role for mankind: as fuel for cooking and heating.

Twentythree years have passed but the situation has not improved much. The efforts made for firewood production through the plantations raised under social forestry/farm forestry programmes have proved insufficient to ease the situation which gets complex due to deteriorating forest productivity and ever increasing human population. The statement made by Spears (1978) 20 years back that "by the turn of the century, at least a further 250 million people will be without wood fuel for their minimum cooking and heating needs and will be forced to burn dried animal dung and agricultural crop residues, thereby further decreasing food crop yields" has come true. Thus, deforestation through a chain reaction threatens productive agriculture. Now, on the degraded forests and wastelands, no more lopping and harvesting practices are followed but mining does take place.

The study group on fuelwood and fodder set up by the Planning Commission estimated the demand during 1991, 1996 and 2001 as 306, 343 and 384 mt respectively. In the rural and urban sectors per capita energy consumption has 68.5 and 45.5 per cent share of firewood (Table 18.4). The

Swaminathan Committee Report (1982) said that during 1975-76 the consumption of fuelwood, agricultural wastes and animal dung was 133, 41 and 73 mt respectively. The availability of fuelwood was only 49 mt leaving a gap of 84 mt between the demand and supply. Demand and supply of industrial and fuelwood in India shows progressive deficit which has become difficult to manage due to the decline in forest productivity and increasing land degradation (Table 18.5).

TABLE 18.4: **Sourcewise Energy Consumption (non-commercial) in the Household Sector**

Energy	Rural per capita energy consumption				Urban per capita energy consumption			
	% share of energy form	Source of supply of each form			% share of energy form	Source of supply of each form		
		Purchased	Collected	Home grown		Purchased	Collected	Home grown
Firewood	68.5	12.7	64.2	23.1	45.5	73.7	14.8	11.5
Animal dung	8.3	5.1	6.2	68.7	3.2	49.1	12.3	38.6
Others	3.4	8.9	61.0	30.1	1.5	71.2	28.8	0.0

Report of the working group on energy policy, Planning Commission, Govt. of India, New Delhi, 1979.

TABLE 18.5: **Demand and Supply of Industrial and Fuelwood in India**

Year	Industrial wood			Fuelwood		
	Estimated demand	Estimated total production	Deficit	Estimated demand	Estimated total production	Deficit
1966	12.5	8.5	4.6	136.6	93.8	42.8
1970	16.3	9.8	6.5	150.0	102.0	48.0
1975	21.2	12.3	8.9	167.0	115.3	51.7
1980	25.0	NA	—	184.0	NA	—
1989	32.6	NA	—	202.0	NA	—
2000	55.0	NA	—	225.0	NA	—

Natarajan, B. 1982: Renewable source of Energy, Instt. of Techno economic studies, Madras, p. 154.

Estimates of fuelwood supply and demand are problematic in terms of rural and urban ratios and also in their temporal dimension. Dwivedi (1994) has reported, assuming an average consumption of fuelwood as 400 kg/head/year, the total consumption to be 265 mt (1991) of which 39 mt was used in urban areas. Annual fuelwood production capacity was only 28 mt and the crop byproducts played an important role in relieving the pressure on public forests for fuelwood consumption (Mukherjee 1994).

Dubey and Agrawal (1997) have estimated the demand and supply position of fuelwood, timber and fodder for Madhya Pradesh for 1991 and reported a shortfall of 93, 69 and 16 per cent respectively. Forests continued to supply Nistar worth Rs. 240.6 million.

Recent studies show that about 85 per cent of the fuelwood consumption was in the rural areas and non-commercial fuels included fuelwood (billets and twigs), crop waste, animal dung, gobar gas and charcoal (NCAER 1985). Another major component of fuelwood is twigs (Table 18.6). In another study Ravindranath *et al.* (1997) have reported for a Karnataka village the domestic requirements including cooking, bathing and lighting of about 79 per cent of all the energy used in the village, virtually all of which comes from biomass sources, mainly firewood and some crop residues, 11 per cent energy goes for commercial purposes, viz. agricultural product processing and brick-making, and 10 per cent for agricultural operations where only commercial energy sources are used.

TABLE 18.6: **Patterns of Non-commercial Energy Use in Rural India**

Activities	Non-commercial energy source	Energy need k cal	Percentage of total energy used
Domestic (Cooking, Household work)	98% (Firewood, cowdung, agro. waste)	7.31×10^{14}	64.0
Agriculture	77% (Human energy, animal energy, cowdung manure)	2.52×10^{14}	22.0
Non-agricultural work (pottery, brick-making, metalwork, blacksmithy)	100 per cent (Firewood, charcoal, human energy)	0.76×10^{14}	7.0
Transportation	100 per cent (Human energy, animal energy, bicycle)	0.35×10^{14}	3.0

Revelle, R. 1976: *Science* 192: 969-74.

The Forest Survey of India estimates of consumption and recorded production of fuelwood show a wide gap (Table 18.7).

The annual availability of fuelwood from the forests in India is estimated at 26.29 m cu m (FSI). It is expected that of this production 20 per cent may not be available due to non-extraction from protected areas. So only 21.8 m cu m (18 mt) could be safely assumed as available from the forests annually. This assumption is based on the removal of annual increments (in reality much more than the annual increment is harvested annually). The present and

TABLE 18.7: **Estimated Firewood Consumption (m cu m) and Recorded Production in India**

Year	Consumption	Production
1953-54	83.3	6.49
1960-61	99.6	8.15
1965-66	109.3	9.16
1970-71	107.9	11.62
1975-76	133.1	19.00

Source: Forest Survey of India (1995).

projected firewood consumption in Indian households thus at 162 mt (1996) will rise to 180 mt and 199 mt in 2001 and 2006, respectively. Thus, the bulk of the supply has to come from non-forest-area plantations since the annual increment is only 18 mt or the overexploitation of the forests has to continue. The situation becomes still serious when the requirement of cottage industries (25), rituals (4.0) and hotels (10) is added up to make it 201 mt. In addition, there is the requirement of an additional 107 m cu m for small timber and implements. The availability of wastelands in the States when contrasted with the requirements of fuelwood indicates the required potential productivity (Table 18.8). It is observed that high production efficiency of 7.2 t/ha/yr is required in Tripura which is easily possible looking to its humid climate. States requiring 3-4.5 t/ha/yr are J&K and West Bengal and those requiring 2-3.5 t/ha/yr are Bihar, H.P., Kerala and U.P. All other States require very low potential. This situation shows a very optimistic sign for undertaking agroforestry on the degraded lands to meet the energy demands.

Due to its ease of production, renewable nature, well-understood use technology and easy availability, wood is considered the cheapest source of energy in the rural set-up. Trees, when managed well, provide energy to the rural households in the most inexpensive manner. Besides, trees are so important for environmental protection and other associated benefits. Thus, large-scale energy plantations have been taken up to meet the deficit of firewood supply. These plantations, besides providing firewood from their lops and tops which is taken as 30 per cent, are the major source for the supply of poles, small timber and pulp wood. Besides the use of wood as fuel in the rural households, massive programmes for the generation of electricity, use in boilers, metal smelters, klins, charcoal manufacture, pottery, etc., are underway in many countries. Species like *Leucaena leucocephala, Casuarina equisetifolia, Prosopis juliflora, Calliandra calothyrsus*, etc., have shot into prominence due to their potential for providing wood energy at the highest efficiency, shorter rotation and also their high adaptability to diverse habitats and climates.

TABLE 18.8: **Wastelands, Firewood Availability and Requirement**

State	Wastelands area Mha*	Annual Fuelwood Consumption Mt*	Availability from Forests Mt*	Balance Need Mt#	Production potential (t/ha)#
Andhra Pradesh	9.665	11.2	1.4232	9.7768	1.01
Arunachal Pradesh	1.195	0.4	3.6584	-3.2584	-2.73
Assam	1.963	4.7	1.4544	3.2456	1.65
Bihar	4.751	13.8	0.4112	13.3888	2.82
Goa	0.214		0	0	0.00
Gujarat	8.553	4.6	0.3504	4.2496	0.50
Haryana	1.443	0.8	0.0072	0.7928	0.55
Himachal Pradesh	1.206	3.1	0.3856	2.7144	2.25
Jammu and Kashmir	1.225	6.3	1.5368	4.7632	3.89
Karnataka	8.277	10.6	1.3376	9.2624	1.12
Kerala	1.228	4.1	0.476	3.624	2.95
Madhya Pradesh	12.715	23.3	3.3896	19.9104	1.57
Maharashtra	7.453	8.9	1.2024	7.6976	1.03
Manipur	1.326	2.1	0.4528	1.6472	1.24
Meghalaya	1.102	1.2	0.5168	0.6832	0.62
Mizoram	1.002	0.6	0.3192	0.2808	0.28
Nagaland	0.821	1.6	0.4568	1.1432	1.39
Orissa	5.802	10.7	1.096	9.604	1.66
Punjab	1.07	1.4	0.0048	1.3952	1.30
Rajasthan	19.001	8.9	0.0696	8.8304	0.46
Sikkim	0.367	0.5	0.184	0.316	0.86
Tamil Nadu	4.111	7.9	0.3344	7.5656	1.84
Tripura	0.295	2.2	0.076	2.124	7.20
Uttar Pradesh	10.105	21.7	1.3968	20.3032	2.01
West Bengal	2.455	10.6	0.104	10.496	4.28
Union Territories	0.085	0.3	0.42	-0.12	-1.41
Total	107.43	161.5	21.064	140.436	1.31

* Draft report of the Working Group on Fodder and Firewood, Planning Commission, Government of India, 1998.

Author's estimates.

5.b. Fodder

Fodder demand and supply position has always been considered in relation to the grazing animal population and the area under forage supply. Most current estimates show a current deficiency of 31 per cent in dry fodder, 23 per cent in green fodder and 47.1 per cent in the concentrates which is likely to be 17.3, 31.0 and 47.6 per cent in the year 2000 respectively (Table 18.9). Considering the rise in livestock population (Table 18.10) it is observed that the population

TABLE 18.9: **Green and Dry Fodder Availability and Requirement (Mt)***

	Availability	Requirement	Deficiency (%)
Current			
Dry Fodder (Straw)	398.88	583.62	31.0
Green Fodder	573.50	744.73	23.0
Concentrates	41.98	79.40	47.1
By 2000 AD			
Dry Fodder (Straw)	523.61	632.61	17.3
Green Fodder	573.50	830.12	31.0
Concentrates	46.18	88.05	47.6

* Draft Report of the Policy Advisory Group on Integrated Grazing Policy, Ministry of Environment and Forests, 1993.

TABLE 18.10: **Livestock Population in India (million)**

Species	Population 1987	Projected Population*				
		1991	1996	2001	2006	% increase over 1987
Cattle	199.69	206.75	216.76	228.36	242.06	21.22
Buffaloes	75.97	84.21	96.32	110.97	128.71	69.42
Sheep	45.70	47.07	48.83	50.66	52.57	15.03
Goat	110.21	119.84	133.11	147.84	164.25	49.03
Total	431.57	457.87	495.02	537.83	587.59	36.15

* For projecting livestock population the cumulative growth rate of the Department of Animal Husbandry, GOI, have been used.

of buffaloes and goats will increase faster compared to cattle and sheep. This will call for a different feeding strategy and also feed quality to sustain them. Based on the animal species, Ranjhan (1994) calculated the nutrient requirements and had observed that in 1996 the annual dry matter requirement would be 904 mt. At the level of 1991 population, thus there was a wide gap in demand and supply of dry matter (4 per cent) digestible crude protein (62 per cent) and total digestible nutrients (49 per cent). The demand and supply of feed and fodder in the year 1991 showed a gap of 13 per cent in feed stuff straw/stover and 18 per cent in green fodder between the availability and requirement.

Increase in the goat population will also require more supply of fodder from tree leaves besides grazing/brousing in the forests.

6. Programmes for Meeting the Demands

6.a. Wood

6.a.1 Multipurpose Trees Programme

In order to solve the problems of firewood supply and also encourage production of other products in the rural setup, plantation of multipurpose trees was encouraged. While identifying such plants, emphasis was on the plants with a wide adaptability to sites including problem soils, ease of establishment, and resistance to abiotic and biotic forces. Other important attributes included nitrogen fixing ability, rapid growth, ability to coppice, wood quality (density and energy value, smoke-free fire), shorter harvest rotations, etc. Such trees are now well identified from the indigenous and introduced tree species (Table 18.10).

TABLE 18.10: **Firewood Properties of Some Forest Species**

Species	Calorific values of oven dry wood samples (cal/g)	Specific gravity (Wt. oven dry & Vol. at green)	Smoke odour
1	2	3	4
Acacia nilotica	5825	0.69	No
Acacia auriculiformis	5755	0.68	No
Azadirachta indica	6943	0.68	Suffocating & irritating to eyes
Albizia lebbck	6360	0.63	Irritating to eyes
Casuarina equisetifolia	6547	0.71	No
Dalbergia sissoo	6197	0.35	Irritating to eyes
Eucalyptus hybrid	6197	0.56	No
Gmelina arborea	5755	0.46	Poor cracking suffocating

(Contd.)

TABLE 18.10 *(Contd.)*

1	2	3	4
Madhuca indica	6221	0.80	No
Moringa oleifera	6407	0.17	No
Melia azadirachta	5778	0.60	Light bad smell & irritating to eyes
Parkinsonia aculeata	6500	0.70	Suffocating & irritating to eyes
Prosopis juliflora	6034	0.73	No
Peltophorum inerme	5755	0.30	No
Syzygium cumini	6174	0.64	No
Sesbania grandiflora	6360	0.53	Suffocating
Terminalia arjuna	6873	0.60	Irritating to eyes
Tamarindus indica	5871	0.56	Irritating to eyes
Zyzyphus jujuba	6104	0.40	No
Acacia lenticularis	6384	0.83	No
Acacia leucocephala	6104	0.57	No
Leucaena leucocephala	6454	0.65	Light pleasing smell
Butea monosperma	5848	0.58	Light pleasing smell
Acacia catechu	6127	0.68	No
Anogeissus latifolia	5568	0.72	Irritating to eyes
Albizia procera	6430	0.47	Suffocating & irritating to eyes
Acacia farnesiana	6547	0.67	Suffocating
Cedrela toona	5172	0.45	No
Terminalia bellirica	5708	0.53	No
Acacia mearnesii	7826	0.55	No
Alnus nepalensis	6127	0.47	Light pleasing smell
Eucalyptus globulus	7550	0.75	No
Toona ciliata	5661	0.61	Bad smell

(after Chaturvedi *et al.*, 1986).

6.a.2 Firewood Plantations

A massive drive for tree plantation on the degraded lands was initiated during 1984 realizing that the country had more than half of its area lying degraded and waste. Although an annual target for afforesting 5 m ha was set it was only partially achieved.

Through the Social Forestry Programme, degraded forest areas, roadsides, canal banks and railway sides were planted with fast-growing tree species by the State Forest Departments. This was intended to meet the fuelwood and small timber demands of the rural people. But these programmes are the Government projects where people's involvement was only at the level of plantation as it was employment generation programme. The aftercare and protection remained partial and consequently many of such plantations withered away. Property ownership and responsibility sharing before the products are ready for harvest is an important issue needing the attention of village institutions. In order to succeed, the plantation initiative should fit into the social, cultural, economic, religious, political and legal framework of the place where it is planned (Anonymous, 1980).

The non-forest wastelands account for 93.69 m ha of saline-alkaline, waterlogged, ravine lands, coastal sands, arid and semi-arid regions etc. A 1,000 ha plantation can provide about 3 MW of power besides providing fuelwood and charcoal which can support the energy needs of 125-150 families. Thus, even 16 m ha if converted into plantation can create a generation capacity of 4,800 MW which can be more than the installed capacity of the country from all the sources. Such installations can cost only Rs. 12,000 per KW (Dayal, 1986).

6.a.3 Wood Conservation

Wood is the fourth target source of energy after petroleum products, coal and natural gas. Wood scarcity has forced its price rise and also needs more time for collection from natural sites. Its effect on wasteful burning of cowdung cannot be overemphasized. To optimize this resource, plantations and agroforestry are considered the viable alternatives. Its careful use and conservation is equally important. This is possible through the improvement in wood-consuming devices.

The energy efficiency of traditional *chulhas* (wood-stoves) ranges between 2-15 per cent and needs improvement. Even a small improvement of 1 per cent will result in a saving of 3 mt of firewood (Vimal and Tyagi 1986). Besides, improved stoves reduce smoke and other health hazards. Many institutions have achieved energy efficiency up to 30 per cent in their cook stoves. The Department of Non-conventional Energy Sources has introduced *chulhas* with an efficiency ranging from 10-25 per cent. The design of the *chulhas* for different regions of the country and the type of food items have been varied. In many areas these *chulhas* have been rejected by the housewives due to the specialized nature of fuel needs and also comparatively less ease of cooking. Therefore it still remains the most vital area for R&D to improve the situation of energy and help the environmental amelioration.

6.a.4 Biogas

In order to check the misuse/wasteful use of cowdung and other organic residues, production of gas through biogas plants is a most profitable alternative compared to direct use. Monga and Lakhanpal (1988) have shown that as against cowdung cake which provides an income of Rs. 387/yr if it is processed through the biogas plant it yields Rs. 1560/year. Besides, cleaner fuel from gas can be used for cooking or lighting most efficiently. Although much is being done to popularize the biogas plant at individual and community level, it has not gained popularity in many areas due to the problems of design and other socioeconomic reasons. Its popularization and more convenient use are an important step in solving the problems of rural energy supply.

6.a.5 Agroforestry as a Strategy for Meeting the Firewood and Forage Needs

Potentiality of agroforestry systems to bridge the gap between demand and supply of forage, firewood and timber is well documented. Pathak and Roy (1995) have attempted to model landuse systems in the Bundelkhand region (7 mha) based on agroforestry interventions like silvipasture, farm boundary plantation, agrisilviculture and alley cropping on rainfed farms, energy plantation and agrohortipastoral systems. The model has shown potential to generate surplus of these items even if these interventions worked at 50 per cent efficiency or on 50 per cent of the available land area (Tables 18.12 and 18.13).

They also prepared a village landuse plan of a conceptual village in the Bundelkhand region based on agroforestry intervention. The allocation to different categories of farmers based on an actual survey data showed that about 15 per cent of the total area under village commons was not available for farming. The production levels are based on the improved interventions at a minimal input level. It is evident from the table that it has a potential to bridge the gap in demand and supply. Besides, the resource conservation value is not shown which has a promise to bring in progressive improvement in the land capability and thus the rural prosperity. The table also shows that about 66.3 per cent of the firewood supply, 30 per cent of timber supply and 4.3 per cent of fodder supply could be assured from village commons. When supply of top feeds from trees is included it can meet up to 10 per cent of the demands.

In another attempt Pathak and Roy (1994) observed that even if applied on just 50 m ha of degraded and wastelands, the annual need of forage and firewood in the country could be met. (Table 18.14).

TABLE 18.12: **Potentiality of Annual Production (M t/yr) in the Bundelkhand Region through Agroforestry Interventions**

Intervention	Forage	Firewood	Timber	Others
Silvipastoral systems				
Degraded forests	4.30	1.63	0.90	Cons., Bio.
Wastelands	5.43	2.05	1.13	Cons., Bio.
Farm Boundary Plantation				
Rainfed croplands	0.07	0.09	0.03	Cons., Bio.
Irrigated areas	0.03	0.04	0.02	Cons., Bio.
Agrisilviculture				
Rainfed farms	0.07	0.29	0.14	Cons., Bio.
Alley cropping				
Rainfed areas	0.98	—	—	—
Energy plantation		1.73	0.85	
Agri-Horti-Pastoral	0.16	0.20	Rs. 2000 per yr	Fruit
Total	11.04	6.03	3.07	

TABLE 18.13: **Potential of Annual Production in a Typical Village of Bundelkhand Region through Agrosilvipastoral Intervention (at the minimum input level)**

Production from	Forage	Crop residues	Total forage	Firewood	Timber	Others
			(in 000 t/yr) (cu m/yr)			
Small farmer	0.70	0.84	1.54	0.10	10	C
Medium farmer	0.85	0.86	1.71	0.16	15	C
Large farmer	1.07	0.86	1.93	0.27	22	C,B,F
Village common	0.23	—	0.23	1.18	20	C,B,F
Total Production	2.85	2.56	5.41	1.71	67	C,B,F
Total requirement			4.64	0.87	30	

Notes: i. Likely forage availability from top feeds has not been accounted in this calculation which is expected to be 410 t/yr.

ii. The timber production calculations are based on short rotation (5-10 years) and long rotation (15-20 years) species.

iii. The requirements are at the present level.

iv. C= Conservation, B= Biodiversity, F= Fruits.

TABLE 18.14: **Present and Expected Returns from a Silvipastoral System on the Degraded Land**

Products	Present		Expected	
	Productivity (t/ha/yr)	Production (M t/yr)	Productivity (t/ha/yr)	Production (M/t/yr)
Forage	0.5-1.0	25-50	4.0-5.5	200-275
Topfeeds	Negligible	—	1.6-2.5	80-125
Firewood	Negligible	—	2.0-3.0	100-150

7. Conclusion

The potential of improved technologies of agroforestry for arresting land degradation and improving the productivity can be realized only if the community lands/common property resources are properly managed. Institutional arrangements to create, manage and utilize the outputs from these lands vary with the sociopolitical and economic situation of the area. Joint Forest Management, Tree Patta Scheme or the shared resource management through Van Panchayats are the options. The village forest committees aim at creating and managing these resources for their efficient utilization. In the areas where stumps of the old trees are available, Assisted Natural Regeneration can serve a better purpose at less than 70 per cent of the cost of the development of degraded lands. Planning for making the project remunerative in the early years and also meeting short- and long-term objectives is essential which can be achieved through enrichment planting of high economic species to be utilized at shorter rotations. Effective marketing and value addition are essential for the surplus disposal and remunerative prices to generate financial resources for meeting the other input and management costs.

In all such programmes, management of forage supply becomes problematic because of its harvesting management during the early years of the silvipasture growth and grazing management within the carrying capacity later. The permission for removing forage headloads from the plantations often does not attract the users due to the distance, easy availability of forage and labour requirements. In these circumstances establishment of fodder banks in villages and protein banks in the plantations for the lean periods can serve as the best alternative. Under the cut-and-carry system choice of forage during different months based on the maturity/seeding potential of grass is very important for the scientific management of the pasture for its sustainable growth and production. It has been observed that users harvest grasses during the monsoon period and legumes during the dry winters followed by tree-lopping/pruning during the summers. Such management schedules develop with proper education of the resource users and also the type of livestock maintained.

Organization of the village institutions, their proper orientation based on the microplan and systems of award and punishment go a long way in assuring the success of the programme. Linkages between different government departments, viz. Forestry, Agriculture, Animal Husbandry and Marketing are essential to ensure the success of this venture. The present implementation of the Panchayati Raj system may have a prime role for village resource management giving equal status to firewood and fodder which are the prime needs of the people.

Acknowledgements

I am thankful to Ms Kranti Pipal for word processing of the manuscript.

REFERENCES

Anonymous. 1980. *Firewood Crops: Shrub and Tree Species for Energy Production*, Washington D.C.: National Academy of Sciences, p. 237.

Abrol, I.P. and P.K. Joshi. 1984. "Economic viability of reclamation of alkali lands with special references to agriculture and forestry", In: Sharma, Kamal (ed.), *Economics of Wastelands Development*, 19-30, SPWD, New Delhi.

Abrol, I.P. and J. Sehgal. 1992. "Degraded lands and their rahabilitation in India". In : Greenland, D.J. and I. Szabolcs (eds.) *Soil Resilience and Sustainable Landuse*, p. 129-144, Presented International Conf. on Soil Resilience and Sustainable Landuse, held at Bucharest (Hungary) (1992).

Akobundu, I.O. 1995. Unpublished (quoted by Mac Dicken *et al.* 1997).

Bhumbla, D.R. and A. Khare. 1984. *Estimate of Wastelands in India*, New Delhi: Society for Promotion of Wastelands Development, p. 8.

Brewbaker, J.L., K.B. Willers and B. Mavklin. 1990. "Nitrogen fixing trees: Validation and prioritization". *Nitrogen Fixing Tree Research Reports*, 8:8-16.

Chaturvedi, A.N., D.N. Bhatt, C.M. Misra and S.L. Singh. 1986. "Firewood properties of some forest species", *U.P. Forest Bulletin* No. 53. p. 12.

Danso, S.K.A., G.D. Bowen and N. Sanginga. 1992. "Biological nitrogen fixation in trees in agroecosystems", *Plant and Soil* 141: 177-96.

Dass, H.C., J.C. Kalla and K.A. Shankarnarayana. 1984. "Economic viability of fruit tree crops and grasses in arid zone", In: Sharma, Kamal (ed.), *Economics of Wastelands Development* 31-36, SPWD, New Delhi.

Dayal, M. 1986. Foreword, In: Vimal, O.P. and P.D. Tyagi (eds.), *Fuelwood from Wastelands*, New Delhi: Yatan Publications, vii-viii, 24, p. 376.

Debroy, R., B.D. Patil and P.S. Pathak. 1978. "Silvipastoral farming for amelioration and increased land productivity of the arid and semi-arid regions", Proc. International Symposium on Arid Zone Research and Development, 345-50.

Dhruvanarayana, V.V. and Ram Babu. 1983. "Estimation of soil erosion in India", *J. Irrig. Drain.*

Engg., ASCE, 109(4): 419-34.

Dhruvanarayan, V.V. and Ram Babu. 1984. "Economic viability of tree/grass crops on highly eroded soils", In: Sharma, Kamal (ed.), *Economics of Wastelands Development* 37-45, SPWD, New Delhi.

Dhruvanarayan, V.V. and Ram Babu. 1990. "Social and economic considerations in the management of soils of hilly regions", In: Abrol, I.P. and V.V. Dhruvanarayana (eds.), *Technologies for Wasteland Development*, 273-284, ICAR, New Delhi.

Dubey, A.P. and S.K. Agrawal. 1997. Tribal society forests and agriculture. *Wastelnnds News* XII (4): 12-15.

Dwivedi, B.N. 1994. "Fuelwood and other energy supply and demand", International Workshop on India's Forest Management and Ecological Revival, New Delhi: Tata Energy Research Institute, p. 38.

Eckholm, E.P. 1975. "The other energy crisis: Firewood". *World Watch Paper 1*. Washington DC: Worldwatch Institute, USA.

Fisher, R.F. and A.S.R. Juno. 1994. "Mechanisms of tree growth in acid soils". In: D.D. Ewans and L.T. Szott (Eds.), Nitrogen Fixing Trees for Acid Soils, Nitrogen Fixing Tree Association, *Nitrogen Fixing Tree Research Reports*, Special Issue, 1995, 1-18.

Forest Survey of India. 1993. "State of Forest Report", FSI, Dehradun, p. 81

Forest Survey of India. 1995. "Extent, composition, density, growing stock and annual increment of India's Forests", FSI, Dehradun, p. 128.

Garrity, D.P., M. Soekardi, M. Van Noordwijk, R. De la Crus, P.S. Pathak, H.P.M. Gunasena, N. Van So, G. Heijun and N.M. Majid. 1997. "The Imperata grasslands of tropical Asia: area, distribution and typology". *Agroforestry Systems* 36 (1-3): 3-29.

Gupta, J.P. and A.K. Sharma. 1994. "Agrihorticulture in arid region for stability and sustainability", In: Singh, P., P.S. Pathak and M.M. Roy (eds.), *Agroforestry Systems for Degraded Lands*, 164-167, New Delhi: Oxford and IBH Publishing Co. P. Ltd..

Gupta, T. and D. Mohan. 1982. *Economics of Trees v.s. Annual Crops on Marginal Agricultural Lands*, New Delhi: Oxford & IBH Pub. Co.

Gupta, R. K. and D.L.N. Rao. 1994. "The potential of agroforestry for sequestering carbon in wastelands and mitigating climatic change", In: P. Singh, P.S. Pathak and M.M. Roy, (eds.), *Agroforestry Systems for Sustainable Landuse*, 90-95, New Delhi: Oxford & IBH Pub. Co. Pvt. Ltd.

Jha, A.K. and J.S. Singh. 1991. "Vascular flora of naturally revegetated coalmine spoils in a dry tropical environment". *Journal of Tropical Forestry* 6: 131-141.

Jha, A.K. and J.S. Singh. 1994. "Rehabilitation of Mine Spoils with particular Reference to Multipurpose Trees", In: Singh, P. , P.S. Pathak and M.M. Roy (eds.), *Agroforestry Systems for Sustainable Landuse*. 237-249, New Delhi: Oxford and IBH Publishing Co. (Pvt.) Ltd.

Kerr, J.M. 1997. "Market failures in natural resources management". In: Kerr, J.M., D.K. Marothia, K. Singh, C. Ramaswamy and W.R. Bantley (eds.), Natural Resource Economics: Theory and Application in India, 185-222, New Delhi: Oxford and IBH Pub. Co. Pvt. Ltd.

Kuligod, V.B., M. Hebbara, S.G. Patil, M.V. Manjunatha and G.D. Radder. 1994. "SEWN-as a tool to evaluate trees for salinity and water logging", In: Singh, P., P.S. Pathak and M.M. Roy (eds.), *Agroforestry Systems for Degraded Lands*, 343-50, New Delhi: Oxford and IBH Publishing Co. P. Ltd.

Lal, R. 1988. "Soil erosion by wind and water: problems and prospects", In: Lal, R. (ed.), *Soil Erosion Research Methods*, Soil Water Conservation. Soc. Amer., Ankeny. IA, USA. p. 1-6.

Lamb, D. 1988. "IUCN Guidelines for Restoration of Degraded Ecosystems, Draft, World Conservation Union IUCN", Gland, Switzerland.

Mac Dicken, K.G., K. Hairiah, A. Otsamo, B. Duguma and N.M. Majid. 1997. "Shade based control of *Imperata cylindrica*: tree fallows and cover crops", *Agroforestry Systems* 36 :131-149.

Misra, R. 1987. "Ecology of grazing land of India", Sri P. M. Dabadghao Memorial Lecture,

Range Management Society of India, IGFRI, Jhansi, pp. 1-29.

Misra, S.M., B.D. Patil and P.S. Pathak. 1982. "Comparative differences in soil properties as a result of growing different grass, legume and tree combinations". *Indian J. Range Management* 3(1 & 2) : 71-74.

Monga, P. and T.N. Lakhanpal. 1988. *Rural Energy Alternatives in the Hilly Areas*, New Delhi: Today & Tomorrow's Printers and Publishers, pp. 197.

Mukherjee, A.K. 1994. "State of India's Forests: concepts, definitions, trends, controversies", Report Ministry of Environment and Forests, Govt. of India, New Delhi.

Muthana, K.D. and K.A. Shankarnarayana. 1978. "The scope of Silvipastoral management in arid regions". *Arid Zone Research in India*, Souvenir, Silver Jubilee, CAZRI, Jodhpur.

National Council of Applied Economic Research. 1985. "Domestic Fuel survey with special reference to kerosene". Vol. I, NCAER, New Delhi, pp. 208.

NWDB. 1987. "Cost models for establishment of silvipasture farms in different regions". Mimeographed, New Delhi: National Wastelands Development Board.

Pachauri, R.K. and P.V. Sridharan (eds). 1998. *Looking Back to Think Ahead, GREEN India 2047*, New Delhi: Tata Energy Research Institute, pp. 346.

Pathak, P.S. 1991. "Economic analysis of silvipastoral systems". In: Thammincha, S., L. Puangchit and H. Woods (eds.), *Forestry Economics Research in Asia*, 41-51, Canada: KaSetsart University Bangkok and IDRC.

Pathak, P.S. and J.C. Dagar. 1998 a. "Agroforestry : a strategy for rehabilitation of degraded lands", In: Gopal, B., P.S. Pathak & K.G. Saxena (eds.), *Ecology Today: an Anthology of Contemporary Ecological Research*, 333-71, New Delhi: International Scientific Publications, pp. XVIII + 472.

Pathak, P.S. and J.C. Dagar. 1998 b. "Traditional agroforestry systems : an over view", In: *Landmarks in Botany in India*, CAS in Botany, BHU, Varanasi (in press).

Pathak, P.S. and T.A. Khan. 1990. "Silvipastoral systems in economic framework". In: Pathak, P.S. and P. Singh (eds.), *Silvipastoral Systems in India*, 1991-199., Jhansi: Range Management Society of India, IGFRI.

Pathak, P.S. and T.A. Khan. 1992. "Economics of minirotation energy plantations on moist wastelands". In: Mathur, A.N., Iqbal Hussain and N.S. Rathore (eds.), *Economics of Energy Plantation*, 1-8, Delhi: Himanshu Publications.

Pathak, P.S. and M.M. Roy. 1994. *Silvipastoral System of Production*, Bulletin, Jhansi: IGFRI, pp. 1-55.

Pathak, P.S. and M.M. Roy. 1995. "Agrosilvipastoral farming systems for optimizing forage and energy resources in rainfed areas, In: (Singh, R.P. ed.) *Forage Production and Utilization*, 154-178, Jhansi: IGFRI.

Pathak, P. S., S.K. Gupta and R. Debroy. 1985. "Biomass accumulation pattern and the productivity of Leucaena minirotations on moist wastelands". *J. Trop. For.* 1(II): 112-123

Pathak, P.S., S.K. Gupta and P. Singh. 1995. IGFRI *Approaches to Rehabilitation of Degraded Lands, Bulletin*, Jhansi: Indian Grassland and Fodder Research Institute (IGFRI), p. 23

Patil, S.G., M.V. Manjunatha, M. Hebbara, V.B. Kuligod and Raj K. Gupta. 1994. "Evaluation of tree species for their biodrainageability in irrigation commands". In: P. Singh, P.S. Pathak and M.M. Roy (eds.), *Agroforestry Systems for Degraded Lands*, 35-356, New Delhi: Oxford & IBH Pub. Co, (Pvt.)Ltd.

Prajapati, M.C. 1979. "Silvipastoral system of production in ravines", *Proc. Summer Instt. on Silvipastoral Production*, Jhansi: IGFRI, pp. 28-40.

Ranjhan, S.K. 1994. "Availability and requirements of feed and fodder for livestock and poultry", Report Animal Husbandry Department, New Delhi: GOI.

Ravindranath, N.H., H.N. Chanakya and J.M. Kerr. 1997. "An ecosystem approach for analysis of biomass energy", In: Kerr, J.M., D.K. Marothia, Katar Singh, C. Ramaswamy and W.R. Bentley (eds.), *Natural Resource Economics Theory and Application in India*, 561-587, New Delhi: Oxford & IBH Publishing Co. Pvt. Ltd.

Sanginga, N., K. Mulonggoy and A. Ayanaba. 1988. "Nodulation and growth of *Leucaena leucocephala* (Lam.) de wit as affected by inoculation and nitrogen fertilizers", *Plant and Soil,* 112: 129-135.

Sanginga, N., K. Marrigue and G. Hardarson. 1991. "Variation in redulation and N2 fixation by the *Gliricidia sepium/Rhizobium,* spp. symbiosis in a calcareous soil", *Biol. Fertil. Soils.* 11: 273-278.

Sehgal, J.L., R.K. Saxena and R.M. Pofali. (1990a). "Degraded soils-their mapping through soil surveys". In: I.P. Abrol and V.V. Dhruvanarayana (Eds.), *Technologies of Wasteland Development,* New Delhi: ICAR Publ., p. 1-20

Singh, D., N.D. Mannikar, N.C. Srivas and D.C. Saxena. 1977. "Changes in soil fertility under long-term cultivation of fodder crops and grasses", *J. Indian Soc. Soil Sci.* 25: 28-32.

Singh, G.B. and P.S. Pathak. 1998. "Agroforestry in India : Retrospects and prospects", *Fifty Years of Forestry in India,* Solan: Indian Society of Tree Scientists, India (in press).

Singh, P., P.S. Pathak and M.M. Roy. 1994. "Agroforestry Systems on degraded lands—An introduction", In: Singh, P., P.S. Pathak and M.M. Roy (eds.), *Agroforestry Systems for Sustainable Landuse,* 1-3, New Delhi: Oxford and IBH Pub. Co. (Pvt.) Ltd.

Singh, R.P. and Y.V.R. Reddy. 1986. "Degradation and rehabilitation of dry lands: Some technical and economic aspects". Paper presented at the regional Workshop for 9 countries of South and Southeast Asia on Economics of Dry Land Degradation and Rehabilitation. August 25-29, 1986, New Delhi.

Spears, J.S. 1978. Quoted by Anonymous, 1980.

Srivastava, A. K. 1994. "Alternate landuses for sustained production in semi-arid vertisols", In : Singh, P., P.S. Pathak and M.M. Roy (eds.), *Agroforestry Systems for Degraded Lands,* 128-133, New Delhi: Oxford & IBH Pub. Co, (Pvt.) Ltd.

Srivastava, S.C., A.K. Jha and J.S. Singh. 1989. "Changes with time in soil biomass C, N and P of mine spoils in a dry tropical environment". *Canadian Journal of Soil Science* 69: 849-855.

Swaminathan, M.S. 1982. Report of the fuelwood study committee, New Delhi: Planning Commission, Govt. of India, p. 81.

Vimal, O.P. and P. D. Tyagi. 1986. *Fuelwood from Wastelands,* New Delhi: Yatan Publications, p. 376.

SECTION 4

INSTITUTIONAL ARRANGEMENTS IN FISHERIES RESOURCES

19 Management of Inland Fisheries Resources under Different Property Regimes

M. Sinha and **Pradeep K. Katiha**

The Indian fisheries date back to time immemorial, but the saga of success has been related to early post-independence years. With renewed accent on optimum utilization of the country's aquatic wealth for fisheries, the Government of India drew up an ambitious programme of mechanization and modernization through upgradation of technology during the early fifties (Jhingran 1991). Therefore, Indian fisheries witnessed an impressive transformation from a highly traditional rural activity to technologically sound, well-developed industry. Its contribution in the net domestic product (NDP) at current prices has increased from Rs. 8.06 billion in 1980-81 to Rs. 98.26 billion in 1994-95. It is much higher than the increase in the NDP of agriculture (four-fold) during this period (Anonymous 1996a). The fish production in India has reached 4.95 million tonnes in 1995-96 from 0.75 million tonnes in 1950-51. For different Five Year Plans, its average annual growth rate ranged between 1.47 and 8.37 per cent. The working group for the Ninth Five Year Plan has set a target of 4.38 per cent annual growth rate for the fisheries sector with 3 per cent for marine and 6 per cent for inland sector (Anonymous 1996b). The inland fish production has increased eleven-fold (0.21-2.28 million tonnes) during 1950-51 to 1997-98. Various factors contributed significantly towards these achievements, but the prime component is the availability of scientific technology for the enormous inland fishery waters in our country. These waters sustain either capture or culture fisheries depending upon the manag ement system adopted. Inland capture fishery is a labour-intensive activity, represented mainly by the traditional fishers, fishing in natural community or common property waters, while the aquaculture in the country witnessed an impressive transformation from highly traditional activity to well-developed industry. There was nearly three-and-a-half-fold increase in the aquacultural fish production, while capture fisheries declined to two-thirds during the past decade (Table 19.1). Despite the significant increase in inland fish production, it seems impossible to meet the projected demand of 12.5 million tonnes by the turn of this century to provide nutritionally required fish quality to the expected populace.

TABLE 19.1: **Contribution of Capture and Culture Fisheries in Inland Fish Production of India. (Modified from Anonymous 1996 b)**

Year	Production (000t)		
	Capture fisheries	Culture Fisheries	Total inland fish production
1984-85	591.74	511.50	1103.24
	(53.64)	(46.36)	
1989-90	396.50	1005.50	1402
	(28.28)	(71.72)	
1994-95	334.03	1762.70	2096.73
	(15.93)	(84.07)	

Figures in parentheses represent the per cent of total inland fish production.

The Central and State Governments have taken a number of steps to improve fish production and productivity, organize the fishermen community and initiate schemes for their development. These have resulted in the formation of 11,440 primary fisheries cooperatives, 72 district/regional-level federations, 15 State-level federations and one national-level federation. The primary cooperative societies have above 12.5 lakh members (Anonymous 1996a). Some of the important schemes are: establishment of Fish Farmers' Development Agency (FFDA), Composite Fish Culture Schemes and Fisheries Research Institutes. These organizations are aimed at improving fish production and productivity through horizontal or vertical expansion, and increase in the adoption of improved technologies. Despite these sincere efforts production from fishery waters is much below the potential, and for some of the capture fishery resources, it is declining. Further, the pace of bringing more and more aqua-resources under the umbrella of culture fisheries also could not gather the expected momentum. The impact of fisheries developmental activities could not be realized as per expectations due to the very nature of resource under-use, which has multiple water-use rights and may be designated as common pool resource (CPR). These are used to meet the day-to-day human requirements, so utilized for different purposes in addition to fisheries. Furthermore, most of the fishing waters belong to State

Governments, excepting some under the private property right. The government authorized various agencies to manage the fishery activities in these waters. These agencies respond differently to the management and exploitation of the available fish stock and have varied impact on the target group, the fishers. In this context, it is pertinent to have an in-depth study of the pros and cons of these management systems. This chapter briefly describes the various Indian inland aqua-resources along with their fishery status, and appraises the existing property rights and management regimes for these resources, with special emphasis on rivers.

I. Inland Fisheries Resources

Indian inland waters include rivers, reservoirs, aquacultural waters (ponds and tanks), estuaries and flood plain lakes. Their description along with the fisheries status is summarized below:

1.a. The Rivers

The river systems in India may be classified into two major groups, namely, Himalayan or extra-peninsular rivers and peninsular rivers (Table 19.2). The general profile of these groups is mentioned below:

1.a.1 Himalayan or Extra-Peninsular Rivers

Originating from the Himalayans to transverse the great alluvial Indo-Gangatic plains, these snow and rainfed rivers are characterized by complicated flood regimes and seasonal variations in the volume of flow. Descending on the plains, they become sluggish and inundate vast land area. These rivers may be categorized into three systems: the Ganga, the Brahmaputra and the Indus. The Ganga river system has a combined length of 12,500 kms and a catchment area of 97.6 million ha. The Ganga, Ghagra, Gomti, Ramganga, Kosi, Gandak, Yamuna, Chambal, Sone and Tons are the major rivers of this system. These rivers are spread over most of the north Indian States (except the hilly States) to extend up to West Bengal through Bihar. In the upland waters of the system commercial fisheries is virtually absent, due to the inaccessible terrain and other exploitation problems. The stretch of the river Ganga from Haridwar to Lalgola is recognized as one of the richest source of capture fisheries in India, comprising highly priced major carps, hilsa and catfishes. Mid September to June are the peak months for fishing. During the lean period of monsoon months the fishing activities generally are confined to the river banks.

TABLE 19.2: **The Profile of Various River Systems in India. (Basedon Jhingran, 1991a and Rao, 1979)**

S. No.	River system	Name of main Rivers	Approxi. length (km)	States
Himalayan or Extra-Peninsular Rivers				
1	Ganga	Ganga	2525	Uttar Pradesh, Bihar, West Bengal
		Ramganga	569	Uttar Pradesh
		Gomti	940	Uttar Pradesh
		Ghagra	1080	Uttar Pradesh, Bihar
		Gandak	300	Bihar
		Kosi	492	Bihar
		Yamuna	1376	Punjab, Haryana, Delhi, Uttar Pradesh
		Chambal	1080	Madhya Pradesh, Uttar Pradesh, Rajasthan
		Tons	264	Uttar Pradesh
		Son	784	Uttar Pradesh
		Ken	360	Madhya Pradesh
2	Brahamputra	Brahmaputra, Dibang, Siang, Lohit, Manas, Buri Dihang, Dhansiri, Kopili	4000	Arunachal Pradesh, Assam, Nagaland, Sikkim, Manipur
3	Indus	Jhelum	400	Jammu & Kashmir
		Chenab	330	Jammu & Kashmir, Himachal Pradesh
		Beas	460	Himachal Pradesh, Punjab
		Sutlej		Himachal Pradesh, Punjab
		Ravi		Jammu & Kashmir, Himachal Pradesh, Punjab
B. Peninsular Rivers				
4.	East Coast	Mahanadi	851	Orissa, Madhya Pradesh
		Godavari	1465	Maharashtra, Andhra Pradesh
		Krishna	1401	Maharashtra, Andhra Pradesh, Karnataka
		Cauvery	800	Karnataka, Tamil Nadu
		Bhima	861	Karnataka
5	West Coast	Narmada	1322	Maharashtra, Gujarat, Madhya Pradesh
		Tapti	720	Gujarat, Maharashtra
		Mahi	583	Gujarat

The combined length of the Brahmaputra river system is 4,023 kms. with a catchment area of 51 million ha. Originating from Tibet, the river flows through the northern slopes of Himalayas to enter India at its north-east corner of Arunachal Pradesh. It has 918 kms. stretch in India, including 730 kms only in Assam. Its northern tributaries Subansiri, Kameng and Manas are large with steep, shallow-braided channels, whereas those on the southern banks—Buri Dihang, Dhansiri and Kopilli—are deeper with meandering channels and a low gradient. The Brahmaputra valley is marked for its abandoned riverbeds (beels) supporting rich fishery. Catfishes, and major and minor carps dominate the commercial catches of the upper middle and lower stretches, while the commercial catch in the lower-middle stretch is primarily composed of catfish and miscellaneous catch.

In the case of the Indus river system, the main Indus river and its tributaries in the upper, and the Beas and Sutlej in the lower reaches are important from the Indian fisheries viewpoint. Its headwaters in the States of Kashmir, Himachal Pradesh and Punjab mainly harbour mahseer, snow trout, some cyprinids and exotic trouts. The rivers Beas and Sutlej contain indigenous carps and catfishes, which are commercially exploited.

1.b.2 Peninsular Rivers

The torrential and rain-fed peninsular rivers have a well-defined stable course. These include two river systems, the East Coast and the West Coast. The East Coast river system has a vast expanse of water in the States of Orissa, Madhya Pradesh, Maharashtra, Andhra Pradesh, Karnataka and Tamil Nadu. The river system has mainly four constituent rivers—Mahanadi, Godavari, Krishna and Cauvery—with a combined length of 6437 kms and a catchment area of 121 million ha. This system drains the entire peninsular India and east of the Western Ghats in the west and south parts of central India. Besides its own fish fauna of several carps, catfishes, murrels and prawn, the system is repeatedly enriched by transplantation of the Gangetic carps.

The combined length of the rivers of the West Coast river system and catchment area is 3,380 kms and 69.16 million ha respectively. The Narmada and the Tapti are the longest rivers of the system along with 600 small rivers. Its rivers are distributed in the States of Gujarat, Maharashtra and Madhya Pradesh. The fish fauna of the system consists of carps, catfish, mahseers, prawns, etc.

The riverine resources had a major share in the inland capture fish production, but during the past few decades the riverine ecosystem has witnessed marked alterations, due to mammoth human interventions in the form of water abstraction, dam construction, sedimentation and irrational fishing. These have had a discerningly disturbing effect on the natural riverine fish production, which has showed continuous declining trends. The studies of the Central Inland Fisheries Research Institute, Barrackpore, reveal that the average yield of major carps from the Ganga river system has declined from 26.62 kg/ha/year during 1958-61 to 2.55 kg/ha/year during 1989-95. The fisheries of anadromous hilsa have declined by 96 per cent above Farakka after the construction of Farakka barrage in 1974. These examples of the Ganga river system may be extended to depict the status of fish production in all the rivers of India. The restoration of riverine fisheries would, therefore, entail an integrated approach encompassing the requirements of fisheries alongwith other uses of land and water.

1.b. The Reservoirs

During the post-independence period, a large number of river valley projects created a chain of impoundments, which are highly amenable for fishery activities. These man-made water bodies created by obstructing the surface flow, by erecting a dam of any description, on a river, stream or any water course, are called reservoirs (Sugunan 1995). These are generally classified into small (<1,000 ha), medium (1,000-5,000 ha) and large (>5,000 ha). The area under these water bodies is continuously increasing with the adoption of more and more reservoirs for fisheries. At present, in India the total area under reservoirs is 3.15 million ha (Table 19.3), out of which small reservoirs occupy 1.49 million ha followed by large 1.14 million ha and medium 0.52 million ha. Among the States, maximum percentage area under reservoirs is in Madhya Pradesh (14.6) followed by Andhra (14.54), Karnataka (13.87) and Tamil Nadu (11.38). Among the different sized reservoirs, maximum annual production is from small reservoirs (49.9 kg/ha) followed by medium (12.3 kg/ha) and large 11.43 (kg/ha) with an overall average of 20.13 kg/ha. Despite the amenability for fish production and a production potential in the range of 50-300 kg/ha, the present yield from reservoirs in India is very low. The large and medium reservoirs are generally managed as stocking-cum-capture fisheries resources. The management policies based on norms of stock manipulation through selective stocking and harvesting operations have been suggested to rectify the imbalances in the species spectrum and increase the fish yield. For small reservoirs, culture-based management is considered the best.

1.c. Aquacultural Water Bodies

By virtue of its goegraphical situation in the monsoonal belt, India is endowed with good rainfall and consequently extensive aquacultural water bodies. The freshwater aquacultural water resources in the form of ponds and tanks have been distributed over almost all the States of India (Table 19.4). These bodies

TABLE 19.3: **State and Size-wise Distribution of Reservoirs in India (Modified from Sugunan, 1995)**

S.No.	State	Small			Medium			Large			Total		
		Area (ha)	% of Total	Yield (kg/ha)	Area (ha)	% of Total	Yield (kg/ha)	Area (ha)	% of Total	Yield (kg/ha)	Area (ha)	% of Total	Yield (kg/ha)
1.	Tamil Nadu	315941	21.27	48.50	19577	3.71	13.74	23222	2.04	12.66	358740	11.38	22.63
2.	Karnataka	228657	15.39	—	29078	5.51	—	179556	15.75	—	437291	13.87	—
3.	Madhya Pradesh	172575	11.62	47.26	169502	32.13	12.02	118307	10.38	14.53	460384	14.60	13.68
4.	Andhra Pradesh	201927	13.58	188.00	66429	12.59	22.00	190151	16.68	16.80	458507	14.54	36.48
5.	Maharashtra	119515	8.05	21.09	39481	7.48	11.83	115054	10.09	9.28	273750	8.68	10.21
6.	Gujarat	84124	5.66	—	57748	10.95	—	144358	12.66	—	286230	9.08	—
7.	Bihar	12461	0.84	3.91	12523	2.37	1.90	71711	6.29	0.11	96695	3.07	0.05
8.	Orissa	66047	4.45	25.85	12748	2.42	12.76	119403	10.47	7.62	198198	6.29	9.72
9.	Kerala	7975	0.54	53.50	15500	2.94	4.80	6160	0.54	—	29635	0.94	23.37
10.	Uttar Pradesh	218651	14.72	14.60	44993	8.53	7.17	71196	6.24	1.07	334840	10.62	4.68
11.	Rajasthan	54231	3.65	46.43	49827	9.45	24.47	49386	4.33	5.30	153444	4.87	24.89
12.	Himachal Pradesh	200	0.01	—	—	—	—	41364	3.63	35.55	41564	1.32	35.55
13.	North-east	2239	0.15	—	5835	1.11	—	—	—	—	8074	0.26	—
14.	Haryana	282	0.02	—	—	—	—	—	—	—	282	0.01	—
15.	West Bengal	732	0.05	—	4600	0.87	—	10400	0.91	—	15732	0.50	—
	Total	1485557	47.11*	49.90	527541	16.73*	12.30	1140268	36.16*	11.43	3153366	100.00	20.13

* Per cent of total area under reservoir in India.

TABLE 19.4: **Aquacultural Water Bodies in India (Based on Anonymous 1996a & b)**

S.No.	State	Total area (lakh ha)		Covered Area (000 ha)	% of State Area covered	Production (t)	Yield (kg) per ha per year)
1.	Andhra Pradesh	5.17	(18.13)	13.72	2.65	26074	1900
2.	Arunachal Pradesh	0.01	(0.04)	0.16	16.40	180	1098
3.	Assam	0.23	(0.81)	3.44	14.97	6368	1850
4.	Bihar	0.95	(3.33)	22.31	23.49	47527	2130
5.	Goa	0.03	(0.11)	—	—	—	—
6.	Gujarat	0.71	(2.49)	30.93	43.57	34027	1100
7.	Haryana	0.1	(0.35)	18.57	185.70	65005	3501
8.	Himachal Pradesh	0.01	(0.04)	0.26	26.30	658	2502
9.	Jammu & Kashmir	0.17	(0.60)	1.56	9.15	2022	1300
10.	Karnataka	4.14	(14.52)	21.70	5.24	31898	1470
11.	Kerala	0.3	(1.05)	4.00	13.34	7202	1800
12.	Madhya Pradesh	1.19	(4.17)	54.96	46.19	86292	1570
13.	Maharashtra	0.5	(1.75)	11.31	22.63	6109	540
14.	Manipur	0.05	(0.18)	1.79	35.82	2507	1400
15.	Meghalaya	0.02	(0.07)	0.03	1.25	18	720
16.	Mizoram	0.02	(0.07)	0.15	7.30	219	1500
17.	Nagaland	0.5	(1.75)	1.16	2.33	1163	1000
18.	Orissa	1.14	(4.00)	39.84	34.95	75698	1900
19.	Punjab	0.07	(0.25)	12.15	173.57	49628	4085
20.	Rajasthan	1.8	(6.31)	4.17	2.32	7211	1730
21.	Sikkim	—	—	0.06	—	196	3500
22.	Tamil Nadu	6.91	(24.23)	12.15	1.76	16521	1360
23.	Tripura	0.12	(0.42)	3.33	27.78	6666	2000
24.	Uttar Pradesh	1.62	(5.68)	69.21	42.72	138410	2000
25.	West Bengal	2.76	(9.68)	98.78	35.79	296349	3000
26.	Pondicherry	—	—	0.07	—	75	1119
27.	Others	0.03	(0.11)	—	—	—	—
	Total	28.52	(100.00)	425.82	14.93	908023	2135

The covered area, production and yield are under farms adopted by FFDA.
Figures in parenthesis represent per cent of total area.

have over 2.85 million ha area, with maximum in the State of Tamil Nadu (0.69 million ha) followed by Andhra (0.52 million ha) and Karnataka (0.41 million ha). These States account for about 57 per cent of aquacultural waters of the country. Despite immense efforts for a horizontal expansion of this industry, only 0.8 million ha area could be brought under scientific fish culture. In the early 1970s, with the World Bank assistance, the Fish Farmer's Development Agency (FFDA) was set up, with the objectives of promotion of pond fish culture and adoption of modern aquacultural techniques to achieve high fish production. This agency has adopted over half of the area covered under fish culture. The maximum percentage of area covered by FFDA was in the States of Punjab and Haryana, where fish farmers were taking more than one crop, as was evident from the higher cropped area than the actual. The productivity was also highest for Punjab at 4,085 kg/ha/year followed by Haryana at 3,501 kg/ha/year. The national average productivity from FFDA-supported ponds has increased from 50 kg/ha/year in 1974-75 to about 2,135 kg/ha/year in 1994-95. Yet a lot of effort is needed to harness the unexploited water bodies. During the Ninth Five Year Plan the stress will be on the strengthening of the technical wings of FFDA to assist fish farmers to adopt various improved packages and practices of aquaculture. It also emphasizes expansion of prawn farming and setting up of medium sized fish feed units (Anonymous 1996b).

1.d. The Estuaries

The estuarine capture fishery forms an important component of inland fisheries. The open estuarine system includes Hooghly-Matlah and Mahanadi estuarine systems (Table 19.5). The Godavari estuary is the main estuary of peninsular India, with Adyar, Mankanam and Mandovi as other estuaries and Chilka, Pulicat and Vembanad as important brackish water lagoons. These estuaries and lagoons are recognized as excellent sources of naturally occurring fish and prawn seed. The fisheries of the estuaries are considered as above the subsistence level. The average yield varies between 45-75 kg/ha.

1.d.1 The Flood Plain Lakes

India has extensive flood plains in the form of oxbow lakes (*mauns, beels, chaurs and jheels*) especially in the States of Assam, Bihar and West Bengal (Table 19.6). These are shallow, nutrient-rich water bodies formed due to a change in the course of rivers. Some of these retain connection with the main river, at least in the monsoons, while others have lost it permanently. Due to their high production potential these are adopted for aquaculture-based capture fisheries. The areas having river connections can be exploited optimally by keeping the deeper central zones exclusively for capture fisheries and renovating the marginal pockets for culture fisheries.

TABLE 19.5: **Important Estuarine Fishery Resources of India**

S. No.	Estuarine system	Estimated area (ha)	Production (t)
1.	Hooghly-Matlah	234000	20000 to 26000
2.	Godavary estuary	18000	c.5000
3.	Mahanadi estuary	3000	c.550
4.	Narmada estuary	30000	c.4000
5.	Peninsular estuarine system	—	c.2000
6.	Chilka lagoon	103600	c.4000
7.	Pulicate lake	36900	760-1370
8.	Vembanad lake and Kerala Backwaters	50000	14000-17000
9.	Wetlands of West Bengal		
	(a) Freshwater Bheries	9600	10-14
	(b) Saline Bheries	33000	c.25500
10.	Mangroves	356500	—

Source: Sinha, 1997.

2. Fishery Management Under Different Property and Management Regimes

The aforementioned inland waters vary significantly in nature and magnitude of their resources. Accordingly, these are managed differently for fishery activities under various property and management regimes. This mechanism has a direct bearing on the socio-economic conditions of ultimate clientele, the fishers. In the following paragraphs an attempt has been made to discuss fisheries management under these regimes for different inland resources, with special emphasis on rivers.

2.a. The Rivers

Traditionally, the rivers are managed as a common property resource. These have multiple uses for riparian area population. The residents of these areas cannot be excluded from its use, as they have the rights and duties in common property regime. They have the customary ownership of the local river stretch as social units with definite membership. The collective management of rivers should ensure that the interests of all its users including the fishers are protected in a sustained way. The key concept to assure it is characterizing the relationship of different users of river for purposes of domestic, commercial,

TABLE 19.6: **The Floodplain Wetlands of India**

S.No.	State	River basin	Local name	Area (ha)
1.	Arunachal Pradesh	Kameng, Subansiri, Siang Dibang, Lohit, Dihang, Tira	Beel	2500
2.	Assam	Brahamputra and Barak	Beel	100000
3.	Bihar	Gandak and Kosi	Mauns and Chaurs	40000
4.	Manipur	Iral, Imphal, Thoubal	Pat	16500
5	Meghalaya	Someshwari and Jinjiram	Beel	213
6.	Tripura	Gumti	Beel	500
7.	West Bengal	Ganga and Ichamati	Beel	42500
	Total			202213

Source: Sinha, 1997.

drainage use, etc. The river being a fluvial resource, the interests of users with domestic and drainage purposes may be safeguarded in a sustainable manner, in the stretches with sufficient width and depth. But the crux lies with the commercial users or the individuals who depend on rivers for their livelihood, e.g. members of fishing community, agriculture (cutting water for irrigation) and sand industry, water transporters, etc. To diffuse this situation, the property regimes must clarify the perceptions of collective use of scarce and valuable or worth protecting resources. It would restrict all the users to exploit the resource in tolerable limits, in order to avoid any encroachment in the interests of other users with same or different purposes. Riverine fish stock, a scarce and valuable natural resource, has followed a declining trend over the past few decades due to human invasion in the interest of fishers through water abstraction, dam construction, river training, sedimentation, etc. It emphasized the need to discuss riverine fish exploitation in the context of all the other multiple water use rights. But, it would be a very cumbersome exercise. For simplicity, fishing alone may be discussed under different property rights and management systems.

As stated earlier, rivers are the State property and various river stretches within or between the States belong to departments of fisheries, revenue, forestry, village panchayats, etc. These departments adopt varied policies for fishing in these stretches. The rivers being fluvial and fish being migratory renewable resource, it is difficult to apportion the fish biomass in territorial limits. From the fisheries viewpoint, most of the rivers are in open access, with some exceptions where these are leased to cooperatives or private parties. A comparative account of fishery activities under these management regimes has been made selecting one stretch in each of these management regimes, i.e. open access, private and cooperatives (Table 19.7), for an in-depth study. These include stretches of river Ganga (Kanpur to Farakka) under open access; river Yamuna (Yamuna Nagar to Panipat) under private (contractor); and river

TABLE 19.7: **Riverine Fisheries under Different Property Right and Management Regimes**

S. No.	Item	System		
		Common Property	Private	Cooperative
1.	River stretch	Ganga, Kanpur to Farakka	Yamuna, Yamuna Nagar to Panipat	Ghagra, Ghagra Barrage to Faizabad
2.	Year	1996-97	1997-98	1997-98
3.	Property right regime	State departments of Revenue/Forestry, Village Panchayat	State departments of Revenue/Forestry, Village Panchayat	State departments of Revenue/Forestry, Village Panchayat
4.	Management system	Individual fisherman/fishermen group	Contractor	Fishermen Cooperative
5.	Whether in multiple uses, if yes in			
	(i) Fishing	Yes	Yes	Yes
	(ii) Bathing	Yes	Yes	Yes
	(iii) Washing clothes	Yes	Yes	Yes
	(iv) Drinking water	Yes	Yes	Yes
6.	Duration of lease	———	One year	One year
7.	Harvesting period	Round the year with lean period in monsoon	Round the year with lean period in monsoon	October to January and March to June
8.	Arrangements for fisheries requisites	Individual/Shared	Self+Contractor	Cooperative
9.	Time and mode of payment	In cash on the day of disposal of catch	Daily/Weekly/ Monthly in cash	Daily/Weekly in cash
10.	Remuneration for the fish catch	Within the group based on pre-decided %age Share	Based on prefixed labour charges/ royalty per Kg of catch	Based on fixed/% of Market price per kg of catch
11.	Distribution of profits	Only as remuneration	Solely of contractor	Among members

Ghagra (Ghagra Ghat to Faizabad) under cooperatives. To have a proper comparison it is necessary to understand these regimes in terms of rights and duties.

In open access, as the name indicates, the riverine fish biomass has a free access to any one. There is a free entry to riverine fishing enterprise, which allows anyone to fish anywhere, anytime. Although, there are regulations under the Indian Fisheries Act for fishing and responsibility of conservation of fish stock lies with the State governments, but due to the unmanageable vast magnitude of this natural resource, institutional arrangements and authority systems inevitably cease in this regime. Under the cooperative management regime, State Governments lease out the stretch to fisheries cooperative societies, and confer all the rights and powers of decision-making regarding fisheries in the stretches on the cooperatives. Generally, the stretches are leased for one year, but the lease is likely to be renewed every year, unless there were some serious complaints about fisheries management by the cooperative. The members of the society have the right to fish and exclude non-members from fishing. The non-members have the duty to abide by this exclusion.

The only difference between the cooperative and private management regimes was that the fishing rights and power to transfer fishing rights and decision-making rested with the individual to whom the stretch was leased out in the latter case. The stretch was leased out for a period of one year based on open auction. As there was an open auction, so, the lease may continue with some person or may be transferred to others, with a higher bid. The lessee or contractor transfers the fishing rights to the fishers on terms and conditions best suited to him. In all the regimes fishing rights rest with fishers, but they have to perform the fishing activities within socially acceptable limits, and allow the non-fishing people to use water to meet their day-to-day requirements.

The studied stretch of river Ganga with open access is recognized as rich in fish biomass, and fishing activities were also intense as compared to stretches of rivers Yamuna and Ghagra under private and cooperative management regimes. The ownership of different portions of the stretch was with various departments, e.g. fisheries, revenue, forestry, village panchayat, etc. Some of these portions were disputed as more than one department claimed the same stretch. Furthermore, since the districts on both banks of a river may also be different, so the conflict on ownership was also to be within the same department operating in different districts. In some stretches the same stretch was leased out by two offices to different parties, which led to great tension in the area. This duplicity of fishing rights and claim of ownership by more than one department led to overall degradation of fishery resources of the river stretch, due to improper monitoring and exploitation of fish stock. All the river stretches have multiple water uses, i.e. for fishing, bathing, washing clothes, drinking water, etc.

Regarding the management regimes, under open access, individual fishermen or groups of fishermen can fish anywhere in the river, but in a few cases, due to declining fish catch, local fishers may prohibit the migrating fishers from fishing in their area. It largely depends upon the mutual relationship between the fishers of different stretches. In the case of cooperatives the member fishers mostly fished in their own stretch. The length of stretches leased to a society varied greatly. Accordingly, the fishing area and time spent by fishermen fluctuated for these cooperatives. For private management regimes, the river stretch was generally leased out to contractors annually. These contractors were mostly the fish traders, who engaged local fishermen or professional fishing parties for fish harvesting. Regarding the level of exploitation and follow-up of conservation measures, the open access and cooperatives adopt mild fishing practices and try to follow the mesh and fish size regulations, as they have to continue fishing over the years, but for contractors under private regime, as the lease period is one year, and there is no certainty for future, the fishing gears used are comparatively less mild. The parties engaged for fish harvesting generally use smaller mesh dragnets to have the maximum catch. The fishing period under all the management regimes is almost the whole year with a lean period or close season during the monsoon months. The only exception was the stretch of river Ghagra. The water level of the river was observed to have high fluctuations over the year, due to the opening of the Ghagra barrage gates, so it reduced the fishing period over the year, as it is difficult and uneconomic to fish under very high water levels. The fishing in the stretch was limited to March to June and October to January.

The fishery requisites under open access and cooperatives were either owned or shared by the fishermen, while in the case of private regime these belonged to fishermen (may also be financed by contractors) or provided by contractors (Table 19.8).

The remuneration for catch and distribution of profits were the best in the case of open access. These were on the basis of the contribution in effort and fisheries requisites. The fishermen having the boat and nets would get a higher share than the fishermen sharing these requisites with him. For private and cooperatives the remuneration and payments largely depended upon the pattern of disposal of catch and the mode adopted for payments by the respective regimes. It may be daily, weekly or monthly. The contractors generally remunerated the catch of local fishers at some fixed rate/royalty per kg. But, in the case of a hired fishing party it may be on the share basis. The contractor being the fish trader himself did not share the profits with the fishers. In the case of cooperatives the remuneration was in terms of per cent of market price, after deduction of commission by the society for rendering the services. The profits are distributed among the member fishers according to

TABLE 19.8: **The Input-Output Profile of Riverine Fisheries under Different Management Regimes**

S. No.	Item	System		
		Common Property	Private	Cooperative
A.	**Input profile**			
1.	Per cent of fishers with type of gears			
(i)	Gill net	67.06	56.27	57.14
(ii)	Drag net	18.14	32.23	17.14
(iii)	Cast net	7.78	5.02	2.86
(iv)	Hook and line	24.37	21.73	34.20
(v)	Other	6.59	5.62	20.00
2.	Per cent of fishers with own boat	79.64	62.13	25.00
3.	Hired labour (Mandays/Year)	—	96.28	—
4.	Annual fishing effort (Mandays/Year)	281.82	293.24	147.63
B.	**Output**			
1.	Catch per family (kg/year)	1431.67	780.02	376.46
2.	Catch per day (kg)	5.08	2.66	2.55
C.	**Costs and benefits**			
1.	Costs			
(i)	Fixed cost (per year)	2907.31	3017.17	1451.48
(ii)	Variable cost (per year)	1712.21	1737.39	285.43
(iii)	Total cost	4619.52	4754.56	1736.91
2.	Benefits			
(i)	Price received (kg)	24.09	18.79	34.82
(ii)	Gross returns (per year)	34488.93	14656.58	13108.34
(iii)	Net returns (per year)	29869.41	9902.02	11371.43
(iv)	Net returns (Rs. per kg)	20.86	12.69	30.21
(v)	Input-output ratio	7.49	2.90	7.55

their share capital.

The pattern of the inputs used, fishing efforts, cost structure and net returns under different regimes are depicted in Table 19.8. Most prevalent gears under all the regimes were gill nets followed by hook and line in the case of open access and cooperatives. For a private regime it was the drag net due to fishing operations by hired professional parties, which generally use this type of net. The highest percentage of crafts was owned under open access followed by private and cooperative regimes. The area of operation was limited for cooperative and private regimes, while it was not so for the open access. To avail of this facility of fishing anywhere, the fishers preferred to have their own fisheries requisites. It increased their degree of freedom for fishing, which influenced their returns. In the case of cooperatives, the member fishers have a limited area of operation and have greater association, thus they preferred to share the requisites, particularly the boats. In the case of a private regime, the remuneration is low, so, fishers do not want to share their catch with anyone, as this would reduce their income. This led them to prefer their own boats and gears. Further, the contractor also provided them finance to purchase the inputs. In the case of cooperatives and open access, credit support from any institution was very rare.

The annual fishing effort was the highest for a private regime followed by open access and cooperatives, while the annual and per-day catch was maximum for open access. The cost structure was almost similar for open access and private regimes, while very low for cooperatives. These observations may be attributed to the intensity of fishing or the fishing effort put in by the fishers under different regimes. Fluctuations and the height of water level and the fish stock present in the river effected these over the year. The lower cost in the case of a cooperative may be due to lower fishing effort and sharing of inputs.

The per kg price received by the fishers may be recognized as the indicator of the impact of these management regimes and fishing rights on the fishers' income. These estimates favoured cooperative regimes the most followed by open access. The lowest values for these estimates were under the private regime. The cooperatives directly dispose of the catch in the local market or at a nearby town. The members of the society themselves do the marketing, eliminating all the market intermediaries, and so received much better prices. In the open access the catches are auctioned in the wholesale markets and fishermen receive the auction price after duduction of the wholesaler's commission. In the private regime, the contractor remunerated the fishers catch in terms of fixed rate/royalty per kg, so they are deprived of the benefits of the market price.

The gross and net annual and per-day returns were maximum for an open access regime followed by the cooperative and private, but the net income per kg of catch favoured cooperatives the most followed by open access, and the least for the private regime. The input-output ratios also indicated the superiority of cooperatives and open access regimes over the private as their value for these ratios were more than two-and-a-half-times of the estimated ratio for the private regime. It depicted the working efficiency and extent of remuneration of fish catch for different management regimes and revealed that privatization of the fishing rights in riverine fisheries would accelerate the process of social disequilibrium to broaden the income inequalities. It would push the downtrodden further down and push the already economically well-off fish traders further up.

2.b. The Reservoirs

The reservoirs are mainly the irrigation or hydroelectric power projects, so they mostly belong to the irrigation department or are under the control of boards or authorities. Most of them were adopted for fisheries after construction and, therefore, the fisheries component was missing during its planning. This resulted in absence of pre-impoundment survey and operations. There are a substantial number of submerged trees, rocks, etc., which hinder fishing activities in the reservoirs. There removal at later stages enhances the management costs. For better fisheries management of the reservoirs on scientific lines, its management board must, therefore, have representation from fisheries. Since these water bodies, if managed properly for fisheries operations, prove to be very effective in enhancing the incomes of rural mass and, in addition, provide them sufficient employment as in the case of the Gobind Sagar and Pong Dam reservoirs in Himachal Pradesh (Katiha 1994). Therefore, it should be mandatory to have fisheries experts on the planning bodies for any river valley project.

The fisheries in these water bodies is considered as a secondary activity, the primary being the irrigation and hydro-power generation. The department of fisheries or other fisheries agencies obtain the fishery management rights from the owners of the reservoirs, either by paying some royalty/nominal amount (Rihand in Uttar Pradesh and Kansbati in West Bengal) or even free (Gobind Sagar and Pong Dam in Himachal Pradesh). Some of the fisheries departments transfer the fishing rights to other government/cooperative/private agency and receive the royalty with/without rendering any fisheries development services.

One of the most important institutional arrangements for the exploitation of fisheries in reservoirs is the leasing system. It depends on the trends of fish production, income and expenditure of the department, socio-economic conditions of the fishermen, government policy towards cooperatives and above all the status of the States' fisheries resources and the concerned reservoir. The leasing system may vary within the State and even for the same reservoir over time. Different leasing systems followed in various Indian States are summarized in Table 19.9. These include departmental fishing, licence fishing, free licence fishing, share system, open auction to cooperative/private party.

The duration of a lease also plays an important role in the fisheries management of a reservoir. The lease period generally varies according to the size of the reservoir due to different best suited fisheries management

TABLE 19.9: **Leasing Systems and Fishing Rights in Reservoirs of Different States (Modified from Anonymous, 1994)**

S. No.	State	Leasing systems and fishing rights
1.	Andhra Pradesh	Department fishing, licensed fishing, free licensing system, share system.
2.	Bihar	Departmental fishing with 50% share of fishers, open auction with 10% concessions for cooperatives society and first year stocking by fisheries department.
3.	Gujarat	Leased to Gujarat Fisheries Development Corporation or Gujarat Fisheries Central Co-operative Association Ltd. with varying rate of royalty and target quota. These bodies either conduct yearly auction to contractors or give their own fixed rates to fishermen. The fisheries department monitors the fish harvesting to control overexploitation.
4.	Haryana	Open auction for fishing only in the month of May.
5.	Himachal Pradesh	Annual lease to local cooperatives on the basis of 15% royalty to department. The fisheries management is done by fisheries department including stocking practices and monitoring of fish harvesting and conservation activities.
6.	Karnataka	Licensing with fee based on types and quantity of nets used.
7.	Madhya Pradesh	Leased to Madhya Pradesh State Fisheries Development Corporation on some fixed royalty per tonne. Corporation collects royalty from fishermen at a fix rate for their catch. Annual contract for fishing based on tenders with highest royalty for different varieties.
8.	Maharashtra	For leasing priority is for cooperatives @ maximum water spread × fixed rate per ha for three years; otherwise the department stocks the reservoir and issues monthly licences to fishermen of different cooperatives; department issues free permits to members of cooperatives and charges royalty on some fixed rate.
9.	Orissa	Leased to cooperative at some fixed rate per sq mile; in absence of cooperatives open auction.
10.	Punjab	Departmental fishing.
11.	Rajasthan	Open auction for one year with 12.5% concession to cooperatives, long-term lease with 5% annual increase in lease amount.
12.	Tamil Nadu	Departmental fishing, lease to State Fisheries Corporation based on royalty or share basis, licencing to fishermen on monthly/yearly basis.
13.	Uttar Pradesh	Open auctionfor (i) one year with size <100 ha, (ii) three years for 100-150 ha, (iii) five years for 500-1000 ha and (iv) ten years for > 1000 ha.
14.	West Bengal	On lease to West Bengal State Fisheries Development Corporation (WBSFDC) on nominal rent. WBSFDC engages fishermen of cooperatives on 50% share basis.

practices for various sized reservoirs. The large and medium reservoirs should be managed as stocking-cum-capture fisheries resources, while for the small reservoirs, culture-based management is considered the best. In some States (Uttar Pradesh and Rajasthan) the reservoirs with an area (i) below 100 ha. are leased for one year, (ii) 100-500 ha for 3 years, (iii) 500-1000 ha for 5 years, and (iv) above 1000 ha for 10 years. The past experience reveals that reservoirs entrusted to State agencies for the monitoring of fish stock through stocking and check on harvesting consistently maintained the good production level, while in the case of reservoirs under the control of private contractors, the results were *vice versa*. If the fisheries management rested with cooperatives, the results were moderate, but required a proper supervision at stocking and fish harvesting stages.

2.c. Aquacultural Water Bodies

Most of the States in India have ponds and tanks as the aquacultural water bodies. Generally, these are the community village ponds (CVP) under the ownership of either Village Panchayats or private parties. Like the rivers, traditionally, these have been under the control of Village Panchayats and managed as common property resources. These have multiple uses for human and animal populations, for day-to-day requirements and all the members of the village have a right to use its water under the common property regime. But, unlike the rivers the quantity and area of water in these bodies is limited, and the multiple uses greatly influence each other's activity. The nature of institutional arrangements or working rules defines the extent of property regimes of CVPs and water resources for aquacultural development (Marothia, 1992). In other words these imply the guidelines for interdependent decision-making in reciprocal and joint efforts to enable each individual to relate himself to other productive efforts. These multiple uses of CVPs influence their productivity and rate of adoption for fish culture. Village Panchayats lease out these CVPs either under the FFDA programme or otherwise to fishermen cooperatives, groups of fishermen or individual fishermen. The leasing is only for fishery activities. The leasing policy of these water bodies varies in different States. But, in most of the cases, the priority for allotment of CVPs is given to local cooperatives, fishermen groups or individual fishermen belonging to the SC/ST category and operating below the poverty line. The lease rent of CVPs varies according to its size, leasing period, ownership, perennial or seasonal water availability, weed population and extent of maintenance. The socio-economic, cultural and political structure and location of pond are also the important factors in fixing the rent of CVPs. The lease period of CVPs differs according to the ownership, the lessee and the size of pond and whether or not covered under the FFDA scheme.

The study conducted by Singh and Bhattacharjee (1991) in West Bengal indicated that the ponds and tanks under common property regimes had a low fish productivity. Depending upon the technical and financial feasibility of aquaculture, the government should promote it on a cooperative basis and provide funds for the restoration of degraded CVPs in addition to provision for technical guidance to fish farmers. The study preferred cooperatives over public or private management as it is considered most appropriate means of ensuring equity, sustainability and satisfaction of co-users of such ponds. The study also advised to involve NGOs for promotion of aquaculture and extending the necessary technical support to aquaculturists. Marothia (1995, 1997) has revealed that the multiple use of CVPs created conflicts and disorder among the fishers and village community as the water of CVPs was not safe for human consumption. The study has also suggested institutional modification over the existing practice, by reserving close-in ponds for common village use and the more distant for aquaculture to resolve the spatial and temporal conflicts. The study has also showed dissatisfaction over the caste-based preferential allotment of CVPs for aquaculture. It has opined that on the one hand such practices reduced the productivity of freshwater aquaculture and, on the other, created socio-economic disorder. The study has favoured management of CVPs by cooperatives.

2.d. The Estuaries

Most of the estuaries in India are in open access regime. The winter migratory fisheries locally known as "been jals" in the lower zone of the Hooghly estuary is a typical example of open access regime in inland fisheries (Paul *et al.* 1997). A large number of fishing groups migrate from different areas of the Hooghly estuary during the winter season and establish transitory fishing camps at suitable spots on the seaface in the lower zone of the estuary and remain engaged in bagnet fishing from the end of October to early February. The share of this fishery increased to over 67 per cent in the total annual catch of the entire estuary during 1984-85 to 1993-94 as compared to 32.7 per cent during 1970-71 to 1974-75. This tremendous rise in the catch may be attributed to the deployment of mechanized boats, large number of bagnets and higher number of fishermen involved in fishing operations during recent years, which was possible only due to the open access system of exploitation. Contrary to the subsistence character of riverine fisheries, winter bagnet migratory fisheries of the lower estuary seem to be a pronounced activity at highly remunerative levels. Considering the intensity of fishing in the winter months this fishery may be termed as seasonal industry. But this open access system in the winter migratory bagnet fishery has proved to be detrimental in the recent past. With an unchecked and unlimited increase in the fishing effort, the catch per unit effort (CPUE) has showed a gradual but continuous decline after 1994-95 (93.72 kg). It was 89.46, 77.24 and 53.12 kg during 1995-96, 1996-97 and 1997-98, respectively. Though the total catch kept on increasing initially (20.8, 28.2 and 35.8 thousand tonnes during 1994-95, 1995-96 and 1996-97, respectively), it showed a sharp decline in 1997-98 (21.2 tonnes). This is an outcome of the open access system and overexploitation. The enormous rise in the fishing effort seems to have already surpassed the maximum sustainable harvest level and, if not checked, would prove detrimental for future fishery.

2.e. Flood Plain Lakes

The flood plain lakes are distributed mainly in the States of Assam, Bihar and West Bengal. In Bihar, most of the lakes are public property barring a few with private ownership (Sinha and Jha 1987). The government had classified them under two categories: (i) lakes with "Makhana" and lotus; and (ii) lakes without "Makhana" and lotus. The fishing rights in both the types of lakes vest with the department of fisheries, although, for the former category of lakes, they are with the revenue department. These are auctioned annually by the fisheries department to local fishermen cooperatives. The auction amount varies according to the area and pattern of the fish catch of the lake. Many of the lakes could not be adopted for fisheries due to unsettled disputes and claims of cooperatives. The recent upsurge in the number of fake cooperatives tends to increase rivalry and litigation. There is an urgent need for effective enforcement of the fisheries and cooperative legislation for the proper fisheries development and conservation of these water bodies.

The short-term leasing policy of the fisheries department also affects the fisheries of these lakes (Jha 1997). Due to the short period of the lease, the lessees are not interested in investment in fisheries development in the lakes. On the contrary, they try to catch out the entire stock of fish, irrespective of the size and species, resulting in further depletion of the fish stock. It would amount to converting these most fragile ecosystems into fishery deserts.

3. Conclusions

The rivers, reservoirs, ponds and tanks, estuaries and floodplain lakes form the inland fishery resources of India. Most of them belong to State Departments and Village Panchayats, while some are under private property regimes. Being the State property, these resources have multiple water use rights, including fishing, to meet the day-to-day requirements. Therefore, these are managed as common property or common pool resources (CPR). For fishery activities, the rights may be open or transferred to cooperatives or private parties. The decision regarding designing the institutional arrangements and management policies for these CPRs depends upon the characteristics of the resource. These include magnitude, quantum of water, lotic or lentic, open or close, seasonal or perennial, source of water, fish production, income and expenses of the department, socio-economic conditions of fishers, government policy, etc. Based on earlier observations, some of the suggestions for institutional arrangements, and management and property regimes are given below to restore and improve the productivity of these inland fishery CPRs.

1. The rivers are the storehouse for enormous flowing water with State ownership. The property rights of the same stretch with more than one department cause many conflicts in the exploitation and management of fish stock. Furthermore, due to the ambulatory nature of fish, it is not possible to apportion the fish stock into physical boundaries. It is, therefore, essential that for fishery purposes, the rivers may be treated as a national property. A Riverine Fisheries Development Authority, at national level, need be constituted for the development of fisheries of the major rivers of the country flowing through two or more States. It is very necessary because in the case of such rivers none of the riparian State is ready to spend for its fisheries development with the benefits also accruing to other(s). Along with this, the fishing rights in the riverine stretches within a State should be transferred to its fisheries department. It may help in overcoming the problems and maintain proper co-ordination for fisheries development.
   The comparative efficiency of different management systems for fishery operations favoured cooperatives the most followed by open access, although there exists an immense scope for improvement. The privatization of fishing rights in rivers has created social and economic inequalities, to the benefit of the affluent fish traders or contractors at the cost of poor fishers. This practice needs to be discouraged for the welfare of the fishing community.
2. The reservoirs have an immense fishery potential, but to harness and manage this potential in a sustained manner, fishery should receive the required emphasis even during the planning stage of such a project. Further, the fisheries management of these waters under the supervision of State agencies like the State Fisheries Department would yield better results.
3. In addition to the activities of FFDA, aquaculture should be promoted with the necessary credit and technical support to fish farming agencies. Necessary changes in the lending norms of banks are a must for an easy flow of credit to the aquaculturists. The preferential allotment of these waters to production oriented cooperatives with sufficient representation of fishers would provide impetus to the development of

this enterprise.

4. The estuarine fishery is a unique example of open access fisheries regimes and is recognized as a profitable proposition with increasing fishing effort and investments on mechanization and infrastructure. It has led to overexploitation of the fish stock, as is evident from the declining catch per unit effort. This may push this activity into the third stage of production. It pinpoints the urgent need to regulate the effort and limit the fish harvest to the maximum sustainable level, through appropriate institutional arrangements.
5. The fishery operations in the floodplain wetlands are either under the cooperative or private management regimes. But, recognition of genuine cooperatives for lease, revitalization of the cooperative spirit in these institutions and increasing the lease period are some of the institutional arrangements necessary to enhance fish production from these nutritionally rich biomes.

REFERENCES

Anonymous. 1994. *Handbook on Fisheries.* Global Fishing Chimes Private Limited, Vishakhapatnam, pp. 45-47.

Anonymous. 1996a. *Handbook on Fisheries Statistics.* Ministry of Agriculture (Department of Agriculture and Co-operation, Fisheries Division), New Delhi: Government of India, 217p.

Anonymous. 1996b. *Ninth Five Year Plan for Fisheries.* Report of the Working Group, New Delhi.

Indian Institute of Management, Ahmedabad. 1985. Inland Fish Marketing in India. Volume 4a & b. New Delhi: Concept Publishing Company, 1184 p.

Jha, B.C. 1997. "Salient Ecological Features of the *Mauns* and *Chaurs* of Bihar and Their Fisheries". In Sugunan, V.V. and M. Sinha (Ed.), *Fisheries Enhancement of Small Reservoirs and Floodplain Lakes in India,* Bulletin 75, Barrackpore: Central Inland Capture Fisheries Research Institute, pp. 167-174.

Jhingran, A.G. 1991. "Indian Fisheries: Milestone of Progress". In: *Glimpses of Science,* Allahabad: National Academy of Science, pp. 49-68.

Jhingran, V.G. 1991a. *Fish and Fisheries of India.* Delhi: Hindustan Publishing Corporation (India), pp. 79-107.

Katiha, P.K. 1994. "Natural Resource Management: A Case Study of Reservoir Fisheries in Himachal Pradesh". Ph.D. Thesis, Unpublished. Department of Social Sciences, Nauni: Dr. Y.S. Parmar University of Horticulture and Forestry, Solan (H.P.). 192 p.

Marothia, D.K. 1992. "Village Ponds and Aquacultural Development: Issues of Inequality in Common Property Regimes". Presented at Third Annual Common Property Conference of International Association for the Study of Common Property, Washington, D.C. September 18-20, 1992.

Marothia, D.K. 1995. "Village Ponds and Aquaculture Development: Is Conflict Inevitable?" Invited Paper presented to the National Workshop on Poultry Fisheries and Food Processing Organised for the Members of Parliament held at the National Academy of Aquacultural Research Management, Hyderabad, July 4-7.

Marothia, D.K. 1997. "Institutional Arrangements for Common Village Fish Ponds". In *Natural Resource Economics*, In: Kerr, J.M., D.K. Marothia, K. Singh, C. Ramaswamy and W.R. Bentley (eds.), New Delhi: Oxford & IBH Press, pp. 463-476.

Paul, S., P.M. Mitra, D.K. De, H.K. Sen, N.C. Mandal and P. Singh. 1997. *Winter Bagnet Fishery of the Hooghly Estuary: An Economic Evaluation*. Bulletin 76, Barrackpore: Central Inland Capture Fisheries Research Institute, 17 p.

Rao, K.L. 1979. *India's Water Wealth: Its Assessment, Uses and Projections*. New Delhi: Orient Logman Limited, pp. 55-102.

Singh, K. and S. Bhattacharjee. 1994. "The Bergram Majhipara Common Pool Fish Pond. In: Kartar Singh, *Managing Common Pool Resources: Principals and Case Studies*. Bombay: Oxford University Press. pp. 288-307.

Sinha, M. 1997. "Inland Fisheries Resources of India and Their Utilisation". In: V.V. Sugunan and M. Sinha (eds.), *Fisheries Enhancement of Small Reservoirs and Floodplain Lakes in India*, Bulletin 75, Barrackpore: Central Inland Capture Fisheries Research Institute, pp. 167-174.

Sinha, M. and B.C. Jha. 1997. *Ecology and Fisheries of Ox-bow Lakes (Maun) of North Bihar—A Threatened Eco-system*. Bulletin 74, Barrackpore: Central Inland Capture Fishereis Research Institute, pp. 37-38.

Sugunan, V.V. 1995. *Reservoir Fisheries in India*. FAO Fisheries Technical Paper No. 345, Rome: Food and Agriculture Organisation, p. 6, 12.

20 Open Water Capture Fisheries: Development Strategies and Policies

P.V. Dehadrai

1. Introduction

Fisheries is all-pervading in the lives of more than 6.5 million fisherfolk in India. It is one community which loves their vocation. It is not only their profession but a way of life. Come rains and cyclones, a certain inner urge drives them to set out for fishing in the sea every morning with renewed enthusiasm and hope. Many a time several of them do not return. Once visiting the Cannanore coast in Kerala along with a colleague we talked to a fisherwoman waiting in her hut for her husband to return from fishing on a devastating cyclone day with the No. 5 danger signal hoisted by the authorities. The fisherwoman's hut had sand as the floor and coconut leaves thatched as a roof with a couple of *tin-pots* as utensils. When asked why many fisherwomen do not wear blouses, she informed that she had only two of them. But the requirements of her two growing daughters were more important so she had given the blouses to them. Witnessing such incidences of the prevalent abject poverty raises the goose flesh at times. Uncertainties of exploiting open water resources in the sea, rivers, streams and lakes aggravates the socio-economic stress on the community which already suffers from lack of resources.

Fisheries and aquaculture in the country have witnessed an impressive transformation from a highly traditional activity to one based on a well-developed and diversified infrastructure with an immense potential for industrialization. The fishery sector, particularly during the recent past, has played an important role in the Indian economy through employment generation, enhanced income and earning valuable foreign exchange.

These developments have encouraged private entrepreneurship with a substantial diversification of investment in the sector. This intervention of resource-rich entrepreneurship in fisheries has caused the avoidable stress on the artisanal fishery sector resulting in incidents of social and economic conflicts. So the question is: what could be the worth of all those development programmes which do not help to upgrade the quality of life of those poorest of the poor in the fisheries sector?

The fishery sector provides full-time or part-time gainful employment to about 3.84 million fisherfolk with an equally impressive segment of the population engaged in ancillary activities associated with fisheries and aquaculture. The fisheries compared to the agriculture and allied sectors offers the maximum equality and opportunity of employment to the womenfolk. The contribution of the fishery sector to the net domestic product has shown an eight-fold increase from Rs. 8.06 billion in 1980-81 to Rs. 67.5 billion in 1993-94 at corresponding current prices when compared to only the four-fold increase in agriculture during the same period. The share of fisheries in GDP from agriculture has almost doubled from 1.97 per cent in 1980-81 to 3.89 per cent in 1993-94 (Anon 1996a).

Increase in productivity and production of fish would be one of the continuing programmes. Based on the projected human population and considering that 56 per cent of the population would be including fish in their animal protein diet and further considering the WHO recommendation of providing a minimum 11 kg of fish per capita annually in human diet, a total fish production of about 6.4 million tonnes is suggested at the end of the century. The individual growth rate for marine fish production at 3 per cent and for inland fish production at 6 per cent should be considered a rational target to achieve a total annual growth rate of 4.38 per cent during the next five years in terms of production. To achieve this growth rate, the sector-wise development strategies and policies for open water fisheries in marine and inland sectors under common property regime are suggested in this chapter.

2. Marine and Inland Fisheries Resources

The country is singularly endowed with a vast expanse of water resources amenable for fishery (Table 20.1). While marine resources are spread in the three oceans encompassing the 8,129 km coastline, the inland waters in the form of rivers, canals, estuaries, lagoons, natural and man-made lakes, backwaters and brakishwater impoundments and mangrove wetlands constitute the bedrock of inland fishery and acquaculture.

2.a. Marine Resources

The Indian Ocean covering the area between longitudes 30° and 150° and

TABLE 20.1: **Water Resources for Fisheries in India**

Oceanic EEZ	2.02 million sqkm
Coastline	8129 km
Continental shelf	0.5 million sq km
Coastal aquaculture area	0.9 million sq ha
Rivers & Channels	1,71,334 km
Reservoirs	2.05 milion ha
Ponds & Tanks	2.9 million ha
Jheels & Swamps	7.9 million ha

Source: Fisheries Statistics, Ministry of Agriculture and Cooperation, Govt. of India, 1998.

from Asian landmass in the north to 50° South has a total area of 51 million sqkm. After the declaration of the Exclusive Economic Zone (EEZ) in 1977, the area available to India is estimated at 2.02 million sqkm comprising 0.86 million sqkm. on the west cost, 0.56 million sqkm on the east coast and 0.60 million sqkm around the Andaman and Nicobar Islands (Table 20.2). With the absolute right on the EEZ, India has also acquired the responsibility to conserve,

TABLE 20.2: **Statewise Marine Fishery Resources of India**

Sl.	States/Uts.	Continental Shelf ('000 Sq.mn)	Number of Landing Centres	Number of Villages	Approx. Length of Coastline (km)
1.	Andhra Pradesh	31	379	409	974
2.	Goa	10	87	91	104
3.	Gujarat	164	773	771	1600
4.	Karnataka	25	28	204	300
5.	Kerala	40	226	222	590
6.	Maharashtra	112	184	387	720
7.	Orissa	24	62	329	480
8.	Tamil Nadu	41	362	442	1000
9.	West Bengal (P)	17	47	652	157
10.	Andamans	35	57	45	2000
11.	Pondicherry	1	28	45	45
12.	Lakshadweep	1	28	45	45
13.	Daman & Diu	0	7	31	27
	Total	504	2251	3638	8129

Source: Annual Reports of State/UT Govts., 1993.

develop and optimally exploit the marine living resources up to 200 nautical miles of our coastline (Anon 1992).

2.a.1 Inland Resources

Rivers, the lifeline of our country, are the vast repository of unmatched biological wealth. With a catchment area of 3.12 million sqkm., the 14 large, 44 medium and innumerable minor rivers are characterized by their highly diverse fish fauna. While the 14 large river systems form 83 per cent of the total drainage areas of the country, the next group of 44 rivers constitute another 7 per cent of the total area. The minor rivers mostly confined to coastal areas, where the width of the land between the mountains and the sea is less than 100 km, constitute the remaining 10 per cent. The total length of the rivers and canals has been estimated at 1.7 lakh km. Various estuarine systems cover an area of over 2.7 million ha and have been identified as important sources of fish and prawn seed. The estuaries are vital for the fisheries health of both riverine and marine ecosystems (Anon 1996b). The floodplain lakes are a continuum of the rivers and the resource constitutes an area of about 2 lakh ha in the Ganga and Brahmaputra basins. These lakes are important as they have a vital bearing on the fisheries and ecology of the river systems (see chapter; Sinha and Katina).

A number of small, medium and large river valley projects have come into existence during the past four and a half decades with the primary objectives of irrigation, power generation and a host of other activities. Consequently a chain of man-made lakes have been created which also include the irrigation tanks. The present live storage capacity of the projects completed has been estimated at 162.47 cukm and with the completion of the projects under construction, this capacity is expected to increase to 239.18 cukm. (Sugunan 1995).

2.a.2 Fisheries Potential

Based on the available scientific information, exploratory surveys, experimental fishing and other data available, the potential harvestable yield of the Indian EEZ has been estimated at 3.9 million tonnes (Anon 1992). This potential has been estimated from three different sources, i.e. inshore fishing (up to 50 m depth) contributing 1.4 mt and the oceans providing 0.3 million tonnes of tuna and other commercial species (Table 20.3). In the inland sector, the resource potential has been estimated at 4.5 million tonnes which takes into account the production from both capture and culture fisheries (Anon 1976). However, excluding the contributions from aquaculture up to about 65 per cent,

TABLE 20.3: **Potential Resources Available, Level of Exploitation and the Potential Available for Exploitation Depthwise within the Indian EEZ**

Depth range (m)	0-50	50-200	200-500	Oceanic	Total
Demersal	1.28	0.625	0.028	—	1.933
Neretic Pelagic	1.00	0.742	—	—	1.742
Oceanic Pelagic	—	—	—	—	0.246
Total %	2.28	1.367	0.028	0.24	3.921
Present level of exploitation	2.08	0.82	Negligible	Negligible	2.9
Available for exploitation	0.20	0.737	0.028	0.246	1.211

Source: Fisheries Report, Ministry of Agriculture, Govt. of India, 1997.

the potential from reservoirs and rivers is immense.

For the effective exploitation of the estimated harvestable resource of 3.9 million tonnes from the Indian Exclusive Economic Zone (EEZ), it would be essential to enlarge our activities in marine fisheries beyond the limits of the area of present exploitation which is mostly within the near shore range. Harnessing of the off-shore waters by the mechanized craft will result in lower pressure on the near shore fishery resources of the continental shelf.

2.a.3 Fish Production

Total fish production in the country has increased from 2.801 million tonnes in 1984-85 to 5.30 million tonnes during 1996-97 of which 2.9 million tonnes was from the marine sector (Table 20.4). The average annual growth rate in fish production during the period 1984-85 (base year for the Seventh Plan) to 1996-97 is 5.6 per cent. The growth rate in the marine and inland sectors has been 5.0 per cent and 6.7 per cent per annum during this period. The average annual growth rate from 1990-91 to 1996-97 is 6.0 per cent. Though fish production has increased at a higher rate than foodgrains, milk and many other food items generally, the consumption of fish among the fish-eating population is still about 8 kg per capita per annum (Anon 1996a).

2.a.4 Fish Export

There has been a significant increase, both in quantum and value of export of marine products, and, for the first time, the value of export of marine products crossed the $ (US) 1 billion mark in 1994-95 (MPEDA 1996). The export of

TABLE 20.4: **Fish Production and Annual Growth Rate**

	Fish Production (Lakh Tonnes)			Percentage Annual Growth Rate		
Year	Marine	Inland	Total	Marine	Inland	Total
1950-51	5.34	2.18	7.53	-	-	-
1960-61	8.80	2.80	11.60	6.48	2.84	5.43
1970-71	10.86	6.70	17.56	2.34	13.93	5.14
1973-74	12.10	7.48	19.58			
1970-81	15.55	8.87	24.42	4.32	3.24	3.91
1981-82	14.45	9.99	24.44	-7.07	12.63	0.08
1982-83	14.27	9.40	23.67	-1.24	-5.91	-3.15
1983-84	15.19	9.87	25.06	6.45	5.00	5.87
1984-85	16.98	11.03	28.01	11.78	11.75	11.77
1985-86	17.16	11.60	28.76	1.06	5.17	2.68
1986-87	17.13	12.29	29.42	-0.17	5.95	2.29
1987-88	16.58	13.01	29.59	-3.21	5.86	0.58
1988-89	18.17	13.35	31.52	9.59	2.62	6.52
1989-90	22.75	14.02	36.77	25.21	5.02	16.66
1990-91	23.00	15.36	38.36	1.10	9.56	4.32
1991-92	23.47	17.10	41.57	6.39	11.33	8.37
1992-93	25.76	17.89	43.64	5.27	4.62	5.00
1993-94	26.49	19.95	46.44	2.83	11.51	6.39
1994-95	26.92	20.96	47.88	1.62	5.06	3.10
1995-96	28.25	21.25	49.50	4.94	1.38	3.38
1996-97	29.00	24.00	53.00	—	—	—

Source: (i) Fisheries Report, CMFRI upto 1970-71.
(ii) Annual Reports of State Govts./UTs.

marine products in terms of value registered a level of Rs. 4,697.50 crores in 1996-97 against Rs. 2,503.02 crores during 1993-94 (Table 20.5). Though shrimp accounted for 35 per cent of the quantity and about 71 per cent of the value of export in recent years, there has been diversification also and the country is now exporting frozen squid, cuttle fish/fillets, etc., in large quantities (Table 20.6). Prospects of export lie in diversified fishing, products and markets. Tuna and caephalopods have been identified as potential export candidates. The trade in frozen fish, fish fillets and surimi is promising and the industry has to be adequately geared and equipped to handle and export them in value-added

TABLE 20.5: **Export of Indian Marine Products during 1990-91 to 1997-98**

Year	Quantity (thousand tonnes)	Value (Rs. in crores)
1990-91	139.4	893.37
1991-92	171.8	1375.89
1992-93	208.6	1767.43
1993-94	244.0	2503.62
1994-95	307.3	3575.27
1995-96	296.3	3501.11
1996-97	378.2	4121.36
1997-98	386.0	4697.50

Source: Marine Products Export Development Authority, 1998.

TABLE 20.6: **Export of Major Commodity Groups of Marine Products**

Commodity Group	Qty.	(Tonnes)	Value (in Rs. million)	
	1995-96	1996-97	1995-96	1996-97
Fr. Shrimp	95724	105429	2356.81	2701.79
Fr. Fish	100093	172627	372.26	632.95
Fr. Squid	45025	40924	319.58	290.45
Fr. Cuttlefish	33845	31778	260.86	272.37
Dried items	7726	10475	46.48	47.03
Live items	1756	2030	21.31	33.97
Chilled items	2773	1956	26.28	22.71
Frozen Lobster	1587	1172	51.06	43.87
Others	7748	11808	40.00	40.11
Total	296277	378199	3501.11	4121.36

Source: Marine Products Export Development Authority, 1997.

packagings. Freshwater species, such as carps, too have a potential market, especially in West Asia. Consumer preferences and product identification need to be done for tapping this market and opening the export base for freshwater fishes. Quality control, exports promotion and marketing strategies need to be pursued more aggressively, keeping in view the contemporary requirements of the export markets.

2.a.5 Fishing Fleet

The Indian fishing fleet comprises 1.91 lakh traditional craft (including about 31,726 motorized traditional craft), about 46,918 mechanized craft and 180 large fishing vessels of 21m OAL and more. As seen from the number of traditional craft and small mechanized vessels, the major fishing activities are still concentrated in the area within 70-80 m depth zone. Industrial fishing is confined to the north-east coast, Visakhapatnam being the base. As compared to the west coast, the concentration of traditional craft is more on the east coast. In the case of motorized and mechanized vessels the trend is reverse (Table 20.7). This distribution pattern is also reflected in the total fish landings of the two coasts (Table 20.8).

TABLE 20.7: **Fishing Craft in Maritime States/UTs as in 1994-95 - by Coasts.**

(Number)

States/UTs	Traditional Crafts	Motorised Traditional Crafts Out of Col (2)	Mechanised Boats	Total
East Coast				
Andhra Pradesh	57,269	3,269	8,911	66,180
Orissa	10,249	2,453	2,453	11,914
Tamil Nadu	32,077	5,340	8,230	40,307
West Bengal	4,361	270	1,880	6,241
A&N Islands	1,340	160	230	1,241
Pondicherry	6,265	365	553	6,818
Total	111,561	11,857	21,469	133,030
West Coast				
Goa	2,000	900	850	2,850
Gujarat	12,653	4,283	8,365	21,018
Karnataka	13,141	1,189	3,655	16,796
Kerala	40,786	12,913	4,206	44,992
Maharashtra	9,888	286	7,930	17,918
Lakshadweep	1,078	298	443	1,521
Total	79,646	19,869	25,449	105,095
Grand Total	191,207	31,726	46,918	238,125

Source: Annual Reports of State/UTs.

TABLE 20.8: **State-wise Marine Fish Production during 1992-93 to 1994-95—by Coasts**

(in '000 Tonnes)

States/UTs	1992-93	1993-94	1994-95	1995-96
East Coast				
Andhra Pradesh	113.07	154.32	150.26	165.00
Orissa	119.38	103.93	122.89	115.00
Tamil Nadu	308.00	317.72	330.50	350.00
West Bengal	145.00	153.00	151.20	147.00
Andaman & Nicobar	24.17	25.08	26.12	26.00
Pondicherry	35.00	37.78	36.75	37.00
Total	744.62	791.82	817.72	840.00
West Coast				
Goa	101.49	102.11	98.46	110.00
Gujarat	589.00	619.84	645.26	632.00
Karnataka	174.19	174.52	173.75	182.00
Kerala	496.24	559.20	548.37	625.00
Maharashtra	387.55	350.40	357.00	380.00
Daman & Diu	13.43	11.53	11.51	15.00
Lakshadweep	9.73	9.41	9.75	11.00
Total	1771.63	1827.01	1844.10	1955.00
Deep Sea Fishing Sector	60.00	30.00	30.00	30.00
Total (East+West+ Deep Sea)	2576.25	2648.83	2691.81	2825.00

Source: Annual Reports of State/UTs.

2.a.6 Fish Stock Exploitation

While the inshore waters have been almost exploited at the MSY levels, the contribution from the deep sea has been insignificant. The thrust of the deep sea fishing industry has hitherto been directed at shrimps only, notwithstanding the other resources. As of today, the deep sea fishing industry is almost 100 per cent shrimp oriented enterprise, faced with overexploitation of the available shrimp resources as well as the fierce competition from the smaller class of vessels.

The further enhancement of fin and shellfish production from the marine sector lies in the deep sea. The estimated groupwise fishery potential of the Indian EEZ is given in Table 20.9. Tuna and tuna-like fish resources which have

TABLE 20.9: **Estimated Groupwise Fishery Potential of the Indian EEZ**

(in '000 tonnes)

Groups	Up to 50 m	Beyond 50 m	Total
Elasmobranchs	65	103	168
Eels	7	-	7
Catfish	60	63	123
Oil Sardine	191	-	191
Other Sardines	96	-	96
White bait	91	-	91
Other clupeids	157	14	171
Bombay duck	104	-	104
Lizard fish	27	21	48
Perches*	114	145	239
Sciaenids	120	22	142
Ribbon fish	95	216	311
Carangids	143	304	447
Silver bellies	82	4	86
Pomfrets	42	12	54
Mackerel	162	62	224
Seer fish	42	-	42
Tunnies	37	242	279
Flat fish	38	-	38
Penaeid prawns	178	**	178
Non-Penaeid prawns	54	-	54
Cephalopods	50	21	71
Priacanthus spp.	-	55	55
Black ruff	-	9	9
Indian drift fish	-	7	7
Deep sea prawns	-	3	3
Deep sea lobster	-	5	5
Oceanic tuna	-	209	209
Bill fishes	-	4	4
Others***	254	189	443
Total	2210	1690	3900

* Predominantly threadfin breams; ** About 4,000 tonnes of potential stock available in 50-100 m depth zone in the N.E. Coast not accounted; *** Includes a variety of low value fish, crabs, etc.

Source: Reports of CMFRI, Cochin, 1996.

an enormous potential in both domestic and export markets are underexploited. Though about 5 lakh tonnes of tuna is estimated, presently about 30,000 tonnes are being caught. Cephalopod resources which include squids, cuttlefish and octopus are put at 1.8 lakh tonnes, but only about 68,000 tonnes are being fished. The world market for cephalopods is fast expanding, but it has limited domestic market at present. Another major resource is finfishes of both pelagic and demersal origin (excluding tuna). Though sardines and mackerels are harvested optimally, anchovies are less exploited. Dried anchovy has a good market and should be exploited. The other promising groups are elasmobranchs, perches, ribbon fishes, silver bellies, catfishes, carangids, etc.

Lack of R&D efforts on fishing vessels best suited to Indian conditions has impeded the growth of this sector. The indigenous ship-building yards are doing very little in improving the situation. Mechanized vessels below 20 m OAL necessitate major inputs in their design not only to increase their voyage endurance period but also facilitate bringing back the catch in as good condition as possible. Adoption of new hull material such as fibre reinforced plastic (FRP) and ferro-cement boats (FCB) have not caught the imagination of the industry, in spite of the subsidy offered by the government. This aspect needs further promotion to reduce the dependence on wood. Similarly, artificial reefs and fish aggregating devices (FADs) which provide a measure for enhancing the food for fishes and also help in protecting the coastal ecosystem for sustainable fishery development need to be taken up in right earnest.

In regard to exploitation of EEZ living resources, the territorial water up to 12 nautical miles (except between Paradip and Nizampatnam where it is 24 nautical miles) is a State subject whereas the rest is with the Central Government. The fishery resources exploitation by the artisanal as well as the small mechanized sector has already extended beyond the territorial waters on the one hand and on the other the activity of large mechanized vessels and those under foreign collaborations exploiting the off-shore fishery have indulged in fishing activities disregarding demarcation of fishing areas. The overlapping interest of various sectors on resource areas has resulted in social and political conflicts. The management of fishery exploitation in the EEZ, therefore, requires close coordination between the Centre and the State with identified agencies to be entrusted with specific responsibilities.

Similarly, while the upgradation of the small mechanized sector to support the entrepreneurial response in the sector should be given high priority, the investment on motorization may not be indiscriminate in terms of number and in terms of putting additional financial burden on the artisanal community with fossil fuel as an expensive input in their operational economics.

2.a.7 Responsible Fishing

A new world order is emerging in global fisheries. Freedom of the seas is being replaced by exclusive access rights. Within coastal zones (Exclusive Economic Zones) extending 200 nautical miles, coastal States have jurisdiction over all the zone's main resources, and under the United Nations Convention on the Law of the Seas, they now control from 80-90 per cent of the global fish stock. This exclusive right has now been punctuated with the concept of responsibility and sustainable development (Code of Conduct for Responsible Fishing). UNCED's Rio Declaration in this regard says that *the right to fish is conditional and accompanied by the duty to manage and conserve resources for present and future generations.* It has, therefore, to be ensured that all programmes aimed towards the development of marine fisheries have in-built components of responsible, sustainable and environment friendly practices.

2.a.7 Marine Capture Fisheries

In pursuance of the objectives set for fisheries development in the country and taking into account the problems and potentialities of the vast and varied marine fisheries sector, the following thrust areas may be considered.

1. Upgradation of fishing capabilities of existing mechanized vessels (below 20 m OAL) by providing them with navigational aids (GPS, Fish Finders, Communication Equipment, etc.) and increasing their fish hold capacity.
2. Introduction of intermediate range of fishing vessels (15-19 m OAL) with capacity to fish at a depth of 70-150 m (or even up to 200 m). These vessels would be combination of trawlers, long liners, purse seiners, etc.
3. Diversification of existing trawlers (wherever there is extra fishing pressure) to long liners, purse seiners, squid jiggers, etc.
4. Continuation of assistance for procurement of patrol boats and their operations for enforcement of MFRA with increased involvement of States.
5. Motorization of traditional craft with OBM/IBM, including the gear component.
6. Introduction of new hull materials such as FRP and FCB for fishing vessels.
7. Provision of Central excise duty exemption on HSD oil supplied to vessels of below 20 m OAL.
8. Inclusion of Turtle Excluder Device (TED) in trawl nets.
9. Utilization of Potential Fisheries Zone forecasting wth increased use of

remote sensing facilities for resource assessment.

10. Setting up of artificial reefs and fish aggregating devices (FAD) for enhancing the resource potential.
11. Improve data base of various aspects of fisheries.
12. Information system for fisheries within an appropriate framework of a network.
13. Fisherfolk-based welfare measures such as on-shore amenities, housing, health, drinking water, insurance and old-age pension.
14. Alternative vocations for the coastal fisherfolks during lean seasons.

2.a.8 Riverine Fisheries

The country is endowed with a very high potential for inland fisheries development. The vast and varied resources, possessing rich ecological heritage and biodiversity are one of the greatest strengths of the country, but their management is difficult and poses the greatest challenge. Inland fish production has increased from 1.103 million tonnes during 1984-85 to 2.4 million tonnes in 1996-97, registering an average growth rate of 6.7 per cent during the period (Anon 1996). Although a potential of 4.5 million tonnes of fish has been identified for the inland sector, in the true sense this has little meaning. Other than the natural resources, such as rivers, estuaries, floodplain and natural lakes, the area under man-made water bodies such as reservoirs, canals, ponds, tanks, etc., is fast increasing and as such the potential would also increase.

Consequent upon the post-independence thrust on overall development, the riverine environment has been subjected to tremendous pressure. Human interference in the form of water abstraction, river training, dam construction, sedimentation, *effluxion* and pollution have produced discerningly disturbing effects. A reappraisal of fisheries of the middle stretches of river Ganga (Kanpur to Bhagalpur) has indicated that the yield of major carps and several other commercial species has fallen during the period 1958-61 to 1980-86. The impact of man-made barriers on the migrating fish species such as *Hilsa ilisha* is also evident from its decline in the upstream waters of river Ganga due to the Farakka Barrage. The example of river Ganga largely illustrates the situation existing in almost all the river systems of the country.

Riverine fisherfolk have been poorest of the lot and they have been denied a fair deal so far. Disruption of environment and creation of man-made lakes on rivers (the reservoirs) have displaced fisherfolk to some extent and also affected adversely their livelihood. The answer lies in raising fish productivity of rivers and streams as productivity in any commodity sector will determine the levels of employment and income. The basic objective in riverine fisheries is to give emphasis to improvement in the water quality and conservation of biological and particularly fishery resources while attempting to optimize the productivity. Yield models need to the developed for the multi species/ multigear fisheries particularly in the wake of modified water abstraction and pollution for industry and agricultural fields. Since water has multiple usufructuaries particularly irrigation and abstraction of water for domestic and industrial uses, a need for reconciling inter-sectoral conflicts is bound to be felt. The requirement of drinking water, irrigation and fisheries are to be treated in a holistic manner. No demands for water from the National Grid has yet been made by the fishery sector.

Ecological investigations covering rivers Ganga and Brahmaputra during the past decades have helped in comprehending the riverine environment and fish catch structure to the advantage of fishermen. But, of late due to the overall environment degradation and man-made interferences in the catchment areas of river basins, there has been a perceptible decline in both fish productivity and production. Therefore, it is necessary to give added emphasis to fish biology vis-a-vis the changed environmental conditions for eco-restoration and evolution of management norms for advising development departments.

The restoration of riverine fisheries would entail a broad integrated approach taking into account the requirements of fisheries with the other uses of land and water in the river basins. It would also necessitate regulation of fishing effort, strict enforcement of closed season, rejuvenation of endangered fish species through stocking programmes, protection of natural breeding grounds and setting up of sanctuaries for restoration of depleted germplasm.

The floodplain lakes, by virtue of their production potentiality, constitute the frontline areas where a judicious combination of culture and capture fisheries can be practised. Being a continuum of the river, the floodplain lakes also have a vital bearing on the fisheries health of the riverine ecosystem and, therefore, need adequate conservation measures besides harvesting of the fisheries resources.

3. Inter State River Management Conflicts and their Effect on Fishery Development

In a federal policy there are in-built strains between the Union Government and States which are independent and co-ordinating authorities, and not subordinates to the Central Government. Entry 14 of List II of Article 246 of the Indian Constitution places agricultural research and education in State List whereas regulation and development of inter-State rivers and river valleys are covered under Entry 56 of List I (Union List). The recent history of the country is replete with inter-State river disputes. As the ownership and rights vest in multiple agencies it becomes difficult to have a co-ordinated approach. Whereas Article 262 provides mechanism for resolving disputes or complaints with regard to use of waters of inter-State rivers and river valleys, no such mechanism exists for the regulation of fisheries of such rivers on a uniform basis. In the case of river Ganga which flows through three States, viz. Uttar Pradesh, Bihar and West Bengal, the exploitation policies are at variance depending upon the importance of riverine fisheries in each State. There is a definite need for taking up stock assessment studies and allied aspects, namely, patterns of breeding and recruitment. Further, the impact of man-made perturbances in the catchment areas of the river basins need to be linked to fish productivity and production. Therefore, creation of a controlling agency, namely, Inter-State Riverine Fisheries Board, should be considered for the formulation of a rational and ecologically sound exploitation policy for the fisheries of inter-State rivers. Management of the Narbada river system and the man-made reservoirs over it need to be reviewed accordingly. Once this is agreed in principle, the modalities can be worked out by a committee of experts. This authority may be on the lines of the National Highway Authority as in the case of surface transport.

3.a. Constitutional Position and Proposals for Legislative Reform

Entry 21 of List II of Article 246 (3) of the Constitution puts fisheries in the State List whereas regulation and development of inter-State river and river valleys figure in Entry 56 of List I (Union List). Present-day conservationists and planners owe a debt of gratitude to Dr. Francis Day who drew attention of the then Government of India in the year 1883 to the widespread slaughter of fish, fry and fingerlings and pleaded the urgency of adopting legislative measures to conserve fishery resources. By 1888 the question again forced its way to the front and it was considered by the Agricultural Conference at Delhi. The Government of India enacted the Indian Fisheries Act, which came into force in 1897. Under Section 3 of this Act the States have been promulgating rules. Under this Act. The regulatory measures generally comprise limited access, licensing of gear, gear restrictions, leasing and auctioning.

The operation of various fishery laws in the country has, however, not yielded the desired results. Although the preambular declarations are very lofty, at the implementation stage hardly anything is achieved. The time is now ripe to have second thoughts on the fishery laws and other allied rules for the development of inland fisheries. The following proposals for legislative reforms merit attention:

(i) The anachronistic Indian Fisheries Act 1897 should be repealed and a new comprehensive Act should be brought after taking stock of all the changes in the last five decades.
(ii) Keeping in view the diverse local conditions, the central law may be of

limited avail but related rules should be promulgated with the basic framework of comprehensive Central Act.

(iii) Inland fisheries should be included in the Concurrent List of the Indian Constitution so that the Union Government can also frame laws.

(iv) Though deterence is not the sole basis of law, the punishment prescribed in fishery laws is very mild. Even in the matter of adulteration of food and drugs it becomes difficult to bring offenders to book. Unfortunately, in fisheries, violation of the rules is not taken very seriously by the people.

(v) An expert group comprising environmentalists, fishery scientists and jurists should examine the possibility of making offences relating to destruction of habitat environment and aquatic life cognisable and non-bailable.

(vi) The enforcement machinery needs strengthening though it may lead to an increase in the financial liability of development departments. Without adequate manpower and social ethics, it is difficult to implement even ideally conceived laws. The duty of conservationists, planners and decision makers does not end by adding a new laws to the statute book unless it is administered properly.

(viii) The river cleaning programme should be closely linked to afforestation of river basins and the overall catchment areas. Further, man-made interferences may push us near to the point of no return if we do not oppose them with an iron will.

In view of the above, the following may be considered for promulgation and implementation:

1. A reliable database on a time series mode to be generated while planning the formulation of development strategies for open water fisheries especially the riverine fishery in the country.
2. To initiate awareness for the conservation of bio-diversity, revival of commercially viable biomass and protection of the habitat programme should be taken up in identified areas.
3. Open water fisheries/riverine fisheries cut across the geographical boundaries of various States in the country. Conservation and sustainable exploitation measures taken in one State need to be complemented by the neighbouring States up or downstream of the rivers following globally agreed principles of responsible fishing. Certain well-thought-out mechanisms for inter-State understanding and coordination would need to be evolved.
4. Indiscriminate fishing of juveniles from secluded pools of water created along the banks of the rivers after the flood recedes has been a major

cause of depletion of commercially important fish stock in the rivers. Therefore, these breeder pools may be protected by declaring them as fish-breeding parks/sanctuaries.

5. Certain identified strategic but manageable high-altitude streams/lakes may be adopted under a conservation of bio-diversity programme through a ban on fishing, protection of habitat through punitive orders and enhancement of natural population with ranching of certain species such as mahseer, snow-tout through hatchery breeding.
6. The existing rules and regulations under the Indian Fisheries Act (1897) have provision to control and monitor the use of gear, mesh size as well as observance of fishing on closed seasons. For an effective implementations of the regulations, following measures may be considered:

    (i) While leasing the riverine stretches to lessees conditions should be clearly stipulated with punitive clauses on violations of conditions.

    (ii) Mesh-size regulation may be monitored by inspecting landing centres for fish size in particular seasons and parties operating the river stretch be made responsible.

    (iii) Riverine stretches to be leased may be enlarged in length to minimize fishing pressure per unit length of the river by the lessee.

    (iv) Lease period should have a flexible component with possibility to extend the period depending upon the performance of the lessee.

7. The river stretches along with their catchment areas may be characterized utilizing GIS facilities for their productivity potentials, exploitable areas and conservational problems.
8. The fishery sector must spell out its water demand from the national grid of water in terms of quantified requirements of water for their various activities.
9. The rights and responsibilities of developing fisheries in various water bodies, irrespective of their primary use, be entrusted to the State fishery departments for their appropriate use in fisheries development.
10. Alternative vocation and activities may be programmed in the form of Fishery Estate, Cluster Based Consortia for post-harvest facilities to benefit the primary producers. Marketing, storage and transport facilities may be considered for the benefit of fisher-folk who are put to difficulties during lean seasons/closed seasons, etc. Even a lean season allowance may be considered for better productivity during operational days.
11. Encourage all women cooperative societies in marketing and post-harvest to indicate support to gender issues.

4. Reservoir Fisheries

A number of small, medium and large river valley projects have come into existence in the past four decades and consequently a chain of impoundments have been created which are highly amenable for fisheries and fish husbandry practices. The Indian reservoirs are estimated to have a fish production potential varying from 50 to 200 kg/ha/yr depending on their size, nutrient status and geographic location. Against this, the present yield is at a staggeringly low level of about 20 kg/ha/year on an average basis. Although there are good examples where production has exceeded 100 kg even in larger impoundments such as the Gobind Sagar (Himachal Pradesh), such examples are very few and need to be replicated.

Reservoirs are a vast resource and their exploitation on scientific lines may improve the socio-economic conditions of fishermen, provided appropriate linkages between research and development are established. Based on research results achieved so far small reservoirs have shown a greater promise as they are more amenable to intense human intervention. Small reservoirs where resident fish population is negligible can be developed more on lines of culture-cum-capture fishery where whatever is stocked is largely extracted. But in large, deep basin reservoirs, management options are limited, i.e. mesh size adjustment, fishing efforts management and observance of conservation norms. Species and stock enhancement, whenever resorted to, are aimed at implanting nuclei of breeding populations. One of the greatest difficulties in conservation measures, such as closed seasons and mesh size observance rules, is the resentment among the fishermen community due to low income levels. Unless sources of subsidiary income are provided it is very difficult to sell the idea of conserving stocks for long-term gains for higher yields. Therefore, cooperatives/corporations which have fishing rights in reservoirs have to create awareness among fishermen with regard to conservation measures which may help them in the long run. The reservoirs could be brought under fisheries development. It would help a sizable quantum jump in fish production as well as help in lessening pressure on landuse for aquaculture.

The research in reservoir fisheries has been mainly confined to morphometry, limnology, biology, production potential estimated on the basis of food resources, and stock manipulation. Except for a few success stories, there has always been a persistent schism between projected potential and actual yield rates due to a number of imponderables. Till today reservoirs are characterized by the prevalence of low fish yield (20 kg/ha/yr.), revenue biased unimaginative exploitation policies, disregard for ecological considerations and low income of fishermen (ranging from Rs 1,000 to 4,000/ yr). The exploitation system comprises open auction, royalty and preferential lease to fishery cooperatives (Dehadrai 1998).

The fast-changing scenario in the water courses of the country, especially through the flow control structures, and inland profile through reclamation, human settlement, construction of roads and other development activities tend to render the fragile aquatic ecology most vulnerable. Soil erosion, pollution, loss of mangroves and forest largely affects the aquatic biodiversity. Drainage of natural fish producing wetlands, swamps, pools and puddles also reduce and affect floodplain fisheries. Intensive agriculture and agriculture related industries discharge directly or indirectly harmful waste material into the aquatic system. Added to this, increased urban and municipal wastes are all detrimental to the aquatic system. The siltation rate is alarming in certain reservoirs, whereas, in different river systems, many fish species are threatened by various anthropogenic interventions.

Unfortunately, the present growth in fisheries production is considerably less than the increase in demand. This gap stimulates intensification of fish capture without much concern for natural recruitment and sustainable population. The overfishing in capture fisheries not only depletes the stock but also results in damaging the ecological system. Efforts to check over-exploitation must be initiated and intensified to achieve sustainable production. The rehabilitation of depleted stocks and adoption of resource conservation strategies are essential to minimize the risk of collapses.

The requirements of food, fodder and industrial raw material may lead to disappearance of some wetlands/derelict water bodies, but this loss may be offset by a judicious exploitation of expanding man-made irrigation network and watershed which are likely to come up in future. This would offer great opportunities to utilize these water bodies for inland fish production.

The strategies necessary for optimum utilization and sustainable development of the reservoir resources and the constraints being faced by them necessitate that all major issues be addressed through a pragmatic approach like.

- — Exploring to lease out reservoirs to private entrepreneurs/public limited companies and reserving certain percentage of profit for welfare activities for fisherfolks.
- — Development of large, medium and small reservoirs for fish yield optimization.
- — Seed rearing/production infrastructure exclusively for stocking/ management of reservoirs.
- — Development of floodplain lakes for ecosystem improvement and fish yield optimization.
- — Impact assessment of river valley projects on fisheries.
- — Monitoring and surveillance of inland and coastal water pollution.
- — Aforestation of the catchment areas of river basins.

4.a. Coldwater Fisheries

A large population in the hilly areas depends for their daily subsistence on manual catch of fish from fast-flowing streams/lakes. The fish fauna in these coldwater streams has depleted to dangerous levels affecting not only the daily catch but also threatening the biodiversity of the nation.

There exists a vast and varied scope for recreational (including ornamental) and coldwater fisheries (including food fish) in the country. This area has, however, remained grossly neglected. Except some effort to set up integrated trout projects through external aid in Himachal Pradesh and Jammu and Kashmir, no major initiative has been made in this direction. Uttar Pradesh, Sikkim, West Bengal (hill districts), Arunachal Pradesh, Meghalaya, Nagaland and Manipur are yet to develop their coldwater resources utilizing the available spectrum of exotic fish species. Research interventions are necessary in standardizing norms for propagation and raising of endemic coldwater fish species such as snow-trout, etc.

At a lower altitude, species such as mahseer have an enormous potential for both food and sports. One of the best game fishes of the world, mahseer population has been on the decline in some of its major habitats in the country. Setting up of mahseer hatcheries for breeding and propagation in the suitable riverine stretches is highly essential, lest the depletion process lead to extinction of the species.

The thrust areas identified for the community-based coldwater fisheries are as follows:

- — Establishment of hatcheries and farms of mahseer species.
- — Development of selected high-altitude lakes and hill streams for food and game fisheries development.
- — Inventory of damaged hill stream/lake habitats and measures for their ecorestoration.

5. Policy Issues

In order to reach the suggested target, socio-economic need is to be identified so as to evolve a suitable policy framework for consolidating the gains of research and technological developments. Technological strides made as a result of massive research efforts rarely receive adequate infrastructural and policy support for accelerating the pace of fishery development. Though government and inter-governmental bodies, financial and research Institutions have been contributing to the cause of fishery development, the existing policies have been more in the nature of piecemeal responses to a particular situation. The focus has been mainly on aquaculture and sustenance of export boom in respect of overheated overseas markets for shrimps. This lopsided approach has resulted in utter neglect of open water fisheries which has been a means of subsistence to millions of fisherfolk population, a class belonging to the poorest of the poor. The fishery is presently characterized by the prevailing low productivity and consequent low incomes. Some of these aspects have been well researched in the last decade.

The exploitation of fishery resources is and has always been managed but it cannot be said to have been well managed. We tend to suppose that to manage affairs is to have an effective control but even then we get into trouble under the mistaken belief that we still exercise control. But the fact is, trouble starts because we have lost control. Nevertheless, when we speak of management of exploitation we do generally intend "effective control of exploitation" even if we are not entirely clear in our minds as to the nature of control, its effectiveness and the objectives towards which it should function.

The complexity of factors involved in the regulations of fisheries both domestic and international is often underestimated. Fishing is largely an activity to harvest the stock of highly ambulatory animals. These animals cannot be fenced in a limited area with marked ownership. This makes fisheries of open waters particularly the sea, flowing rivers and streams a "Common Property Resource" with its related problems. Apparently rivers and streams may look to be poor similarities of seas but they have been cradles of major river valley civilizations. The essence of tragedy resides in our foolhardiness of treating our rivers as dumping grounds for domestic and industrial wastes. In recent years an ever-rising demand for fish and fish products has led to an appreciable increase in fishing intensity in open waters through the development of more efforts in terms of nets, boats and hours of fishing. The implications of greater application of labour and capital in familiar grounds are not clearly understood. However, human intervention in the capture fisheries is bound to be less intense as compared to site-based aquaculture. Yield rates in large sheets of water often display voilent fluctuations even if the efforts in terms of layout and capital are kept constant. No research system aiming at enhancement of fish production in open waters like rivers, reservoirs, lakes and floodplain wetlands can provide insulation against variation in fish production. However, fishery regulation rarely concerns itself with a situation where stocks are threatened with extinction.

With the emphasis on the overall development of fisheries for employment and income generation and export earnings, the sector suffers from a weakness in the most essential component of organized marketing, both domestic and, to some extent, export. The fish farmer/fisherman as the primary producer needs to be provided remunerative prices, on the one hand, and the consumer needs to be provided fish products at reasonable rates, on the other. It is pathetic that fish is sold on the roadside even today. The export-oriented fishing industry has not gained any confidence from the weak domestic marketing mechanisms. This grey area needs adequate attention.

In the marine sector, utilization of the by-catch and diversification in both harvest and post-harvest activities need priority attention. On the export front, the future accent has to be on development of new products through value addition. While fish shall continue to provide the valuable protein to the masses, its role in pharmaceuticals, industrial, chemical and medical fields also needs to be promoted.

To propel Indian fisheries into the 21st century, the quality, technical skills and management of fisheries manpower must improve in consonance with the rapidly changing needs of our society, both nationally and internationally. Human resources development for raising a cadre of experts at various levels to support research and vindicate a sustained development of the fishery sector is critically important to India. Moreover, to maintain the pace of growth witnessed by the fisheries sector in the recent past, the efforts may have to be probably larger and faster by several times than made earlier. For such an effort adequate funding to strengthen and streamline organizations, infrastructure and manpower would be the basic requirement.

In the development of fisheries, preoccupation with bio-physical processes at the expense of social process would be detrimental to the overall progress. Man should remain at the centre stage and the benefits of various development programmes should percolate to the poor fisherfolk and fish farmers. In regard to gender issues, the fishery sector compared to the agriculture and allied sectors offers the maximum equality. The participation of women in post-harvest and marketing activities needs to be supported and if possible organizationally through the cooperative medium. Exclusive all-woman cooperatives need encouragement. Linkages of fisheries and aquaculture development with ongoing rural development programmes would help in providing the weaker section of the society an easy access to the socially compatible vocation for better income.

6. Outlook

Does the Maritime Zone of India, Fishing by Foreign Fishing Vessels Act (1980), and the rules thereunder (1982) help in encouraging entrepreneurship in the marine sector? Non-implementation of the Acts and the rules is causing conflicts between resource-rich entrepreneurs and the traditional sector in marine fisheries. Basic rights such as fishing off the coast of neighbouring maritime States are being resented for loss of political benefits rather than for economic benefits almost amounting to suggest balkanization of States in the country. Conservational measures to effectively manage the multi-species stock and avoid overexploitation of particular species as well as varied rules in regard to allocation of fishing zones to fishing vessels of different capability from State to State are certainly not healthy for the judicious growth of marine fisheries as a common property resource.

Will the legislative support help us in arresting deterioration in the riverine environment so as to protect aquatic flora and fauna? Without going into details of civil or criminal jurisprudence, the basis of implementation of laws in a civilized society is habitual obedience that emanates from inherent respect for the country's laws by majority of the citizens. What is important is the quality of citizens who display responsiveness to the country's needs. Fishery development will be on the sound footing if a proper mix of appropriate policy instruments along with production incentives is contemplated. Development presupposes identification of core areas and thereafter prioritization with resource allocation. The Inland fishery sector is yet to be shorn of its subsistence character. Management of openwater fisheries under a common property regime calls for greater ingenuity and vision to solve its intricate problems. Individual entrepreneurship, community management or governmental control are some of the choices for the effective utilization of these national resources with location specific relevance.

REFERENCES

Anon. 1992. "National Commission on Agriculture Fisheries", Vol. VIII. Planning Commission, Govt. of India.

Anon. 1992. "Eighth Five Year Plan for Fisheries"—Report of the Working Group, Ministry of Agriculture and Cooperation, Govt. of India.

Anon. 1996a. "Handbook of Fisheries Statistics". Ministry of Agriculture and Cooperation, (DOAC-Fisheries Division), Govt. of India.

Anon. 1996b. "Ninth Five Year Plan for Fisheries"—Report of the Working Group, Ministry of Agriculture and Cooperation, Govt. of India.

Dehadrai, P.V. 1997. "Riverine Fisheries Management". Proceedings of the Workshop on Riverine Fisheries Management organised by U.P. State Department of Fisheries, 8-9 January 1997, Lucknow.

Dehadrai, P.V. 1998. "Policies for Development of Inland Fisheries in India". Experience Sharing Workshop for Fisheries Development for the State of Gujarat, 22-23 September, 1998. Govt. of Gujarat, Ahmedabad: Indian Institute of Management.

MPEDA. 1998. "Statistics of Marine Products Exports". Marine Products Export Development Authority, Cochin, Govt. of India.

21 Impact of Modern Shrimp Farming on Common Property Resources in Coastal Zones of Tamil Nadu

C. Ramasamy, C. Sekar and S. Selvam

1. Background

Global concern for the environment was formally proclaimed at the First United Nations Conference on the Human Environment held in Stockholm in 1972. The conference adopted an Action Plan for Human Environment, including the General Principles for Assessment and Control of Marine Pollution. In 1992, on the 20th anniversary of the conference, the United Nations Conference on Environment and Development (UNCED) adopted a comprehensive action plan called Agenda 21. Chapter 17 of the Action Plan enumerates a number of management-related activities within the programme area for integrated management and sustainable development of coastal and marine areas. Over the two decades since the Stockholm meeting, the coastal zone has become a key area of attention because of its rapidly growing share of human population (McManus 1993). In recent years, the Integrated Coastal Zone Management (ICZM) has gained momentum among the international community. ICZM is a dynamic process in which a co-ordinated strategy is developed and implemented for the allocation of environmental, socio-cultural and institutional resources to achieve the conservation and sustainable multiple use of the coastal zone (Clark 1989). It is an iterative process that is subject to modification as dictated by feedbacks from its components which are ever changing. The integrated management is also concerned with the economics of the use and development of resources in the coastal zone, the socio-cultural and legal institutional structures, all of which interact to determine the way the coastal zone is used and altered. The goal of ICZM is not conservation, *per se*. The goal is to utilize resources in perpetuity and, therefore, realize inter-generational equity. The only rational way to sustain its utilization of resources is to take stock of the way environment responds to their use and added pressures and to incorporate such indices in planning and implementing economic development. The convergence between economics and environment is achieved when long-term use of, and access to, resources, i.e. across many generations, becomes the overriding theme. The management of common property resources (CPR) in the coastal zones is critical for not only preserving the environment but also to derive large-scale economic benefits.

In view of the multifarious uses of coastal CPRs, viz. fishing, recreation, aquaculture, resorting, waste disposal, salt panning, etc., the coastal CPR environmental issues are also highly composite and have a distinct spatial magnitude, requiring rational decisions to facilitate appropriate strategies. In the coastal zones, main attractions to the tourists are coastal water quality and beauty of the beach. Problems of coastal pollution are unique in India which require dedicated efforts and action to conserve coastal CPRs. Coastal shrimp industries have contributed greatly to the deterioration of environment because of the disposal of waste water into natural waters. The quality of coastal water during certain periods of the year has been identified as not suitable for drinking, irrigation and even swimming. Degradation of water quality is caused by discharging of waste water from shrimp farms into coastal waters. This degraded coastal water quality results in damaged coral reefs. Shallow wells utilized by the local people in the vicinity of the waste disposal site are heavily contaminated. Residents getting water from wells are very often reported to be suffering from gastro-intestinal diseases. Highly contaminated coastal water poses health hazards to farmers and agricultural labourers. But it was difficult to get data about this type of health effects since the incubation periods and immediate reactions of the infecting organisms are not known for assessment.

The major pollutants of the coastal resources are sewage waste, solid waste, organic and inorganic wastes from industries, acids and bases, radioactive substances, oilspills, wastes from shrimp farms and so on. The various pollutants have made several species of fish, crops, trees and other micro flora and fauna extinct. Human beings dependent on these resources for their day-to-day existence are exposed to health hazards by the consumption of polluted coastal resources which besides affect the recreational atmosphere on the seashore. In addition to the damage posed by industrial effluents, oilspills are an ever present threat to our surface waters (Karpagam 1991). The remains of radioactive materials released from the nuclear device testing by the developed nations are also found in all oceans and coastal zones. The encroachment of coastal CPRs by influential resource mongers is not uncommon now-a-days. Mismanagement, overextraction and use, free-riding attitudes and open access to the community or society lead to the "Tragedy of

Commons". Low productivity is observed in coastal CPRs due to continuous exploitation, overusage, lack of control, non-availability of caretakers, free-riding behaviour, etc. The coastal eco-systems like mangroves are under severe stress due to deforestation, sustained flooding of wastes all along the coastal region, pollution and other extraneous factors. Following the conversion of the cultivable lands and mangroves into prawn farms in recent years, the coastal inhabitants, particularly women, are not getting adequate employment. Due to the seepage of effluents from the prawn farms, undergroundwater in many villages has become polluted. Their survival itself is in question because of the over-use and indiscriminate exploitation of good quality water to maintain the pH level of the prawn farms. There is also shortage of land area for constructing houses as the available land has already been acquired for prawn farming. At a time when food production needed an impetus, aquaculture farms, which are mostly cent per cent export-oriented units, have threatened the coastal CPR ecosystems. The specific objective of this chapter is to study the economic and ecological consequences (like clearing of mangroves) of shrimp farming, change in employment and income and to examine the externalities and environmental impacts due to shrimp farming.

2. Coastal Resources and their Importance

A coastal zone comprises the coast, beach and the near shore and sometimes the whole Exclusive Economic Zone. Sorensen *et al.* (1989) viewed the term coastal Zone as the area including the shoreland influenced by the sea, the water column and the seabed extending the edge of the continental shelf. The coastal zone provides an opportunity for multi-disciplinary activities owing to a variety of natural resource systems and habits. Indian beaches are attracting tourists from all over the world. Now-a-days coastal eco-systems are places of hectic human activity. It is understood that two out of three people live in the coastal regions of the world. In the world as a whole, it has been estimated that about 75 per cent of human population will by the year 2000 live in a narrow strip, up to 60 km, along the shores of the continents. Some of the major cities of the world are situated along the coast and in South East Asia, 65 per cent of the cities having a population of over 2.5 million inhabitants, are located along the coasts. The coastal resources have a definite role in maintaining the economic efficiency, ecological sustainability and socio-economic equity. The coastal zone, as an interface between land and marine systems, constitutes a valuable resource and it serves multiple functions. It is also a productive food source. Villagers in coastal areas have to eke out their livelihood through fishing and selling fish. Agriculture has been the main occupation apart from fishing in those areas.

The total length of the coastline of mainland India, Lakshadweep island and Andaman and Nicobar islands is 7,516.16 km. This provides livelihood for over 100 million population. Over a dozen ports are situated along the Indian coasts. Tamil Nadu has a coastal length of 1,000 km. Coastal wetlands rescue the rainfall from flowing into sea. While the east coast of India is low-lying with lagoons, marshes, beaches and deltas, the west coast is dominated by rocky shores. Islands of Lakshadweep, like those of Maldives, are composed of atolls while the Andaman and Nicobar islands arise from a submerged mountain chain and are volcanic in origin. India is among the few countries in the world to exploit the fish wealth from the coastal CPRs. There are also historically important coastal CPR sites located along the coast of Tamil Nadu like the mangroves at Pitchavaram, the Pulicat lake, the swamps at Vedaranyam and the bird sanctuary at Point Calimere. The Tamil Nadu Coast has generally been known to have been clean for centuries and only in the last three decades, in the wake of urbanization and commercialization of aquafarming, has the ecological disorderliness resulted.

Coastal areas in the country are home to some of the richest, most diverse and fragile of natural resources. In the Coastal Zone, terrestrial, marine and atmospheric ecosystems interact in complex, dynamic and often unknown ways. Coastal habitats like mangroves play an important role in the coastal water quality and protection. The coastal zone as an economic entity provides sites for a wide range of activities. Such as agriculture (e.g. rice, coconut plantations, bananas), forestry (e.g. mangrove), fisheries and aquaculture, human settlements, manufacturing and extractive industries (sand mining for oil mineral), waste disposals, ports and marine transportation, water control and supply projects, shore protection and tourism and recreation. Indian beaches are attracting tourists from all over the world. Coastal areas are a magnet for tourists as is evident from the fact that the Mediterranean littoral alone attracts one-third of world tourism (Swaminathan 1993).

Coastal ecosystem has a long-standing fraternity with mangrove forests. Mangroves along the coastline not only provide food for fish and other habitats but also help stabilize the physical environment by dissipating wave action, buffering salinity changes and by stabilizing sediments. By acting as a fender against coastal tides and waves, it protects valuable coastal resources from erosion, and sea water intrusion. In the coastal ecosystems, the presence of perennial trees and mangroves along coastal zones supply fodder to livestock, fuelwood and timber to the local residents. Mangroves are also important in nutrient cycling as a source of organic matter to increase coastal productivity and as breeding grounds, nursery area or a general habitat for many commercially important fishes, crustaceans and molluscs (Machintosh 1982 and Turner 1977). Mangroves, if used within the assimilative capacity, offer services (economic, ecological and social functions) to humankind. Productivity of commercially important shrimp fisheries appear to be positively correlated to the abundance of mangrove forests adjacent to fishing grounds (Primavera 1991). Mangrove removal may cause coastal erosion (Carter 1959) and changes in the patterns of sedimentation and shore live configuration (Snedaker and Getter 1985) and make it more vulnerable to storm damage. For example, the damage caused by the 1991 cyclone in south-eastern Bangladesh would have been worse but for the existence of mangroves (Anonymous 1991). Similarly in the Mekong delta, loss of mangroves is already causing some dramatic changes in coastal erosion (Mekong Secretariat 1992). The economic effects of such impacts ultimately can be very significant and may outweigh short-term benefits from activities such as conversion to shrimp ponds. Nevertheless, market forces nearly always operate to favour conversion of mangroves for specific uses. Dixion (1989) has emphasized that conversion of mangroves to shrimp ponds can lead to a shift from a multi-use system to a single-use, with the net benefits shifting to a fewer users. Mangrove forests supports a wide variety of goods and services, including timber, thatching material, fuel wood and various food stuffs such as honey (Hamilton and Snedaker 1984). Sirisup (1988) reports that in Chantaburi district, fishermen have reported a decline in catches, linked to restricted access to previously accessible mangrove areas. The same problem but on a wider scale is the basis of major conflicts between coastal fishermen and shrimp farmers in Ecuador (Odum and Arding 1991).

According to Saleth (1997), the coastal ecosystem has four major components: (i) salt marshes in the temperate zone, (ii) mangroves in the tropical zone, (iii) estuaries, and (iv) coral reefs and sea grasses. He has identified four major coastal activities like fishing, farming, logging and developmental activities. Under each of these activities he has categorised mangrove-dependent groups and sectors, viz. fish pond owners, fishermen. Farmers, rural groups, businessmen, scientists, industries, etc.; uses of mangrove systems like collection of fodder, fuel wood, tanning, fish catch, wood cutting, resorts, recreation, research, preservation, mining, salt production, etc.; output/products derived from mangroves, viz. cattle feed, household cooking fuel, crop output, fishery product, building materials, foreign exchange earning, aesthetic satisfaction, knowledge, biodiversity, mineral products, employment and so on (also see Table 21.1). Operation of all these activities under the various systems either in isolation or in joint action ultimately led to a reduction in the coastal mangrove population and gradual disappearance from the coastal sites, causing economic inefficiency, ecological unsustainability and income inequality. As only individual short-term economic benefits (like high sale price of shrimps, poor gestation period for the pay back of investment on shrimp farming, etc.) are given priority, ignoring the long-term social gain, the mangrove forests are marching towards disappearance. In such a situation property rights structures in the coastal area

TABLE 21.1: **Human-Mangrove Interactions: Economic Benefits and Ecological Impacts**

Activity	Mangrove-dependent groups/sectors	Uses of mangrove ecosystem	Output/products	Stress on mangrove ecosystem
Fishing	a) Fishpond owners	a) Creating fishpond	Fishery products	Cleared area
		b) Fry collection for stocking	Fishery products	Forested area
	b) Fisherfolk	a) Collection of adult fish, shrimp, etc.	Fishery products	Forested area
		b) Fish for consumption	Household nutrition security	Forested area
		c) Tanning collection	Increased durability of fish nets	Forested area
Farming	a) Farmers	a) Rice cultivation	Higher rice yield	Cleared area
		b) Manure	Substitute for chemical fertilizer	Damage (2) (Qty)
		c) Soil and water Pollution	Agricultural output	Damage (Qlty)
		d) Coastal protection	Land saved from coastal protection	Forested area
	b) Other rural groups	a) Feed for cattle	Energy for farm operation, milk, etc.	Damage (2) (Qty)
		b) Fuelwood collection	Energy for household use	Damage (?) (Qty)
		c) Honey & herbal medicine	Additional income and income saving	Forested area
Logging	a) Business people	a) Commercial wood cutting	Building materials, charcoal, etc.	Damage (Qty + Qlty)
	b) Other rural groups	b) Wood cutting for own household needs	Building materials	Damages(?)
Developmental activities	a) Industry	a) Wastage disposal	Industrial products	Damage (Qlty)
		b) Oil spillage	Oil products	Damage (Qlty)
	b) Urban development	a) Ports	Enhanced trade	Cleared area*
		b) Roads	Communication	Cleared area
		c) Housing	Houses	Cleared Area*
		d) Sewage disposal	Cost saving	Damage (Qty + Qlty)
	c) Recreational	a) Beach hotels & resorts	Foreign exchange earnings	Cleared area*
		b) Conoeing, bird watching, etc.	Aesthetic satisfaction, recreation, etc.	Forested area
	d) Scientists	a) Research	Knowledge	Forested area
		b) Preservation	Biodiversity	Forested area
	e) Others	a) Mining	Mineral products	Damage (Qty + Qlty)
		b) Salt production	Salt & employment	Cleared area*

Notes : *Destructive uses whose ecological impact is a function of the scale of operation.

can play a vital role in restoring the coastal ecosystem.

3. Property Rights Regimes in Coastal Zones

Property Rights Regimes (PRRs) offer the basic structure from which appropriate avenues and opportunities for using and managing resources are derived. Basically, it has got two components, viz (i) Property rights, the rights and duties in the use of a particular resource and (ii) property rules, rules under which the rights and duties are exercised (Bromley 1991). By determining privileges and duties in the use of resources, Property Rights Regime act as a co-ordinating mechanism and an organizing factor between man and the natural environment. The performance of a property rights regime is generally measured in economic, social and ecological dimensions, which are interactive, interconnected and embedded in a system. Like any other natural resource, coastal zone resource property rights regimes also link ecological systems to human systems. Market-based property rights regime, usually in the form of an exclusive permit, licence, lease, etc., are often used in the management of CPRs like community grazing yards, forests, fisheries, wildlife, etc. Although there has been an increase in the use of market approaches in forest, fishing, grazing, pollution control, etc., the increase has been marginally slow because market-based property rights systems rely on the incentive of guided self-interest more than command and control system do, their effectiveness is a function of the value of the tradable rights (Young and McCay 1995). Like many multiple use CPRs (Marothia 1997), coastal zones entangle an overlap of property regimes. Open access and common property regimes exist on the seaside, while private and State property regimes can be found on the landside. Hence evolution of institutions of management of the coastal zone get extremely complex (also see Kurien 1997). Currently existing institutional mechanisms also do not provide any guarantee or incentive to the non-polluters. For instance, under the existing property regimes and institutional structures of coastal CPRs, individuals will not have any incentive to conserve coastal reserves like mangroves, as the uncut trees left will just be cut by somebody, since there in no restriction on the exploitation of the coastal CPRs, which requires serious consideration. The inherent difficulty in defining formal property rights regimes and lack of attitude towards conservation and optimal use of coastal CPRs by individual economic agents have led to the gradual depletion and ultimate extinction. This is primarily due to the divergence between private and social values. Hence, depending upon the outcome derived and the interactions of the coastal CPRs with economic, ecological and social dimensions, the institutional systems may be modified through changes in the property rights regimes to ensure sustainable use of coastal CPRs.

4. Coastal Shrimp Farming in India—Recent Trends

India has a traditional system of coastal aquaculture as practised in the estuaries. The coastal areas with the estuaries, mangroves and nearshore waters are generally rich in fishery resources. Traditionally, these resources have been cropped by the artisanal sectors to meet their livelihood demands on a sustainable manner. Technological advancement, remunerative international market prices and quick recovery or payback of investment by aquaculture farming made the system highly commercialized and export-oriented. The development of brackish water shrimp farming on commercial and scientific lines started in India during the mid eighties only with the demand for shrimps from the export continuing to rise and the shrimp production from captured fisheries has remained stagnant. Consequently, Indian seafood exporters have resorted to develop brackish water shrimp farming on the lines of South East Asian countries. Rapid and swift growth in the aquaculture industry, once initiated and encouraged to utilize the vast stretches of coastal land, has led to a severe ecological and environmental crisis. It is estimated that 1.4 million hectares of brackish water area is available along the coast, out of which one million hectares are found suitable for aquafarming. However, at present, only about 1,00,000 hectares are being utilized in the coastal States of West Bengal, Kerala, Andhra Pradesh, Orissa, Tamil Nadu, Karnataka and Goa for shrimp culture (Anonymous 1995). In fact, nearly 70-80 per cent of the shrimp produced for export is from the aquaculture sector. Commencing in the early seventies, several development programmes of brackish water aquaculture were introduced by the Government of India to be implemented by the State Governments. These were the Pilot Project Centres of the Fifth Five Year Plan (FYP), the Area Development Scheme of the Sixth Five Year Plan and the Integrated Brackish Water Fish Farm Development Scheme of the Seventh Five Year Plan. To provide extension support, district-level Brackishwater Fish Farmers Development Agencies (BFDA) were organized in the States. To provide research support, the Indian Council of Agricultural Research (ICAR) implemented the All India Co-ordinated Research Project on Brackishwater Fish Farming during 1972-85 and, in 1987, the ICAR established Central Institute of Brackishwater Aquaculture for carrying out research (Alagarswami 1993a).

Coastal shrimp farming has shown a dramatic development particularly in the coastal areas of Andhra Pradesh and Tamil Nadu but in a haphazard manner without any regulation. Due to the vast potential offered by this sector, the pace of development has been fairly rapid and, over the last one decade, several companies, including large corporate groups, have been setting up aquaculture projects. Experience has indicated that whenever such investment opportunities open up in sectors of the economy with similar high growth potential and promise of high yields, there is an unhealthy proliferation of projects tending to concentrate in a few specific localities, leading to an unbalanced growth as well as severe pressure on the environment. The corporate firms, Balaji group, DCM, Hindustan Lever, ITC, Kirloskar, RPG, Shriram, Tatas, Thapars and SPIC which have hitherto been concentrating on industrial ventures have made forays into aquaculture by taking up large-scale integrated projects. As a consequence of coastal zone shrimp farming, the export of marine products from India rose from 89,263 tonnes in 1986 to 2,23,663 tonnes in 1993-94. Among this, the share of shrimp products is 36 per cent. In value terms, export earnings from marine products in 1995-96 were placed at Rs. 1,860 crores, which is nearly three times the exports in 1988-89. By 1996-97, production of cultivated shrimp was reported to be 78,000 tonnes (Selvam and Ramasamy, 1996).

On the one hand, economic liberalization policies of the government since 1991 have favoured mushrooming of shrimp farms as they are cent per cent export-oriented units. The Marine Products Export Development Authority (MPEDA) has introduced subsidy schemes for new farm development, establishment of shrimp hatchery, manufacture of shrimp feed and establishment of brood stock. Concessions in the customs duty on imported shrimp feeds have also been declared by the Government of India (GOI) as an incentive to promote export of shrimps. State Governments have also liberalized leasing policies and taken necessary steps to lease out brackish water lands available in the coastal areas for shrimp farm development.

5. Shrimp Farming, People's Movement and Government Intervention

On the other hand recently apprehension have been expressed at various forums about the undesirable impact of shrimp farming on agricultural activities and on common property resources in rich coastal areas. People of the Nagapatinam and Karaikal regions of Tamil Nadu and Union Territory of Pondicherry, especially peasants and fisher folks, have demonstrated their collective protest against the negative externalities due to shrimp farming and want to establish rights for survival and prevent the environmental degradation. Due to the movements against shrimp farming, the Tamil Nadu Government enacted a bill providing for regulation of coastal aquaculture in 1995. This bill was not in consonance with the Ministry of Environment and Forestry notification issued in 1991 as it allows the construction of aquaculture units within 500 metres of the High Tide Line (HTL) of the sea.

Consequent to the proliferation of shrimp farming and its negative externalities on environment, the Supreme Court, in its order of March 27,

1995, directed NEERI (National Environmental Engineering Research Institute) team of technical experts to inspect the shrimp farms in the coastal areas of Andhra Pradesh and Tamil Nadu, and to submit the investigation report on various farms and suggest remedial measures, if necessary, for environmental restoration to the Hon'ble Supreme Court, Accordingly, a 13-member team of scientists constituted by NEERI inspected the shrimp farms situated on the ecologically fragile coastal areas in the States of Andhra Pradesh and Tamil Nadu in April, 1995. The coastal areas in the Union Territory of Pondicherry were also inspected by the team because of their proximity to Tamil Nadu. The Ministry of Environment and Forests (MEF) notification dated February 19, 1995, stipulates that the aquaculture farms on the coastal areas should not be constructed within 500 m from the High Tide Line (HTL) of the seas. The hatcheries, however, may be constructed between 250 and 500 m from HTL of the sea.

The inspection team observed during field investigations that the MEF's norms for the location of aquaculture and hatcheries have neen violated in the States of Andhra Pradesh, Tamil Nadu, and the Union Territory of Pondicherry. The current practice of the installation of coastal aquaculture farms within 500 m of HTL violates the fundamental rights to life and livelihood security of people in the States and Union Territory inspected by the team.

Andhra Pradesh has adopted 20-point guidelines as *ad hoc* measures for scientific management of aquaculture in the district of Nellore. These guidelines are not adequate. Furthermore, these guidelines have not been made mandatory in Andhra Pradesh as a whole. The State Government of Tamil Nadu has enacted a Bill to provide for the regulation of coastal aquaculture on April 10, 1995. This Bill is not in consonance with the MEF's notification dated February 19, 1991, as it allows the construction of aquaculture units within 500 m of HTL of the sea. There is an urgent need to ensure scrupulous implementation of the provisions made in the MEF's notification dated February 19, 1991, in the States and Union Territory inspected by the team. In addition, the damage caused to the land and water ecosystems by coastal aquaculture activity, as detailed in the report, must be repaired to its original ecological state. The cost for eco-restoration of the coastal fragile area must be borne by individual entrepreneurs of the coastal aquaculture farms in keeping with the Polluter-Pays Principle.

Further, no activity of commercial coastal aquaculture should be undertaken even beyond 500 m HTL unless a comprehensive and scientific Environmental Impact Assessment (EIA) study has been conducted by the entrepreneur, and the Environmental Management Plan approved by the respective State Departments of Environment, Pollution Control Boards, Shore Development Authority, and also by the Ministry of Environment and Forests. Appropriate terms of reference for EIA have been incorporated in the report. A socio-economic assessment of aquaculture in the ecologically fragile coastal areas in the States of Andhra Pradesh and Tamil Nadu conducted by the NEERI team also indicate that the cost of ecological and social damage far exceeds the benefits that accrue from coastal aquaculture activities (Anonymous 1995).

But this investigation report was criticized by MPEDA, the nodal agency to promote shrimp farming in India. To overcome these types of controversies there is an urgent need for in-depth studies on the socio-economic and environmental consequences of shrimp farming in the Coromandal coast to develop policy guidelines for negating or minimizing the adverse environmental impact of shrimp farming practices and their future expansion.

The integrated projects of shrimp farming have been producing significant quantities of both organic and chemical waste discharges which have put severe pressure on the environment. Proliferation of projects in select localities besides ruining the environment have had a suicidal effect on the projects themselves as the chances of a disease outbreak, loss of crop and quality are higher in such projects. Apart from the direct effects of aquaculture operations on environment, the industry would also have to reckon the social effect. The change in occupation of the small farmers and change in the use of land would have a long-term impact, which needs to be viewed from a broader perspective.

6. Externalities

Although aquaculture was considered to be an environmentally viable production system in the early days of its expansion, it has been observed only subsequently that it could cause ecological degradation, if adequate appropriate measures are not taken. The major damage due to shrimp farming has been to the coastal mangrove forests, which are fast getting depleted. Moreover, pollution due to chemicals, food and faecal matter in ponds and release of this polluted water into adjacent natural water bodies has been causing general pollution and public health hazards. Hyper nitrification of ponds and subsequently natural water bodies has also been causing general pollution. This situation is an externality. The operation of shrimp farms in the coastal belt has a social cost due to increased waste disposal imposing an externality or an external cost to the society.

7. Pollution of Groundwater

The trend of using groundwater for aquaculture to maintain salinity is not unusual. Excessive pumping of saline water in the case of borewell-water-dependent shrimp farms and sweet water in the case of coastal shrimp farms results in a fall in the groundwater table. In several cases, it leads to subsidence of land. Salinization of adjacent fertile lands, either directly or through seepage of seawater, has polluted the lowered groundwater table. The salinated groundwater affects the drinking water source of the coastal villages. Aquaculture companies want to tap the good quality water from the deeper aquifer to dilute sea water from 34 ppt (parts per thousand) to 28 ppt where the growth level of shrimp is optimum. The abstraction of freshwater from underground aquifers for shrimp farming in Taiwan, Philippines and Thailand has resulted in saltwater intrusion and salinization of fresh water aquifers (Liao 1992 and Primavera 1991). This salinization has resulted in degradation of potable and agricultural water supplies which combined with the land subsidence has caused significant conflicts between local shrimp farmers and coastal residents. Communities near shrimp farms in Cebu province have experienced complete drying up or salinization of shallow wells meant for domestic and agricultural uses (Primavera 1991).

Release of saline water from shrimp ponds has been reported to cause salinization of fresh water supplies in several countries including Thailand (PSU 1991). Bangladesh (Mahmood 1986), India and Philippines (SEAFDEC 1989). In India, shrimp farmers have deliberately tampered with saline control barriers and irrigation canals to bring saltwater in land much to the detriment of other agricultural users. A survey of two districts in Thailand showed that 16-22 per cent agricultural farms were affected by saline intrusion linked to shrimp farm expansion (PSU 1993). The practice of discharging farm effluent directly into rivers renders them unsuitable for irrigation and domestic uses. Shrimp farming not only causes increased salinity of surface waters but the waste water discharged from shrimp farms also has a high content of nitrogen, phosphorus, carbon compounds, organic matters, feed residue, shrimp excretion, plankton, chemicals and antibiotics. If the shrimp farmers directly discard waste water into a public canal or coastal area without treatment or dilution, river, canal and shore would be polluted (Grusmee 1995).

In coastal CPR, freshwater supplies are scarce and deliberate utilization of fresh water for shrimp farming seems hardly justified in social and economic terms. Supply of shrimp seed for the commercial farming is itself a source of environmental damage. Alagarswami (1993) estimated that by 1997-98, India would need one billion shrimp seeds. Experience with aquaculture species in general indicate that a number of problems may arise following the introduction of new species. Habitat changes and disruption of host communities may lead to emergence of new predators, genetic changes, introduction of diseases and parasites and adverse socio-economic effects. It is also reported that non-native shrimps are escaping from shrimp culture facilities into natural waters which lead to transmission of diseases from cultured shrimp into wild stocks (Selvam and Ramasamy 1998). Primavera (1991) reported that the introduction of exotic species and gene pool alteration by interbreeding of cultured and wild stocks are potentially irreversible with ecosystem wide repercussions. To feed the shrimp ponds, extensive shrimp collection is going on from mangroves, estuaries and lagoons and it may have a greater impact on other fisheries.

Removal of shrimp seeds in billions will have dire consequences not only on the estuarine ecosystem but also on coastal resources and bio diversity. The fry of shrimp come to estuaries and backwater for feeding, growing and passing the juvenile stage and get back to the sea from where they came. This would enrich the shrimp resources of the inshore and offshore sea. But when they are transferred to shrimp culture farms, the sea is deprived of its legitimate supply of prawns. Shrimp farming in East Godavari, Krishna, Nellore and Prakasam districts of Andhra Pradesh have caused depletion of marine shrimp stocks in the sea owing to exploitation of wild shrimp seed (Rao 1995).

8. Waste Disposal and Environmental Consequences

Nutrient and organic wastes produced by intensive shrimp pond culture consist of solid matter mainly uneaten feed, faeces, phytoplankton and colonizing bacteria and dissolved metabolites such as ammonia, urea, carbon-di-oxide and phosphorus (Mohanty 1989). The wastes include amino acids, proteins, fats, carbohydrates, fibre, minerals and bacteria (Boyd 1989). When a high proportion of nitrogen and phosphorus is added to a shrimp pond, feed is wasted. Ramanamurthy (1995) has reported that discharge of shrimp pond effluent can bring about one or few of the following pollutive effects of receding waters: (i) hypernutrification or eutrophication, (ii) fall in dissolved oxygen, (iii) increase in sanitary indicator bacteria, (iv) increased algal blooms, (v) increased suspended solids, (vi) increased turbidity, (vii) deposition of solids, (viii) discoloration of water, (ix) smell, (x) bad taste of fish, (xi) changes in the benthic fauna, and (xii) deteriorated fishery and fish kills. Antibiotics such as chloramphenicol, oxy-tetracycline, furazoline, streptomycin and nitro furanzone are applied in shrimp hatcheries and grow-out ponds to treat and prevent outbreaks of disease. Aoki (1992) has reported that antibiotic residues can be extremely persistent in marine sediments and may lead to development of bacterial antibiotic resistance. According to Brown (1989), transfer of such resistance to human pathogens could have serious human health implications. Unwanted species are being eradicated by applying copper sulphate as algicide, plant-based bio degradable pisicides such as tobacco dust (nicotine), tea seed cake (Saponin), derris root extract (rorenone) as well as organo-pesticides such as mollusc acides which include chlorinated hydro carbons (DDT, endrin, aldrin, thiodan) and organotins (brestan and aquatin). These organo pesticides are of particular concern due to their toxicity and persistence and their potential implications for product quality and human health.

Effects on coastal habitats due to salinity is another potential problem stemming from the release of saline pond effluent. Salinity has a direct effect on both marine and freshwater organisms. Zonation along estuaries and marshes is determined by the length of time and organisms are exposed to altered salinity and by the magnitude of the salinity differential. The species and quantities of both land and aquatic flora and fauna may be changed as a consequence of salinity change in the local receiving environment. The flora and fauna not adopted to a more saline environment would tend to be replaced by other species. However it may take more than 10 years before the new ecological niche could be established (Grusmee 1995). Moreover, over-exploitation of shrimp seeds from natural waters, indiscriminate use of unwanted and uneconomical seeds in catches and overexploitation of large shrimps as brood-stock for hatcheries have upset the delicate ecological balance. Improper management of water quality in the ponds and creeks has resulted in an outbreak of diseases in natural shrimp farms. For instance, in Andhra Pradesh, which shares 25 per cent of India's total shrimp production, mass mortalities have resulted in losses amounting to Rs. 500-600 crores worth of shrimp exports (Anonymous 1995a). It is suggested that the NEERI team of scientists visit coastal zones in other States and Union Territories to conduct investigations in the ecologically fragile coastal areas and make recommendations for the restoration of these areas, if necessary. This study will require two months for its completion.

9. Socio-Economic Consequences

Since shrimp ponds cover extensive coastal areas by conversion of rice lands, salt pans, coconut and sugar plantations, casuarina plantations, abandoned lands, etc., the coastal ecosystem is heading for a worse disaster. Shrimp production in the ASEAN countries is projected to reach two lakh tonnes by the end of this century (Selvam and Ramasamy 1996). Excess production of shrimp by the turn of the next century will lead to a fall in the price and only those farms with large capital investment base and low production cost due to economies of scale will survive. This means that many small and marginal farms will have to necessarily abandon their operations. Thus it will widen the already existing social inequality. Tropical shrimp farming has been found to have largely negative social consequences because its benefits in terms of profits or protein supply do not favour coastal inhabitants, who are semi-skilled or unskilled. A study conducted in the Philippines (Anonymous 1989) to investigate the drawbacks of aquaculture farms shows the displacement and further marginalization of small-scale farmers and fishermen in the communities, where these farms are established.

Experience indicates that the benefits (both economic and social) of shrimp farming did not trickle down to the coastal residents, but remained with the entrepreneurs and traders only. Instead of improving the living standards and village welfare, shrimp farming brought about social displacement, marginalization of fishermen and income inequality. The loss of earnings of riverine fishermen (i.e. reduction in fish catch) is reported due to influx of untreated toxic chemical effluents into the streams, rivers and sea. The use of antibiotics has given birth to several issues of human health, water quality and environmental sustainability. Recent studies have shown that antibiotic residues are extremely persistent in marine sediments and may lead to the development of bacterial antibiotic resistance. There is also a concern that transfer of resistance to human pathogens will have serious human health implications in future. The introduction of exotic species and gene pool alteration by inter-breeding of cultural and wild stocks are potentially irreversible. This will have serious repercussions on CPRs and environmental sustainability.

10. Results of a Case Study

10.a. Backdrop

A study conducted by the authors (C. Ramasamy and S. Selvam) in shrimp farming areas of the Coromandal coast of South India revealed mismanagement of CPRs and environmental consequences of shrimp farming. The study has critically analysed the emergence of the shrinking coastal common property resources and their impact on the welfare of the coastal inhabitants, externality effects, etc. Out of the 1,750 km Coromandal coast, Nagapattinam district of Tamil Nadu and the Karaikal region of Pondicherry cover a length of 110 km. In this region 6,000 hectares of cultivable croplands have been acquired for shrimp farming by 10 major companies. Besides, about 150 medium and small shrimp farms have come up in recent years. Hence, it was proposed to take up the study in Coromandal coast. Selection of study sites was accomplished as given below.

10.b. Methodology

The Space Application Centre, Indian Space Research Organization, Ahmedabad, has identified two areas of the Coromandal coast for coastal land mapping for brackish water aquaculture. They are:

(i) Three kilometres north-west of Manapad (58 L 3) in Tuticorin district of Tamil Nadu.

(ii) Area between Keezhavanjiur and Pattinacherri (58 N 13) in the Karaikal region of Union Territory of Pondicherry.

On comparing the two sites, the latter was selected for this study because a number of small and big shrimp companies and agricultural farms existed side by side and also there were a few study reports about the shrimp farming issues. The reports were helpful in identifying and sharpening the key issues for further research. Shrimp farming areas of the Coromandal coast were the universe of the study. The area between Keezhavanjiur and Pattinacherri in the Karaikal region was purposefully selected (see Figure 21.1). The area lies in Akkaraivattam and Keezhavanjiur villages and it was targeted as the problem relating to emergence of shrimp farming was most discernible in these villages. Purposive sampling was used for selecting respondents. The total sample size of the respondents was fixed at 120, encompassing 30 agricultural farmers, who sold their lands to shrimp farming, 30 shrimp farmers whose land is affected by shrimp farmers and 30 non-affected farmers. The population of the study villages has different groups like (i) marine fishermen, (ii) riverine fishermen, (iii) crop farmers, (iv) livestock farmers and (v) others based on their occupational status. The data collected pertain to the agricultural year 1994-95 and the survey was conducted between September and December, 1995. Some of the key findings of the study are presented below.

Karaikal, the second important region of Union Territory of Pondicherry, is spread over an area of 160 sq. km. It lies at the tail-end of the "Cauvery delta", 16 km north of Nagapattinam. The total geographical area of the study villages, viz. Keezhavanjiur and Akkaraivattam as per village papers, is 661.96 and 567.74 ha, respectively. The total cropped area was 231.88 ha and 227.34 ha, respectively, in Keezhavanjiur and Akkarivattam villages. The Karaikal region has only 20 km stretch of coastal area which is environmentally significant as the area and its environs have creeks and lagoons, beaches with sand dunes, coastal plains, natural reeves and flood plain.

10.c. Landuse Pattern and Soil Quality

With the spread of shrimp cultural activities, a large part of the common and private land in the area is submerged for most of the year. The common land was previously used as grazing field and the private land was used for crop production. Rice stubble in the cultivated land and grass found on the common lands formerly provided forage for livestock. Shrimp farming has led to reduction in the maintenance of the number of livestock largely due to shrinkage in the common grazing land. The cost of cow's milk production

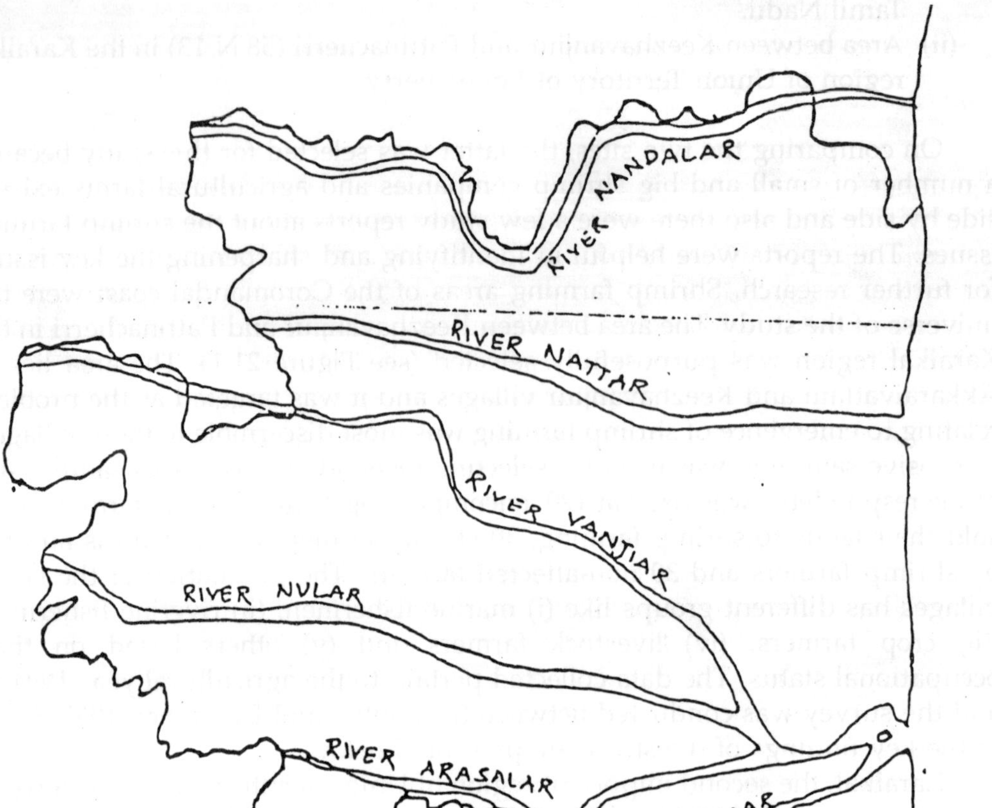

Fig. 21.1: Location of the Study Region—Karaikal

before shrimp farm establishment was Rs. 1.51 which rose to Rs. 3.42 per litre after the introduction of shrimp farming. The higher cost was largely due to shrinkage of grazing lands and increase in the cost of dry and green fodder. Conversion of agricultural lands into commercial aquaculture farms is rampant in the study area. Most of the shrimp farmers bought fertile agricultural lands for expansion of shrimp farming but used only a portion leaving the remaining as fallow, thereby causing reduction in the agricultural output. For instance, in the study area, out of 1,230 ha of reporting area, 250 ha were converted into shrimp farms, of this only 110.50 ha were used for shrimp production and the remaining 139.50 ha were kept unutilized. These lands were previously used to cultivate crops like paddy, sugarcane, etc. The introduction of shrimp farms also led to perceptible changes in the use of natural resources in the coastal belts. According to villagers, the shrimp farms have encroached upon the common "porompoke lands" near the seashore areas of the study villages.

The mismanagement of CPRs created displacement of labourers and small farmers as their cattle dependent on grazing lands could not be maintained. The other consequences are the shortfall in supply of cheap fuel (cowdung), organic manure and milk. Natural phenomenon of absorbing excess water during heavy rain or draining of excess surface water into the river is now interrupted by the construction of artificial bunds near the coast. This has resulted in poor flow of rainwater across different plots. Besides, sea water enters and floods the lands which was not the case earlier. Flow of natural saline canal is being obstructed by prawn farming activities and has resulted in the spread of brackish water resulting in salinization which has affected fresh-water ponds in the study region. Out of 30 shrimp farms surveyed, it was found that many of them had cleared a large number of trees in the coastal belt resulting in deforestation. Thus, forest, which acted as a natural barrier to cyclones, is lost. When such natural barriers are lost, people living in the adjoining coastal belts became more vulnerable to cyclones. In addition, deforestation also led to coastal soil erosion. The details of the annualized external cost due to shrimp farm production are furnished in Table 21.2.

10.d. Encroachment and Extinction of Traditional Fish Species

Encroachment of common grazing lands was also reported by the farmers. In the study area around 38 per cent of the common grazing lands are encroached upon by prawn farmers. Out of 14.50 ha of common grazing lands available, 5.50 ha were encroached upon by prawn farmers. Families involved in grazing of livestock are constantly intimidated by shrimp farmers. Encroachment of the coastal lands which were traditionally enjoyed by the fishing population has resulted in denial of access to use. This also denies passage to women fish vendors. Because of the encroachment and fencing in and around the shrimp

TABLE 21.2: **Annualised External Cost due to Shrimp Production**

Item	External Cost (Rs./ha)
Loss of Potable Water	7037.10
Loss due to Salinization of Adjacent Lands	2972.30
Loss of Human Health	950.00
Loss of Fishing Income	122929.14
Loss of Fishing Net	23457.01
Loss of Manpower due to Non-approachability of fishermen to Seashore Directly	316669.68
Loss of Agricultural Production	15970.59
Total Loss	555968.17

farms, the coastal women have to walk longer distances to reach the fish market and the fishermen to reach the fishing yard. Thus there was a growing social disharmony between the coastal poor and the shrimp farmers. The introduction of exotic fishes has caused severe damage to the local population either by hybridizing with them or by outcompeting them, leading eventually to extinction. It is also learnt that a few species of fishes are steadily depleting. They are Valai (Rabbon), Vaval (Pomfret), Kannan Keluthi (Mackerel) and Vanjaram (Seer). And certain other species have become extinct. The unusual odour created by the effluent flowing from shrimp farms into sea water keeps away catchable fish from the shore which was not the phenomenon earlier. The traditional fishing of Anchory (Nethili), a commercially viable species caught with shore seine nets along the seashore, is significantly affected by the construction of powerful jetties to pump the seawater to feed the shrimp ponds. Shore seine net fishing needs uninterrupted coastline but the activity is severely affected.

10.e. Groundwater Pollution and Health Risk

The groundwater reserves of the study region is severely affected by shrimp farming. Sweet water aquifer is about 4 to 8 m deep. There is no other potable aquifer. This water source cannot be exploited continuously since it takes time to replenish and poses danger of sea water intrusion. Only hand pumps are being used to tap this water at present. It is in this context that the coastal zone is posed with the serious danger of losing quality groundwater due to the unscrupulous use of groundwater for shrimp rearing. There is also no possibility for recharging mechanisms as the nearby wetlands and common pool resources are already converted into aquafarms and these areas have lost their functions of aquifers recharging. Aquaculture companies in the study region want to tap the good quality water from the deeper aquifers to dilute seawater from 34 ppt (parts per thousand) to 28 ppt at which level, growth of shrimp is optimum. The extraction of good quality water from the aquifers would lead to land subsidence and loss of potable waters.[1] In the study, using the replacement cost approach, it has been estimated that shrimp farming has added an annualised external cost of Rs. 7,037 per ha of shrimp farm due to groundwater pollution. The flow of natural saline canals is being obstructed by the prawn farming activity which has resulted in the intrusion of brackish water into agricultural farms, common grazing lands, resulting in salinization. In this study, loss of adjacent lands due to salinization by the shrimp farming was estimated by the replacement cost approach.[2] The above action created an external cost of Rs. 2,972 per hectare of shrimp farming (Table 21.1). Shrimp farmers do not bear this cost but it adds to the social cost. Aquaculture companies in the study region tap the good quality groundwater for their salinity control. This has led to loss of potable water to the coastal zone residents. The dispersion of salt has created an external cost of Rs. 2,972 per hectare. The shrimp farming directly causes external cost to the society through health risks.[3] Prevalence of bilhazaria and lepto-spirosis was found to be common in the coastal zones. Formalin and Malachite green used as prophylactics are found to be the potential carcinogens to the humans. Increased salinization of drinking water leads to gastro-intestinal disorders. An external cost of Rs. 950 per ha of shrimp farming was estimated through the preventive cost approach.

10.f. Decline in Income Loss of Mandays and Agricultural Production

The construction of permanent jetties for a water supply system to shrimp grow-out ponds, especially the seawater-fed shrimp, has eliminated the shore seine net fishing. This action leading to loss of fishing income to the fishermen to the tune of Rs. 1,22,930 per hectare assessed by the change in productivity method of shrimp production is a social cost.[4] Similarly the external cost due to loss of fishing net is Rs. 23,457 per hectare.[5] Construction of ponds for an aquaculture unit in the coastal area with fencing in and around has resulted in the blockage of free access for the fishermen to seashore and led to loss of mandays in fishing activities. This has created an external cost of Rs. 3,16,670 per ha.[6] Thus, development of shrimp farm in the coastal zone of the Coromandal coast has created an external cost of Rs. 5,55,968 per ha of shrimp farming to the society. It is found that the annualized external cost per hectare of shrimp farm was Rs. 36,675, which is higher and significant. The National Environmental Engineering Research Institute (NEERI 1995) has also assessed that the total damage due to aquaculture was Rs. 423 crores against an income of only Rs. 280 crores. That is, the cost of ecological and social damage far exceeds the benefits that accrue out of coastal aquaculture activity.

11. Conclusion

Environmental problems caused by the expansion of shrimp farming and mis-management of coastal CPRs have become a matter of serious concern in the recent past. Proliferation of shrimp farming has led to displacement of labour force who are economically weak and marginalized and whose livelihood, largely, depends on marine fishing. It has caused startling and irreparable damage, particularly to the livelihood security of indigenous coastal fishing inhabitants. Pumping out of brackish water and indiscriminate use of sub-terranean fresh water for hatcheries by shrimp farms causes salinization of soils as well as fresh water aquifers and the salt water intruding into fresh water has become unfit for irrigation and human and animal consumption needs. So ecological sustainability may be restored only through proper regulations and management of inputs like chemicals, treatment of effluents and expedient use of resources like soil, water, mangroves, etc. Shrimp farming within the coastal environment has direct and indirect effects on the marine ecosystems and other resource-based economic sectors operating in the vicinity of the area. Hence shrimp farming should be allowed to function only with adequate monitoring and mitigating measures as well as with minimal conflicts in multiple resource use areas. Therefore, what is required at this stage for the development of coastal CPR zones is a multi-sectoral, combined and holistic approach as also to ensure wise and judicial use of the scarce coastal CPRs.

The coastal CPR information system should be strengthened for consistent monitoring of the usage of the coastal CPRs, the status of environment, etc., and the information guided institutional systems may be thought of for regulation and harmonious use of coastal CPRs by coastal inhabitants. The advanced data information systems involving Coastal System Capability Research analysis, GIS (Geographical Information System), ILWIS (Integrated Land and Water Information Systems) may be employed to map out distribution, the change in the area under coastal CPRs, etc.

Externalities or external effects to CPRs result from the technological interdependence among the economic agents and free-riding behaviour that persists because of the failure of market to evaluate these external effects. The imposition of tax on pollution will internalise an externality and obtain an optional allocation of resources. For the economy and the society as a whole, a pollution tax may be far better. Taxing the firms with source specific emissions above the limit set would be an ideal solution and the tax will compel the polluting shrimp farms to reduce aggregate emissions from these farms. Severe punishment for trespassing resource use rights, in terms of social, economical and even natural sanctions against misusers by community based CPR management groups, will be helpful. At this juncture, what is essential is consideration of people's needs and ecological dimensions and not the immediate monetary benefit alone. At least, at this stage, it would be appropriate to closely look at CPRs with a view to designing an agenda which may be central to the development programme.

The coastal CPR use can be improved upon by government intervention. Areas for intervention include regulation of pollution, zoning of landuse, collection and dissemination of information regarding geology, topography, effective regulation of entry to fishing grounds, etc., for further exploitation and resource sustainability. The government should monitor regularly the spatial and temporal changes of environmental parameters on a regional basis. Conducting frequent environmental impact and social benefit cost analysis studies in the coastal zone, probing the change in quality of water, emission levels of aquaculture farms, composition of the mangrove system, etc., should be strengthened for mitigating anthropogenic pressures on coastal CPR eco-systems. Special zones for shrimp farming may be determined in the coastal areas after a detailed investigation through remote-sensing and ground truth data for the preparation of thematic maps to minimize ecological unsustainability. The government should also take appropriate measures to allow shrimp farms to function in higher grounds found beyond the mangrove ecosystem as the mangroves are the bloodline of coastal inhabitants, particularly the fisherfolk, and one should also ensure that the coastal aquaculture should aim at improving the domestic nutritional status by producing more for the indigenous markets.

Extensive planning should be made to provide a conceptual, methodological and institutional framework to internalise the shrimp farming externalities progressively. The prudent use of CPRs is of absolute importance and its sustainable exploitation is obligatory to correct distributional imbalances. Since coastal CPRs have become the victims of mindless modernization, a new development paradigm should be evolved to focus on the optimal use of resources for efficiency, equity and sustainability. An equitable balance between the socio-economic, cultural and environmental needs of the present as well as future generations needs our urgent attention. Focus on proper management of CPRs, restoring ecosystem and increasing the efficiency of CPRs will enable coastal inhabitants to meet their local needs in an environmentally sustainable manner. Since the CPR milieu has become a sensitive issue, Non-Governmental Organizations (NGOs) have an important role to play and they may be permitted to develop location-based technologies.

The recurring effects of CPR overuse are a matter of great concern and it warrants a comprehensive policy to ensure sustainability of CPR,. Creating awareness about the coastal CPRs property rights regimes and institutions through information package, education, training and mass media to the user groups as well as shrimp farmers by the government will be an essential ingredient to minimize social externalities of shrimp farming. In short, the development and economic invulnerability in relation to coastal shrimp farming should consider the prudent and efficient use of biological coastal resources, use of environment friendly technologies of production, conservation and sustainability of coastal CPR environment, trade off between domestic and export market, improvement of the people's nutritional status and finally the livelihood security of the coastal inhabitants.

NOTES

1 The external cost due to loss of potable water was estimated by multiplying the quantum of good quality water used per hectare per year and treatment cost per m^3. The treatment cost per m^3 was Rs. 30 (also see NEERI 1995).

2 The reclamation cost is the better approximation to cost of damaged asset, namely, land. The Assistant Agricultural Chemist, Department of Agriculture, Government of Tamil Nadu, provided the reclamation cost of saline soil. It was about Rs. 2,346 per ha (also see Anonymous 1979).

3 NEERI has estimated that at least two persons required medical assistance per hectare of shrimp farm and medical assistance cost per person was about Rs. 450 (also see NEERI 1995).

4 The loss of fishing income was computed by using information such as boat equivalent of fish catch per hectare of shrimp farm, number of fishermen per boat, fish catch per fisherman, cost of fish catch and fish catch period during the year.

5 External cost due to loss of fishing net due to shrimp farming activity was estimated by multiplying the number of fishing nets damaged by per hectare of shrimp farming per year by computing the actual cost of fishing net.

6 External cost due to non-approachability of fishermen was calculated using information such as boat equivalent of fish catch per hectare of shrimp farms, loss of mandays for fish catch activity due to the construction of aquaculture units, fishermen in each boat, fish catch per fisherman, cost of fish and total fish catch during the year.

REFERENCES

Alagarswami, K. 1993. "Planning for Augmenting Shrimp Seed Production", *Fishing Chimes*, 13(1) pp. 27-30.

Alagarswami, K. 1993a. "Sustainable Management and Development of Coastal Aquaculture", In: M.S. Swaminathan (Ed.), *Sustainable Management of Coastal Eco-Systems*. Chennai: M.S. Swaminathan Research Foundation.

Anonymous. 1979. "The Project on the Reclamation of Saline and Alkaline soils in Chengalpat

District Under Massive Programme", *Project Report*, Department of Agriculture, Government of Tamil Nadu, p. 5.

Anonymous. 1989. "Aquaculture for Genuine Development?", *Aqua Farm News*, 8(3-4): 1-14.

Anonymous. 1991a. "World Shrimp Farming 1991", *Aquaculture Digest*, San Diego, U.S.A.

Anonymous. 1991b. "Fight for Survival Turns into Bloodshed", *The Bangkok Post*, 26th May.

Anonymous. 1995. "Aquafarming may cause Severe Ecological Crisis", *Economic Times*, 8th February.

Anonymous. 1995a. *NEERI Report on Aquaculture*, NEERI, Nagpur.

Aoki, T. 1992. "Chemotherapy and Drug Resistance in Fish Farms in Japan". In: M. Sheriff, R.P. Suhasinghe and J.R. Arthur (Ed.). *Diseases in Asian Aquaculture I, Fish Health Section*, (Asian Fisheries Society, Manila, Philippines), pp. 519-529.

Boyd, C.E. 1989. "Water Quality Management and Aeration In Shrimp Farming", *Fisheries and Allied Aquaculture*, Dept, Series No. 2: Alabama: Aubum University, USA.

Bromley, D.W. 1991. *Environment and Economy : Property Rights and Public Policy*, Oxford: Basil Blackwell.

Brown, J. 1989. "Antibiotics : Their Use and Abuse in Aquaculture". *World Aquaculture*, 20(2):34-43.

Carter, J. 1959. "Mangrove Succession and Coastal Changes in SW Malaya", *Trans Institute Br. Geor.*, 26:79-88.

Clark, J. *et al.* 1989. "The State of Integrated Coastal Zone Management: A Global Assessment", Preliminary *Summary Report* of a Workshop convened at Charlestow, U.S.A.: South Carolina, July 4-9.

Dixion, J.A. 1989. "Valuation of Mangroves", *Tropical Coastal Area Management*, 4(3):1-6.

Grusmee, Banchong Tienson. 1995. "Environmental Issues of Shrimp Farming: South East Asian Experience", Paper Presented in the Technical Session of *"INDAQUA 95"* January 27-30, 1995, Chennai, India (Marine Products Exports Development Authority, India) p. 15.

Hamilton, L.S. and Snedaker, S.C. (eds.). 1984. *Hand Book for Mangrove Area Management*, UNESCO/IUCN/UNEP East West Centre. Environment and Policy Institute, Honolulu, Hawai: East West Centre.

Karpagam, M. 1991. *Environmental Economics—A Text Book*, New Delhi: Sterling Publishers Private Limited.

Kurien, J. 1997. "Environmental Issues Along Coastal Zone", In: Anil Agarwal (ed.), *The Challenge of the Balance*, Delhi: Centre for Science and Environment.

Liao. I.C. 1992. "Marine Prawn Culture in Taiwan 1992", In: A.W. Fast and L.J. Leaster (eds) *Marine Shrimp Culture: Principles and Practices Development in Aquaculture and Fisheries Science*, Volume 23, Elsevier, Amsterdam, pp. 653-675.

Machintosh, D.J. 1982. "Fisheries and Aquaculture Significance of Mangrove Swamps with Special Reference to the Indo-west Pacific Region", In: J.F. Muir and R.J. Roberts (eds.), *Recent Advances in Aquaculture*, Volume 1. pp. 3-85, London: Croom Helm.

Mahmood, N. 1986. "Effect of Shrimp Farming and Other Impacts on Mangroves of Bangladesh", In: R.H. Mepham and T. Peter (eds.), Papers contributed to the Workshop on Strategies for Management of Fisheries and Aquaculture in Mangrove Ecosystems, 23-25 June, 1986, Bangkok, Thailand, 1986. pp. 46-66.

Marothia, D.K. 1997. "Property Rights, Externalities and Environmental Pollution: In Anil Agarwal (ed.). *The Challenge of the Balance*, New Delhi: Centre for Science and Environment.

Me Manus, Liana T. 1993. "Training Needs in and Teaching Curricula for Coastal Zone Management in theAsia-Pacific", In: John E. Hay and Chou Loke Ming (ed) Report of the *First NETTLAP Resources Development Workshop* for Education and Training at Tertiary Level in Coastal Zone Management, *NETTLAP Publication No. 7.*

Mekong Secretariat. 1992. "Fisheries in the Lower Mekong Basin—Interim Committee for the Co-ordination of Investigations of Lower Mekong Basin", Bangkok, Thailand.

Mohanty, A.N., P. Ravichandran, T. Rajalakshmi and S.M. Pillai. 1989. "Rate of Ammonia Excretion in *Penalus monodon* (fabricius)", *Journal of Aquaculture in the Tropics 4*, pp. 93-95.

National Environmental Engineering Research Institute (NEERI). 1995. *Investigation Report* on "Impacts of Aquaculture Farming and Remedial Measures in Ecologically Fragile Coastal Areas in the States of Andhra Pradesh and Tamil Nadu", (NEERI, Nehru Marg, Nagpur).

Odum, H.T. and J.E. Arding. 1991. "Energy Analysis of Shrimp Mariculture in Ecuador", Working Paper Prepared for the Coastal Resource Centre, USA: University of Rhode island, Narragansett.

Prasada Rao, P.V.S.V. 1995. "A Study on Impact of Aquaculture on Environment in Coastal Andhra Pradesh", In: Parthasarathy, G. and J.V.H. Dixitu (eds.), *Blue Revolution and Public Policy*, Hyderabad: Booklinks Corporation, p. 154.

Primavera, J.H. 1991. "Intensive Prawn Farming in the Philippines: Ecological, Social and Economic implications", *Ambio*, 20(1):28-33.

PSU "Pak Panang Bay". 1991 and 1993. Coastal Resource Institute (CORIN), Prince of Songkhla University.

Ramanamurthy, K.V. 1995. "Shrimp Cultures and Environmental Issues", In: Parthasarathy, G. and J.V.H. Dixitulu (eds.), *Blue Revolution and Public Policy*, Hyderabad: Booklinks Corporation, p. 154.

Ramasamy, C. and C. Sekar. 1997. "Groundwater Exploitation and its Impact on Environment in Western Tamil Nadu", In: Anil Agarwal (ed.), *The Challenge of the Balance*, New Delhi: Centre for Science and Environment.

Saleath, Maria. 1997. "Sustainable Management of Mangrove Resources in India: Strategies and Options", In: Anil Agarwal (ed.), *The Challenge of the Balance*, New Delhi: Centre for Science and Environment.

Sathia Sundari. 1997. "Practical Methods to Protect the Ecosystem of the Bhavani River Basin", Paper Presented in the Meeting organised to offer suggestions to preserve Bhavani River held at Coonor. May, 1997.

Snedaker, S.C. and C.D. Getter. 1985. "Coastal Resources Management Guidelines, Renewable Resources Information Services". *Coastal Management Publication 2*. Colombia: Research Planning Institute. Inc.

Selvam, S. and C. Ramasamy. 1996. "Socio-economic and Environmental Consequences of Shrimp Farming in Coramandal Coast of South India", (*Research Report*, CARDS, Coimbatore: Tamil Nadu Agricultural University.

Sirisup, S. 1988. "Socio-economic Change in the Course of Commercialisation", *Coastal Aquaculture in Chanthabun*, Bangkok, Thailand.

Sorensen, J.C., S.T. Mc Creary and M.J. Hershman 1989. *Institutional Arrangements for Management of Coastal Resources*, South Carolina, Washington: Research Planning Institute Inc., Columbia.

Swaminathan, M.S. 1993. "Building an Integrated Ecological and Livelihood Security System for the Coastal Zone", In: M.S. Swaminathan (ed.). *Sustainable Management of Coastal Eco-systems*, Chennai: M.S. Swaminathan Research Foundation.

Turner, R.E. 1977. "Inter Tidal Vegetation and Commercial Yields of Penaeid Shrimp", *Trans American Fish Society*, 106: 411-416.

Young, Michael D. and Bonnie J. McCay. 1995. "Building Equity, Stewardship and Resilience in to Market Based Property Rights Systems", In: Susan Hanna and Mohan Munasinghe (ed,), *Property Rights and the Environment—Social and Ecological Issues*, Washington: The Beijer International Institute and the World Bank.

SECTION 5

BIODIVERSITY AND INSTITUTIONAL STRUCTURES

22 Sacred Groves as Common Property Resources: An Exploratory Study

Kailash C. Malhotra

In the present day Indian society, as elsewhere in many parts of the world, there are a number of communities that practise many forms of nature worship. One such significant tradition of nature worship is that of dedicating and according protection of patches of forests to ancestral spirits/deities. These vegetation patches have been designated as "Sacred Groves" (SGs). Although there is a variation in the way these groves have been described/defined, most of the scholars emphasize the natural climax nature of the vegetation and the preservation of vegetation through local taboos and sanctions that entail spiritual and ecological values. Thus SGs are segments of landscape, containing vegetation and other forms of life and geographical features that are delimited and protected by human societies under the belief that to keep them in a relatively undisturbed state is an expression of important relationship to the divine or to nature (Hughes and Chandran 1998). Diverse cultures perceive this relationship in different ways, and institutionalize various rules of behaviour (taboos) in regard to the sacred space and its elements. But wherever SGs occur, they are of an immense cultural and ecological interest.

The institution of SGs has been fairly well studied in India from anthropological as well as biological conservation points of view (for an overview on anthropological studies, see Roy Burman 1995, Gupta 1998, Malhotra 1998, Das and Malhotra 1998, and for biological conservation related studies see Chandrashekara & Sarkar 1998, Deshmukh *et al.* 1998, Pushpangadan *et al.* 1998, Gokhale *et al.* 1998, Ramakrishnan 1998, and also see Ramakrishnan *et al.* (eds.), 1998—this publication contains several articles on the subject.

A review of the literature pertaining to SGs in India, however, suggests that SGs have not been studied and analysed within the framework of the concept of Common Property Resources (CPRs).

In this chapter, therefore, an attempt has been made to examine whether the concept of CPRs could be extended to the institution of SGs. The material used in this chapter is the published literature on SGs as well as our own field studies conducted in Orissa and West Bengal. The material is described and discussed in three parts. Part I provides a descriptive overview of SGs in India with a focus on those features of SGs that have a bearing on the concept of CPRs. Part II examines the various features described in Part I within the framework of CPRs. Part III is devoted to a discussion and conclusions.

1. Descriptive Overview of SGs

The material in this part has been described under the following heads and draws heavily on an earlier review article of Malhotra (1998).

(i) Antiquity of SGs
(ii) Spatial distribution of SGs in India
(iii) Number and size distribution of SGs
(iv) Ownership pattern and management of SGs
(v) Ethnicity and SGs
(vi) Gender and SGs
(vii) Interface between people and SGs
  (a) Sacred (Religious)
  (b) Socio-cultural and economic
  (c) Harvesting of biomass from SGs
  (d) Political dimensions of SGs
(viii) Biological and ecological value of SGs

1.a. Antiquity of SGs

Several scholars have noted that SGs are a very ancient and widespread phenomenon in the old-world cultures (Hughes and Chandran 1998). According to Kosambi (1962) the institution of SGs in India is very ancient and dates back to the pre-agrarian hunting stage, before humans had settled down to raise livestock or till the land (also see Vartak and Gadgil 1981).

1.b. Spatial Distribution of SGs in India

The sacred groves are widely present in different parts of the country. They have been reported from Rajasthan, Maharashtra, Karnataka, Kerala, Tamil Nadu, West Bengal, Bihar, Madhya Pradesh, Andhra Pradesh, Orissa, Uttar Pradesh, Meghalaya, Sikkim and other north-eastern States (see among others Brandis 1897, Hughes and Chandran 1998).

The groves, as would be expected, are known by different names. For example, in central India they are known as *jankor, sarana,* in West Bengal as *jaher,* in Rajasthan as *orans,* in Kerala as *kavus,* in Maharashtra as *deorai,* in Kodagu (Karnataka) as *Devarakadus,* in Meghalaya as *lakyntang,* in Karnataka as *kans,* etc.

However, sacred groves have not been reported from Jammu and Kashmir, Gujarat, Punjab, Haryana and the Andamans and Nicobar islands. It is likely that studies have not been carried out in these States in respect of sacred groves, or may be groves are absent in these States. It is important to note that except for the States of Kerala, Meghalaya and some regions of Karnataka (Kodagu district), Maharashtra (Western Ghats) and Orissa (Koraput district), our knowledge regarding the presence or absence of sacred groves in other parts of the country is scanty and rather inadequate.

1.c. Number and Size Distribution of SGs

As noted above, although sacred groves have been reported from many parts of the country, however, we as yet do not have even an estimate of the number of such groves in India. In Table 22.1, available data in terms of numbers of groves in India is given. Somewhat detailed inventories are only known for certain regions of the country. Gadgil and Vartak (1981) report 483 groves in Maharashtra. Actually they reported only 233 groves, but the total area of 3,570 ha. included areas from Ratnagiri district also. Godbole *et al.* (1998) report the existence of over 250 groves in Ratnagiri district. Thus adding these 250 and 233 gives the total of 483 groves. Kalam (1996) reports 1,214 groves in the Kodagu district of Karnataka. In Meghalaya 79 groves have been listed by Tiwari *et al.* (1998). Rajendraprasad (1993) reports the existence of over 2,000 well-preserved sacred groves in Kerala. In one block, Semiliguda of Koraput district in orissa, Malhotra *et al.* (1997) surveyed all the 220 villages and found in 169 villages 322 sacred groves. Pooling together these groves and other listed in Table 22.1, at least 4,125 groves have been reported so far.

It may be pointed out here that this figure of 4,125 is only an indication of the extent and magnitude of the presence of SGs in the country. It is certainly difficult to make a guess regarding the total number of SGs in the country, but the known presence and pattern of distribution of sacred groves in Madhya Pradesh, Bihar, Andhra Pradesh and several north-eastern States for which inventories are not available, we strongly feel that the number of SGs in India is likely to be between 100,000 and 150,000.

The limited data that are available suggest the existence of inter-district (region) variation in the extent of presence of SGs. Thus, an examination data of Gadgil and Vartak (1981) and Godbole (1998) pertaining to Maharashtra reveals: (a) that the number of groves in the Western Ghat districts of

TABLE 22.1: **Reported Area of the Sacred Groves in India**

Location	No. of Sacred Groves	Area (ha)	References
Maharashtra[1]	483	3,570	Gadgil and Vartak, 1981
Kodagu	1,214	5,947	Kalam, 1990
Meghalaya[2]	79	26,326	Tiwari *et al.*, 1998
Kerala[3]	2,000	500	Rajendraprasad, 1995
Tamil Nadu	10	127	Swamy *et al.*, 1998
Rajasthan	1	83	Singh and Saxena, 1998
Rajasthan	8	158	Jha *et al.*, 1998
Uttar Pradesh	1	5,500	Sinha and Maikhuri, 1998
Orissa	322	50	Malhotra *et al.*, 1998
West Bengal	7	2	Malhotra *et al.*, 1998
Total	4,125	39,063	

1. Includes districts of Thane, Kolaba, Jalgaon, Pune, Satara, Kolhapur, Yeotmal, Bhandara, Chandrapur and Ratnagiri; Gadgil and Vartak, however, estimate that the total area in Maharashtra under sacred groves is likely to be 5,000-10,000 ha. Godbole *et al.* (1998) report existence of over 250 groves in Ratnagiri district, these have been added to 233 reported by Gadgil and Vartak.
2. Khiewtám and Ramakrishnan (1989) reported 21 sacred groves in Cherrapunji and adjoining areas in Meghalaya. The total area under protection was estimated as about 5,000 ha. (50 km²). It is not clear whether in the 79 groves reported by Tiwari *et al.* (1998) includes these 21 groves.
3. Rajendraprasad (1995) estimated about 2,000 well-preserved sacred groves in Kerala. However the area is based on only 360 groves which obviously is in underestimate of the area under sacred groves in Kerala.

Maharashtra (see Table 22.2) is much bigger compared to Khandesh (Jalgaon district) and Vidarbha in eastern Maharashtra, (b) even the six districts of the Western Ghats show considerable variation, the observed range is from a minimum of 15 in Kolaba to a maximum of 250 in Ratnagiri district; and (c) there seems to be a gradient of increase in the number of groves from north to south, thus while in Thane and Kolaba districts the number of groves are 21 and 15 respectively, further south in Pune and Kolhapur district, the number is 70 and 97 respectively and the southernmost Ratnagiri district has over 250 groves. We certainly cannot take this inter-district variation at the face value, since we do not know whether the density of groves is a function of the size of geographical area and number of villages and their ethnic composition in different districts, or it is a function of the intensity of the institution in itself. Only future well-planned studies in the region will clarify the situation.

Literature review and our own studies in Orissa and West Bengal suggest

TABLE 22.2: **The Size Distribution of Sacred Groves in Maharashtra, Inter-district Variation**[1]

District	No. of Sacred Groves	Size of Sacred Groves in ha.				
		up to 2	2-5	5-10	10-15	>15
Thane	21	9.5	33.4	14.3	4.7	38.1
Kolaba	15	6.7	0.0	20.0	20.0	53.3
Pune[2]	66	81.8	9.1	3.0	4.6	1.5
Satara	16	93.7	0.0	6.3	0.0	0.0
Kolhapur	97	82.5	11.3	4.2	1.0	1.0
Jalgaon	4	100.0	0.0	0.0	0.0	0.0
Vidarbha[3]	7	85.7	0.0	0.0	0.0	14.3
Total	226	71.7	10.6	5.7	3.6	8.4

1. Data given by Gadgil and Vartak (1981) in Appendix I has been reanalysed to examine inter-district variation in the number and size distribution of sacred groves in Maharashtra.
2. Out of 70 sacred groves, area for four was not available thus reducing the total to 66.
3. Sacred groves from Yeotmal (n=3), Bhandara (n=3) and Chandrapur (n=4) have been pooled together; however, area for only 7 groves was available.

that the size of the groves varies considerably from a cluster of a few trees to several hectares. Unfortunately, not many scholars have given the sizes of individual sacred groves. However, pooled total areas are available for some States/regions/localities. In Table 22.1 we have documented the available data in terms of the area under SGs in different parts of the country. The data reveal that there exists a vast inter-State variation in the extent of area under SGs. It appears that SGs in Western Ghats, Kodagu, Meghalaya, Tamil Nadu and Rajasthan are relatively larger compared to the groves in Orissa and West Bengal. Data in terms of area are available for 4,125 sacred groves. These groves cover an estimated area of 39,063 ha.

According to Gokhale *et al.* (1998) the total area of SGs in India as a whole would be about 33,000 ha. or 0.01 per cent of the total area of India. There seems to be some error in this estimate as just 4,125 SGs reported so far cover over 39,000 ha. Although based on the rather imcomplete data it is not possible to come up with a reasonable estimate. However, it can safely be said that the area under SGs will be many times more than Gokhale *et al.*have estimated.

As noted above, there also exists inter-State/region variation in the number as well as size of SGs. It is likely that there also exists an intra-State variation in the size of the groves. The inventory prepared by Gadgil and Vartak (1981) provides an excellent opportunity to examine this aspect. These authors documented SGs in nine districts of Maharashtra. This data is reanalysed by the author to capture the inter-district variation. The results are presented in Table 22.2. It is evident that the size of the groves depicts considerable variation between the districts. Thane and Kolaba districts have much larger groves compared to the adjacent southern districts of Pune, Satara and Kolhapur. Over 80 per cent of the groves in these latter districts are up to only 2 ha, while in the former districts such groves are less than 10 per cent. Likewise there are a significant number of groves measuring above 10 ha. in Thane and Kolaba (20 out of 36, i.e. 55.6 per cent) in the southern districts they are only 6 out of 179, i.e. 3.4 per cent.

Further, there seems to be an inter-regional variation in the size of the groves in Maharashtra; compared to the groves on the Western Ghats, the groves in eastern Maharashtra are much smaller in size. Similar inferences can be drawn from the data reported by Deshmukh *et al.* (1998) for 14 districts in Maharashtra.

A gradient of increasing number of SGs from north to south in the Western Ghats was observed. In terms of the size of the groves, interestingly the reverse pattern is seen, i.e. the number of groves with larger size show an increasing trend from south to north (see also Deshmukh *et al.* 1998).

The data available on the number and size of individual groves are rather scanty and often in many studies ethnicity of the localities is not described (Kalam 1996, Godbole *et al.* 1998, Gadgil and Vartak 1981, Pushpangadan *et al.* 1998). From the available data the following tentative observations can be made:

(i) The distribution of over 2,000 SGs in Kerala is almost entirely found in districts having very little tribal population. Therefore, it can be inferred that SGs in Kerala seem to be strongly associated with different Hindu castes. However, from the data it is not clear with which castes are the groves associated;
(ii) In Kodagu also it seems that the groves are primarily associated with non-tribal Hindus, but the caste-affiliation cannot be inferred;
(iii) In the Western Ghats region of Maharashtra the groves are associated with both tribals (Mahadeo Kolis) and non-tribals (Kunbis and several other castes) (Vartak and Gadgil 1981, Roy Burman 1996);
(iv) In south of West Bengal and in Koraput district the groves are associated predominantly with the tribals;
(v) In Meghalaya the groves are associated with the Khasi tribals;
(vi) In Rajasthan the groves have been reported among the Bishnois and Rajputs;
(vii) The only grove reported from Garhwal (Sinha and Maikhuri 1998) is associated with Hindus; and
(viii) The sacred groves reported from Tamil Nadu are associated with non-tribals.

1.d. Ownership Pattern and Management of SGs

Literature on this aspect though sparse and scanty suggests the existence of a vast variation in the legal status and management of SGs in the country. An understanding of these aspects, i.e. who owns a particular grove, is a prerequisite and crucial in not only interpreting the present cultural and biological status of the groves but also in initiating long-term conservation strategies of these sacred sites.

It appears that in terms of the legal tenurial rights, the sacred groves fall under three categories:

(i) under the control of State forest departments;
(ii) under the control of revenue and other government departments; and
(iii) privately owned.

A large number of SGs in Maharashtra are under the control of the Forest Department. Gadgil and Vartak (1981) have documented 233 such groves. Legally all sacred groves in Meghalaya are under the control of District Councils (Tiwari *et al.* 1998).

Kalam (1996) reports that *devarakadus* in Kodagu district of Karnataka are under the control of the Revenue Department. Godbole *et al.* (1998) and Roy Burman (1996) mention that many SGs in western Maharashtra are under the control of the Revenue Department. Roy Burman further mentions that a few thousand temples and their groves in western Maharashtra were brought under the scrutiny of the government by forming the Paschim Maharashtra Deosthan Prabodhan Samiti in the 1960s.

There are also several SGs owned privately—owned by a family, a group of families, a clan(s), a village, a cluster of villages, etc. Chandrashekara and Sankar (1998) give examples of groves in Kerala like Ollur Kavu owned by a single family, like S.N. Puram *kavu* owned and managed by several families and a *kavu* like Iringole managed by the Temple Trust.

In terms of management of the sacred groves, i.e. upkeep, protection, performance of rituals and festivals and harvesting of biomass, etc., also there exists vast variations. To cite a few examples: Orans in Rajasthan are usually managed by the Gram Panchayats (Jha *et al.* 1998); the Haryali grove in Garhwal is managed by a temple committee made up from members of three villages (Sinha and Maikhuri 1998), Roy Burman (1996) mentions that among the Mahadeo Kolis of Pune district, the management is usually vested with the clan elders, whereas among the Kunbis of Kolhapur district the groves are managed by village elders; the Kantabanshini Thakuramma SG in Koraput district is managed by two clans of the Proja tribe (Hemam *et al.* 1997); clan-based management appears to be a widespread practice among the Santhals,

Oraon, Munda, Kharia and other tribes of central and eastern and north-east India.

1.e. Ethnicity and Sacred Groves

The processes of peopling of India stretching over indeed a long period brought in not only different human biological traits, but also a variety of cultural, religious and technological characteristics. Contemporary India is an agglomeration of over 40,000 endogamous groups (Malhotra 1984). An estimated 37,000 groups are structured in the Hindu caste system. Each group (caste) belongs to one of the five *varnas*: Brahmin, Kshatriya, Vaishya, Sudra and Puncham. The remaining 3,000 groups constitute different tribes, religious communities and other historical migrant populations like Parsis and Siddis. In other words, there is a bewildering heterogeneity in the Indian society in terms of religious beliefs, culture, language and pattern of livelihoods.

In this section an attempt is made to examine if there exists any pattern in terms of association of the institution of sacred groves and ethnicity.

A few tentative inferences in terms of association of sacred groves with different ethnic groups that can be drawn from the materials described earlier are: (i) that sacred groves are found among both tribals and non-tribals; (ii) there is regional variation in terms of ethnic association; (iii) the association with castes of different *varnas* is not clear; (iv) in States like Bihar, MP, Orissa, West Bengal, etc., where we have both tribals and non-tribals the presence or absence of groves in the non-tribal areas is not clear, i.e. whether districts with no tribals or districts away from the tribal areas in these States depict presence of sacred groves comparable with districts with higher tribal populations; and (v) whether the institution is found in the regions/villages inhabited by Christians, Muslims and other religious communities.

1.f. Gender and SGs

The role of gender in sacred groves can be analysed at least at four levels. Firstly, the gender of the deity associated with the sacred groves, secondly, the gender of priesthood serving the groves, thirdly, the nature and extent of access to men and women in various rituals, festivals and ceremonies that take place in the groves, and harvest of biomass from the groves, and fourthly, who has a say in the management of the sacred groves.

A random literature search reveals that by and large a majority of the sacred groves are associated with female deities. Gadgil and Vartak (1976) found, among 21 sacred groves in Maharashtra, 15 associated with goddesses ad 5 with male deity (phallic worship) and one with ancestor worship. Chandran (1995) reports occurrence of both male (Bhutappa, Jatakappa) and female (Choudamma) deities associated with sacred groves in Karnataka. In south-west Bengal and in Koraput district of Orissa, the deities are mostly female (Hemam *et al.* 1997, Malhotra *et al.* 1998).

Regarding the gender of the priest, it appears that without an exception the priesthood rests with males (see, among others; Vartak and Gadgil 1981, Roy Burman 1996, Godbole *et al.* 1998, Sinha 1989). However, this aspect needs to be further studied, as many studies do not provide explicit details on the gender of priests. Of great interest will be the situation among the matrilineal populations such as Nairs in Kerala, Khasis and Garos in north-east.

The data in terms of access to sacred groves by women are also very scanty. It appears, as could be inferred from some studies, that women are not permitted into the groves after attaining puberty. Roy (1912) while describing sacred groves, known as *sarana* or *jaher* among the Oraon of Chottanagpur, mentioned that the main festival associated with *sarna* is *sahrul*. However, women are not allowed in the *sarana*, but take part in dance at the *akhara* which is located close to the grove (also see Fernandes 1993, for more details). Roy Burman (1996) has reported a similar phenomenon among the Mahadeo Kolis of Pune district and among the Kunbis of Kolhapur district in Maharashtra. Malhotra *et al.* (1998) has observed taboo against entry of women in the sacred groves among the tribes of south-west Bengal and among the tribes of Koraput district of Orissa.

Although many studies have mentioned about harvesting of a certain type of biomass from the sacred groves, it is not clear whether women are allowed to gather the same (see, among others, Unnikrishnan 1990, Mitra and Pal 1994, Viji 1995).

Lastly, nothing is known at all about the kind of role women play in decision-making regarding management of the sacred groves. It will be of immense value to examine whether women are represented in numerous trusts that are managing sacred groves, in particular in Maharashtra, Karnataka and Kerala. The limited information that is available from our own field observations in West Bengal and Orissa suggests practically no role of women in the management of the sacred groves.

1.g. Interface between People and Sacred Groves

In this section we shall try to examine the role of sacred groves in the lives of the people from four aspects: (a) sacred (religious); (b) socio-cultural and economics; (c) harvesting of biomass from SGs, and (d) political dimensions of SGs.

1.g.1 Sacred (Religious)

There is a category of SGs among many communities that are associated with a certain deity(ies). In such groves annual rituals and ceremonies are performed to propitiate the deity. During these rituals sacrifices of animals (such as fowl, goat, pig, buffalo) are made. In other 'sanskritized' groves offerings of vegetarian items are made. These rituals are performed for the well-being of the inhabitants, animals, crops, etc. Anthropological literature is full of such detailed accounts (see, among others, Roy 1912, Gurdon 1914, Biswas 1956, Nath 1960, Kosambi 1962, Vidyarthi and Rai 1977, Patil 1982, Hembram 1983, Danda and Ekka 1984, Sinha 1989, Hemam *et al.* 1997).

The presiding deities not only look after the well-being of the people, but also protect the groves by punishing (mostly death) the offenders. The practises of oath/vow taking in the groves is fairly widespread in the country (among others see Roy 1912, Sisodia and Malhotra 1963, Kalam 1996). People take vows for wish-fulfilment when there is a crisis, particularly bearing on health, and offerings mostly of terracotta of animals, birds, humans, etc., are made. We observed in some of the groves of West Bengal heaps of such terracotta offerings of elephants and horses (Malhotra and Ketaki unpublished).

There seems to be a hierarchy of sacred groves in terms of their geographical influence. At least five such hierarchical levels are discernible (Table 22.3): village/hamlet level where only inhabitants of the village/hamlet or even different ethnic groups/different castes in multi-ethnic situations have their own groves. Roy Burman (1996) reports existence of such groves for different castes in villages of Kolhapur and Pune districts. Malhotra *et al.* (1997) observed in Kendua village of Jamboni taluk of Midnapore district where tribals Kora and Santhal have their separate groves. Such a pattern seems fairly widespread among the tribes of central India, Bihar and Orissa. Such groves are mostly managed by the local community(ies)—a family, group of families, clan, or an entire village.

TABLE 22.3: **Hierarchical Levels of Sacred Groves in India, A Tentative Framework**

Hierarchical Levels of Sacred Groves		Management of Sacred Groves
V	Pan India	By trust
IV	Regional	By trust
III	Local	By whole village/community/local committees
II	Village	By whole village
I	Intra-village	By separate communities

The local-level groves are where people from somewhat larger geographical areas usually couple of districts come to worship a particular grove. Examples of such groves are Iringole in Kerala and Kantabanshini

Thakumaa in Orissa (Hemam *et al.* 1997). Such groves are usually managed by local community and/or committees.

The regional-level sacred groves are where people from several districts/ States participate. Such an example is of the Sabarimala sacred grove in Kerala. Such groves are usually managed by temple trusts.

The next level of sacred groves are of Pan Indian character in which people from many parts of the country participate. The example of such a grove could be the Hariyali sacred grove in Garhwal Himalayas (Sinha and Maikhuri 1998). Such groves tend to be larger and managed by temple trusts.

Another category of sacred groves are those that are considered abodes of ancestral spirits. Often these groves are, in fact, burial grounds. Such groves have been reported from a number of places. A few illustrative examples are: Vidyarthi (1963) reported such groves called Masani among the Maler of Bihar; Godbole *et al.* (1998) report several such groves (e.g. in the villages of Muradpur, Hativ, etc.) in Sangameshwar tehsil of Ratnagiri district in Maharashtra; Unnikrishnan (1990) mentions that the *theyyam* ritual in north Kerala is ancestor worship; Fernandes (1993) mentions about Sasan sacred groves as burial grounds among the Chottanagpur tribes; Nath (1960) reports such groves among the Bhils of Ratanmal. It may be mentioned that sometimes a grove may serve both the functions, i.e. deity worship and ancestor worship. Unlike the groves associated with deity(ies), the groves associated with ancestor worship, in particular burial grounds, do not seem to have a hierarchical pattern.

1.g.2 Socio-cultural and Economic

Several scholars have reported that besides the sacred functions associated with the sacred groves, in these places several festivals are also performed. The literature on this subject is indeed very vast and detailed accounts of socio-cultural functions performed are described in several earlier ethnographic studies. Just to mention a few as illustration: Nath (1960) mentions that once a year on the occasion of Deepavali, offerings of food and liquor are made in groves among the Bhils of Ratanmal; Deb and Malhotra (1997) report that, among the tribals of south West Bengal, gatherings take place in these groves on the occasion of Salui and Karam festivals, as well as wedding ceremonies; Vidyarthi and Rai (1977) report that different tribes of Bihar celebrate their major festivals at the sacred groves; sacred groves among the Mahadeo Kolis of Pune district play a significant role in their social life, such as marriage ceremonies; Fernandes has stressed the role of sacred groves in the socialization of youth among the tribes of Chottanagpur; Godbole *et al.* (1998) report that festivals like Holi, Navaratri, Devdiwali are performed in village sacred groves in Ratnagiri district of Maharashtra; Kalam (1996) mentions offering of miniature cows and buffaloes to the deity when cattle take ill in Iyappa Devarakadu in Kodagu; Troisi (1978) mentions that the association of a village with *jaherthan* expresses the unity of the group. No two villages share the same Jaher, and this serves as an important criterion to ascertain village membership and geographical boundary; Paranjpye (1989) highlighted that the function of the sacred grove is to maintain a hierarchical order within the community; Roy Burman (1996) observed in western Maharashtra that while among the Mahadeo Koli tribes the sacred groves play the role of maintaining the clan control over the resources, among the Kunbi caste they assist in maintaining social hierarchy based on caste and social status.

The purpose and meaning attached to various rituals, ceremonies and functions performed in SGs are summarised in Table 22.4.

TABLE 22.4: **Non-economic Services Provided by SGs**[1]

Typologies		Functions provided by SGs
1. Sacred	—	Propitiation of deity/spirits
	—	Propitiation of ancestral spirits
	—	Propitiation of totemic objects—biotic and abiotic
2. Profane/Secular		
2.1 Cultural	—	Provides cultural space to the community as a CPR
2.2 Social	—	Assertion of group identity
	—	Assertion of group solidarity
	—	Establishing new alliances
	—	Gift exchange
2.3 Health	—	Well-being of crops and animals
	—	Well-being of community
2.4 Economic	—	Good rainfall
	—	Good agricultural production
	—	Success in hunting
2.5 Psychological	—	Moral support, guidance
	—	Fertility and paternity
	—	Well-being of individual/family

1 After Malhotra *et al.*, 1998.

1.g.3 Harvesting of Biomass from SGs

There is a general belief that biomass resources from the sacred groves are not harvested. This is certainly true in many sacred groves found across the country. Gadgil and Vartak (1976), Roy Burman (1995) and Godbole *et al.* (1998) report several such groves in the Western Ghats of Maharashtra. Malhotra *et al.* (1998) report such groves in south-west Bengal and in Koraput district in Orissa. Pushpangadan *et al.* (1998) report existence of numerous groves in Kerala from which plants and animals are not harvested while Swamy *et al.* (1998) report such groves in Tamil Nadu.

However, there are many groves in the country from where certain biomass is extracted, and thus the local communities derive certain direct economic benefits from the groves. A few illustrative examples are given here: Singh and Saxena (1998) and Jha *et al.* (1998) report that in many Orans people graze their animals; Godbole *et al.* (1998) report collection of dead wood and dried leaf litter and harvesting of certain species of trees (*Caryota urens* and *Mangifera indica*) from groves in Ratnagiri district of Maharashtra; Malhotra *et al.* (1998) report 192 out of 322 groves from Koraput district from which dead wood and several NTFP are gathered; Unnikrishnan (1990) in the context of certain sacred groves in Kerala observed that certain plant species provide livelihood to many artisans; Gadgil and Vartak (1975) report that villagers of Tunbad in Kolaba district use the bark of *Entada phaseoloides Merr.* for the treatment of cattle against snakebite; from many groves dedicated to ancestor worship wood is extracted for cremation (Mitra and Pal 1994).

1.g.4 Political Dimensions of SG

Roy Burman in a series of articles (1992, 1995, 1996) has demonstrated the political dimensions of sacred groves in the local and regional context. This section has drawn heavily on the material synthesised by Roy Burman.

Sontheimer (1989) showed linkages of forest deities of the Western Ghats with the pastoral nomads as a means of drawing their territorial affinity. Kosambi (1962) observed that sacred groves are usually found along the pre-agrarian trade routes and cross-roads. Sawant (1990) wrote that the sacred groves at Phondaghat in Sindhdurg district of Maharashtra was a resting place for traders and that the troops of Shivaji passed through it while depredating the coastal townships. Roy Burman (1996) described that at Jhnji mahal sacred grove in Kolhapur district, Shivaji had taken shelter before attacking Shayasta Khan in Pune. This grove has been a hiding place for the troops and also their training centre. Sacred groves have often been supported by the local rulers. Sahu Chatrapati, the king of Kolhapur, use to support a sacred grove dedicated to Amba Devi (Roy Burman 1992). Kalam (1996) has mentioned about the State patronage of sacred groves in Kodagu district of Karnataka. Roy Burman (1993) mentions about the strategic location of sacred groves along the trade routes in Meghalaya where the moral authority of the priests-chiefs guided the free flow of commodity. As noted earlier, among the Santhals the sacred groves serve as an important criterion to ascertain village membership and geographical boundary (Troisi 1978). Hembram (1983) states that through the Sarna Dharma (religion) discrete ethnic groups in Chottanagpur were brought to a common platform for asserting their rights to self-determination. The Sarna Dharma, in fact, helped them in consolidating their common identity and solidarity between the Christian and non-Christian tribes of the region. Mitra and Pal (1994) observed that Sarna was one of the basic factors that stalled the Koel-Karo dam project in Bihar a decade ago. Roy Burman (1995) has also highlighted this aspect of self-assertion among the Gonds of Gadchiroli district of Maharashtra. The Gonds have revived the Danteswari sacred grove to assert their identity and right of self-determination. Self-assertion of the tribes through sacred groves is not always strong. D.N. (1990) interprets the construction of temples in the groves or replacing the local deities by the idol of Hanuman as reflecting subjugation and marginalisation of the tribal communities by "the mainstream Hindu civilization".

1.h. Biological and Ecological Value of SGs

A number of scholars have studied the biological and ecological value of SGs in India. The literature is too vast to be reviewed in this chapter. We shall, therefore, only mention some of the main findings as illustrations.

1.h.1 Biological Value

As noted earlier, a number of studies have emphasized that SGs harbour vegetation in its climax formation and probably constitute the only representation of forests in a near natural condition in many parts of India. Such a scenario can be seen in many parts of the Western Ghats; Koraput and Kalahandi districts of Orissa; south-west Bengal, etc. (among others, see Gadgil and Vartak 1975, Pushpangadan *et al.* 1998, Tewari *et al.* 1998). Several studies have shown that many groves, especially the ones that are somewhat larger like in the north-east (Tiwari *et al.* 1998), in Kerala (Chandrashekara and Shankar 1998), in Maharashtra (Gadgil and Vartak 1976), in Himachal Pradesh (Singh *et al.* 1998) harbour rich floral and faunal biodiversity, Pushpangadan *et al.* (1998) reviewed the existing literature on this subject and concluded that the biological spectrum of SGs in Kerala closely resembles the normal spectrum of tropical forest, and that the groves were rich in floral biodiversity. For example, the 90 sq. km. Silent Valley encompasses 960 species of angiosperms compared to 722 species in only 1.4 sq.km of the area occupied by SGs. Often SGs harbour endangered and rare species; Haridason and Rao (1985) reported at least 50 such species in the SGs of Meghalaya. Out of the 416 bird species found in the entire district of Uttara Kannada (Karnataka State), 107 species were recorded in SGs by Chandran and Gadgil (1993). Deb *et al.* (1997) reported similar observations in SGs of south-west Bengal.

1.h.2 Ecological Value

Several ecological functions performed by SGs that have been reported in the literature are: since many SGs are located in the catchment area of major rivers and rivulets they act as micro-watersheds (Pushpangadan *et al.*, 1998); the soil moisture retention capacity of SGs is higher compared to the adjacent areas (Rajendraprasad 1995); SGs are often associated with fresh water ecosystem meeting the water needs of the local communities; SGs also reduce temperature on a small scale and build up a humidity regime; Khiewtam and Ramakrishnan (1993) have carried out extensive studies in the sacred grove in Cherrapunji in Meghalaya and reported that four keystone species are found there; SGs act as refugia for birds and the birds check the insect and pest population; insect flora, particularly the bees, make their hives in SGs and facilitate cross pollination of many plant species (Malhotra *et al.*1998); SGs have played a significant role as "seed banks" for the restitution of biodiversity in Koraput district of Orissa, and when SGs occur in abundance, they provide ecological security (Malhotra *et al.* 1998).

2. Sacred Groves as Common Property Resources

From the foregone description, the following main points emerge regarding SGs in India:

(i) the institution of SG is rather ancient and probably dates back to the pre-agrarian hunting stage;
(ii) SGs are found widely distributed in many parts of the country;
(iii) the number of SGs in India is likely to be between 100,000 and 150,000;
(iv) the estimated area covered by SGs is likely to be between 1-2 per cent of the total area of the country;
(v) although SGs are found among both tribal and non-tribal populations, it seems the association of a particular type of SGs is stronger among the tribals;
(vi) there exists vast variation in the legal status and management of SGs in the country;
(vii) the institution of SGs serves multifarious functions—cultural, social, economic, health, psychological, religious and political;
(viii) SGs usually represent climax vegetation, are rich in floral and faunal biodiversity, often harbour rare, endangered and keystone species, and perform a variety of vital ecological functions.

In order to analyse SGs from the CPRs perspective it is essential that we briefly describe the salient features of CPRs.

Although CPRs have been defined quite differently in literature, the following features seem to have wider acceptance:

(i) ***Use rights***: That the resources are controlled by an identifiable group and are not privately owned by individuals or managed by government;
(ii) ***Boundary Condition or Exclusion Principle***: That there exist rules concerning who may use the resource as against who may not use the resource; and
(iii) ***Use Rules***: That there exist rules regarding how a resource is used by the group.

In the vast literature that exists on CPRs, there seems to be an emphasis on resources that accrue economic benefits to the community (group of people that collectively use a resource). In the literature the examples of CPR often cited are water, wildlife, fish, forests and pastures. The concept has, however, been extended to some other resources like public parks, highways and oil pools (Oakerson 1986), radio wavelengths (Ostrom 1986). The deep seabed and Antarctica are cited as examples of global commons.

Let us now examine whether the traditional institution of SGs as described in Part I satisfies the above mentioned features of CPRs.

(i) ***Use rights:*** As noted earlier, a wide variety exists in terms of ownership of SGs in the country;

(a) ***SGs owned and managed by single or joint family:*** Such groves are found mostly in Kerala and Bastar district of M.P.. It may be noted here that in these groves both land and fauna and flora belong to the families. These are thus examples of privately owned and managed groves and, therefore, cannot be treated as CPRs.
(b) ***SGs owned and managed by temple trusts:*** There are groves that are associated with temples. Usually like in (a) above, both land and fauna and flora are privately owned and managed by the temple trusts. Such groves are found in Maharashtra, Kerala, Karnataka, U.P., etc. Like (a) above, these groves are also privately owned and managed and, therefore, do not fall under the category of CPRs.
(c) ***SGs managed by communities:*** There are numerous SGs where although the land usually is owned by the Forest Department or the Revenue Department, or other State agencies, the right of use of resources and management rest with the communities. Such groves

could be owned and managed by a clan, different ethnic group in a village or the entire village. These are the classic examples of community-managed SGs. Such groves are found throughout the country, but especially in Orissa, Bihar, West Bengal, Meghalaya, parts of Maharashtra, Karnataka, Andhra Pradesh, Rajasthan, etc.

Although the number of such groves is not known, based on the limited data available, it is certain that their number is several times greater than the types mentioned in (a) and (b) above. It may be mentioned that just in one block of Semiliguda of Koraput district there are 322 such groves (Malhotra *et al.* 1998); in Kodagu district of Karnataka there are over 1,000 (Kalam 1966); a majority of the 953 groves reported from Maharashtra belong to this category (Deshmukh *et al.* 1998).

It is of immense interest here to point out that there seems to be a strong association between the three types of SGs mentioned above and the ethnicity; type (a) and (b) are mostly associated with Hindu castes, while type (c) is most often associated with numerous tribal communities.

It is thus evident that based on the use rights, some SGs do not fall under CPRs, whereas a large number of them, primarily found among different tribal communities, confirm to the definition of CPRs. Therefore, the other two features of CPRs have been examined only for those SGs that conform to CPRs.

(ii) ***Boundary condition or the exclusion principle:*** On the basis of this principle at least three types of SGs are observed:

(a) A village having only one SG. In such cases the whole village is affiliated to the grove. Occasionally a village may have more than one grove (serving different purposes), in such situations also the whole village is affiliated to both (or more) the groves. Persons from other villages cannot be affiliated to such village-owned and managed groves;

(b) Sometimes in multi-ethnic villages each ethnic group may have a separate grove of its own. In other words, each ethnic group manages its own SG; and

(c) Sometimes people from neighbouring villages may participate in a village having SG. Such a situation occurs when the neighbouring villages do not have their own SGs and have moved out from the parent village to establish new villages/hamlets.

It is thus seen that all SGs have well-defined boundary rules.

(iii) ***Use rules:*** There are well-established rules in terms of use of resources from SGs. Broadly speaking two types (although there is scope to further refine this) of use patterns are witnessed: (a) groves from where collection of any form of biomass is forbidden, and (b) groves from where dead wood, leaf litter, medicinal plants and other NTFP are harvested. In other words, from groves of type (a) no tangible economic benefits are derived, while from the type (b) some tangible economic benefits are derived.

It is thus evident that the (c) type of SGs conform to all the three characteristic features of CPRs.

3. Discussion and Conclusions

From the foregone description and analysis, it is evident that the institution of Sacred Groves is not a homogeneous category, and instead encompasses a variety of systems ranging from truly privately owned and managed groves to community-owned and -managed groves. Therefore, further discussion will be limited only to those SGs that are community-owned and -managed.

Unlike many CPRs studies reported in the literature like pastures, forests, fisheries, water, etc., which provide tangible economic benefits to the communities, not all SGs in contrast provide such tangible economic benefits. In this regard SGs, therefore, differ markedly from other CPRs. In fact a majority of SGs provide a variety of, strictly speaking, non-economic functions—cultural, social, political and religious—to the individuals, clan and communities. It is highly noteworthy, as noted earlier, that a number of ceremonies are performed and festivals held annually in the groves. All households affiliated to a grove contribute their share in cash for the purchase of sacrificial animal and other materials. Thus, in fact, instead of deriving any economic benefits the community spends a considerable amount to propitiate the deity.

Therefore, SGs should not be viewed as CPRs providing tangible economic benefits to the community but instead providing a common socio-religious space which the community uses to establish cohesiveness, identity, solidarity and well-being of the inhabitants as also of crops and animals.

As noted earlier, irrespective of the type, all SGs harbour varying degrees of natural biodiversity. The biodiversity in the groves is preserved on religious grounds and not because of economic benefits. However, several studies show that because of the weakening of traditional religious beliefs, the cultural and biological integrity of many groves is threatened.

However, it is not always clear as to which type of groves are under threat, i.e. the privately owned (family-owned or owned and managed by temple trusts) or the community-owned (the ones from where biomass is harvested or the ones from where biomass cannot be harvested). It is often also not explicitly stated whether the degree of threat is associated with the hierarchical levels of SGs.

In order to develop suitable intervention strategies for the conservation of SGs, it is abundantly clear that no single approach or strategy will be applicable to all the groves. Instead grove-type specific approaches will have to be developed.

In this context it is appropriate that we briefly examine the analytical models developed in relation to CPRs. It is outside the scope of this chapter to examine critically the various models, so we shall limit our observation to the overall relevance of such models to SGs. Also, it is not the purpose of this chapter to suggest any alternative models appropriate to SGs, instead the purpose is to raise issues and look for major constraints in the existing models.

Singh (1994) gives an excellent account of theories of collective action in managing common pool resources. Some of the theories and models mentioned are: Prisoner's dilemma game, the chicken or the hawk-dove game, tender trap game, threat to survival theory, theory of participative behaviour, Olson's theory, Buchanan and Tullock's theory, etc. All these theories are based on an important assumption that CPRs provide economic benefits to the group managing a CPR. Since a majority of SGs do not provide tangible economic benefits, instead provide a variety of non-economic services, most of these theories in their present form cannot be applied to analyse the threats faced by SGs.

Similarly the seven principles of design for self-organized systems of resource management advanced by Ostrom (1990, 1992) cannot be applied in their present form to an analysis of SGs.

To conclude, for a better understanding of the changes that are taking place in the institution of SGs, we need to develop approaches and models that are primarily not based on economic principles, instead include a variety of services—cultural, social, political and religious—provided by SGs. These models should help us analyse the nature of threats, both internal (those that emanate from within the community) and external (those that come from outside the community) that are likely to weaken the institution of SGs. We need to understand the processes, identify the factors that trigger shift in the traditional value and belief system.

REFERENCES

Biswas, P.C. 1956. *Santhals of the Santhal Parganas*, Bharatiya Adimjati Sevak, Delhi.

Brandis, D. 1897. "Indigenous Indian Forestry: Sacred Groves", In: *Indian Forestry Working*, Oriental Institute, pp. 12-13.

Chandrashekara, U.M. and Sankar, S. 1998. "Structure and Function of sacred groves: Case studies in Kerala", In: Ramakrishnan, P.S., K.G. Saxena and U.M. Chandrashekara (eds.) *Conserving the Sacred for Biodiversity Management*, New Delhi: Oxford and IBH Publishing Co., pp. 323-36.

Chandran, M.D.S. 1995. "Peasant perception of Bhutas, Uttar Kannada", In: B. Saraswati (ed.) *Integral Vision: Primal Element of Oral Tradition*, New Delhi: D.K. Publishers.

Chandran, M.D.S. and M. Gadgil. 1993. "Sacred groves and sacred trees of Uttara Kannada" (a pilot study). *Mimeograph.*

Danda, A.K. and W. Ekka. 1984. *The Nagesia of Chattisgarh*, Calcutta: Anthropological Survey of India.

Deb, D. and K.C. Malhotra. 1997. "Interface between Biodiversity and Tribal Cultural Heritage: An Exploratory Study", *J. Human Ecology* 8: 157-63.

Deb, D., K. Deuti and K.C. Malhotra. 1997. "Sacred grove relics as bird refugia", *Current Science*, 73: 815-17.

Deshmukh, S., M.G. Gogate and A.K. Gupta. 1998. "Sacred groves and biological diversity: Providing new dimensions to conservation issue", In: Ramakrishnan, P.S., K.G. Saxena and U.M. Chandrashekara (eds.) *Conserving the Sacred for Biodiversity Management*, New Delhi: Oxford and IBH Publishing Co., pp. 397-414.

Das, K. and K.C. Malhotra 1998. "Sacred groves among the tribes of India: A literature survey of ethnographic monographs", *Mimeograph.*

D.N. 1990. Women and forests, *Economic and Political Weekly*, April 14.

Fernandes, W. 1993. "Forest and tribals, informal economy: Dependence and management decisions", In: Miri (ed.), *Community and Change in Tribal Society*, Shimla: Indian Institute of Advanced Study.

Gadgil, M. and V.D. Vartak 1975. "Sacred groves in India: A plea for continued conservation", *Journal of Bombay Natural History Society*, 72: 314-20.

Gadgil, M. and V.D. Vartak 1976. "Sacred groves in Western Ghats in India", *Economic Botany*, 30:152-60.

Gadgil, M. and V.D. Vartak 1981. "Sacred groves in Maharashtra—An inventory", In: S.K. Jain (ed.) *Glimpses of Indian Ethnobotany*, New Delhi: Oxford & IBH Publishers, pp. 279-294.

Godbole, A., A. Watve, S. Prabhu, J. Sarnaik 1998. "Role of sacred groves in biodiversity conservation with local people's participation: A case study from Ratnagiri district, Maharashtra", In: Ramakrishnan, P.S., K.G. Saxena and U.M. Chandrashekara (eds) *Conserving the Sacred for Biodiversity Management*, New Delhi: Oxford and IBH Publishing Co., pp. 233-46.

Gokhale, Y., R. Velankar, M.D. Subhash Chandran and M. Gadgil 1998. "Sacred woods, grasslands and waterbodies as self-organized systems of conservation", In: Ramakrishnan, P.S., K.G. Saxena and U.M. Chandrashekara (eds) *Conserving the Sacred for Biodiversity Management*, New Delhi: Oxford and IBH Publishing Co., pp. 365-98.

Gurdon, P.P.T. 1914. *The Khasis*, London: MacMillan and Co.

Gupta, A.K. 1998. "Policy and institutional aspects of sacred groves: Tending the spirit, sustaining and sacred", In: Ramakrishnan, P.S., K.G. Saxena and U.M. Chandrashekara (eds) *Conserving the Sacred for Biodiversity Management*, New Delhi: Oxford and IBH Publishing Co., pp. 397-414.

Haridason, K. and P.R. Rao. 1985. *Forest Flora of Meghalaya*, Vol. 1, Bishen Singh, Dehradun.

Hemam, S.N., K.C. Malhotra and S. Stanley 1997. "The bamboo sacred grove, Katabaushini Thakurmaa of Sindipad village, Koraput district", Orissa, Unpublished.

Hembram, P.C. 1983. "Return to the sacred groves", In: K.S. Singh (Ed.) *Tribal Movements in India*, New Delhi: Manohar Publications, Vol. 2, pp. 87-91.

Jha, M., H. Vardhan, S. Chatterjee, K. Kumar and A.R.K. Sastry. 1998. "Status and role of Orans (Sacred Groves) in Peepasar village (district Naguar) and Khejarli village (district

Jodhpur), Rajasthan", In: Ramakrishnan, P.S., K.G. Saxena and U.M. Chandrashekara (eds) *Conserving the Sacred for Biodiversity Management*, New Delhi: Oxford and IBH Publishing Co., pp. 263-276.

Hughes, J.D. and M.D. Subhash Chandran. 1998. "Sacred groves around the earth: An overview", In: Ramakrishnan, P.S., K.G. Saxena and U.M. Chandrashekara (eds) *Conserving the Sacred for Biodiversity Management*, New Delhi: Oxford and IBH Publishing Co., pp. 69-86.

Kalam, M.A. 1996. *Sacred Groves in Kodagu District of Karnataka (South India): A Socio-Historical Study*, Pondichery: Institut Francais de Pondichery.

Khiewtam, R.S. and P.S. Ramakrishnan. 1989. "Socio-cultural studies of the sacred groves at Cherrapunji and adjoining areas in north-eastern India", *Man in India*, 69:64-71.

Kosambi, D.D. 1962. *Myth and Reality: Studies in the Formation of Indian Culture*, Bombay: Popular Press.

Malhotra, K.C. 1984. "Population structure among the Dhangar caste cluster of Maharashtra, India", In: J.R. Lukas (ed.) *The People of South Asia*, New York: Plenum Press, pp. 295-324.

Malhotra, K.C. 1998. "Anthropological dimensions of sacred groves in India: An overview", In: Ramakrishnan, P.S., K.G. Saxena and U.M. Chandrashekara (eds.), *Conserving the Sacred for Biodiversity Management*, New Delhi: Oxford and IBH Publishing Co., pp. 423-38.

Malhotra, K.C., K. Das 1998. "Interface between faunal biodiversity and cultural heritage in south-west Bengal, in India", In: Fujiki, N. and Macer, R.J. (eds.), *Bioethics in Asia*, Japan: Eubois Ethics Institute, pp. 346-51.

Malhotra, K.C., S. Stanley, N.S. Hemam and K. Dass 1997. "Biodiversity conservation and ethics: Sacred groves and pools", In: Fujiki, N. and R.J. Macer (eds.) *Bioethics in Asia*, Japan: Eubois Ethics Institute, pp. 338-45.

Malhotra, K.C., N.S. Hemam, S. Stanley and K. Das 1998. "Cultural and Ecological Value of Natural Sacred Biodiversity Sites in Orissa, India: Threats and Opportunities", In press: Proc. volume of International Symposium on Natural Sacred Sites—Cultural Diversity and Biological Diversity, UNESCO, Paris, 1998.

Mitra, A. and S. Pal. 1994. "The spirit of the sanctury", *Down to Earth*, January 31, 1994.

Nath, Y.V.S. 1996. *Bhils of Ratanmal*, Baroda: Maharaja Sayajirao University.

Oakerson, R.J. 1986. "A model for the analysis of common property problems", In: *Proceedings of the Conference on Common Property Resource Management*, Washington DC: Natural Academy Press, pp. 13-30.

Ostrom, E. 1986. "Issues of definition and theory: Some conclusions and hypothesis", In: *Proceedings of the Conference on Common Property Resource Management*, Washington DC: Natural Academy Press, pp. 13-30.

Ostrom, E. 1990. *Governing the Commons: The Evolution of Institutions for Collective Action*, New York: Cambridge University Press.

Ostrom, E. 1992. *Crafting Institutions for self-Governing Irrigation Systems*, San Francisco, California: Institute for Contemporary Studies.

Paranjpye, V. 1989. "Deorai (sacred grove): An Indian concept of common property resources", In: Jayal, N.D. (ed.) *Deforestation and Drought*, New Delhi: INTACH.

Patil, S. 1982. *Dasa-Sudra Slavery*, New Delhi: Allied Publishers.

Pushpangadan, P., M. Rajendraprasad and P.N. Krishnan. 1998. "Sacred groves of Kerala—A synthesis on the state of art of knowledge", In: Ramakrishnan, P.S., K.G. Saxena and U.M. Chandrashekara (eds) *Conserving the Sacred for Biodiversity Management*, New Delhi: Oxford and IBH Publishing Co., pp. 193-210.

Rajendraprasad, M. 1995. "The Floristic, Structural and Functional Analysis of Sacred Groves of Kerala", Ph.D. thesis, Thiruvananthapuram: University of Kerala.

Ramakrishnan, P.S. 1998. "Conserving the sacred for biodiversity: The conceptual framework", In: Ramakrishnan, P.S., K.G. Saxena and U.M. Chandrashekara (eds.) *Conserving the Sacred for Biodiversity Management*, New Delhi: Oxford and IBH Publishing Co., pp. 3-16.

Ramakrishnan, P.S., K.G. Saxena and U.M. Chandrashekara (eds). 1998. *Conserving the Sacred for Biodiversity Management*, New Delhi: Oxford and IBH Publishing Co.

Roy, S.C. 1912. *Munda and their Country*, Calcutta: City Book, Soc.

Roy Burman, J.J. 1992. "The institution of sacred grove", *Journal of Indian Anthropological Society*, 27: 219-38.

Roy Burman, J.J. 1995. "The dynamics of sacred groves", *Journal of Human Ecology*, 6: 245-54.

Roy Burman, J.J. 1996. "A comparison of sacred groves among the Mahadeo Kolis and Kunbis of Maharashtra", *Indian Anthropologist*, 26: 37-46.

Sawant, V. 1990. "Phondaghat: Ughwai Parisar", *Maharashtra Times*, 22 December.

Singh, G.S. and K.G. Saxena 1998. "Sacred groves in the rural landscape: A case study of the Shekhala village in Jodhpur district of desert Rajasthan", In: Ramakrishnan, P.S., K.G. Saxena and U.M. Chandrashekara (eds) *Conserving the Sacred for Biodiversity Management*, New Delhi: Oxford and IBH Publishing Co., pp. 277-88.

Singh, G.S., K.S. Rao and K.G. Saxena. 1998. "Eco-cultural analysis of sacred species and ecosystems in Chhakinal watershed, Himachal Pradesh", In: Ramakrishnan, P.S., K.G. Saxena and U.M. Chandrashekara (eds) *Conserving the Sacred for Biodiversity Management*, New Delhi: Oxford and IBH Publishing Co., pp. 301-14.

Singh, K. 1994. *Managing Common Pool Resources: Principles and Case Studies*, Delhi: Oxford University Press.

Sinha, A.P. 1989. *Religious Life of Tribal India*, New Delhi: Classical Publishers.

Sinha, B. and R.K. Maikhuri. 1998. "Conservation through 'socio-cultural'—religious practices in Garhwal Himalayas: A case study of Hariyali sacred forest", In: Ramakrishnan, P.S., K.G. Saxena and U.M. Chandrashekara (eds) *Conserving the Sacred for Biodiversity Management*, New Delhi: Oxford and IBH Publishing Co., pp. 289-300.

Sisodia, V. and K.C. Malhotra. 1963. *Terracotta Motifs among the Warlis of Dharampur*, East and West, 14: 97-105.

Sontheimer, G.D. 1989. *Pastoral Deities in Western India*, New Delhi: Oxford University Press.

Swamy, P.S., S.M. Sundarapandian and S. Chandrasekaran. 1998. "Structure and function of sacred groves: Case studies in Tamil Nadu", In: Ramakrishnan, P.S., K.G. Saxena and U.M. Chandrashekara (eds) *Conserving the Sacred for Biodiversity Management*, New Delhi: Oxford and IBH Publishing Co., pp. 357-64.

Tiwari, B.K., S.K. Barik and R.S. Tripathi. 1998. "Sacred groves of Meghalaya", In: Ramakrishnan, P.S., K.G. Saxena and U.M. Chandrashekara (eds) *Conserving the Sacred for Biodiversity Management*, New Delhi: Oxford and IBH Publishing Co., pp. 253-62.

Troisi, J. 1978. *Tribal Religion: Religion and Practice among the Santhals*, New Delhi: Manohar Publishers.

Unnikrishnan, E. 1990. *Part played by the Sacred Groves in Local Environments*, New Delhi: Centre for Science and Environment.

Vidyarthi, L.P. 1963. *Maler: A Study in Nature-Man-Spirit Complex of a Hill Tribe of Bihar*, Calcutta: Bookland Pvt. Ltd..

Vidyarthi, L.P. and B.K. Rai. 1977. *Tribal Culture of India*, New Delhi: Concept Publishers Company.

Viji, C. 1995. The sacred groves, *The Hindu*, 5 September.

23 Medicinal Plants Revisited: An Institutional Inquiry in the Common Property Resource Regime

M.G. Chandrakanth, Ravishankar, A, Rangesh Parmesh and **M.S. Suneetha**

1. Preamble

The adage *"JASYA deshasya yo janthuhu tasya tadhitham aushadham"* indicates that for the treatment of diseases in an area, the required medicinal plants are available in the same habitat. This is the reason for most of the flora to have some medicinal property or the other and is reinforced by another adage *"Jagath yeivam anoushadham, nasthi kinchith vidyathe"*: there is no plant on the earth without any medicinal property. "Jivaka", physician of the Buddha's period when asked by his Guru to trace herbs, which are not medicinal, returned empty-handed and this stands testimony for the medicinal nature of most flora. Thus, we find the use of over 7,000 species of plants in the folk tradition, for medicinal uses in India. It is believed that Lord Dhanwanthari who emanated during the "Samudra Mathana"—churning of the ocean by "Suras" and "Asuras" brought the knowledge of "Ayurveda" —the art and science of healthy and spiritual living. Pre-historical evidence of the use of plants for medicinal purposes is documented in the "Oushadhi Sukta" of the *RigVeda*. In the Agneya Kanda of *Yajurveda Samhitha*, "Sri Rudram" — a set of hymns praising Lord Rudra highlights Rudra as "Prathamo Daivyo Bhishg" meaning the first Vaidya (doctor) to treat animals with plant medicines. *Ramayana*, the great epic, highlights the frantic efforts of "Hanumantha" in search of "Sanjeevini" to save Lakshmana's life. All these are pointers to the potential of medicinal plants in life-saving and also the tradition of use of medicinal plants in India.

The *Caraka Samhitha* (1500 BC- 400 AD) has the earliest description of medicinal uses of plants[1]. The first historical evidence of a medicinal plant garden in India dates to the reign of Emperor Ashoka who established a garden of medicinal plants in 260-258 BC[2]. While the Emperor himself emphasized the establishment of medicinal plants garden as a governmental fiat, for the sake of the public and livestock, such endeavours have not attracted adequate attention of our planners. However, an exception to this is the establishment of a series of medicinal plant gardens by the Karnataka State Forest Department in recent years[3].

2. Common Property Resources and Medicinal Plants

The land-based common property resources (CPRs) are the repositories of medicinal plants. The process of conservation and sustainable use of medicinal plants is inextricably linked to the conservation of our CPRs. Medicinal plants have been escaping the attention of both researchers and policy-makers while addressing the land-based CPRs. The loss of medicinal flora entails huge transaction costs and intra- and inter-generational inequities. The issue that degradation or destruction of the commons affects the conservation of medicinal plants is both true and false, as it has to be examined in the context of the habit and habitat of the medicinal plant species.

In this chapter we attempt to provide positive and normative insights into the management of common property resources influencing the medicinal plants. All through we have adopted an inter-disciplinary approach. This becomes inevitable in order to understand the multifarious dimensions and an array of issues associated with medicinal plants. Here the focus is not confined to the "economics" of medicinal plants but is spread across other disciplines also. In fact, the economic component is underplayed in the overall fabric of medicinal plants. An overall perspective at the national level relating to medicinal plants and health care is attempted and supported by examples from the southern states of Karnataka, Kerala and Tamil Nadu. We have used the terms traditional medicine, ayurvedic medicine, herbal medicine synonymously. To understand and appreciate the problem of scarcity of medicinal plants, following issues/dimensions have been identified:

(i) The transaction costs of educating the public with regard to medicinal plants are prohibitive since (a) cost of convincing the public regarding the medicinal value of plants native to their habitat and (b) cost of educating regarding uses of medicinal plants are both colossal. The components (a) and (b) are different because unless one gets convinced, he/she would not want to be educated. The cost of the former is more than that of the latter as people have an in-built bias towards the modern medicine.

(ii) The survival value of medicinal plants and their knowledge is directly related to the survival value of common property resources.

(iii) The demand for medicinal plants is the factor (derived) demand for medicinal plant products.

(iv) The economics of health care in the traditional system of medicine is the opportunity cost of health care in the modern system of medicine. And the economics of medicinal plant cultivation or gathering are weak representations of the economics of health care in the traditional system since their valuation and contribution are grossly underestimated. In this sense market imperfections in the cost of health care are discernible when compared with market imperfections in the trade of medicinal plants.

(v) It is not as much the physical availability of medicinal plants as the knowledge of medicinal plants (source of availability, identification, recognition, belief and end use) which is eroding and vanishing.

(vi) The quality of medicinal plant products, which are heavily advertised and have a large market share, is under suspicion.[4]

(vii) Threats to current supplies of major medicinal plants (by quantity) sourced by industry are modest in comparison to endemic and economically scarce medicinal plants and medicinal plants which are substitutes.

(viii) Natural factors—forest fire, elephants and other calamities—are the causes of degradation of medicinal plants in the heavily wooded forests rather than anthropocentric forces.

(ix) Market imperfections in medicinal plants are manifested due to lack of transparency in the trade, prices, margins, existing knowledge base, skewed distribution of services of traditional medicine, doctors and retail outlets.[5]

(x) Majority of the weeds in non-forest areas have medicinal properties which can be gathered to augment the supplies of medicinal plants and incomes of farmers.

(xi) Majority of the endemic medicinal plants are economic substitutes for other medicinal plants.

(xii) Knowledge of medicinal plants and their uses are dwindling among the villagers and tribals' as they are switching to the modern system of medicine.

We may recall the issue that the economics of health care in the traditional system of medicine is the opportunity cost of health care in the modern system of medicine. And the economics of medicinal plant cultivation or gathering are weak representations of the economics of health care in the traditional system since their valuation and contribution are grossly underestimated. In this sense market imperfections in the cost of health care are discernible when compared with market imperfections in the trade of medicinal plants. Thus, the subject of the economics of medicinal plants is intricate, intriguing, puzzling, opaque and esoteric. In fact, market imperfections in medicinal plants are overplayed in relation to the valuation of medicinal plants. This needs to be appreciated in the light of the fact that most medicinal plants are low-priced in relation to their true value in health care, health cure and overall health security. When we consider alternative systems of health care, the transaction costs involved shape the relative demand for medicinal plants. In the herbal-based system, ecological and economic scarcity overlap and hence complicate estimation of resource scarcity. In this article a modest attempt is made to de-mystify a few of the issues involved in the economics of medicinal plants in the framework of the common property resources.

The cost of health cure and health care the world over is skyrocketing and thereby health consciousness is now at the centrestage. Unfortunately, in India, our continuing obsession with food security has relegated health-security and related aspects to the back stage. Even though, modern medicine has increased life expectancy at birth and the average life, the numbers suffering from chronic and crippling diseases and the investment to manage the diseases are increasingly rising. This is resulting in serious inequities for the have-nots who can ill-afford to invest in their health security even under conditions where food security is not at stake. Though food security and health security are the two faces of the same coin and have synergistic relationships, overemphasis on food security at the cost of nutritional and health security has resulted in the predicament of poor health of the masses. A major transaction cost of overemphasis is the heavy drain on the exchequer for the maintenance of public health care system. A major segment of the poor, and who suffer from poor health security, depends excessively on the public health care system. The education of the poor and those with poor health regarding the economics of health care under different systems of medicine will pave the way for reducing the financial drain on the exchequer. The investment thus saved can be channelled to have a population with health security.

3. Effective Demand for Medicinal Plants and Medicines

The effective demand for medicinal plants and medicines is caught in the rigmarole of sourcing, valuation, pricing, trade, consumer or patient response, which are directly related to the level and degree of information regarding the medicinal plants, their products and their uses. The institutional and economic dimensions involved (Table 23.1) in the use of herbal medicines mould the effective demand for herbal medicines. The efficacy of herbal medicines depends on the desired level of "patience" of the patient. This factor weighs heavily in favour of modern medicine, since the foremost instinct of any patient or sufferer is that he or she gets "instant" relief. This is reinforced by the nature of occupation which demands how fast the patient needs to be relieved from the illness so that he or she is fit for work. The experience as a patient treated under different systems of medicine influences the degree of acceptance and shift towards herbal medicine.

TABLE 23.1: **Dimensions and Factors shaping the Effective Demand for Herbal Medicines**

Factors	Dimensions				
	Social	Psycho-logical	Cultural	Economic	Institu-tional (Working Rules)
1. Patience, self-control and diet restrictions (*pathya*)	X	X	X		
2. Nature of occupation				X	
3. Income	X		X	X	X
4. Personal experience as a patient			X	X	X
5. Access to information	X			X	
6. Availability and accessibility to herbal medicine practitioners and medicine outlets		X		X	
7. Influence of mass media	X	X	X	X	
8. Stage of illness					X
9. Type of illness					X

Note: 'X' denotes that the respective dimensions shape the respective factors.

There are nine factors that influence the effective demand for medicines. Each of these factors is in turn shaped by the interaction of five dimensions. Take the case of the factor "nature of occupation". It is distinctly influenced by the "income" dimension. If the daily wage earners (low-income group) are considered, they need to get instant relief in order to get back to work immediately to earn their bread. Often the takers of herbal medicines are those who have experienced most other systems of medicine and as a last resort turned to the herbal medicines. Therefore, efficacy not only depends upon the type of illness but also the stage at which the patient turns to the herbal medicine. This is dictated by the access to information, availability and accessibility to herbal medicine practitioners, influence of mass media and so on.

Hence, converts to herbal medicine are more in relation to the captive population as a result of shift from the conventional to modern medicine.

Further, a critical mass of takers is an essential component for renaissance of the traditional medicine. It is a paradox that even though 80 per cent or more of the population is cared by traditional medical practitioners and birth attendants the demand for the modern medicine is increasing by leaps and bounds despite the prohibitive costs—of consultation, health care, health cure, health education and externalities.

4. Habit and Habitat of Medicinal Plants

It is estimated that the quantity available in the forest areas is about 40 per cent out of which 75 per cent are medicinal trees and the remaining 25 per cent other types (Table 23.2). Though it is estimated that the quantity of medicinal plants available in non-forest areas (in the vast stretches of 75 per cent of our rainfed lands plus wastelands, grazing lands, bunds, road-sides) is as high as 50 per cent, the quantity gathered is as low as 5 per cent. The principal reasons for this are : (i) absence of forward (from farmers) and backward (from medicinal plants industries) linkages; (ii) sparse distribution of medicinal plants rendering it difficult to economically gather bulk quantities from several spots / places; (iii) even though 75 per cent of the weeds found in rainfed lands have medicinal properties, they are not identified and recognised by farmers and pharmaceutical companies.

TABLE 23.2: **Estimates of Distribution and Availability of Medicinal Plant Species in Forest and Non-forest Areas in India (%)**

Availability	Distribution		
	Forest areas	Nonforest areas	Cultivated
1. Number of species	70 to 90	30 to 10	<10
2. Quantity available	40	50	10
3. Quantity gathered	30	5	10

It is estimated that[6] on an average, an acre of dry land under weeded condition yields 4 to 8 quintals of weeds. Under unweeded condition, an acre of dry land yields 20 to 24 quintals of weeds. This shows that the ratio of grain to weeds is around 1:2 in dry lands when weeded and 1:5 when not weeded. Considering the fact that 75 per cent of the weeds are medicinal plants, this amply demonstrates the huge potential for mere gathering (not cultivating) of the medicinal plants, with least effort in the non-forest CPRs and (iv) lack of adequate knowledge regarding medicinal plants in non-forest areas. Lack of knowledge base is largely due to erosion of the traditional medicinal knowledge base due to popularity of the modern medicines. Experiments have shown that medicinal plants grown in different habitats have different quantities of active ingredients. For instance, the active ingredient in Glodiosa plants is found to vary from 0.1 per cent to one per cent in different habitats. This variation will complicate the process of manufacturing herbal medicines and hence influence the efficacy rates and the quality control. Scientific cultivation of medicinal plants may help reduce this variation[7]. While such a variation is welcome from the diversity angle, a great deal of sophistication in the science of medicinal plants will become a prerequisite to harness the full potential of their diversity.

Empirical evidence from natural tropical dry deciduous forest[8] (Muddumalai, Tamil Nadu) suggests that the major causes of habitat destruction of medicinal plants are the elephant, fire and other calamities. In their study Sukumar *et al.* (1997), have monitored the population of 43 medicinal plant species over a period of five years (1988-93). Around 30 species (70 per cent) have recorded negative rates of annual population change. The population of medicinal flora, viz. *Bambusa arundinaceae, Kydia calicina* and *Helicteres isora* have been alarmingly reduced by more than 50 per cent thus vindicating the stance that the non-anthropocentric factors are the major reasons for the habitat destruction in the forest areas.

In a primary survey of the flora of Tumkur District, Karnataka (Table 23.3), there were 901 plant species of which 464 species (52 per cent) were having medicinal properties. Out of the 464 medicinal species, 229 (44 per cent) were herbs, 106 (23 per cent) were trees, 70 (15 per cent) were shrubs and 59 (12 per cent) were creepers[9].

TABLE 23.3: **Common, Frequent and Rare Medicinal Plants in Tumkur District, Karnataka**

Habit	Number	Frequency			Potential		
		Common	Frequent	Rare	Common	Frequent	Rare
Herbs	229	134	79	16	43	63	123
	(43.9)	(58.5)	(34.5)	(7.0)	(18.8)	(27.5)	(53.7)
Trees	106	43	40	23	39	26	41
	(22.8)	(40.6)	(37.7)	(21.7)	(36.8)	(24.5)	(38.7)
Shrubs	70	38	29	3	21	8	41
	(15.0)	(54.3)	(41.4)	(4.3)	(30)	(11.4)	(58.6)
Creepers	59	33	22	4	19	7	33
	(12.2)	(55.9)	(37.3)	(6.8)	(32.2)	(11.9)	(55.9)
Total	464	248	170	46	122	104	236
	(100)	(53.4)	(36.6)	(10)	(26.3)	(22.4)	(51.3)

Source: Adapted from Kushalappa, C.G., 1996.

Considering all the tree species, 106 (83 per cent of a total of 120) were found to have medicinal properties. Out of the 464 medicinal plant species, 46 (10 per cent) were found to be rare. From among the 46 rare medicinal plants, 23 (50 per cent) were found to be rare medicinal trees. Hence medicinal trees are more vulnerable to extinction and suitable strategies need to be evolved to preserve them.

5. Ecological or Economic Scarcity?

Considering the habit and habitat of medicinal plants species (Table 23.4), 36 per cent are trees, 21 per cent are shrubs, 28 per cent herbs and 15 per cent are others (climbers/lianas). Here, we have estimated the type of scarcity, viz. economic, ecological and /or both economic and ecological. Further, the substitutability of these medicinal plant species is also indicated.

The issue of scarcity of medicinal plants, ecological or economic or both, is a challenge and provides an excellent research opportunity for natural resource economists. Here, the ecological scarcity is often not reflected in or transmitted to economic scarcity. Hence the relevance of these two types of scarcity becomes all the more pertinent. The availability or renewable flow of medicinal plants (excluding endemic and endangered) can cater to the short-run domestic and export demands. In addition, considering the demand for the top three medicinal plants by quantity (in Kerala—*Sida sp., Tinaspora cordifolia* and *Phyllanthus emblica*) and in Karnataka (*Terminalia chebula, Terminalia belerica* and *Phyllanthus emblica*), Sida species can be gathered from rainfed lands, and the other four can be cultivated and supplied, the economic scarcity is modest. This scenario holds largely for major medicinal products which are required in bulk where the above five ingredients are common and are used in most Ayurvedic formulations. However, the economic scarcity of the remainder of 400 and odd species of medicinal plants which are used in Ayurveda needs to be estimated. Though, the process of estimating the economic scarcity is vexed, it is a fertile ground for researchers.

In South India, 19 per cent (68) of the 357 medicinal plant species[10] are endemic which is reflective of ecological scarcity. About 46 per cent (29) of the 68 endemic medicinal plants are trees. If we can further add another layer of scarcity considering the non-substitutability of the endemic medicinal plants, we estimate that 40 per cent (27) of the 68 endemic medicinal plants have no substitutes making them further vulnerable. Among the 68 medicinal plants, 32 per cent (22) are ecologically and economically vital and scarce. A comprehensive list of trees having a medicinal value along with their distribution in Karnataka and their potential to cure various diseases is provided in Table 23.5.

Ecological scarcity of medicinal plants is due to their endemic nature, while

TABLE 23.4: **Scarcity of Endemic Medicinal Plants in the Southern States**

Sl. No.	Botanical Name	Habit	Parts Used	Whether Substitutable	Medicinal Use	Type of Scarcity
1.	Achyranthes aspera (Uttarani)	Herb - weed	Whole plant	Not known	Skin diseases	Ecological & Economic
2.	Adhatoda beddomei	Shrub	Whole plant	YES	Cough, cold	Ecological
3.	Aerva wightii	Shrub	Whole plant	YES	Not known	Ecological & Economic
4.	Amorphophalus commutatus	Herb	Corm	YES	Piles	Ecological
5.	Ampelocissus araneosa	Climber (W)	Roots			Ecological
6.	Artocarpus hirsutus	Tree	Leaves	NO		Ecological & Economic
7.	Asparagus rottleri	Herb	Roots	YES		Ecological
8.	Calaphyllum apetalum	Tree	Resin and Seed	YES		Ecological
9.	Cinnamomum macrocarpum	Tree	Bark	NO	Carminative	Ecological
10.	Cinnamomum sulphuratum	Tree	Bark	NO	Carminative	Ecological
11.	Cleome burmanni	Herb	Whole plant	YES	Skin diseases	Ecological
12.	Coleus vettiveroides	Shrub	Stem	NO	Anti-stress	Ecological & Economic
13.	Curcuma pseudomontana	Herb	Rhizomes	YES		Ecological
14.	Cyclea fissicalyx	Climber (W)	Roots	YES		Ecological
15.	Dalbergia horrida	Climber	Bark	YES		Ecological
16.	Decalepis hamiltonii	Liana	Roots	NO	Skin diseases, blood purifier	Ecological & Economic
17.	Dendrobium ovatum	Herb	Whole plant	NO	Adultrant in drugs	Ecological
18.	Diospyros candolleana	Tree	Root, Bark	NO		Ecological & Economic
19.	Diospyros paniculata	Tree	Root, Bark	NO		Ecological & Economic
20.	Dipterocarpus indicus	Tree	Stem, Oleoresin	NO		Ecological & Economic
21.	Dysoxylum malabricum	Tree	Wood	NO	Reducing tension	Ecological & Economic
22.	Eulophia cullenii	Herb	Tubers	YES		Ecological & Economic

TABLE 23.4 *(Contd.)*

Sl.No.	Botanical Name	Habit	Parts Used	Whether Substitutable	Medicinal Use	Type of Scarcity
23.	Eulophia ramentacea	Herb	Tubers	NO		Ecological
24.	Garcinia gummigutta	Tree	Resin	YES	Food supplement, urine stones & gout	Ecological & Economic
25.	Garcinia indica	Tree	Seeds	NO	Food supplement, urine stones & gout	Ecological & Economic
26.	Garcinia rubro-echinata	Tree	Seeds	NO		Ecological
27.	Garcinia talbotii	Tree	Seeds	YES	Food supplement, urine stones	Ecological
28.	Garcinia travancorica	Tree	Seeds	YES	Food supplement, urine stones	Ecological
29.	Glycosmis macrocarpa	Shrub	Fruits	NO		Ecological
30.	Gymnema khandalense	Climber (W)	Leaves	YES		Ecological
31.	Gymnema montanum	Climber (W)	Leaves	YES		Ecological
32.	Heliotropium keralense	Herb	Roots	YES		Ecological
33.	Heracleum candolleanum	Herb	Whole plant	YES		Ecological
34.	Heracleum rigens	Herb	Seeds	NO	Carminative	Ecological & Economic
35.	Humboltia vahliana	Tree	Stem/Bark	YES		Ecological
36.	Hydnocarpus macrocarpa	Tree	Seeds	NO	Skin diseases	Ecological & Economic
37.	Hydnocarpus pentandra	Tree	Seeds	NO	Skin diseases	Ecological & Economic
38.	Janakia aralpatra	Shrub	Roots	NO		Ecological
39.	Kingiodendron pinnatum	Tree	Wood, resin	NO		Ecological
40.	Knema attenuata	Tree	Fruits	NO		Ecological
41.	Lamprachaenium microcephalum	Herb	Wood	NO		Ecological

TABLE 23.4 *(Contd.)*

Sl. No.	Botanical Name	Habit	Parts Used	Whether Substitutable	Medicinal Use	Type of Scarcity
42.	Luffa umbellata	Climber (H)	Seeds	YES		Ecological
43.	Madhuca diplostemon	Tree		YES		Ecological
44.	Madhuca insignis	Tree		YES		Ecological
45.	Myristica malabarica	Tree	Seeds	YES		Ecological
46.	Niligianthus ciliatus	Shrub	Leaves/Roots	NO	Nervous disorder	Ecological & Economic
47.	Ochreinauclea missionis	Tree	Bark	NO		Ecological
48.	Paphipedilum druryi	Herb	Fruits	NO		Ecological
49.	Piper barberi	Shrub		YES		Ecological
50.	Piper nigrum	Shrub	Fruits	YES		Ecological
51.	Plectranthus nilgherricus	Herb	Whole plant	NO		Ecological
52.	Pterocarpus santalinus	Tree	Wood	NO	Herbal cosmetics	Ecological & Economic
53.	Pterospermum xylocarpum	Tree	Wood	YES		Ecological
54.	Semecarpus travancorica	Tree	Fruits	YES		Ecological
55.	Shorea tumuggaia	Tree	Resin	YES		Ecological
56.	Smilax wightii	Herb	Roots	YES		Ecological
57.	Strychnos aenea	Climber (W)	Fruits	YES		Ecological
58.	Strychnos minor	Climber (W)	Leaves, Roots	YES		Ecological
59.	Swertia lawii (Chirayata)	Herb	Whole plant	NO	Hepatitis	Ecological & Economic
60.	Syzygium travancoricum	Tree	Bark	YES		Ecological
61.	Tragia bicolor	Climber (H)	Roots	YES		Ecological
62.	Trichopus zeylanicus	Herb		NO	Immuno-modulator, adaptogenic	Ecological & Economic
63.	Trichosanthes anaimalaienis	Liana	Roots	YES	Immuno-modulator, adaptogenic	Ecological & Economic

TABLE 23.4 (*Contd.*)

Sl. No.	Botanical Name	Habit	Parts Used	Whether Substitutable	Medicinal Use	Type of Scarcity
64.	Uvaria hookeri	Climber (W)	Whole plant	YES		Ecological
65.	Valerina lechenaultii	Herb	Roots	YES		Ecological
66.	Vateria indica	Tree	Resin	YES	Dysentery, bleeding disorders	Ecological & Economic
67.	Vateria macro carpa	Tree	Resin	YES	Dysentery, bleeding disorders	Ecological & Economic
68.	Vepris bilocularis	Tree	Wood	NO		Ecological

Note: The scarcity has been estimated based upon discussion with the industry, research organizations and experts in Ayurveda.

TABLE 23.5: **Use and Distribution of Medicinal Trees Distributed in Karnataka**

Sl. No.	Botanical Name	Common Name	Disease Cured	Distribution Frequency	
				Forest areas	Non-forest areas
1.	Acacia concinia*	SEEGE MARA-SOAPNUT	Skin disease	XXXX	XX
2.	Acacia leucophloea	BILIJALADAMARA	Heart pain	XXXXXX	
3.	Acacia nilotica*	KARIJALA	Stomach, toothache & Skin disorder	XXX	XXX
4.	Aegle marmelos	BILWAPATRE/BILWA	Gastric problems & Bodypain	XXXXXX	
5.	Albizia amara	SUJJALU	Dog bite	XXXXX	X
6.	Albizia odoratissima*	BILAWARA	Diarrhoea	XXXX	XX
7.	Anogeissus latifolia*	DINDIGA	Diarrhoea with blood	XXXXX	X
8.	Azadirachta indica	BEVU, NEEM	Ear ache, skin ailments, intestinal worms	XX	XXXX
9.	Bauhinia racemosa	BASAVANAPADA CAMEL'S FOOT	Diarrhoea	XXXXX	X
10.	Bombax ceiba	BURUGADA MARA, SILKCOTTON TREE	Boils	XXXXX	X
11.	Butea monosperma	MUTTUGA, FLAME OF THE FOREST	Diarrhoea	XXXX	XX
12.	Caesalpinia bonduc	GAJJIGA, FEVER NUT	Stomach ache	XXX	XXX
13.	Cassia fistula	KAKKE, INDIAN LABURNUM	Stomach ache, Laxative & Diarrhoea	XXXX	XX
14.	Citrus medica	HARALEKAI, CITRON	Headache	XXXXXX	
15.	Dalbergia latifolia	BEETE, ROSEWOOD	Chest cough	XXXXXX	

TABLE 23.5 *(Contd.)*

	Botanical Name	Common Name	Disease Cured	Distribution Frequency	
				Forest areas	Non-forest areas
16.	Dalbergia paniculata	PADASA	Stomach pain	XXXXXX	
17.	Diospyros montana	JAGALAGUNTI MARA	Joint pains	XXXX	XX
18.	Dodonaea angustifolia	BANDARIGE	Anteseptic	XXX	XXX
19.	Eucalyptus tereticornis*	NEELAGIRI, EUCALYPTUS	Fever	XXX	XXX
20.	Feronia limonia	BELADA MARA	Heat exhaustion	XXXXXX	
21.	Ficus religiosa*	ASHWATHA, PEEPUL	Fever	XXX	XXX
22.	Ficus viren*	BASARIMARA	Mouth Ulcer	XXX	XXX
23.	Flacourtia indica*	SALIRAMARA		XXXXX	X
24.	Glochidionvelutinum	ULIPMARA	Diarrhoea	XXXXXX	
25.	Helicteres isora	YEDAMURI	Leg deformities & intestinal worms	XXXXX	X
26.	Holarrhena pubescens	ALEMARA	Intestinal worms	XXXX	XX
27.	Holoptelea integrifolia	TAVADASAMARA	Body aches and pains	XXX	XXX
28.	Jatropha tanjorensis	BETTADA HARALU, CANDLE STICK	Antiseptic, toothache & Diarrhoea	XXX	XXX
29.	Justica adhadota	ADUSOGE	Diabetes, earache	XXX	XXX
30.	Lantana camara	CHADURNAGA, LANTANA	Wounds	XXX	XXX
31.	Madhuca logifolia	HIPPE, MAHUA	Skin disease	XXX	XXX
32.	Maytenus emarginata	TONASE	Vomiting & dizziness	XXXXX	X
33.	Mitragyna parviflora	KADAGADAMARA	Diarrhoea	XXXX	XX
34.	Phyllanthus emblica	BETTADA NELLI, GOOSEBERRY	Dizziness	XXX	XXX

TABLE 23.5 *(Contd.)*

Sl. No.	Botanical Name	Common Name	Disease Cured	Distribution Frequency	
				Forest areas	Non-forest areas
35.	Phyllanthus reticulatus*	KARIHULIMARA	Spider bites	XXX	XXX
36.	Pithecellobium dulce*	SEEME HUNISE, MADRAS THORN	Dizziness & Vomiting	XXX	XXX
37.	Premna tomentosa*	EJEMARA	Fever	XXXXX	X
38.	Scheichera oleosa	SAGADEMARA	Skin problem	XXXXX	X
39.	Shorea roxburghii	JALADAMARA, TALOORA LAC TREE	Cold	XXXXX	X
40.	Strebulus asper	MITTALA	Diarrhoea	XXXX	XX
41.	Syzygium cumini*	JAMBU NERALE, BLACK PLUM	Diabetics & Diarrhoea	XXX	XXX
42.	Tamilnadia ulingosa	INDASEMARA	Pregnancy after care	XXXXX	X
43.	Terminalia bellirica	TARE MARA	Immobility in children	XXXXX	X
44.	Terminalia chebula	ALALEKAI MARA	Toothache & Headache	XXXXX	X
45.	Ziziphus mauritiana*	BARE/ELACHI MARA, INDIAN JUJUBE, BER	Chest Pain	XXX	XXX
46.	Ziziphus rugosa	CHOTTE MARA	Diarrhoea	XXXX	XX

Note: "X" indicates the relative distribution in the forest and non-forest areas. This table is adapted from Clare V Bostock Wood, *Trees in society in rural Karnataka*, India. Overseas Development Administration and Natural Resources Institute, UK, November 1992.

economic scarcity is due to (i) non-availability of substitutes, (ii) the type of diseases/disorders cured, and (iii) the commercial importance. It is to be noted that 41 per cent of the ecologically and economically scarce medicinal plants are trees (12). These species require a great deal of attention since their present population is deceptive and their distribution is sparse. Because their natural propagation is difficult and (perhaps) ecologically linked with species of fauna, their regeneration capacity is time-consuming and is associated with uncertainty. This analogy can be extended to those medicinal plants which are substitutes since their potential medicinal uses are often not fully explored. Also, because of their very nature as substitutes, thus receive inadequate attention. This calls for distinct and differential strategies for the conservation of ecologically and economically vital medicinal plants.

6. Trade-related Issues and Market Imperfections in Medicinal Plant Trade

The domestic market for Ayurvedic products in India is estimated at Rs. 8,000 million per year (1977). The global market for herbal medicines is Rs. 315,000 million and is expected to reach Rs. 1,400,000 million by 2010, at a compound growth rate of 12.15 per cent (*The Economic Times*, 29th Oct.1997). The potential in the European market is Rs. 94,500 million[11]. Considering the quantity and value of medicinal plants exported, China tops with an average annual export of 1,21,900 tonnes worth $ 264.5 million and India stands second with an export of 32,600 tonnes ($ 45.9 million). Hongkong imports the highest quantity of 77,250 tonnes of medicinal plants ($ 133.7 million). Japan imports 43,500 tonnes of medicinal plants ($ 114.5 million). Germany imports 42,800 tonnes ($ 96.25 million). USA imports 35,000 tonnes of medicinal plants ($ 95.2 million) (DGCIS, Calcutta,1997). The largest imports by Hongkong may be for exports as medicinal plant products.

The *Plantago* species (Isabgol) tops the exports from India (Table 23.6) among the medicinal plants (70 per cent, Rs. 1,040 million), followed by Ginseng roots (*Withania somnifera*—Ashwagandha, Rs. 142 million), Ayurvedic and Unani herbs (Rs. 103 million), *Vinca rosea* (Rs. 4.8 million) and others, totalling Rs. 1,470 million during 1994-95. The highest compound growth rate of exports (between the period 1987 and 1994) is in the case of Sarsaparilla roots (*Hemidesmus indicus*) which registered 87 per cent per annum, followed by *Psyllium* (Isabgol) which registered 68 per cent.

Other promising medicinal plants for exports are *Zedovary* roots (33 per cent), ginseng roots (27 per cent) and *Piper cubeba* (25 per cent). One of the reasons for large exports of Isabgol abroad is due to the problem of constipation. This can be attributed to the consumption of low-fibre food which is complicated by the sedentary work habits and consumption of junk food.

TABLE 23.6: **Exports of Medicinal Plants from India**

Plant	1987 Price Per Kg	Apr 87-Mar 88			Apr 94-Mar 95			Computer GR of value
		Quantity (Kg)	Value (Rs.)	Propor-tion	Quantity (Kg)	Value (Rs.)	Per cent of Total Value	
PLANTAGO SP (PSYLLIUM-ISABGOL)	36.48	8903634	324806327	75.94		1.0E+09	70.75	18.08
OTHER GINSENG ROOTS	21.96	1222638	26852448	6.28		1.4E+08	9.71	26.94
AYURVEDA & UNANI HERBS	11.61	1932807	22437360	5.25		1.0E+08	7.04	24.41
PSYLLIUM SEED	1.00	2265159	2265159	0.53		8.7E+07	5.92	68.40
CASSIA SENNA (LEAVES AND PODS)	6.63	5270409	34947468	8.17		8.3E+07	5.68	13.24
VINCA ROSEA (HERB)	23.37	407064	9514280	2.22		4793800	0.33	9.33
OPIUM POPPY FLOWERS	30.39	134047	4074051	0.95		3182400	0.22	3.47
TUKMARIA	9.29	69088	641998	0.15		1848400	0.13	16.31
HEMIDESMUS INDICUS (SARSAPARILLA) ROOTS	7.74	2596	20092	0.00		1597100	0.11	86.84
PIPER CUBEBA (CUBEBS ?)	19.30	5340	103038	0.02		488200	0.03	24.89
ZEDOVARY RTS	7.71	8000	61647	0.01		463500	0.03	33.40
NUX VOMICA				0.00		375700	0.03	
SWERTIA CHIRAYATA	28.62	58502	1674464	0.39		278900	0.02	22.59
LIQUORICE RTS				0.00		182500	0.01	
RAUWOLFIA SERPENTINA (ROOTS)				0.00			0.00	
OPIUM POPPY (HUSK)	10.42	11500	119776	0.03			0.00	
KUTH ROOT	46.19	490	22632	0.01			0.00	

TABLE 23.6 (*Contd.*)

Plant	1987 Price Per Kg	Apr 87-Mar 88			Apr 94-Mar 95			Computer GR of value
		Quantity (Kg)	Value (Rs.)	Propor-tion	Quantity (Kg)	Value (Rs.)	Per cent of Total Value	
KAEMPHARIA GALANGA	6.41	2000	12820	0.00			0.00	
RHIZOMES/ROOTS								
BELADONA LEAVe	44.13	3700	163264	0.04			0.00	
UNAB				0.00			0.00	
GINSENG ROOT	15.79	300	4738	0.00			0.00	
TOTAL		20297274	427721562	100	0		1.5E+09	19.28

Source: Director General of Foreign Trade Statistics, Government of India (Various issues of the *Monthly Bulletin of Foreign Trade Statistics*).

Though India is the second biggest exporter of medicinal plants and is next to China, it also imports (Table 23.7) a host of medicinal plants. *Glycyrrhiza glabra* (Liquorice - Athimadhura/Jyeshta madhu) imports are Rs. 54 million (48 per cent of the value of total imports of Rs. 111 million) followed by Kuth roots (*Saussurea lappa*) Rs. 28 million (25 per cent), Ayurveda and Unani herbs Rs. 11.44 million (10 per cent) and others.

Regarding, imports of medicinal plants, the highest compound growth rate of imports is for Galang roots (71.5 per cent) followed by Poppy flowers (52 per cent) and Athimadhura (42 per cent). The Kuth roots cost Rs. 1997 per kg followed by Ginseng roots Rs. 1,672 per kg and Rs. 714 per kg for Liquorice.

There are about 87 medicinal plant species being sourced by the drug manufacturing industries, in quantities more than 10 tonnes each per annum. Other medicinal plants being sourced are less than 10 tonnes each per annum by the industry. There are around 220 firms involved in manufacturing Ayurvedic drugs in Karnataka, 700 in Andhra Pradesh, 800 in Pondicherry and 800 in Kerala. According to the Drug Licensing Authority of Ayurveda in Karnataka, on the basis of turnover, around 10 per cent of the firms are large scale (turnover of more than Rs. 80 lakhs per year), 20 per cent of the firms are with Rs. 30 to 40 lakhs, and 70 per cent of the firms are small with a turnover of Rs. 2 to 5 lakhs.

7. Domestic Prices of Medicinal Plants

The people of Kerala have a tradition of using medicinal plants (Kashtoushadhas-plant based medicines) in most of their medicines. The price data from Kerala can be taken as a reflection of the price data of medicinal plants in Southern India. In contrast, the mineral (Rasoushadha) and herbo-mineral preparations are popular in the north. Considering the 66 common medicinal plants used by the medicine manufacturers in Kerala (Table 23.8), *Sida* sp. (Bala) tops with an annual requirement/use of 2,750 tonnes (45 per cent of total quantity and 27 per cent of total value) by the medicinal plant firms at a unit price of Rs. 11 per kg. In Kerala, the *Sida* sp. is so popular that any plant-based medicine doctor is referred to as "*Kurunthoti Vaidyan*" (parallel to *Alalekai Vaidya* in Karnataka) implying that if any doctor has the knowledge of *Sida* sp., he/she can cure most of the ailments.

Other medicinal plant species required are *Tinospra cordifolia* (Amrithaballi) (requirement 275 tonnes), *Phyllanthus emblica* (Amalaki) (255 tonnes), *Vetivera zizanoides* (Khus grass) (175 tonnes), *Terminalia chebula* (Alalekai) (168 tonnes) and others. It is to be noted that among these top five medicinal plants, Phyllanthus and Terminalia are gathered from the forests. The other three can be relatively easily obtained from non-forestlands. Without loss of generality, it can be inferred that the top five medicinal plants in Kerala do not face threat of

TABLE 23.7: **Imports of Medicinal Plants**

Name of the Plant	1987 price per kg	April 1987-March 1988 Qty. (kg)	% to tot qty	% to Val. (Rs.)	1994 price per kg	April 94-March 95 Qty. (kg)	Proportion	Value (Rs.)	Proportion	Compound growth rate of value
GLYCYRRHIZA GLABRA (LIQUORICE)	5.21	899355	34.04	4681263	714.42	75290	10.37	53789000	48.36	41.73
KUTH ROOT	42.75	195261	7.39	8347634	1997.16	14070	1.94	28100000	25.27	18.93
AYUR & UNANI HERBS	10.05	633086	23.96	6363798	34264.97	334	0.05	11444500	10.29	8.75
PYRETHRUM	21.65	84000	3.18	1818969	63.53	120000	16.54	7623600	6.85	22.72
GALANG ROOTS	13.54	6810	0.26	92175	11.79	341308	47.03	4025100	3.62	71.52
GINSENG ROOTS	24.33	70919	2.68	1725424	1672.92	2160	0.30	3613500	3.25	11.14
CHIRATA	7.42	163606	6.19	1213950	14.90	152180	20.97	2268000	2.04	9.34
POPPY FLOWERS	4.17	3400	0.13	14189	13.62	19820	2.73	270000	0.24	52.33
PSYLLIUM HUSK			0.00		149.09	550	0.08	82000	0.07	
SENNA LVS&PDS			0.00				0.00		0.00	
OTHER GNSNG RTS	31.56	401702	15.20	12676451			0.00		0.00	

TABLE 23.7 (*Contd.*)

Name of the Plant	1987 price per kg	April 1987-March 1988 Qty. (kg)	% to		1994 price per kg	April 94-March 95				
			tot qty	Val. (Rs.)		Qty. (kg)	Propor-tion	Value (Rs.)	Pro-portion	Compound growth rate of value
NUX VOMICA	1.91	163118	6.17	310948			0.00		0.00	
UNAB	7.73	20741	0.79	160424			0.00		0.00	
SARSAPARILLA			0.00				0.00		0.00	
TOTAL		2641998		37405225		725712		1.11e+08		

Source: Director General of Foreign Trade Statistics, Government of India (Various issues of the *Monthly Bulletin of Foreign Trade Statistics*).

TABLE 23.8: **Quantity, Price and Value of Medicinal Plants Used in Kerala in 1993 (Rupees per kg)**

Sl. No.	Part of the Plant	Scientific name of Medicinal plant	Common Name in Malayalam	Required /Yr. in Kgs	Per cent to total quantity	Value of Med. plants in 1993 000 Rs	Per cent to total value	Nominal price in 1990 Rs/Kg	Nominal price in 1993 Rs/Kg	C.G.R. in price
1	2	3	4	5	6	7	8	9	10	11
1.	ROOTS	SIDA SPECIES	KURUMNTHOTI	2750000	44.79	30250	27.53	6.5	11	14.06
2.		TINOSPORA CORDIFOLIA	CHITTAMRITH	275000	4.48	688	0.63	1	2.5	25.74
3.	HUSK	PHYLLANTHUS EMBLICA	NELLIKKA	255000	4.15	1658	1.51	5	6.5	6.78
4.		VETIVERIA ZIZANOIDES	RAMACHAM (LAVANCHA)	175000	2.85	10500	9.56	7	60	71.11
5.	HUSK	TERMINALIA CHEBULA	KADUKA DRY (ALALEKAI)	167500	2.73	1675	1.52	7.5	10	7.46
6.	TUBERS	KAEMPHERIA GALANGA	KACHOLAM	145000	2.36	23925	21.77	24	165	61.93
7.	ROOTS		MOOVILA	125000	2.04	1625	1.48	6.5	13	18.92
8.	TUBERS	ASPARAGUS RACEMOSUS	SHATHAVARI	125000	2.04	625	0.57	3	5	13.62
9.	ROOT	DESMODIUM GANGETICUM	ORILA	95000	1.55	1235	1.12	7	13	16.74
10.	PSUDOSTEM		KATTUVAZHATHANDU	95000	1.55	143	0.13	1.5	1.5	0.00
11.		CURCUMA AROMATICUM	KASTURIMANJAL	87500	1.43	2363	2.15	6.5	27	42.76
12.	ROOTS	BOERHAVIA DIFFUSA	THAZHUTHAMA	77500	1.26	581	0.53	5	7.5	10.67

TABLE 23.8 (Contd.)

1	2	3	4	5	6	7	8	9	10	11
13.	ROOT	ADHATHCDA VESICA	ADALODAKOM	77500	1.26	504	0.46	3	6.5	21.32
14.	ROOTS	RICINUS	VELLUTTHAVANAKKU	77500	1.26	504	0.46	3	6.5	21.32
15.	ROOTS	SROBILANTHUS	KARINKURINJI	77500	1.26	465	0.42	4	6	10.67
16.	HUSK		THANIKKA	77500	1.26	310	0.28	3	4	7.46
17.		CYPERUS ROTUNDUS	MUTHANGA	77500	1.26	271	0.25	3	3.5	3.93
18.	WHOLE		KADUKA	65000	1.06	455	0.41	4	7	15.02
19.	GRADE I		KUNDARIKAM (SAMBRANI)	62500	1.02	3386	3.08	24	54.17	22.57
20.	TUBERS	PLUMBAGO INDICA	KODUVELI	57500	0.94	633	0.58	24	11	-17.72
21.	WHOLE DRY	TRICHOSANTHES	PADAVALAM	55000	0.90	1650	1.50	16	30	17.02
22.	FRESH	PHYLLANTHUS EMBLICA	NELLIKKA	48500	0.79	315	0.29	3.5	6.5	16.74
23.	ROOTS	PIPER LONGUM WLD	KAATUTHIPPALI	47500	0.77	570	0.52	5	12	24.47
24.	ROOTS		KUMIZH	46000	0.75	184	0.17	2	4	18.92
25.			KOLLARAKKU	45000	0.73	3825	3.48	35	85	24.84
26.	SEEDS		NEERVALA	45000	0.73	1125	1.02	18	25	8.56
27.		ACORUS CALAMUS	VAYAMBU	45000	0.73	563	0.51	9	12.5	8.56
28.			MARAMANJAL	45000	0.73	405	0.37	6.5	9	8.48
29.			MARAMANJAL	45000	0.73	405	0.37	6.5	9	8.48
30.	TUBER		PALTHUKAM	45000	0.73	158	0.14	2.5	3.5	8.78
31.		ANDROGRAPHIS	KEERIYATH	36500	0.59	4380	3.99	70	120	14.42
32.			KATTUPAYAR DRY	36000	0.59	540	0.49	9	15	13.62
33.			PACHOTTITHOLI	36000	0.59	468	0.43	6.5	13	18.92
34.	WHOLE	SROBILANTHUS	KARINKURINJI	36000	0.59	144	0.13	3	4	7.46

TABLE 23.8 (*Contd.*)

1	2	3	4	5	6	7	8	9	10	11
35.		PIPER BRACHYSTACHYUM	KAATUKURUMULAKU	32500	0.53	1365	1.24	23	42	16.25
36.		HEMIDESMUS INDICAINDICUS	NARUNEENDI	26500	0.43	1193	1.09	35	45	6.48
37.	WHOLE	INDIGOFERA TINCTORIA	NEELAMARI	26500	0.43	663	0.60	12	25	20.14
38.	SEEDS		MULLILA	26500	0.43	371	0.34	7	14	18.92
39.	TUBER	HOLOSTEMMA KODIEN	ADAPATHIYAN	26000	0.42	1820	1.66	240	70	-26.51
40.	ROOTS		KATTUMULAGU	26000	0.42	143	0.13	4	5.5	8.29
41.			NAIKORUNNUPARIPPU	25500	0.42	459	0.42	12	18	10.67
42.	ROOTS	SIDA SPP	VANKURUNTHOTI	25000	0.41	175	0.16	5.5	7	6.21
43.			ATTITHIPPALI	24500	0.40	294	0.27	8	12	10.67
44.	ROOTS		CHERUTHEKU	24500	0.40	172	0.16	5	7	8.78
45.	TUBER		PADAKIZHANGU	24000	0.39	840	0.76	14	35	25.74
46.			KATTUPUNNAKAI	24000	0.39	216	0.20	3.5	9	26.63
47.	FRESH		CHANGALAM-PARANDAM	22500	0.37	45	0.04	2	2	0.00
48.		RAUWOLFIA SERPENTINA	AMARPORI-RED	22000	0.36	1430	1.30	50	65	6.78
49.	FRUIT		KAKKUMKAI	18500	0.30	130	0.12	4	7	15.02
50.	OIL	MADHUCA LATIFOLIA	MAHUA OIL	18000	0.29	990	0.90	45	55	5.14
51.	ROOTS	SOLANUM ANGUIVI	PUTHARICHUNDA	18000	0.29	225	0.20	6.5	12.5	17.76

TABLE 23.8 (*Contd.*)

1	2	3	4	5	6	7	8	9	10	11
52.			CHITTELAM	12750	0.21	1148	1.04	45	90	18.92
53.	TUBER DRY	ALPINIA GALANGA	CHITTARATH	12500	0.20	375	0.34	20	30	10.67
54.	SEEDS		KUZHANJI	12500	0.20	281	0.26	19	22.5	4.32
55.			THETTAPARAL	12500	0.20	138	0.13	8	11	8.29
56.	FRESH	PHYLLANTHUS NIRURI	KEEZHARNELLI	12500	0.20	125	0.11	8	10	5.74
57.			GARUDAKKODI DRY	12500	0.20	125	0.11	6	10	13.62
58.	GRASS		DHARBAPUL	12500	0.20	113	0.10	5	9	15.83
59.			PUNNAPOOVU	12500	0.20	100	0.09	4	8	18.92
60.			PINNARI DRY	12500	0.20	100	0.09	4	8	18.92
61.	FRUIT DRY	PHYLLANTHUS EMBLICA	NELLIKKA	12500	0.20	75	0.07	4	6	10.67
62.	ROOTS	HIBISCUS	CHEMBARATHI	12500	0.20	50	0.05	3	4	7.46
63.	WHOLE		THANIKKA WHOLE	12500	0.20	38	0.03	3	3	0.00
64.			IDAMPIRI	12000	0.20	84	0.08	7	7	0.00
65.	ROOTS	OCIMUM AMERICANUM	KAATUTHUASI	9000	0.15	63	0.06	6	7	3.93
66.		RAUWOLFIA SP	AMARPORI-WHITE	1000	0.02	12	0.01	7.5	12	12.47
			TOTAL	6139250		109879				

Source: Ayurvedic Drug Manufacturers' Association of Kerala, Thrissur, 1996.

extinction. And even if there is, while *Sida* sp. and *Vetivera* sp. are available as weeds on rainfed lands, *Phyllanthus emblica* (Amalaki), *Terminalia chebula* and *Tinospora cordifolia* can be cultivated and supplied, as long as there is an effective market.

Our inquiries with a leading local dealer of medicinal plants in Bangalore[12] revealed that the Triphala (*Terminalia chebula, Terminalia belerica* and *Phyllanthus emblica*) are the three top medicinal plants in great demand in Karnataka. These fruits are usually gathered from trees in the forests of BR hills, Bandipur, and the surrounding areas.

8. Interplay of Property and Patent Regimes for the Conservation of Medicinal Plants

With the advent of the New Economic Policy (NEP) and the World Trade Organization (WTO) regime, the conservation and use of medicinal plants in India will increasingly be influenced by the interplay of the property regime and the patent regime and their enforceability. A heuristic scenario of the interplay indicates that in the open access resource regime, patent rights will help in declaring national sovereignty over the flora and fauna (Table 23.9). Australia, Peru, Costa Rica and a few other countries have declared national sovereignty over their germplasm (flora and fauna) by legislation. India is also contemplating in this direction.

Sustainable use and conservation of medicinal plants will depend on the interplay between the property regime/s and patent regime/s. The property regime may vary from open access to private property. Likewise we can have a three-case patent scenario (i.e. strong, feeble and lack of IPRs). Take the case of farmers —they cultivate medicinal plants (raw plant material) but they need protection from patent laws and hence are exempt from IPRs. Even the TRIPS clause in the WTA recognizes this and has a crucial provision "Farmers Exemption".

The proposed Bio-Diversity Bill of the Ministry of Environment and Forests, Government of India, has made provision for such a legislation. This will pave the way for sovereign rights of our nation on all naturally occurring flora and fauna against the likely patent threats from outside. This will provide an institutional shield for all the national flora and fauna until the new patent regime comes into force. In the State property regime, in the forest areas, the sustainable use of raw medicinal plant materials will be aided and complimented by a strong IPR (Intellectual Property Rights Regime) regime to prevent gene trafficking and bio-piracy. This also provides State control and generates revenue which can be further used for conservation. For final products, a strong IPR regime would be desirable only for life-saving drugs, for the purposes of equity[13]. In the common property regime, in the forest areas,

TABLE 23.9: **Interplay of Property and Patent Regimes desirable for Sustainable Use of Medicinal Plants**

Patent regime (PR)	Property Regime						
	Open access resource (O)	State property (S)		Common property (C)		Private property regime (P)	
		Raw medicinal plant material (RM)	Final medicinal plant product (Fp)	Forest areas (FA)	Non forest areas (NFA)	Farmers (Fs)	Drug manu-facture (DM)
1. With strong PR regime (with national sovereignty, royalty payment & enforcement)	1 O	1 S To prevent bio-piracy for equity	1 Fp only for vital drugs	1 SRM FA	NA	NA	1 DM Fp
2. With feeble IPR regime	NA	NA	NA	NA	2 CRM NFA	NA	NA
3. Without IPR	NA	NA	NA	NA	NA	3 RM Fs1	NA

strong IPR jells with the forests to be treated as State property. The medicinal plants in the non-forest can have a common property nature with a feeble patent regime with usufructury rights with the users, facilitated by co-management. Medicinal plants in the farmers' fields need no patent regime, whereas for the drug manufacturers a strong IPR regime will promote R&D and entrepreneurship.

9. Market Imperfections

Hypothesizing about market imperfection in medicinal plants and plant products rather than market perfection is a question the economist needs to address, since both the supply side and the demand side market imperfections are apparent in medicinal plants. *The bottomline for market perfection is marginal cost pricing*. If there is a wide gap between marginal cost and price and the gap is unaccountable by the market functions, then there is a *prima facie* case for market imperfection. Market imperfections are implicit in the trade of any natural resources and medicinal plants are no exception to this phenomenon due to (i) absence of well-defined property rights, (ii) complexity in arriving at a convincing patent regime, (iii) uniqueness, uncertainty and irreversibility and (iv) knowledge of medicinal plants is limited to certain population.

Another problem in bridging the supply and demand is the lack of *buy back arrangements* between the medicinal firms and the suppliers. On the one hand the medicinal plant dealers complain that they are not getting the cooperation of the State Forest Department in allotment of areas for harvesting medicinal plants, while on the other farmers say they are willing to cultivate to supply any quantity of the required medicinal plants as long as they are assured of the market.

9.a. "Niche Market"

Further, the shallow knowledge base of consumers regarding medicinal plants, the "niche" market for medicinal plants and products, the difference between the proprietary and classical preparations, oral tradition and "Goupya" (desirable secrecy's), shallow knowledge about the practitioners, availability and accessibility of medicinal plants and plant product outlets add to the complexity of imperfection. One of the litmus tests of imperfection in the Ayurvedic medicine, for instance, is the huge gap between the price of gathered medicinal plants and the Ayurvedic drug. This gap can be appreciated only if the procedures followed in preparing the drug are monitorable by an authority like "drug control inspectorate" so that the consumers are assured of quality.

9.b. Multi Ingredients—Multi Processes

It is to be noted that a large number of Ayurvedic drugs have multi-ingredients and involve multi-processes, both of which are difficult to monitor/supervise[14]. In Ayurveda, a drug inspector may be able to verify whether an ingredient is present in a formulation or not, but cannot quantify whether the ingredient has gone into the formulation in the required quantity. Further, when the efficacies of plant-based medicines are compared with the alternative systems of medicine like allopathy, there are some treatments in Ayurveda for which there is no substitute in other systems of medicine, for which there can be no relative economics. This is also a market imperfection, since the opportunity cost of treatment with traditional system of medicine is so huge that it is difficult to be valued[15].

9.c. Dietary Restrictions and Patience

Patience (waiting period) and self-control ("Pathya" or the "diet restrictions" for instance) are the prerequisites for the efficacy of plant- based medicines and medicinal products. These are also the major factors influencing market imperfections. The difference in the price of the gathered medicinal plant and that of the cultivated medicinal plant also adds to market imperfection.

9.d. Quality Control[16]

The demand for establishing new herbal/ayurvedic firms (in Karnataka) is governed by strict quality control, though there is a great difficulty in monitoring the verification of drug formulations. For instance, it is difficult to monitor 150 formulations of a firm, each formulation having 40 ingredients. In contrast, in allopathy, there is/are single/few ingredient/s and the checks are relatively far easier as standards are established. With all the complexities and inherent imperfections in the plant-based medicines, according to the Drug Licensing Authority of Ayurveda in Karnataka, the quality of Ayurvedic formulations has been largely maintained by the efforts as quality control by the Government.

9.e. Practice of Allopathy and Other Systems of Medicine by Ayurveda Doctors

On the basis of a discussion with the Ayurvedic practitioners and first-hand experience, it is disheartening to note that several Ayurveda Vaidyas are practising allopathy and other systems of medicine and are unable to convince their patients that some diseases can be more effectively cured by Ayurveda.

This not only tarnishes the reputation of Ayurveda, but also smashes the confidence of the public in Ayurveda.

9.f. Wide Variations in Practice of Ayurveda

A reconnaissance of a few patients of Ayurveda revealed that there is wide variation in (1) the way the Ayurvedic drugs are prescribed and (2) the consultancy charges. We found one class of Ayurvedic doctors who would prepare medicines themselves and therefore would not write a prescription. This made the patients to exclusively depend on the doctor and in the case of emergency or any contingency the possibility of self-medication was totally ruled out. The patients said that even though self-medication is dangerous, at times of emergency, since the number of Ayurvedic pharmacies is limited[17] and the number of alternative Ayurvedic doctors is also limited, it becomes extremely difficult for the patients to depend on such Ayurvedic doctors who provide their medicinal preparations and hesitate to give prescriptions. Obviously, this system breaks down and even the patients who are committed to Ayurveda shift to modern medicine. In addition, the patients feel that there is no transparency in the drug preparations. An urban patient who is literate is obviously interested to know the ingredients in each drug preparation. Some patients have apprehensions that doctors may add steroids or cannabis (Bhang) to provide instant relief which is harmful in the long run.

We found a second class of doctors who were relatively well settled in their profession, giving out prescriptions. In this system, patients did not have to depend on doctors in the case of a contingency and this system increased the transparency, since patients could buy the drugs from medical stores and find out the ingredients. Regarding consultancy charges, there were wide variations, depending upon whether the doctors themselves would provide the drugs or whether they would writeout only the prescriptions. In the first category, the range of fees charged was large. In the second category, the variation was small.

10. Overcoming Market Imperfections

Overcoming market imperfections is easier said than done. Nevertheless we have attempted to provide a few plausible measures which might solve a few of the imperfections :

10.a. Convincing and educating the public regarding the efficacy of Ayurvedic medicines and products[18]

Firms need to be educated regarding the availability of medicinal plants in vast stretches of drylands mostly considered as weeds. The firms can utilize the services of agricultural extension workers in educating farmers to gather medicinal plants from farms and other common lands for supplying to the firms. In addition, firms needing medicinal plants in bulk will benefit richly from buy-back arrangements with the growers to supply medicinal plants.

10.b. Institutional Involvement

In Kerala, the Department of Agriculture initiated in 1995 a scheme for cultivation of medicinal plants in every Gram Panchayat. In this scheme, the planting materials (seed or seed material) of various species are supplied to interested farmers in the Panchayat at a nominal fee. The technology of cultivation and harvest is provided to farmers. Arya Vaidya Sala of Kotakkal in Kerala has a garden of eight acres growing one thousand species of medicinal plants to partially meet their requirements of "kashtoushadhas". A few species of medicinal plants namely *Kaemphaeria galanga, Adathoda vasa, Indigofera tinctoria* (Neeli Bringadi) are being commercially cultivated by farmers and are sold to firms who extract medicines from them. Otherwise a large number of species are not cultivated, but are only gathered / collected by the tribals and supplied to the manufacturers through market channels which are totally opaque, difficult to extract information and hence add another dimension to the market imperfection.

10.c. Having appropriate but differential property and patent regimes for medicinal plants

Suitable property and patent regimes are the *sine qua non* for conservation and wise use of medicinal plant resources. These regimes are contextual and differ with the type of resource, width of applicability, degree of enforceability, transferability and exclusion (Table 23.11).

10.d. Valuation

Proper valuation of the contribution of medicinal plants and Ayurvedic medicines in curing chronic as well as common diseases will help to widen the demand for medicinal plants. This will also educate the public regarding the savings they can make by adopting plant-based medicines and medicinal products when compared with modern medicines.

10.e. Pricing

Pricing of medicinal plants should include not only the cost of gathering/

cultivation, but also the ecological cost of irreversibility, uncertainty and uniqueness, so that the resource gets duly valued. Often, most medicinal plants (the raw materials) are priced cheaply due to the ignorance and the social stigma associated with the medicinal plant gatherers.

10.f. Transparency in drug therapy

To serve the cause of Ayurveda, it is desirable for the Ayurvedic doctors to introduce transparency by providing prescriptions to the patients so that they can know the ingredients in the formulation. In cases, where the prescribed drugs are of poor quality, the doctor can arrange to prepare the drugs to administer. This also can be followed in case where fresh preparations have to be provided to patients. However, in places where Ayurvedic drug stores are non-existent or are inaccessible due to distance, the Ayurvedic doctor may prefer to provide medicines himself / herself again by honouring transparency.

10.g. Practice of Ayurveda by Ayurvedic doctors instead of doctors of other systems of medicine

It is unfortunate that many Ayurvedic doctors trained in the four-year degree programme are practising allopathy and other systems of medicine. Unless these doctors build confidence in the patients about Ayurveda, the system cannot survive and this will be a self-deceiving mechanism. Though the Ayurvedic doctors may have to struggle to survive in the beginning, they should be able to prove after a few years of struggle that they too can establish on their own.

10.h. Export promotion

It is to be realized that many of the Ayurvedic medicinal plants and trees can be cultivated, if there is a conscious effort in developing (1) propagation techniques and (2) buy-back arrangements. The Government of India has banned the export of some 50 or more medicinal plants like Jatamansi (*Nardostachys jatamansi*), Guggula (*Commiphora mukul*), Katuki (*Picrorrhiza kurrha*), and the drugs like Livomin, Liv 52, Mentat, Rymanyl, Rhumayog, Becamine, Traquinyl and Obenyl (to reduce obesity) (among propriety drugs). Mahayogiraja guggula, Kanchanara guggula (used to cure thyroid, ovarian and breast tumour), Kaishora guggulu, Dasha moolarishta, Arjunarishta and others. Unfortunately most of the medicinal plants used in many of these preparations which have been banned can be cultivated and the country can reap precious foreign exchange. Obviously this promotes smuggling of Ayurvedic preparations out of the country since the exports have been banned without carefully examining whether there is any real scarcity of medicinal plants[19].

11. Transaction Costs

The transaction costs (read cost of information, contract and enforcement) in the economy of medicinal plants and plant products arise because of inherent market imperfections and due to the very nature of medicinal plant resource and the science and art of Ayurveda (Table 23.10). It is a pity that "Ayurveda", the art and science of health which was developed in India, now has to fight for its own survival. People who are skeptical about Ayurvedic medicines have perhaps forgotten how this system has contributed to the health of the masses since time immemorial. While the modern system of medicine has the advantage of providing a fast cure or instant relief which is apt for the people who have eke out their living everyday, patients need to realize that, in addition to instant relief, sustainability of that relief is harmful in the long run. Hence a pluralistic approach to health is crucial.

12. Policy Issues

Even after 50 years of India's Independence, conservation of medicinal plants in common property lands continues to escape the attention of policy makers and planners. Even where programmes are devised for the conservation of CPRs, nowhere there is recognition of the vast and invaluable treasure house of medicinal plants and their knowledge. This is the bane of the country's culture which can be described by the adage in Kannada—Hittalagida Maddalla (the plant in the backyard is not medicinal). Conservation and sustainable use of medicinal plants are inextricably linked to the survival of our commons. Towards this end, policies that shape the conservation and wise use of medicinal flora in forest CPRs and those in non-forest CPRs have to be carved differently considering the ecologically fragile nature of forest CPRs. Further, policies need to consider ecologically and economically scarce medicinal plants within the forest and non-forest CPRs. In addition, a desirable policy matrix has to capture the interplay of property and patent regimes (Table 23.11).

The policy approaches to achieve conservation and sustainable use of medicinal plants can be institutional, economic and technological (R&D).

Education of the farming community, general public and gatherers regarding medicinal plants is vital for two counts: first, to check the erosion of existing indigenous knowledge regarding medicinal plants by other systems of medicine; second, to educate the new generation regarding the uses of medicinal plants for several illnesses and diseases. The declining trend is that villagers and tribals who have ample opportunities to practise the use of

TABLE 23.10: **Comparative Analysis of Transaction Costs in Traditional and Modern Medicine**

Transaction costs	Systems of medicine	
	Traditional (Ayurveda)	Modern (Allopathy)
1. Relief	Long waiting time leads to high transaction costs	Low transaction costs due to instant relief.
2. Side effects	Not apparent	Increasingly becoming apparent which is also promoting the cause of traditional medicines.
3. Availability of practitioners and retail outlets	High transaction costs since relatively few practitioners and retail medical stores are available	Low transaction costs since access to services or practitioners and medical stores is easier.
4. Restrictions as institutions	High transaction costs due to restrictions on diet and mind in terms of several do's and don'ts while administering medicine. Incidentally these common do's and don'ts are so popular that a common man feels constrained to live without them (example, fried foods, coffee, tea, ice-cream, etc.). In addition, it is difficult for the patient to appreciate the requirements of the Ayurvedic system, unless the patient has 'patience' culture.	Low transaction costs due to modest restrictions on diet and mind. The system permits the patient to be relatively flexible with respect to food and other habits, which is a key factor for the popularity.
5. Ease of drug administration	High transaction cost since the process is relatively inflexible. More than the drug *per se*, the knowledge of method of use is crucial in Ayurveda. For instance, formulations are commonly required to be taken with hot milk/honey/cow's ghee and so on at a certain time.	Low transaction cost as the process is relatively easy and flexible. For instance capsules/pills can be conveniently carried and used to cure an illness.

TABLE 23.11: **Policy Matrix for Sustainable Use and Conservation of Medicinal Flora**

Habitat	Policy Approach		
	Technological	Economic	Institutional
Medicinal plants in forest CPRs	Devising sustainable methods of harvesting/gathering. Developing the processes for vertical integration	Lessen market imperfections in gathering. A corpus fund has to be established by the industry to promote research	Regulation of gathering, promotion of gatherers' cooperatives; ICAR-SAU network to establish *in situ* sites, and encouraging NGOs in documenting.
Medicinal plants in non-forest CPRs	Devising sustainable methods of harvesting/gathering. Developing the processes for vertical integration	Promote buy-back arrangements between medicinal plant processors and gatherers/sellers	Regulate buy-back arrangements, monitor NGOs, education of rural folk in recognition of medi-cinal plants for various uses by KVKs, schools, and educational institutions.
Medicinal plants in cultivation	Launch breeding programmes and evolve package of practices with support from Government and industry for research	Promote buy-back arrangements between medicine processors and gatherers/sellers and provide other incentives.	Promote Growers cooperatives & credit flow.

medicinal plants are giving them up and are preferring the use of modern medicine. Education will add to the "existence value" of medicinal plants by imparting reverence/sacredness to the medicinal plants and to that extent conservation of medicinal plants will be promoted. By conservation and sustainable use of forest CPRs, not only the *in situ* medicinal plant populations, genes and their chemical properties are preserved, but also the cost incurred otherwise in *ex situ* cultivation efforts is contained. The ICAR-SAU system may establish gene banks for preserving germplasm of medicinal plants.

Breeding efforts in medicinal plants parallel to those in cultivated food crops will emphasize health security in relation to food security. A careful observation reveals that after achieving food security, cost of health care is skyrocketing. Hence development of medicinal plant medicines and effective home remedies will hopefully provide vast savings to the public and save them from heavy expenditure involved in modern systems of medicine[20]. With the growing demand for herbal and Ayurvedic medicines, it is imperative that the supply side economics plays a crucial role in providing signals for entrepreneurs involved in the herbal medicinal industry. The supplies of medicinal plants can be augmented if market forces transcend signals to farmers/growers encouraging them to cultivate/gather from their own dry lands/common property lands/wild lands. As the supplies of medicinal plants are difficult to be promoted, the survival value of medicinal plants is directly related to the survival value of our forests and non-forest common property resources. Thus the CPRs need to be protected by checking the rate of degradation due to several causes.

13. Conclusion and Implications

A host of dimensions *inter alia* social, psychological, cultural, economic, institutional shape the effective demand for herbal medicines and their products. The information or knowledge base regarding medicinal plants is a vital factor and a key for market perfections, the benefits of which can reach all those involved in traditional health care. In the context of the new economic policy and the regime of WTO, conservation and sustainable use of medicinal flora will be directed and enforced by the interplay of property and patent regimes. While market imperfections are inherent in both traditional and modern health systems, it may be easier to value them in modern health systems since the procedures and practices are relatively standardized and the number and type of medical facilities offered are regulated. Supply and demand factors which influence modern medicine can be assessed, due to relatively large numbers of consumers, registered doctors, pharmaceuticals and industries.

Research in the economics of traditional medicine are plagued by opacity which is responsible for modest research efforts by economists. Two reasons stand out for this: first, the recognition of market imperfections and transaction costs are deceptive; second, their measurement is an onerous task. The trade-related aspects of herbal medicines and products are shrouded in secrecy. Therefore, an analysis of the magnitude and dimension of trade and trade-related benefits and costs is difficult, unless great efforts are made to unearth them. Policy prescriptions concerning the conservation and sustainable use of medicinal plants should be location and context specific. The approach must consider the synergistic relations among the economic, institutional and technological factors which determine the conservation and propagation strategies of medicinal plants in forest CPRs, non-forest CPRs and in cultivated lands. *The policy domain and the valuation of the contribution of medicinal plants should be pluralistic, i.e. the approach should appreciate that different systems of medicine for different types and degrees of illnesses are complementary and not competitive.* For instance, sports and aviation medicines ought to provide instant relief, when compared with common and chronic illnesses. It is to be noted that 90 per cent of the illnesses faced by human beings are chronic and crippling and only 10 per cent of the diseases require immediate attention. In this regard plant-based medicines and Ayurveda offer an immense scope in reducing the costs of health security.

The rainfed lands of India forming 70 per cent of the total cultivated area and the non-forest CPRs are the rich repositories of common medicinal plants and the repertoire of indigenous knowledge base of traditional medicines with 70 per cent of the population. These offer tremendous opportunities for the renaissance of the accessible - affordable - apt system of medicine. Westerners are increasingly inclining to herbal medicines and India can richly benefit from these opportunities from the export of both plant medicines and services of plant-based medicine doctors. It is worthwhile to note that 41 out of 63 medical colleges in the USA have recognized the need for traditional systems of medicine in their curricula. The threat to medicinal plants in forest CPRs is grave and is induced by deforestation and habitat destruction. It is estimated that between half a million and two million plant species accounting for 15 to 20 per cent of the total natural flora could be extinguished by 2000 AD. The process of planning, therefore, should bestow due attention on the conservation and wise use of medicinal plants in our CPRs. In addition to the ecological threat which physically endangers the medicinal flora, the policy should not ignore the threat to the rich repertoire of intellectual property with regard to the medicinal plants in India.

The historical importance of medicinal plants in India needs to be emphasized in the contemporary context since the cost of health security with modern medicines is spiralling. The rich and diverse indigenous knowledge systems of medicinal plants provide a ray of hope to those who feel the pinch of the prohibitive cost of modern medicine. In this regard, it is pertinent to examine the cost of health security in different systems of medicine and then make a sincere attempt to evaluate the medicinal plants considering their rich and potential contribution to the health security in India. The economics of traditional health care system offers excellent opportunities as also challenges for the evaluation of the contribution of medicinal plants and products to health. Research efforts in this direction are modest, since the signals from the market for research are oriented towards economics of modern medicine through sponsorship from pharmaceuticals and a wide host of interested partners[21]. Market forces alone cannot be relied upon for offering a desirable orientation in the economics of traditional health. It is in order to recall the seminal contribution of Kautilya (*c.* 310 BC) through his *Artha Shastra* which is the first text in "Institutional Economics" in the world. It is to be appreciated that Kautilya wrote and imposed his codes of conduct regarding conservation and wise use of natural resources at a time when there was absolutely no ecological or economic scarcity of natural resources. In these days of ecological and economic scarcity induced by population explosion and inequity, such institutional economic approaches are all the more relevant. Neo-classical economic approaches will address only the tip of the iceberg of the economics of traditional healthcare which is dominated by the medicinal plants, mineral and herbo-mineral preparations. Pluralism of approaches leading to a blend of institutional economics (also called as transaction cost economics) and natural resource economic approaches with the help of concepts like survival value, safe minimum standard of conservation, scarcity rents, existence value, intrinsic value, externalities and transaction costs provide a framework for understanding and unravelling the intricate issues in the economics of medicinal plants and health security[22].

NOTES

1. For a succinct treatment of the knowledge of medicinal plants, please refer to P.M. Unnikrishnan, An insight into Ayurveda's knowledge of medicinal plants, *Amruth*, Aug 1997, pp. 1-26. Appendix I provides a historical list of classical texts in Ayurveda.
2. Rock Edict II of Emperor Ashoka, Girnar.
3. It is in order to acknowledge the efforts of Sri A.N. Yellappa Reddy, IFS (Retd), who pioneered this novel scheme through Dhanwanthari Vana in Bangalore, Pavitra Vanas in Ramanagaram, Bakkala and other centres in Karnataka.
4. Based on discussion with experts in Ayurveda, we understand, for instance, that the contents of leading brands of popular Ayurvedic food supplements with a massive market share and advertisement do not reflect the ingredients that they ought to contain .
5. Following hypotheses provide a stepping guide to further studies on the economics of medicinal plants:

a. The real price of forest-based medicinal tree parts is increasingly reflecting their economic scarcity.
b. With the degradation of natural forests, the bases of medicinal trees are eroded, resulting in difficulty in the availability of certain medicinal trees, long delays in their availability, longer distances involved in their gathering, and total non-availability of certain medicinal trees.
c. The medicinal preparations do not have some or all of the natural ingredients in their preparations due to:

    (i) inadequacy and non-availability of certain medicinal trees,
    (ii) high costs of gathering the medicinal trees,
    (iii) general public non-response, due to a high degree of belief.

d. The policy environment provides a lopsided support to "proprietary medicines" with the result that the "classical preparations" and their quality are dwindling, undermining the holistic approach of the philosophy of Ayurvedic medicine.
e. The price spread between the gatherers and the final consumers does not reflect the competitive marketing costs of functionaries.
f. The information about the source of availability of medicinal trees, the gatherer, the processor, the intermediaries, the final traders and the prices charged by them is imperfect. In many cases these are guarded secrecies.
g. Unclear property and patent rights and imperfect knowledge regarding privileges of collection of forest-based medicinal trees have resulted in lower margins for the gatherers, since they can always be threatened with illegal removal from natural forests, making rent-seeking rampant.
h. The livelihood of medicinal plant gatherers is now diversified and consequently they are less dependent on gathering medicinal plants from forests than before.
i. Production of proprietary and other branded Ayurvedic products has increased with no institutional check on their quality.
j. With a gradual erosion of the forest base, there is a shift in the dependence on sources of cultivated medicinal plants.

6. Based on the discussion with Dr. T.V. Ramachandra Prasad, Professor of Agronomy, All India Coordinated Research Project on Weed Control, UAS, Bangalore.
7. Scientific communication with Dr. R.N. Kulkarni, Scientist, Central Institute for Medicinal and Aromatic Plants (CSIR), Bangalore and Dr. Farooqui, Professor of Medicinal Plants, Department of Horticulture, University of Agricultural Sciences, Bangalore.
8. R. Sukumar, H.S. Suresh, H.S. Dattaraja and N.V. Joshi, "Diversity and Dynamics of Tropical Forests in Southern India, in *Sustainable Development and Bio-diversity*, background material for Indian Forest Service Officers, Centre for Ecological Sciences, Indian Institute of Science, Bangalore, 20-24, Jan 1997.
9. V. Bhaskar and C.G. Kushalappa, *Germplasm exploration for plants of horticultural and Silvicultural importance from the forests in Tumkur District*, Karnataka (forthcoming).
10. The Foundation for Revitalization of Local Health Traditions (FRLHT), Bangalore, has prioritized a list of 352 medicinal plants in South India reflecting ecological scarcity. This list includes the medicinal plants species which are endemic in nature. Endemic plants are those which grow in a specific area and have a restricted distribution. Such endemic species are the special concern of Conservation biologists due to their vulnerability to becoming endangered.
11. S. Chandrashekar, Ayurveda turns an old leaf in Europe, *Economic Times*, 30 Oct., 1997.
12. Information provided by the owner of Amruth Kesari Depot, Avenue Road, Bangalore, for sharing this information on 8.11.1997.

13. To illustrate the point, suppose a private drug company is able to produce a vital life-saving drug for an endemic disease like TB or Malaria, the State should prevail to provide an easy access at a reasonable cost for the masses.
14. This is also one of the reasons why our exports are not as high as expected. The European market does not permit import of multi-ingredient Ayurvedic drugs.
15. One illustration is that of a patient who suffered from paralysis of the right vocal chord, since he was involved in teaching. The allopathy system of medicine suggested him to be in voice rest for five years, and this meant a total loss of around Rs. 3.5 lakhs in terms of salary (@Rs. 5,000 per month). On the other hand the "Pancha karma" treatment in Ayurveda helped the patient to manage his chord paralysis at a cost of Rs. 1,000 for one month. There may be several other similar examples. This is a pointer to the huge disparities in the valuation between the different systems of medicine.
16. Input supplied by Dr. Gopalakrishna, Inspector, Drug Control Authority of Ayurveda, Karnataka.
17. For the entire Metropolis of Bangalore, with a population of six million, there are not more than 30 stores which exclusively sell Ayurvedic drugs. In the State of Karnataka, there are 15,000 practitioners of Ayurveda, Siddha and Unani, among whom Ayurvedic doctors are 11,000. India has around 1.5 million Ayurvedic doctors.
18. The efforts of the Ayurvedic Academy, 236, 4th Main, Chamarajpet, Bangalore-560 018 in educating the public through bringing out a monthly *Ayurvijnana* and conducting regular classes to educate the public about Ayurveda are laudable.
19. Our interaction with Shri Vaidya Bhagwan Dash, a reputed Ayurvedic vaidya and author of several books on Ayurveda, indicated that in Italy where he practises Ayurveda, there is a great demand for Ayurvedic medicines and all the banned medicines are available to patients. In addition, there is a great demand for Ayurvedic medicines and their practitioners in Europe.
20. It is heartening to note that the Government of India has recently recognized the Ayurvedic medicinal system by introducing Ayurvedic medicine for patients through the Central Government Health Scheme hospitals countrywide. However, even though several committees have recommended introduction of an Ayurvedic chair, in the Central Institute of Medicine, regrettably the Government of India has not yet responded positively. The age-old system of "Ayurveda" which has proved its efficacy deserves full attention.
21. Marothia, D.K. "Property Regimes in Medicinal and Aromatic Plant Resources" (Some Policy Issues). Keynote Paper presented at National Conference on Health Care & Development of Herbal Medicines, held at Indira Gandhi Agricultural University, Raipur, 29-30 August, 1997.
22. Marothia, D.K. & W.S. Phillips. "Analysis of Natural Resources: Problems Using a Synthesis of Neoclassical and Institutional Economics", *Asian Journal of Economics and Social Studies* (Vol. 4, No. 4), 1985, pp. 263-81.

REFERENCES

Bostock Wood, C.V. 1992. *Trees in Society in Rural Karnataka*, India, Overseas Development Administration, Natural Resources Institute, Karnataka Forest Department, Kent, UK.

Chandrakanth, M.G. 1995. "Market imperfections, transaction costs and economic scarcity of forest based medicinal plants and plant products in Karnataka, India", Invited paper for discussion at the Research seminar on Environmental Economics, organized by The Beijer Institute, Royal Swedish Academy of Sciences, Kotakinabalu, West Malaysia, 16-19 May.

Chandrashekar, S. 1997. "Ayurveda turns an old leaf in Europe", *Economic Times*, (Bangalore ed), 29th Oct.

Government of India. *Trade year book of Directorate General of Foreign Trade Statistics* (various issues), Calcutta.

CSIR. *Journal of Aromatic and Medicinal Plant Abstracts,* Council for Scientific and Industrial Research, various issues.

Kushalappa, C.G. 1996. "Germ Plasm Exploration for Plants of Horticultural and Silvicultural Importance from the forests in Tumkur District, Karnataka", Ph. D. thesis (Unpublished), Department of Forestry, Bangalore: University of Agricultural Sciences.

Marothia, D.K. 1997. "Property Regimes in Medicinal and Aromatic Plant Resources: Some Policy Issues", Keynote Paper presented at National Conference on Health Care and Development of Herbal Medicines, held at the Indira Gandhi Agricultural University, Raipur, 29-30 August, 1997.

Marothia, D.K. and W.E. Phillips. 1985. "Analysis of Natural Resources Problems using a Synthesis of Neoclassical and Institutional Economics", *Asian Journal of Economics and Social Studies* (Vol. 4, No. 4), pp. 263-281.

Panchabhootha Bhagirathi Association. 1983. *Glossary of Medicinal Plants of Karnataka* Bangalore: Incorporating Ayurvedic Pharmacological Properties.

Ravishankar, A. 1997. *Intellectual Property Rights and Indian Agriculture : Some Issues,* Policy Brief No. 4, NCAP - ICAR, Sep 1996, pp. 1-4.

Shankar Darshan. 1997. "Conserving a National Resource: Need for National Policy and National Program on Medicinal Plants Conservation". Paper presented in the course on Sustainable Development and Biodiversity for IFS officers, Bangalore: Center for Ecological Sciences, Indian Institute of Science, 20-24, Jan.

Sukumar, R., H.S. Suresh, H.S. Dattaraja and N.V. Joshi. 1997. Dynamics of a tropical deciduous forest: Population changes during 1988-1993 in a 50 hectare plot at Muddumalai, Southern India. Paper presented in the course on Sustainable Development and Biodiversity for IFS officers, Bangalore: Center for Ecological Sciences, Indian Institute of Science, 20-24, Jan.

Unnikrishnan, P.M. 1997. "An insight into Ayurveda's knowledge of medicinal plants", *Amruth,* Supplement to Vol. I, Issue 10, Aug., pp. 1-26.

Ved, D.K. 1997. Trade in medicinal plants: The State of Our Ignorance, *Amruth*, Vol. I, Issue 10, Aug., pp. 2-8.

APPENDIX I

Sources of Classical Literature on Plants

Sl. No.	Text name	Chronology	Author	Region	No. of plants referred
1.	Charaka Samhita	1500 BC-400 AD	Agnivesa Charaka Drdhabla	Himalaya Kashmir	12850
2.	Sushruta Samhita	1500 BC-500 AD	Susruta Nagarjuna	Kasi Sindhudesa	9650
3.	Ashtanga Sangraha	500 AD	Vagbhata	Sindhudesa	20500
4.	Ashtanga Hrdayam	600 AD	Vagbhata	Sindhudesa	9900
5.	Ashtanga Nighantu	800 AD	Vagbhata		2100
6.	Paryayaratnamala	900 AD	Madhava	Silahrda	1900
7.	Dhanvantri Nighantu	200 AD-1000 AD	Unknown	Unknown	3250
8.	Chakradatta	1075 AD	Chakrapanidatta	Vanga desa	12300
9.	Dravyaguna Sangraha	1075 AD	Chakrapanidatta	Vanga desa	320
10.	Madhavadravyaguna	1250 AD	Madhava	Unknown	750
11.	Sarngadahara Samhita	1300 AD	Sarngadhara	Devagiri	4200
12.	Nighantu Sesa	1200 AD	Hemachandra	Unknown	2950
13.	Siddhmantra	1210 AD-1247 AD	Kesava	Unknown	950
14.	Hrdayadipaka Nighantu	1260 AD-1271 AD	Bopadeva	Unknown	820
15.	Madanapala Nighantu	1374 AD	Madanapala	Kashthanagara	3000
16.	Bhavaprakasha	1550 AD	Bhavamisra	Kasi Kanyakubja	11200
17.	Bhavaprakasha Nighantu	1550 AD	Bhavamisra	Kasi Kanyakubja	2600
18.	Raja Nighantu	1700 AD	Naraharipanda	Kasmira	7300
19.	Saligrama Nighantu	1896 AD	Saligramvaisya	Muradabad	4200
20.	Siddhabhesajamanimala	1896 AD	Krshnaramabhatta	Jayapura	620

24 Biodiversity: A Key Issue for Commons Management in the Himalayan Region

Vir Singh

1. Introduction

Biodiversity is an important common property resource and a potent option for development of sustainable economies. For the marginal and remote areas characterised by an overwhelming feature of common property resources, sustainability cannot be operationalised without an efficient management of biodiversity. In the highly patronised areas in the plains, production systems are now based on monocultures of crops and CPRs have almost vanished. Diversity or heterogeneity in these areas, therefore, is hardly an issue. But, in the mountains of the Himalaya, biodiversity reigns both in the privately owned cropland and in the community lands. The natural diversity in this region would be an important issue for the whole region for its sustainable development.

Community forests and grazing lands spread over vast stretches of Civil-Soyam and Panchayat lands are the most important CPRs in the Himalayan mountains. During recent years these CPRs have been conventionally managed mainly for fuelwood and fodder supplies. For the fulfilment of these two basic needs, the CPRs in many mountain areas generally cover only a limited variety of plants and in many cases they simply exhibit monocultures of pine trees due to which a considerable loss to biodiversity has occurred. In the mountains of Indian Western Himalaya (Jammu and Kashmir, Himachal Pradesh and the Himalayan part of Uttar Pradesh) area under forest cover is 55,592 sq km which is far more than that the cropped area, i.e. 31,010 sq km (GOI 1995). By a sound management of these CPRs, a diversity of benefits can be accrued to the community. Apart from fuelwood and fodder, CPRs can provide plentiful foods (fruits, nuts, pods, vegetables, edible flowers, buds, seeds, roots and leaves, honey, edible oils, fibre, medicinal and aromatic plants, spices and condiments) and raw material for small-scale village industries. In order to ensure these gains on a sustained basis, biodiversity consideration must be central to CPR management strategies.

A biodiversity-rich area does not only ensure plentiful supplies of a very large number of products of special consumptive use value, but also makes many more functions, e.g. maintenance of local hydrological cycle, moisture circulation, nutrient flows, soil conservation, etc., which are vital to the sustainability of production systems (Singh 1991, 1995). Moreover, the biodiversity in the CPR areas has a tremendous bearing on the agriculture of the area (Partap 1993). Production flows through agriculture are a manifestation of the health of forest ecosystems in the mountain region which, in turn, is the manifestation of the degree of diversity in these woodlands. In the context of the ecological stability of the mountains, viable economy, energy efficiency, resilience, farmers' security and social justice have been considered as the main indicators of sustainability (Singh 1995).

Examining the biodiversity-sustainability linkages, this chapter attempts to emphasise the central role of diversity as the key issue in the management of commons with special focus on the mountain areas of the Indian Himalayan region.

2. A Panorama of Biodiversity in the Mountains

Mountain areas represent an extreme degree of heterogeneity which, according to Troll (1988), is a function of interactions of different factors such as elevation, altitude, geologic and edaphic conditions, steepness and orientation of slope, wind and precipitation, mountain mass and relief of terrain. Diversity acts as a positive attribute for the inter-linked activity patterns and should serve as the true basis for assessing mountain areas' carrying capacity (Jodha *et al.* 1992).

Marginally, inaccessibility and fragility are the negative attributes associated with the mountain areas. This leads to the impression that this region's contribution to the overall economy would be non-significant. But diversity, "niche" or comparative advantages and human adaptation mechanisms inextricably linked with the mountain agriculture (Jodha 1990) are the positive attributes indicative of a very high potential the mountain areas offer for the local, national and global economies. Partap (1996) opines that the marginal lands would be the focus of the 21st century's agriculture, mainly because of the fact that the mountains' agro-economy, by and large traditional, is built upon the local biodiversity managed within farming systems.

The mainstream agriculture largely revolves round cultivated land, while the mountain agriculture embraces common lands (mainly the forests and grasslands) and it is holistic as a sustainable agroecosystem should be. The mainstream agriculture is dependent on the external inputs, especially the chemical fertilizers and synthetic pesticides, but the mountain agriculture is self-dependent, being nourished by the inputs grown and prepared within the system. Nearly 65 per cent of the organic matter that nourishes the cultivated land grows in common forests (Singh *et al.* 1995). The mountain farming system is self-contained and tends to be self-reliant. This multi-component farming system, having forests, cropland, livestock and human beings as the integral parts of it, represents an overwhelming feature of the solar-powered agriculture. The system also uses natural subsidy in the form of forest biomass and recycled nutrients. The biodiversity—rich mountain agriculture, in ecological terms, may be referred to as nature-subsidised solar-powered agriculture.

The diversity rich multi-component farming system is altogether different from the one operating in the plains under the Green Revolution cover. In the latter, organic linkages among various components are virtually missing. Forests are almost absent and draught animal power has been replaced with fossil-fuel-powered machines. Inputs in the form of chemical fertilizers and synthetic pesticides to be used massively in crops are supplied from outside. This agriculture is bound to strongly depend on the free capitalistic market system.

Relying completely on renewable sources of energy—inexhaustible sunlight, forest biomass and crop residues, human and animal muscle power, and microbial decomposition processes in the soil (indicative of soil fertility)—the mountain farming system embraces the characteristics of sustainability. The Green Revolution agriculture, on the contrary, relies on precious and finite energy sources and such a food production system cannot guarantee sustainability.

The performance of the mountain farming system is influenced enormously by the measure of diversity stocked in the forest ecosystems under the domain of CPRs, for this component is a natural "fertilizer factory" for the agriculture, and well-being of the agriculture depends on the well-being of the forests.

According to the Forest (Conservation) Act of 1988, 60 per cent of the land area in the hills should be under forest cover, while for the country as a whole, it should be 33 per cent. The total forest cover in the Indian Himalaya is only 30.44 per cent which ranges from 9 per cent in Jammu and Kashmir to 82 per cent in Arunachal Pradesh. Hence the Himalayan areas are much deficient in forest cover. The dense forest cover (crown density 40 per cent and above) is only on 23 per cent area in the Indian Himalaya ranging from 5 per cent in Jammu and Kashmir to 65 per cent in Arunachal Pradesh. Thus, except for Arunachal Pradesh, forest cover is nowhere near 60 per cent in any Himalayan State of India (Table 24.1).

Operating site factors, e.g. altitude, slope direction, temperature, humidity, rainfall, availability of irrigation water and distance from the snowline or plains, are the driving forces for the diversification of agriculture into various farming situations. From the Outer Himalayan area to the Greater Himalaya, as many as eleven farming situations have been identified (Singh 1995). Each situation is characterised by a specific niche vital for specific botanical composition, cropping patterns and for specific activities and products.

TABLE 24.1: **Forest Cover in Indian Himalaya**

(Area in sq. km.)

Himalayan State/Area	Geographic Area	Dense Forest[a]		Open Forest[b]		Total		Scrub[c]
Jammu & Kashmir	222235	11020	(4.96)	9413	(4.24)	20433	(9.14)	3087
Himachal Pradesh	55673	9565	(17.18)	2936	(5.27)	12501	(22.5)	1845
U.P. Himalaya	51125	17615	(34.5)	5043	(9.86)	22658	(44.3)	567
Darjeeling (W.B.)	3149	1091	(34.65)	357	(11.35)	1448	(45.98)	1
Sikkim	7096	2424	(34.16)	703	(9.91)	3127	(44.07)	437
Arunachal Pradesh	83743	54176	(64.7)	14445	(17.3)	68621	(81.9)	354
Indian Himalaya	423021	95891	(22.64)	32897	(7.78)	128788	(30.44)	6291

Compiled from GOI (1995).

Note : Figures in parentheses are percentage forest cover to geographical area.

Crown Density : a—40% & above; b—10% to less than 40%; c—less than 10%.

Traditionally, four cropping systems in the Lesser Himalayan region are maintained. The kitchen garden around homesteads serves to supply fruits and vegetables for home consumption. Irrigated land cropping system is devoted to rice and wheat cultivation. The upland or rainfed cropping system is dominantly occupied by millets and pulses, while the summer-camp cropping system is commonly devoted to pseudocereals (amaranth and buckwheat) and beans (mainly the kidneybean). These diverse cropping systems have been designed by the farmers in tune with varying micro-ecological niches suiting to the cultivation of specific crops and crop combinations.

The responses of mountain plants to their environment are due to a complex mixture of genetic and environmental influences. There is evidence that some mountain plants have evolved in response to their particular altitudinal environment. In comparison to their lowland counterparts, the mountain plants have an increased ability to fix CO_2 from lower than sea-level concentrations, use high irradiance levels more efficiently, photosynthesize and grow at lower temperatures and have intrinsically lower growth rates (Friend and Woodward 1990). Farmers' interactions with plants, animals and their environment and their protection, selection, domestication and cultivation of native plants, introducing and improving exotic plants have all given rise to an enormous genetic diversity in the mountain environments. The crop plant genetic resources of the world can be more or less assigned to the specific centres of diversity identified by Vavilov (1951) on the basis of varietal diversity, homologous variation, endemism, dominant allele frequencies, and disease resistance (Khoshoo 1996). In India, there are eight sub-centres, namely, (i) Western Himalaya, (ii) Eastern Hamalaya, (iii) North Eastern Region, (iv) Gangetic Plains, (v) Indus Plains, (vi) Western Ghats, (vii) Eastern Ghats, and (viii) Andaman and Nicobar (Arora and Nayar 1984). The first three of these fall in the Himalayan belt. According to Arora and Nayar (1984) there are around 399 species of wild relatives of crop plants belonging to 90 genera in the Western, Eastern, and North-Eastern Himalayas. The Himalayan region has especially been the source of several cereals, pulses, fruits, oil-yielding plants, spices, tuberous vegetables and sugar-yielding plants and their close wild relatives which number 155 (Arora and Nayar 1984). A list of wild relatives of economic plants in the Himalayan region is presented in Table 24.2.

TABLE 24.2: **Wild Relatives of Economic Plants in the Indian Himalayan Region.**

	A. North-West and Northern Himalayas
Cereals and Millets :	*Aegilops tauschii; Avena barbata, A. fatua var. fatua; A. ludoviciana; Digitaria sanguinalis; Elymus dahuricus, E. dasystachys, E. nutans, E. distans, E. orientale; Hordeum glaucum, H. spontaneum, H. turkestanicum; Pennisetum orientale.*
Legumes :	*Cicer microphyllum; Lathyrus aphaca; Moghania vestita; Mucuna capitata; Trigonella emodi, Vigna capensis, V. radiata var. sublobata; V. umbellata.*
Fruits :	*Elaeagnus hortensis; Ficus palmata; Fragaria indica; Morus spp.; Prunus acuminata, P. cerasoides, P. cornuta, P. napalensis, P.* prostrata, *P. tomentasa; Pyrus buccata; P. communis, P. kumaoni; P. pashia; Ribes glaciale, R. nigrum; Rubus ellipticus, R. fruticosus, R. lanatus, R. lasiocarpus, R. moluccanus; Zizyphus vulgaris.*
Vegetables :	*Abelmoschus manihot (tetraphyllus forms); Cucumis hardwickii, C. callosus; Luffa echinata, L. graveolens; Solanum incanum, S. indicum; Trichosanthes multiloba, T. himalensis.*
Oilseeds :	*Lapidium capitatum, L. draba, L. latifolium, L. ruderale.*
Fibre :	*Linum perenne.*
Spices & Condiments :	*Allium rubellum, A. schoenoprasum, A. tuberosum and other species; Carum bulbocastinum.*

TABLE 24.2 (*Contd.*)

Miscellaneous :	*Saccharum filifolium; Miscanthus nepalensis.*
	B. Eastern and North-Eastern Himalayas
Cereals and Millets:	*Digitaria cruciata; Hordeum agricrithon.*
Legumes :	*Atylosia barbata, A. scarabaeoides, A. villosa; Canavalia ensiformis; Mucuna bractearata; Vigna umbellata, V. radiata var. sublobata, V. pilosa.*
Fruits :	*Fragaria indica; Morus spp.; Myrica esculenta; Prunus acuminata, P. cornuta, P. jenkinsii, P. nepalensis, Pyrus pashia, Ribes glaciale, Rubus lineatus, R. ellipticus, R. lasciocarpus, R. moluccanus, R. reticulatus, Citrus assamensis, C. ichangensis, C. indica, D. hookeriana, Eriobotrya angustifolia, Mangifera sylvatica, Musa balbisiana complex, M. manii, M. nagensium, M. sikkimensis, M. superba, M. velutina.*
Vegetables :	*Abelmoschus manihot-pungens forms; Luffa graveolens, Neoluffa sikkimensis; Cucumis hystrix, C. callosus, Momordica dioica, M. cochinchinesis, M. macrophyllata, M. subangulata, Trichosanthes cucumerina. T. dioica, T. dioaelosperma, T. khasiana, T. ovata, T. trumcata, Solanum indicum and tuber types; Allocasia macrorhiza, Amorphophallus bulbifer, Colocasia esculenta; Dioscorea alata, Moghania vestita, Vigna capensis.*
Oilseeds :	*Brassica trilocularis types.*
Fibres :	*Gossypium aboreum (primitive types).*
Spices and Condiments :	*Allium tuberosum, A. Sublobatum, Curcuma zedoaria, Alpinia galanga, A. speciosa, Amomum aromaticum, Curcuma amoda, Piper peepuloides.*
Miscellaneous :	*Saccharum langisetosum, S. sikkimensis, S. ravennae; Erianchus spp., Miscanthus nudipus; M. nepalensis; M. taylorii, Naranga fallax, Camellia spp.*

Source: After Arora & Nayar (1984).

3. Biodiversity and Food and Nutrition Security

Conventionally, the management of agro-biodiversity is regarded as the only key to solve the problem of food and nutrition security. But, in the mountains, CPRs, especially the natural forests, offer an enormous scope for providing edibles of high nutritive value.

In the Henwal Valley of the Garhwal Himalaya, as many as 189 different species of plants offer edible products while people cultivate only 92 different food-producing plants on their arable land. If we compare this scenario with that of the plains' agriculture in the foothills of the Himalaya, we find that farmers depend only on 33 plant species for their survival. Thus, from the point of view of plant species diversity offering food articles, CPRs are the richest sources (Table 24.3). A list of common plant species of high consumptive use value found in the commons and cultivated area of Garhwal's Henwal Valley is presented in Tables 24.4 and 24.5.

TABLE 24.3: **Number of Plant Species in Mountain Ecosystems and the Plains' Agriculture providing Edible Products**

Edible Product	Mountain Ecosystems*		Plains Agriculture**
	CPRs	Cropland	
Fruits	24	18	6
Vegetables	14	32	10
Cereals, Millets & Pseudocereals	—	12	4
Pulses	—	10	5
Oilseeds	—	7	4
Medicinal & Aromatic Plants	99	4	—
Fodders	52	9	4
Total Species	189	92	33

* Figures are based on a survey of Henwal Valley in the Garhwal Himalaya.
** Figures are based on a survey of the plains (foothills of the Garhwal Himalaya).

TABLE 24.4: **Plants of Different Consumptive Use Values in the Commons of the Garhwal Himalaya (A Case of Henwal Valley)**

Edible Fruits, Flowers and Buds	*Benthamida capitata, Myrica esculenta, Ficus auriculata, F. palmata, Bauhinia purpurea, Morus serrata, Celtis australis, Indigofera gerardiana, Phyllanthus emblica, Rhododendron arboreum, Aesculus indica, Rubus ellipticus, R. lasiocarpus, Pyrus pashia, P. lanata, Fragaria vesca, Pyracantha crenulata, Grewia sapida, Holboellia latifolia, Bombax sp., Debregeasia longifolia, Carissa opaca, Elaeagnus parviflora, Pinus gerardiana.*
Wild Vegetables	*Diplazium frondosum, Utrica ardens, Chenopodium album, Diascorea belophylla, D. bulbifera, Solena amplexicaulis, Nasturtium officinale, Flemingia procumbens, Fagopyrum dibotris, Bombax sp., Indigofera gerardiana, Celtis australis, Kholya or sisua (local name), mushrooms.*
Leaf Fodders	*Adina cordifolia, Aesculus indica, Artocarpus lakoocha, Bassia butyraceae, Bauhinia purpurea, B. Vahlii, B. variegata, Boehmeria platyphylla, B. rugulosa, Brassiopsis hainla, Budleja asiatica, Castanopsis hystrix, C. indica, C. tribuoides, Celtis australis, Choerospondias axillaris, Debregeasia salicifolia, Erythrena arborescens, Eurya acuminata, Ficus auriculata, F. fabberrima, F. infectoria, F. neriifoli, F. religiosa, F. semicordata, F. subincisa, Geruga pinnata, Grewia optiva, helectecteres isora, Holmskioldia sanguinea, Kydia calycina, Lespediza eriopcarpa, Lithocarpus elegans, Litsea monopetala, Mallotus philippensis, Maoutia putya, Melia azedarach, Melletia auriculata, Morus alba, Myrsina capitellata, Porana paniculata, Premna latifolia, Prunus armeniaca, P. serasoides, Pterespermus acerifolium, Quercus glauca, Q. lamellosa, Q. lanata, Q. leucotrichophora, Q. semecarpifolia, Spermedictyon suaveolens, Woorfordia fruticosa.*

Note : Apart from the above there are 99 medicinal and aromatic plants found in the area.

TABLE 24.5: **Plant Diversity in the Agroecosystems of the Garhwal Himalaya (a case of Henwal Valley)**

Cultivated Fruits:	*Prumus armeniaca, P. amygdalus, P. demestica, P. avium, P. persica, Malus pumila, Juglans regia, Pyrus communis, Citrus reticulata, C. sinensis, C. aurantifolia, C. limon, C. medica, Mangifera indica, Aegle marmelos, Musa paradisiaca, Litchi sinensis, Embilica officinalis.*
Cultivated Vegetables:	*Solonum tuberosum, S. melongena, S. lycopersicum, Capsicum annum, C. frutescence, Colocasia esculenta, Alocasia macrorrhiza, Cucurbita pepo, C. moschata, Langenaria siceraria, Luffa acutangula, L. aegyptiaca, Trichosanthes anguina, Cucumis sativus, Raphanus sativus, Spinacia oleracia, Momordica charantia, M. dioca, Daucus carota, Pisum sativum, Lablab perpureus, Amaranthus sp., Fagopyrum sp., B. juncea, B. oleracca, B. rapa, Trigonella foenumgraecum, Beta vulgaris, Allium cepa, A. sativum, Vicia faba, Phaseolus vulgaris.*
Cereals & Pseudocereals:	*Oryza sativa, Triticum aestivum, Hordeum vulgare, Zea mays, Sorghum sp., Pennisetum typhoides, Eleucine coracana, Echinochloa frumentacea, Setaria italica, panicum millaceum, Amaranthus sp., Fagopyrum sp.*
Pulses:	*Glycine max, Vigna mungo, Macrotyloma uniflorum, Vigna umbellata, V. angularis, V. radiata, Phaseolus vulgaris, Cajanus cajan, Lense culinaris, Cicer arietinum.*
Oilseeds:	*Brassica juncea, B. campestris, B. napus, Sesamum indicum, Arachis hypogea, Helianthus annuus, Perilla frutescence.*
Spices:	*Zingiber officinale, Curcuma domestica, Coriandrum sativum, Ammomum oramaticum, Trigonella foenumgraecum, Cleaome viscosa.*

When glancing at the food spectrum of prehistoric man, we come to know that man embraced at least 1,500 species of wild plants, while over 500 vegetables were utilised by the ancient civilization. However, in contemporary times, human nutrition is derived from not more than 30 plants, with three crops—wheat, rice and maize—accounting for 75 per cent of our cereal consumption and 20 more vegetable species are encountered in field cultivation (SAM 1984).

From the above, it is clearly inferred that human societies have steadily been running towards a state of food poverty. In the plain areas this situation has been triggered by a decline and degradation of CPRs coupled with cultivation practices based on monocultures of a fewer varieties of a limited number of species.

Compared to these "food poor" plain areas, the Himalayan mountain areas are truly "food rich" and it is mainly because the livelihood systems in these areas are built upon the diversity-stocked CPRs. The quality of our food should fundamentally be decided by the number of plant-sources we derive our food ingredients from. This is particularly true of the vegetarians who should incorporate in their diet food from as many edible plants as possible. Dependence on a limited number of plants for food will carry a potential risk of malnutrition and underdevelopment. The quantity and quality of food available for the rural poor is far below the standard one. The fact is that they cannot, and they should not, rely upon agricultural crops alone for their adequate and balanced diet (Singh 1991). In sharp contrast is the health status of the people living in the natural bounty of forests, anywhere in the world. Where there are natural forests, there exist woodlands, rivers, lakes and even medicinal herbs supplying massive amounts of carbohydrates, proteins and other nutrients. Apart from these, the daily harvests of fruits, nuts, leaves, twigs and bark supply a variety of dietary ingredients.

CPRs are often appreciated for their contribution as fuel, fodder, timber, etc. That they provide the most basic necessity of humans, i.e. a variety of foods, is seldom appreciated. While cultivation of the annual crops should continue and it should even be diversified to enhance sustainability, CPR's potentialities of providing numerous types of foods (fruits, nuts, seeds, pods, bark, leaves, twigs, flowers, buds, honey, etc.) should be recognised.

The conventional food production policies that seek food security only through bulk production of foodgrains and often compromise with the quality of food also give way to bringing more and more forest areas under plough, for that is necessary to feed the increasing number of bellies. The food production system solely dependent on cultivation of foodgrain crops is not a sustainable one, for it creates an imbalance among various farming system components (forests, grasslands, cropland, etc.) by weakening the linkages among them. The food production policy must, therefore, take the uncultivated CPR areas into consideration for food and nutrition security. Focussing the forests as the potential areas for food production ought to provide a dimension of sustainability to our food production strategies. At the time of adversity (e.g. during drought periods) CPRs especially provide protection to the local community.

4. Biodiversity and Sustainability

There are strong linkages between biodiversity and sustainability. In the case of agriculture, the variety of plant species may not be an essential input for sustainability, but for the commons' management it is. Sustainability in the context of CPRs, as akin to the one elaborated by Jodha (1990), would mean ability of these resources (e.g. forests or grasslands) to maintain a well-defined level of performance over time without external biochemical, biophysical and other forms of subsidisation.

In the fragile mountains, ecological stability of the system should be the foremost criteria for sustainability. The greater the measure of biodiversity in a forest ecosystem the higher the degree of stability of a system. For example, climax community of oak (*Quercus leucotrichophora*) with maximum diversity of associated species at this juncture of nature's biological evolution in the Middle Himalaya provides very high stability to the mountain-farming system. Biodiversity-rich support area (the forest) to supply massive amounts of nutrients through fodder to livestock (see Table 24.4) and cropland and maintain the local hydrological cycle, owing to its contribution to stability (Singh 1991, 1995), continues to be an essential feature of the mountain agriculture, though much degradation of such forests has already occurred in many areas of the mountains, and such areas are facing grim consequences. In addition to maintain the quality of the resource base, the biodiversity contributes to enhance the vitality of the entire agro-ecosystem which is best ensured when the soil is well managed. Farming systems' management practices involve the use of one ecosystem's produce as a subsidy for the other component (e.g. forest biomass, particularly the tree leaves, is used as livestock feed which, when turned into dung and manure, nourishes the cropland). Biodiversity thus helps strengthen linkages between and within various components. This contribution is vital for maintaining the ecological integrity of the whole system.

That biodiversity is the key issue for designing and developing a viable agrarian structure is reflected in the potential of this diversity stocked in the diverse ecological niches spread over a wide range of land use. This diversity is of great consumptive, productive, existence and option value. It ranges from forestry species, including medicinal and aromatic plants, to life-support landraces of minor crops, to off-season vegetables. There are several low-volume high-value crops and animal products derivable from mountain diversity. Given that the carrying capacity of the biophysical resource base is not over-reached, the mountain farming system, owing to its diversity, ought to be capable of fulfilling most of the basic needs (e.g. food, fibre, shelter, water, medicines, etc.) and also of providing work to all residents with the guarantee of their satisfactory living standards. Dependence on outside will be only for those articles which cannot be cultivated or manufactured within the system. At the same time, many things extractable from local diversity (e.g. Ayurvedic medicines, condiments, etc.) might be exported (Singh 1995).

Conventionally, the direct marketable farm produce, i.e. yield, is considered as a major economic indicator. But in order to understand how the system functions, it should be measured in terms of the energetic efficiency of a system as a whole, of its subsystems, of individual crop or animal, or of a crop variety or animal breed. Energetic efficiency of the whole system relying on internal renewable resources contributed by diversity must naturally be very high. On the other hand, energy efficiency of the so-called high production homogeneous systems developed at the risk of biodiversity and depending heavily on external inputs from non-renewable energy sources is generally poor. For example, 5 calories of energy produce only 1 calory of energy in apple production in Garhwal (Singh and Dankeleman 1993).

The natural ecosystems endowed with diversity are extremely resilient (Quinney 1984). Diversification, flexibility and interlinkages among different production activities, input use practices and consumption patterns impart a degree of resilience to the traditional farming system in the fragile mountain areas (Jodha 1990). Landmass fragility of the mountains increases catastrophically if the diversity and complexity of the system are reduced. Whereas inaccessibility, fragility and marginality characteristics of the mountains correlate negatively with the resilience, the diversity, niche and adaptation characteristics are positive attributes to resilience against shocks.

Biodiversity creates barriers against any natural calamity (e.g. drought) and pest epidemics. Some living organisms may be host to certain insects or diseases, some may be little more prone to weather extremes or other natural calamity, but a complex mix of naturally occurring (in CPR areas) organisms will do away any chances of widespread loss to the farmers.

Biodiversity is also the base of a socially just system. Reserve forests, grasslands, alpine pastures, village commons and several kinds of marginal ecosystems are open to a community's usage. Mountain farmers, in addition to exercising their rights of resource ussage, can have opportunities to participate in decision-making, especially with regard to the management of village commons. In fact, biodiversity in the commons and social justice are closely linked with each other.

5. Conclusions

Livelihood systems of the mountain people are built around CPRs, especially the common forests. The production capacity and sustainability of CPRs depend mainly on the degree of biodiversity, especially the varieties of plants and their genotypes. The commons' biodiversity has an enormous bearing on the agro-biodiversity due to CPR-cropland linkages. The mountain regions are ecologically more fragile and hence special attention and differential strategy with a focus on CPRs management is the need of the hour. There is a strong linkage between CPR biodiversity and sustainability. Ecological, economic and equity are the various dimensions of sustainability. The efficient management of CPRs, with biodiversity considerations at its heart, and coupled with cropping activities, can take care of food and nutrition security to a great extent, supply many basic necessities of life, elevate the economic standard of people, provide favourable ecosystem services and infuse sustainability in the whole production system. Biodiversity should, therefore, be the most important fundamental issue of our policies relating to CPR management in the Himalayan mountains.

REFERENCES

Arora, R.K. and E.R. Nayar. 1984. *Wild Relatives of Crop Plants in India*, New Delhi: NBPGR.

Friend, A.D. and F.I. Woodward. 1990. "Evolutionary and Physiological Responses of Mountain Plants to Growing Season Environment". In: Begon, M; Fitter, A.H. and Macfaden, A. (eds.), *Advances in Ecological Research*, Vol. 20, London: Academic Press.

GOI (Govt. of India). 1995. *The State of Forest Report*, Dehradun: Forest Survey of India.

Jodha, N.S. 1990. *Mountain Agriculture: Search for Sustainability*, Mountain Farming Systems Discussion Paper No. 2, Kathmandu: ICIMOD.

Jodha, N.S., M. Banskota and T. Partap. (eds.). 1992. *Sustainable Mountain Agriculture*, New Delhi: Oxford and IBH and ICIMOD.

Khoshoo, T.N. 1996 "Biodiversity in Indian Himalaya: Conservation and Utilization", In: Pei Shengji (ed.) *Banking on Biodiversity*, Kathmandu: ICIMOD, 185-255.

Partap, T. 1990. "Biological Diversity of Genetic Resources: Some Issues for Sustainable Mountain Agriculture". Paper presented at the *International Symposium on Strategies for Sustainable Mountain Agriculture* at ICIMOD, Kathmandu, September 10-14, 1990.

Partap, T. 1993. "Biological Diversity Issue and Sustainable Mountain Development", In: Singh, V. (ed.) *Eco-crisis in the Himalaya: Causes, Consequences and Way Out*, Dehradun: IBD.

Partap, T. 1996. "Mountain Agriculture Biodiversity Perspectives and Framework for Management", Paper presented at the *Expert Meeting on Mountain Agriculture Biodiversity Perspectives and Issues in the HK-Himalayan Region* at New Delhi, July 18-19, 1996.

Quinney, J. 1984. "Designing Sustainable Small Farms". *The Mother Earth News*, July-August.

SAM. 1984. *Seeds and Food Security*. Penang: Sahbat Alam Malaysia.

Singh, V. 1991. *Ecological Impact of Apple Cultivation in the Himalaya*. Dehradun: IBD.

Singh, V. 1995. "Biodiversity and Farmers: Experiences from Garhwal Himalaya, India", Paper presented at the *Beijer Research Seminar*, Kota Kinabalu, Sabah, Malaysia, May 16-19, 1995.

Singh, V.. 1996. Diversity in Mountain Agriculture. *ILEIA Newsletter*, January-March.

Singh, V. 1997. *Draught Animal Power in Sustainable Development of Mountain Agriculture: A Study of Perspectives and Issues in Central Himalaya, India*, Kathmandu: ICIMOD.

Singh, V. and I. Dankelman. 1993. "Energy Audit of Apple Cultivation", In: Rajwar, G.S. (ed.) *Garhwal Himalaya: Ecology and Environment*, New Delhi:Ashish Publishers, 153-170.

Singh, V., R.J. Sharma and A. Kumar. "Perspectives on the Utilisation of Forest Fodders in the Himalaya, In: Singh, V., R.J. Sharma and A. Kumar (eds.) *Ecological Carnage in the Himalaya*, Dehradun: IBD.

Troll, Carl. 1988. "Comparative Geography of High Mountains of the World in View of Land Scale Ecology: A Development of Three and a Half Decade of Research and Organisation", In: Allan, N.J.R., G.W. Knapp and C. Stadel (eds.) *Human Impacts on Mountains*. New Jersey: Rowman & Littlefield.

Vavilov, N.I. 1951. "The Origin, Variation, Immunity, and Breeding of Cultivated Plants". *Chronica Botanica* 13: 1-364.

25 Ecotourism in Sikkim: Contributions toward Conservation of Biodiversity Resources

Eklabya Sharma, Nandita Jain, S.C. Rai and **Renzino Lepcha**

1. Introduction

Tourism has become the most important civil industry in the world. Its contribution to the Global Gross Domestic Product (GGDP) is about 10 per cent involving nearly 7 per cent of the workforce to make it the world's largest creator of jobs. The total global capital investments (10.7 per cent), worldwide consumer spending (10.9 per cent), and the world's international trade in goods and services (6.8 per cent) make tourism one of the three top categories of trade (WTTC 1995). Understanding its high multiplier effect, the governments around the world are taking more proactive roles to attract more tourists, recognizing tourism as an effective tool for economic diversification where traditional industries are failing and as a source of foreign exchange earnings and better employment opportunities. World Travel and Tourism Council (WTTC) says that tourism earnings by 2005 AD will be double its current gross income and generate 90 per cent more jobs. Its capital investment is expected to increase three-fold to US$ 1.7 trillion, and attract more than twice the current level of consumer spending amounting to US$ 4.6 trillion.

For a number of developing countries their natural environments continue to be a source of significant economic benefits, attracting international and domestic visitors often in search of an authentic natural and, to a lesser degree, cultural experience. Detailed information on the numbers of visitors visiting natural areas and the amount of resultant economic activity in the developing countries is both difficult to obtain and often unreliable. Tourism associated with natural and protected areas has been and continues to be a growing sector in the global tourism industry (Whelan 1991, Brandon 1996). Of the estimated $55 billion in tourism receipts in the Third World, a significant portion of this in the early 1990s was the result of nature tourism activities (Whelan, 1991). Although not always concerned with protected areas, it is estimated that annual global expenditure on adventure-related travel amount to $110 billion (Adventure Travel Society 1998). Conservative estimates of the growth in demand for nature-related tourism range from 10 to 15 per cent while more optimistic forecasts go up to 30 per cent (Brandon 1996), the variation due primarily to differences in the definition of the types of tourism included. Although difficult to generalize, for many developing countries, their natural heritage is a primary attraction for international visitors and the increasing numbers of domestic tourists.

Associated with the growth of the nature-related travel sector is the notion of ecotourism that the Ecotourism Society (Lindberg and Hawkins 1993) defines as "responsible travel that conserves natural environment and sustains the well-being of people". In other words, ecotourism is the symbolic relationship between tourism and environment which benefits the socio-economic condition of local inhabitants and at the same time promotes tourism and protects the environment. By harbouring environmental awareness both among local people and visitors, and by linking tourism to social and economic development, it is potentially possible to conserve the natural and cultural heritage of an area, and to improve the living standards of host region inhabitants. Ecotourism, if developed responsibly and managed properly, can become a powerful instrument/strategy for the biodiversity conservation. It is a form of tourism that promotes positive tourism-environment linkages, and at the same time, the host regions can take pride in what they have to offer for their people and the tourists.

Tourism development in India, given its federal character, remains a State subject and, therefore, the politics of the States concerned have a greater bearing on the aspects of policy implementation. The Eighth Five Year Plan (1992-97) document of India lays emphasis on tourism sector promotion. The national action plan for tourism development has emphasized enhancing of the socio-economic status of the people, increase in employment opportunities, diversification of the tourism product and preservation of cultural heritage and environment.

The Hindu-Kush Himalayan region is a unique area in the world offering rich biodiversity, culture, socio-economic traditions, history and lifestyles. Since time immemorial lofty mountain ranges of the Himalaya have attracted tourists, pilgrims, naturalists, explorers, trekkers, mountaineers and other various adventure travellers. Tourism as a livelihood option is important next to farming in the Himalayan region. It can play a key role in the development of the remote mountain areas. Development of tourism activities may help in the diversification of the mountain economy, and provide viable alternative livelihood opportunities for the mountain people.

Most of the ecotourism activities in Sikkim are either in protected areas or cultural sites. Protected areas are the State properties where ownership, control and management of resources and claims rest with the government, however, usufructuary rights for tourism purposes are with a variety of users including local entrepreneurs, communities, commercial tour operators (residents and also from outside the area and sometimes region) and government agencies such as the Forest and Tourism Departments. Permits are often issued by the Tourism and Forest Departments of the State Government with the intention of generating revenue and regulating visitor flow. Cultural sites of tourism interest such as monasteries and their sacred forests are under the control of local institutions. There is a unique example of Khecheopalri sacred lake where the legal rights lie with the State Government but the operational rights seem to be with a local institution, viz. Khecheopalri Holy Lake Welfare Committee.

The eastern Himalaya is a recognized global site of high biodiversity value, and is facing growing threats from mass tourism. Sikkim is growing in popularity, and likely to attract increasing numbers of tourists interested in the cultural sites and protected areas of high biodiversity value. Tourism is a highly seasonal activity in the State—October through November and March through June being the two peak seasons. Since income and employment are dependent on the tourist flow, the income earned during the tourist season has to compensate for the lean tourist seasons. The seasonality factor, therefore, makes it more important to link tourism to local production systems.

As concern grows over the loss of natural heritage in the area, it appears this is an ideal time to facilitate ecologically and socially responsible tourism at key destinations to conserve the biological diversity of the area. Therefore a collaborative project of The Mountain Institute and G.B. Pant Institute of Himalayan Environment and Development with other collaborators, namely, the Travel Agents Association of Sikkim (TAAS), the Green Circle and local NGOs with communities is being implemented in the west district of Sikkim. The Government of Sikkim has also played a key role at the various stages of the project implementation. The activities and roles of each stakeholder have been presented in Table 25.1. At the heart of the project are participatory approaches that link enterprise operation with conservation action, while merging traditional cultural practices.

2. Overview of Regional Tourism Development

The tourist visiting the Himalayan region has been growing very fast during recent years. The data on tourist flow in the Himalayan region is not properly recorded and maintained, though its implications and contribution in mountain economy is quite significant. The share of domestic tourism in the

TABLE 25.1: **Role, Responsibilities and Activities of Different Groups in Sikkim Biodiversity and Ecotourism Project**

Activities	Tour Operators	Community/NGOs	Government	TMI	GBPIHED
Role	To cover issues of conservation, policy and infrastructure development and management of Tourism industry. TAAS/PTDA as key agencies	Preservation of natural and cultural heritage. Local stakeholders use natural resources. KCC is local NGO	Government of Sikkim responsible for policy formulation and resource control and management	Dedicated to conserve mountain environment and cultural heritage through education, conservation and development working with the community. To develop participatory and scientific monitoring	Focal Institute to advance scientific knowledge to evolve and demonstrate integrated management strategies for resource and sustainable development. To develop participatory and scientific monitoring, and pursue applied research
Activities/Responsibilities					
Product and site enhancement	Fuel-wood reduction, trekking hut, garbage, litter and sanitation management, health and safety measures	Community forest management, conservation education and village beautification	Infrastructure development and promotion of health and safety measures	Enterprise destination enhancement	Technical input in choice of species and planting techniques
Entrepreneurial skills and product development	Trekking staff training, new product development	Study tours for guides, lodge management, promotion of local food, micro-enterprise development	Tourism Departments participation in training	Training inputs and organization	Green house vegetable production, composting and indigenous food promotion
Ecotourism marketing	Market trend survey to design and implement marketing strategies	Help in implementation of tourism promotion activities	Quality tourism development	Provide international experts	Provide local experts, study tours and workshop

(Contd.)

TABLE 25.1 *(Contd.)*

Activities	Tour Operators	Community/NGOs	Government	TMI	GBPIHED
Planning, monitoring and applied research	Policy review, business survey and participatory monitoring	Community resource management	Policy review and implementation	Policy workshop	Participatory, biological, socio-economic and enterprise monitoring
Biodiversity preservation	Threatened habitats and areas are not exposed to tourists	Avoid disturbance and negative impact to wildlife	Signboard about vulnerable species and implement law	Plan activities with no negative impact	Carry out impact studies and monitoring
Cultural preservation	Trekking staff to inform visitors about culture and values	To be aware and feel pride about culture and tradition	Cultural site planning for tourism	Support in managing cultural sites and museums	Support in the management of cultural sites

TAAS—Travel Agents Association of Sikkim; PTDA—Pelling Tourism Development Association; KCC—Khangchendzonga Conservation Committee; TMI—The Mountain Institute; GBPIHED—G.B. Pant Institute of Himalayan Environment & Development.

economy of the region is overwhelming in the total tourist arrivals. The western, central and eastern Himalayan region hosts about 96 per cent domestic tourists of the total visitor flow (AME 1995a, 1995b, Rai and Sundriyal 1997). A similar situation prevails in other parts of the Hindu-Kush Himalayan region. But in smaller economies of the region such as Nepal and Bhutan, the concept of domestic tourism is not properly accounted. The magnitude of tourist flow may testify to the increasing economic importance of tourism. This sector contributes about Rs. 200 to 250 crores annually to the economy of Himachal Pradesh. Similar values for the U.P. hills were Rs. 250 to 275 crores and for Sikkim about 5 crores (AME 1995a, 1995b, Rai and Sundriyal 1997). There is a general perception that the majority of the tourists come for recreation (about 60 to 80 per cent). But in the case of U.P. hills, there is a predominance of pilgrimage (60 per cent). Now ecotourism has emerged as an important activity in the Himalayan region which includes trekking, mountaineering, river rafting and other nature-oriented activities.

The number of tourists in Sikkim has been showing an increasing trend from 1980 onwards. Until 1980, the State hosted only about 1,000 visitors, which eventually increased to more than ten times by 1997 (Fig. 24.1) which constitute 0.3 per cent of the total tourist arrivals in the country. It is expected that by the end of this century it may reach about half a million (Rai and Sundriyal 1997). There has been a tremendous increase in the number of international tourists coming to Sikkim during the period 1990 to 1997 comprising the following nationalities: UK (14 per cent), Germany (13 per cent), France (10 per cent), USA (9 per cent), Japan (6 per cent) and Switzerland (5 per cent). The majority of domestic tourist arrivals are from West Bengal (65 per cent) (Rai and Sundriyal 1997). Although Sikkim has gained popularity in recent years as a prime mountain destination for nature lovers, there exists considerable competition with similar sites in Nepal and Bhutan.

3. Components of Ecotourism and Conservation

The Sikkim Biodiversity and Ecotourism Project focuses its work in three key areas that link conservation with ecotourism enterprises. As part of a strategy of biodiversity conservation, the project has sought to increase stakeholder participation in tourism development and natural resource conservation through activities in the following areas. The working hypothesis is that if income generation is dependent on the continued availability of biodiversity as is the case with certain tourism activities in Sikkim, then those entrepreneurs and stakeholders will have to act upon economic incentives to conserve the resources (protected areas and other natural features) on which income depends.

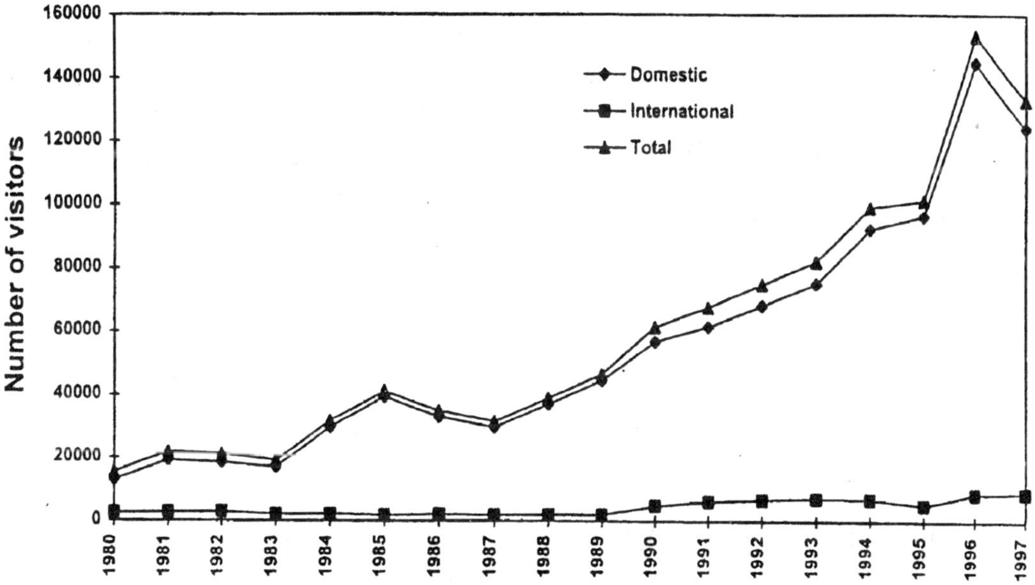

Fig. 25.1: The Number of Domestic and Foreign Tourists in Sikkim during 1980-1997

Increasing Community and Private Sector Biodiversity Conservation Initiatives

Activities include:

— Community ecotourism plans covering site-enhancement, and trail and site maintenance.
— Natural resource management and monitoring and conservation education.
— Supporting fuel-wood reduction measures by trek operators and local lodges.
— Supporting local NGOs working in ecotourism and conservation.

Increasing Economic Returns from Community-based and TAAS Ecotourism

Activities include :

— Training in ecotourism services, e.g. for guides, lodge-owners, cooks, porters.
— Supporting new community ecotourism enterprises, i.e vegetable growing indigenous food promotion, fuel-wood saving equipment hire for treks.

— Developing marketing strategies for community-based ecotourism and TAAS ecotourism activities.
— Conducting market research and developing new ecotourism products, e.g. off-season activities, and indigenous food products.

Improving and Contributing to Policy-making on Conservation and Ecotourism

Activities include :

— Scientific and participatory monitoring of project activities and impacts.
— Applied research on conservation and ecotourism.
— Sharing of research and monitoring findings among policy-makers, communities and the private sectors.
— Promoting public-private sector dialogue through workshops, exchanges and policy review.

4. Project Sites and Approach

Khangchendzonga National Park and the communities residing in the surrounding areas of the protected area in West Sikkim are the focus of the project activity. Within the park are Sikkim's major trekking routes, the Yuksam-Dzongri-Goecha La trail, and exhilarating hikes through dense forests and past impressive mountain views. The forests and alpine meadows are some of the most biologically diverse areas in India, and contain over 36 species of Rhododendrons, 400 species of Orchids and many other flowering plants. The park and surrounding areas also contain a large proportion of the 81 mammals, 300 birds, and 400 butterflies recorded in the State of Sikkim.

The spiritual and physical focus of the area is Khangchendzonga, the world's third highest mountain peak (8,598 m) and revered as the protective deity of Sikkim. At the trailhead is Sikkim's first capital, Yuksam. From Yuksam, visitors can take short walks to several archaeological ruins and to Dubdi, Sikkim's oldest monastery. A number of different groups, including Limbus, Lepchas, Bhutias and Nepalese, as well as Tibetan refugees, live in this culturally and historically rich area. Most pursue traditional agricultural livelihoods, while some have added tourism in recent years. The other project sites include Khecheopalri, one of Sikkim's most sacred and popular lakes, and Pelling, a settlement near Pemayangtse monastery.

4.a. Participatory Ecotourism Planning

Innovation and empowerment through learning and skills development feature strongly in the project. Participants in community ecotourism plans, training courses and conservation management are all using and developing new participatory learning tools that build upon best practices and positive attributes of Sikkim's natural and cultural heritage. A combination of Appreciative Inquiry[1] and modified Participatory Learning and Action (PLA)[2] tools provides the basis for planning, implementing and evaluating community ecotourism activities. Using the same approach, the project is exchanging experience and expertise with mountain people and affiliated projects in Nepal, and other parts of India.

4.b. Community Ecotourism Planning at the Project Sites

A critical element of planning and subsequent actions in ecotourism is a focus on appreciative inquiry; finding and building upon positive attributes and values in local environments and groups of stakeholders. Unlike traditional rural development efforts that incorporate PLA techniques and focus on problem identification and solving, the approach taken in Sikkim asks: "What is that you value in your community and environment, what excites you most about where you live, what is the most positive vision you have of your environment and community in the future, what do we need to do to get to your vision of the future"? The focus is on finding the causes of success and motivation rather than failure as the basis for community planning. PLA tools have been modified to help investigate these questions—trend lines of attributes such as garbage, wildlife, forest cover, etc., are projected to 10-20 year horizons, schematic maps of future community and natural resources status, mapping of current and potential ecotourism resources, ranking of ecotourism attributes, e.g. sites, services, etc. A similar approach is adopted during the evaluation of community conservation and ecotourism activities, when the focus is on "What worked well, and what needs to be improved".

In May, 1996, participatory community ecotourism planning was conducted in Yuksam. The team of five project staff and six local residents worked with local community members to gather information and generate site-specific ideas for linking tourism-related income-generating activities to conservation efforts, with a view to encouraging visitors to extend their stay in the village and conserve natural resources in the area. Local community members felt that the opportunity for increased income generation lay in trying to extend the stay of visitors to the area. On an initial experimental basis, team members used a framework of appreciative inquiry and modified participatory learning techniques to suit the purposes of ecotourism planning.

The critical element of planning and subsequent actions in ecotourism is the focus upon positive attributes and values of local environment. All participants were asked to "Discover" the elements in their environment and community that represent the best of what they are and what they do.

Positive attributes identified by villagers:

— Lots of greenery
— Community unity seen in actions to help others
— Meeting tourists from many different countries
— Fresh air
— Dense forests
— Yuksam is the first capital of Sikkim
— Historical importance of Yuksam

Participants were then asked to "Dream"; to think of what the best vision of Yuksam might be in 10 years time.

What would you like to see in Yuksam 10 years from now:

— More forest cover
— More tourists in Yuksam
— No litter in Yuksam and along the trails
— Local conservation groups or NGOs
— More income from tourism
— Yuksam as a "little Switzerland".

The next phase was to use PLA tools to collect some of the information needed to design a plan for achieving the common dream, one that was inclusive of participants' aspirations, and more focussed on the issue of increasing income from existing tourists.

A preliminary report was prepared by participants and included:

— a listing of environmental and community attributes
— ecotourism resources maps
— local stories about sites and history
— maps and analyses of the availability and use of forest resources
— socio-economic analyses of tourism benefits.

The final step was to identify actions to be taken in the next three to six months that would start to deliver the vision. Thus, in addition to the report, specific outputs from the planning exercise included a set of actions to be undertaken in the following four to six months including:

— village beautification activities, e.g. planting of native tree species, clean-up campaigns.
— training courses for lodge-operators, naturalist guides.
— collection of material to be used for a promotional brochure about Yuksam and its attractions.

In addition to the activities identified in May, in October, 1996, 28 village members organized their own clean-up campaign of the major trekking route, generating a small initial amount of funds for further activities through recycling bottles and tins.

In December, 1996, a participatory evaluation of activities since May was conducted and a plan developed for 1997. In addition to the use of PLA tools such as pair-wise ranking, and standard ranking to assess activities, narrated stories of community action in conservation were also documented. Yuksam residents have readily accepted the principle of local contributions to project activities and enthusiastically attended the training courses, as well as showed a keen interest in enterprises such as low-cost covered vegetable production. As a result of the lodge-operators training, participants have developed an agreed tariff and standardized menus. Operators now maintain visitor registers and issue receipts to customers. Community-wide events connected with income-generation through extended visits, such as clean-ups and afforestation, were particularly well attended.

Based on the evaluation, local community members and project staff also prepared an action plan for 1997 using tools and outputs such as mapping and future maps of the village as the framework for designing and deciding activities. The final plan outlined activities, responsibilities, dates and indicators of success.

A critical element developed by village participants during the use of the methodology was the commitment to an action during the planning exercise itself, demonstrating as the villagers say themselves "that we go beyond talk and can do something". In the first exercise it was a clean-up of the village by teachers, school children and other villagers. In the second session, villagers committed to raise funds for garbage management and visitor education. By March, 1996, three signboards and six garbage bins could be found in Yuksam.

Community-identified activities for 1997 included:

— Garbage management in the village and along the trail
— Trail repair by local residents
— Plantation work and management
— Training for porters, lodge-operators, guides, pack animal operators, trek cooks
— Conservation education of visitors and residents
— Completion of the Yuksam promotional brochure

Other results of community ecotourism planning in Yuksam:

— During May to December, 1996, a series of project and other events catalysed community members to form a local conservation organization, the Khangchendzonga Conservation Committee (KCC).

KCC has developed a Code of Conduct for visitors to follow in the area. Signboards with the code and paid for by KCC have been erected in Yuksam, and visitors now receive a copy of the code at the lodges.

— Yuksam community members participated as resource persons for a community ecotourism planning effort at nearby Khecheopalri Lake.

5. Participatory Conservation Practices

Despite all the claims of good governance and sustainable management, it is clear that the tremendous growth of nature-based tourism has not been matched by official efforts to adequately plan, implement and monitor developments through an administrative and legal mechanism. A critical element developed by the community participants during participatory planning was conservation-related activities, viz. clean-up campaign, site beautification and tree plantation in and around their village. In the first phase a local clean-up of the village was done by school teachers, children, community members and the project staff while during the second phase, villagers proposed to raise funds for garbage management and environmental awareness drive for visitors as well as for the community members. In the ensuing next three months, three signboards and six garbage bins were placed at strategic locations with the assistance from the project and initiated by the Khangchendzonga Conservation Committee (KCC), a village-based NGO. The positive reaction generated among the village community members was evident as shopkeepers and Sunday market hawkers collected their trash and burned all the refuse. The shops have been advised to minimize the use of plastic bags, mineral water bottles and to keep trash bins for collection of garbage. In addition to the activities identified by the local community members, the Khangchendzonga Conservation Committee organized their own clean-up campaign of the major trekking route, generating an initial fund for further activities through the sale of bottle and tins collected during the clean-up campaign (Table 25.2).

TABLE 25.2: **Participation of Local Communities in Conservation Related Activities**

Activities	Place	Total participants
Clean-up campaign	Yuksam	105
Tree plantation	Yuksam	114
Clean-up campaign	Yuksam-Dzongri trekking trail	26
Tree plantation	Khecheopalri lake	17
Tree plantation	Yuksam lake	22

In order to beautify the surrounding locality, indigenous fruit and flower-bearing species were sorted out and planted with the active participation of schoolchildren and the village community. The choice of the species was participatory. Such an afforestation programme was successfully carried out on a number of occasions at different places of the project site. Through the initiative of the community-based NGO, KCC, the department of tourism provided cast-iron benches which were placed in different locations for the convenience of the visitors. At Tsokha, located at 3,040 m along the trekking trail, the village community contributed significantly in constructing a toilet, mainly for the porters and trekking support staff.

These activities which were initially triggered off by the project have been readily accepted and appreciated by the local community. These actions over time are slowly being adopted and carried out by some enthusiastic village people and KCC is playing a leading role with the active support from the Panchayat. The evaluation of these activities that were done annually reflected the pride taken by the local people and ensured their continuity.

6. Skill Development Training Programme

Ecotourism programmes are based on tourism management plans developed in consultation with the local people. The community identified the different training programmes and these were designed at the project sites with inputs from different stakeholder groups. Some of the major training imparted by the project to the local people and the operators were naturalist guides training, lodge operation, trek cooks and porters and ecotourism product marketing exclusively for the operators.

The Sikkim Biodiversity and Ecotourism (SBE) project has organized training programmes in the field of skill development since 1996 (Table 24.3). On every occasion, a nominal registration fee was charged to ensure full-time and meaningful participation. The naturalist guides training curriculum included map reading, first aid, guiding techniques, fuel-wood reduction, and environmental awareness.

The porters' training highlighted the responsible role played by the porters in trekking and mountaineering and how they could significantly contribute to conservation by observing and practising. The impact of the porters' training was quite significant as the porters adopted responsible practices and earned recognition by the government, tourists and different stakeholders. In a particular incident, a porter-cum-guide refused to collect firewood for a group of trekkers up in the mountains. He was a trained person and hence his conservation effort was later appreciated and highlighted in the national papers. This example of conservation effort being made at the project sites has been exemplary.

TABLE 25.3: **Skill Development Training Programme**

Training type	Duration (day)	Participants		
		Male	Female	Total
Porters	2	120	4	124
Cooks	8	31	4	35
Trek cooks	4	20	-	20
Lodge operators	7	26	14	40
Green vegetable production	4	7	2	9
Seed production and vegetable growing	4	13	10	23
Naturalist guide	6	17	2	19
TAAS guide	4	11	2	13
TAAS marketing course	2	13	3	16
Institutional strengthening	2	6	4	10

Trek cooks' training emphasizes menu planning, incorporation of indigenous food in the trekking menu, use of alternative fuel, safety, hygiene and sanitation. Lodge operators were trained in house-keeping, managing the accounts, menu planning, use of alternative fuel for heating and cooking purposes, hygiene and sanitation and preparation of local cuisine. To boost the local economy of the farmers, poly-house technology, bio-composting and vegetable seed production training was imparted. In one case a farmer exhibited an outstanding performance and produced vegetable seeds of indigenous mountain varieties and was running a successful enterprise. The local Panchayat recognizing the effort and success of this farmer has engaged him as a resource person for informal night school teaching.

7. Study Tours and Exchanges

Study tours and exchanges have been a very effective means of learning the positive and negative impacts of tourism and protected area management. The project was able to organize several such tours within and outside Sikkim for different levels of stakeholders. One such tour for the vegetable growers was organized at St. Alphonsus Social and Agriculture Centre at Kurseong, where the farmers were exposed to poly-bed vegetable growing technique and farm-based resource composting apart from piggery, poultry, cattle rearing and bio-gas production. This exposure trip boosted the enthusiasm and knowledge of the farmers who later successfully adopted some of the above techniques. The farm produce would basically cater to the requirements of the tourists at the project sites.

To understand the various impacts of tourism on mountain environments, to learn about the cultural and traditional practices of a similar site in Nepal, a mixed group of community participants from Sikkim was taken to Langtang, Nepal. This trip was successful as the participants could learn how the people of Langtang had devised mechanisms for conservation of their natural and cultural resources. It was not only learning from the Nepal experience but also exchanging the expertise developed in Sikkim in vegetable growing and bio-composting which was appropriate at higher altitudes in Langtang.

A policy-level study tour was organized in early 1998 to Buxa Tiger Reserve and Royal Chitwan National Park in Nepal where the group comprised government officials from the Planning and Tourism Departments, the private sector and community members. This was an opportunity to learn about conservation and tourism-related issues in and around the protected areas. The visit provided an excellent opportunity for interaction among the participants to learn about community forest management for ecotourism purposes and to meet the natural resource requirements of the people. During the tour different issues on tourism and protected area management were looked into for the possibility of their incorporation into the management of the Khangchendzonga National Park in Sikkim.

As part of the projects' objective to increase income from responsible ecotourism, the trade association of Sikkim, Travel Agents Association of Sikkim (TAAS) was encouraged to build links with an equivalent association in Nepal, the Trekking Agents Association of Nepal (TAAN). Two reciprocal visits were organized for TAAN and TAAS where on both occasions workshops were held on mountain tourism management which culminated in signing of an MOU between the two associations on cooperation and collaboration on ecotourism.

8. Tourism Policy and Monitoring

For the first time in Sikkim the project created a common platform for a private and public sector dialogue on tourism and biodiversity conservation. The sectoral approach of different departments was inadequate in addressing the management aspect in a holistic manner. The various private sector stakeholders who were engaged in tourism operation had their own problems and expected incentives from the government. Occasion did not exist for the public and private sector stakeholders in tourism to sit together and discuss matters of concern, which would be beneficial in the long term for both.

The above two prime stakeholder groups were involved by the project right from the planning phase of the project since April, 1995. The local community, which is an integral component of ecotourism development, had a limited approach with the government, but this was significantly strengthened during the implementation of the project. In due course of time the local community-based conservation group KCC has been empowered by various agencies to monitor and implement conservation activities. The monitoring skills of KCC have been strengthened by the project through continuous interaction and presentations.

It was fortunate that the master plan for tourism development in Sikkim was in its conceptual stage during the project inception and thereby over time the project provided meaningful inputs and played an important role in its formulation. Workshops and meetings have increased the level of public and private sector interaction and awareness of tourism and conservation-related issues. The State Government has incorporated some of the policy issues in the master plan addressed by the project.

The project developed a strong biological and participatory monitoring plan. In the biological monitoring, a comprehensive applied research has been incorporated to monitor the impact of tourism on biological resources and ecosystem functioning. Khecheopalri, a sacred lake with a surrounding watershed, is monitored for its longevity in terms of its health. Constant fuel-wood removal at various points along the trekking Yuksam-Dzongri trail has degraded the forests changing the habitat that is monitored for vegetation type, structure, species regeneration, and bird and butterfly richness. The impact of tourism specially on the camping sites and high-altitude pastures by pack animals is extensive. The monitoring of apline meadows and various campsites for the impact of grazing has been established for looking into the carrying capacity and vegetation composition. One of the monitoring aspects is to analyze and look into the benefits from ecotourism services available to the local community by their involvement in different tourism-related activities. The internal project monitoring and the evaluation by the donors have been a constant feature of the project.

Conservation requires a range of interventions, and while the enterprise approach will be a key component of future programmes in Sikkim, it will not necessarily be the only one. For entrepreneurs to undertake and continue conservation actions that support their livelihoods, it seems critical that they have some level of decision-making power over the resources in question. It appears that unless this is possible, economic benefits from an enterprise are unlikely to be effective as incentives to conserve.

In Sikkim, there was little decision-making power over natural resources among the range of entrepreneurs participating in the project, and thus there would seem a little chance of economic incentives turning into actions to conserve biodiversity on which tourism depends.

However, for the project, the value of the enterprise-based approach to conservation in Sikkim, especially tourism, lies in introducing the concept as part of a long-term strategy to support conservation and one that implies greater participation by key stakeholders in natural resource management. In Sikkim, the natural resources have for the most part been managed by the State Government with permits and rights for subsistence extraction given by State departments. Little exists in the way of community management of forests. But, by engaging stakeholders in a debate over the value of biodiversity in the State economy and the most efficient way this can be conserved, local stakeholders at the project sites are now participating in the on-going discussions over how biodiversity conservation can be conducted. The traditional decision-makers, such as government, are now increasingly highlighting the important role that local institutions can play. This shift in approach is based, in a large part, on the success of the project in supporting local organizations to take action in local conservation efforts, and also is the result of project efforts to facilitate stakeholder dialogue where such issues have been debated.

The experience in Sikkim suggests that agencies and organizations perceived to be neutral are most successful in promoting and engaging stakeholders in an open debate over who manages natural resources. If these are not present, then it seems that the dialogue is not always productive. In the case of Sikkim, the most important feature of the enterprise-based approach was to provide a framework in which to analyze and develop the potential of tourism for more than one type of stakeholder. Furthermore, it provided a means to argue that long-term benefits from tourism would be possible only if those whose income depended on the activity had a greater decision-making power in natural resource management.

As part of an approach to biodiversity conservation, ecotourism, defined as environmentally and socially responsible tourism, clearly has a role to play in India. As the numbers of visitors both domestic and international increase, the need to be proactive on promoting and supporting a responsible tourism ethic among consumers, suppliers and producers alike is imperative. The Sikkim Biodiversity and Ecotourism Project has shown that collaboration between public and private sectors, as well as local communities, and a participatory design can produce results that contribute to conserving biodiversity assets that are of global significance.

9. Acknowledgements

The authors are grateful to the G.B. Pant Institute of Himalayan Environment and Development and The Mountain Institute. The authors were associated with the Sikkim Biodiversity and Ecotourism Project which received support from the collaborating institutions and communities, donations and grants obtained from the United States Agency for International Development including support from the Biodiversity Conservation Network (a programme of the Biodiversity Support Programme, a consortium of World Wildlife Fund, the Nature Conservancy and the World Resources Institute), and the Bureau of Humanitarian Response.

NOTES

1. Appreciative Inquiry is an approach to the field of Organizational Development. Useful initial introductions to the approach can be found in OD Practitioner, 1996, Vol. 28, and in Cooperrider, D.L., (1990) *Positive Image, Positive Action: The Affirmative Basis of Organizing*, in Srivastava, S., D.L. Cooperrider and Associates, (eds.) *Appreciative Management and Leadership*. Jossey-Bass, San Francisco.
2. Participatory Learning and Action attempts to go beyond Participatory Rural Appraisal (PRA) into planning for action and evaluation by participants. For more details, contact International Institute of Environment and Development, Sustainable Agriculture, 3 Endsleigh St., London WCI, UK.

REFERENCES

Academy for Mountain Environics. 1995a. *Mountain Tourism in Himachal Pradesh and the Hill Districts of Uttar Pradesh: An Overview*. MEI Discussion paper series 95/6, Kathmandu: ICIMOD.

Academy for Mountain Environics. 1995b. *Mountain Tourism for Local Community Development, Report on Case Studies in Kinnaur District, H.P. and Badrinath Tourist Zone, U.P.*, MEI Discussion paper series 95/13, Kathmandu: ICIMOD.

Adventure Travel Society. 1998. Press Release—Adventure Travel Congress, Colorado.

Brandon, K. 1996. "Ecotourism and Conservation: A Review of Key Issues", Environment Department Papers, No. 33, Washington D.C.: The World Bank.

Lindberg, K. and D.E. Hawkins (eds.). 1993. "Ecotourism: A Guide for Planners and Managers", North Bennington VT., The Ecotourism Society.

Rai, S.C. and R.C. Sundriyal. 1997. "Tourism and Biodiversity Conservation: The Sikkim Himalaya", *Ambio*, Volume 26, Issue 4, pp. 235-42.

Whelan, T. (ed.). 1991. *Nature Tourism: Managing for the Environment*, Island Press, Washington D.C., USA, xii+223 pp.

World Travel and Tourism Council. 1995. *Travel and Tourism's Economic Perspective*, Brussels: WTTC.

26 Nature Conservation Areas: Who Will Protect Them ?[1]

Ashish Kothari

1. The Crisis

1.a. Introduction

India's biodiversity is mostly contained in its vast common property resources, viz. forests, wetlands, coastal and marine areas, grasslands, and other habitats that are under the control of government agencies or village bodies. For the past few decades, legal and administrative protection to these ecosystems and to notified animal and plant species has been the main strategy for biodiversity conservation in India. The declaration of national parks, sanctuaries, and other categories of protected areas (PAs) under the Wild Life (Protection) Act, 1972, has resulted in protecting a large number of areas from certain destruction by commercial, industrial, or biotic forces. Legal protection against hunting and capture, given under the same Act to listed species, has also helped to safeguard threatened and rare species. Related legislation like the Forest (Conservation) Act has also helped to curb diversion of natural habitats for non-conservation purposes.

But increasingly, chinks in the armour of this strategy are being exposed. Public and political support for conservation is falling everywhere, State Governments are trigger-happy about sacrificing notified protected areas for so-called developmental activities, illegal hunting and tree-felling has been hard to curb in many areas, and conflicts between wildlife officials and local people living in and around PAs are getting more common. Several species, whose existence had been relatively well secured over the past 2-3 decades, are once again facing the threat of extinction. It is clear that unless there are significant attempts to respond to such issues, including changes in the policy and legal direction of conservation, wildlife and biodiversity will remain in deep trouble.

A centralized, bureaucracy-dominated approach to conservation is doomed to failure in the new circumstances that India finds itself in. Firstly, new macro-economic policies, responding to the globalization process that is sweeping the world, are essentially in contradiction to conservation and sustainable use of natural resources. The same government which declares a PA is now willing to sacrifice it at the altar of "development" and "economic growth". Second, a new political dynamic has empowered State parties and governments much more than before, and the Central Government is unable to wield its environmental clout as before. Third, government controls are generally loosening under the impact of the private corporate sector, both domestic and foreign, which has far more clout to influence policies now than just a few years ago. Fourth, local communities everywhere are no longer willing to take things lying down; they want, and rightly so, a voice in making the decisions that affect their lives. This relates as much to top-down development processes as to conservation measures taken by governments. Privatization and decentralization are powerful forces, and they militate against the form of centralized control that conservation and natural resource management has enjoyed over the last century or so.

The conservation movement has yet to organize itself to respond to these new challenges. In a sense, this failure has a lot to do with history: in the past, urban conservationists found favour with a tiny section of the political elite which was sympathetic to wildlife conservation, and able to wield power with State governments. However, little attempt was made to broad-base the movement, so that when the political support at the top ended, conservationists were suddenly left out in the cold.

The differing ways of looking at the same natural ecosystem. . . as wildlife habitat, as industrial raw material, as survival base for rural people, as catchment. . . have led to the inevitable question: whose resources are such ecosystems and their wildlife? Many would argue, with some justification, that the first right on these areas belongs to the wild inhabitants themselves, for they preceded humans on the scale of time, and are heavily dependent on such ecosystems. The question is, however: who amongst humans will help them to obtain and maintain such a right? Surely not a handful of elites for whom it is a burning commitment, but who are simply too insignificant to matter in the larger processes of their countries, and who will never have the resources to do the task?

The only thing that can save the conservation movement, and make it effective, is to move away from its elitist base to a much broader base of local community members, academics, NGOs, and sensitive government officers. Together, these constituents can defeat the destructive forces engulfing natural habitats; divided, they will be powerless against (or even support) these forces.[2]

1.b. Ignoring People's Needs, Rights and Knowledge

Conventional conservation policies and programmes in India have been characterized by an amazing ignorance or deliberate neglect of the integral relationship between rural communities and natural habitats. The majority of the country's population still depends *directly* on natural resources. This is even more true of PAs than elsewhere, for the simple reason that they are predominantly inhabited by highly ecosystem-dependent people. A study by the Indian Institute of Public Administration in the mid and late 1980s revealed that 69 per cent of surveyed PAs had human population living *inside*, and 64 per cent had rights, leases, or concessions. to extract fuel and fodder, to graze, or to carry out other activities (Kothari *et al.* 1989). The situation has not substantially changed, since in the past decade or so not so many people have been moved out of PAs, nor have so many adjacent communities been provided alternatives. A rough extrapolation of the same data suggests that there are at least three million people living *inside* PAs, and several million more using them from adjacent settlements. Official policy never came to grips with this reality, with the result that legal and administrative structures of restriction and denial of access to resources were imposed on every area which became a PA. While actual displacement of communities has fortunately not been very prevalent, curtailment of rights to resources has been commonplace. Simultaneously, restrictions on hunting (perhaps usually justified from the conservation point of view) have denied communities a means of self-defence against wild animals which attack livestock or humans and damage crops.

Short-sighted was the neglect of the enormous knowledge of ecosystems and wildlife that India's local communities had, and in many cases still have. This knowledge and the associated practices of prudent resource use and conservation have been documented by several people (Gadgil, Berkes and Folke 1993, Sen 1992, Deeney and Fernandes 1992, Gokhale *et al.* 1997, Ramakrishnan 1998). Even where pieces of traditional knowledge were used in conservation programmes (as is often done by sensitive officers), the community as a whole continued to be alienated from its natural context (see, e.g. Baviskar 1998). Almost never were community members (even the much-celebrated Bishnois, or the Irulas, or other communities which official wildlife pamphlets pay lip-service to) asked to be in any decision-making or planning capacity.

The result of the above aspects of conservation strategy has been the following:

1. Communities, even those which continued to practise sustainable or conservationist resource use, were increasingly alienated from natural habitats, resulting in a break-down of traditional practices, erosion of

knowledge, and loss of the desire to protect resources from degradation (the "why should we protect *sarkari* tigers?" syndrome).

2. Hostility towards official conservation efforts and officials, manifested in a range of responses including non-cooperation (e.g. during a fire incidence or illegal timber cutting incidents); outright violence against officials (e.g. against the former director of the Ranthambhor Tiger Reserve, Shri Fateh Singh Rathore); deliberate destruction (including poaching and setting fire to forests); undermining of regulations by obtaining political and other patronage (Saberwal 1998); and demands for denotification of PAs.

What is particularly tragic is that conventional conservation dogma has not even been based, often, on sound scientific grounding. Evidence from various parts of the world suggests that limited human use may not only be possible to absorb within ecosystems, but that in many cases it may enhance local biodiversity levels; and indeed that many of the so-called "pristine" wildlife habitats that we want to preserve in their "virgin" character (the Amazonian forests, the American prairies, the African savannah, freshwater wetlands in India) actually owe their current levels of diversity *partly* to a long history of human use (Gomez-Pompa and Kaus 1992, Bush and Colinvaux 1994, Adams and McShane 1992, Arhem 1985, Saberwal 1996), and further, that stoppage of human activities (including grazing and fire) from such ecosystems could actually reduce biodiversity levels and even make the habitat worse for the species sought to be conserved (Ali and Vijayan 1986, Vijayan 1991, Naithani *et al.* 1992, Pandey and Singh 1992, all citing cases from India). It would of course be dangerous and foolish to extrapolate from these examples and suggest that all human use is compatible with biodiversity conservation, but surely they do indicate that a blanket policy either way is unscientific and potentially detrimental to conservation objectives.

1.c. Conflicts and Cooperation

The current conservation scenario is confusing in its complexity, making any generalizations hazardous. For example,

— In some areas, local villagers/communities are totally rejecting the official concept of PAs and consequently are even willing to sacrifice the forests and wildlife for immediate gains. In the Narayan Sarovar Sanctuary of Gujarat (western India), many villagers have welcomed the recent denotification of the sanctuary to make way for a cement factory. This phenomenon has received a major boost due to the recent haphazard and insensitive processes of settlement of rights that have been launched in all States, as a result of a Supreme Court order in a case that WWF-India is fighting. In Udaipur district, a *sarpanch* has filed a case asking for the denotification of the Phulwari-ki-Naal Sanctuary, arguing that the settlement process is violative of his rights.

— Commercial forces are invariably very strong and often influence industrial States to reverse their own conservation measures. In 1991, the government of the Himalayan State of Himachal Pradesh denotified the Darlaghat Sanctuary to make way for a cement factory; the same purpose drove Gujarat to denotify the Narayan Sarovar Sanctuary in coastal Kutch. In 1994, Karnataka gave fresh mineral prospecting leases inside the evergreen forest habitat of the Kudremukh National Park.

— In many areas, local people on their own or sometimes with the help of sympathetic forest officers or NGOs are struggling to conserve these areas. In Sariska Tiger Reserve in Rajasthan, villagers have fought against mining, using the help of forest officials and the Wild Life (Protection) Act and going all the way to the Supreme Court to seek redressal. Inhabitants of two villages in the Alwar district of Rajasthan have declared several hectares of forest as the Bhairodev Dakan "Sonchuri", and promulgated their own set of rules and regulations which allow no hunting (Shrestg, in press).

— At several places, bold forest officers and NGOs are also standing in the way of destructive commercial interests. For example, at the Radhanagari Sanctuary, part of the evergreen forests of Maharashtra, when local forest officers dug up the road leading to a proposed mining site, local NGOs campaigned to get the mining lease cancelled, and a Bombay-based NGO obtained a stay order on further mining.

— Many governments, or individual officers, are realizing that either the survival needs of communities must be allowed to be met from PAs, or acceptable alternatives must be provided in place. In Uttar Pradesh, a government order has made it possible for villagers around the Rajaji National Park to once again legitimately collect *bhubbar* grass for rope-making (though the Park management has not been so forthcoming in implementing this).

While some of these examples show continuation of serious conflicts, others show the existence of significant opportunities for more effective conservation in the future. There are many instances of conflicts being resolved, dialogues opening up new partnerships, communities protecting habitats on their own steam or with support from officials, forest officers entering into informal arrangements with communities for conservation and access to livelihood resources, and so on.

1.d. Ecodevelopment: Is it an Adequate Response?

In the last few years, realization of the impossibility of saving wildlife in the midst of hostile and dispossessed humans has grown considerably. Perhaps the single most ambitious official response has been *ecodevelopment*. Advocated as a strategy even as far back as the National Wildlife Action Plan (1983), ecodevelopment aims at providing alternative livelihood options to villagers, thereby weaning them away from dependence on natural ecosystems. Typical ecodevelopment inputs include employment opportunities like dairying, horticulture, handicrafts, etc., energy-saving devices such as more efficient stoves, and market linkages such as roads and transportation. A Central Government scheme has disbursed funds for ecodevelopment to various States since 1990; in addition, the World Bank in association with other groups has funded ecodevelopment in several reserves (notably Great Himalayan National Park and Kalakad-Mundantharai Tiger Reserve over the past four years), and approved a large Global Environment Facility (GEF) loan to implement ecodevelopment in another seven PAs.

There is, unfortunately, no systematic account available of the earlier attempts at ecodevelopment. Some NGO accounts suggest that eco-development inputs (pressure cookers, roads, etc.) do not match the requirements of the poorer sections of the villages, and that there is little evidence of the work having benefited the Park (Baviskar 1998). On the other hand, official and donor accounts from some areas suggest that the people's livelihood status in many villages has improved, pressure on the PA has come down, and financial management by village committees has been successful (World Bank n.d., Melkani and Venkatesh 1998).

But while it is undoubtedly a serious effort at tackling the conservation-people conflict, and certainly more people-oriented than conventional conservation programmes, ecodevelopment continues to have the following major weaknesses:

1. Since the major objective remains that of reducing the people's "pressure" on natural habitats, its dominant model is still one of "separation" or "exclusion" rather than "integration" or "inclusion". In other words, ecodevelopment advocates would still much rather alienate local communities from the natural habitats which are sought to be officially protected (giving rise to the risk that their stakes in its conservation may actually go down), rather than find ways of integrating their livelihood needs and their traditional practices into the conservation of the area.
2. It is *not* a model of participatory planning and management of the PA as a whole. Even the new ecodevelopment project, funded by the GEF,

separates the "Improved PA management" component (exclusively carried out by existing bureaucracies) from the "Village ecodevelopment" component (which involves villagers in planning and implementation) (World Bank 1996).

3. It largely limits itself to working within the existing framework of law, essentially the Wild Life Act and related legislation (though some of its proponents do advocate some legal changes). It cannot, therefore, tackle the conflicts that are sometimes created by arbitrary and rigid application of the law.
4. There is very little attempt to build on available local community institutions, knowledge, and practices, even though some conceptual documents related to ecodevelopment suggest this as a part of the strategy. Typically (though not always), the use of traditional knowledge has been restricted to PRA mapping exercises and building up ethnobiological checklists (see, for instance in the case of Great Himalayan National Park, Baviskar 1998).
5. Though the GEF project talks about "leveraging" the inputs (including finances) of other government agencies working in and around the identified PAs, available accounts suggest that this has rarely happened. State governments have not bought the idea, and have, therefore, made little attempt to reorganize their plans and allocations in such a way that all official agencies would cooperate with wildlife officials in providing conservation-oriented developmental inputs.
6. It is not yet clear whether the strategy of diverting the people's pressure by providing alternatives does actually help wildlife conservation. Recent evidence from Integrated Conservation and Development Projects from Indonesia suggests that there is no necessary correlation, and some conservationists have argued that rapid development of the peripheries of PAs could attract many more people from further away to come in, thereby increasing pressure.
7. Finally, and perhaps most important, ecodevelopment does not attempt to reverse the historical process of State take-over of community lands, and the common (though not universal) denial of rights and tenurial security over resources for local people. It has taken the important step of involving the people in planning the development inputs they want, but there is a continued denial of the revival of people's resource rights within and around PAs.

In theory, ecodevelopment could overcome these shortcomings in its future planning. Indeed, World Bank officials or Indian consultants who have been questioned about their support to ecodevelopment have said that the GEF project has built-in processes of self-correction. However, given that many of the above issues require far more planning, organization and re-orientation amongst all stakeholders, it is doubtful that they can be built into a process that is already going ahead full-steam, and where the reigns are still tightly held by the government.

1.e. Towards a New Paradigm

Non-official responses to the crisis facing India's wildlife and the conflicts mentioned above have ranged from an advocacy of more stringent, military-like protection of habitats and species (the "animal rights" lobbyists), to strident voices arguing that the people's rights should prevail over wildlife interests (the "human rights" lobbyists). Somewhere in between these two extremes has been a group of people who argue that both wildlife *and* human rights are critical, and that given appropriate changes in attitude and policies, this can well be achieved.

A series of dialogues and other events over the 1990s have helped considerably to build bridges between hitherto warring factions, and this has been further aided by the perception of a common enemy, the rampant "development" process which bulldozes both natural habitats and local communities. In three successive consultations between wildlife conservationists and social activists (1997 and 1998, at Bhikampura, district Alwar, Rajasthan and 1999, at Bhopal, M.P.), a common declaration was adopted, asserting the need to protect both wildlife and human rights, to oppose forcible displacement in the name of conservation, to protect threatened species even against use in traditional practices, and to use other means to both conserve wildlife and ensure sustainable livelihood rights. The plea for joint or participatory management of PAs was strongly made at these and other meetings, as was the appeal to jointly monitor and check poaching, timber smuggling, encroachment, etc.

2. Resolving the Crisis

If people's participation is indeed part of the answer to the crisis, what is the precise nature of this solution? (para) As a group of people affiliated to the Indian Institute of Public Administration and Kalpavriksh, we have carried out a series of case studies, and been involved in work on the ground, relating to the people's participation in conservation. While case studies have been conducted in India, lessons have also been learnt from other countries of South Asia, and currently we are helping to coordinate field studies in Pakistan, Nepal, Sri Lanka and Bangladesh (Kothari et al. 1997, Kothari et al. 1999). In addition, we have been involved in a series of consultations and workshops mentioned above, and in responding to the periodic crises that natural habitats (including PAs) and resident communities face in various parts of India.

This involvement over the past few years, in addition to the experience of a number of other groups and individuals, has provided a number of critical lessons which need to be heeded in our quest for participatory conservation methods. These lessons are described below.

2.a. Research/Information/Monitoring

Despite decades of existence, India's protected area network and other natural habitats remain considerably understudied. Information on several individual areas (including PAs) and many species, is thus severely lacking, and it is no wonder that management is more often than not piecemeal and haphazardly planned.

There are several specific aspects to this:

(i) A ***historical understanding*** of the area or species to be conserved is needed. This would include assessment of the changes in ecological conditions, land and water use, political and economic relations, legal status, and other parameters, over at least a brief historical period. Both documentary and oral evidence is needed to piece together this picture.

(ii) An ***ecological understanding*** of the area, especially the impacts of various human activities on elements of local biodiversity and on the ecosystem as a whole, is also weak in most areas, especially amongst the managers of PAs. Indeed, on inquiry we have found that the vast majority of management decisions, including those to curb human use, have been made on the basis of assumptions and generalizations, not solid research or evidence from site-specific circumstances. Long-term research has shown these decisions to sometimes be mistakes (e.g the ban on grazing in the Keoladeo National Park; see Ali and Vijayan 1986, Vijayan 1991). Much greater emphasis is needed on ecological assessments.

(iii) The ***indigenous/local community knowledge*** base, where relevant, needs to be built upon in the management of these areas and species, including in the research mentioned above. Even though local communities are rapidly losing their traditions, we have found considerable evidence of the continuation of their knowledge base, especially amongst the elderly members (e.g. in Kailadevi Sanctuary of Rajasthan, Dalma Sanctuary of Bihar, Melghat Tiger Reserve of Maharashtra, tribal and non-tribal communities in many Reserve and Protected Forests of the country, fishing communities in the Andaman and Nicobar Islands, Lakshadweep, and others). Given that we have in our studies only scratched the surface, what is potentially available amongst the villagers is probably quite substantial. This knowledge could be critical in better managing the area, though certainly it alone would not be adequate.

Mutual learning exercises between forest staff, local villagers and NGOs are urgently needed, especially to understand local and other forms of knowledge in their own contexts, and to use these in synergistic ways. Some of this is happening in PRA exercises, however PRA itself has become a caricatured substitute for more deeply participatory and long-term research, which could be self-defeating.

(iv) ***Access to available information*** must be enhanced to all stakeholders. At the Kailadevi Sanctuary (Rajasthan), for instance, we found that even the front (ground) staff of the Forest Department was ignorant about the nature of the massive ecodevelopment plan that had been launched for the PA; and the villagers had simply not heard of it. Moreover, what little information exists for most such areas is often in English or the State language and, therefore, often inaccessible to the local villagers.

Greater networking and sharing of information could be done in various ways, including exchange visits of personnel and community members. Relevant management plans, research reports, and other documents from one conservation area should also be more easily available to another area than is currently the case.

There is also a need for a participatory method of conducting research and investigation, which would yield information which is acceptable to all.

(v) ***Monitoring of ecological and social parameters*** in and around the conservation areas and relating to protected species needs to be instituted as a systematic management activity. It is very weakly developed in India's protected areas (not to speak of other areas of conservation significance), with the exception of the periodic census of some animal species in PAs, some biodiversity monitoring (such as in a few PAs in Maharashtra), and some ecological monitoring in ecosystems outside PAs (e.g. some JFM areas). Even many externally aided ecodevelopment programmes have this weakness; some attempts are being made to plug it in the GEF-funded ecodevelopment project, but it is too early to tell their effectiveness. With an inadequate database, it will in any case be difficult to judge the impact of management and ecodevelopment plans. Such monitoring should assess the impacts of human activities and management strategies on the ecological status of the PA and surrounds, and on the social and economic conditions of the local communities (for example, see Bhatt 1998 and Lele *et al*. 1998). There is also an urgent need for some good qualitative and quantitative indicators (including some that may emerge from local knowledge) to be used, and for simple monitoring procedures with local community involvement to be put into place.

2.b. Institutional Structures

Current centralized, top-heavy institutional structures for conservation of natural habitats and species are clearly unable to fulfil their responsibility for reasons mentioned in Part I above. Changes in this system have already been made with reference to forest lands under JFM (Poffenberger and McGean 1996), or village lands in the case of some ecodevelopment projects (e.g. Kalakad-Mundantharai Tiger Reserve, see World Bank n.d.). However, there is still considerable resistance to such changes in the case of standing forests (especially Reserve Forests), PAs, and protected wetlands or marine areas. Some changes are beginning even here, e.g. the Forest Department has recognized Van Suraksha Samitis in the Kailadevi Sanctuary. Several different aspects of the present conservation effort are striking:

(i) Far more openness is needed in the official system to recognize *existing institutions amongst local communities,* and strengthen them towards meeting the needs of conservation and livelihood security. In the case of the Dalma and Kailadevi Sanctuaries, and in initiatives at Mendha (Lekha) (Maharashtra), Jardhargaon (U.P.), and Bhaonta (Rajasthan), there are extremely innovative structures established by the villagers in the form of Forest Protection Committees, which are obvious candidates for devolving management functions such as patrolling, fire prevention and control, and catching or reporting offenders (Kothari *et al.* 1999). To some extent, the Forest Department appears to recognize this, but it also lacks the flexibility to allow for local variations in the structure and functioning of these bodies. So in Kailadevi, it has started its own Van Suraksha Samitis, which (with a single exception) appear to work less effectively than the villager-initiated Forest Protection Committees (Das 1997).

A potentially powerful opportunity for utilizing local institutions for conservation and resource management is the 73rd Constitutional Amendment related to *panchayati raj* bodies. In particular, the extension of this amendment to Scheduled (tribal) Areas through a specific enactment in 1996 has opened up the possibility of devolving more resource controls to communities while ensuring conservation responsibility and accountability. It is not yet clear how the provisions of these enactments relate to PAs or other government lands such as Reserve Forests (in Maharashtra, for instance, the relevant State legislation has exempted PAs from some clauses such as tribal ownership of "minor forest produce", but certainly they can be used to promote community-based conservation. By the same token, they can also be used by vested interests to subvert conservation programmes, so it would be well worth the while of conservationists to study and utilize its potential before the enemies of wildlife do so.

(ii) To involve people at more than their village scale, there is a need for *institutional structures covering the entire conservation area or substantial parts of it.* At the moment, even where village-level committees have been set up under

JFM or ecodevelopment schemes, the overall management of the conservation unit or protected area remains exclusively in the hands of a government agency, with no formal involvement of the local communities. While an immediate change in such a process may not be feasible, as a first step, advisory bodies comprising various stakeholders should be established for each of these PAs. This proposal has already found partial acceptance in the draft new Wild Life (Protection) Act which is currently under consideration by the Central Government; it provides for advisory bodies in the case of sanctuaries.

Eventually, however, there needs to be a gradual shift towards joint or participatory management institutions, which involve the Forest Department and local communities as equal partners in decision-making and implementation. These would, of course, only be relevant where local communities have a substantial stake in the conservation and/or sustainable use of the area or species in question. We have even suggested such a joint structure for the ongoing procedure of settling the people's rights, which is being urgently and rather haphazardly carried out by State governments (primarily district collectors) under directions from the Supreme Court. It is only through such a participatory process that a fair and sustainable settlement will be worked out.

(iii) Most tricky but absolutely crucial is the need for institutional structures, which could ensure regular *coordination within and amongst the various governmental departments* which have a bearing on the habitats or species sought to be conserved. In all the PAs and other areas studied so far, we found a severe lack of interaction and joint planning between the Forest Department on the one hand, and other government agencies on the other. The serious shortage of water inside the Kailadevi Sanctuary (a severely drought-prone area) must have been common knowledge with the forest staff, yet the district administration appeared unaware of the situation in several villages when we were conducting research in 1997. In Dalma, the Bihar Irrigation Department appeared to have taken decisions (e.g. the alignment of the Subarnarekha canal) without consulting the sanctuary authorities. In the case of many areas, e.g. at Kailadevi, there are also significant complaints of a lack of coordination within the Forest Department itself, between the wildlife wing and the territorial wing.

Indeed, and this applies to the current ecodevelopment project, it is our contention that if all government agencies working in an area were to coordinate their activities according to a regional land/water use plan, within which were nestled areas earmarked for conservation, there would be little need for foreign funding. And if this is not done, conservation will in any case be difficult, as development plans will keep pulling in directions away from those set by the wildlife agencies. Such coordination was for a few years achieved by an enterprising district officer in the case of the Melghat Tiger Reserve (Pardeshi 1996), and in the case of the forests in Harda district by an equally enterprising forest officer (Rathore 1996), so there appears little reason why it cannot be done elsewhere if appropriate orders were to be issued by State governments.

An interesting example from the forests of central India illustrates that, here too the people's empowerment and participation may be one potential key to achieving inter-governmental coordination. In the village of Mendha (Lekha), Gadchiroli district, villagers are so well-organized and self-empowered that they have been able to call all government departments to the village and organize a joint meeting to pool their funds together (Pathak in press).

(iv) A basic problem plaguing India's conservation programmes seems to be the absence of any *institutionalised dialogue* among the various stakeholders, and in particular between wildlife authorities and local communities. What little interaction that exists is strongly one-sided, with the Forest Department being dominant; or else it is confrontationist. The result is that each group is rather misinformed about the other's position and justifications and circumstances.

Regular and open dialogue, with neither side assuming the position of supremacy, could considerably ease tensions between wildlife officials and local communities. This has become clear from the experiments at achieving a more participatory process going on in various places, whether initiated by officials, NGOs, or community members: Rajaji National Park (Rathore 1996), Kalakad-Mundanthurai Tiger Reserve (Melkani and Venkatesh 1998), Kailadevi Sanctuary (Das 1997), Dalma Sanctuary (Christopher 1997), and dozens of JFM areas (Poffenberger and McGean 1996).

(v) The institutional *role of outsiders* (NGOs, government officers other than local conservation authorities, the judiciary) are also often critical. In many areas, local or national NGOs or individuals have been instrumental in mediating between villagers and wildlife officials, gathering data and doing research, helping local communities to organize for their rights, and keeping a watchdog eye on local activities.

Given the important role played by such "outside" parties so far, one question naturally arises: in any process of participatory or joint management, what should the role of these parties be? Should it be in a controlling and decision-making capacity, equivalent to that of the government and the local communities, or should be more advisory? While certain flexibility may be required in deciding on a case by case basis, it is our opinion that *the role of such parties should be mainly advisory and mediatory*. This is because NGOs (as distinct from community-based organizations like the FPCs) have no direct stake in the resources, nor any formal responsibility, nor any formal accountability to anyone. They cannot claim to represent the communities (though they can, and do, act as central supporters), as this would only perpetuate a system in which villagers themselves continue to be sidelined. However, groups or individuals who are very active/knowledgeable may be co-opted onto the overall multi-stakeholder management body (as advocated above).

Caution is also needed against agencies and individuals who have vested interests in continuing conflicts or using local people as covers for exploitative activities.

2.c. Benefit-sharing Mechanisms and Rights

The realization that in the absence of tangible benefits emanating from the protected area, local communities are not likely to become a strong support base for the area, has resulted in the search for innovative mechanisms of generating and sharing the benefits. Perhaps the most powerful stake is the continued and guaranteed access to survival resources, including biomass, as a matter of traditional right and not merely concession by the State. Linked to this is secure tenure over land and other resources; not, however, to unsustainably sell off to the highest bidder, but to assume the responsibility for conservation and sustainable use.

Conservationists have conventionally believed that PAs cannot yield substantial benefits for local people, hence they are unlikely to have the incentive to participate in conservation (e.g. Singh 1996). This view is based on the assumption that (a) biomass resources are the primary benefits that local people require and this is not possible to give since (b) human activities would inevitably degrade ecosystems. Therefore, the conclusion is, protected areas must generally be off-limits to human use. Neither of these assumptions is necessarily valid. As stressed above in Part I, some forms and levels of human use do not cause irreversible damage to biodiversity, and indeed may even locally enhance it, though it would be dangerous and invalid to extrapolate this to all activities and all ecosystems. Moreover, substantial benefits may accrue from non-biomass based use of the PAs, even though biomass resources will remain a major component (for a fuller discussion, see Pathak and Kothari 1998).

Possible benefits that a PA (or natural habitat outside the PA system) can yield include *subsistence* resources (fuel, fodder, non-timber forest produce, timber, and fish/other aquatic produce); *economic/livelihood* gains (forest/aquatic/grassland produce, value enhancement of traditional products, employment, returns from commercial use of local knowledge/resources, tourism revenue, compensation for wildlife damage/opportunities lost, and appropriate development inputs); and *social/cultural/political* benefits (protection of cultural values, social recognition, and empowerment/control).

Many JFM and wetland areas provide adequate proof that a range of biodiversity values can coexist with sustained generation of benefits for local populations.

In our work in the field, some striking features have emerged in relation to benefits:

(i) *Access to regenerating and protected biomass resources* is seen by local people as being critical. In Kailadevi and Dalma, villagers stress this as a traditional benefit; in Rajaji, they are more vocal in arguing that such access should be considered a customary and legally defensible right. In several community-initiated conservation efforts, such access is secured through *de facto* control. The provision of *bhabbar* grass to villagers around Rajaji, by an order of the Chief Wildlife Warden of Uttar Pradesh on May 8, 1995 (Vania 1997), though not amounting to such a right, is nevertheless a welcome step in that it recognizes the need to share the resources of the PA as benefits to local communities. So is the order of June 26, 1996, of the West Bengal Government, under which Ecodevelopment Committees are to be set up for PAs, and resources within the PAs can be shared with villagers in return for conservation functions (Government of West Bengal 1996). Several other states have subsequently passed such orders.

In many areas, conservation actually increases the biological resources (fish, fodder, medicinal plants, etc.) which local communities can harvest, yet sometimes they are not quite aware of this. In the Sunderbans Tiger Reserve, for instance, fish stock in the surrounding areas has reportedly increased due to protection of breeding grounds inside the Reserve. Lack of awareness of such benefits could be simply because they do not have actual access to these regenerating or multiplying resources; or it could be because, though access is available, the connections with the conservation programmes are not evident. This happens, for instance, with the increase in water availability as hydrological cycles improve with conservation of forests. In such situations conservation authorities and NGOs could play a significant role in highlighting the connections, thus also building a stake amongst local communities.

The sticky issue that remains is one of whether the access so granted should be a *legal right or merely a concession* offered by the government. Communities everywhere are saying that they do not want to be at the mercy of a fickle government, which one day will allow access and the next day ban it (e.g. what happened with grazing in Keoladeo National Park, Rajasthan). They would much rather take on conservation responsibilities if they are guaranteed some security of access, in other words tenurial rights.

Benefits must be considered not as acts of charity by the government, but as a matter of right for people who have otherwise "sacrificed" for the PA. Undoubtedly also, conservation responsibilities must go in tandem with these rights, a point that many local communities themselves (though not so many social activists!) will stress.

(ii) Though in relation to countries like Kenya, India's *returns from wildlife tourism* are miniscule, nevertheless they are substantial in some PAs and non-PA areas (e.g. mountains). Without at this stage judging the ecological or social advisability of these levels of tourism, it is a shame that the revenue being earned from it does not go back to the PAs or the local communities. Reportedly this is now being considered in the case of Keoladeo National Park, Rajasthan (where detailed studies have shown the potential of benefiting the local villagers from this source of income; see, for instance, Murty 1996). India would do well to learn from experiments such as the Annapurna Conservation Area Project in Nepal, where local communities and NGOs are completely managing the enormous trekking tourist flow, and generating very substantial returns from it and trying to ensure that it is ecologically sustainable.

(iii) Villagers themselves often have very *innovative ideas for benefit-sharing*. One, mooted by villagers of Kailadevi, was that the penalties imposed by the Forest Department on offenders whom the Village Forest Protection Committees (FPC) help to catch, should be returned to the village (Das 1997). In addition, compensation for damage by wild animals to crops, livestock, and humans must both be enhanced, and paid with simpler procedures. This is a universal demand from the affected communities all over India. A suggestion made by the Kailadevi villagers in this regard is to accept the recommendations of the FPC with regard to individual compensation claims, rather than insisting that a doctor or official certify the damage, a process which not only consumes time but also often forces villagers to bribe officials to obtain a favourable report. Another innovative attempt is by some NGOs (such as Corbett Foundation and the WWF through its Tiger Conservation Programme), which quickly detect cases of livestock kills and pay compensation equivalent to the difference between the market rate and what the government provides, or have given vehicles to the Forest Department to quickly reach villages reporting such cases (see *Tigerlink*, Vol. 4, No. 2, September 1998).

(iv) Benefits linked to natural resource related *knowledge and innovations* that the local people have are a part of the global debate on biodiversity. The protection of indigenous knowledge through appropriate (non-monopolistic) community and individual *intellectual rights*, and the generation of benefits from the use of these knowledge, are now being considered all over the world, especially in the wake of the Convention on Biological Diversity (CBD). The CBD mandates countries to protect such knowledge, seek permission from its holders before using it, and equitably share any benefits that come out of such use. India too is considering National and State-level Biodiversity Funds, which could be used to give incentives to communities and individuals who promote conservation and sustainable use. There are several possible methods of doing this (Nijar 1995, Posey and Dutfield 1996, Shiva *et al.* 1997, Gupta 1997,

Pathak and Kothari 1998), which should be considered for use in conservation programmes.

Researchers in the formal sector should be particularly aware of such issues. Academics get extremely upset if someone takes their information or ideas without due acknowledgment; indeed, the person can even be sued for plagiarism. It is strange then that the same yardsticks are not applied by most of us when using local people as guides, informants, etc.; how many Ph.D. dissertations, research reports, forest working plans, PA management plans, and other such documents actually name the villagers who have provided information that has gone into these documents?

(v) Even those *basic survival and developmental needs* of communities, which are seemingly unconnected to wildlife conservation requirements, are equally vital to address. Indeed, it may well happen that some rural areas, which were earlier neglected by the government, receive some attention because of the establishment of a PA or conservation scheme in their region. In Kailadevi, because of its status as a sanctuary, the serious water shortages are now being tackled by both NGOs and government agencies (including the district administration and the Forest Department), and communities are re-organizing themselves to participate in this. The institutional capacities and partnerships which are thus built up may help ultimately in conservation too. To some extent, ecodevelopment also aims to do this.

(vi) Finally, and this is a point that social activists are often loath to admit, many benefits being derived by communities from PAs may already be causing irreversible damage to ecosystems or species. Others that are being demanded may do the same. There is, therefore, a critical need for *assessment* of all such *unsustainable activities*, and the search for on-site or other *alternatives* (ranging from modifications in these activities to completely unrelated alternatives) where they cannot possibly be in harmony with the conservation objectives of the area. Ecodevelopment activities are essentially aiming at this. Both the assessment and the search for alternatives, however, are likely to be much more effective if conducted in a participatory manner; otherwise, they run the risk of either being biased or inaccurate, or being rejected by the affected communities. In several successful community-based conservation efforts, unsustainable activities of the community itself have been curtailed when villagers have been convinced that they are destructive (Kothari *et al.* 1999).

2.d. Intra- and Inter-Community Dynamics

Both social activists and conservationists often assume the local community to be a homogeneous entity. In India, it is far from that, especially in non-tribal areas. Official programmes of involving people in forest regeneration (JFM) and PA conservation (ecodevelopment), as also many NGO projects, have generally failed to disaggregate the community by class, caste and gender. Even when they are aware of it, these agencies have been reluctant to address the rather thorny issues of inequities and power play within and between communities, hoping that general prescriptions for community participation will sort these problems out on their own. But this does not happen.

In particular, the way in which inequities in social status, political power, economic standing, and other attributes influence conservation, does not appear to have been well studied, with a few exceptions (Sarin 1998; Baviskar 1995; Saberwal 1998). We have been especially mindful of this factor while studying the potential for the people's participation in protected areas. Some important results which have emerged are:

(i) ***Women continue to be disprivileged*** in conservation programmes, both in those initiated by communities themselves as also in officially-sponsored ones. For instance, women are generally unrepresented in the Forest Protection Committees of Kailadevi, though in Dalma they are at times represented, which may be a reflection of the generally more equal status of women in tribal societies. In Kailadevi, women complained that the forest protection work of the FPCs (which were male-dominated) caused greater hardships for them, at least in so far as fuelwood collection had become harder (though they also admitted that fodder shortage had eased as a result of the forest protection). Most villagers, including men, agreed that there was a need for greater women's participation in decision-making, but they also strongly felt that this could not be achieved merely through formal reservation of seats in the local institutions (as has already happened with village *panchayats* in many parts of India). There was a need to build the capacity amongst women to be able to confidently speak and make their opinions matter, which, given the centuries of male domination in the area, would not be an overnight development. This is of course also true of the Forest Department and other line agencies of the government; Sarin (1996) reveals that out of 2,576 Indian Forest Service officials in the country in 1995, only 72 (i.e. 3 per cent) were women.

(ii) ***Landless people, lower castes, minority communities, and other disprivileged sections*** within a community are often left out of the decision-making process. However, in some other cases, there have been conscious attempts on the part of the village community to have representation of all these sections in the decision-making body. Villagers themselves increasingly realize the need to resolve the inequities in representation on decision-making bodies, and also admit that government or NGO intervention may at times be necessary to make this happen.

An interesting initiative comes from the village of Saigata, Maharashtra, which consists of tribals and non-tribals, the latter split into several castes. Forest revival and village mobilisation has been led by a 'lower' caste person, and decision-making involves all sectors (Khobragade n.d.).

Indifference towards this issue could doom the conservation effort in the long run, for people left out of the process are likely to consciously or accidentally undermine it. In the Great Himalayan National Park, Baviskar (1998) reports that the ecodevelopment process does not really reach benefits to the poorest sections of the villages, those who in fact are most dependent on the Park's resources. Such people will continue to "steal" into the Park for survival and livelihood, and chances are they would abandon whatever sustainable use practices they may have earlier employed in the quest to "cut and run" as fast as possible.

Such issues can of course also be misused by politicians and others for populist purposes, and it often becomes very tricky to determine whether majority or minority views should prevail. Sustained dialogue, coupled with NGO and official monitoring processes, could help to avoid such misuse.

(iii) ***Inter-community inequities*** could also strongly influence the success or failure of the people's participation in conservation attempts. In Kailadevi, Dalma, Bhonta-Kolyala, and other initiatives the forest protection efforts of some villages were often thwarted because adjacent villages did not undertake the same responsibility, and allowed their forest patches to be degraded/cut down, with detrimental effects on the protected patches. This brings into focus the need for larger level coordination bodies which can mediate between different villages, between villages and the protected area authorities, and among other stakeholders. The Baragoan ki Panchayat (council of 12 villages) in Kailadevi, created to bring together people of 12 villages who have a common interest in forest protection, is one such example. PA-level advisory committees, proposed under the draft new Wild Life (Protection) Act which is currently under consideration, could be another such initiative.

2.e. Intra- and Inter-Departmental Dynamics

It is interesting that while the inequities and differences within and between local communities are increasingly being focused on by researchers, the internal dynamics of government agencies responsible for conservation is not yet well studied, much less seriously tackled. The problems are severe :

(i) There is little *vertical interaction among the various levels of the PA authorities*; the experience of the ground situation being gained by the frontline staff (forest guards, foresters, daily wagers) has no systematic way of getting to the "higher" officials, and there is little reverse flow of the policy/ programmatic priorities being fixed by the latter. In Kailadevi, the Project team found that very little was known amongst the frontline staff about the ecodevelopment scheme. Recent management planning exercises in Dalma and ecodevelopment planning exercises in Kailadevi, and the stakeholder meetings being organized in Rajaji, are giving an opportunity to partially increase vertical interaction, but it is too early yet to tell if they will result in a systemic change.

(ii) At the same time, *horizontal coordination among the various wings/ divisions of the Forest Department* is also seriously deficient. There were, for instance, complaints by the wildlife staff in Kailadevi about the programmes of the territorial staff around the sanctuary, which, they claimed, had an adverse impact on the habitat. The wildlife officials also appeared to feel less powerful compared to their counterparts in the other wings of the Department. In many States, even PAs have not been fully handed over by the territorial wing of the Department to its wildlife wing, sometimes because it is felt that the latter does not have the resources to manage them, but more often because the former simply does not want to relinquish control.

(iii) Finally, ***coordination between the Forest Department and other departments/agencies of the government*** is far from satisfactory, as noted above.

There is, therefore, a need for serious introspection by the Forest Department on their internal problems, and by the State governments on the need for inter-departmental coordination, followed by appropriate restructuring to improve coordination and motivation. This could include, for instance, interaction workshops between the senior and frontline staff of the wildlife wing, held in a neutral surrounding where participants could be more open and frank; and similar workshops and joint practical exercises among the various wings of the Forest Department and among the various government departments active in the area.

Other needs are well known, though not yet fully addressed: *training of conservation staff* in wildlife/habitat management, *better facilities* for the ground staff and for their families, and others.

2.f. Legal Measures

Many of the steps described above are possible within India's current policy and legal framework governing conservation. For instance, the Uttar Pradesh order concerning grass harvesting from within PAs (including within national parks which are supposed to be devoid of human presence), was passed using the Wild Life Act's provisions concerning management activities which are beneficial to wildlife: it was argued that grass harvesting would help in fire prevention.

However, these spaces within current legislation only go a certain distance. There is inadequate legal mandate, and indeed a barrier, where it comes to steps such as setting up joint management committees for PAs and other areas, or providing tenurial rights (or custodianship) to people in national parks even if conservation would be better served by this. Settlement procedures for rights remain vague, and large loopholes exist with regard to the entry of large development and commercial projects into conservation areas. Perhaps most important, the laws do not have the flexibility which would allow their constructive and creative use for a variety of ecological and social situations.

Both the Wild Life (Protection) Act and the Forest Act are currently (as of late 1998) under review, and citizens have strongly urged the government to make the changes necessary to facilitate participatory conservation. This has also been argued in the context of the proposed Biodiversity Act (being promulgated as a follow-up to India's ratification of the Convention on Biological Diversity), and the *panchayati raj* legislation (Pathak and Kothari 1998).

Mainly, three kinds of thrusts are required in the new legislation (Kothari 1997):

(i) Strong provisions against the use of conservation areas and threatened species for industrial or large-scale commercial purposes;
(ii) Provisions empowering local communities to participate in management of such areas; and
(iii) Provisions enabling resource-dependent communities to receive, as rights, appropriate benefits from such areas, in a way that is not detrimental to their conservation values.

Also suggested is a larger system of PA categories (renamed "conservation areas" since they are not strictly protectionist), which would allow the flexibility of accommodating different kinds of ecological and social situations without compromising conservation values or livelihood rights. Bhatt and Kothari (1997) have suggested four additional categories to the two existing ones of national parks and sanctuaries: Strict Nature Reserve, Resource Reserve, Biosphere Reserve and Community Reserve.

Of these, the categories of Biosphere Reserves (this concept, which has the potential of harmonizing conservation and human livelihood objectives over large land/waterscapes, has not really been applied in its full meaning in India), and of Community Reserves (which would provide a legal backing to communities who are trying to protect their sacred groves, catchment forests, village tanks, etc.), are particularly important. Proposal amendments to the Wild Life Act have included two new categories: Community Reserves, and Conservation Reserves.

We would argue that with such an expanded set of categories, and using a much more inclusive range of conservation areas, India's PA network could increase to well over 10 per cent of its landmass (over double the present). This could in fact also include over 1 per cent of its landmass under totally inviolate areas, jointly decided by government agencies and local communities, and including uninhabited islands, forests with no human use, sacred landscapes, etc.

Another major legal issue to be tackled is the role of *customary law*. Traditionally, communities have managed resources through the use of customary rules, regulations and institutions, but these have eroded over time or been replaced by formal legal structures. In some areas customary law has been revived (e.g. the cases mentioned here, of Kailadevi Sanctuary, Rajasthan, and Mendha-Lekha village, Maharashtra), and are proving more effective than formal laws. The challenge is to build flexibility into the legal regimes to enable such customary legal mechanisms to function.

2.g. The Larger Context of Land/Water Use

Most habitats of wildlife significance in India are not only themselves inhabited by humans, but are also surrounded by human settlements, private lands and developmental infrastructure. What happens in these adjoining areas has a significant bearing on the ecological status of the wildlife habitat, e.g. the enormous fuelwood demand from Jamshedpur (Bihar) appears to be putting an unsustainable pressure on Dalma Sanctuary's forests (Christopher 1997). In addition, economic and social policies and programmes at the state, national, and international levels also have strong impacts on the PA. The decision to make a major dam at Tehri town, in the Garhwal Himalaya of Uttar Pradesh, has had a detrimental impact on far-away Rajaji National Park, as people to be displaced by the project have been resettled in the middle of the elephant corridor adjacent to the Park. In India as a whole, the ongoing phase of "liberalization", has led to demands to denotify or alter the boundaries of several PAs, to enable commercial-industrial activities in these areas (Kothari *et al.* 1995). The entire coastline and marine areas of India are threatened by plans to increase the export of fishery products (entailing the spread of polluting aquaculture and destructive trawlers), and to locate tourism and shipping facilities and industries.

While national and international forces cannot be tackled at the level of each conservation area, there is an urgent necessity, and possibility, of carrying out *integrated landuse plans* for the whole region within which a critical wildlife habitat is embedded. One view is to declare the conservation area and its surrounding region as a special management unit, and set up an institutional structure to build up a detailed land/water use plan and manage this whole area. This is somewhat akin to the Special Area Development Authorities set up in many parts of India, but with an orientation towards conservation in this case. Examples of participatory management from across the world reveal that such an approach is increasingly being taken by many countries (Suri 1997). To a certain extent, Tiger Reserves are attempting this, by handing over a substantial buffer area around the designated national park or sanctuary to the wildlife authorities. However, coordination amongst government agencies active within this area has not yet been very heartening, and community involvement remains very weak. What is, therefore, also needed is a close re-examination of the impacts of several State/national policies and programmes, on the ecological health of wildlife habitats in India.

In addition, it is vital to get away from an almost exclusive protected area focus. True, representative and rich biodiversity sites need special attention, but this is not an excuse to neglect the need for conservation in non-PA sites. As is well-known, considerable wildlife (including many of the "flagship" species of Indian conservation, the so-called charismatic mega-fauna) is found outside PAs, including in human-dominated ecosystems, and its only protection is what the Wild Life Act provides rather ineffectually, or what local people themselves are providing. A range of incentives to local communities where these species exist, or encouragement of beliefs and practices which allow them to thrive, would perhaps be the most effective way of protecting such wildlife.

Eventually, it would be critical to ensure some level of conservation across the entire range of human land/water uses, rather than focus exclusively on a small percentage of biodiversity-rich areas.

Many *grassroots movements* are providing their own responses to this challenge. Several million fisherfolk across India's coastal areas have successfully protested the introduction of destructive trawling in the seas; in so doing, they have not only protected traditional fishing livelihoods but also rich marine ecosystems. The same is true of the widespread protest against industrial aquaculture along our coasts. Chipko, Appiko, and other peasant-based movements have protected forests over large landscapes in the Himalaya, the Western Ghats, and other regions. Several dams, power projects, and other so-called development projects which would have gobbled up rich biodiversity areas have been stalled by popular local opposition. Many movements are also devising alternative ways of generating water, energy, and other benefits, which are far less destructive and more equitable. Such movements are allies in the struggle to conserve India's wildlife and biodiversity, though unfortunately urban conservation groups and officials do not often see them as such.

3. Conclusion—Hurdles and Opportunities

India's conservation policy and programmes are moving increasingly towards more participatory processes. Rather than resist such a move, conservationists must see this as an opportunity to do what we have not been able to do for decades: make the conservation movement truly broad-based and grassroots rather than restricted to a small and increasingly ineffective elite. *Indeed, it is only if we see village communities as conservationist in their own right, albeit with often different motives, and only if we see the legitimacy of their rights to survival and livelihood resources, will we be able to make conservation a sustainable effort.* Some compromises may appear necessary (by both urban conservationists and local communities) to make these new alignments and strategies possible: some wildlife habitats may be lost, some communities may have to give up cherished traditions (such as mass hunts in areas with considerably depleted wildlife). But in the long run, a range of options in which co-management and community-based conservation figure prominently offers a much surer vision of conservation than the one that has dominated over the past few decades.

The basic assertions made above can be summarized as follows:

1. The conventional method of protecting wildlife, especially the creation of PAs, has undoubtedly saved many habitats and species from destruction, but also caused severe hardships for local communities dependent on these habitats and species.
2. The alienation of these communities from their resource base, which has been the result of exclusionary conservation policies and strategies, is both unjust and shortsighted, for wildlife cannot survive in the midst of dispossessed and hostile populations. A strategy of exclusion is in any case unviable, given the extent of dependence of several million people on wildlife habitats and the impossibility of finding alternative lands and resources for all of them. Political ways will always be found by many such people to undermine official strategies, if these strategies are not beneficial to them.
3. People, especially those who have traditionally subsisted on local resources, have a continuing right to these resources, except where they are causing irreversible ecological damage, in which case viable alternatives have to be provided.
4. Official and non-governmental conservation agencies, which were always somewhat weak, are becoming increasingly ineffective in the face of declining political support and mounting "developmental" pressures. Such agencies have inherent limitations of human, financial, technical and political resources.
5. Both wildlife and local communities are threatened by a third party: the urban-industrial sector which is bent on gobbling up natural resources as raw material and rural dwellers as cheap labour. Only a partnership between conservationists and communities/social activists, and the empowerment of ecosystem-dependent communities, can withstand this destruction, as can be seen at dozens of sites across India.

6. Changes are, therefore, needed in conservation policy, law and administration, to allow for a much more participatory system, one which is respectful of both the needs of wildlife and the rights of humans. Such changes will have to bring in several factors previously ignored or only weakly integrated: relevant community knowledge and practices, customary laws and local institutional structures, vertical and horizontal integration within government agencies, land/water use planning in a regional context within which special areas for wildlife protection are supplemented by incentives for conservation across the spectrum of human resource uses, mutual learning sessions amongst various stakeholders, open access to information, and so on.
7. Decisions regarding conservation should be based much more on ecological, historical, and socio-economic research than is currently the case, research that is participatory and integrates the informal paradigms of local communities with the formal approaches of ecologists and wildlife scientists.

There are, undoubtedly, several hurdles to cross in achieving such a redirection of conservation strategy. These include:

— the rapid erosion of community knowledge, practices and laws;
— loss of sustainability due to increases in human and livestock population and changes in lifestyle;
— social inequities at various levels;
— continued resistance from those who have power to share it with those who don't;
— severe distrust between government officials and local people;
— inappropriate development paths and national laws/policies;
— political interference;
— corruption; and
— lack of capacity amongst all stakeholders.

But for each of these hurdles, there are also examples of people having overcome them and creating opportunities:

— revival of community-level knowledge, practices, institutional structures and laws, relevant to conservation (such that, according to one recent official estimate, upwards of 7 million hectares of forests are being protected by communities in India today);
— voluntary reduction of livestock numbers and/or regulations on free grazing by several communities;
— willingness to accept family planning if adequate incentives are

available and where women are empowered;
- — decentralization opportunities created by recent constitutional amendments;
- — informal and formal arrangements between communities and government agencies/officers for conservation and sustainable livelihood options;
- — challenges to destructive development processes by traditional fisherfolk, forest-dwellers, peasants and others;
- — politicians taking up cudgels on behalf of conservation (e.g. to save Bhitarkanika and Balukhand Sanctuaries in Orissa from "development" projects);
- — reduction in the incidence of corruption where people's organizations have empowered themselves; and
- — increasing awareness and capacity amongst different stakeholders to handle the complex job of managing natural resources.

The opportunities are there, and I believe that if the urban conservation community can respond adequately, and in time, to seize these opportunities, it will help to forge a new path of conservation. If it does not, it risks becoming increasingly redundant as larger forces take over.

NOTES

1 This paper is based on a larger one presented at the National Seminar on Wildlife Conservation, Research and Management, Wildlife Institute of India, Dehradun, 10-13 August, 1998. Thanks are due to Neema Pathak, Sunita Rao, Bansuri Taneja, and Simronjit Singh, for useful inputs.

2 These aspects are explored in more detail in Kothari, Singh, and Suri 1995; Kothari 1996; Rangarajan 1996; and Tucker 1991.

REFERENCES

Adams, J.S. and T.O. McShane. 1992. *The Myth of Wild Africa: Conservation Without Illusion.* London and New York: W.W. Norton and Company.

Ali, Salim and V.S. Vijayan. 1986. *Keoladeo National Park Ecology Study: Summary Report 1980-85.* Bombay: Bombay Natural History Society.

Arhem, K. 1985. *Pastoral Man in the Garden of Eden: the Maasai of the Ngorongoro Conservation Area, Tanzania.* Sweden: University of Uppsala.

Baviskar, A. 1995. *In the Belly of the River: Tribal Conflicts over Development in the Narmada Valley.* New Delhi: Oxford University Press.

Baviskar, A. 1998. "The Community and Conservation: The Case of Ecodevelopment in the Great Himalayan National Park, India". Paper presented at the 7th Conference of the International Association for the Study of Common Property at Simon Fraser University, Vancouver. June 10-14, 1998.

Bhatt, Seema. 1998. "Conservation Through Community Enterprise". In: Kothari *et al.* (ed.).

Bhatt, Seema and A. Kothari. 1997. "Protected Areas in India: Proposal for an Expanded System of Categories". In: Kothari *et al.*

Bush, M.B. and P.A. Colinvaux. 1994. "Tropical Forest Disturbance: Paleoecological Records from Darien, Panama". *Ecology* 75: 1761-1768.

Christopher, K. 1997. "Dalma Sanctuary, Bihar: Prospects for Joint Management". In: Kothari *et al.*

Das, P. 1997. "Kailadevi Wildlife Sanctuary, Rajasthan: Prospects for Joint Management". In: Kothari, *et al.*

Deeney, J. and W. Fernandes. 1992. "Tribals: Their Dependence on Forests, Their Traditions and Management Systems". In: Fernandes, W. (ed.). *National Development and Tribal Deprivation*. New Delhi: Indian Social Institute.

Gadgil, M., F. Berkes, and C. Folke. 1993. "Indigenous Knowledge for Biodiversity Conservation". *Ambio* 23: 151-156.

Gokhale, Y., R. Velankar, M.D. Subhash Chandran and M. Gadgil. 1997. "Sacred Woods, Grasslands and Waterbodies as Self-organized Systems of Conservation in India". *Paper* presented at the Regional Workshop on the Role of Sacred Groves in Conservation and Management of Biological Diversity, KFRI, Peechi, 8-11 December, 1997.

Gomez-Pompa, A. and A. Kaus. 1992. "Taming the Wilderness Myth". *Bioscience* 42: 271-279.

Government of West Bengal. 1996. Resolution No. 3841-For/FR/0/11M-7/95, dated 26 June, 1996, on setting up of Ecodevelopment Committees. Also reported in *JPAM Update 12: News on Action Towards Joint Protected Area Management*, New Delhi.

Gupta, A. "Getting Creative Individuals and Communities Their Due". Paper presented at the South and Central Asian Regional Workshop on Community-Based Conservation: Policy and Practice. New Delhi: Indian Institute of Public Administration, 9-11 February, 1997.

Khobragade, S. Undaved. Ek Gaon Saigata: Van Saueakshanasathi Gram Sabhecha Sanghareh ('A Village Saigata: One Village Assembly's Struggle to Protect Forests'). Unpublished note in Marathi, Facilitated by H.B. Ingle.

Kothari, A., P. Pande, S. Singh and D. Variara. 1989. *National Parks and Sanctuaries in India: A Status Report*, New Delhi: Indian Institute of Public Administration.

Kothari, A., N. Singh and S. Suri. 1995. Conservation in India: A New Direction. *Economic and Political Weekly*, Vol. XXX, No. 43, October 28.

Kothari, A. 1996. "Is Joint Management of Protected Areas Desirable and Possible?" In: Kothari, A., N. Singh and S. Suri (eds.). 1996. *People and Protected Areas: Towards Participatory Conservation in India*. New Delhi: Sage Publications.

Kothari, A. 1997. "New Directions in India's Wildlife Legislation". In Kothari *et al.* 1997.

Kothari, A., N. Pathak, R.V. Anuradha and B. Taneja. (eds.). 1998. *Communities and Conservation: Natural Resource Management in South and Central Asia*. New Delhi: UNESCO and Sage Publications.

Kothari, A., N. Pathak and F. Vania. 1999. *Where Communities Care: Community Wildlife and Ecosystem Management in South Asia*. Kalpavriksh, Pune, and IIED, London.

Kothari, A., F. Vania, P. Das, K. Christopher and S. Jha (eds.). 1997. *Building Bridges for Conservation: Towards Joint Management of Protected Areas in India*. New Delhi: Indian Institute of Public Administration.

Lele, S., K.S. Murali and K.S. Bawa. 1998. "Community Enterprise for Conservation in India: Biligiri Ranganaswamy Temple Sanctuary". In: Kothari *et al.*

Melkani, V.K. and A. Venkatesh. 1998. "Attempts Aiming at Reduction of Anthropogenic

Pressures on Resources of 'KMTR' Through Ecodevelopment Strategy". *Paper* for presentation at the workshop on Collaborative Management of Protected Areas in Asia, Nepal: Royal Chitawan National Park, 25-28 May, 1998.

Murty, M.N. 1996. "Contractual Arrangements for Sharing Benefits from Preservation: Joint Management of Wildlife". In: Kothari *et al.*

Naithani, H.B., J.D.S. Negi, R.C. Thapliyal and T.C. Pokhriyal. 1992. Valley of Flowers: Need for Conservation or Preservation. *Indian Forester* 117:371-378.

Nijar, G.S. 1995. *Developing a Rights Regime in Defence of Biodiversity and Indigenous Knowledge.* Malaysia: Third World Network.

Pandey, C.B. and J.S. Singh. 1992. Influence of Rainfall and Grazing on Herbage Dynamics in a Seasonally Dry Tropical Savanna. *Vegetatio* 102: 107-124.

Pathak, N. with V. Gour-Broome In press. Tribal Self-Rule and Natural Resource Management: Community-Based Conservation in Mendha (Lekha), Maharashtra, India. Kalpavriksh, Pune and IIED, London.

Pathak, N. and A. Kothari. 1998. "Sharing The Benefits Of Wildlife Conservation With Local Communities: Legal Implications". *Economic and Political Weekly* XXXIII(40): 2603-2610.

Pardeshi, P. 1996. "Conserving Maharashtra's Biodiversity Through Ecodevelopment". In: Kothari *et al.*

Poffenberger, M. and B. McGean (eds.). 1996. *Village Voices, Forest Choices: Joint Forest Management in India.* New Delhi: Oxford University Press.

Posey, D. and G. Dutfield. 1996. *Beyond Intellectual Property Rights.* Ottawa: International Development Research Centre.

Ramakrishnan, P.S., K.G. Saxena and U.M. Chandrashekhara (eds.). 1998. *Conserving the Sacred for Biodiversity Management,* New Delhi: Oxford and IBH.

Rangarajan, M. 1996. "The Politics of Ecology: The Debate on Wildlife and People in India, 1970-95". *Economic and Political Weekly,* 31: 2391-2409.

Rathore, B.M.S. 1996. "Joint Management Options for Protected Areas: Challenges and Opportunities". In: Kothari, A., Singh, N. and Suri, S. (eds.). *People and Protected Areas: Towards Participatory Conservation in India,* New Delhi: Sage Publications.

Saberwal, V. 1996. "Pastoral Politics: Gaddi Grazing, Degradation, and Biodiversity Conservation in Himachal Pradesh, India". *Conservation Biology,* Vol. 10, No. 3, June.

Saberwal, V. 1998. *Pastoral Politics: Shepherds, Bureaucrats, and Conservation in the Western Himalaya.* New Delhi: Oxford University Press.

Sarin, M. 1996. "Who is Gaining? Who is Losing? Gender and Equity Concerns in Joint Forest Management". *Working Paper,* National Support Group for JFM, Society for Promotion of Wastelands Development, New Delhi. Shorter version titled Gender and Equity Concerns in Joint Forest Management, in Kothari *et al.* 1998.

Sen, G. (ed.). 1992. *Indigenous Vision: Peoples of India, Attitudes to the Environment.* New Delhi: Sage Publications.

Shiva, V., A.H. Jafri, G. Bedi and R. Holla-Bhar. 1997. *The Enclosure and the Recovery of the Commons.* Research Foundation for Science, New Delhi: Technology and Ecology.

Shresth, Swati, with S. Devidas, In Press. Forest Revival and Water Harvesting: Community-Based Conservation at Bhaonta-Kolyala, Rajasthan, India. Kalpavriksh, Pune and IIED, London (in Press).

Singh, S. 1996. "India". In: Dompka, V. (ed.), *Human Population, Biodiversity, and Protected Areas: Science and Policy Issues.* Washington D.C. : American Association for the Advancement of Science.

Suri, Saloni. 1997. "People's Involvement in Protected Areas: Experiences from Abroad and Lessons for India". In: Kothari *et al.*

Tucker, R.P. 1991. "Resident Peoples and Wildlife Reserves in India: The Prehistory of a Strategy". In: West, P.C. and S.R. Brechin (eds.). *Resident Peoples and National Parks: Social*

Dilemmas and Strategies in International Conservation. Arizona : University of Arizona Press, Tuscon.

Vania, F. 1997. "Rajaji National Park: Prospects for Joint Management". In: Kothari, A. *et al.*

Vijayan, V.S. 1991. *Keoladeo National Park Ecology Study: 1980-90, Final Report*. Bombay: Bombay Natural History Society.

World Bank. 1996. *Staff Appraisal Report, India Ecodevelopment Project*. Report No. 14914-IN. August 3. South Asia Department II, Agriculture and Water Division, Washington D.C. : The World Bank.

World Bank. Not dated. *Conserving Biodiversity Through Ecodevelopment*. South Asia Brief, Washington D.C. : The World Bank Group.

27 Shared Management of Protected Areas: Possibilities and Constraints in Keoladeo National Park, Bharatpur

Kanchan Chopra

1. Introduction

Protected areas extend to around 5 per cent of the geographical area of India, and consist of both national parks and sanctuaries. They are managed solely for conservation under the statute of law. However, in developing countries such as India, in particular those with high densities of population, protected areas tend to impact closely the livelihoods of local communities living in and around the park. In turn, they are affected by the continued existence of rights of the local people, mainly arising out of a continuation of conventional arrangements. It was found in a study covering 32 national parks and 138 sanctuaries[1] in India that

(a) 56 per cent of the national parks and 72 per cent of the sanctuaries had settlements of human population within the protected area,
(b) 83 per cent of the parks and 87 per cent of the sanctuaries had a population adjacent to the protected area,
(c) 43 per cent of the parks and 68 per cent of the sanctuaries accorded and accepted rights of local communities such as to grazing by livestock, harvesting of timber and collection of minor forest produce.

Use is, therefore, never totally irrelevant. In the case of some protected areas such as wetlands, use is an integral part of conservation even as seen by international conventions governing them.[2] Ecological studies have in some cases confirmed the scientific basis of some kinds of traditional use patterns. Finally, of course, tourists use these parks for recreation and education and scientists for research. Each of these uses creates a set of stakeholders with limited rights to the protected areas.

Simultaneously, however, the responsibility for conservation rests only with the government and the line department. Large expenditures are incurred on maintenance and upkeep, resulting in implicit subsidies for the users. This chapter argues, using Keoladeo National Park (KNP) as a case in point, that biodiversity conservation can be both more effective and less resource consuming if stakeholders are involved in a meaningful way in the management of the park. This is particularly true in cases where stakeholders differ in terms of their access to resources such as money, time and knowledge. The following sections shall

(a) Identify stakeholders in KNP,
(b) Put together evidence on cost-benefit flows accruing to different groups,
(c) Determine their perceptions with respect to value accruing from the park. In particular, the nature of tourists' demands for the services of the park are identified using a travel cost approach and ordinal ranking of different kinds of value as perceived by stakeholders analysed using the multi criteria approach.
(d) It is argued finally that guidelines for joint management can be laid down. Based on areas of complimentarity in cost-benefit accruals and value perceptions. This is attempted in the last section.

2. Keoladeo National Park: An Introduction

The Keoladeo National Park located in the Indo-Gangetic Plain near the town of Bharatpur (27°13´N, 77°32´E)[3] is a Ramsar and a designated World Heritage site since 1985. (Map 27.1) It is a resting place for many migratory birds including the Siberian crane. Located within easy access from a number of other tourist sites, it has a very high tourist value. The Keoladeo National Park (KNP) is a 29 sqkm mosaic of monsoonal wetlands, seasonally flooded grasslands and thorny woodland. The wetland area of the park covers a central depression of about 8.5 sqkm which is divided by dykes into a number of compartments or blocks. These blocks are interconnected by gates or bunds. In some of the blocks small mounds have been constructed and planted with *Acacia* trees to provide nesting and breeding sites for the heronry species. Though the maximum potential depth of water in the blocks is about 2 m. the mean maximum depth is usually around 1 to 1.5 m. The variety of habitats available, i.e. wetland, part grassland, and part semi-arid forested grassland give an idea of the multitude of niche present within the park's area. The wetland itself is at places grassy meadows, reed beds and open water regions with submerged plants, and within the canal, free flowing deeper water

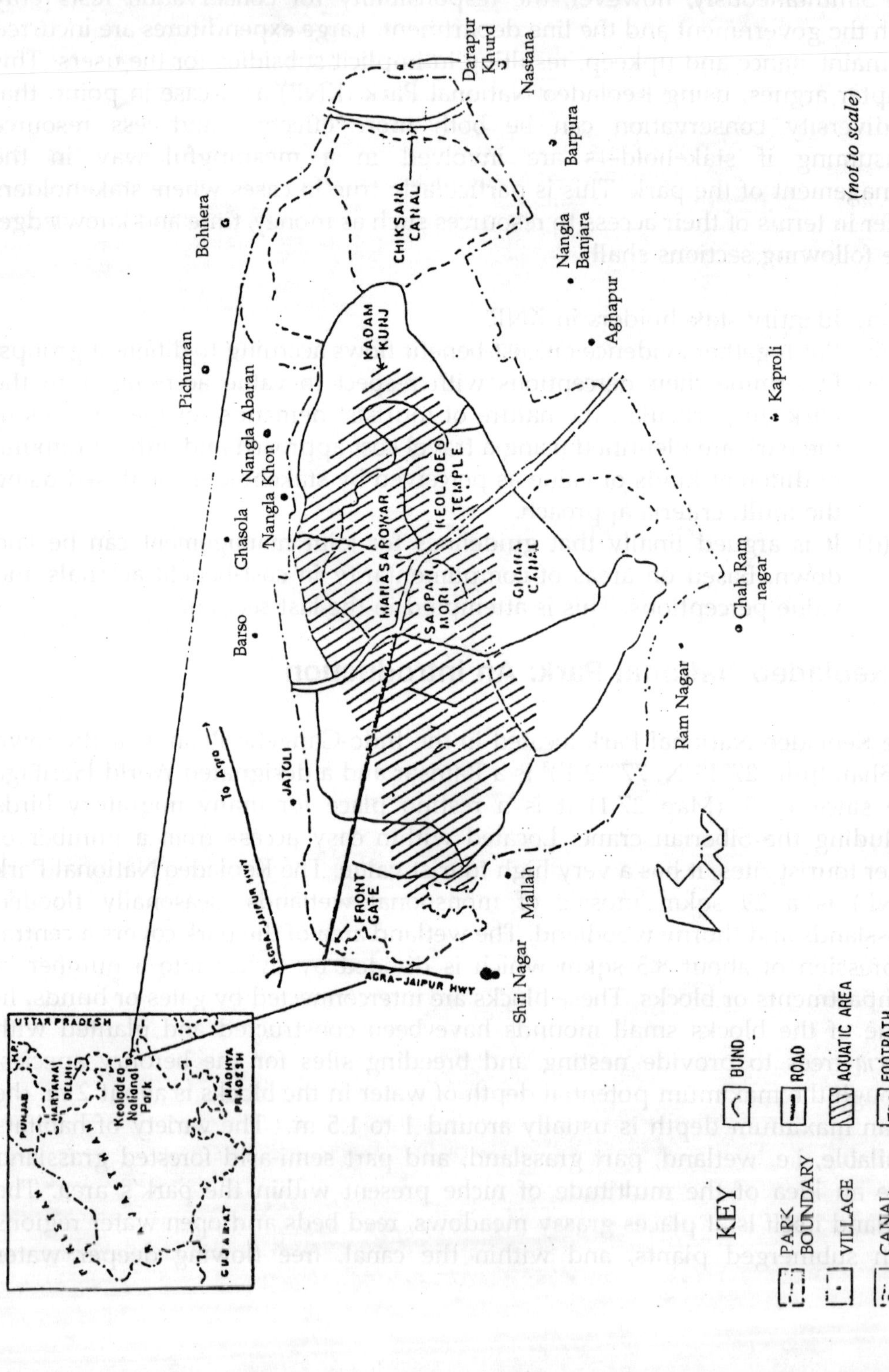

Map 27.1: Keoladeo National Park

teeming with fish. A variety of organisms inhabit these niche, and it is especially favoured as waterfowl habitat. Studies have been carried out throughout these diverse regions on the plants, insects, animals and birds of the park.

KNP is part of the Yamuna sub-basin floodplains. The vegetation with many species of terrestrial and aquatic fauna is characteristic of the north Indian floodplains. The destruction and fragmentation of natural floodplain habitat due to its use for agriculture, housing and industry has made such systems unique, but along the immediate floodplains of the rivers remnants of similar habitat are found. Along the river Yamuna throughout its stretch from the city of Delhi, small, temporary monsoonal wetland habitats exhibit similar vegetative communities and even some of the avifauna found in Keoladeo during the winters. As such KNP is one of the few surviving typical floodplain wetland systems found in the region with the characteristic annual floods and hot summers.

The unique character of the Keoladeo National Park arises from the fact that it was created by humans. The construction of the succession of tanks and the intricate system of water movement used the natural topography and hydrology of the area to provide for the requirements of the numerous species naturally found in the floodplains. The administrator of Bharatpur State at the turn of this century was instrumental in getting this system constructed. The area was first flooded in 1901 and for a long time was treated as an important duck shooting area by the Maharaja of Bharatpur. During this period, local people living in villages nearby were permitted to graze their cattle inside the park, except from December to March. They also collected fuelwood, and a variety of grasses that had economic value. Therefore, ever since the park came into being, the notion of use has been an integral part of its existence.

The area was taken over by the Rajasthan Government in 1956. A significant change in the management came in 1982 when KNP was declared a National Park and officials of the Forest Department were required, by law, to end all human interference within the its boundaries. There followed a period of conflict, at times marked by violence, between the villagers and the management of the park.

The next important watershed in the park-people interaction was a 1985 report of the Bombay Natural History Society (BNHS) which concluded that grazing per se was not damaging to the ecology of the park. On the contrary, the excess growth of *Paspalum* an important grass species (which was earlier grazed on and controlled by cattle) caused difficulties for bulb, tuber and root feeding avifauna such as the Siberian crane. As a consequence, permits for grass removal were given on a regular basis to people living in villages around the park since 1986. Use by local people, albeit limited, is, therefore, a part of the management strategy of this park. They have an important stake in the park and its sustainable use.

The large number of visitors to the park makes the management (the Forest Department) and the government perceive it as a significant locale. Tourists probably constitute the most important stakeholders from the official point of view. The number of tourists has increased from 95,000 to 1,25,000 in the past three to four years. This has meant that a large and growing tourism industry has developed in Bharatpur town, with the accompanying income generation benefits to the region. The urban economy of the region benefits from this growth and has a stake in the efficient management of the tourist traffic into the park. Indirectly they have an interest in the ecological health of the park, which ensures the continued accrual of this income. *Use value accruing from the tourism industry is, to some extent, complementary with the maintenance of the park as a healthy wetland system.*

While the management of KNP has seen phases of a significant change, it is important to note that the government has been subsidising the park. The magnitude of this subsidy varies from year to year. In 1995-96, it was about Rs. 13 lakhs. An important issue from the management's point of view and also from a macro economic viewpoint relates to the reduction of these subsidies.

The single largest item of expenditure for the park authorities was the creation of open water bodies. Such open water spaces are the required habitat for several bird species, including the Siberian crane. However, in recent years, the aquatic area of the park has been shrinking due to the uncontrolled growth of weeds like the water hyacinth and *Paspalum distichum*. Though several methods like bulldozing, cutting and burning have been tried to control the growth of these weeds, they have met with only limited success. Hence, some observers like Vijayan (1987 and 1988) have recommended that grazing by a limited number of buffaloes be re-introduced into the system. Though there are several people who empathize with the view that the local communities should have a stake in the management process, how far such models of people's participation will be permitted in KNP, however, still remains undecided.

Ecologists view KNP as a manmade wetland with a high ecological value. Existence value is probably high in their scheme of things. However, the park has also been used extensively for research and analysis, which is a kind of use value to the community of scientists.

2.a. Stakeholders in KNP and Values they Derive

The stakeholders in the park can be identified as given below:

— the local rural population which derives a use value from the park, mainly through the collection of grasses, fuelwood and fish;

— the local urban population which benefits from incomes generated by the hotel and tourism industries;
— the tourists who enjoy services of recreation, education and tourism;
— the management which is responsible for the maintenance of the ecological health of the park at such a time that the economic benefits continue to accrue;
— the community of scientists and ecologists who put a premium on existence value of the wetland ecosystem;
— non-users in the rest of India and elsewhere who value the existence of national parks and protected areas such as these.

Non-users in the rest of India and in other parts of the world who value the contained existence of avian habitats such as these constitute another category of stakeholders.

From the foregoing discussion it is clear that each category of stakeholders benefits from the unique ecology of the park. This is a clear situation in which total economic benefit is associated positively with preservation of the ecology. Its distribution between users and the extent to which users are able to reap the benefits depends on:

(a) the pressures created on the ecology by continuous use and the resultant changes in ecology.
(b) the manner in which the management allocates rights to the benefits accruing from the park.

3. Economic Impact of KNP on Local Population: A Cost-Benefit Approach

The Murty-Menkaus (1994) study estimated the costs and the benefits accruing from preserving KNP to all the concerned groups, namely, tourists, local population, government, and non-users (Table 27.1). The methodology used combines contingent valuation tachniques with survey-based techniques to arrive at the estimates of value. It is maintained that non-use value accruing to the tourists is also captured by the contingent valuation survey. This is, however, only a partial capturing of non-use value, more in the nature of option value as the tourists, having visited the park, are not, strictly speaking, non-users. The present approach considers the non-use value mentioned in the Murty-Menkaus study as option value and treats scientists and non-Bharatpur residents as non-users who are to be considered a separate category of stakeholders.

In spite of the apparent benefits, it seems that the bulk of the costs of preserving KNP have been borne by the local villagers. The reason lies in the

TABLE 27.1: **A Summary of the Benefit and Cost Flows from KNP during the Year 1992-93.**

(Rs. in million at 1992-93 prices)

1. Primary Benefits		
1.1	Recreation benefits	8.950
1.11	Domestic nationals	7.791
1.12	Foreigners	1.159
1.2	Income from forest produce	0.057
1.3	Non-use value	40.886
1.31	Domestic nationals	25.173
1.32	Foreigners	15.713
2. Secondary Benefits		
2.1	Hotels and restaurants	31.160
2.2	Transporters	18.330
2.3	Employment to locals	1.905
3. Transfers		
3.1	Visitor charges	2.126
3.11	Domestic nationals	0.261
3.12	Foreigners	0.793
3.13	Others	1.163
3.2	Compensation to locals	0.000
4. Costs		
4.1	Income losses to locals	18.330
4.2	Govt. Investment expenditures	3.895
4.3	Operating expenditures	2.250

Source: Murty and Menkhaus, 1994.

fact that, prior to 1982, KNP and its resources were freely available to the villagers for their use. The villagers used to graze their cattle in the area, and also extract several resources from it. However, once the area was declared a National Park in 1982, a ban was placed on all extractive activity, in accordance with the Wildlife Protection Act. Though there is reason to believe that the villagers do still collect several resources illegally from the park, such as grass, fuelwood, and minor forest products like fruits, this is obviously lesser than the amount collected in earlier periods.

The case of fodder is illustrative. The local rural economy seems to be at a disadvantage even after some extraction is allowed through the system of permits. The total annual demand for fodder by the rural households in the pre-1982 era was to the tune of Rs. 21.23 million (at 1992-93 prices). At that time, KNP used to supply Rs. 20.01 million worth of fodder annually. At present, under the permit system, the households are allowed to collect Rs. 1.78 million worth of fodder annually. Therefore, "the net loss to the rural households is Rs. 18.23 million from the denial of grazing rights to them". This has increased the dependence on the market; "on an average, a household uses annually Rs. 3,866 worth of fodder for dairying, out of which 64 per cent comes from the market, 21 per cent from the Park and 15 per cent from the home-grown stock".

The ban on grazing introduced in 1982 had the effect of altering the entire occupational structure in the region. Earlier, dairying was the predominant income-earning activity of the people. In 1993, each household owned, on the average, 6 cattle. Murty and Menkhaus have estimated that the cattle strength in the pre-1982 period was 2.5 times the currently observed levels. Due to the denial of grazing rights, however, the importance of dairying as an income-earning activity has waned over time. As the study reports, "among the three main sources of income currently available to the people (agriculture, dairying and other activities), dairying occupies the last position in terms of its contribution to household annual income".

As already mentioned, employment is an important direct benefit that the park provides to the villagers. It provides employment to some local people, as forest and cattle guards, rickshaw-pullers, guides, casual workers, etc. It was found in 1992-93 that the park provided direct employment to 131 people, including 2 rangers, 10 foresters, 30 forest guards, 65 cattle guards, 8 clerks and 4 supporting staff. It was noted that many of the employees of the park in the lower categories were local villagers. The wages and salaries to all 131 employees amounted to Rs. 2.25 million in 1992-93. Murty and Menkhaus have also reported that there were 16 guides registered with the park at that time. The total annual employment benefits for the 16 guides were estimated at Rs. 3,16,800.

The rise of tourism in Bharatpur due to the park has also impacted the villagers beneficially in some indirect ways. For instance, the large number of hotels and restaurants have created an assured market for perishable commodities like milk and vegetables. Murty and Menkhaus report that "the monthly demand for vegetables by hotels and restaurants serving the tourists in Bharatpur increases from 39 quintals per month in the off-peak tourist season to 72 quintals per month during the peak tourist season. The demand for milk also increases from 2.6 kilolitres in the off-peak season to 3.98 kilolitres in the peak season. Thus tourism in Bharatpur contributes to incremental monthly demand of 33 quintals of vegetables and 1.8 kilolitres of milk during the winter months".

4. Costs and Benefits accruing to the Urban Economy

The growth of transport services and the rise of hotels and restaurants in Bharatpur have created employment opportunities for several people in the city. There are a large number of hotels and restaurants catering to the needs of tourists in Bharatpur. Murty and Menkhaus have carried out a survey of 22 hotels and restaurants in Bharatpur city and found that the total park-induced investment expenditures on hotels and restaurants in Bharatpur are nearly Rs. 40 million at 1992 prices.

The returns to the hotels and restaurants from tourism in Bharatpur are substantial. They are also found to be subject to great variations over the year, being significantly higher in the peak tourist season. Murty and Menkhaus have concluded that "66 per cent of the annual income from room rent and 65 per cent of the annual income from catering services have originated during the peak tourist season". These incremental incomes can be said to have originated solely due to the presence of the park. The increase in these hotels and restaurants has benefited the urban economy of Bharatpur in various ways. Besides the wages and salaries, they also spend on goods like vegetables, fuel and other provisions Based on all this, Murty and Menkhaus have reported that "the net annual benefits accruing to the urban economy of Bharatpur due to park-induced investments on hotels and restaurants are estimated at Rs. 20.15 million at 1992 prices".

4.a. The Cost-Benefit Analysis for KNP

The Murty-Menkhaus study basically represents an attempt to conduct a CBA of the Keoladeo National Park. The time horizon taken in the analysis is 50 years, starting from 1982, when the area was first declared a national park. The cost-benefit exercise conducted by Murty and Menkhaus brought out the following salient points :

(1) The existing distribution of benefits and costs from KNP is such that the gainers are mainly people from higher income classes, i.e. the domestic and foreign tourists while the losers are the local communities, who belong to the lower income classes. However, if equity considerations are not considered important, the net present benefits from KNP are in the neighbourhood of Rs. 184 million.

(2) If the income distribution aspects are taken into account in the analysis (this can be done by using income distributional weights to weight the costs and benefits accruing to the different groups), the Net Present Social Benefit (NPSB) of the park turns out to be negative under the existing system of zero-redistribution.

(3) However, when redistribution efforts are incorporated in the analysis, NPSB turns out to be positive. Thus, Murty and Menkhaus conclude that "the redistribution of net benefits from recreational tourists to compensate local populations increases the net present social benefit of Keoladeo National Park".

As indicated by the cost-benefit analysis conducted by Murty and Menkaus, tourists seem to be the group that gains from the manner in which the park is being managed. However, the nature of demand for tourism services generated by the park has to be examined before a shared management can provide pointers towards a feasible policy change. This is what the next section aims at doing.

5. The Travel Cost Method (TCM) for Valuing Tourism Services

Methods for valuation by stakeholders can be based on revealed preferences or stated preferences. When preferences are expressed on a market, it is easy to estimate the demand for a good or service. The price used must be the appropriate one. For subsidized public goods such as national parks, the price of admission cannot be used as an indicator of the true value of the site. What TCM does, therefore, is to use the travel costs incurred by the individual to reach the site as a surrogate for the price of the site. Since the travel costs will vary across individuals living at different distances from the site, this data can be used to derive a demand curve for the services provided by it. The visitors are divided into zones (generally, these zones are defined by political boundaries such as counties, states, or countries), and the visitation rate, which is the number of visitors from a zone as a proportion of its total population, is calculated for each zone. Statistical demand functions are then estimated, regressing the visitation rate upon the travel cost, the availability of substitute sites, as well as income level, literacy and any other socio-economic factors that may, *a priori*, be expected to affect visitation.[4]

A version of TCM was applied to determine the value of tourism and nature of demand for it. Data was collected regarding tourists' travel and stay expenses, duration of stay, and various socio-economic characteristics. The respondents were also asked how much they would be willing to pay for the preservation of the Park.[5]

The final set of usable responses consisted of 111 respondents, of which 68 were Indians and 43 foreigners. Each respondent gave information on the number of members in his group/family. Hence, the total number of tourists covered in this manner were 305 consisting of 235 Indians and 70 foreign nationals.

Demand functions for tourism are set up making the probability of visiting

KNP depend on the *amount spent on travel, either by way of total cost or by way of local cost, opportunity cost of time* spent (which in turn reflects *household income*), *educational levels* and *reason for visiting the park*.

The above exploration using a semi-log demand function (both in its total and local cost specifications) indicates that the travel cost is a valid proxy variable for price in determining the demand for tourism services. Further, estimates of consumer's surplus and demand elasticities can help in the formulation of policy with respect to management of these areas.

Table 27.2 gives the consumer's surplus as estimated from the semi-log form of the function relating visitation rate to travel cost, both its total and local variants. This gives an estimate of willingness to pay for preservation. At the level of average travel cost, the area under the demand curve and above the line of average cost represents the consumer's surplus enjoyed by the tourist. This is a measure of willingness to pay for the services provided.

TABLE 27.2: **Area under the Demand Curve and Consumer Surplus**

Model Specification	Total Area	Consumer surplus per visit (Indians)	Consumer surplus per visit (Foreigners)
Set I: Using Total Travel Cost Variable			
Semi-Log Model	19,257.30	18,689.09	11,027.32
Set II: Using Local Cost Variable			
Semi-Log Model (Log of Dep.)	505.44	427.04	431.99

Note: The consumer surplus estimates obtained from both the quadratic models were understated.

As expected, the consumer's surplus using total travel cost is higher. In view of the joint product nature of the services provided by the park, it is considered more appropriate to estimate the consumer's surplus from the local cost estimates. This amounts to about Rs. 427.04 per visit by Indians and Rs. 432 per visit by foreigners.

The demand functions were also used to estimate price elasticities of demand at the mean value of the variables. Table 27.3 gives these estimates for the five zones. The demand for the services of KNP turns out to be inelastic. Using the function based on TTCPP (Set I), the price elasticity is between -.07 and -.03 for most cases whereas the elasticity range from -0.24 to -0.01 obtained from the functions of Set II. The values obtained from Set I are higher for zone 5 (non-Indians), being in the range of -.63 to -.80 in three of the four cases.[6]

However, in Set II the values are comparatively lower for the tourists from Zone 3 but higher than for Zone 5.

The inelasticity of demand for recreation with respect to its price has been observed in other studies as well (Navrud and Mungatana, 1994, for Kenya). Walsh (1986) gave an overview of the price elasticities of demand for various activities. The elasticity for 23 cases of outdoor recreation activities varied from -0.12 to -0.32. Low elasticities can be attributed to the following:

(i) the expenditure on the good is a small part of total income, and
(ii) the service in question provides a specialized kind of recreational experience.

TABLE 27.3: **Elasticity of Demand for Tourism Services: Zone-wise**

MODEL	ZONE 1	ZONE 2	ZONE 3	ZONE 4	ZONE 5
Set I: Functions Based on TTCPP					
Quadratic*	-0.0391	-0.0753	-0.0912	-0.0172	-0.9015
Semi Log	-0.0288	-0.0583	-0.0681	-0.0130	-0.5958
Set II: Functions Based on TLCPP					
Semi Log	-0.1405	-0.0727	-0.2366	-0.0778	-0.1130

* Model with EDU variable.

All indications seem to suggest that the Indians visiting the park belong to the better educated group with higher levels of household income. Expenditure incurred on the visit is probably a small part of their household income. In this scenario, an increase in the entrance fee could probably be recommended as one part of management.

In the context of tourism, a related issue that needs to be studied is: what is the optimum number of tourists that can be taken in without affecting the ecosystem adversely. This requires information on the effect of levels of disturbance on the ecosystem (effect on different species, on the grass, wetland, etc.). Such a study would enable a shift in the direction of eco-tourism.

6. Perceptions of Value of Different Stakeholders

As part of the surveys carried out to determine the value of the presence and preservation of the Keoladeo National Park rankings of different aspects of value by stakeholders was generated.[7] The questions were designed in accordance with the uses of the park perceived to be important for different sections of the population. Stakeholders include people residing in other parts of the country as they too perceive the benefits from the park, and are willing to rank the advantages they receive as non-users.

The respondents from each group were asked to rank aspects of the park, which benefited them the most. The following aspects cover most of those uses: ecological functions provided, consumption of different goods, livelihood provided, existence or presence of unique or rare species, aesthetic or recreational value, future use, providing different kinds of services, ritual and cultural value.

The uses of the park and the values of the park as perceived by different stakeholders were expected to differ. The uses of the park framed in the questionnaire were of the kind given in Table 27.4.

TABLE 27.4: **Kinds of Uses Ranked by Stakeholders**

S.No.	Uses	Stakeholders asked to give Ordering
1.	Ecological	Scientists, Village Residents, Non-users
2.	Consumption	Scientists, Villagers and Non-users
3.	Livelihood	Scientists, villagers and Non-users
4.	Rarity	Scientists and Tourists
5.	Aesthetic	Scientists, Tourists and Non-users
6.	Future	Scientists and Non-users
7.	Existence	Scientists, Tourists and Non-users
8.	Services	Scientists, Tourists and Villagers
9.	Ritucul	Scientists and Non-users

The categories of functions mentioned in Table 27.4 are defined as given below:

Ecological Function:	The existence of biodiversity helps to keep ecosystems stable and functioning, and wetland ecosystems perform many important ecological functions for the humankind, e.g. flood control, regulation of water and nutrient cycles, etc.
Consumption:	Plants and animals provide many goods which satisfy human needs, e.g. timber, wool, medicines, fodder, etc. Also, the use of water in irrigation and for domestic purposes.
Livelihood:	Providing livelihood for people.
Rarity:	Presence of unique or rare species.
Aesthetic:	Aesthetic or recreational value for the respondent.
Future:	Possibility of new uses for it in the future, e.g. scientists may find a cure for cancer from a plant variety.
Existence:	The existence of diverse plant and animal species and every living creature have a right to live, regardless of their use to us.

Services:	The park provides different kinds of services like tourism, educational value to the visitor, cattle grazing, requirement of permits of longer duration for collection of fodder grass to the villager, etc.
Ritucul:	It has ritual and cultural value in the lives of many people.

It may be pointed out that the manner in which each of these questions was canvassed in different schedules varied. This was done to ensure that the respondent was able to respond in a meaningful manner.

For each stakeholder, the aspects of the park are taken as "Alternatives" (along the row) and individual respondents as "Effects" (along the column) while creating an Effects Table. Each respondent was given equal weightage, irrespective of his individual perception of different "Alternative" uses of the park, and the ordinal values given by the respondent to the uses were the inputs into the Effects Table.

The perception of these stakeholders—scientists, villagers, non-users (residents of Delhi) and tourists (Indian and foreign)—as obtained by Multi Criteria Analysis (MCA) is detailed below. Alternative techniques can be used for arriving at the scores given to different aspects of value.[8] When the data set is of an ordinal nature, the regime method is one of the preferred techniques. The "effects" are compared in a pairwise fashion in order to arrive at an aggregate score.

Table 27.5 shows the scores for alternative kinds of value found to exist according to the perception of the scientists group, some of whom have carried out certain studies on the park. The set included people who had specialized in different disciplines including biology, ecology and hydrology all of which have some bearing on KNP. Further, some of them have conducted research studies in KNP. Their value perception, therefore, reflects the impact of a particular kind of use to which such national parks can be put, for example, research and study.

TABLE 27.5: **Scientists Perception of Value**

Rank	Options	RM-Score	Kind of Use
1	VRARE	1.00	Rarity
2	ECOFUN	1.00	Ecological function
3	VPRES	0.83	Existence
4	VCONS	0.50	Consumption
5	VLIVE	0.33	Livelihood
6	VFUTU	0.67	Future
7	VSERV	0.17	Services
8	RITCUL	0.25	Ritcul
9	AESTHETIC	0.00	Aesthetic

The scores obtained indicate that alternative sources of value can be divided into three categories: rarity, ecofunction and existence values with scores of 0.80 and more are on top: consumption, livelihood and future use with scores between 0.5 and 0.8 come next and value generated by provision of services such as tourism, ritual and aesthetic value come at the bottom in the value indicators.

The tourists surveyed included both Indian and foreign nationals.[9] Table 27.6 gives the value rankings based on the perceptions of the complete sample, Indians and foreigners both.

TABLE 27.6: **Value Scores from Tourists' Perception**

Rank	Options	RM-Score	Kinds of Use
1	ASREC	0.80	Aesthetic
2	ASCUR	1.00	Curiosity
3	ASDIVER	0.60	Existence
4	ASEDU	0.40	Services
5	ASUNIQ	0.20	Rarity
6	ASOTH	0.00	Others

It is found that tourists as a group value the aesthetic, curiosity and existence aspects of the park, with existence getting a score less than the other two. The services and rarity-related values figure low in their way of viewing the park. There does not seem to be much difference between the value perceptions of Indian and non-Indian tourists. This is expected. The two groups do not differ much in terms of their education and awareness levels.

Perceptions of village residents are based on a participatory rural appraisal study conducted by the WWF in six villages located around the park.[10] The villages are: Aghapur, Darapur, Ramnagar, Ghasola, Mallah and Baraso (Map 27.1). In all the cases, the villagers were requested to rank their requirements from the park. These requirements are presently being met only to some extent. The ranked requirements are perceptions of the villagers' requirements from the park. It is to be noted that the ranking was done on the basis of options that the respondents could relate to. Later, correspondence was found between the categories selected by villagers and our categories, as indicated in Table 27.7. These ranks were put together and the following result was obtained.

It is seen that value is perceived to accrue by the villagers from a number of alternative services such as grazing of cattle and longer duration permits for grass collection. One had to be selected in order to derive a score for value. This was done by means of a statistical test of the differences between them. The testing of difference of means, obtained for the two options of the same use

TABLE 27.7: **Value Perceptions of Village Residents.**

Rank	Option	RM-Score	Kinds of Use
1	Open Grazing	0.86	Services/livelihood
2	Longer Permits	0.64	Livelihood/Services
3	Employment	0.71	Livelihood
4	Gates	0.64	Others
5	Water	0.50	Ecological function
6	DD Wood	0.36	Consumption
7	Revenue	0.29	Others
8	INCR Wall	0.00	Others

Note:

Open Grazing — means the requirement of allowing cattle into the park for grazi[illegible] as was allowed previously. It is a service related to livelihood.

Longer Permits — means the duration, under the present circumstances, of four month permits for the removal of fodder grass should be increased.

Employment — need for better employment opportunities related to expansion of tourism.

Gates — requirement of more gates as they have to jump the wall to enter the park.

Water — regulation of water by the wetland for irrigation and domestic purposes.

DD Wood — fuelwood and other deadwoods.

Revenue — revenue collected by the park authorities should be shared.

INCR Wall — height of the wall surrounding the park should be increased so that wild herbivores cannot eat their crops.

value, was done by applying t-test.[11] The hypothesis of no significant difference in the means was accepted in both the cases at 5 per cent level of significance. This implies that for the villagers the two types of *services* were of equal importance and therefore, either one of the scores could be taken as an input into the combined *Effects Table*. Similarly, the two items of *consumption* were also equally important and the score for deadwood was selected as the input into the combined *Effects Table*.

Differences in value perceived from KNP by different stakeholders are illustrated clearly by the results obtained from villagers' perceptions. The Value obtained from livelihood provided and services rendered in that connection come out on top as having the highest value scores. Ecological function is next and all other sources of value are grouped together at the bottom of the preference profile.

Non-user perception was identified on the basis of a pilot survey of Delhi residents drawn from areas with differing kinds of environmental situations and differing population densities.[12]

The perception of these people regarding the main reason for the park conservation and preservation reveals that from their point of view the park should be preserved for maintaining ecosystem stability. Ecological functions and consumption value featured prominently in their ranking of sources of value of KNP as illustrated in the scores tabulated in Table 27.8. Interestingly, preservation for future generations, existence value and livelihood generation capability came next. Ritual, cultural and aesthetic values were at the bottom of the scale.

Table 27.9 classifies value scores of different stakeholders into three categories, in accordance with the significance accorded to them, with Category 1 being the one with the highest significance and Category 3 the one with the least.

Though a fair degree of conflict is inherent in the above rankings, it is important to note the areas of agreement. Ritual cultural and so-called aesthetic values seem to be pretty low down in the preference pattern of three of the four categories of stakeholders. This is probably due to the fact that they have found a reflection in other ways such as in the ecological function and existence values concepts. Alternatively, it may mean that the value system itself has undergone a process of change.

TABLE 27.8: **Non-users' Perception of Value**

Rank	Option	RM-Score	Kinds of Use
1	ECOL	1.00	Ecofun
2	GOODS	0.87	Consumption
3	AESTH	0.13	Aesthetic
4	RIGHT	0.62	Existence
5	FUTGEN	0.75	Future
6	FUTUSE	0.38	Future
7	LIVE	0.50	Livelihood
8	REC	0.25	Aesthetic
9	RITCUL	0.00	Ritual-cultural

Both classes of non-users, the scientists and the non-users, seem to realize the significance of livelihoods generated by KNP. This provides some common ground for policy making. The ecological function of the wetland in preserving the water and nutrient flows seems to be given a high value by scientists, villagers and non-users outside the park. Such perceived congruence in value perception is an important point of take-off for policy.

7. Government as the Manager of KNP

While the existence and different forms of management of KNP have resulted in significant changes in its management, it is important to note that the government has been subsidizing the park. Table 27.10 gives an indication of the magnitude of this subsidy.

TABLE 27.9: **Classification of Perception of Value**

Category	Scientists	Tourists	Village residents	Non-Users
I. High Value	Rarity, Ecological function, Existence	Aesthetic, Curiosity	Livelihood and related services, employment	Ecological function, Consumption
II. Medium	Consumption, Livelihood, Future	Existence	Ecological function	Existence, Future, Livelihood
III. Low	Services, Ritual cultural, Aesthetic	Services, others	Others including Ritual Cultural	Ritual Cultural, Aesthetic

TABLE 27.10: **Revenue and Expenditure of KNP.**

Year	Revenue (Rs.)	Expenditure (Rs.)
1990-91	10,97,836	17,48,162
1991-92	17,37,712	14,79,042
1992-93	18,63,630	2,30,339
1993-94	20,27,825	19,79,443
1994-95	19,76,480	22,91,024
1995-96	24,52,000	37,07,400

An important issue from the management's point of view and also from the macro economic viewpoint relates to the reduction of these subsidies.

From the main heads of expenditure for the year 1995-96, it can be seen that the single largest item of expenditure for the park authorities was the creation of open water bodies. Such open water spaces are the required habitat for several bird species, including the Siberian crane. However, in recent years, the aquatic area of the park has been shrinking, due to the uncontrolled growth of weeds like the water hyacinth and *Paspalum distichum*. Though several methods like bulldozing, cutting and burning have been tried to control the growth of these weeds, they have met with only limited success. Hence, some observers like Vijayan (1987 and 1988) have recommended that grazing by a limited number of buffaloes be re-introduced into the system. Though there are several people who empathize with the view that the local communities should have a stake in the management process, how far such models of people's participation will be permitted in KNP, however, still remains inconclusive.

In conclusion, it can be said that there exists a case for significant changes in the management of the park. While some of these changes are concerned with low-income users such as villagers in the surrounding regions, reduction in subsidies to the park by tapping the spending capability of high-income users such as tourists is a step in the right direction. It is important in this context to examine the nature of demand for tourism services generated by the park. In other words, the economic value as expressed in the market needs to be determined in order to take appropriate measures that help to make park management independent of subsidization. This source of income can be used profitably to protect the ecology of the park as well.

8. Towards Joint Management with Stakeholder Participation

Some policy implications of the study in the context of joint management of protected areas, in particular wetlands, are recapitulated below:

1. Cost incurred locally is a better index of the price paid by tourists to visit the Keoladeo National Park than the total travel cost. This is primarily on account of the location and the joint product nature of the services provided. The demand for the Keoladeo National Park tourism services is fairly insensitive to price.
2. If a redistribution of the benefits and costs from the Keoladeo National Park were attempted through an increase in the entry fee, among other things, the demand would not be affected.
3. Stakeholders other than tourists value livelihood and ecological functions of the park highly as indicated by the scores obtained from multi-criteria analysis. Aesthetic and ritual value is quite low in their ranking.

"Wise Use" needs to be identified at the wetland level for specific sites. To begin with, this could be done for major wetlands identified as Ramsar sites. The following policy directions to determine levels of sustainable use can be suggested:

1. Bring together all stakeholders in the wetland in a local area institution[13]: elicit views on the wise use and use it as a forum for increasing awareness,
2. Simultaneously, commission studies by wetland specialists to determine the levels of extraction and use that are compatible with the maintenance of the ecological health of the wetland.
3. Examine the outcome of 1 and 2 and arrive at a policy for use in

consultation with stakeholders, which include all local-level development agencies.

4. Ensure an environmental impact analysis of all development projects undertaken in the area, defined to include the catchment. Projects with an adverse impact on the health of the wetland would need to be reviewed to include abatement measures.

In the context of KNP, for instance, increased use of pesticides by agriculturists in the catchment has had adverse consequences for birds in the park. Industries located in the catchment also have an effect on the water in KNP. A policy to counter this needs to be worked out at the local level in consultation with the agriculturists themselves.

Another issue relates to the optimum amount of grazing in the park. The legal position with respect to national parks insists on total elimination of human intervention. However, as discussed at length earlier, expert opinion on the levels of extraction of grass with or without grazing differs. The official position on this needs to be spelt out, perhaps changed in the interest of "wise use", cost effective management of the park and welfare of local communities.

Wetlands differ in stakeholders' market linkages. Some areas are with a large tourist presence. Policies with regard to tourism need to address the following issues:

1. Impact of the magnitude of tourists and of the manner in which they use the wetland on its health needs to be determined. The questions to be addressed in each context relate to determining the form of eco-tourism and the limit, if any, on tourist numbers in the interests of the wetland ecosystem.
2. Determining the extent to which cross substitution between different categories of stakeholders can improve the financial management of the wetland. In particular high-income tourists, scientists and others with a stake in preservation could pay for it and/or compensate for the loss in the income of low income stakeholders incurred due to the limiting of use and extraction to sustainable levels.
3. Where the above is not possible, the magnitude of subsidy required to maintain the wetland in a healthy state needs to be determined and sources of government or non-government funding found for it. This may be at national or international levels.
4. Conservation enthusiasts, both within and outside the country, may be willing to pay for the up-keep and maintenance of wetlands, if proper institutions are in place for their management.

Determining the sound management practices is helped if the nature of demand for the services of the park is spelt out. In the case of KNP, for instance, this study shows that the demand for tourism services is quite inelastic and it seems possible to implement a policy of cross subsidization. This is attributable to the specific nature of demand for its services. Willingness to pay by non-users exists to a limited degree and is conditional on the introduction of accountability and transparency in management.

Institutions need to be set up, spelt out and made accountable at different levels. Some methods of doing this are spelt out below:

1. The nodal organization is the "Committee of Stakeholders" at the local level. This committee could be a subcommittee of the local panchayat or urban municipality as the case may be in order to give it a legal standing. It has to be defined for each wetland area to include representatives of
   (a) all persons who have an interest/stake in it, in particular local populations who have traditionally been using the wetland and the managers, such as the Forest Department,
   (b) all plan or project implementing departments in the area whose activities may impinge on the health of the wetland, and
   (c) representatives of the private sector units whose activities affect the wetland.

2. The Committee of stakeholders works in collaboration with local scientists and universities to determine whether a convergence exists between indigenous perceptions and scientific knowledge. At times, this collaboration may have to be worked out with institutions outside the area.
3. Plans for wetland conservation, management and use evolve from the deliberations of these local-level institutions and are presented and discussed at the appropriate State and Central Government ministries levels. Here they are viewed in the larger context of the conservation and development needs of the nation. It is important that at these levels as well, all development implementing agencies of the government are fully represented and involved.
4. It may be useful to aim at setting up these procedures for a few sites initially, possibly the Ramsar sites or those where information or experience exists. A phased plan for all wetlands could then be drawn up.

NOTES

1. See IIPA (1993) and Kothari (1989).
2. See, for instance the insistence on "wise use" in the Ramsar Convention for wetlands (IUCN 1971)..
3. See Map 26.1 for location and other details with respect to Keoladeo National Park.
4. For a description of the methodological details of the travel cost method, the assumptions it makes and likely problems, see chapter 10 of the report (Chopra *et al.* 1997).
5. See Appendix of Chapter10 of the report for the tourists scedule canvassed. (Chopra *et al.* 1997) See also Maerud and Mungatena (1994) and Ward and Loomis (1986.
6. The functional form with logarithms of the independent variables gives a lower value as expected.
7. See Appendix Chapter X of the report for the schedule canvassed (Chopra *et al.* 1997).
8. The software called DEFINITE has been used for this exercise. See Jansen (1994) and Jansson and Van Herwijnen (1994) for details of the technique used.
9. About 400 individuals were represented by the sample of 111 respondents who were interviewed.
10. See WWF (1996) for details of the study.
11 The calculated t-values for Services and Consumption were 1.27 and 0.61 respectively with 10 df in each case.
12 see Chapter for details with respect to the results of this survey (Chopra *et al.* 1997).
13 This could be a new institution or an existing legal institution such as a panchayat or an urban local body.

REFERENCES

Chopra, Kanchan *et al.* 1997. *Economic Valuation of Biodiversity-status Paper* (Part I) and *A Case Study of Keoladeo National Park,* Bharatpur (Part II), Institute of Economic Growth, December, 1997.

IIPA. 1993. Wildlife Management in India. *Mimeo,* New Delhi: IIPA, June 1993.

IUCN. 1971. "The Ramsar Convention. The Final Act of the International Conference on the Conservation of Wetlands and Waterfall", *IUCN Bulletin 2, Special Supplement,* pp. 1-4.

Jansson, Ron. 1994. "Multiobjective Decision Support for Environmental Management". *Environment & Management,* Vol. 2&3. The Netherlands: Kluwer Academic Publishers, Dordrecht.

Jansson, Ron and Marjan van Herwijnen. 1994. *DEFINITE: A System To Support Decisions on a FINITE Set of Alternatives: User Manual.* The Netherlands: Kluwer Academic Publishers, Dordrecht.

Kothari, A. *et al.* 1989. *Management of National Parks and Santuaries in India, A Status Report,* New Delhi: IIPA.

Murty, M.N. and Susan M. Menkhaus. 1994. "Economic Aspects of Wildlife Protection in the Developing Countries: A Case Study of Keoladeo National Park, Bharatpur India". *Mimeo,* Delhi: Institute of Economic Growth.

Navrud and Mungatana. 1994. "Environmental Valuation in Developing Countries : The Recreational Value of Wildlife Viewing." *Ecological Economics,* Vol. 11, pp. 135-151.

Vijayan, V.S. 1987. "Keoladeo National Park Ecology Study". *Report January to June 1987.*

Bombay Natural History Society.

Vijayan, V.S. 1988. "Ecology of Keoladeo National Park". *Annual Report 1988*. Bombay Natural History Society.

Walsh, R.G. 1986. *Recreation Economic Decisions: Comparing Benefits and Costs*. USA: Venture Publishing, State College, PA.

Ward, F.A. and John, B. Loomis. 1986. "The Travel Cost Demand Model as an Environmental Policy Assessment Tool : A Review of the Literature." *Western Journal of Agricultural Economics*, Vol. 11, pp. 164-78.

WWF. 1996. "Participatory Management Planning for Keoladeo National Park", Bharatpur, India. New Delhi: WWF India.

28 Management Issues of Aquatic Resources Including Wetlands

Brij Gopal

The rapid depletion and degradation of natural resources have been a matter of concern for several decades. It is widely recognized that the problems related to the natural resources (and environment) are multifaceted and hence, the solutions to them also require multi-disciplinary attention. Earlier, the degradation of natural resources was perceived and analysed mainly as physical and biological processes accentuated by anthropogenic activities. Much emphasis was laid on the ever-growing human population, and the rate and patterns of resource consumption as the major factors causing degradation. During the past few decades, the social scientists have also contributed significantly to the resolution of the problems of natural resources' degradation and their management by examining the problem from a sociological perspective. In this context, the economists have begun recognizing the differences between the traditional economics of human generated products and that of the natural resources. Consequently, there has emerged a new discipline of natural resources economics which seeks to provide fresh perspectives to the policy and management aspects through various methods of economic analysis (Kerr *et al.* 1997).

The natural resource economists are examining the natural resources and their management in terms of property rights regimes. It is widely held that the management of a natural resource, used collectively by a community or a group of communities, depends upon the appropriate property rights structures (regimes), institutional arrangements and authority systems (Singh 1997). Thirty years ago, Hardin (1968) in his classic essay, "The Tragedy of the Commons", had expressed the view that any resource to which several individuals have common access is apt to be overused and exhausted. The subject has been extensively debated with numerous examples in various parts of the world.

Water is one of the most valuable resources on which the very survival of humans depends. It has often determined the progress and fate of civilizations, kingdoms and societies, and yet it has nearly always been treated as an open access resource. This did not affect the resource appreciably until the uses and needs were limited. The people had open access not only to water but also to all the biological resources (such as fish) in some areas such as rivers and lakes whereas at some places the waterbodies such as village ponds and fish tanks were held as common pool resources. Today, water has become a scarce and highly polluted commodity which is threatening not only human activities but the very survival of humans as well as other life, and the aquatic biological resources have declined sharply.

The issues related to the property rights regimes of aquatic resources and their management are far more complicated than those of the terrestrial resources with which the resource economists have so far been largely concerned. In this chapter, I present some aspects of this complexity and my thoughts on the management of the inland aquatic resources, particularly wetlands, and the applicability of the concepts of property regimes to them.

1. Inland Aquatic Resources

The inland aquatic resources comprise various kinds of natural and man-made water-bodies such as streams, rivers, lakes, reservoirs, ponds, tanks, etc. During the past four decades, another term "wetlands" has come into common use for a wide spectrum of aquatic habitats. The ecological characteristics, values and human use of these aquatic resources depend greatly upon their size (area and depth), shape and the surrounding landscape. Besides water, a distinctive feature common between the rivers, lakes, reservoirs, wetlands and all other aquatic resources is that they are an integral part of the landscape unit called watershed (UNEP and WI 1997). A major part of the precipitation over a watershed runs off down the slope into the streams and rivers, which carry it to another watershed or to the sea, or accumulates in depressions, the lakes. The flow in a stream or over the land surface is often checked by humans by constructing dams (reservoirs). The seasonal variability in precipitation and the amount of surface runoff primarily determine the amount of water in the streams, rivers, lakes, reservoirs and other shallow depressions. Accordingly, land areas adjacent to these waterbodies become flooded for different durations and to various depths. Such areas, which experience periodic exposure and flooding, and generally lie at the interface between the upland (terrestrial) and open water (for example, the river floodplains and shallow marginal areas of lakes and reservoirs) are typically identified as wetlands. They also include shallow waterbodies with large water level changes, even if not associated with a river, lake or sea (Mitsch and Gosselink 1993).

Water itself is a multiple-use resource for humans. It has both consumptive and non-consumptive uses. The consumptive uses include drinking, food production (irrigation) and industrial use. The non-consumptive uses include bathing, recreation (water sports), industrial and other cooling, transport, energy generation (hydropower) and waste disposal. However, water is also essential for all other life some of which are directly important for humans. A large diversity of plants and animals occurs in water or depends on aquatic resources at least for a part of their life-cycle. Of these many such as reeds, fish, frogs and ducks are directly utilized by the humans while others are of indirect value. Further, water has also a direct and dominant influence on the macro- and micro-climate.

Thus, the aquatic resources such as rivers, lakes and wetlands are not simply a resource with multiple uses but a complex system of multiple resources many of which have multiple uses. In fact, Pearce and Turner (1990) have called wetlands as "multifunctional resources".

1.a. Resource vs Multiple Resource Systems

It is important to recognize the distinction between the individual resources such as minerals, plants or fish, and the multiple resource systems which indeed are whole ecological systems. Rivers, lakes and wetlands are ecological systems, which have, besides water, many biological resources. These biological resources and water interact with each other in such a complex manner that the use of any one of them affects the other to some extent. The very existence of the biological resources is dependent upon the availability, quantity and quality (in terms of physical and chemical characteristics) of water. In turn, the biological resources also exert influence on the water, particularly its quality. Further, the use of one biological resource often affects the others, generally adversely. Therefore, water and the biological resources cannot be considered separately and individually as resources under particular property rights regimes.

The issues, related to aquatic resources are further complicated for two additional reasons. First and foremost, as pointed out earlier, all aquatic systems, being an integral part of their watersheds, receive their water moving through the surrounding terrestrial landscape (Fig. 28.1). Without their respective watersheds, the waterbodies have no existence. Further, all watershed-based human activities exert demand on water and/or contribute to the degradation of water quality (influx of silt, nutrients and other pollutants from land with surface or subsurface runoff) and affect the amount of water in the system through reduced flows and increasing siltation of the water body.

Second, multiple uses and demands of water differ from the multiple uses of terrestrial resources. Many of the multiple uses of water are quite incompatible with each other. The demands for various uses are often met without proper allocation. Consumptive uses such as drinking water supply,

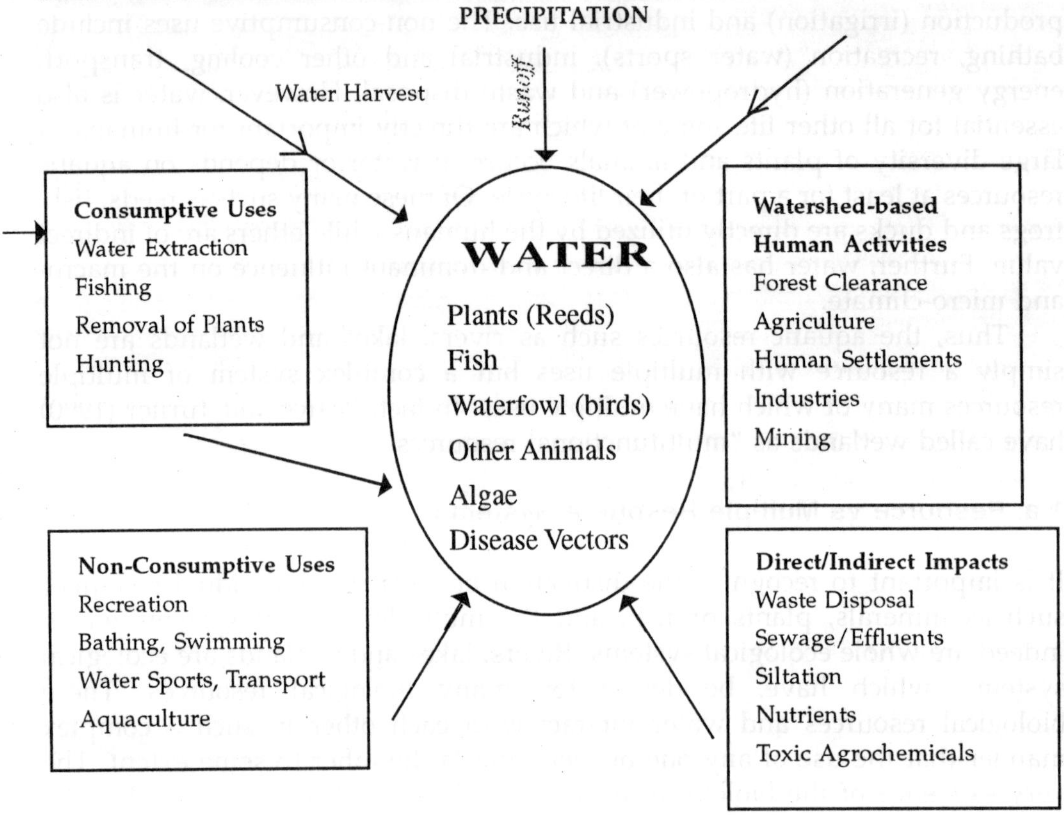

Fig. 28.1: Impacts of consumptive and non-consumptive uses of aquatic resources and the human activities in their watershed on various aquatic resources.

irrigation and industrial use adversely affect the availability (e.g. for fisheries, and hydropower generation) besides degrading the water quality indirectly (waste inflow/discharge). Non-consumptive uses such as fisheries and aquaculture, bathing and recreation, and transport render the water quality unfit for drinking supplies and increase the costs of treatment. These multiple demands on water have direct consequences for the availability and quality of water for all the biological resources.

The values of wetlands are not confined to the above-mentioned direct uses by humans alone. The natural functions such as storage of excess (flood) water, recharge of aquifers, protection of shorelines (and riverbanks) against erosion, protection against cyclonic storms (e.g. by mangroves), bring indirect benefits to humans. The wetlands together with other aquatic resources provide habitat and necessary resources for a large diversity of plant and animal life which itself is important for the direct and indirect values attached to the aquatic resources and for a sustainable Earth. These functions and values have been discussed in many recent publications, for example, Pearce and Turner (1990), Constanza *et al.* (1993), Gopal (1995).

1.b. Degradation and Loss of Aquatic Resources

All water-bodies are subjected to natural processes of change, though over different time scales. The lakes get filled with incoming sediments and autochthonous organic matter and become shallower or turn into dry uplands over centuries or millennia (Moss, 1988). Coastal lagoons become brackish or freshwater as their interaction with the sea is stopped by the gradual deposition of sand at their mouth. Rivers often meander due to the deposition of alluvial mineral matter, leave cut-off portions of their channels, and sometimes change their course completely (Petts and Amoros, 1996). However, various anthropogenic activities in and around the waterbody and in the entire watershed cause rapid degradation and loss of these aquatic resources (Gopal 1995).

Rapid losses occur by draining and/or filling of the waterbody in order to reclaim land for economically more lucrative uses (residential, industrial and commercial). Diversion of flows for irrigation, channelization and construction of dams have converted the rivers and streams into reservoirs or dried them up. These activities directly reduce the river floodplains and alter their vegetation and fauna. Changes in the interaction with the river water affect the fertility of the floodplain for agriculture and its use for grazing, and in turn affect the rural and tribal human populations dependent upon them.

Intense human activity, especially deforestation and agriculture, on a large scale throughout the watershed of the waterbody results in the erosion of sediments and increased runoff which carries the nutrients and other agrochemicals to the waterbodies. This leads to their rapid siltation and eutrophication with consequences for both the aquatic plant and animal communities (Fig. 28.1).

Over-exploitation of resources, particularly of biological resources such as food, feed, fibre and fuel, causes not only degradation of other aquatic resources but many organisms may be lost for ever. Overgrazing by domestic cattle adversely affects the stream bank integrity, increasing siltation and runoff with a consequent loss of fish in the river.

The disposal of partly treated or untreated domestic sewage and industrial effluents (also other organic and toxic wastes) affect the water quality and the organisms. The eutrophication often results in excessive growth of undesirable aquatic vegetation which has adverse consequences for many uses of the aquatic resource.

The waterbodies often support a variety of organisms (insects, molluscs, leeches, etc.) which are vectors of important human pathogens. The use of herbicides and pesticides to control nuisance growth of weeds and disease vectors within the waterbody and/or in its watershed is another major cause of degradation.

1.c. Management Problems of Multiple Resource Systems

The complex interactions between water and biological resources on the one hand and their interactions with the watershed on the other cause conflicts between various uses of different resources, particularly when the management by the humans, under any particular property regime, seeks to maximize two or more incompatible uses in the waterbody and its watershed. Pearce and Turner distinguish between "natural" and "created" uses which cause conflicts and lead to inefficient management and degradation. The "created" uses need not be a new use but also the maximization of one of the "natural" uses. The numerous human activities in the watershed continue to aggravate the problem of using the waterbody sustainably. It is also readily forgotten that the rivers, lakes and wetlands have many functions and values but neither any one of these systems can perform all the functions nor all the systems can perform the same function. For example, all lakes and wetlands cannot be used for waste disposal without grave consequences, all wetlands cannot be used for drinking water supply and the same lake or river cannot be used for waste disposal as well as for recreation and fishing.

Extending the consideration further to the watershed brings to light many more problems. How can an individual or a community be the owner of a waterbody which lies embedded in a watershed owned by others and derive its water as well as minerals from the entire catchment area. How can one exercise his rights over the water which may be prevented from flowing into the waterbody by a user of the watershed. This conflict extends today to disputes between the upper and lower riparian administrative units—states and nations, not just individuals or village communities. The conflict does not end there with the water alone because the water-body also influences and often supports the resources in the watershed. A large variety of animals including fish, birds and turtles migrate across the continents seasonally to utilise the aquatic resources lying within the watersheds separated totally from each other. The international Convention on Migratory Species enjoins upon the member nations to protect not only the migratory species but their habitats and resources along the migration routes. How can the right-holders to the aquatic system and its resources under any particular property rights regime use or manage the resources without regard to the international obligations?

The conflicts that arise between the multiple uses of an aquatic system, and between the use of the aquatic system and its watershed, cannot be resolved simply by allocating a part of the resource for different uses (sharing of a common pool resource by various stakeholders). Whereas in terrestrial systems it is possible to allocate land for various uses (settlements, industry, agriculture, forestry, conservation, etc.) and in a manner so as to minimize the adverse impacts of one activity on the other, an aquatic ecosystem cannot be divided into zones for different uses without impacts on all the activities. Similarly, zonation (core and buffer zones) is practised in protected areas where certain human activities and resource extraction are permissible beyond the "core area for conservation". Such a zonation within an aquatic ecosystem is generally meaningless. In case of rivers, the interconnected network of tributaries and the flow regimes make zonation for multiple uses extremely difficult. The uses along the length of a river must ensure that the upstream activity does not affect the downstream use.

2. Aquatic Resources and Property Regimes

The rivers, lakes and wetlands have remained until recently an open access resource particularly for their non-consumptive uses such as bathing and recreation. Until the human population pressure was relatively small and the demand for aquatic biological resources was limited to the local communities, everyone in the community had an open access. With an increasing demand for water and other resources as well as an increase in the categories of stakeholders, the property regimes had to be changed through an intervention of the government. Whereas certain sections of the river continue to be an open access resource, the reservoir(s) built on it become the State property. Similarly, large lakes and many wetlands were open access resources until their uses became partially regulated by the State. Smaller wetlands such as village ponds, fish ponds and temple tanks were and continue to be common pool resources owned and managed by the local communities.

The concept of property regimes needs to be re-examined in the context of the aquatic resources. A lake or a reservoir or even a river cannot be treated simply as a State property because there are many stakeholders (government agencies/departments). The common pool resources are owned and managed collectively taking into consideration the interests of all stakeholders. However, the aquatic resources such as lakes, reservoirs, wetlands or even rivers are neither owned nor managed collectively. The stakeholders include the departments of irrigation, hydropower, municipal water supply, fisheries, tourism, revenue, agriculture, forests and wildlife, health, waste disposal, industries, and a host of other smaller ones. Every stakeholder tries to maximize the benefits without caring for the others and without owning a responsibility. As pointed out earlier, several other agencies operating in the catchment continue activities with total disregard to the impacts on the aquatic resources. Thus, majority of the aquatic resources including wetlands cannot be fragmented into individual components for ownership or management.

3. Wetlands as Common Pool Resources

It is widely recognized that the wetlands were managed in the past by traditional local communities which treated them as common pool resources, and that the change in property regimes and management practices have degraded the wetlands. In fact, many wetlands have been used for centuries as an open access resource system. However, this is only partly true as far as the wetlands (including ponds, temple tanks, etc.) are considered in isolation of their surrounding landscapes. Let us examine the management issues of the aquatic systems with a few better known examples of wetlands which will demonstrate that the degradation has resulted from a suit of many more factors than those invoked by the concept of property regimes.

First, we should understand the evolution of the wetlands over time as a system whose values are now being recognized for specific purposes. In general, all wetlands have co-evolved with humans who have interacted with them for many millennia. Agriculture started in the alluvial floodplains of the rivers where periodic flooding provided enough nutrients and soil moisture for raising crops. Humans also started their settlements along the rivers, lakes and wetlands which allowed ready access to water, aquatic biological resources (plant and fish) and facilitated both agriculture and transport. There is little doubt that in the beginning the aquatic systems were used as open access resources and only gradually turned into common pool resources which were defended by the user communities against additional users. Probably the conflicts between multiple uses were resolved by the experience gained with time and the dependence on the resources in the absence of mobilization of resources from other areas. The degradation of the resources did not occur because of the low human population which may have even moved to other areas when necessary. However, it is impossible to peep into the past for a glimpse of the diversity of resources and their value perceived by early societies. However, the place of wetlands and their biota in the Indian culture and ethos and innumerable references to them in the ancient Indian literature reflect the close association between humans and wetlands as well as a respect for the resources.

3.a. Lake Kolleru Wetland

Lake Kolleru occupies a large area (900 sq.km) of periodically flooded lowland—a system of large ponds in the middle of the deltas of rivers Godavari and Krishna on the eastern coast of India. It has a catchment area spread over 5,000 sq.km. There were about 70 villages in the bed of the shallow lake (average 1 m deep) and about 120 village settlements in the surrounding area. The villagers (about 15,000) utilized and managed the area as a common pool resource. They cultivated rice, farmed ducks, grew bananas and caught fish. Palms, reeds, cattails and other resources were used for navigation, housing, etc. Molluscs were harvested, shelled and stored for feeding ducks. The community disposed its wastes into the waterbody. Additional 40,000 people around the lake depended on the fish and paddy cultivation in the area. There were also hunters which lived on hunting waterfowl. Yet, it was a productive wetland with very high biodiversity. It provided subsistence to a large local community, supplied fish to the neighbouring areas of the State, and served as an important refuge for a very large population of migratory waterfowl (Seshavatharam 1978, Gopal 1990).

The Government of Andhra Pradesh saw potential in the area for developing into fish tanks for increasing the income of the community, State revenue and possibly other benefits. The cooperative fish farming was promoted by an official order, and the fish farms were started by converting the natural wetlands through dredging. Fishery yields increased at the cost of duck farming, waterfowl and other biodiversity, and other natural resources. Natural vegetation was replaced by eucalyptus raised on the bunds of large fish tanks. This did result in social conflicts and criminal activity as well. There was institutionalization of the management of the system for a specific resource. The natural system is now almost completely lost. The wetland is no more a CPR although the fish tanks owned and managed by the cooperatives could be called a common property. The resource degradation has been the result of a change in the property regime imposed by the government, and neither due to a normal decay of the traditional institutions nor due to over-exploitation of the natural resource by the local communities.

The periodic flooding was seen to be detrimental to the economic potential of the area. It was considered more profitable to use the large amounts of water for raising culture fisheries by storing it in large deep tanks. The value of the duck farming, and the subsistence of the village communities was underestimated and the value for wildlife, particularly the waterfowl, was ignored. Now that the wetland conservation is becoming an international topic, the remaining few small isolated pockets of naturally waterlogged or flooded areas are being projected as the Kolleru Lake in need of conservation. The impact of water harvesting on the catchment area for agriculture and human settlements, and of the chemical pollution from the agriculture and fish tanks is being overlooked.

In sum, a natural resource managed earlier also as a CPR has been degraded and lost by mismanagement under another property regime due to the emphasis on monetary economics and not because it became an open access resource.

3.b. Keoladeo Ghana National Park

If open access to a resource leads to overexploitation without responsibility for its management, management by the property holder without understanding the nature and characteristics of the resource can also result in its degradation. This is best exemplified by the example of the Keoladeo Ghana National Park at Bharatpur. The area now under the Park was once a floodplain of rivers Gambhir and Banganga, two tributaries of river Yamuna. As the area is geomorphologically a saucer-shaped basin in which Bharatpur township (a former princely State) is located, periodic heavy flooding caused serious damage to the agriculture and the settlements. The erstwhile Maharaja constructed an earthen dam (Ajan bund) to isolate the area from a large reservoir where water could be stored and carried through a network of canals (passing through the Park) for irrigation on the other sides. As the undulating area comprising a mosaic of shallow depressions and forest escaped from deep short-term flooding and the depressions retained water for longer periods, it attracted huge flocks of waterfowl including many migratory species. The Maharaja then converted it into a private reserve but allowed an almost open access to the villagers for fuelwood, Vetiveria grass and cattle grazing. The Park area remained a common property resource for use by the villagers and their cattle even after independence although it was declared a wildlife sanctuary. The change in the status of the area did not affect the rights of the villagers to use the resources—fuelwood, water and grass. The use as well as the activity inside were considered detrimental to the goals of conservation of the area without understanding the system. A ban on human use and grazing has created many difficulties for the park, and a degradation is clearly visible. The overgrowth of grass affects the same waterfowl for which grazing was banned. The ban on fuelwood removal has caused fire accidents, and now management for fire, as well as rapid terrestrialization of the system. (For detailed information on the Park, its resources and problems, see Vijayan 1991 and L. Vijayan 1994).

The problems have also arisen due to the changes in the interaction of the Park with its watershed outside the Park boundary. The rapid strides in agriculture with the use of fertilizers and pesticides have increased the demand for water for irrigation. The water is no more supplied to the villages on the other side through the canals. In years of extreme drought such as 1978 and 1979, the water scarcity is perceived as a major problem for the management of the wetland. In fact, the supply of a small amount of groundwater extracted from deep borewells dug inside the Park (1979) had created a major problem of the dense growth of cattails in a part of the area which had to be cleared by bulldozers.

Water has been perceived a problem because the Park depends on water from outside through a system of canals and sluice gates. The increasing demand of water in the watershed area has reduced the availability for the Park (except in 1998 when excessive unseasonal rains brought in enough water into the Park). A change in the institutional arrangements together with the emphasis on the resource to be used/conserved has degraded the whole system.

3.c. Lake Chilka

Lake Chilka on the east coast of India is a large lagoon which exchanges water with the sea (Bay of Bengal) through a mouth. It receives freshwater on its northern side from two major rivers, Daya and Bhargavi, besides several smaller streams draining the catchment on the west. The oceanic currents transport huge amounts of silt which tend to narrow down or close the mouth. The lagoon is estuarine in character, with the northern side being more freshwater while the southern part is saline. The lower influx of sea water through the mouth lowers the salinity in the southern part whereas the northern freshwater part is prone to filling due to increased siltation from the catchment. A change in the salinity regimes is one of the major problems. The lagoon has been the major source of livelihood for a large population of local fishing community which has used the lake since centuries as a common pool (or open access) resource for the highly valued prawn fisheries. The yields have greatly declined in recent years. This decline and high economic returns from prawns led to the development of aquaculture along the margins. Recently efforts were initiated also to develop commercial aquaculture farms on the eastern side near the mouth. Increase in the fishing effort together with extensive recreational facilities, and increased siltation have led to the excessive growth of aquatic vegetation which comprises only a few species of macrophytes and some algae. The growth of human settlements, tourism-related activities, and processing of prawn fisheries are also contributing to the pollutional load. The published information on Lake Chilka has been reviewed in detail by Bandyopadhyay and Gopal (1991) and Ram *et al.* (1994).

The degradation of the resources of Lake Chilka is apparently the result of just not the overexploitation alone but the State-sponsored aquaculture activity on the one hand, and the degradation of the catchment itself, on the other. The natural forces of ocean currents also contribute to it. Efforts are being made to keep the mouth open by dredging to facilitate marine water enter the lagoon. In the absence of enough freshwater inflow (due to extraction in the catchment), there is a risk of an increase in the salinity and consequent change in the values of the system.

3.d. Loktak Lake

The Loktak Lake in Manipur is a large shallow lake on the west of river

Imphal. Hydrologically, the lake receives its water, besides runoff from the adjacent hills, from the river during high water period (flood) through a connecting channel, the Khordak cut. During the dry season, the lake drains into the river through the same channel. Thus, the lake experiences large water level changes, and serves as a nursery for the fishes whose fingerlings migrate from the downstream into the lake. The large mass of aquatic vegetation produces floating islands, the phumdis, and the local communities use the lake for fishing, cultivation of makhana (*Euryale ferox*), etc. The southern shallow part of the lake basin (Keibul Lamjao) also serves as the only habitat of the brow antler deer, an endangered species. There is no recorded account of degradation of the wetland or its resources as long as the local communities used it as an open access (or common pool) resource. In the 1970s, the government decided to convert Loktak Lake into a permanent lake by constructing a barrage on the Khordak cut (Ithai barrage) for exploiting the water for hydropower generation and irrigation on the other side of the hills. The change in the hydrological regime has adversely affected the whole system and its stakeholders. The phumdis have increased and covered a larger water surface, interfering with fishing and water extraction. The fish migration has ceased and the fisheries declined. The agricultural fields around the lake become flooded during the rainy season causing economic losses, makhana cultivation is no more possible in the lake, and water quality has deteriorated. The brow antler deer is also facing problems because of the change in its habitat. Once again the degradation of the wetland is not the result of over-exploitation or the failure of earlier institutional arrangement. The details of the lake, its resources and management problem are available in Tombi Singh and Singh (1994).

3.e. Village Ponds and Tanks

There are hundreds of thousands of small and large ponds scattered throughout the country. Most of these ponds have been constructed for various purposes such as irrigation, religious functions (temple tanks) or fish culture. However, they have multiple uses which also include washing, bathing, recreation, and sometimes domestic uses. Marothia (1997) has discussed the institutional arrangements of their management. Whereas some ponds have been private properties, majority of them have been managed as common pool resources. The uses were regulated by Village Panchayats which avoided conflicting uses to a great extent. For example, use for fish culture (often on lease to an individual or a group of fishermen) did not allow inputs such as agrochemicals and feeds which adversely affect other uses. The introduction of the Fish Farmers Development Agency for promoting increased fish yields and economic status of fishing community created problems for other stakeholders and consequently social conflicts. These issues have been discussed at length by Marothia (1997) who demonstrated that village-level institutions ensured fish production with low social conflict but the FFDA-sponsored aquaculture which focused on large external inputs affected other uses and increased social tensions. The same impacts have been pointed out above also in the case of Lake Kolleru. The promotion of fisheries in village tanks, primarily used for irrigation, has created similar conflicts between other uses of the aquatic resource.

4. Issues for Policy Initiatives

The foregoing examples show that the wetland resources have continued to be degraded irrespective of the property regimes of their management. Therefore, in all these cases, the property regimes and institutions alone cannot be blamed for the degradation of the valuable resource systems. Singh (1997) has pointed out, in a different context though, that "Theoretically, all of these systems of ownership (private, public and collective) are equally good or bad... No system of management will work successfully in all situations and at all times. The choice of a system will depend on the particular resource and setting in question, and often requires an interdisciplinary approach...." Clearly, as discussed above, the aquatic resources are multiple use systems where emphasis on one or the other use adversely affects other uses and hence the stakeholders. Further, the functions and values of aquatic resources depend upon the catchment basins. In simple words, there are many more stakeholders with an interest in the aquatic resources beyond its physical boundaries and their activities influence the multiple resources. The concept of property regimes, which suits best specific terrestrial resources, cannot be applied to the aquatic resources without taking the entire watershed into consideration.

Two concepts related to property regimes are those of participatory management and traditional practices. The participatory management is not the same as common property regime because the ownership lies with the State or a different organization which also determines primarily the management objectives. This does not ensure that the activities outside the area or their impact on the resource are taken into account. There is growing appreciation of the importance of traditional practices in the management of natural resources. These practices were regulated, explicitly or implicitly, by the almost total dependence of the communities on a particular resource. The access gained and/or provided to the resources from distant areas has also reduced the dependence and hence, the traditional practices got gradually abandoned. At the same time the misplaced development has also driven away the communities from traditional practices. The cost-benefit analyses have followed a narrow sectoral approach, and in the process ignored almost totally the indirect and intangible benefits from the natural resources as well as the indirect costs (externalities).

Unfortunately the natural resource management policies have followed a sectoral approach, focusing separately on one or the other resource of immediate interest. Even the so-called followers of the watershed approach tend to focus on soil and water conservation in the area for a particular goal (using water for the settlements or agriculture or natural vegetation). This is reflected in the measures taken such as construction of check dams and ponds or contouring the slopes and/or raising of soil binders (Chopra *et al.* 1988; Singh 1994). While these activities often have beneficial impacts on the downstream aquatic resources, the policy and planning initiatives do not take into account the interests of the stakeholders elsewhere in the downstream watersheds. The policy makers must consider the whole riverbasin as one watershed for which an integrated planning has to be made keeping in mind the multitude of resources and stakeholders as well as the cascading effect of activities in the upper riparian areas (upstream watershed) on the downstream areas. The institutional arrangements, at the level of a Village Panchayat or the State, must take cognizance of all the individual resources and various stakeholders in the entire sub-watershed instead of fragmenting it into small units for maximizing the use for one resource at a time, as well as the impacts of their activities on the downstream areas.

In conclusion, the management of aquatic resources including wetlands on a sustainable basis requires an integrated river-basin wide watershed approach, and sectoral policies and planning under any specific property regime or their combinations are not suitable for these resources.

REFERENCES

Bandyopadhyay, S. and B. Gopal. 1991. "Lake Chilka". In: Gopal, B. and V. Asthana (eds.) *Aquatic Sciences in India*, 117-172, New Delhi: Indian Assoc. Limnol. Oceanogr.

Chopra, K., G.K. Kadekodi and M.N. Murty. 1998. *Sukhomajri and Dhamala Watersheds in Haryana: A Participatory Approach to Management*, Delhi: Institute of Economic Growth.

Constanza, R., W.M. Kemp and W.R., Boynton. 1993. Predictability, scale and biodiversity in coastal and estuarine ecosystems: Implications for management, *Ambio* 22: 88-96.

Gopal, B. 1990. "Wetland (mis) management by keeping people out: two examples from India". pp. 352-59. In: Marchand, M. and H.A. Udo de Haes (eds.). *Proceedings of the International Conference on People's Role in Wetland Management*. Leiden, The Netherlands: Center for Environmental Studies Univ. of Leiden.

Gopal, B. (Compiler). 1995. "Handbook of Wetland Management", New Delhi: WWF-India.

Hardin, G. 1968. The tragedy of the commons, *Science* 162: 1243-1248.

Kerr, J.M., D.K. Marothia, K. Singh, C. Ramasamy and W.R. Bentley (eds.). 1997. *Natural Resource Economics: Theory and Application in India*, New Delhi: Oxford & IBH, 636p.

Marothia, D.K. 1997. "Institutional arrangements for common village fish ponds", In: Kerr, J.M.,

D.K. Marothia, K. Singh, C. Ramasamy and W.R. Bentley (eds.) *Natural Resource Economics: Theory and Application in India,* 463-76, New Delhi: Oxford & IBH.

Mitsch, W.J. and J.G. Gosselink. 1993. *Wetlands,* New York: Van Nostrand-Reinhold.

Moss, B. 1988. *Ecology of Freshwaters,* Oxford, U.K.: Blackwells.

Petts, G.E. and C. Amoros. 1996. *Fluvial Hydrosystems,* London: Chapman & Hall.

Pearce, D.W. and R.K. Turner. 1990. *Economics of Natural Resources and the Environment.* USA: The Johns Hopkins University Press, Baltimore, MD.

Ram, R.N., K.V. Rama Rao, and A. Ghosh. 1994. *Chilka Lake.* New Delhi: WWF-India, p. 69.

Singh, Kartar. 1994. *Managing Common Pool Resources: Principles and Case Studies,* New Delhi: Oxford Univ. Press.

Singh, Kartar. 1997. "Property rights and tenures in natural resources". In: Kerr, J.M., D.K. Marothia, K. Singh, C. Ramasamy and W.R. Bentley (eds.) *Natural Resource Economics: Theory and Application in India,* 131-59, New Delhi: Oxford & IBH.

Tombi Singh, H. and R.K. Shyamananda Singh. 1994. *Loktak Lake.* New Delhi: WWF-India, 69 p.

UNEP & WI. 1997. *Wetlands and Integrated River Basin Management: Examples from Asia and the Pacific,* UN Environment Programme, Nairobi, and Wetlands International-Asia Pacific, Kuala Lumpur.

Vijayan, L. 1994. *Keoladeo National Park,* New Delhi: WWF-India, 77 p.

Vijayan, V.S. 1991. *Keoladeo National Park: Ecology Study 1980-1990,* Summary, Bombay: Bombay Natural History Society, p. 25 + plates.

SECTION 6

COMMON POOL KNOWLEDGE

29 The Enclosure and Recovery of the Biological and Intellectual Commons

Vandana Shiva

1. Plant Genetic Resources and Intellectual Property Rights (IPRs)

The biological diversity of India has always been a common resource for lakhs of our traditional communities, who have utilised, protected and conserved their biodiversity heritage over centuries. Their collective and cumulative innovation has been the basis of local culture and local economies, which constitute the dominant economies in terms of the livelihoods provided and the needs met. In fact, their traditional knowledge of medicine, agriculture and fisheries is the primary base for meeting their food and health needs. For them, conserving biodiversity means to conserve the integrity of the ecosystem and species, the right to resources and knowledge and the right to the production systems based on biodiversity. Therefore, biodiversity is intimately linked to the traditional indigenous knowledge systems as well as the people's right to protect their knowledge and resources.

However, nature's diversity and the diversity of knowledge systems are undergoing a major process of destabilisation with the expansion of patents and IPRs into the domain of biodiversity, via the Trade-Related Aspects of Intellectual Property Rights (TRIPs) agreement of World Trade Organisation (WTO). The whole notion of TRIPs has been shaped by the objectives and interests of trade and Trans National Companies (TNCs). Through the instrument of TRIPs, TNCs have posed a potential threat to the biological and intellectual heritage of our diverse communities by appropriating and privatising their knowledge. For their commercial interests, biodiversity itself has no value, it is merely a "raw material" for the production of commodities and for the maximisation of profits (Shiva, Jafri, Bedi and Holla-Bhar 1997).

Biodiversity and knowledge of its utilisation are a common pool resource which have been maintained through institutional mechanisms and value systems over millennia. These subtle systems of maintaining the biological and intellectual commons have largely been ignored because an analysis of Common Property or Common Pool Resources (CPRs) has largely focussed on land as a resource, not so much on what grows on it. This is largely due to the fact that while land has been owned by the better-off sections, biodiversity has provided the survival base for the poorest. The neglect of biodiversity as a commons is thus related to the neglect of the poor.

Biodiversity came into focus in the 1990s as a result of the commercialisation of genetic resources, largely due to the emergence of the new technologies. This in turn has promoted the expansion of industrial property concepts such as patents to cover life forms. The broadening of the concept of patenting of IPRs to apply to genetic resources or living resources is in effect the enclosure and privatisation of the biological and intellectual commons.

While most intellectuals and experts treat such an enclosure as inevitable, I am compelled to resist it on epistemological, ethical and political grounds.

2. Why Patents on Life are Illegitimate—Epistemological Reasons

Patents are granted for inventions which are novel in non-obvious ways. However, life is not an "invention" in the way mechanical artifacts are. Nor is the knowledge of utilisation related to genetic resources always novel as the case of patenting of neem, basmati, turmeric, pepper, etc. makes clear. There is no inventiveness involved in the patent claims based on biopiracy. There is no epistemological basis of the claim of novelty. There is merely a sociological basis in the hierarchy of knowledge practitioners. The West is assumed to be more innovative than the non-West. A scientist trained in the Western science in non-Western societies is assumed to be more scientific and innovative than the one trained in the indigenous knowledge systems. On the basis of this assumed superiority, claims based on piracy by Western science or Western-trained scientists are interpreted as inventions. A social hierarchy is thus falsely mutated into an epistemological process (Shiva 1996).

The principle that plant *P* is useful for *U* is, therefore, existing knowledge, and cannot be treated as novel. Further, given this principle, small variations in processing *P* for *U* are an obvious step. How then does such knowledge get patented and qualify as "novel" and "non-obvious"?

The false claim to novelty is based on the existence of diverse and pluralistic knowledge systems. It is based on the fact that while such knowledge might exist in knowledge system Ki, it does not exist in the Western knowledge system *Kw*. The lateral transfer of knowledge with no epistemic value added, i.e. mere translation of the knowledge that plant *P* is useful for the purpose of *U* from system *Ki* to system *Kw* is taken as an innovation (Fig. 29.1). Translation of $Ki \rightarrow Kw$ in a hierarchical perspective suggests a "higher" level of knowledge content. Translation is misconstrued as the "creation" of knowledge (Fig. 29.2).

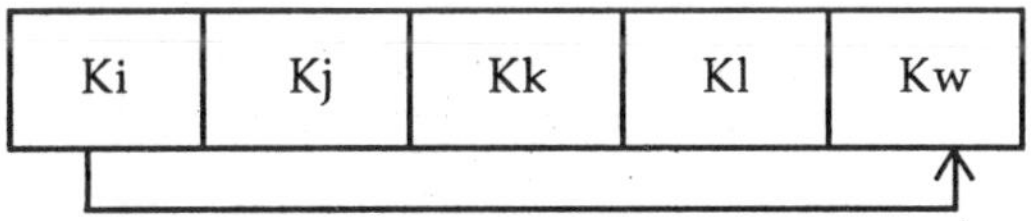

Fig. 29.1: Knowledge Transfer

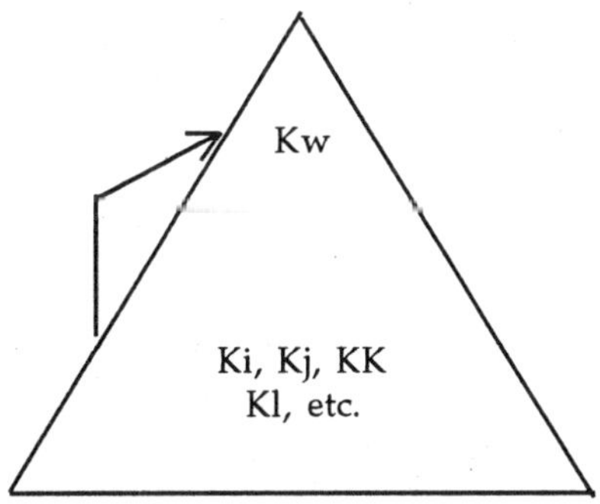

Fig. 29.2: Knowledge Hierarchy

A sociological shift is thus fallaciously treated as an epistemological shift. This fallacy of sociological and cultural displacement as an epistemological shift generating new knowledge is made possible because knowledge pluralities have been transformed into knowledge hierarchies as a result of colonial biases which have treated Western knowledge as exclusively scientific and non-Western knowledge systems as unscientific.

However, the difference in epistemological foundations does not make indigenous knowledge systems inferior, it just makes them different.

This diversity of knowledge needs to be recognised and respected, and a pluralistic IPR regime needs to be evolved which makes it possible to recognise and respect indigenous knowledge, and protect the indigenous knowledge systems and practices and livelihoods based on it.

Schematically, what is being proposed is that we need to recognise that there are diverse knowledge systems *Ki*, each with its own epistemological foundations and its own scientific community of practitioners *Ci*. We, therefore, need diverse legal regimes *Li* to protect the diverse *Ki* and the diverse *Ci*. *Li* being universalised through TRIPs and WTO being restricted to *Lw*, IPR systems reflect the interest of the dominant economic systems of the west, the TNCs.

The criteria on which *Lw* is based fails to recognise *Ki* where *i* is not Western, i.e. non-Western knowledge systems. It is only when an element of *Ki* (*i* is not *w*) is transferred to *Kw* that it is recognised, and it is then treated as an innovation in *Kw*. As a corollary, the interests and rights of *Ci* (*i* is not *w*) find no place in *Lw*, and are transferred to *Cw*, the scientific practitioners of Western knowledge system *W*, in particular those backed by corporate capital.

It is the inappropriateness of existing IPR regimes like patents for the protection of traditional knowledge systems and biodiversity, and the absence of a legal framework that protects the integrity of indigenous knowledge systems that leads to IPRs in their present restrictive forms becoming the mechanisms for piracy.

The protection of indigenous knowledge systems as systems of innovation and the prevention of piracy require a widening of the legal regimes beyond the existing IPR regimes such as patents. In this context, it becomes clear that what are referred to as "strong IPR regimes" from the perspective of economically powerful corporations of Western countries are actually weak regimes from the perspective of the people of countries like India with a rich biodiversity heritage and an ancient intellectual heritage of indigenous knowledge systems. What we need to evolve is a strong legal framework for biodiversity protection and the protection of our intellectual heritage. "Strong" and "weak" are, therefore, not absolute qualifications for IPR regimes but are relative to the social and economic objectives (Shiva 1996).

A "strong" IPR system from the perspective of protection of biological resources as common property would have major areas of exclusions from patentability on grounds of basic needs, human rights, ethics and prior innovation. It is such strong systems that protect biodiversity as CPRs which need to be evolved in our Biodiversity Laws and Plant Variety Laws.

3. The Unethical Universe of Patents on Life

Patents on life are unethical at two levels. Firstly, patents allow the owning of other species which are our kin, fellow members of the Earth Family, *Vasudhaiva Kutumbkam*. The artificial dualism between humans and other species that is a characteristic of the Western thought does not exist in our philosophies. One would not appropriately "own" a family member, and in our context plants are members of the earth family. Hence patents on plants are unethical from the pluralistic perspective of Indian philosophies.

Secondly, patents on life are unethical because they are based on the piracy of indigenous knowledge systems and hence privatisation of a common resource or common good to which individual resource users have collective goods as co-users of an interdependent group. Every member has equal access and claims on the benefits of resource use. These "use" rights are not private property rights, but usufructuary rights and are hence ethically consistent with the mutual interdependence philosophy of *Vasudhaiva Kutumbkam*.

There are major differences between ownership of resources shaped in Europe during the enclosures movement and during the colonial takeover, and "ownership" as it has been practised by tribals and farmers throughout history across diverse societies. The former is based on ownership as private property, based on concepts of returns on investment for profits. The latter is based on entitlements through usufruct rights, based on concepts of return on labour to provide for ourselves, our children, our families, our communities. Usufruct rights can be privately held or held in common. When held in common, they define common property.

Equity is built into usufruct rights since ownership is based on returns on labour. The poor have survived in India in spite of having no access to capital because they have had guaranteed access to the resource base needed for sustenance—common pastures, water and biodiversity. Sustainability and justice are built into usufructuary rights since there are physical limits on how much one can labour and hence inequity is built into private property based on ownership of capital since there are limits on returns on investment of labour and return on investment. Inequity is built into private property based on ownership of capital since there is no limit on how much capital one can own and control and invest. Today, the economy of financial capital has become a "virtual economy"—sixty times larger than the "real" economy of goods and services produced in the world. One trillion dollars move around daily in the global economy, and this virtual economy grows exponentially, generating an unprecedented inequality.

Because of the inherently inequitable nature of ownership through capital, "ceilings" have been put on ownership through capital, to ensure equity. Land reform laws such as "land ceilings" are an instrument for limiting monopoly control over resources. "Land to the tiller" policies, such as operation Bargha in West Bengal, are examples of re-introduction of juridical concepts of ownership based on return on labour, rather than a return on capital. Not only are juridical systems based on usufruct more equitable, they are also more sustainable since usufruct ownership means resources are held in trust for future generations, so that the rights of future generations are not undermined for short-term profits.

4. IPRs as Political Polarisers

IPRs on plant genetic resources or products derived from them convert the survival resource held in common by the poor into a monopoly of the rich and powerful. It thus polarises society into haves and have-nots on the basis of appropriation of the biological and intellectual commons. Often this appropriation is done under project for "bioprospecting".

This bioprospecting is being promoted as the model for relationships between corporations, which commercialise indigenous knowledge, and the indigenous communities which have collectively innovated and evolved the knowledge. It is being presented as an alternative to biopiracy. However, bioprospecting is merely a sophisticated form of biopiracy. Bioprospecting, in effect, leads to the enclosure of the biological and intellectual commons. It takes the biodiversity and intellectual heritage of indigenous communities and converts it into commodities protected by IPRs (Shiva, Jafri, Bedi and Holla-Bhar 1997).

The much celebrated case of "benefit sharing" under bioprospecting arrangements between Tropical Botanical Garden and Research Institute (TBGRI) and the Kani has now been exposed: it has neither protected the "intellectual property rights" of the Kani nor brought them any benefits from the commercialisation of "Arogyaparcha" (Anonymous 1998).

Structurally, no benefit can come to the community if the commons on which they survive are enclosed and privatised and they are pushed off the commons. Any enclosure of the common resource is a theft from the people who hold the resource in common, and results in their deprivation. Such mechanisms of deprivation cannot be called "benefit sharing". The only legitimate benefit-sharing arrangements for the use of the commons are the common and equal access arrangements characteristic of "common property resources" or "common pool resources".

5. Agenda for the Recovery of the Commons

As we enter the third millennium, we need to find ways to protect the biological diversity and intellectual heritage of India for the future of her people. On the one hand, the emergent ecological concern for the conservation of biological diversity provides a new opportunity to value our biological and intellectual wealth, and use and conserve it for the needs of our people. On the other, the emergent forms of private property in knowledge and life forms threatens the continuity of our biodiversity and related knowledge for the poorer two-thirds of India. The incentive to conserve comes from commitments India has made in international conventions and agreements such as the Convention on Biological Diversity (CBD). The threats to our rich biological and intellectual heritage come from the expansion of Western style "intellectual property rights" regimes to biodiversity and to all countries through the TRIPs agreement of GATT/WTO.

In the context of this existing reality of CBD and TRIPs, we can go in two different directions—privatisation of the biodiversity commons or defence and recovery of the biodiversity commons. The recovery of the commons also requires the re-invention of sovereignty.

The re-invention of sovereignty has to be based on the re-invention of the State so that it is made accountable to the people. Sovereignty cannot reside only in centralised State structures, nor does it disappear when the protective functions of the State with respect to its people start to wither away. The new partnership for national sovereignty needs empowered communities which assign functions to the State for their protection. Communities defending themselves always demand such duties and obligations from State structures. On the other hand, TNCs and international agencies promote the separation of the community interests from State interests and the fragmentation and divisiveness of communities.

Sovereignty over biological resources and indigenous knowledge has been recognised by CBD specifically in Articles 3 and 15. This recognition has changed the open-access regime that was prevalent under colonial systems in which the third World genetic resources were treated as the "common heritage of mankind" available freely, while plant varieties and products developed from this rich biodiversity were treated as the intellectual property of northern corporations.

The recovery of the commons is different from the open access systems of "common heritage of mankind". Commons are based on community control and community management and are not open-access systems. In fact, community control over common resources is the only real mechanism for ensuring sovereign control over natural resources.

The recovery of the commons requires that in our legal systems related to biodiversity and knowledge, we recognise the rights of communities, and not merely the rights of corporations. In the IPRs context, this requires that we evolve categories of community intellectual rights (CIRs) related to biodiversity to balance and set limits and boundary conditions for IPRs, and on the monopolies of TNCs which they are designed to create.

The legal precedence of biodiversity as commons has already been established by the Provisions of the Panchayats (Extension to the Scheduled Areas) Act which came into effect in December, 1996. This Act represents ground-breaking legislation in that, for the first time in India's juridical history, a community (in this case a community of tribals in scheduled areas) has been granted recognisable collective rights over its own community resources, and the power to manage its own affairs. The Act accepts two important premises: firstly, that the community is the basic building block of the system and, secondly, a formal system can be built on the firm foundation of the tradition and custom of the tribal people. The new provisions for the Scheduled Areas mark a break from the impasse in which the formal system refused to recognise the vibrant tribal community which has been managing its own affairs in accordance with its traditions through the ages, meeting effectively the challenges which have been coming in its way. The new Act not only formally recognises the community, which is designated as Gram Sabha, but treats the same as the pivot of the system of self-government in the Scheduled Areas (Sharma 1996).

The new law marks the beginning of a new chapter in the history of democracy in our country, perhaps in the world. The ground is clear for participatory democracy in the face-to-face setting at the village level (Sharma 1996).

This Act demonstrates the existence of juridical innovation for the recognition and protection of the indigenous knowledge of the tribals in parts of the country. What must follow from this is an expansion of such rights to cover all communities within India.

Further juridical innovation is, therefore, needed, which would achieve three tasks simultaneously:

1. It would protect the biodiversity and cultural integrity of indigenous communities, and allow them to continue to use their resources and knowledge freely as they have done since time immemorial.
2. It would prevent the piracy and privatisation of indigenous biodiversity and indigenous knowledge through IPRs, nationally and internationally.
3. It would carve out a public domain of commons in the area of biodiversity and knowledge.

To reflect the collective and community nature of the innovation and rights related to indigenous biodiversity utilisation, we call these rights "community intellectual rights" (CIRs).

IPR systems evolved in industrialised countries reflected in the TRIPs agreement only recognise Western knowledge systems as scientific and formal and non-Western knowledge systems are regarded as unscientific and informal. The creation of monopoly rights to biodiversity utilisation through its claim to the creation of "novelty" can have serious implications of erosion of national and community rights to biodiversity and devaluation of India's indigenous knowledge. TRIPs gives countries the option of formulating its own *sui generis* regime for plants as an alternative to patent protection. Collective rights can be a strong candidate for such *sui generis* systems for agricultural biodiversity and medicinal plant biodiversity. Therefore, it is crucial that community-held and-utilised biodiversity knowledge systems are accorded legal recognition as the "common property" owned by the communities concerned.

Community rights provide for the protection of India's biodiversity by keeping resources and knowledge of its utilisation in the community. Colonisation of India's genetic resources and indigenous knowledge systems have been going on for too long. Therefore, India must now take steps to prevent further usurpation of its heritage before it is too late, by means of protecting community innovations from biopiracy and ensuring benefits from usurped resources reach the communities from which they were taken (at present the State is not even collecting royalties on the genetic resources taken by non-Indian interests nor is it insisting that a transfer of technology be carried out from the research conducted by the bioprospecting countries).

5.a. The Essential Steps

In concrete terms, the following steps need to be taken to protect our sovereignty, our biodiversity and our knowledge systems.

All IPR regimes, be they copyright, design, patents trademarks or breeders' rights, should have a section on CIRs which allows collective claims to be registered by communities as areas of exclusions from the logic of privatisation and monopolisation and which allows communities to challenge IPRs on grounds of "prior art" of commonly held and practised knowledge.

When TRIPs comes up for review in 1999, India and other G-77 countries should insist that the "effective *sui generis*" systems have to be effective in reflecting the human rights of indigenous communities to their indigenous knowledge and their environmental rights to their biodiversity. This implies that any IPR regime in any country that relates to biodiversity has to have a mechanism of institutionalising CIRs for respecting indigenous people, protecting biodiversity and preventing biopiracy.

It is quite evident that there is a lack of fit between the structure of commons and communities, and the structure of Western, especially US, concepts of rights and property.

If commons and communities do not fit into the narrow, non-sustainable and parochial framework of eurocentric jurisprudence, then it is that framework that needs changing rather than the collective nature of rights of communities.

This is the context in which we propose a right and responsibilities framework which reflects the values of India's composite culture, and protects all such biological and cultural heritage.

The collective rights framework is not aimed at changing the common, traditional practices of indigenous communities, or overburdening the people with new State interference in their daily use of biodiversity for their survival needs. The legal framework is aimed at protection of indigenous communities and societies *externally* by regulating the access and rights of powerful commercial interests. The communities themselves would then be left free *internally* to organise their biodiversity utilisation and knowledge exchange on the basis of their own values, beliefs and epistemologies, which would be explicitly recognised and respected, though not regulated by State structures and commercial interests.

The society of self-regulation and self-organisation would dispense with the need of communities having to remould themselves into Western judicial frameworks based on individualism, private property and value based or expropriation alone. One the other hand, a Western-based regulatory system would form an interface with external access to their knowledge and resources and externally imposed rights and this would protect their rights from external abuse (Shiva, Jafri, Bedi and Holla-Bhar 1997).

The challenge at the end of 500 years of colonialism and 50 years of independence and the threshold of the third millennium is to evolve a millennium perspective on the environment, and on the people's rights instead of being enslaved by the colonial paradigms that have emerged over the last 500 years of colonial rule.

REFERENCES

Anonymous. 1998. "Biological accused of stealing tribal knowledge", SUNS No. 4270, Friday 7th August.

Sharma, B.D. 1996. "Tide Turned: The Makings of Tribal Self-Rule in the First Central Law in the Wake of the Bhuria Committee Report", New Delhi.

Vandana Shiva. 1996. *Protecting our Biological and Intellectual Heritage in the Age of Biopiracy".* New Delhi: RFSTE.

Vandana Shiva, Afsar H. Jafri, Gitanjali Bedi, Radha Holla-Bhar. 1997. *The Enclosure and Recovery of the Commons: Biodiversity, Indigenous Knowledge and Intellectual Property Rights*, New Delhi: RFSTE.

30 Recognizing and Rewarding Common Pool Knowledge Resources

Madhav Gadgil

1. Knowledge is Power

Over the last 10,000 years humans have come to dominate the earth thanks to the large pool of knowledge and of artefacts produced on the basis of this knowledge. Creation, transmission, use of knowledge is essentially a social activity; knowledge is shared through action followed by imitation, through oral discourse, or with the help of symbolic records, be they rock inscriptions or files transferred over computer networks. Many social animals already show evidence of incipient pools of knowledge maintained through imitation. Perhaps the most famous example is that of the Japanese Macaque troupe in which Imo, an innovative female, discovered that wheat could be separated from sand by floatation on water. The knowledge of this technique slowly spread through her troupe. But it was the invention of complex symbolic communication through language that has permitted humans to transcend here and now, to develop elaborate concepts and to create a body of knowledge, or systematically organized information. Such knowledge can grow by being shared and by being put to use. Indeed over known human history the pool of knowledge has continually expanded by being shared by larger and larger numbers of people, and by being put to use in ever newer contexts, in particular through fabrications of a variety of artefacts from simple stone axes to modern computers or rockets.

Knowledge is important in shaping how people relate to people, in deciding who dominates whom. In other words, knowledge is power. So while sharing and widespread use is the key to growth of knowledge, establishing monopoly over knowledge and restricting its use is the key to deploying knowledge to serve interests of individuals, or limited groups of individuals. There is, therefore, a tension between sharing of knowledge and monopolizing it, between formation of common, open pools vs. private, limited pools of knowledge.

2. Social Organization

Humans may have discovered a complex, symbolic language in its present form 60,000 or more years ago, thereby making a beginning of development of knowledge in the modern form. At these early stages, till the beginning of agriculture and village society some ten thousand years or less ago in different parts of the world, human populations were organized into largely autonomous endogamous tribes of perhaps two to ten thousand people each. There would be considerable social intercourse within a tribe, but little across tribes, who would often speak mutually incomprehensible languages. There would then be common pools of knowledge limited to individual tribes; pools of different tribes may greatly diverge with little in common. But even within tribes there may be people, such as "Shamans", especially concerned with development and systematic management of knowledge, in charge of pools of specialized knowledge such as that of movements of celestial bodies or march of seasons, or of herbal remedies. The Shamans may share this knowledge only with a few selected individuals. Such restrictions are analogous to what are now termed as "Intellectual Property Rights (IPR)". IPRs may then date right from the hunting-gathering stage. The way in which these were enforced is analogous to the institutions of "trade secrets" of today.

With the beginning of agriculture and animal husbandry, human societies changed radically, with a breakdown of boundaries between erstwhile endogamous tribal groups. This must have let to an amalgamation of their many distinct knowledge pools. Along with this there may have developed a variety of specialized groups of people concerned with management of pools of knowledge, such as that dealing with fashioning of tools or use of herbal medicines. Ayurveda, the traditional Indian system of primarily plant-based medicines took advantage of the ongoing amalgamations. A verse in the *Sushruta Samhita*, for instance, urges a healer to absorb the knowledge of medicinal plants from herders and hunters, sages and other forest dwellers.

3. Fragmentation of Knowledge

Such merging of knowledge pools and their usage in newer and newer contexts may then have led to a rapid expansion of the total pool as the hunter gatherer societies transformed into agrarian ones. But the Indian agrarian society again became partitioned into a larger number of endogamous caste-based groups, a process that seems to have been completed by the 7th century of the Christian era. Castes tended to follow relatively narrowly defined functions and patterns of earning livelihoods. The specialized function of systematizing, organizing knowledge was assigned to Brahmanical upper castes in this system. Other livelihood activities of the Brahmans included those calling for deployment of systematized knowledge such as practice of Ayurveda, priesthood and formal administration; but excluded activities requiring manual labour, such as collection of forest produce.

The caste society with these fragmented pools of knowledge also elaborated devices for maintenance of monopoly of limited groups of people over particular bodies of knowledge. Thus, the *Vedas,* and other sacred texts in the Sanskrit language were to be a monopoly of Brahman males, specialized techniques of metal working those of the artisan castes and so on. The systematized knowledge of herbal medicines embodied in Sanskrit texts such as *Charaka Samhita* and *Sushrut Samhita* was also by and large the monopoly of Brahman males, though there were some special exceptions as in Kerala. But these Brahman males would not be expected to engage in activities such as manual collection of medicinal herbs; or slaughtering of goats or handling of human cadavers. Those dispensing herbs as medicines would then have little knowledge of these plants under natural conditions, or of mammalian or human anatomy. Those collecting the herbs to be used as medicines, would not, at the same time, have access to the pool of systematized knowledge about the medicinal uses of these plants.

4. Slow Track Knowledge

This fragmentation would evidently have consequences for maintenance and growth of the knowledge pools. Validation of pieces of knowledge is more than anything else a matter of checking against empirical facts, and of logical consistency amongst different components of the knowledge pool. But in the arrangements put in place in the caste society Brahman medicinemen would have limited familiarity with many relevant empirical facts. This would limit their ability to define the various entities they would be dealing with, as well as to establish cause-effect relationships. Thus, Ayurvedic pharmacopeias, or Nighantus, many times use the same name for very different plants. Shankhapushpi is a plant with a conch-shaped flower, and the name is applied to as many as seven very different plant species. The maladies too are characterized by very broad, somewhat fuzzy categories. Nor does Ayurveda have rigorous methods of establishing that a specific remedy is effective against a particular malady. Given the difficulty of carrying out well-defined empirical tests, Ayurveda tends to rely heavily on old, well-established authorities such as the Samhitas of Charaka and Sushruta.

One may term such a knowledge pool, knowledge on slow track. Knowledge may grow through practice by defining new categories, by discovering new relationships, by replacing old elements. Very limited contacts with the empirical world, fuzzy categories and procedures of verification, and reliance on long-standing authorities would all tend to slow down the growth of the knowledge pool. Indeed Ayurveda has grown exceedingly slowly following its initial development culminating in the works of Charaka and Sushruta 2,000 years ago. Of course, newer and newer Ayurvedic Nighantus have been composed, and plants newly introduced to India, such as tomato, been incorporated. But there is no progress in the basic theoretical formulation, nor in better definitions of categories such as plant species. Good illustrations of plants and animals do appear in medieval Persian manuscripts, and were sponsored in India by the Mughals. Dara Shukoh, Aurangzeb's elder brother, had, for instance, commissioned whole albums of such animals and plants illustrations. But none of the Nighantus include illustrations of the plants mentioned therein.

The pool of Ayurvedic knowledge was initially put together by amalgamation of the many pools of medical knowledge held by large numbers of tribe-like human groups, complemented by systematization of the knowledge by Brahman specialists. The resultant pool was largely, but not entirely, monopolized by the Brahmans of the subcontinent; noteworthy exceptions to this monopoly include the lower caste Ezhava physicians of Kerala. Their acquaintance with Ayurveda is primarily through Vagbhata's seventh-century text, Ashtangahrdya. Vagbhata follows Charaka and Sushruta by several centuries. He was attracted to a Buddhist school; since Buddhism had not accepted the fragmentation of the knowledge pool under the Hindu caste system and had retained a more active Ayurvedic tradition. Vagbhata was from Sindh and was rejected by his own Hindu society because of his Buddhist contacts. So he migrated south and was welcomed in Kerala which probably had an on-going active tradition of herbal medicine largely based on local practices. Vagbhata then added many Kerala plants to the repertoire from Charaka and Sushruta largely based on Himalayan plants and composed texts that gave entry to systematized Ayurvedic knowledge not only to the Brahmans, but also to non-Brahman caste groups such as Nairs and Ezhavas.

Ezhavas engaged in manual labour, toddy-tapping was an important component of their livelihood, they collected medicinal plants with their own hands. It is then likely that the pool of knowledge of herbal medicine, complemented by systematized Ayurvedic knowledge, remained more alive and growing with Ezhavas. Indeed we know that one Ezhava physician, Etty Achyuthan, played a significant role in the development of a quite different knowledge pool, that of modern botany.

Ancient and medieval Europe had a history of its knowledge pool that parallels in some ways that of India. The early agrarian societies of Greece, around the time of Charaka and Sushruta, had a vibrant community of people specializing in systematizing and growing knowledge. But this slowly ceased with the coming in of Christianity around the same time as the crystallization of a rather rigid caste society. Christian priesthood then assumed the function of managing the pool of systematized knowledge, and insisted on acceptance of authority, rather than recourse to verification with reference to the empirical world. So the European knowledge pool remained stagnant, indeed regressed till the 13th-14th centuries. By this time Europe had suffered extensive deforestation and soil erosion; to which was added the Little Ice Age that commenced around 1300 A.D.

5. Knowledge on Fast Track

The resulting difficulties prompted Europeans to actively seek new resources, new lands. This needed new knowledge, such as that of navigation over open seas. The whole range of forces thus unleashed led Europeans to elaborate a system of actively growing knowledge, of putting knowledge on the fast track. This is the system that now goes by the name of scientific methodology. It is a system that requires precise definition of the various entities and of the relationships amongst different entities. It is a system that has elaborated rigorous procedures of establishing cause-effect relationships. It is also a system that has rejected the need to accept any authority. In modern science everybody is supposed to be free to challenge and to verify all claims being made. All claims are expected to be specified in sufficient details so that all others, at least those with requisite knowledge base, should be in a position to test them, to reproduce the observation. Observations that cannot be reproduced are supposed to be rejected, however venerable the authority that has made the claim.

Of course, such a methodology is still practised by people who have their own inclinations and prejudices, their own narrow interests. Nevertheless, modern fast track science is indeed a rather special common pool of knowledge. Its very wide accessibility, its rejection of authority, its invitation to all who wish to challenge, modify, add to it has led to its phenomenal pace of growth.

One of its requirements is the need to specify the various entities with ever greater precision. Species of plants, including medicinal plants, are amongst such entities. All societies have names for many species of plants, especially those used as sources of food, cosmetics or medicines, or those that are a nuisance such as weeds. But the names vary from locality to locality, so that the same plant species may go by different names; or the same name may specify very different species. Thus, the English name mango comes from Tamil Mangai; it is Mavu in Kannada, Amba in Marathi and Aam in Hindi. And Shankhapushpi is seven very different species. Fast track science attempts to devise a single standard name for each distinct species, so that mango is called *Mangifera indica* and nothing else. This is a system devised by Carl Linnaeus, of whom it is said that "God created the world, Linnaeus ordered it". Linnaeus was inspired by an earlier work, called *Hortus Malabaricus* (Plants of Malabar) by a Dutchman called Van Rheede. This Van Rheede was an official at a Dutch post near Cochin in Kerala and was greatly interested in the medicinal uses of local plants. So he worked with three Ayurvedic physicians of Cochin, amongst them Etty Achyuthan, an Ezhava. He systematically noted the medicinal uses of various plants trying to assess their efficacy in curing various defined maladies. He described the plants, including illustrations, in his treatise, considered a pioneering work of modern botany. He used a system of nomenclature of these plants based on the Ezhava system that he learnt from Etty Achyuthan. This Ezhava system, as interpreted by Van Rheede, inspired Linnaeus to devise the system that is now an important component of fast track science.

6. Selective Acceptance

Just as Charaka and Sushruta were involved in systematizing and evolving a knowledge pool that amalgamated the many smaller and less systematized knowledge pools of hunters and herders, so has fast track science incorporated many smaller and less systematized knowledge pools such as the Ezhava system of plant classification. The fast track science has been exceedingly successful in further building upon such knowledge. A striking instance of this comes from development of rockets. This technology initially evolved in China from where it reached India and was part of Tipu Sultan's military repertoire. Tipu employed rockets against the British in his first war taking the enemy completely by surprise. The result was a victory for the Indians. But following the war, the British machinery of fast science swung into action. While running away they had collected some unexploded rockets. These were sent to the Woolwich Arsenal in Britain, and became the focus of a concerted research and development effort. The result was that the British were well prepared to face Tipu's rockets at the next war; indeed they could respond with superior rocket power, leading to Tipu's defeat. Tipu himself, living in a slow knowledge, society, had made no progress in the military technology employed by him in the intervening years.

But the British were not equally receptive to the contents of all pools of slow knowledge from India. For instance, they had little interest in the knowledge of how to manage living resources prudently, on a sustainable basis. An element of such prudent management in Indian tradition is a system of refugia, or localities where living organisms receive total protection, even though their populations may be harvested elsewhere. Thus in Himachal Pradesh no fishing is permitted in the sacred pools along the rivers called "Machiyals". Excellent fishing is, however, available downstream of Machiyals beyond a zone of 200 metres. A similar network of sacred forests and grazing lands called "Orans" once covered much of Rajasthan, and a series of sacred groves protected forests of the Western Ghats. Immediately following the final defeat of Tipu Sultan in 1799, British East India Company asked one of its surgeons, Francis Buchanan, to survey the natural resources of his domains. Buchanan discusses the sacred groves, but has no thought for their possible role as a management tool. Instead he condemns them as a device to keep East India Company from claiming its rightful property.

Establishment of property rights then remains a prime consideration in societies with knowledge on the fast track or on the slow track. Knowledge of rocketry was appropriated as helpful in expanding the wealth of the East India Company; knowledge of ecologically prudent resource management practices rejected as a hindrance to establishing claims over forest resources. Inevitably, European societies putting knowledge on the fast track were conscious of rights over intellectual property as well. But they had to confront a contradiction. Traditionally intellectual property rights were maintained through the route of trade secrets; of refusing to share the knowledge widely. But fast track knowledge depended on widespread sharing of information, of involving all comers in challenging and verifying accepted conclusions. So growth of knowledge depended on rejection of trade secret type of protection. The solution that has been arrived at is the system of patenting. Patent literally means laying open something that everybody may examine. In the context of intellectual property rights patenting is granting of monopoly rights for a limited period over some new and useful knowledge, in return for the innovator laying open the discovery for all to see. A patent may be granted only when accompanied by a disclosure statement that is sufficiently detailed for anybody else well versed in the arts to reproduce it.

7. Patents

This then is the device arrived at by the fast track knowledge to keep the knowledge pool open to everybody to hasten its growth, yet create incentives for private parties to profit from their innovations. The arrangement, however, requires that a new element of knowledge entering the common pool does it through the very special route of patenting if it is to enjoy the benefits of its commercial utilization. If it does not take this special route, but is transmitted to others in any other normal way, by way of a lecture, or an article in a newspaper or a scientific journal, then it is deemed to have entered the common pool forever with no special claim on the benefits accruing from its commercial use.

The well-known case of attempted U.S. patenting of use of turmeric paste to heal wounds illustrates this situation. Knowledge of such a use is common in India, transmitted orally, as well as through inscriptions and in writing for centuries as a part of the common pool of the slow track knowledge. Fast tract knowledge has absorbed this kind of information effectively, through numerous documents beginning with early ones like *Hortus Malabarius*, leading to the 19th century Watt's *Dictionary of Economic Products*, to modern electronic data bases such as NAPRALERT—natural products alert—at Chicago. Any person may access this information, add to it an innovative step, however trivial, and then claim a patent over the process or product. This is what was attempted in the patent claim filed. Our Council for Scientific and Industrial Research was successful in contesting this claim and have the patent rejected. But the rejection merely amounts to the Patent Court agreeing that there was no innovative step beyond what was already in the knowledge pool open to all public. It does not amount to any provision for arranging for benefits of commercial utilization of such public domain knowledge being shared with, let us say, practitioners of Ayurveda, or with the Indian Council of Medical Research.

Knowledge on the slow track is today faced with serious challenges. Fast track knowledge has absorbed many of its elements of value, and then outstripped it in its own reach. Consider, for instance, Ayurveda. Some of its remedies, such as use of Sarpagandhi, *Rouwolfia serpentina,* for treatment of hypertension, have been taken over by allopathy. Allopathy has then gone ahead and more precisely characterized a molecule, resperpine, as responsible for the useful property and taken up its commercial manufacture. All the profits of this commercial utilization have gone to fast tract knowledge based enterprises. Meanwhile the slow track knowledge system of Ayurveda has failed to appreciate and assimilate the innovations of fast track science. For instance, till this date there is no serious work on the precise identity of plants used in Ayurvedic pharmacopoeias in terms of the system of nomenclature adapted by modern science. So Ayurvedic knowledge pool stands still, while its practice is declining under competition from allopathy. The large number of smaller knowledge pools of village or tribe-level practice of herbal medicine are eroding even more rapidly as fewer and fewer people from younger generation acquire the knowledge. The knowledge pools of ecologically prudent management of the natural resources are also on the decline, with manifold assaults from the State machinery managing these resources.

8. Two Approaches

Can these pools of slow track knowledge be saved from steady erosion and appropriation without due credit? We have before us two, and rather different approaches to dealing with the challenge. The first, to my mind, is a reactive approach, grounded in a rejection of modern fast track science. It seeks to revive the conditions under which small-scale tribal and rural communities lived self-sufficient lives, untouched by the products of modern technology, unaffected by the now pervasive market forces. In this approach Western science, transnational corporations, intellectual property rights regimes all have uniformly undesirable attributes and, therefore, must be rejected. I am quite unable to see how this approach can ever be put into operation. The other approach, which I would like to advocate, accepts, firstly, that fast track science, transnational corporations, modern intellectual property rights regimes are powerful forces we cannot escape and must learn to live with; and secondly, that in fact they each have certain positive features which we must build upon. The positive features of fast track science are its openness, its rejection of authority and willingness to permit all parties to engage in challenging its conclusions and come up with new ones. If we wish to nurture it, slow track knowledge must absorb these features, rejecting secrecy and authoritarianism and accepting to open it to being made public and challenged by all comers. Fast track science has its deficiencies as well, and amongst these is an arrogance bred of success and an attitude of contempt towards slow track knowledge. This is a distortion, incompatible with the spirit of openness of modern science and must be given up. So modern science must accept with humility that it has made little headway in dealing with complex systems such as natural ecosystems or human mental health. In these contexts the particular knowledge accumulated by slow track systems, be they traditional resource management practices such as protection of sacred ponds or groves, or of dealing with mental health such as yoga is still of great value and often superior to that arrived at by fast track science. This has to be accepted by modern science, replacing its current rejection of such knowledge as superstitions. Modern intellectual property right regimes too embody very positive features in insistence on full disclosure in place of the secrecy prevalent in the traditional intellectual property rights arrangements. But these regimes must be reformed to devise arrangements for sharing of benefits with the public domain foundation of the innovations which are sought to be protected. An important advance in this direction has been made by the International Convention on Biological Diversity, in force since December, 1993. This convention seeks to ensure sharing of commercial benefits of utilization of knowledge of living resources with the indigenous holders of such knowledge.

9. Benefit Sharing

This is a complex issue which may be illustrated through a pioneering initiative of Tropical Botanical Garden and Research Institute (TBGRI) at Thiruvananthapuram in Kerala. Scientists of this research institute learnt of the value of a plant *Trichopus zeylanicus* in keeping people from getting tired during physical exertions. This information was imparted to them by two Kani tribals as a traditional practice of their community. TBGRI subsequently developed a tonic formulation of potential commercial value by conducting further researches. This formulation has been passed on to a pharmaceutical concern which has made an initial payment of Rs. 10 lakhs to TBGRI. TBGRI has decided to share half of this, Rs. 5 lakhs, with the Kani tribes, whose pool of slow track knowledge was the basis of the further innovation.

But the scheme has run into difficulties. It is not clear who the beneficiaries of the Rs. 5 lakh should be. Should it be the two individual Kanis who first provided the information? Should it be all Kanis of Kerala State? Should it also include Kanis in the neighbouring State of Tamil Nadu? Should it include other tribal groups of the region who may also have shared this knowledge with the Kanis? How should the money be disbursed? Should it be simply equally divided amongst all individuals considered eligible, or all households considered eligible? Or should it be given to Kani panchayats for activities aimed to benefit all members of the community? Given the difficulties of resolving such issues the funds are simply sitting in a bank account.

We must then think through appropriate mechanisms for benefit sharing. I feel that it is important to link these to the step of disclosure in the patent application. We must make it mandatory that all patent applications specify the public domain foundation, both publications in modern scientific literature, and knowledge in the slow track system of the innovation that is sought to be protected. It would then be mandatory for a patent application such as use of turmeric paste for wound healing to specify that such use is a well known traditional practice of India, and then demonstrate that there has been a further innovative step. This, however, requires that slow track knowledge also goes beyond its traditional routes of oral transmission, and its penchant for secrecy and like fast track science takes to publicly available written documentation.

10. Biodiversity Registers

I have been involved in one experiment of managing slow track knowledge—folk knowledge of living resources, their management and uses—adopting such an approach involving publicly accessible documentation. This has been a cooperative endeavour of a large number of friends from the NGO and academic sector working with local people in 52 clusters of villages distributed over the States of Rajasthan, Himachal Pradesh, Bihar, Assam, Orissa, Karnataka, Maharashtra and the Union Territories of Andaman and Nicobar Islands. The documents generated have been called "People's Biodiversity Registers". The documentation is completely voluntary; it does not seek to persuade people to indicate any particular practice against their inclination. People, however, have the option of recording a claim, for instance, that a certain individual, or a clan is aware of a very effective remedy against, say, epilepsy. Such documentation may serve a variety of purposes. It may serve to guard against erosion and permanent loss of this knowledge as the younger generation loses interest in continued use of herbal medicine, or of traditions such as protection of sacred groves. It may permit amalgamation of the knowledge in the larger pool and enrich it. It may help direct positive incentives for conservation and continued use of such knowledge to appropriate individuals or communities. It may serve as a tool for decentralized, flexible locality and time specific, knowledge intensive management of living resources in a transparent and participatory fashion.

Access to such documentation, which may be maintained either as written material or in electronic form, may not be totally open, but could be appropriately regulated. Those accessing it for possible commercial use may be charged access fees, and may be required to agree to pay further fees if they put the information to commercial use. If this material is made part of a searchable electronic database, then all parties filing patent applications could be required to acknowledge pertinent records as prior art, and some mechanism worked out for appropriate sharing of commercial profits. The State may directly reward excellence in preparing such documentation to encourage long-term conservation of such information.

It may be very difficult to organize a good system of direct payment of royalties in relation to recording of such information. In that case the government may merely create a fund based on excise duty or other taxation on the sale of products such as biodiversity-based pharmaceuticals or cosmetics and provide awards to communities or individuals in recognition of their contribution to the knowledge pool.

People's Biodiversity Registers would also serve as valuable tools for good locality specific management of resources such as medicinal plants. Today these resources are being used in a thoroughly unregulated fashion, often leading to their exhaustion. There is no adequate database on their status with any agency, be it Forest Departments or pharmaceutical industry. The only people knowledgeable about what is happening to the medicinal plant resources in any detail are those who collect them in the field. Of course these people know very little of what goes on outside their own localities, either in terms of resource stocks or market value of these plants. Good management of the resources must be based on properly recording and collating the information with these people, informing them of the real value of the resources, and involving them in sustainable harvests. People's Biodiversity Registers could be very useful tools for such a purpose.

11. Possible Pitfalls

It is of course important to anticipate two possible dangers in this whole exercise and work out measures to contain them from the very beginning.

These are that the availability of easily accessible databases may promote over-harvest and depletion of biodiversity resources and usurpation of knowledge of uses of biodiversity resources without equitable sharing of benefits. It may, however, be pointed out that both these processes are rampant today. A pertinent example turned up during the preparation of a PBR in village Mala in Dakshina Kannada district of Karnataka. Mr Kunjeera Moolya is the most knowledgeable of the dispensers of herbal medicines in Mala; he does not charge for his services, but makes a living as a farm labourer. Moolya was approached in March 1995 by an agent of some pharmaceutical firm to disclose his knowledge of local medicinal plants. He went around the forest for two days and shared this information, for which he was paid a sum of Rs. 220 (US $ 6), equivalent to his normal earnings over four to five days. This agent evidently represented some pharmaceutical company engaged in screening Indian plant resources for possible commercial products. Commercial interests are also able to locate resources, e.g. medicinal plant stocks such as *Mappia foetida* of the Western Ghat or *Taxus buccata* of Himalayas, and prompt their overexploitation. But in the total absence of organized information we are unable to monitor these trends. The information on stocks of biodiversity resources contained in the PBR would facilitate such monitoring and institution of measures to check them.

12. Conclusions

To conclude, it is now important to create systems of fusion of the vast pools of locality specific slow track knowledge of complex natural systems with those generated through fast tract science. Documents such as People's Biodiversity Registers that take advantage of the crucial methodological advances of fast track science to confer dignity on and enhance the utility of slow track knowledge could serve as very useful tools in such an endeavour. Of course, full benefits of such a fusion would flow only when supported by systems of open, public participation in the management of natural resources and a just sharing of benefits flowing from relevant commercial applications.

Acknowledgements

I am grateful to a larger number of friends in academic institutions and in NGOs, as well as amongst farmers, fisherfolk and herders who have participated in the development of ideas discussed above. I apologise for not being able to mention them all; but would like to record my special debt of gratitude to the following: Ashwini Chhatre, Anirban Ganguly, Utkarsh Ghate, P. Pramod, P. R. Sheshagiri Rao, Darshan Shankar, K. C. Malhotra, M. K. Prasad and M. S. Valiathan. This work has been generously supported over years by the Ministry of Environment and Forests, Government of India.

REFERENCES

Gadgil, M. 1997. "A framework for managing India's Biodiversity". *RIS Biotechnology and Development Review* 1(1):1-14.

Gadgil, M., F. Berkes and C. Folke. 1993. "Indigenous knowledge for biodiversity conservation". *Ambio* 22:151-156.

Gadgil, M., and P.R.S. Rao. 1995. "Designing incentives to conserve India's biodiversity". In: S. Hanna, and M. Munasinghe, (eds.). *Property Rights in a Social and Ecological Context.* Washington D.C.: The Beijer International Institute of Ecological Economics and The World Bank, pp. 53-62.

Gadgil, M., M.D.S. Chandran, P. Pramod, G. Utkarsh, Y. Gokhale, W. Thomas, and P. Menon. 1996. "Peoples biodiversity register: A record of India's wealth". *Amruth* (Oct. 96) Spl. Suppl.:1-16.

Gadgil, M. and other colleagues from Srishti Jigyaasa Pariwar. 1998. "Let the people speak". *The Hindu Survey of Environment,* 1998, 101-137.

Posey, D.A. and G. Dutfield. 1996. *Beyond Intellectual Property: Towards Traditional Resource Rights for Indigenous People and Local Communities.* Ottawa: International Development Research Centre.

Sukh Dev. 1997. "Ethnotherapeutics and modern drug development : The potential of Ayurveda". *Current Science* 73 (11):909•928.

UNEP, 1992. *Convention on Biological Diversity.* Nairobi, Kenya: United Nations Environment Programme.

SECTION 7

PROPERTY RIGHTS, INSTITUTIONAL CHANGE AND POLICY PROBLEM

31 Alternative Governance in Common Pool Resources

Dinesh K. Marothia

A sizable proportion of the people in rural India depend directly for their livelihood and welfare on natural resources like forest, soil, water, fisheries and wildlife. These are the flow common pool resources (CPRs) with critical minimum levels below which a decline in the flow may have the irreversible consequences. In India nearly 40 per cent rural poor are suffering from poverty and largely depend on CPRs. Nearly 30 per cent of the total land, 40 per cent of the total forest and bulk of the water resources and fisheries are CPRs and traditionally have been used by the rural poor (Singh 1994). One of the major causes of the rural poverty in India is the unequal access and control of the poor on CPRs (Jodha 1986, Singh 1994). Depletion of CPRs has also been a major cause of the displacing of a large number of rural people and reducing their status to environmental refugees. Sustainable management of these resources largely depends on the attributes of the resource ecosystem, resource users' local knowledge and technology, pattern of institutional arrangements, property rights regimes or resource governance structures, and authority systems (Oakerson 1992, Marothia 1993, Folke and Berkes 1995). Institutional arrangements are the determinants that provide resource users or a group of resource users or communities with rules to manage natural and environmental resources. Property rights regimes are part of the institutional arrangements through which resource users sometimes convert natural resources and environmental services into human-made capital or inputs of production (Berkes and Folke 1992, 1994, Folke and Berkes 1995). A resource regime is an explicit or implicit structure or institutional arrangement or working rules of rights and duties characterizing the relationship of co-users to one another with respect to a specific natural resource (Bromley 1989, Bromley and Cernea 1989). According to Bromley (1989 and Ostrom 1990) property rights regimes or resource management regimes in resources can be classified under four possible categories: state property (where the secure claim rests with the government); private property (where the claim rests with an individual or corporation); common property (individuals have claims on collective goods as members of an organized group); and open access (or no property regime with no secure claims). The basic requirement for any property regime is an authority system that can guarantee the security of expectations for the rights holders. When the authority system breaks down, a particular resource regime degenerates. Under such a situation, new institutional arrangements are used to define the resource regimes over natural resources and the authority systems protect the interests of those holding the rights under a particular regime (Bromley and Cernea 1989, Gibbs and Bromley 1989, Marothia 1992 a,b, 1993, 1997a,b,c). These concepts have their roots in institutional economics (see Commons 1950, Ciriacy-Wantrup and Bishop 1975, Bromley 1989, Marothia and Phillips 1985, Marothia 1989a).

Renewable CPRs have been managed and controlled under different management regimes in India. These resources can be managed sustainably under State or common or private property regimes and are also subject to being degraded. There are many overlaps and combinations of State (public), community and private management systems or governance structures in managing resources or the eco-system. In other words often resources are managed at the interface of different property regimes. Enough evidence is available in India when resources managed under a common property regime degrade into open access due to weak property rights regimes, inadequate institutional arrangements and breakdown of the authority system. Examples are also available when renewable resources degraded under an open access system brought under a State or private or community management regime through appropriate changes in the institutional arrangements (Arnold and Stewart 1991; Marothia 1992b, 1993, 1997a, 1997c). Many researchers and policy makers have suggested privatization or State control of resources as a solution to arrest degradation of these resources and the ecosystem. However, it has been widely experienced that Government or State control over natural resources has shown a relatively weak record (Marothia 1993, 1997a). In turn, resource management under common and private property regimes has increasingly come to be seen as better alternatives to State management regime. However, there are two important arguments against "pure" private or "pure" common property regimes. First, the government has the larger ecological and bio-diversity concerns that extend many times beyond a sectoral management concept of a particular resource and interest of local community; and second, there is no guarantee that the local communities/resource users will organize themselves into an effective authority system to design rules for managing a particular resource (Townsend and Pooley 1995, Marothia 1993, 1998, 1999, Singh 1994). Dissatisfaction with traditional failure of "pure" community natural resource management and "pure" government control has led to great interest in distributed governance. State or government control with active local communities' involvement has recently been identified as a feasible option in managing CPRs (Marothia 1998). Local communities may be able to design and administer institutional arrangements that are workable with least transaction costs. The local communities have cumulative traditional knowledge about the resources and the well-tested local technologies that may be useful in designing effective institutional arrangements. Locally enforced institutional arrangements may have the advantage of greater acceptability; and hence may face less resistance in implementation than the institutional arrangements designed by the external agencies and imposed externally on the resource users in a particular eco-system (Townsend and Pooley 1995, Singh 1994, Marothia 1998). These alternative perspectives suggest that distributed governance or shared management might prove more effective than any form of "pure" government or "pure" local community management. Townsend and Pooley (1995) recently extended the standard classification of property rights regimes (State, private, common and open access) to recognize that management can be shared among the State (or government), local communities (resource users) and private enterprises in various ways. Alternative management approaches have recently been used by several researchers to achieve distributed governance, i.e. how rights and responsibilities are distributed among and within the State, local communities and resource using institutes (Townsend and Pooley 1995). A large number of the resource development programmes in India failed or could not yield anticipated outcomes due to lack of understanding on the part of the researchers, administrators, planners about the issues related to distributed governance or shared management and institutional arrangements and their application in the socio-economic network of village life (see Marothia 1993, 1997a and Gupta, 1995 for the importance of local institutional arrangements in managing CPRs). In recent years, particularly in the eighties several developmental programmes for water, forestry, fisheries and rehabilitation of waste and wetlands resources have been introduced and a few of them were managed under the distributed governance or shared management system. In these projects local communities/resource user groups and the State or local government shared the responsibility of managing CPRs by combining appropriate institutional skills of local resource users/local committees and technical, administration and financial resources available with the States. In this chapter an attempt has been made to discuss the outcomes of the CPR-based development programmes implemented under different property regimes for the upliftment of the rural poor in the Chhattisgarh region of Madhya Pradesh (M.P). The chapter argues in favour of distributed governance for managing CPRs through alternative approaches of management.

1. Common Pool Resource-Based Development Programmes and Alternative Governance

In this section, capsule descriptions of instructive experiences about the role of institutional arrangements, types of property rights regimes and authority systems in managing CPRs are discussed based on the studies conducted in the Chhattisgarh region of M.P. Readers are referred to Marothia (1992a,b 1993, 1996a,b,c 1997a) and Marothia and Gauraha (1996) for fuller accounts. These case studies highlight the assessment of alternative management systems or alternative governance structures in managing CPRs. Some CPR-based programmes have been managed under a particular property regime while others under distributed governance structures.

It is important to recognize that the governance can be shared among States, communities and private interest groups in various ways. In other words, distributed governance is the extended version of the standard regimes of property rights (State, common and private property, open access). Distributed management system involve a share of authority among different groups/ agencies at different decision-making levels. (Townsend and Pooley 1995). Distributed governance involves external institutional arrangements among the government and local communities or resource users as well as internal institutional arrangements within local community institutions or resource users. Government, local communities and private parties utilizing common pool resources each brings different interests, capabilities and understanding to the resource management process (Townsend and Pooley 1995). These alternative institutional perspectives shape the decision-making process among the government and local resource user communities and within members of the local community for managing a resource by converting unorganized structures into the organized ones or going concern (Marothia and Phillips 1985).

An external governance structure has essentially three alternatives of management systems (Townsend and Pooley 1995), namely, *rights-based management* (the government grant usufruct rights to individual resource users/ party under well-specified constraint conditions and assumes the role of monopoly over the resource base and retains all responsibility/authority for conservation decision), *co-management* (the government and local communities share ongoing responsibility for decision-making over all or most of the resource management decisions) and *contracted management* (to transfer a large part of the decision-making process to local bodies). These systems have been functional in various parts of India in general and Chhattisgarh in particular to manage CPRs. These alternative management systems have their inherent strengths and weaknesses (see Marothia 1996a, 1996b, 1998 for the evolution process of external institutional arrangements in managing NTFPs in the Chhattisgarh region of M.P.).

Three alternative internal institutional arrangements (Townsend and Pooley 1995) have closely been associated with the concept of distributed governance—*self-organizing institutions* (institutional and organizational decisions remain with the local communities and the government may use the institutional building capacity to support and gain strength from self-organization), *communal management* (to reduce the existing authority of state and vest more localized interest), *cooperative management* (membership is limited with well-defined working rules for collective governance) and *corporate* (under the corporate governance the owners and shareholders of the corporation would operate under governance rules typical of private corporations (see Townsend 1995 and Townsend and Pooley 1995 for a detailed analysis of external and internal institutional arrangements). The degrees of authority that the government could grant to local organization varies with the internal governance structure (see Marothia 1993 and 1997a for the importance of internal institutional arrangements in managing village commons like common wastelands, water bodies and small irrigation tanks). If management is to be most effective and efficient, two features should be characterized distributed management. Firstly, institutional arrangements for local community and government be clearly defined and the potential for prolonged and costly disagreements among resource user groups and government administration be minimized. Second, the decision-making structure should be shared at different levels of administration so that costs and benefits of any decision are internalized within some cohesive decision-making unit (Townsend and Pooley 1995). To this end, we discuss alternative governance systems managing (a) micro-minor irrigation tanks (MMITs), (b) Village Woodlots (VWLs), (c) Community Fish Ponds (CFPs) and (d) Non-Timber Forest Resources (NTFRs).

1.a. Micro-Minor Irrigation Tanks

The State Department of Agriculture (SDA), Government of Madhya Pradesh, introduced the micro-minor irrigation tanks (MMITs) programme, *Dabri Yojna,* through its soil conservation wing in 1977-78 to provide irrigation facilities to increase foodgrain production, generate employment and minimize migration due to soil moisture stress. MMITs were constructed on government-owned wastelands across the natural water courses to store rainfed run-off for irrigation. The command area of MMITs is generally below 50 hectares. After construction, the panchayats were given ownership rights of MMITs and these were expected to be managed under a common property resource regime by group(s) of the farmers within the command area of a particular tank.(See Marothia 1986,1992b for details and Table 31.1).

The MMITs programme was introduced in all districts of the Chhattisgarh region with the conventional assumption that contributions of farmers in different types of resources-labour, materials and capital will be forthcoming, once it is determined that the benefits of MMITs are significant to farmers and panchayats. This assumption has largely been proven false in the case of MMITs by the users. Due to lack of legislative and administrative powers, panchayats

TABLE 31.1: **Silient Features of Alternative Governance in MMITs, VWLs, CFPs, NTFPS Resources**

SN	Characteristics	MMITs	VWLs	CFPs	NTFPs
1.	Resource Management Programme (RMPs)	Dabri Yojna	VWLs Scheme	FFDA	NTFPs Coop.
2.	Objectives of RMPs	Life saving irrigation to kharif crops and minimizing migration	Increase fuel, fodder and timber supply	Reliable and equal access to water to increase fisheries productivity	Provide market for nationalized and non-nationalized NTFPs, minimize exploitation of members
3.	Sponsoring Authority	SDA	SDF	SFD/FFDA	SDF
4.	Year of Initiation	1977-78	1986	1981-82	1988-89
5.	No. of Case Studies	18 (Tanks)	3 (Sites)	10(CFPs)	8(PMFPCs)
6.	Social structure of users and organization	Multicaste	Multicaste	Fisheries Communities, SC/ST	Tribal dominant
7.	Size and boundary	Well-defined boundaries of tanks and command areas	Well-defined area of common wastelands	Well-defined boundaries of CFPs	Well defined boundries of collection centres
8.	Original Ecological Status	Natural depressions, degraded Panchayat lands	Degraded/grazed village lands	Natural catchment, degraded private lands	Protected and reserved forest
9.	Original PRR	Panchayat	Village Panchayat	Private (Zamindars, Malgulars)	State
10.	Current PRR	Owned by VPs but open access status	Usufructury right to SFD (5-6 years)	CPR under cooperative governance/formal groups of fishermen	Usufructury rights to collect NTFPs
11.	Authority Sharing Arrangement	Absent	SFD control over project period	Internally dominated	Distributed governance (three-tier organizational set-up)

(Contd.)

TABLE 31.1 (*Contd.*)

SN	Characteristics	MMITs	VWLs	CFPs	NTFPs
12.	External Institutional Arrangements	Initially managed by SDA, handed over to Panchayat	Implementation of project for (5-6) years by SFD.	External support –FFDA-	Financial, Technical and Infrastructure support at different levels
13.	Internal Institutional Arrangements	Unorganized-weak authority system	Absent – No involvement of local community	Self-Cooperative formation/group formation	Cooperative structure with well-defined rules.
14.	Outcomes	High returns to individual users, without sharing labour, material and capital inputs Inequitable distribution of water and income Unsustainable use of tank water	In some cases fodder is available Babul sticks as tooth brush Unsustainable use of wasteland Conflict between SDF and Village Panchayat	Fish sale Wages paid to members Common Pool fund for fish rearing assests Social conflict between users and non-users over use of common village ponds	· Proper and timely wages · Commission on total collection · Equal access to the NTFPs · FDT investment for regeneration of NTFPs biomass

Source: Table based on the synthesis of inferences drawn from NTFPs Cooperative (Marothia, 1996a 1996b; Marothia and Gauhara 1996), CFPs Marothia 1993, 1997). MMITs (Marothia, 1986, 1992), VWLs (Marothia 1993,1996c).

Note: SDF: State Department of Forest, PMFPCs: Primary Minor Forest Product Primary Cooperatives, SFD: State Fisheries Department, FFDA: Fish Farmers Development Agency, SDA: State Department of Agriculture, VPs: Village Panchayats, CFPs: Community Fish Ponds, PRR: Property Rights Regimes, FDT: Forest Development Tax.

could not manage MMITs under the common property regime. One reason for the poor management was that MMITs have extremely poor excludability, i.e. it is difficult to exclude non-contributors in labour or capital resources from taking advantage of the water use in the absence of a well-defined structure of rights and duties for the users and breakdown of the local authority system to ensure that the expectation of the water users can be met through panchayats. All MMITs were provided with iron sluice-gates. Water runs continuously in most of the cases. Water distribution is based on the crude negotiable rules. Despite the fact that field-to-field irrigation water distribution method is operating within the command area, it has minimum external effects in terms of time and location due to the small size of the command area of MMITs. Poor maintenance of MMITs, lack of field channels and poor water control are most pressing problems. Inadequate labour and capital share, non-payment of irrigation fees by the water users indicate their non-committal attitude towards the sustainable development of MMITs as they yet have to develop a sense of belonging to the common pool MMITs (see Marothia 1986, 1992b for details). Simple working rules of keeping the sluice-gate closed on rainy days, control operation of the sluice according to the water requirement of the crop, introducing water measuring devices and appointing water operators can increase the water use efficiency. In the absence of MMIT Management Authority with appropriate administrative and legislative powers, the goal of sustainable management of MMITs may not be achieved. This has resulted in an unsustainable resource base for future users. MMITs are common property resources and their operation and management should be based on community action on the basis of rules and regulations which influence water control and resource base. The Panchayat system broke down due to lack of a well-defined structure of water rules, regulations and acts; and the common property (*res communes*) MMITs ultimately degenerated into open access (*res nullius*).

To bring back MMITs under a common property regime it is necessary to develop incentives and sanctions that promote long-term participation and involvement of the water users and panchayats in the management of MMITs. These incentives, which may be economic or social in nature, should either reward those farmers or panchayats who are diligent in fulfilling their obligations, or penalize those who are delinquent. Such incentives and sanctions should constitute the major focus for management of MMITs. Currently, MMITs are poorly managed in the absence of well-structured rights and duties or incentives and sanctions and MMIT management authority. Research on irrigation tanks in M.P. (Marothia 1986, 1992b), ICRISAT (Von-Oppen and Subba Rao 1980a,b, Von Oppen 1985) and elsewhere (Palanisami and Easter 1984, Rao and Chandrakanth 1984. Also see Shah *et al.* (chapter in this book) has shown that tank irrigation efficiency may be improved with effective institutional arrangements under a shared resource management regime. In a series of studies conducted in Chhattisgarh, Marothia (1986,1992b,1993, 1996c) has suggested the formation of a Tank Management Authority with distributed responsibility and rights structures to be shared by the government (State Department of Agriculture); Panchayats; Tank Users' Association, and farmers and villagers (users of the tank water for domestic purposes). A cooperative management system of governance may be adopted to restore MMITs, which are currently operating under the open access regime, where the government (panchayats) and village communities (water users) share on-going responsibilities for decision-making over MMITs management decisions.

1.b. Village Woodlots

The State Department of Forest (SDF) undertook village woodlots (VWLs) plantation as part of its social forestry programme on village common grazing lands for a period of five years in various areas of M.P. Based on studies conducted in Kura, Kathadih and Saragaon villages in Raipur district of M.P. (Marothia 1993, 1996c) it was concluded that the programme had utterly failed as it was implemented without having a clear understanding of the sociological context, institutional arrangements (including property rights), insufficient consultation and involvement of the local people who depend upon the grazing land, on which woodlots was developed (see Marothia 1989b for socio-economic interpretations of afforestation programme). For the entire project period of five years, village communities, particularly shepherds, were excluded through fencing and a watchman to guard the area. After the second year naturally grown grass was available in the project area in large quantities. However, grass cutting was not allowed even for stall feeding. In the opinion of the village community, surpanch and panches, the transfer of common grazing lands for woodlots was a losing proposition both in terms of shrinking grazing area for 5-6 years and conflicts generated between SDF and village communities over the use of village commons. Village woodlots have resulted in poor patterns of interactions and inefficient, inequitable and unsustainable use of the village common grazing lands, besides dissatisfaction among the villagers (see Table 31.1). The village panchayat was in the process in 1993 of getting back grazing land under its control to develop collective fodder grounds.

1.c. Community Fish Ponds

Freshwater aquaculture, or fish farming is an important component of India's rural ecosystem and economy. The Central Government introduced the Fish Farmers Development Agency (FFDA) in 1973 to improve the productivity and income from aquaculture in village ponds and tanks. The network of FFDA has also been expanded in Chhattisgarh villages, along with other States of the country with the financial assistance from the World Bank in 1979. FFDA has been specifically responsible for ensuring that all publicly owned ponds were leased for fish culture and that all lease payments were made besides creating a supportive infrastructure for promoting aquaculture in community ponds.

Prior to the FFDA programme, panchayats did lease out a few specific community ponds for fish culture to the highest bidder from the village's fishing community, with the understanding that water quality in the village's other community ponds would be maintained for domestic use of the villagers. The fish were sold and consumed locally, and rents more or less reflected profits realized from the fish culture. If conflicts arose between fishermen and villagers, the Panchayat resolved the issue. Community ponds have multiple uses for the human and animal population of the village; they traditionally have been controlled and managed as common property resources by the village panchayats. Under this system they are governed not only by a well-defined set of institutional arrangements concerning who may or may not use the resource but also by rules concerning the conduct of accepted users. The relationship of villagers with each other in respect to domestic and livestock uses on the one hand and to fish production on the other was bounded by formal and informal codes of conduct (Marothia 1993,1977a). FFDA now has assumed many of these duties. It arranges the fishing leases between the village panchayats and individuals, small groups, and registered cooperatives. Pond size, lease sources, duration of leases, and the financial capacity of lessees are the major factors in deciding to whom the ponds are leased. Fishing cooperatives are generally given preference in the leasing of large ponds; two or more fishermen often pool their resources to lease community ponds under 2 ha; and individual fishermen normally lease those under 1 ha. (Srivastava et al. 1993).

Based on a study conducted in three villages of Chhattisgarh (Marothia, 1997a) a few lessons are distilled here. Since the implementation of the FFDA leasing policies, the method of selecting beneficiaries and the privatization of fishing rights in community ponds has generated social conflicts between the leaseholders and other villagers. This has affected the productivity of fish farming and created inequalities in the management of community ponds. Under FFDA programmes, these ponds are normally leased to either members of the Scheduled Castes and Tribes or fishing communities, individuals, or groups. To enhance their income, the rents are fixed so low that they have no relation to the profits received for fish farming (Srivastava et al.1991, Marothia 1997a). This creates conflicts with other villagers, especially other fishermen, who would have been willing to pay more for the right to fish but were excluded on the basis of community (Marothia 1997a). Privatizing fishing rights of community ponds often generates conflicts between their owners (panchayats) and fishermen. Community members at large are losers in terms of poorer water quality and increased water scarcity in the water stress years, a loss for which they receive little compensation. Thus the process of privatizing the water resources of community ponds creates social and economic inequalities (Srivastava 1988, Marothia 1997a). Poaching, restrictions on using medicines, feeds, manure and class conflicts were the greatest problems the fisherman community faced. On the villagers' side, skin irritations were reported due to substantial quantities of manure and feed added to water for fish culture. The greatest constraints were imposed in the case of individual fishermen, followed by fishing cooperative societies and fishermen's groups. These constraints created inequalities of income, yield and employment distribution in the management of the community ponds.

Before FFDA became involved, aquaculture in the study villages had been managed as a common property resource. Under FFDA, aquaculture now represents private property for the leaseholders. Like many development projects, the FFDA programmme was implemented with no clear understanding of how restructuring of property rights regime and its institutional arrangements would affect social stability and economic productivity. On the one hand, it has reduced the productivity of freshwater aquaculture and, on the other, socio-economic disorder has been created. Some of the ponds' many uses are reduced or obstructed and the mechanisms for leasing ponds and selecting leaseholders are unsatisfactory. The magnitude of the disorder is more serious when the ponds are managed by groups of fishermen or individuals than when they are managed by cooperatives. FFDA, in reality, has replaced the authority of the village panchayat, but it has not been able to ensure the stream of benefits to the leaseholds. The study suggest to redesign the existing institutional arrangements for CFPs that influence how they are used and maintained by the leaseholders and villagers alike. New institutional arrangements or modifications of existing arrangements – such as reserving close-in ponds for common village use and more distant ponds for aquaculture – may resolve spatial and temporal conflicts. But only organized institutions can reliably regulate behaviour since these institutions impose working rules that define how resource users interact with respect to the common property regimes. They do so by imposing a minimum cost on those whose behaviour or actions require modifications or by providing financial incentives to induce behaviour consistent with socially desired results. Cooperative management with correct distribution of rights and responsibilities at different decision levels seems to be the better option for implementing new institutional arrangements (Marothia 1997a).

1.d Non-Timber Forest Products

Non-timber forest products (NTFPs) play a vital role in the socio-economic, ecological, cultural and political environments of the State of M.P. For managing NTFPs, the SDF has used several alternatives of distributed governance systems in the post-colonial period. These varied from *contract management system* to monopoly arrangement with *purchaser-agent system* (See Marothia 1996a, 1996b for detailed discussion of alternative property regimes in managing NTFPs). However, a few nationalized NTFPs, namely, tendu leaves, sal seeds and gums, are being managed under distributed governance using the Cooperative Management System (Marothia, 1996a, 1996b; Marothia and Gauraha, 1996). Other non-nationalized NTFPs are collected under usufruct rights systems and sold in weekly local markets at prices generally dictated by middlemen. (Marothia and Gauraha 1992, Marothia 1994).

Cooperative governance is the most frequently suggested internal governance structure for managing NTFPs at community levels. The cooperative governance operating in M.P. has both external and internal institutional arrangements reflecting the core concept of distributed management. Recognizing the problems associated with nationalisation or creation of private monopolies by assigning private traders exclusive rights of collection and marketing, and to eliminate the middlemen totalty, cooperative management of NTFPs was initiated in 1988 with the formation of Madhya Pradesh Minor Forest Produce Trade and Development Co-operative Federation (MFPFED) at the apex (State level), District Minor Forest Produce Unions (MFPDUs) at the secondary (district) level and Primary Minor Forest Produce Co-operative Societies (PMFPCs) at the primary level respectively. The organizational structure and external and internal institutional arrangements at different management levels are discussed in Marothia (1996a, 1996b). See also Table 31.1 of this chapter.

For an effective implementation of the cooperative management of NTFPs at MFPFED, MFPDU and PMFPCs bye-laws have been prepared for each level and made effective. The bye-laws clearly spell out the working zones, objectives, functions, responsibilities, organizational, administrative and financial set-up, duties and rights of members of the governing bodies operating at the apex, secondary and primary levels. These bye-laws reflect the relationships between external and internal institutional arrangements for distributed management.

An analysis of the eight PMFPCs conducted by Marothia (1996a, 1996b) indicates that given the resource and resource users' characteristics on the one hand, and the internal decision-making environment, on the other, some pattern of interaction had emerged. PMFPCs can effectively restrict the free riders or non-members and have framed internal institutional arrangements for regularizing different operations and payments to members. Still the financial, technical and administrative control is unevenly distributed at different levels of management, for example, PMFPCs has not been assigned any significant role for procuring and marketing of nationalized and non-nationalized NTFPs. In the past few years, owing to a collective pressure from PMFPCs, MFPFED made certain adjustments in the external institutional arrangements to allow some non-nationalized NTFPs collection and marketing by PMFPCs. However, owing to financial constraints at PMFPCs, significant achievements have not been recorded in this effort. The external institutional relationship for distributed management is well defined (see Table 31.1). However, for self-governance of PMFPCs, the internal institutional arrangements have to be redefined for the greater involvement of local resource users in managing NTFPs.

2. Conclusions and Policy Implications

The foregoing analysis has obvious policy implications for the governance of CPRs and welfare of the rural poor but the analysis also suggests a general approach for policy designing in CPRs management. Institutional arrangements (both external and internal) are important factors in CPRs management under different property rights regimes. Institutional movements have redefined the property rights structure in a number of CPRs development programmes aimed at reducing rural poverty. This transition of institutional arrangements became a major source of eco-system degradation in many cases due to lack of understanding of the policy makers about the social economy and ecological linkages, users' participation in the programmes and patterns of interactions. For example, institutional transition in the case of village woodlots has redefined the property right regime by converting common property into State controlled for undertaking social forestry programmes and created social tensions as well as replaced the customary institutional arrangements to conserve the resource and eco-system. As a result the grazing area of the village was reduced and villagers developed negative attitudes towards plantation programmes due to the policing culture in the implementation of social programmes. Similarly, MMITs have been created on village wastelands but due to weak local governance and absence of well-defined institutional arrangements for common property regimes they have ended up in an open access resource regime. Experiences from management for fisheries have shown that multiple uses of CFPs are capable of creating social tensions even if effective institutional arrangements are designed, keeping in view the number of users. Unless an effective authority system is in place the social disequilibrium cannot be corrected. The findings of NTFPs cooperatives clearly indicate that the cooperative management system still has uneven distributed governance and too much State control visible even at PMFPCs level. The members still remain mere wage-earners and their participation is almost negligible in the decision-making process. The important clue is that the State may use the local institutional building capacity to support and gain strength for making PMFPCs self-governing organizations at local levels.

The outcome of these case studies suggests that the policy designers of institutional arrangements for CPRs development programmes in the rural areas should have an in-depth understanding of the strength and weakness of alternative property rights regimes. Pure State, pure community-based and pure private have more negative outcomes in a large number of cases. Distributed governance seems to be most appropriate for designing CPRs management programmes. Promoting exploration of distributed governance as an acceptable model for institutional innovation to local situations should be reflected in the policy and administration for greater involvement of resource users. However, this involves a major shift in the role of policy makers and administrators to share power for promoting greater involvement of local people in decision making and administration. Serious theoretical and empirical research efforts are needed for testing the efficacy of alternative models of distributed governance in managing CPRs.

REFERENCES

Arnold, J.E.M. and W.C. Stewart. 1991. *Common Property Resource Management in India*, Tropical Forestry Paper No. 24, Department of Plant Sciences, Oxford Forestry Institute, University of Oxford, U.K.

Berkes, F. and C. Folke. 1992. "A Systems Perspective on the Interrelations between Natural, Human-Made and Cultural Capital". *Ecological Economics* 5:1-8.

Berkes, F. and C. Folke. 1994. "Investing in Cultural Capital for Sustainable Use of Natural Capital". In: Jansson, A.M., M. Hammer, C. Folke and R. Costanza (eds.) *Investing in Natural Capital: The Ecological Economics Approach to Sustainability*, Washington, D.C.: Inland Press.

Bromley, Deniel W. 1989. "Property Relations and Economic Development: The other Land Reform". *World Development*, 17:867-77.

Bromley, Daniel W. and Michael M. Cernea. 1989. *The Management of Common Property Natural Resources: Some Conceptual and Opetational Fallacies*, Discussion Paper 57, The World Bank, Washington, D.C., U.S.A.

Ciriacy-Wantrup, S.V. and R.C. Bishop. 1975. "Common Property as Concept in Natural Resources Policy", *Natural Resources Journal*, 15:713-728.

Commons, J.R. 1950. *The Economics of Collective Action*, New York: Macmillan Company.

Folke, C. And F. Berkes. 1995. "Mechanism that link property rights to Ecological System". In: Susan Hanna and Mohan Munasinghe (eds.) *Property Rights and the Environment —Social and Ecological Issues*, Washington, D.C.: The Beijer International Institute of Ecological Economics and World Bank.

Gibbs, C.J.N. and D.W. Bromley. 1989. "Institutional Arrangements for Management of Rural Resources: Common Property Regimes". In: F. Berkes (ed.) *Common Property Resource: Ecology and Community-Based Sustainable Development*, London: Belhaven Press.

Gupta, A.K. 1995. "Sustainable Institutions for Natural Resource Management: How do we Participate in People's Plans ?" In: Syed Abdus Samad, Tatsuya Watanabe and K. Seung Jin (eds.) *People's Initiatives for Sustainable Development: Lessons of Experience*, Kaula Lumpur: APDC.

Jodha, N.S. 1986. "Common Property Resources and Rural Poor in Dry Region of India". *Economic and Political Weekly*, 21:1169-81, July 5.

Marothia, D.K. 1986. "Tank Irrigation in Chhattisgarh Region: Management and Policy Issues", *Indian Journal of Agricultural Economics*, 41(4): 56-58.

Marothia, D.K. 1989a. "Resource Ownership and Human Interaction: A Theoretical Exposition", *Annals of Arid Zone*, 28, 165-80.

Marothia, D.K. 1989b. "Socio-Economic Reationales of Wastelands Afforestation", *Journal of Tropical Forestry*, Vol. 5, No. 4, pp. 343-350.

Marothia, D.K. 1992a. *Village Ponds and Aquaculture Development: Issues of Inequality in Common Property Regimes*, Contributory Paper, Third Conference of the International Association for the Study of Common Property, Washington, D.C., September 18-20

Marothia, D.K. 1992b. "Village Irrigation Tanks: Institutional Design for Sustainable Resource Use", *Agricultural Situation in India*, 47:479-487.

Marothia, D.K. 1993. "Property Regimes and Institutional Arrangements: Concepts and their Relevace in Managing the Village Commons", *Indian Journal of Agricultural Economics*, 48, 557-65.

Marothia, D.K. 1994. *Decentralised Planning for Bastar District: An ACRP Approach*, Planning Commission Project (GOI) Raipur: Indira Gandhi Agricultural University Publication, (M.P.).

Marothia, D.K. 1996a. "Co-operative Management of Minor Forest Products in Madhya Pradesh". In: Katar Singh and Vishwa Ballabh (eds) *Co-operative Management of Natural Resources*, New Delhi: Sage.

Marothia, D.K. 1996b. "Co-operative Management of Nontimber Forest Products: Issues of Property Rights and Institutional Structures", In: Rajgopalan, R. (ed.) *Rediscovering Co-operation: Strategies for the Models of Tomorrow* (Vol. 2), Anand: Institute of Rural Management, November.

Marothia, D.K. 1996c. *Designing Institutions for Self Governing System of Common Pool Resources*, Technical Paper No. 25, Ahmedabad: Agro-climatic Regional Planning Unit of Planning Commission, Govt. of India, ARPU.

Marothia, D.K. 1997a. "Institutional Arrangements in Common Fish Ponds". In: Kerr, J.N., D.K. Marothia, K. Singh, C. Ramasamy and W.R. Bentley (eds.) (1997). *Natural Resource Economics: Theory and Application in India*, New Delhi: Oxford & IBH Pub. Co.

Marothia, D.K. 1997b. "Agricultural Technology and Environmental Quality: An Institutional Perspective: Keynote Paper", *Indian Journal of Agricultural Economics* 52, 473-487.

Marothia, D.K. 1997c. "Property Rights, Externalities and Environmental Pollution", In: Anil Agrawal (ed.) *The Challenge of the Balance*, New Delhi: Centre for Science and Environmental.

Marothia, D.K. 1998. "Shared Management in Nontimber Forest Resources", Invited paper present in the International Workshop on Shared Resources Management in South Asia—The Next Step, held at Institute of Rural Management, Anand (India), February 17-19, 1998.

Marothia, D.K. 1999. *Distributed Governance in Common Pool Resources*, keynote address presented to the National Conference on Environment organized by Paschim Banga Vigyan Manch, WBPCB, Deptt. of Environment, Govt. of West Bengal at Science City, Calcutta, Feb. 2-5, 1999.

Marothia, D.K. and A.K. Gauraha 1992. "Marketing of Denationalised Minor Forest Products in Tribal Economy", *Indian Journal of Agricultural Marketing*, Vo1. 6 No. 2, pp. 84-91

Marothia, D.K. and A.K. Gauraha. 1996. "Cooperative Management of Tendu Leaves: A Micro Analysis", *Indian Journal of Agricultural Economics*, 51, 760-766.

Marothia, D.K. and W.E. Phillips. 1985. "Analysis of Natural Resource Problems Using a Synthesis of Neoclassical and Institutional Economics", *Asian Journal of Economics and Social Studies*, 4, 263-81.

Oakerson, R.J. 1992. "Analysing the Commons: A Framework", In: D.W. Bromley (ed.) *Making the Commons Work*, San Francisco: ICS Press.

Ostrom, E. 1990. *Governing the Commons: The Evolution of Institutions for Collective Action*. New York: Cambridge University Press.

Ostrom, E. 1992. *Crafting Institutions of Self Governing Irrigation Systems*, San Francisco: Institute for Contemporary Studies Press.

Palanisami, K. and K.W. Easter. 1984. "Irrigation Tanks of South: Management Strategies and Investment Alternatives", *Indian Jounal of Agricultural Economics*, (39): 214-222.

Rao, V.M. and M.G. Chandrakant. 1984. "Resource at the Margin, Tank Irrigation Programme in

Karnataka", *Economic and Political Weekly* (Review of Agriculture Number) A 54-A54.

Singh, Katar. 1994. *Managing Common Pool Resources: Principles and Case Studies*, New Delhi: Oxford University Press.

Srivastava, U.K. 1988. *Marine and Inland Fishery Sectors in India: Issues Arising out of Privatization of Common Property Resources for Accelerating Production*. Working Paper No. 742. Ahmedabad: Indian Institute of Management.

Srivastava, U.K., B.H. Dholakia, S. Srinivas Rao and S. Vathsala. 1993. *Freshwater Aquaculture in India*. New Delhi: Oxford & IBH Publishing Company.

Srivastava, U.K., B.H. Dholakia, S. Vathsala, and K. Chidambaram. 1991. *Fishery Sector of India*, New Delhi: Oxford & IBH Publishing Company.

Townsend, R.E. 1995. "Fisheries Self-Governance: Corporate or Cooperative Structures?" *Marine Policy*. 19:39-45.

Townsend, R.E. and S.G. Polley. 1995. "Distributed Governance in Fisheries", In: Susan Hanna and Mohan Munasinghe (eds.) *Property Rights and the Environment—Social and Ecological Issues*. Washington, D.C.: The Beijer International Institute of Ecological Economics and the World Bank.

Von Oppen, M. 1985. *Tank Irrigation in South India—Adapting a Traditional Technology to Modern Socio-Economic Conditions*, Irrigation Symposium on Traditional Irrigation Scheme and Potential for their Improvement. Berlin, Federal Republic of Germany, 109-118.

Von Oppen, M. and K.V. Subha Rao. 1980a. *Tank Irrigation in Semi-arid Tropical India, Part I: Historical Development and Spatial Distribution*, ICRISAT Economics Programme Progress Report 8, Patancheru, A.P. India.

Von-Oppen, M. and K.V. Subha Rao. 1980b. *Tank Irrigation in Semi-arid Tropical India, Part II: Technical Features and Economic Performance*, ICRISAT Economics Programme Progress Report 8, Patancheru, A.P., India.

NOTES ON CONTRIBUTORS

Anil Agarwal is a leading environmental advocate, journalist and analyst in India. His work has had both global and national impact. In 1980, he founded the Centre for Science and Environment at Delhi, one of India's first environmental NGOs. Since 1982, the Centre has published a pioneering *Citizens' report on the State of India's Environment* which provides an overview of the level of environmental degradation and its impact on the people of India, especially its poor. In 1986, Prime Minister Rajiv Gandhi invited him to address a meeting of the Union Council of Ministers on the importance of the relationship between environment and development and subsequently all the 27 Parliamentary Committees attached to various Union Ministries. During this period, Agarwal also chaired the world's largest network of environmental NGOs based in Nairobi, Environment Liaison Centre. In 1998, Agarwal was invited to join the World Water Commission to develop a vision for water management in the 21st century. Agarwal has written or edited over 15 books on the challenges of sustainable development facing India. In 1992, Agarwal founded and continues to edit *Down To Earth*. India's first science and environmental fortnightly. He has received several national and international awards for his work, including the A.H.Boerma Award from the Food and Agricultural Organization in 1979, Padma Shri from the Government of India in 1986, Padma Bhushan in 2000, the Global 500 Honour Roll from the United Nations Environment Programme in 1987. Recently he has also received Global Environment Facility's Year 2000 Global Environment Leadership Award.

R. Balasubramanian is currently working as Assistant Professor in the Department of Agricultural Economics at Tamil Nadu Agricultural Unversity, Coimbatore. He was previously working as Assistant Professor in the research project on tank irrigation funded by the Ford Foundation, New Delhi. He holds a Ph.D. in agricultural economics. His current research interests include economics of environment and sustainability in agriculture issues concerning management of common property resources and economics of natural resources.

Vishwa Ballabh is a Professor at the Institute of Rural Management, Anand. He holds a Ph.D. in Agricultural Economics from the Indian Agricultural Research

Institute, New Delhi. He has been a post-doctoral fellow at the International Crop Research Institute for Semi-Arid Tropics, Patencheru, India, a Visiting Scholar at the Workshop on Political Theory and Policy Analysis, Indiana University, Bloomington, USA, and a Visiting Scientist at the International Rice Research Institute, Los Bonos, Philippines. He has presented several invited papers on natural resources management at national and international workshops and conferences and was presented the DK Desai Award in 1991 for a research article published in the *Indian Journal of Agricultural Economics* and Best Paper Award in 1995 for a paper published in *Indian Dairyman*, co-authored with other colleagues.

M.G. Chandrakanth completed his Ph.D. in Forest Resource Economics during 1981 and began his carrier as an Assistant Professor in Agricultural Economics in the Institute for Social and Economic Change, Bangalore. After two years of teaching and research in the Institute he joined the University of Agricultural Sciences (UAS), Bangalore, as an Associate Professor in Agricultural Economics. He completed three years of post-doctoral research in the University of California at Berkeley as a Ciriacy-Wantrup fellow in institutional economics of natural resources during 1987-1990. He has published in the field of agricultural and resource economics in the *Indian Journal of Agricultural Economics, Natural Resources Journal, Agroforestry Systems*. Currently he is heading the Team of Excellence in Natural Resource Economics at UAS, Bangalore. He is conducting research in the field of economics of groundwater irrigation in hard rock areas, economics of medicinal plants and existence value of sacred groves.

Kanchan Chopra, presently Professor at the Institute of Economic Growth (IEG), Delhi, received her Ph.D. degree in 1969 from the Delhi School of Economics. She worked on different aspects of water management, agricultural economics and project evaluation before venturing into the field of environmental and resource economics in the early 80's. Having taught graduate and post-graduate students for 13 years in Miranda House, University of Delhi, she joined as an Associate Professor at IEG in 1980. Since then her research has been into the area of natural resource in particular forest and water, participatory planning process, evaluation of environmental resources and the linkages between environment and development. She has authored and co-authored several books in the area including a recent one on *Operationalising Sustainable Development: Ecological Economic Modelling in Developing Countries* published by Sage in 1999. In addition, she has published in national and international journals in the area. She has a long experience in conducting training programmes for professionals. Presently, she is the Chairperson of a training committee for practising economists and non-economists in the World Bank Under Capacity Building Programme in Environment Economics. She is also a member of the Expert Committee set up to oversee the working of this programme. Additionally, field work at the grassroot level has kept her in touch with several non-government organizations working in the area of land and water management. Among them are the society for Hill Resource in Bihar, Obeshwar Vikas Mandal and Seva Mandir in Udaipur. Her current interests are focused on seeing a vibrant environmental policy evolve in the context of development: a policy based on extensive and painstaking research into different facets of critical issues.

P.V. Dehadrai holds a Ph.D. from Delhi University a and post-doctoral from the Fisheries Research Board of Canada (1963-65). Dr. Dehadrai joined the National Institute of Oceanography, where as a founder member of the institute, he has initiated an estuaries coastal oceanography programme. Later he joined the Indian Council of Agricultural Research (ICAR) in 1971 as Project Coordinator of an all-India coordinated project in aquaculture and for 10 years was involved in the overall research and development of aquaculture in the country. In 1981 he joined as the first Commissioner of Fisheries Development with the Ministry of Agriculture, Government of India, and was responsible for the development of marine and inland fisheries. After completing a five year tenure, he returned to ICAR as first Deputy Director General, Fisheries, wherein for 10 years he was responsible for the overall development of the fisheries sector and establishment of new fisheries research institutions. All through his involvement in national-level fisheries research and development, the nation today has a well-established network in the fisheries area. Dr. Dehadrai has been published widely and chaired sessions in national and international conferences.

R.S. Deshpande is presently Professor and Head of Agricultural Development and Rural Transformation (ADRT) Unit in the Institute for Social and Economic Change (ISEC), Bangalore. Earlier he had served in Gokhle Institute of Politics and Economics, Pune. Professor Deshpande holds a Ph.D. in Economics from Marathwada University, Aurangabad, Maharashtra. He has published a number of papers in referred journals and edited books.

Madhav Gadgil, M.Sc. (Bombay 1965), Ph.D. (Harvard 1969) has been an IBM Fellow and a Lecturer in Biology at Harvard University, a Visiting Professor at Stanford and a Distinguished Visiting Lecturer at the University of California, Berkeley. Since 1973 he has worked at the Indian Institute of Science, Bangalore, where he is now a Professor at the Centre for Ecological Sciences established through his initiative in 1983. His research interests include population biology, conservation biology, human ecology and ecological history and he has to his credit over 170 research papers (two of them recognized as Citation Classics) and four books, *This Fissured Land, Ecology and Equity, Diversity: the cornerstone of life* and *Nurturing Biodiversity: an Indian agenda.* He regularly writes for newspapers and broadcasts over radio in English and Indian languages, and has been working with the people's science movements and environmental NGOs. He is actively involved in a network of educational institutions working towards monitoring the biodiversity of the Western Ghats, and a countrywide network of voluntary agencies engaged in the preparation of *People's Biodiversity Registers*. He received the National Environmental Fellowship in recognition of his field research on the people-environment relationship on the hill chain of the Western Ghats, where he has been involved in the establishment of India's first biosphere reserve. He was a member of the Science Advisory Council to the Prime Minister of India from 1986-90 and in 1995, a Vice President of the Scientific Advisory Body to the Convention on Biological Diversity. Since July 1998 he is chairing the Scientific and Technical Advisory Panel of Global Environment Facility. He is a Fellow of the Indian National Science Academy, Third World Academy of Sciences, a Foreign Associate of the U.S. National Academy of Sciences and an honorary member of the British Ecological society. A recipient of Shanti Swarup Bhatnagar and Vikram Sarabhai awards, he was conferred the Padma Shri by the President of India.

Brij Gopal, Associate Professor in the School of Environmental Sciences, Jawaharlal Nehru University, New Delhi, is an aquatic ecologist, well known for his contributions to the ecology and management of wetlands, and for his book on waterhyacinth. Dr. Gopal obtained his Ph.D. in plant ecology from the Banaras Hindu University in 1968. He briefly served as Lecturer in Agra College, Agra, before joining the Rajasthan University as Assistant Professor. He moved to his present position in 1986. Dr.Gopal was a Humboldt Fellow at the Max Planck Institute of Limnology in Germany during 1982-83, and a Visiting Professor at the Swiss Federal Institute of Technology, Zurich, during 1984. He has published more than 150 research and review papers besides many general articles, and has authored or edited 28 books. He is Editor or a member of the editorial board of several international journals, including the *International Journal of Ecology and Environmental Sciences, Journal of Aquatic Ecosystem Health, Hydrobiologia, Wetlands Ecology and Management*, and *Regulated Rivers: Research & Management* . Dr. Gopal is the first recipient of the Science Academy Medal for Young Scientists (1974) of the Indian National Science Academy, New Delhi. He also received the second International Fellow Award (1997) of the Society of Wetland Scientists, USA. He has served on several national and international committees including UNESCO, UNEP, SCOPE and IUBS. Among many other positions, Dr. Gopal is currently chairman of the SIL Committee on Limnology in Developing Countries, and Secretary General of the National Institute of Ecology (India.)

Sudarshan Iyengar, Ph.D. (MSU, Baroda) is currently Director , Gujarat Institute of Development Research (GIDR), Ahmedabad. He has also served as Professor in the GIDR, Ahmedabad. He has worked in the areas of decentralized local level planning, resettlement and rehabilitation of the displaced population. His main areas of interest are: rural development, natural resources management and sustainable development.

Nandita Jain is a Regional Programme Manager of the Mountain Institute. She has wide-ranging experience in ecotourism and environmental planning and management in mountain regions. She has carried out consultancies for agencies such as the World Bank and GEF. Dr Jain has an academic background in Agriculture (UK), Resource Management and Policy (M.Sc and a Ph.D from the University of Michigan, USA) with a doctoral thesis on Trekking Tourism and Protected Area Management in Nepal.

Narpat S. Jodha is Policy Analyst with the Mountain Enterprises and Infrastructure Division at the International Center for Integrated Mountain Development (ICIMOD) Kathmandu, Nepal. Formerly he has worked in the Social Policy and Resettlement Division of the Environment Department at the World Bank in Washington, D.C., International Crop Research Institute for Semi-Arid Tropics (ICRISAT) and International Institute for Tropical Agriculture (IITA). His Professional interests include agriculture and natural resource management in fragile areas. He has done pioneer work in common property resource management in India.

P.K. Joshi is presently Principal Scientist at the National Centre for Agricultural Economics and Policy Research. He is associated with research programme on technology policy. Earlier he worked with the International Crops Research Institute for the Semi Arid Tropics. He has contributed in the fields of economics and policy issues related to soil salinity, waterlogging, soil erosion and other environmental externalities in agriculture. Dr. Joshi holds a Ph.D. from G.B.Pant University of Agriculture and Technology, Pantnagar. He has published a number of research articles, books and edited several proceedings. He is a member of the editorial board of the *Indian Journal of Agricultural Economics* and Secretary of the Agricultural Economics Research Association.

Amalendu Jyotishi is presently a Ph.D. Fellow in the Ecological Economics Unit, Institute for Social and Economic Change, Bangalore. He holds an M.A. in Economics from Sambalpur University, Orissa, and is published in the area of water management and biodiversity.

Jagdeesh C. Kalla, retired as Director, National Academy of Agricultural Research Management, Hyderabad. Dr. Kalla also worked as Agricultural Economist, Central Arid Zone Research Institute (CAZRI), Jodhpur, and as a faculty member at Rajasthan Agricultural University, Udaipur. Besides serving on several important committees of ICAR, he was Chairman of the Research

Advisory Committee, CAZRI, Jodhpur. He had guided several Ph.D. students. After retirement Dr. Kalla worked as Consultant (Agricultural Economics) with the European Union assisted Aravalli Project, Gurgaon, Haryana. He made a significant contribution in the field of socio-economics and has authored several research papers and monographs.

Pradeep Kumar Katiha, presently Senior Scientist of Agricultural Economics at Central Inland Capture Fisheries Research Institute, Barrackpore, West Bengal. He holds a Ph.D. in Agricultural Economics from Dr. Y.S.Parmar University of Horticulture and Forestry, Nauni, Solan, Himachal Pradesh. He is published intensively in the area of inland fisheries and is currently working on the national and international projects on the techno-socio-economic status of inland fisheries in several agro-climatic conditions in India. He is a life member of the Indian Society of Agricultural Economics, Indian Society of Agricultural Marketing, Agricultural Economics Research Association and Inland Fisheries Society of India.

R.N. Kaul, retired from the Indian Forest Service as Chief Conservator of Forests, and Secretary, Forests, Government of Arunachal Pradesh. His earlier assignments were Head, Division of Plant Sciences, Central Arid Zone Research Institute, Jodhpur. Director and Central Silviculturist, Directorate of Forestry Research, Forest Research Institute and College. Dehra Dun. Joint Commissioner, Soil Conservation, Government of India, Ministry of Agriculture, New Delhi. Besides serving as Consultant with UNESCO, FAO, UNEP, UNU and UNCCD, he was UNESCO Project Manager from 1968 to 1975, UNDP/UNESCO Project Institute for Applied Research on Natural Resources in Baghdad. Iraq. Kaul was also consultant to the National Wastelands Development Board, Ministry of Environment and Forests, and as Technical Assistance Coordinator with the European Union assisted Aravalli Project, Gurgaon, Haryana. He was appointed by the Supreme Court of India as member of the High Power Committee for the North East to look into matters related to exploitation of forests. He has been twice recipient of the Brandis Award for his outstanding contribution to forestry research in 1999. The Soil Conservation Society of India has honoured him with a Gold Medal for his outstanding contribution to soil and water conservation. In addition to numerous research papers, Kaul has published 10 monographs including two Nursery Manuals and a book: *Afforestation in Arid Zones*, Dr. W. Huk N.V. Publishers. The Hague, Netherlands.

Ashish Kothari, a founding member of Kalpavriksh, a youth environmental action group which has been active for the past 20 years. Currently he is coordinator of the Technical and Policy Core Group to formulate India's National Biodiversity Strategy and Action Plan. A former Lecturer in Environment at the

Indian Institute of Public Administration, New Delhi, he is active in a number of environmental movements, including the Narmada Bachao Andolan. He has coordinated an action research project on local community participation in wildlife conservation in South Asia. He is a member of several governmental committees, including the Expert Group on the Biodiversity Act, the committee to revise the National Wildlife Action Plan, the Environmental Appraisal Committee for River Valley Projects, and others. He is also member of two Expert Commissions of IUCN-The World Conservation Union, and Head of the IUCN Inter-commission Task Force on Local Communities and Protected Areas. He has authored or edited 8 books, and over 100 articles on environment/development issues.

Renzino Lepcha is India Project Officer of the Mountain Institute. He is a native of Sikkim, with a decade of experience in the tourism sector in the State and region. Before joining TMI, he established and managed one of Sikkim's largest travel and trekking agencies and participated in the design of SBE as a travel operator. He is a trainer for international tourism training courses. He has undergraduate and graduate degrees in botany and ecology from Sikkim and the North East Hill University, India.

I.C. Mahapatra is an international consultant and has worked for international organizations including IFAD, CGIAR, FAO, World Bank, UNDP, IRRI, IITA, ICRISAT, WARDA, ADB, IADS, AFC, CWD and ICAR organizations. He holds a Ph.D. in Agronomy from Louisiana State University, Baton Rouge, Louisiana, USA (1966). Dr. Mahapatra's professional career as an agronomist spreads over 45 years encompassing teaching, research, extension, planning, monitoring and evaluation of agricultural research and development programmes, coordination, management and administration in national and international agricultural projects and institutions. He has served as Vice-Chancellor, Birsa Agricultural University and Orissa University of Agriculture and Technology. He has worked as Expert Witness and Chief Consultant in Agriculture for the Cauvery Water Dispute Tribunal. Dr. Mahapatra has been the life member and President of the Association of Rice Research Workers (1981-84), life member and Secretary of the Indian Society of Agronomy (1973-74) and life member of the Indian Society of Soil Science, Indian Society of Coastal Agriculture. He was awarded D.Sc. degree (honoris causa) by the World Development Parliament, and elected as member of Phi Kappa Phi honor society, USA (1966), and fellow of Bihar Academy of Sciences (1982), Indian Society of Agronomy (1990), and Indian Society of Coastal Agriculture (1998). He has published over 293 papers in national and international journals and presented over 170 papers in national and international seminars, symposia and conferences. He has authored ten books and bulletins and sixtyfive technical reports. Dr. Mahapatra's main contributions have been in the fields of crop production, soil fertility and fertilizer use, rice agronomy, multiple cropping, integrated farming systems and sustainable agricultural development involving research, extension, education, rural development, institution building, coordination, management and administration.

Kailash C. Malhotra is currently Professor of Anthropology at the Indian Statistical Institute (ISI), Calcutta. Malhotra obtained his Ph.D. in Anthropology from Poona University in 1966. He served as a faculty member in the Poona University during 1966-68 before joining ISI as senior lecturer in 1969. Since then he has been with ISI. He has received Fellowship from the Indian Academy of Science and Indian National Science Academy and served as UGC National Lecturer. He has also served as Chairman, Division of Science and Technology (DST), New Delhi, member/chairperson on several committees of DST, Ministry of Environment and Forest (MOEF), Planning Commission, Wasteland Board, Ministry of Human Resource Development (HRD), etc. He is Member of Academic Council of several institutions. He was honored as President, Indian Society of Human Genetics, President, Anthropology Section of Indian Academy of Social Sciences, Vice President, International Dermatoglyphic Association, Vice President, Indian Anthropology Society, Calcutta. He has delivered LD Sanghvi, Verrier Elwin, Salim Ali, S. S. Sarkar, D. Panchanan memorial lecturies. He has published over 350 articles including 12 books/monographs. He has travelled extensively in North and Central American, European, South East Asia and Pacific, Japan and other countries for presenting papers and delivered lectures. Dr. Malhotra has attended over 100 international conferences and 500 in India and served as consultant to World Bank, USAID, FAO, UNESCO, SIDA, etc. He is interacting with over 250 NGOs in the country, and has considerable experience and expertise in project development, monitoring and evaluation.

Dinesh K. Marothia holds an M.Sc. (Agricultural Economics) from G.B. Pant University of Agriculture and Technology, Pantnagar, and a Ph.D. from the University of Alberta, Edmonton, with specialization in natural resource economics. Dr. Marothia is the recipient of Canadian Commonwealth Scholarship for Ph.D. degree. Having served as Assistant and Associate Professor at J.N.Agricultural University, he joined Indira Gandhi Agricultural University, Raipur, in 1987 where he is now Professor and Head of the Department of Agricultural and Natural Resource Economics established through his initiative in 1988. This was the first Department under State Agricultural University system in India where teaching and research on natural resource economics was initiated. He has held positions of Member and Chairman with the Commission for Agricultural Costs and Prices, Ministry of Agriculture, Government of India. He had a short stint as (founder) Director of India Natural Resource Economics and Management Foundation, Anand. He is on the panel of guest faculty and member of research advisory committee in a number of universities and management institutions. He has served on several national committees and working groups including as member of Agro-climatic Regional Planning and high powered committee on sugar industry. He was founder editor-in-chief of the *Journal of Agricultural Issues* and member of the editorial board of *Indian Journal of Agricultural Economics*. Currently he is member of the editorial board of the *Agricultural Economics Research Review*. Among many other professional positions, Dr. Marothia was president (Agricultural Sciences) of the Indian Academy of Social Sciences, founder member of the steering committee and Treasurer of Indian Society for Ecological Economics, member of executive committee of Indian Society of Agricultural Economics and currently he is Vice President of the Indian Society of Agricultural Economics. Dr. Marothia is a life member of several professional societies and written extensively on institutional economics, property rights and management of renewable resources. He has participated in and presented several papers and keynote addresses at national and international conferences and chaired technical sessions. He has co-edited the *Natural Resource Economics: Theory and Application in India* with John M. Kerr, Katar Singh, C. Ramasamy and William R. Bentley. Currently Dr. Marothia is involved in a number of national and international projects related to renewable natural resource management in the tribal, backward and hilly areas.

V.K. Misra is presently Executive Director of the Society for Promotion of Wastelands Development, New Delhi. He was Managing Director (1988-97) of the National Tree Growers' Cooperatives Federation (NTGCF) under the aegis of National Dairy Development Board (NDDB) and was responsible for general management, strategic leadership and boundary maintenance. He initiated a pilot project on the Tree Growers' Cooperatives started with the financial assistance of the Swedish International Development Agency and the Canadian International Development. During his tenure NTGCF grew from an organization to an institution to address India's resource regeneration and sustainable development. The first Village Level System for Natural Resource Accounting was developed by IRMA/IGIDR during his tenure. Mishra has also worked as Senior Executive/Deputy Director and Project Manager (1978-88) of the NDDB planned and supervised fodder development programmes under "Operation Flood-I', and Tree Growers' Cooperative Project. He has published a number of technical and professional articles on fodder seed production, fodder development, tree growers' cooperative and sustainable development. His current areas of interest include common property resource management, bio-diversity conservation, gender issues, environmental education, promotion of non-conventional sources of energy and natural resource accounting systems.

M.V. Nadkarni, presently Vice-Chancellor of Gulbarga University. He served for several years as Professor and Head of Ecological Economics Unit at the Institute for Social and Economic Change (ISEC), Bangalore, and also Editor of the *Journal of Social and Economic Development*. He is both an agricultural economist and an environmental economist. He was Conference President of the Indian Society of Agricultural Economics in 1995. He has many books and papers to his credit. Among his well-known books are *Farmers Movements in India* and *Political Economy of Forest Use and Management*.

Sunita Narain is currently the Deputy Director of the Centre for Science and Environment, New Delhi, and Director of the Society for Environmental Communications and publisher of the fortnightly magazine, *Down to Earth*. In her 18 years at the Centre, she has worked to analyse and study the relationship between environment and development and to create public consciousness about the need for sustainable development. She has also developed the management and financial support systems for the institution. Her research interests range from global democracy to solving global environmental problems, with a special focus on the climate change, to the need for local democracy to solve forest and water-related issues. She has travelled across the country to understand the people's management of natural resources and in 1989 co-authored the publication, *Towards Green Villages,* which advocates local participatory democracy as the key to sustainable development. In the early 1990s she got involved with global environmental issues and continues to work on these both as a researcher and advocate. In 1991, she co-authored the publication, *Global Warming in an Unequal World,* and in 1992 *Towards a Green World: Should environmental management be built on legal conventions or human rights*. Since the Kyoto Protocol in 1997, she has worked on a number of articles and papers on issues related to flexibility mechanisms and the need for equity and entitlements in climate negotiations. In 1997, pushing the need for rainwater harvesting, she co-edited the book, *Dying Wisdom: Rise, fall and potential of India's water harvesting systems*. Since then she has worked on a number of articles on the policy interventions needed for ecoregeneration of India's rural environment and poverty reduction. In 1999, she co-edited the *State of India's Environment: The Citizens' Fifth Report*. Narain remains an active participant in the national and international civil society. She is on the boards of different organizations and on government committees and has spoken at many forums across the world on issues of her concern and expertise.

Y.S. Negi is Associate Professor at the Dr.Y.S. Parmar University of Horticulture and Forestry, Nauni, Solan, Himachal Pradesh. He obtained his Bachelor's degree in Agriculture from the Himachal University, Shimla, and specialized in the field of Agricultural Economics for his Master's and M.Phil. After a brief stint at the

Agro-Economic Research Centre, Shimla, he started teaching at the Himachal Pradesh Agricultural University, Palampur, till his joining the present institution in 1985. He has a Ph.D. in Wildland Resource Science (Forest Economics and Policy) from the University of California, Berkely. He has more than 60 publications to his credit in the field of agricultural and natural resource economics. Currently, Dr. Negi is also Coordinator of the Mountain Women Development Centre at this University.

K. Palanisami, presently Director of Water Technology Centre at Tamilnadu Agricultural University (TNAU), Coimbatore. He has also served as Professor of Agricultural Economics in the same University for several years. He holds a Ph.D. from TNAU and a post-doctoral from the University of Minnesota and International Rice Research Institute. He is the recipient of Indian Council of Agricultural Economics (ICAR) Fellowship, Fulbright Fellowship and Robert McNamara Fellowship. Dr. Palanisami is published in national and international journals on tank management and has been consultant to the World Bank, USAID and FAO for water management projects.

Rangesh Parmesh is a consultant in Ayurveda at the Himalaya Drug Company, Bangalore. He had an illustrious carrier as a Reader in Ayurveda (Dravya Guna) at the Government College of Ayurvedic Medicine, Bangalore, for 15 years. He is a celebrated teacher and has received laurels from his students and colleagues. He is well known for his contributions in research in Ayurveda. He has been responsible for the establishment of Ayurvedic colleges in Europe. He is actively associated with the Ayurveda Academy, Bangalore, an institution concerned with the promotion of Ayurveda.

Prem Shankar Pathak, presently Director at the Indian Grassland and Fodder Research Institute (IGFRI), Jhansi. He holds a Ph.D. from the Banaras Hindu University. He has almost 30 years' experience in the fields of Agroforestry (including Multipurpose Trees (MPTs), Agrosilvipastoral systems, Silvipastoral systems, Growth and Production Modelling of Trees, Wastelands reclamation and development, Range Management. He has worked as Assistant Director General (Agroforestry) in the Natural Resource Management Division of the Indian Council of Agricultural Research, New Delhi. He has also worked as Principal Scientist and Head of Agrosilvipasture Division at IGFRI, Jhansi. He was associated with the development, implementation, supervision, administration of several international projects as principal investigator in the area of silvipastoral system of production for development of wastelands. He was elected as member of the Steering Committee of the International MPTs Research Network of Winrock International (1992) and National Research Committee of MPTs Network in India (1991), Organizing Committee of the Third International

Rangelands Congress (1988) and International Conference on Sustainable Development of Degraded Lands through Agroforestry in Asia and the Pacific (1994). He was also Elected Fellow of the National Institute of Ecology, 1989, National Academy of Agricultural, Sciences, 1999. Dr. Pathak was Vice-President, Indian Society of Agroforestry and Editor, *Range Management & Agroforestry* (1980-1994). He is member of the Editorial Board of *International Journal of Ecology & Environmental Sciences* (1997), *Journal of Tree Sciences, Advances in Biological Research.* He is Treasurer of the National Institute of Ecology since 1997 and Executive Vice-President of Science and Environmental Education Society. He has visited several countries and participated in international meetings and field trips related to Agroforestry, MPTs development and development of degraded lands. Dr. Pathak has published 265 papers and edited 14 books.

S.C. Rai is an M.Sc and Ph.D in Geography (Regional Planning) from the Banaras Hindu University, India. His research interests are nutrient dynamics of lake ecosystem, mountain hydrology, micro-level planning, watershed management and ecotourism. He has specialized in remote-sensing and GIS. He is a Scientist in the G.B. Pant Institute of Himalayan Environment and Development, Sikkim unit.

R.K. Rajput obtained his M.Sc.(Ag.) degree from Agra University (1959) and Ph.D. from P.G. School, IARI, New Delhi (1965). He obtained his Post-Doctoral training in Soil and Water Management in the Universities of South West, U.S.A. as well as from the International Rice Research Institute, Philippines. Dr. Rajput started his career as Agricultural Assistant with the Government of Madhya Pradesh and later joined the Indian Council of Agricultural Research as Assistant Agronomist (Soil and Water Management). He was associated with the AICRP on Water Management in coordinating, planning, monitoring and evaluation of multidisciplinary research on water management throughout the country, first as Irrigation Agronomist (1971-76) and then as Project Coordinator (1977-90). Dr.Rajput steered the AICRP on Water Management to the status of Directorate and was its founder Director from October, 1990 till superannuation in October 1996. He has made notable contributions in Irrigation Water Management especially in the "On-Farm Water Management" involving collaboration between research scientists, water managers and the end users—the farmers. He has been consultant to the World Bank, Ministry of Water Resources, ICAR, WAPCOS, Cauvery Inter State Water Dispute. He was an expert member of many high-level committees/working groups/panels of the Ministry of Water Resources, ICAR, Planning Commission, INCID, Bureau of Indian Standards. He is the Life Member of many professional scientific societies and has the distinction of serving them either as President, Vice-President, honorary Secretary or Executive Council member. He has been elected as Fellow of the Indian Society of

Agronomy. Dr. Rajput has contributed over 160 scientific papers in national and international journals of repute besides contributing chapters for books and preparation of scientific reports.

C. Ramasamy is currently Director at the Centre for Agricultural and Rural Development Studies, Tamil Nadu Agricultural University (TNAU), Coimbatore. He has been teaching and undertaking research in Agricultural Economics for nearly three decades in TNAU. He was a visiting Research Fellow to the International Food Policy Research Institute, Washington, DC, International Rice Research Institute, Manila, Philippines and ICRISAT, Hyderabad. He has acted as Resource Person to the Asian Productivity Council. He is the Awardee of Ford Foundation Fellowship for his Ph.D. in University of Minnesota, USA. He has won the Best Researcher Award of TNAU in 1995 and produced several Ph.D. and Masters students in the field of Agricultural Economics and Management. He has also been a consultant to the World Bank on the NATP project and to TAHAL Consultants of Israel on Agricultural Development of Tamil Nadu. Currently, he is serving as a member of the Editorial Board, *Indian Journal of Agricultural Economics*. Dr. Ramasamy has published books in the area of rural policy, infrastructure, green revolution and natural resource economics besides a number of book chapters and articles in leading journals.

M.S. Rathore is a Senior Fellow at the Institute of Development Studies, Jaipur. Apart from several important academic positions, he has served two international institutes, namely, International Centre for Integrated Mountain Development (ICIMOD), Kathmandu (Nepal), and International Crop Research Institute for Semi-Arid Tropics (ICRISAT), Hyderabad (India). He has also been FAO Consultant at Oman and Visiting Fellow at the Institute of Development Studies, University of Sussex, Brighton, UK. His doctoral thesis was selected for the Jawaharlal Nehru Award of the Indian Council of Agricultural Research (ICAR). Dr. Rathore has published extensively on environment and development issues.

A. Ravishankar is presently Scientist (Agricultural Economics) at the National Centre for Agricultural Economics and Policy Research (NCAP), New Delhi. He holds a Ph.D. from the Indian Agricultural Research Institute, New Delhi. He has published several articles in leading research journals on conservation of plant genetic resources and intellectual property rights.

N.C. Saxena, currently Member Secretary, Planning Commission, Government of India, New Delhi. He has also served as Secretary to the Government of India in the Department of Rural Development and Director, Lal Bahadur Shastri National Academy of Administration, Massoorie. Saxena holds a Ph.D. in

Forestry from Oxford. He has written extensively on natural resource management in national and international journals. His books include *To the Hands of the Poor*, written jointly with Robert Chambers and Tushaar Shah; *India's Eucalyptus Craze; Farm forestry in South Asia; Forests, People and Profit*; and *The Saga of Participatory Forest Management in India*. He has taught and lectured on rural development and community forestry in both India and abroad. Dr. Saxena was a Visiting Fellow at the Institute of Development Studies, Sussex (U.K), and at CIFOR, Indonesia.

R. Seenivasan works with PRADAN/DHAN Foundation, Madurai

C. Sekar is Associate Professor with the Department of Agricultural Economics at Tamilnadu Agricultural University (TNAU), Coimbatore. He holds a Ph.D. in Agricultural Economics from TNAU. His current areas of interests are solar, wind and biogas, producer gas components, common property resources, soil and water conservation research.

S. Selvam, presently Assistant Professor with the Department of Agricultural Economics at Soil and Water Management Research Institute, Thanjavur, Tamil Nadu. He holds a Ph.D. in Agricultural Economics from Tamilnadu Agricultural University and his current area interest includes natural resource management.

Tushaar Shah was formerly Director of Institute of Rural Management Anand (IRMA), and is now Research Leader (Policy, Institution and Management) at International Water Management Institute at Colombo, Sri Lanka. He has previously worked at the National Dairy Development Board as a economist and subsequently as a member of the Faculty at IRMA. He has published extensively in the field of groundwater markets, management of natural resources, and farmers' organizations. Shah's publications include *Water Markets and Irrigation Development: Political Economy* and *Making Farmers' Co-operatives Work: Design, Governance and Management*.

C.R. Shanmugam works with PRADAN/DHAN Foundation, Madurai

Eklabya Sharma is currently Scientist-In-Charge of the G.B. Pant Institute of Himalayan Environment and Development, Sikkim unit. His background is in forest ecology and biodiversity conservation. He holds an M.Sc. and Ph.D. in botany from the Banaras Hindu University, India. He is coordinator of a biodiversity project and principal investigator in biosphere reserve, watershed management and agroforestry programmes in Sikkim. Dr. Sharma is published widely in the area of natural resources and community participation.

Vandana Shiva is trained as a physicist and did her Ph.D. in the subject *Hidden*

Variables and Non-locality in Quantum Theory from the University of Western Ontario. She later shifted to inter-disciplinary research in science, technology and environmental policy which she carried out at the Indian Institute of Science and the Indian Institute of Management in Bangalore. In 1982, she founded an independent institute, Research Foundation for Science, Technology and Ecology in Dehra dun dedicated to high quality and independent research to address the most significant ecological and social issues of our times, in close partnership with local communities and social movements. In 1991, she founded Navdanya, a national movement to protect the diversity and integrity of living resources, especially native seeds. Dr. Shiva has been a visiting professor and lectured at the Universities of Oslo, Norway, Schumacher College, U.K., Mt. Holyoke College, U.S.A., and lecture at York University, Canada, University of Lulea. Sweden, University of Victoria, Canada, and organisations and institutions worldwide on environment, feminism and economic development. Besides her academic and research contributions, Dr.Shiva has also served as an adviser to the governments in India and abroad as well as NGOs such as the Intrnational Forum on Globalization, Women's Environment and Development Organization and Third World Network. She is recognized for her contributions to the fields of women and environment biodiversity, biotechnology and intellectual property rights and ecological issues related to agriculture. Her books include *Staying Alive, Ecology and Politics of Survival, Ecofeminism, Violence of the Green Revolution, Monocultures of the Mind, Biopiracy*. For her contributions to the deepening of the ecological paradigm, and for linking research to action, Dr. Shiva has received many awards including the Order of the Golden Ark, 1993, Global 500 Roll of Honour, 1993, Earth Day International Award, 1993, Alternative Nobel Prize (Right Livelihood Award), 1993, VIDA SANA International Award, 1993, "Pride of the Doon" Award from Doon Citizen Council, Dehra Dun, India, 1995. The Golden Plant Award (International Award of Ecology), Denmark, 1997, Alfonso Comin Award, 1997, Barcelona, Spain.

Nimisha Shukla, M.A., M.Phil. (Gujrat University) is Reader in Gujrat Vidyapith. She has a bright academic career and long teaching experience in the undergraduate and post-graduate classes.

Katar Singh is currently Director and Reserve Bank of India Chair Professor at the Institute of Rural Management, Anand (IRMA), and teaches post-graduate courses on 'Common Pool Resources Management' and 'Rural Development'. He earlier taught at the Department of Agricultural Economics, G.B.Pant University of Agriculture and Technology, Pantnagar, for over twelve years. He has a Ph.D. in Agricultural Economics from the University of Illinois, and has been Visiting Associate Professor at the Department of Agricultural and Resource Economics, Oregon State University, Corvallis. He has conducted and coordinated numerous multi-disciplinary research projects sponsored by both national and international agencies and has a large number of notable publications to his credit, including *Rural Development: Principles, Policies and Management* and *Managing Common Pool Resources*. He has served as a member of the Editorial Board and Panel of Reviewers of the *Indian Journal of Agricultural Economics* and is a member of many national and international professional associations and societies, including the International Association for the Study of Common Property and the Society for International Development. Dr. Singh was elected as conference president of the Indian Society of Agricultural Economics in 1988.

Vir Singh is an Associate Professor at the G.B. Pant University of Agriculture and Technology, Hill Campus, Ranichauri, Tehri Garhwal, India. Dr. Singh has nearly two decades' experience of teaching, research and extension in the Indian Himalayan region and has specialized in mountain farming systems and animal nutrition. He has been awarded many scholarships, including Research Fellow Recognition by the Americal Biographical Institute and the prestigious ICIMOD (International Centre for Integrated Mountain Development, Kathmandu, Nepal) Research Fellowship. He has seven books, several research papers and numerous popular articles to his credit. He actively participates in ecological movements and advocates Himalayan ecological renaissance and sustainable development of mountain economy. Dr. Singh also runs Friends of Eco-philosophy, an informal network of the people concerned with the State of Earth.

Maniranjan Sinha, currently Director, Central Inland Capture Fisheries Research Institute (CICFRI), Barrackpore. He has been devoted to the research and development of Inland Fisheries in India for the past over 39 years, is widely recognized as a expert in riverine and estuarine fisheries as well as aquaculture and carried out extensive studies and prepared long-term plan for fisheries development in M.P. and North Eastern regions. He has significantly contributed in the pioneering research effort on riverine spawn prospecting and fishery biology. He has the distinction of successfully breeding four species of freshwater fishes for the first time in India. He has provided able leadership to the trail blazing research on biology, production dynamics and migratory habits of hilsa on account of which the country is now poised for formulating strategies for recovering the lost hilsa fisheries of the Ganga. He is a founder-member of the Asian Fisheries Society and the present Vice-Chairman of its Indian Chapter. He has been conferred the Honorary Fellowship of a number of scientific societies in the country. 'Kheti Puraskar' of the ICAR was awarded to him for 1986-87. He was honored with the prestigious 'Param Krishi Vaigyanik Award 1996-97 by the Indian Society of Agricultural Chemists. Dr. Sinha has published over 100 research papers in national and international journals apart from a book, numerous book chapters, bulletins, popular articles and extension pamphlets.

M.S. Suneetha holds a Ph.D in the field of IPRs and medicinal plants from the University of Agricultural Sciences (UAS), Bangalore. She completed her Master's in agricultural eocnomics at UAS, bagging three gold medals. She wrote her dissertation on the Economics of Medicinal Plant Trade in Kerala. Her interests are in the field of equity in sharing the benefits from medicinal plants with the owners of indigenous knowledge and the role of IPRs.

P. Thomas is Programme Officer at Christian Aid, London. Prior to joining Christian Aid, he was a faculty member at the Institute of Rural Management, Anand. He holds a Master's Degree in Economics from the Gokhale Institute for Politics and Economics, Pune, and a Ph.D. in Developmental Studies from the School of Development Studies, University of East Anglia, Norwich. He has been closely associated with NGOs engaged in organizing people for development and changes in southern Maharashtra and northern Karnataka. His current research interests include: organizing communities for development, process of rural change, political economy of development, rural poverty and poverty alleviation programmes, rural livelihood systems and sustainable management of natural resources.

M.P. Vasimalai works with PRADAN/DHAN Foundation, Madurai.

INDEX